AESTHETICS AND CRITICISM IN ART EDUCATION

AESTHETICS
and CRITICISM in
ART EDUCATION

Problems in Defining, Explaining, and Evaluating Art

edited by

RALPH A. SMITH

University of Illinois

RAND McNALLY & COMPANY   *Chicago*

142345

RAND MCNALLY EDUCATION SERIES

B. OTHANEL SMITH, *Advisory Editor*

Broudy and Palmer, *Exemplars of Teaching Method*
Broudy, Smith, and Burnett, *Democracy and Excellence in American Secondary Education*
Burns and Lowe, *The Language Arts in Childhood Education*
Dupuis, *Philosophy of Education in Historical Perspective*
Evans and Walker, *New Trends in the Teaching of English in Secondary Schools*
Foshay, ed., *Rand McNally Handbook of Education*
Gauerke and Childress, eds., *Theory and Practice of School Finance*
Haines, *Guiding the Student Teaching Process in Elementary Education*
Kimbrough, *Political Power and Educational Decision-Making*
Krumboltz, ed., *Learning and the Educational Process*
Lewenstein, *Teaching Social Studies in Junior and Senior High Schools*
Lieberman and Moskow, *Collective Negotiations for Teachers*
Michaelis, ed., *Teaching Units in the Social Sciences,* 3 volumes
Parker, ed., *Rand McNally Curriculum Series*
    Ford and Pugno, eds., *The Structure of Knowledge and the Curriculum*
    Parker and Rubin, *Process as Content*
    Wellington and Wellington, *The Underachiever*
Perrodin, ed., *The Student Teacher's Reader*
Phi Delta Kappa, *Education and the Structure of Knowledge*
Phi Delta Kappa, *Improving Experimental Design and Statistical Analysis*
Rollins and Unruh, *Introduction to Secondary Education*
Shulman and Keislar, eds., *Learning by Discovery*
Smith, ed., *Aesthetics and Criticism in Art Education*
Smith and Ennis, eds., *Language and Concepts in Education*
Taba and Elkins, *Teaching Strategies for the Culturally Disadvantaged*
Trump and Baynham, *Focus on Change: Guide to Better Schools*
Vassar, ed., *Social History of American Education,* 2 volumes
Wolf and Loomer, *The Elementary School: A Perspective*

Also published by Rand McNally
Gage, ed., *Handbook of Research on Teaching* — A Project of the American Educational Research Association

FOREWORD

Knowledge accumulates, but there is no progress unless new insights are interpreted and their relevance indicated for the processes of schooling. Indeed, if the humanization of knowledge fails to keep pace with social change, then schooling grinds along out of gear with social realities. Hence, educational workers must constantly strive to weave new ideas into the fabric of teaching and learning. For this purpose the anthology can provide a convenient form, and wisely used it can help speed pedagogical reform. It is hoped that the writings collected in this volume will in some measure serve this end.

PREFACE

Art education today is engaged in clarifying its conceptual foundations and in defining its relations to other disciplines of thought and action. In no formal sense a theoretical discipline itself,[1] the profession of art education has structured its field on the metaphor of the child as a creative artist and on the language and insights of psychology. Accordingly, a popular image in the field has the pupil achieving personal integration and identity through the manipulation of expressive art materials.

Now this image of the pupil-artist creatively expressing himself is undeniably persuasive. It is to be appreciated, moreover, as part of the reaction by progressive schoolmen against the restrictive formalism of an earlier day. The introduction into the classroom of art practices which permitted pupils to work with concrete materials was a sound corrective to the abstract verbalism and meaningless exercises often urged on pupils in the older conceptions of teaching. And by underlining the readiness and interests of pupils as motivating factors, advocates of art instruction in the schools reasserted proven pedagogical principles, truisms which hold that effective teaching adapts its materials to the pupil's rate of maturation and level of ability. The exponents of public school art instruction in this century have served education well. It is through their efforts that the study of art is now a standard item in many elementary curricula, and from the elementary level it is moving into the secondary grades where it is certain to become more pervasive.

But if an important contribution has been made, and if that contribution is now acknowledged, it is time to review the shape and style of the achievement. And when this is done, it is discovered that the image of the pupil as a creative artist, as well as an excessive devotion to the cultivation of the inner life of the

---

[1]For discussions of the meanings of "discipline" see John Walton and James L. Kuethe (eds.), *The Discipline of Education* (Madison: University of Wisconsin Press, 1963), esp. pp. 47-71. For responses to the question "Is There a Discipline of Art Education?" see statements by Manuel Barkan, Frederick M. Logan, Irving Kaufman, Elliot W. Eisner, and David W. Ecker, in *Studies in Art Education*, Vols. IV, No. 2 (Spring 1963); V, No. 1 (Fall 1963); and VI, No. 2 (Spring 1965).

child, encourage a subjectivism that fosters neglect of other significant aspects of learning in the arts. By stressing the centrality of the teacher's psychological insight into the needs of pupils, theorizing in art education has paid less attention not only to the structure of subject matter the pupil manipulates in the course of his learning but also to the logical operations he performs on specific items of content. Teaching mastery of an appropriate cluster of topics and ideas, therefore, has been subordinated to the use of art activities to engender personal and social growth. The favored terminology set the tone and theme of the approach; it stressed moving forward from a subject-matter-centered to a child-centered definition of the curriculum in which the release of creative potentialities and attainment of inner equilibrium would be placed above the understanding of content. A popular slogan of the movement — "art is less a body of subject matter than a developmental activity" — expressively conveyed the character of pedagogical strategy foremost in the minds of many teachers during the formative period of the new art education.

The foregoing, of course, does not exhaust the objectives which have been formulated for art instruction.[2] Still, the influence of an "expressionist" theme cannot be denied;[3] and it is clear that a great deal of public school art instruction exemplifies a theory which asserts that the purpose of art is to organize the various psychological functions in persons having art experiences.

A new climate of thought and speculation now promises not so much to reject previous achievements and assumptions, but rather to build upon them. That is to say, the field of art education is undergoing redefinition,[4] and in the process a new style is being forged whose outlines are becoming discernible. In contradistinction to earlier ways of talking, the new language urges moving toward an effective integration of child-centered and discipline-centered con-

---

[2]See the variety of aims discussed in Frederick M. Logan's *Growth of Art in American Schools* (New York: Harper and Brothers, 1956).

[3]For a brief but critical account of the expressionist theme in progressive education, see Lawrence A. Cremin, *The Transformation of the School* (New York: Alfred A. Knopf, Inc., 1961), pp. 204-7.

[4]In addition to a number of articles in art education literature, a series of conferences and seminars are sowing the seeds of change and reform. Most of these conferences are being supported with funds made available through various titles and sections of recent federal legislation. The first conference devoted to the visual arts was held at New York University in 1964. See Howard Conant, *Seminar on Elementary and Secondary School Education in the Visual Arts*. Cooperative Research Project No. V-003 (New York: New York University Printing Office, 1965). This was followed in 1965 by a Developmental Activities Program conducted at The Ohio State University (David W. Ecker, Program Coordinator), and a Seminar in Art Education for Research and Curriculum Development, held at the Pennsylvania State University (Edward L. Mattil, Seminar Coordinator). References for these last two meetings were not available at the time of writing. For a discussion of legislation devoted to the arts, see Stanley A. Czurles, "Federal Legislation and the School Art Program," *Art Education,* Vol. XVIII, No. 7 (October 1965), pp. 3-6. For two statements exemplifying the mood of transition, see Manuel Barkan, "Means and Meaning," *Art Education,* Vol. XVIII, No. 3 (March 1965), pp. 4-7; and Elliot W. Eisner, "Toward a New Era in Art Education," *Studies in Art Education,* Vol. VI, No. 2 (Spring 1965), pp. 54-62.

ceptions of the curriculum.[5] Instead of emphasizing developmental activities "above" content, the concern is to see the teaching of important ideas in relation to the child's characteristic outlook at a given time in his cognitive and affective career.[6] To repeat, this way of viewing matters is not a return to the older formalism. It is more properly interpreted as an attempt to build a philosophy of art education that recognizes both the psychological demands of pupils and the logical demands of content.

To understand the reasons for stressing the mastery of unifying topics, or for grasping the so-called structure of a subject, it is necessary to examine the character of new challenges besetting society at this time in history. It is not only that the wise use of abundance and leisure demands a renewal of the ideals of excellence and self-cultivation. Heightened powers of discrimination and judgment are also necessary to control the streams of impressions that flow endlessly from the mass media. The critical temper is further required to counteract those who in various ways would impose constraints on the conditions of artistic freedom and creativity and thereby undermine fundamental tenets of a liberal and free society. Finally, the study of the arts as a source of personal meaning and value orientation in a technologically interdependent society demands greater degrees of aesthetic mastery than one generally observes. In view of such imperatives arising primarily from new social forms, but also from traditional ideals, the need is now being recognized for placing renewed emphasis on the nature of significant content in art instruction and on the logical operations by means of which content is meaningfully manipulated.

The major content of art instruction is constituted by what may be called central topics and organizing ideas, which subsume clusters of related ideas and concepts. The active learning of important ideas, concepts, rules, and principles enables the pupil to regard aesthetically not only works of fine art but also the whole world of sensible things. It is thus, for example, that the concepts of materials, medium, form, content, subject matter, expression, representation, and style (to mention only some of the more important ones) come to function within the pupil as he practices organizing his aesthetic responses to various kinds of stimuli.[7] By logical operations are understood the processes of defining, explaining, valuating, conditional inferring, etc., opera-

---

[5]The influential work, of course, has been Jerome Bruner's *The Process of Education* (Cambridge: Harvard University Press, 1960). See also, Philip H. Phenix, "Key Concepts and the Crisis in Learning," *Teachers College Record,* Vol. LVIII (December 1956), pp. 137-43.

[6]For classifications of educational objectives in the cognitive and affective domains, see Benjamin S. Bloom (ed.), *Taxonomy of Educational Objectives: Handbook I: Cognitive Domain* (New York: David McKay Co., Inc., 1956); and David R. Krathwohl, Benjamin S. Bloom, and Betram B. Masia, *Taxonomy of Educational Objectives: Handbook II: Affective Domain* (New York: David McKay Co., Inc., 1964).

[7]These concepts are common ones in aesthetics and philosophy of art. This set is from Virgil C. Aldrich, *Philosophy of Art* (Englewood Cliffs, N. J.: Prentice-Hall, Inc., 1963).

tions which, it is pointed out, are independent of any particular subject-matter area.[8]

Once again, contemporary speculation is beginning to assert that only the systematic building of relevant cognitive and evaluative maps in the various contexts of art instruction is likely to develop aesthetic sensibility and to promote the habits and dispositions necessary to counteract the purely emotional appeals made to the individual in a modern mass democracy. Another way of saying this is that unless the pupil through art education fortifies himself with basic aesthetic disciplines,[9] he will be unprepared to judge invidious forms of propaganda, whether expressed in debased popular art or in the pointless posturings of the pseudo-avant-garde. Lest the foregoing sound too general, it will be helpful to indicate some ways in which the essays contained in this volume cast light on problems that have been neglected in art education.

Recent studies of classroom discourse reveal that the level of dialogue between teacher and pupil seldom exceeds that of common sense, with the result that opportunities to develop disciplined patterns of thought are left unexplored.[10] Research into classroom discourse about art is only beginning,[11] but personal observation and experience afford a similar conclusion. Now, since a work of art is a phenomenon that generates a plethora of puzzling questions, it is unfortunate to observe teachers and pupils failing to structure intelligently issues which frustrate efforts to understand the nature of art. Even college instruction is often deficient. Since the necessary knowledge and linguistic skills have not been acquired which would render problematic aspects of the concept of art more manageable, it is not surprising that high degrees of linguistic dissonance are recorded in art instruction. Accordingly, it is perhaps understandable that some variant of the remark — "People who try to explain pictures are usually barking up the wrong tree" — is often invoked to circumvent problems of language. Discourse about art is not unique, of course, in obeying the law of least cognitive strain, but remarks like the preceding (it is Picasso's) are meaningless out of context. Indeed, such utterances are more properly regarded as invitations to inquire into the "concept" of art itself, or the conditions under which we "explain" anything, including works of art. The following will make this point clearer.

Every generation or so, and lately in much shorter periods of time, some

---

[8]See B. Othanel Smith, "A Concept of Teaching," in B. Othanel Smith and Robert H. Ennis (eds.), *Language and Concepts in Education* (Chicago: Rand McNally & Co., 1961). See, also, Smith's essay, this volume.

[9]For a conception of art, or the discipline of aesthetic form, as (a) the discipline of aesthetic confrontation, (b) the discipline of aesthetic construction, and (c) the discipline of aesthetic criticism, see Solon T. Kimball and James E. McClellan, Jr., *Education and the New America* (New York: Random House, 1962), pp. 301-3.

[10]Smith, *op. cit.*

[11]Robert D. Clements, "Art Student-Teacher Questioning," *Studies in Art Education,* Vol. VI, No. 1 (Autumn 1964).

form of the question "What is _____ art?" arises in the classroom. The question most heard recently, of course, is "What is 'op' art?" How do teachers handle this query? Is the pupil simply told the meaning of the terms contained in the question? That is to say, is op art given some sort of definition? If so, then what kind? Definitions may take a variety of forms. Or does the teacher give an account of events and forces which were responsible for bringing about op art? That is, does the teacher respond by giving a historical explanation? Or still further, does the teacher explain a given work of op art by seeing it as an "instance" of a general theory? Or is the question brushed aside with a value judgment that asserts op art is not really art at all, or at least not good art? If this is the case, then what kinds of reasons are given in support of the judgment? The range of possibilities, of course, could be expanded, and it requires little imagination to envisage the interest that might be generated in a properly conducted classroom discussion. Whether the pedagogical potential of such questions is appreciated and exploited will depend on whether the teacher seizes opportunities to help the pupil with logical problems involved in understanding the structure of concepts in general and the structure of the concept of art in particular.

Morris Weitz, in an essay reprinted in this volume, indicates that whether a particular object should be experienced as a work of art always requires a decision on our part, that the question is, in other words, a *decision* question and not a *factual* one. To understand this is to realize that the structure of the concept of art is fundamentally different from the structure of concepts representing such things as books and chairs. But confusion has often resulted from treating the concept of art as if, logically, it were of the same stripe as concepts symbolizing ordinary objects. This matter is clarified in different essays in this volume, and hence it is not necessary to say more here. It is enough to note that the handling of such questions involves a special strategy on the part of the teacher and pupil, a strategy that derives from a proper understanding of the uses of language. It should also be pointed out that dealing effectively with the question "Is X a work of art?" requires that for the moment both teacher and pupil function more as critical reflective beholders than as creative artists. And therein lies at least one limitation of the analogies indicated by the creative metaphor in art education.[12]

It is seen that the teaching of art involves, as do other realms of instruction,

---

[12]For an analysis of educational statements containing definitions, slogans, and metaphors, see Israel Scheffler, *The Language of Education* (Springfield, Ill.: Charles C. Thomas, 1960); and B. Paul Komisar and James E. McClellan, "The Logic of Slogans," in B. Othanel Smith and Robert H. Ennis, *op. cit.* For some remarks on slogans and metaphors in art education discourse, see Ralph A. Smith, "Art Education: Criticism," *Art Education*, Vol. XII, No. 2 (February 1964), and "Images of Art Education," *Studies in Art Education*, Vol. VII, No. 1 (Autumn 1965). David W. Ecker has analyzed educational slogans in "Some Inadequate Doctrines in Art Education and a Proposed Resolution," *Studies in Art Education*, Vol. V, No. 2 (Spring 1963).

the intelligent use of language which in turn entails a careful scrutiny of statements. This kind of behavior—also a form of "activity" or "doing"— suggests that there are important verbal as well as nonverbal learning contexts in art education. And it is not to be expected that the necessary skills will be cultivated without significant changes in the structure of both attitudes and content in the preparation of art teachers.

In addition to having a significant linguistic aspect, the teaching of art turns out to be a multidimensional enterprise in which much more is at issue than having pupils emulate artistic behavior. The renewed emphasis on self-cultivation and connoisseurship particularly means devoting more attention to the nature of what has been called enlightened preference and justification.[13] New objectives for art instruction further stimulate questions about the meaning of aesthetic insight or ways of "knowing" other than scientific knowing.[14]

Finally, new objectives call for inquiries into the relation of language and the verbalization of concepts and standards to the apprehension of nondiscursive forms of expression and communication. Now so long as pedagogical assessment looks toward the evaluation of interior feeling states, the pupil, at least on theoretical grounds, is not required to regard things discerningly at all. Nor is he expected to give an explanation of a work's merit in terms of a critical theory. But it should be obvious that knowing how to defend aesthetic judgments is a radically different affair than merely allowing art to elicit personal feeling responses. It is not that imaginative constructive activities or affective feeling responses are unimportant. All that is being said is that backing up an aesthetic evaluation has distinctive linguistic aspects and that art instruction should be cognizant of them. At this point another example will give concreteness to the substance of the discussion.

As previously noted, studies of classroom discourse reveal a low level of competence in the logical manipulation of content. It was also discovered that only a small percentage of instruction is devoted to value questions which characteristically arise in the appreciative area of learning. Now, it is pointed out that the proper handling of such questions requires an understanding of valuative concepts. A valuative concept is one which expresses a person's attitudes and preferences toward objects, qualities, events, or experiences. That is to say, a valuative concept is used in an individual's rating of things as opposed to his naming, describing, or explaining them. A typical act of evaluation consists of (1) something to consider, (2) a set of criteria incorporating preferences, (3) facts which indicate that the criteria are relevant to the

---

[13]Harry S. Broudy, B. Othanel Smith, and Joe R. Burnett, *Democracy and Excellence in American Secondary Education* (Chicago: Rand McNally & Co., 1964), p. 215.
[14]For an interpretation of knowing and the object of knowledge in aesthetic studies, see Philip H. Phenix, *Realms of Meaning* (New York: McGraw-Hill Book Co., Inc., 1964), p. 142. See, also, the essays by Broudy and Dworkin, this volume.

situation, and (4) a judgment.[15] Any given value judgment may not exhibit this order, but an illustration will indicate the need to understand the logic of evaluation.

Consider the case of Brown who reports that his pupils have made some interesting designs, implying by "interesting" that the designs in question are "good." Upon being asked why the designs are interesting, Brown replies, "Well, they please me." In the language of aesthetics Brown has given what, in this volume, Monroe C. Beardsley calls an *affective* reason in support of his evaluation. An affective reason is one that refers to the peculiar feeling responses evoked in a viewer by an art object, as opposed to a *genetic* reason, which refers to antecedent conditions of a given work, or an *objective* reason which refers to properties of the product itself. Brown no doubt could have been helped to understand, or perhaps helped to recall from his instruction, that while affective responses are part of any evaluation, they do not provide a good basis for ascribing merit. If only affective responses were to be encouraged, then perceptiveness with regard to the qualities of works of art would not be developed to any great degree. A pedagogically more relevant reply by Brown, given, that is, certain assumptions about the proper mode of judgment relevant to works of art, would have involved asserting *objective* reasons, and, in addition, stating facts, rules, or principles by which the value of the designs was decided. Now formulating objective reasons and asserting rules and principles are *logical* rather than *psychological* actions. We might also say that Brown's response exemplified the *attitudinal* but not the *theoretical* or justifying component of evaluation.[16] Since pupils can hardly be expected to master the logic of evaluation if teachers themselves are not alert to the issues, the implications for teacher education, once again, should be obvious.

To summarize: The present state of thinking in art education shows increasing concern for (1) the key topics and important ideas comprising art instruction, and (2) the logical operations by means of which ideas are manipulated. At the same time thinkers in the field are trying to identify the relations of art education to neighboring disciplines of thought and action. The unity of this volume derives from these efforts. The reason for presenting essays by outstanding authorities in philosophy of education, art history, aesthetics, and criticism is to provide models of scholarship from these various disciplines. Readers are invited to consider whether the strategies used by these thinkers can be translated into procedures for teaching art in the classroom. While these exemplars of scholarship exhibit a variety of concerns, readers are encouraged to examine the special ways in which the problems of defining, explaining, and evaluating works of art are explored.

---

[15]Broudy, *et. al., op. cit.,* p.215.
[16]*Ibid.,* p. 147.

In conclusion, a few words are in order about how this volume may be used. It is designed primarily as supplementary reading material for courses in elementary and secondary art education at both the undergraduate and graduate levels.[17] Art teachers in the schools may also find the volume helpful in dealing with those questions which inevitably arise in instruction and which are predominantly linguistic and logical in nature. Secondary school teachers in humanities programs may turn to the essays for assistance in clarifying many of the theoretical problems that occur in integrated arts approaches. The writings could also help the curriculum designer in making decisions concerning the selection of content. It should be evident, however, that this volume is not an introduction to aesthetics, philosophy of art, or art history. This is not to say that the essays could not be used profitably in the college introductory art course where matters of definition, explanation, and evaluation are not always dealt with in a manner satisfactory to either instructor or student. Finally, it should be noted that the section devoted to film is intended to be illustrative of an area of specific application for the operations of defining, explaining, and evaluating art.

It is with pleasure that I express my gratitude first of all to Professor B. Othanel Smith of the University of Illinois who initially supported the idea for this volume. Without his encouragement I should have had more reservations about undertaking an anthology of this kind. I am also happy to acknowledge my indebtedness to Professor Harry S. Broudy, also of the University of Illinois, whose writings and lectures have stimulated my interest in the relation of aesthetic theory to problems of art instruction. A special note of thanks is further due to the members of the Rand McNally College Department for their courteous assistance, and to Ray Perlman of the University of Illinois Graphic Design Department who designed the text. The many authors who kindly gave permission to reprint their works have, of course, made this volume possible, and to them and their publishers I am most deeply indebted.

R. A. S.

---

[17]To those who might claim that the readings in this volume are either irrelevant or too advanced for elementary school majors, it may be pointed out that they are no less difficult or irrelevant than are readings in physical theory for the elementary teacher who must teach science. Just as the elementary teacher needs physical theory to teach science concepts in a rudimentary form, so aesthetic theory is needed to make sense out of what goes on in the art unit.

CONTENTS

I. AESTHETICS AND LANGUAGE IN ART EDUCATION

II. THE PROBLEM OF DEFINITION

III. THE PROBLEM OF EXPLANATION

IV. THE PROBLEM OF DEFINING, EXPLAINING, AND EVALUATING NEW MEDIA: FILM

Appendix IV

Robert Gessner

I

AESTHETICS AND LANGUAGE

IN ART EDUCATION

Introduction

Philosophers do not agree on the proper business of aesthetics. As an area of special investigation, aesthetics has been variously defined as the theory of sentient knowledge, as general philosophical inquiry into the arts, and, more recently, as the philosophy of criticism, that is, the discipline devoted to the scrutiny of critical statements made about works of art. To the teacher and student of art this lack of consensus might seem to constitute grounds for skepticism regarding the usefulness of aesthetic inquiries as a source of knowledge for art instruction. The reality of the disputes notwithstanding, it is F. E. Sparshott's contention that a pattern can be discerned in the efforts of thinkers even of divergent philosophical persuasions. This unity of aesthetics, it is claimed, derives from a study of four interdependently related questions: (1) the meaning and viability of the concept of art, (2) the function of art, (3) the character and language of aesthetic judgments, and (4) the proper method of analysis of works of art.[1]

In "The Case for Aesthetics," reprinted as the first selection of this volume, Sparshott indicates that neither the art historian nor the critic can avoid asking these questions and that often the artist feels prompted to deal with them in his written comments. Indeed, says Sparshott, "One cannot describe a work of art without showing what one thinks important in it." And hence "even a description presupposes a system of evaluation, and such a system when articulated and defended is an aesthetic theory."[2] Reflection will reveal not only the logic of this assertion but also its pedagogical import. For it should become clear that

---

[1]F. E. Sparshott, *The Structure of Aesthetics* (Toronto: University of Toronto Press, 1963), p. 434.

[2]Many philosophers, of course, are concerned to make the same point. Thus Harold Osborne writes that "A theory of the nature of artistic excellence is implicit in every critical assertion which is other than autobiographical record and until the theory has been made explicit the criticism is without meaning" (*Aesthetics and Criticism* [London: Routledge and Kegan Paul, Ltd., 1955], p. 3). It may also be noted that in view of the dominant theme pervading the present volume of writings the quotation from Lucian in Osborne's work (p. 5) is felicitous; that is, "A work of art requires an intelligent spectator who must go beyond the pleasure of his eyes to express a judgement and to argue the reasons for what he sees." Finally, Donald W. Arnstine, in a discussion about ideas for research in art education, writes that "If one is not prepared to say what he thinks art is, he could have no idea of what to look for when he inquires into art education. For without some definitions, how shall one recognize what he is looking for?" ("Needed Research and the Role of Definitions in Art Education," *Studies in Art Education*, Vol. VII, No. 1 [Autumn 1965], p. 7.)

if art historian and art critic can ill afford to neglect aesthetic theory, neither can the teacher or student of art. The teacher's judgment on matters such as the concept and function of art, as well as on the proper mode of analysis and evaluation relevant to art objects, will determine what can be said and thus taught about art, a point underlined in the second essay of this section.

In "The Structure of Knowledge in the Arts," for example, Harry S. Broudy remarks that if it is thought that works of art do *not* communicate anything significant, then this belief certainly will influence the character of a curricular justification. But it is Broudy's argument that some works of art do say something, and often something important. The problem lies in what is said and how communication is accomplished.

Broudy first points out that there is no disputing the presence of some types of knowledge in art study. We may speak of the artist's knowledge of his subject matter, knowledge of techniques, and historical knowledge about art. But the difficulty resides in the nature of aesthetic experience and in what is thought to be disclosed or revealed through it. According to Broudy, genuine aesthetic experience has three major characteristics. The first is that aesthetic experience involves instances of perception rather than distinctively discursive reasoning or memory. The second is that the qualities of sensory elements and formal relations are attended to and enjoyed for their own sake and not as clues to practical action. Third, aesthetic experience has an interpretive phase in which perceived qualities and relationships organize into the representation of feelings, emotions, ideas, or some combination of these. These images of feeling or thought are not literal resemblances to things outside the work of art, but are meanings present within it, which is to say such meanings are ultimately traceable to the work's sensory, formal, and expressive aspects. Just how these meanings are communicated is not well understood, but Broudy subscribes to the possibility that in the interpretive phase of aesthetic experience communication occurs by virtue of imaginative schemata. These schemata are root metaphors which either by nature or nurture are shared by the members of a culture. Through such archetypal images art conveys important information about life which cannot be expressed in discursive language. It should be noted that Broudy does not claim to have established the cognitive status of aesthetic experience. Rather he stresses the "similarities between the creative attitude, the ground rules for the aesthetic experience, and an ideal of knowledge in which formal identity between the knower and the known is achieved." That is to say, "the descriptions given of the aesthetic experience, both in appreciation and creation, have a structural affinity with the classical paradigm for knowing." In brief, Broudy holds that as objects of perception works of art persistently manifest meanings by presenting an image of an idea or feeling or some combination of these. Such meanings, while not statements or assertions themselves, are capable of providing clues from which inferences that are assertions can be made.

The remainder of the essay is devoted to elucidating the nature of art theory and criticism and to discussing the issues attending the inclusion of art study in the program of general education. It is worth remarking that the significance of Broudy's analysis is not completely dependent on its interpretation of knowing. Its value lies in its systematic articulation of the *problem* of knowledge in the arts, and for this reason it is accorded a strategic position in this volume.

Another important essay is B. Othanel Smith's "The Logic of Teaching in the Arts." If Broudy clarifies the nature of content in art education, Smith explains what it means to manipulate this content through the use of characteristic logical operations.

Teaching, says Smith, is describable in terms of what teachers do and not in terms of prescriptions supplied by philosophy and psychology, historically the major sources of teaching directives. Smith's essay is indicative of a new look at teaching from the point of view of the logic of teaching. When teaching is observed and studied, it is discovered that it consists primarily of the teacher (a) showing how to do something, and (b) telling or saying something, with the latter carrying the heavier pedagogical burden. In examining teaching in terms of verbal behavior, Smith and his associates distinguished three major types of language actions: directive, admonitory, and logical. Included in logical language actions are twelve distinct operations: defining, describing, designating, stating, reporting, substituting, valuating, opining, classifying, comparing and contrasting, conditional inferring, and explaining. Since teaching performance consists largely of the manipulation of subject matter, Smith concludes that to increase the teacher's effectiveness in performing logical operations is directly to improve teaching.

The relevance of these logical operations to art instruction may be seen in the handling of appreciation questions. Smith distinguishes between *appreciation* and *liking*. To appreciate a work of art is not only to make a decision about the work's value but also to give evidence in support of one's judgment. This requires, as remarked in the Preface, the stating of facts and rules or principles. Otherwise statements containing value judgments cannot be defended or justified. Appreciation, in other words, has a logical character. On the other hand, no one is required to give reasons for merely liking or enjoying. Liking is a personal and psychological affair. Once again, the fact that Smith emphasizes the cognitive aspects of art instruction, as does this whole volume, does not imply that the creative, imaginative dimensions of teaching and learning art are unimportant. But it is difficult to escape the conclusion that intellectual understanding and knowledge about art often make a marked difference in the improvement of taste, and that a sufficient degree of rational understanding seems prerequisite to significant participation in a work's qualities. And as Smith points out, there is no evidence that the intellectual processes drive out the emotions.

Finally, Edmund B. Feldman in "Research as the Verification of Aesthetics," notes the failure of art educators to exploit the realm of aesthetics as a source of hypotheses for guiding art practice in the classroom. Distinguishing the speculative discipline of aesthetics, or disinterested analysis and comprehension, from the normative and practical domain of art education, Feldman urges teachers to realize that often their instruction is influenced by unarticulated assumptions about the nature of art. He thus asks for an understanding of how plans, motives, and goals for teaching art may be clarified by appealing to the insights of aesthetics.

The four essays in this opening section set the basic tone and theme for the anthology, that is, the nature of content and its uses. Subsequent sections deal specifically with the issues of defining, explaining, and evaluating art, three of the most important operations of art instruction.

The Case for Aesthetics

F. E. SPARSHOTT

*　　*　　*

The general complaint of the cultivated man, that aesthetics should not be attempted because it must consist of generalizations about art, whereas works of art are unique so that one cannot generalize about them, is self-refuting: the statement that each work of art is unique is itself a generalization about art, and the explanation of the sense in which each work was unique and why its uniqueness was such as to preclude further generalizations would constitute a theory of aesthetics (cf. Meager 1958). The kindred complaint of the tender-stomached reader that aesthetics makes dull work of the thrilling business of art stems from simple confusion, and was met by Reid (1785, 721): "A philosophical analysis of the objects of taste is like applying the anatomical knife to a fine face. The design of the philosopher, as well as of the anatomist, is not to gratify taste, but to improve knowledge."[3] Indeed, as DeWitt Parker

From F. E. Sparshott, *The Structure of Aesthetics* (Toronto: University of Toronto Press, 1963), pp. 10-25. Reprinted by permission of the author and the University of Toronto Press.
[3]Cf. Frye (1957, 29): "The strong emotional repugnance felt by many critics toward any form of schematization in poetics is again the result of a failure to distinguish criticism as a body of knowledge from the direct experience of literature, where every act is unique, and classification has no place." Note that it is one thing to attribute uniqueness and unclassifiability to experiences (though even here one does not quite see what is meant and feels inclined to say that "uniqueness" need not be alleged, since classification is inappropriate rather than impossible) and quite another to attribute them to works of art.

observed (1920, 129-30), although one cannot be simultaneously rapt and critical, any aesthetic rapture is likely to arise from the spontaneous exercise of a trained judgement, critical standards, and knowledge painfully acquired.

Critics and historians of art despise aesthetics at their peril, for their task requires of them some general theory of art. If they refuse to acknowledge this, and hence to think out the presuppositions of what they are doing, they are likely to adopt quite uncritically (even unconsciously) an aesthetic theory of extraordinary naivety, as undeliberately as they would catch a cold, and alternately appeal to it as final arbiter and ignore it completely, as the fancy takes them. Thus the great Bernard Berenson, who complains (1950, 25) of the remoteness of aesthetics from experience, and feels it necessary to apologize (1896, 41) for "seeming to wander off into the boundless domain of aesthetics," commits himself to a peculiarly simple-minded version of the theory of empathy (e.g. 1896, 40) and uses it to justify his condemnation of styles which his sensibility leads him to dislike (1950, 58). On a lower level is Mrs. Margaret Hattersley Bulley, whose loud contempt for aesthetic theories is combined with a wholehearted commitment to at least the terminology of R. G. Collingwood, of which she does not acknowledge and perhaps does not recognize the source, and which she embellishes with some claptrap of her own. Presumably she regards the result not as inchoate aesthetic theory but as self-evident truth (Bulley 1952, *passim*).

Critics may not need elaborated theories about art, but they must make theoretical assumptions in their work. People sometimes speak as if a critic were a man who went around saying "This is good," "This is bad," "I like this," and "I don't like that." And it is true that, etymologically, a critic's function is to give verdicts. It is also true that the book reviews and film reviews in most daily papers are meant and used to save people the trouble of deciding what to read or see. But etymology is not a safe guide to reality; nor are the daily papers. In reality, any critic nowadays held worthy of the name describes what he criticizes and says what it is that in his judgement makes one work better than another. Indeed, evaluation is most effective when it flows naturally out of description and analysis. So Professor Richards writes (1929, 11):

There is, it is true, a valuation side to criticism. When we have solved, completely, the communication problem, when we have got, perfectly, the experience, the mental condition relevant to the poem, we have still to judge it, still to decide upon its worth. But the later question nearly always settles itself; or rather, our own inmost nature and the nature of the world in which we live decide it for us.

In fact, the final assertion of merit or demerit may not be made or even implied, any more than after reading a book one has to decide whether one liked it or not, except in so far as the labour spent is itself a token of esteem for the work on which it is lavished.[4] Even if a critic were to confine himself to saying what was good or bad, these assertions would be pointless unless they were based on some principle of judgement. If the critic had no other criterion than the likes and dislikes he found himself happening to have, his use of them as criteria would show that he had a theory about art: the theory that no artistic standards were in principle capable of formulation. And this is a debatable proposition. More precisely, the practice of calling "good" without amplification whatever happened to please the critic, and still more the shoddy habit of saying "Your reviewer liked this" and leaving it at that, imply one theory if the critic ascribes the importance of his judgements to his innate superiority (cf. Hutcheson 1725), and a different theory if he ascribes it to his experience and training (cf. Reynolds 1776). For in either case the fact that he prints or otherwise circulates his opinions shows that he thinks them important, and he must presumably believe that he has some ground for thinking them so.[5] Even if his justification for promulgating his preferences is not that his taste or training is superior but that he is so ordinary that what he likes other ordinary people will like too, his reliance on this justification shows adherence to a theory of the nature and function of art – perhaps that of Tolstoy (1898) or that of Mr. Shaw (1956).

It might seem that a critic could avoid the necessity for theoretical presuppositions by confining himself to an estimation of the artist's success in achieving whatever end he may have set himself. But this is not so. In attempting such estimation a critic shows what he considers to be possible ends for an artist to envisage, and this is no light matter. Then the critic is himself responsible for the decision that the work he is considering must be related to certain of these possible ends and not to others. For he is not likely to have the artist at his elbow to tell him what he was after; and if he had, the artist would probably be unable to formulate in any helpful way the ends that he was pursuing; and if the artist were able, he would probably be unwilling; and if the artist were able and willing, the critic would probably not believe him.

Can a critic then shed his theoretical load by just describing the work before him? No. One cannot describe a work of art without showing what one thinks important in it. Thus even a description presupposes a system of evaluation, and such a system when articulated and defended is an aesthetic theory. One can describe a painting as portraying three darling little kittens in an old boot; or one can describe it as forming a system of intersecting cones. Similarly, in

---

[4]The extreme form of this use of the term appears in Professor Frye's definition of criticism as "the whole work of scholarship and taste concerned with literature which is a part of what is variously called liberal education, culture, or the study of the humanities" (Frye 1957, 3). It's a question of who is to be master, that's all.

[5]This does not, of course, apply to those who are not responsible for bringing their own judgements into prominence – not, for example, to reporters told off by their editors to "do" the Royal Academy. But I see no need to take account of those who disclaim responsibility for their own actions.

music, one can describe a passage from a symphony in terms of feelings, like this, which is from an anonymous commentary on Tchaikovsky's Fifth Symphony: "A bassoon, its voice issuing from the cavernous depths of its lower register, starts us off on our journey of frustration and pain." Or one can represent it as a conflict between personified musical forces, as Vaughan Williams did in the famous programme note he wrote for the first performance of his Sixth: "When the episode is over the woodwind experiment as to how the fugue subject will sound upside down but the brass are angry and insist on playing it the right way up, so for a bit the two go on together and to the delight of everyone including the composer the two versions fit. . . ." Or one can get right down to business like this (Larsen 1956, 195, on Mozart's "Jupiter"): "The first subject and the transition are linked together as follows: the first subject ends with a striking half-close which suggests a first half-period; the transition begins (bar 24) as a second half-period, but then glides into modulating sequences, in preparation for the dominant." Whether all, or some, or none of these ways of describing are appropriate depends on what kind of a business music is.

It seems then that critical activities of all kinds presuppose theories, in the sense that they are reasonable things to do only if certain theories are true. A critic may be too busy, or lazy, or stupid, to find out what these presupposed theories are; but that is no reason for him to despise those who are prepared to take the trouble.

Historians are related to aesthetics in much the same way as critics are. In elaborating this remark I hope I shall be forgiven if I state the obvious: objectors to aesthetics often presume the untruth of the obvious. Just as history in general must always be written in the light of some social or political philosophy, however little thought the historian may have given to it (cf. Geyl 1955), so art history is necessarily always written as if its author held some theory of the nature of art, however rudimentary that theory might be. For history cannot be the mere discovery and recording of facts: the facts must be selected and ordered, and that selection and ordering must proceed on some principles (cf. Wellek and Warren 1949, 28). At the very lowest level, the art historian must within his chosen period follow some sequence. Is this to be the chronological order of individual works? Or that of artists? Or is he to deal with artists by schools, or to take the school itself as a unit? And if the latter, should he take the schools chronologically or in some other order? Even if the choice of one of these seems to the historian a mere matter of convenience, or to be determined by the nature of the material, each possibility corresponds to a different notion of what art is, as is shown by those works (e.g. Malraux 1953) which deliberately make a selection of sequence their principal means of promoting a theory.

Aesthetic problems are more obviously raised by questions of selection and emphasis. Is one to stress what seemed important in its own day, or what seems so now? Is one to support a history of the visual arts by references to contemporary literature, or include in a history of the fine arts a survey of humbler artefacts, or not? Once more, each decision would correspond to an arguable, and argued, theory of the nature of art.

Questions of principle are more notoriously involved in the decision whether to include in a history of art mention of social and economic developments; and, if so, which, and with what emphasis. A comparison of Antal's (1948) treatment of Florentine painting after the Black Death with Meiss's (1951) reply to it, and of both with Berenson's account of the same artists (1896, §§ II and III), will show that this is not a matter of greater or less ignorance of fact, but of what is considered *a priori* to be possibly relevant. Here as elsewhere history has to do with change, change in the behaviour of human beings. As Panofsky points out (1955, 20-1), the historian's account will reflect his judgement of what kinds of motivation might lead to such changes, what reasons there might be for the human decisions they reflect.

It must describe the stylistic peculiarities . . . as that which bears witness to artistic "intentions". Now "intentions" can only be formulated in terms of alternatives. . . . Thus it appears that the terms used by the art historian interpret the stylistic peculiarities of the works as specific solutions of generic "artistic problems" . . . . Upon reflection it will turn out that there is a limited number of such primary problems. . . .

Panofsky seems to imply that all historians and theorists will be forced by the facts to agree as to what these "primary problems" are; but if he really thinks that, he is an optimist.[6]

Different ways of answering such questions as these are implicit in different ways of writing the history of art, whether the questions are openly faced or burked.[7] And one is inclined to feel that questions are better faced than burked. To say this is not to suggest that art historians should do aesthetics, or devote

---

[6]Professor Frye makes an analogous supposition about criticism. The evident coherence of and progress in the study of literature are explicable only on the assumption that there is "a coherent and comprehensive theory of literature, logically and scientifically organized, some of which the student learns as he goes on, but the main principles of which are as yet unknown to us" (Frye, 1957, 11). In both Panofsky and Frye this postulation of a grand undiscovered theory rests on the demand that the studies they profess should be recognized as objective and be accorded the status of science, the hallmark of which they take to be a coherent systematic structure.

[7]Take for example Professor Brieger's history of English art in the thirteenth century. He analyses the art of the period into three phases, corresponding to changes of style; these changes he attributes to social changes in the patronage of art. He also discerns three successive modes of sensibility: aspiration, display, and a *fin-de-siécle* elaboration and melancholy. No precise account is given of why or how this succession of modes occurs, nor is it correlated with the sequence of patron-dependent styles, but it is ascribed generally to a change in the atmosphere of the period. Within this general pattern, local traditions and fashions of symbolism are recognized. Throughout, material is selected on the basis of originality, so that the history becomes one of the *development* of art, not a mere chronicle of practice; and the author passes judgement in terms of a formal aesthetic, taken as absolute, whereby some designs are praised and others condemned on the basis of their proportions and disposition of masses. (Brieger 1957, esp. 271 ff.)

more than a moment's thought to its problems; only that they should recognize that the problems exist and are relevant to what they themselves are doing. For none of the arguments I have used show that aesthetics has any substance. They show only that it has authentic problems. It remains quite possible that discussion of these problems should be futile, either because the answers are too easy or because there is no way of agreeing on what constitutes a good reason in aesthetics, so that one can never progress beyond expressions of conflicting opinion. That fruitful discussion is possible can only be shown by discussing fruitfully. All I claim to have shown is that the attempt is worth making.

Aesthetics is probably not necessary to the artist as it is to the critic and the historian; but at least it is innocuous. We are apt to think of the artist as being pestered by aesthetics and pleading to be left alone to get on with the job. But this is silly. The subject may not help him, but it will not bite him; if he finds a book irritating or disturbing or uninteresting, he can put it down. One has heard it said that artists have been led astray by reading bad aesthetics. I doubt it; I should suspect that anyone feeble enough to be thus corrupted had the seeds of his corruption in him anyway; but if it is indeed so, it would presumably be equally possible for an artist to be put on the right track by reading good aesthetics, were such written.[8] The alternative is to suppose that it is bad for artists to reflect at all upon what they are doing, that the true artist's mind is all in his hands and he should think only *in* his painting, not *about* it. That seems hard to believe. Innovating artists are great ones for manifestos; the renaissance painters were energetic theorists. Sir John Rothenstein indeed maintains that the reason why Steer and Orpen, to name but two, painted less well than they should is that they preferred not to think (Rothenstein 1952, 73 and 221-2). However, it is possible that the kind of intellectual work that painting involves has no connection with the discursive reasoning of art theory; indeed, it is widely believed. And I suppose it is possible that, as some people seem to be suggesting, artists are all so sick or immature that the equilibrium of their working minds can be upset by nasty theories, and they are too innocent to realize this; but to me it seems unlikely. If it is true, it is plainly the duty of aestheticians to mark their books clearly "To be kept out of the reach of artists."[9]

The objection that art theories are so unlike what artists say about their own

---

[8] Professor Arnheim (1933, 14) asserts confidently that "The postulates, reasonable or otherwise, of art-theorists have always had more influence on the work of the creative artist than is generally conceded. The views taken in various ages of the functions of art have always had their immediate effect on the works of art of that period." Can one be sure that these theories were not reflections of incipient practical tendencies? Perhaps not. But it seems likely that such tendencies may be encouraged by articulate verbal formulation and hampered by lack of it.

[9] There is a full discussion of whether artists ought to be exposed to aesthetics, and to what kind if to any, in Munro (1956, 302-23).

work and experience that they are unworthy of consideration is untenable: art theories produced by artists, which abound (cf. Goldwater and Treves 1945), have no common qualities that distinguish them from theories of others.[10] Such protests of irrelevance must then not be directed in the name of the artist's experience as such against those who lack this experience, but equally against the reflections of other artists on their own experience. One might actually say that most writers on aesthetics have known too much about the arts and liked them too well: they tend to have privileged ways of describing their own intense reactions, stylistic axes to grind, canons of excellence to which they would have all art conform. Confident in their taste and knowledge, they do not take seriously the fact that others have other tastes and know other things.

The implication of the objections to aesthetics made by artists, or more usually made by sentimentalists on their behalf, is that if aesthetics is irrelevant to the artist's practical problems it cannot be worthy of attention. But of course these are not the problems it tackles. Art is a public affair: even if the artist can or even should work as for himself alone, his public has its own interests.

The objections to aesthetics raised by philosophers were mostly stated in such a way as to suggest the answers to them; but the answers had better be made explicit.

In so far as contempt for aesthetics is the product of a mere change in generations, it should be ignored. The fact that people are not doing something does not prove that they should not be doing it. Ignoring problems — and we have already seen that aesthetics at least has problems — does not solve them. If one could be certain that no one would ever raise such problems again, one could reasonably ignore them, on the plea of having better things to do. But we do not have this certainty. On the contrary, we can be sure that they will go on being discussed, since they are directly raised by continuing activities. The

---

[10]Professor Gilson writes (1957, 214): "What philosophers can say about art is too abstract to fit the subject . . . what they say is not art, it is philosophy." The latter statement is of course true. But it supports the former only on the supposition that one ought to say nothing about art at all, except (if I understand Gilson) about methods of production. Gilson appears to be maintaining three positions. First, that when artists discuss painting they always discuss methods of painting and never the subjects or merits of completed paintings (cf. *ibid.*, 216); painters who describe the subjects of paintings (*ibid.*, 224 n.) are presumably not painters but philosophers in false beards. Second, that if philosophers discuss other aspects of paintings it is because of their "inveterate mentalism" (*ibid.*, 34 n.), and not because there may be a legitimate interest in the thing made as opposed to the manner of its making. Third, that paintings cannot be described because in their concreteness they evade verbal abstractions (*ibid.*, 214, 224). But, as Professor Arnheim observes (1954, vi), language is no more limited in dealing with art than in dealing with any other object of experience: it cannot duplicate what it describes, but that is not its function. "If we see and feel certain qualities in a work of art yet cannot describe or explain them, the reason for our failure is not that we use words but that our eyes and thoughts do not succeed in discovering generalities able to do the job. Language . . . is not a foreign medium, unsuitable for visible things. It fails us when and because visual analysis breaks down. But fortunately visual analysis can go far and can also call forth the potential capacity to 'see', by which we reach the unanalyzable."

question is only whether they will be discussed sensibly or foolishly, and whether philosophers will be among those discussing.

Objections to aesthetics on the ground of its association with romantic and existentialist thought are less easily rebutted. These are the philosophies which are preoccupied with the nature of man and his place in the world's order. Philosophy with such preoccupations is indeed the most popular kind, the kind from which alone the general educated public claims to get stimulation, illumination and comfort; but the intellectually scrupulous claim that the illumination is hallucinatory, the comfort narcotic, the stimulation intoxicating. Such philosophies are disreputable in scholarly circles because of their arbitrariness, their reliance on a combination of rhetorical persuasiveness and appeals to the readers' or writer's intuitions. The renunciation of such writing, as its renouncers well know, may involve that of all that has usually been thought of as philosophy. But it is not the mere sourgraping of academic nobodies. Perhaps the knowledge and sophistication of our age are such that philosophers must choose between beating the big drum and saying what their knowledge and wisdom entitle them to say. If this is so, the standards to which philosophy has always purported to adhere dictate the latter choice. The abandoning of this territory by philosophy would not be fatal to aesthetics, since its problems are not tied to such grandiose projects. But it is only in the context of such "philosophies of man" that aesthetics has seemed worth spending much time on. For one may recognize that a problem exists and still not think it worth the solving. Perhaps, though, the philosophies of man have been too hastily dismissed: it seems likely that even the purest "linguistic" philosophies of our own day either stem from or are tending towards a view of man's nature.[11] And whenever such philosophies come back they are certain to bring aesthetics with them.

The attack on aesthetics as defiled by overmuch pitch-touching often goes with the attack on it for eluding the methods of analytic philosophy, the subject's non-existence being inferred from the unfruitfulness of such methods when applied to it. Taken in isolation, that unfruitfulness would not seem to reflect more on aesthetics than on the methods. In any subject, to take limitations imposed by one's ways of proceeding as indicating the nature of what is under investigation is hazardous, though common. Philosophy above all must be preserved from methodological asphyxiation; for by common consent problems which elude the methods of other disciplines are left for philosophy to tackle. Philosophers can't be choosers. If they will not handle these residues, the result will be that all the elusive and interesting problems

---

[11]Dr. D. P. Gauthier has argued persuasively to this effect in a lecture on "Is the Revolution in Philosophy a Philosophy of Revolution?", delivered at University College, Toronto, in 1959. Cf. also Hampshire (1959, 234).

will be left to enlightened amateurs — among whom, indeed, the best philosophers have often in the past been found.

The complaint that aesthetics is dull whereas art is thrilling, and that the dullness is due to excessive generality, is not peculiarly philosophical, but it is often heard from philosophers, who tend to quote in its support authors who in fact turn out to be attacking not aesthetics as such but aesthetics badly done. Professor Passmore, in a well-known article on "The Dreariness of Aesthetics" (1951), ascribes the dreariness to an "attempt to impose a spurious unity on things" and conceal their incompatibilities (44), and in particular describes the use of the term "beauty" in aesthetics as "the refuge of the metaphysician finding a home for art in his harmonious universe, attempting to subdue its ferocity, its revelations of deep-seated conflict, its uncompromising disinterestedness, by ascribing to it a 'Beauty' somehow akin to goodness" (*ibid.,* 50). But how can this be taken as an attack on aesthetics as such? The general ascription of ferocity and disinterestedness to art is itself the germ of an aesthetic theory which would require extensive development and vindication. Passmore in turn ascribes the thesis that aesthetics is always dull to Professor Wisdom (1948). But Wisdom does not say that: what he says is that some books on art and some books on ethics are dull, and others are not; and concludes (1948, 211) that "it is possible to make in ethics or aesthetics remarks which are general and still not worthless. This happens when some value is temporarily undervalued or perhaps has always been undervalued." Apparently Passmore is using, and takes Wisdom to be using, "aesthetics" as a term of abuse: writing about art that is not dreary is for that very reason not to be called "aesthetics." It almost seems that he shares the assumption that Professor Hampshire (1952) apparently makes and Mr. Kennick (1958) certainly does, that aesthetics essentially consists of attempts to provide answers in one sentence to the question "What is art?"[12] Now, this is certainly the way aesthetic theories are often remembered, especially by those who know them only through histories or compendia; but it is not the way they are ever written. Whether or not Passmore shares this assumption, his argument certainly seems to rest on the belief that broad generalizations are always boring, and that to point out similarities is necessarily to suppress differences. This belief is widely shared, but seems odd on reflection. If a man says that a triangle is a three-sided rectilinear plane figure one does not censure him for being dull or for attempting to gloss over the interesting differences between triangles and "to impose a spurious unity on them." If generalizations in aesthetics neglect important distinctions, they do not differ in this from other generalizations to

---

[12]It is true that the particular statements which Passmore selects for ridicule do not have this character; but neither do they illustrate or support any of his general charges. The vigour of his remarks has perhaps distracted the attention of the philosophical world from the incoherence of his argument.

which no one objects. One is not deterred from saying that sufferers from migraine tend to dress neatly and prefer Bach to Brahms by the fact that one is thus neglecting important differences among the afflicted, for example that some are male and some female, and each is in fact an unique individual. If the charge means no more than that the likenesses are less striking than the differences, the answer must be that what seems noteworthy (and what seems dreary or boring) depends upon what one's interests at the moment happen to be, and that the ability to concentrate on differences often means only that likenesses have been taken for granted. Nor is it true, of course, that most works on aesthetics consist entirely of statements about all art. Many (e.g. Greene 1940, Langer 1953) are more notable for the distinctions they draw than for their statements of likeness.

The fact seems to be that there is in English academic circles a prejudice against aesthetics based on impermeable ignorance and naivety. So Professor Hampshire (1952) is able complacently to represent as an attack on aesthetics as such what is really an attack on Croce in the name of certain fashionable clichés about art whose truth and adequacy are taken for granted; and Father Turner, making the same equation of Croce with aesthetics, won great applause in the English weeklies for an article on "The Desolation of Aesthetics" (1958) which had the effect of reassuring the complacent that only topics made the subject of examinations at the Ancient Universities really exist.

The next philosophical objection to aesthetics, that the subject has no order, is stronger. But the impression of disorder arises largely because aesthetics, being quite rightly thought of as a marginal subject, is given only a small place (if any) in most courses of instruction, so that a knowledge of its bibliography and of the organization of its problems is not widely diffused among philosophers. No doubt more good ethics has been written than good aesthetics; but certainly as much rubbish has been written on ethics as on aesthetics. It is simply that in ethics the tripe is more widely recognized for what it is. As for the confusion of problems, the greater orderliness of the problems of ethics and other better-known philosophical disciplines may well be due to artificial simplification: classroom usage results, since all lecturers and tutors were once students, in a certain standardization of questions and answers which the subject-matter may not in fact warrant. There is less traffic in standard packages of pre-digested aesthetics.[13]

Aesthetics, thus unsimplified, seems to be a babel of arbitrary assertions and all-embracing disagreements. This is largely because so many different problems arise and can be approached in such various ways. Opinions that seem at first to contradict each other often turn out to be concerned with different

---

[13]The classification of theories used by Professor Rader in his justly famous textbook (1934) has passed into general use in America; but the basis of that classification is obscure, and the results of its adoption have not been happy.

problems or even different subject-matters, so that each might be reasonable in its own sphere. People who are talking about the same thing agree with each other to about the same extent, and in much the same ways, as other philosophers. Of the disagreements that remain, some are due to mere misunderstanding of terminology. The terms "expression" and "emotion" have given much trouble of this kind . . . Thus too when Mrs. Bulley (1952) uses "organic" as a term of abuse and Mrs. Langer (1953) as a term of praise, there is little at issue between them: Mrs. Bulley praises in other terms what Mrs. Langer calls "organic," and herself means by "organic" much what other people mean by "unrestrained." In so far as there is a real difference of opinion between the learned ladies, it is that they take different kinds and aspects of living things as typical.

Such disputes in aesthetics as cannot be resolved in these simple ways usually arise when one disputant excessively emphasizes what the other wrongly ignores. In such cases, both sides of the dispute are usually worthy of attention. No one bothers to set up a theory except to rebut a falsehood. And no falsehood is deemed worthy of such rebuttal if it is not felt to be a dangerous half-truth — dangerous because of the followers it may gain and thus prevent from seeing the other half of the truth, and half true because otherwise it could win no followers. The excessive emphasizing is a reaction to the ignoring, and generally takes the form of pretending that one fact about something is *the* fact about it. Such a pretence naturally has a perverse look. Thus Professor Frye observes (1957, 332) that "To say 'art communicates' is . . . to be content with an obvious plurality of functions: to say 'art is communication' forces us into circular wrangling around a metaphor taken as an assertion." But quite obviously there would be no point in making the milder, more acceptable statement if you were protesting against a doctrine that the artist need work for himself alone, that "eloquence is *heard*, poetry is *over*heard" (Mill 1833, 71). So the appearance of perversity often disappears when one recalls the dispute in the course of which a remark was made or a tract published. The literature of art theory, like philosophical and theological literature generally, is very largely polemical. But in aesthetics the polemics are often directed not so much against other theorists as against rival practitioners of the arts and their advocates, so that it is easy for a purely theoretical discussion to neglect them. Thus, for example, Véron (1878) is widely referred to as a proponent of the thesis that art is essentially the expression of emotion. But on reading his work one finds that it is an explicit and sustained attack on the notion that artists need to depend on "des recettes académiques," and appeared in a series of books designed to attack traditional authorities in the name of advanced ideas — and this in the context of French painting of the 1870's.

An extravagant general thesis may seem less strange when the circumstances of its origin are recalled, but that does not mean that it should never be considered out of its historical context. If one wishes to arrive at a whole truth there is much to be said for having two opposing half-truths forcibly argued. Perhaps, indeed, one should abandon oneself to each half in turn, as Professor Pepper argues (1938, 4-7): it is merely confusing to try to combine or reconcile positions which one has never fully grasped in their distinction. Professor Frye complains (1957, 19) that "there are no definite positions to be taken in chemistry or philology, and if there are any to be taken in criticism, criticism is not a field of genuine learning." But Professor Abrams rejoins (1953, 4-5) that criticism cannot in any case be scientific, since its aim is not the prediction but the ordering of experience; and, moreover, that since critical principles may affect practice a multiplicity in the former may guard against monotony in the latter. The criterion of the validity of a critical theory, he continues, "is not the scientific verifiability of its single propositions, but the scope, precision and coherence of the insights that it yields into the properties of single works of art and the adequacy with which it accounts for diverse kinds of art." Now, he goes on, there is no reason why there should not be several such theories, not necessarily mutually compatible; and any such theory may make one aware of aspects of art to which one was hitherto blind.

Ultimately, of course, mutually contradictory statements cannot both be maintained; either they must be reconciled, or one must be abandoned. Let our guide be Pascal (1670, I, §9):

When we wish to correct with advantage, and to show another that he errs, we must notice from what side he views the matter, for on that side it is usually true, and admit that truth to him, but reveal to him the side on which it is false. He is satisfied with that, for he sees that he was not mistaken, and that he only failed to see all sides. Now, no one is offended at not seeing everything; but one does not like to be mistaken, and that perhaps arises from the fact that man naturally cannot see everything, and that naturally he cannot err in the side he looks at, since the perceptions of our senses are always true.

Our task would be easier than it is if Pascal were right in supposing that people would readily admit failure to see all sides. As it is, we must be content if we can detect such failure in others. Meanwhile, those who press half-truths on each other do at least agree on what are the important problems. Thus, though there are conflicting views on the function of "psychical distance" or "self-identification" in drama, no one denies that the problem is important, and while there are different views as to the relation between "imitation" and "design" in the visual arts, and even whether the distinction between the two can meaningfully be made, no one supposes that it doesn't matter. In fact, from much reading in aesthetics a pattern emerges, though not a simple one. My chief purpose in this book is to articulate that pattern.

Aesthetics, it is claimed, is a recent and gratuitous addition to philosophy. But philosophical interest in art and beauty is by no means new, no newer than Plato. What is true is that it was not till the eighteenth century that the subject was given a name and its problems systematically examined. A good many problems assumed new forms at that time, and are usually thought to be all the better for it. And a great many things are nowadays given names of their own and treated systematically that used not to be. In every case but that of aesthetics, this is taken to be a sign of progress. But the mere fact that so many learned and in other respects intelligent philosophers have written what they and their readers took to be aesthetics does not prove that there really is such a subject any more than it is proved spurious by the still more recent tendency to scorn it. As for the gratuitousness of aesthetics, we have seen that its problems arise inevitably once the arts are chronicled and criticized. But it is quite arguable that the chronicling and criticizing are themselves undesirable activities, sustained ultimately by the greed of dealers. And even if the problems are inevitable, that would not prove that they cohered to form a separate field for investigation or speculation. Even at the end of this book, the viability of the subject will remain imperfectly established. Meanwhile, are there any general considerations that may make the undertaking seem *a priori* worthwhile?

As I have remarked elsewhere (Sparshott 1958, §2.1), if we accept the traditional division of human activities into thinking, doing and making—and it seems a reasonable enough division—aesthetics seems to arise as naturally out of reflection on making as ethics out of reflection on doing. Moreover, the problems of ethics have their counterparts in aesthetics. First, to the general consideration of man's nature as agent (Aristotle's main theme in his *Nicomachean Ethics*) corresponds the general consideration of man's nature as maker or creator. Second, to the issue of the balancing of freedom with law in morals corresponds the aesthetic problem of the respective places of originality and tradition. Third, to the basic division between the ethics of duty and the ethics of goodness corresponds the tension between the claims of function and the claims of pure form. To the various modes of relating judgements of moral goodness to other judgements of goodness, and of relating such goodness to goodness metaphysically conceived, correspond ways of relating "beauty" in art to "beauty" in nature or to a "transcendental" beauty. And in both fields there is a similar inquiry into the logical character of the judgements involved and into the meaning or use of characteristic terms. Professor Hampshire stigmatizes as "alexandrian" the supposition that there ought to be such a subject as aesthetics because a place can be found for it in an abstract scheme (1952). But we have seen that the problems of aesthetics are not, and historically they were not, called into being to fill a theoretical gap: indeed, the charge we thought we had to meet was that the problems were real enough but not systematically related. Both charges cannot be made to stick, for they are incompatible. Is it too much to hope that to have shown independently that there are problems and a place for them is to have refuted both? Hampshire also asserts, however (*ibid.*, 168-9), that ethics is necessary but aesthetics is not, because art is gratuitous but action is not. Moral principles must be formulated and defended to exclude intolerable actions, but intolerable works of art can just be ignored and no harm done. As I have said, this is undoubtedly the reason, and a perfectly valid one, for the comparative neglect of aesthetics. But it is only half true. For in fact nations and municipalities go to great trouble, and put their taxpayers to great expense, to support national theatres, art galleries, ballets, symphony orchestras and the like, in the belief that these activities are of public importance. Immediately, no doubt, the motive is often the enhancement of prestige through means that have become conventional. But what makes these activities prestigious? Whatever the answer may be, to treat the arts as gratuitous personal expressions of artistic egos is, as Tolstoy pointed out, ridiculously at odds with the nature of our artistic institutions.

If in one way aesthetics and its problems seem analogous to ethics, in another way there is an analogy between aesthetics and the philosophy of religion. Each takes its rise from an aspect of human activity which is so widespread as to be virtually universal, but for which no practical justification is obvious; and from a kind of experience in which many have thought to find the deepest significance. One might equally well be startled into reflection by the intensity of the experience or by the universality and diversity of the practice (cf. Farmer 1954, ch. I, and Sparshott 1961).

Artistic creation is a permanent activity of the human spirit and any comprehensive philosophical system must contain a theory of art and aesthetic, integrated into the system. . . . A permanent activity of the human spirit cannot be a matter of indifference to the philosopher. (Copleston 1946, 141.)

To those who do not think that philosophy ought to be systematic this will not seem important. But it remains true that every known people practices art of some form or other, and some civilizations, such as our own and the Chinese, place a very high value upon artistic activity. This fact in itself is surprising, and should arouse the wonder in which (it is said) philosophy begins. Even if we cannot appreciate the products of alien arts, we can usually recognize them as such. In thus "recognizing" works of art as such we may be imposing our own categories on the material. But if we are, this practice is itself indisputably a matter for philosophical inquiry: how is such imposition made possible? What is the meaning of this term "art"? Even if the specific problems suggested by the (discovered or invented) "universality" of art all demand the attention of sociologists and anthropologists rather than philosophers, the legitimacy of such an imputation of universality itself presents a problem of the only kind which no one has yet denied to be peculiarly philosophical.

As to the peculiar force of aesthetic experience, whether one wishes to make philosophical capital out of that will depend on the kind of philosophy one affects. Most may be willing to abandon consideration of such matters to psychologists. In so far, however, as we are interested not merely in the causes of certain effects in us but in our reasons for regarding experiences in certain ways, we must consider our interest to be philosophical.

19

All in all, then, there seem *a priori* to be good but not compelling reasons for taking aesthetics seriously as a study. Objections to doing so seem in the long run mostly to reduce to the romantic reluctance to subject one's raptures or their objects to intellectual scrutiny.

Works Cited

Abrams 1953. Abrams, M. H.: *The Mirror and the Lamp: Romantic Theory and the Critical Tradition* (1953). New York: Norton, 1958.

Antal 1947. Antal, Frederick: *Florentine Painting and its Social Background.* London: Kegan Paul, 1947.

Arnheim 1933. Arnheim, Rudolf: *Film*. London: Faber, 1933.

_____1954. *Art and Visual Perception*. Berkeley: University of California Press, 1954.

Berenson 1896. Berenson, Bernard: *The Florentine Painters of the Renaissance* (1896). In his *Italian Paintings of the Renaissance*. London: Phaidon Press, 1952.

_____1950. *Aesthetics and History*. London: Constable, 1950.

Brieger 1957. Brieger, Peter: *English Art 1216-1307*. Oxford: Clarendon Press, 1957.

Bulley 1952. Bulley, Margaret H.: *Art and Everyman*. Two volumes. London: Batsford, 1952.

Copelston 1946. Copelston, F. C.: *Arthur Schopenhauer, Philosopher of Pessimism*. London: Burns, Oates & Washbourne, 1946.

Elton 1954. Elton, William, ed.: *Aesthetics and Language*. Oxford: Blackwell, 1954.

Farmer 1954. Farmer, H. H.: *Revelation and Religion*. London: Nisbet, 1954.

Frye 1957. Frye, Northrup: *Anatomy of Criticism*. Princeton University Press, 1957.

Geyl 1955. Geyl, Pieter: *Use and Abuse of History*. New Haven: Yale University Press, 1955.

Gilson 1957. Gilson, Etienne: *Painting and Reality*. New York: Pantheon Books, 1957.

Goldwater and Treves 1945. Goldwater, Robert, and Treves, Marco, eds.: *Artists on Art*. New York: Pantheon Books, 1945.

Greene 1940. Greene, T. M.: *The Arts and the Art of Criticism*. Princeton: Princeton University Press, 1940.

Hampshire 1952. Hampshire, Stuart: "Logic and Appreciation" (1952). In Elton 1954.

———1959. *Thought and Action*. London: Chatto and Windus, 1959.

Hutcheson 1725. Hutcheson, Francis: *An Inquiry into the Original of our Ideas of Beauty and Virtue*. London, 1725.

Kennick 1958. Kennick, William E.: "Does Traditional Aesthetics Rest on a Mistake?" *Mind* LXVII (1958), 317-34.

Langer 1953. Langer, S. K.: *Feeling and Form*. London: Routledge, 1953.

Larsen 1956. Larsen, Jens Peter: "The Symphonies." In Landon, H. C. R., and Mitchell, Donald, eds.: *The Mozart Companion*. London: Rockliff, 1956.

Malraux 1953. Malraux, André: *The Voices of Silence*. New York: Doubleday, 1953.

Meager 1958. Meager, R. L.: "The Uniqueness of a Work of Art." *Proceedings of the Aristotelian Society* LIX (1958-9), 49-70.

Meiss 1951. Meiss, Millard: *Painting in Florence and Siena after the Black Death*. Princeton: Princeton University Press, 1951.

Mill 1859. Mill, John Stuart: *Dissertations and Discussions*. vol. I. London: Parker, 1859.

———1833. "Thoughts on Poetry and its Varieties" (1833). In Mill 1859.

Munro 1956. Munro, Thomas: *Toward Science in Aesthetics*. New York: Liberal Arts Press, 1956.

Panofsky 1955. Panofsky, Erwin: *Meaning in the Visual Arts*. New York: Doubleday Anchor Books, 1955.

Parker 1920. Parker, DeWitt H.: *The Principles of Aesthetics*. Boston, etc.: Silver, Burdett, 1920.

Pascal 1670. Pascal, Blaise: *Pensées* (1670). Trans. W. F. Trotter. London: Dent (Everyman), 1908.

Passmore 1951. Passmore, J. A.: "The Dreariness of Aesthetics" (1951). In Elton 1954.

Pepper 1938. Pepper, Stephen C.: *Aesthetic Quality: A Contextualist Theory of Beauty*. New York: Scribners, 1938.

Rader 1934. Rader, M. M., ed.: *A Modern Book of Esthetics*. New York: Holt, 1934.

Reid 1785. Reid, Thomas: *Essays on the Intellectual Powers of Man*. Edinburgh, 1785.

Reynolds 1835. Reynolds, Joshua: *Literary Works*. Two volumes. London: Cadell, 1835.

_____1776. *Seventh Discourse* (1776). In Reynolds 1835.

Richards 1929. Richards, I. A.: *Practical Criticism*. London: Kegan Paul, 1929.

Rothenstein 1952. Rothenstein, John: *Modern English Painters: Sickert to Smith*. London: Eyre & Spottiswoode, 1952.

Shaw 1956. Shaw, Theodore L.: *Precious Rubbish*. Boston: Stuart Art Gallery, 1956.

Sparshott 1958. Sparshott, F. E.: *An Enquiry into Goodness*. Toronto: University of Toronto Press, 1958.

_____1961. "The Central Problem of Philosophy." *University of Toronto Quarterly* XXXI (1961), 1-19.

Tolstoy 1924. Tolstoy, Lev: *Tolstoy on Art*. Ed. and trans. A. Maude. London: Oxford University Press, 1924.

_____1898. *What is Art?* (1898). In Tolstoy 1924.

Turner 1958. Turner, Vincent, S. J.: "The Desolation of Aesthetics." In Todd, John M., ed.: *The Arts, Artists and Thinkers*. London: Longmans, Green, 1958.

Véron 1878. Véron, Eugene: *L'Esthétique* (1878). Second edition. Paris: Reinwald, 1883.

Wellek and Warren 1949. Wellek, René, and Warren, Austin: *Theory of Literature* (1949). New York: Harcourt, Brace (Harvest Books), 1956.

Wisdom 1948. Wisdom, John: "Things and Persons." *Proceedings of the Aristotelian Society*. Supplementary Volume XXII (1948), 202-15.

The Structure of Knowledge in the Arts

HARRY S. BROUDY

William Carlos Williams once wrote:
    It is difficult
    To get news from poems,
    Yet men die miserably every day
    For lack
    Of what is found there.[1]

That sums up the paradoxical situation with respect to the question of knowledge in the arts. Although by the customary interpretation of the customary criteria art appreciation cannot qualify as knowledge, the conviction persists that some works of art are "saying" something and often something important. The problem, both with respect to a particular work of art and art in general, has to do with what is being "said" and how the communication is being accomplished.

In education the problem of the structure of knowledge in the arts is important for several reasons:

From Stanley Elam (Ed.), *Education and the Structure of Knowledge,* Fifth Annual Phi Delta Kappa Symposium on Educational Research (Chicago: Rand McNally & Company, 1964), pp. 75-106. Reprinted by permission of the author and Rand McNally & Company.
[1]William Carlos Williams, *The Desert Music and Other Poems* (Random House, 1954).

a. If art does not add to the knowledge of the pupil in any important sense, then the justification and methods for teaching it must be found in a change of attitude or behavior of which the work of art is presumably a cause.

b. The answer to question (a) determines what can be said *about* art in art education of one kind or another. At least some statements commonly made about art, namely, statements about what the work of art purports to say, would be ruled out if the work of art, in fact, says nothing.

c. If the school is to choose among works of art as more or less "good," there will have to be defensible criteria for making the choice. If works of art say nothing important about what is important, then this criterion, at least, is ruled out.

Types of Knowledge in Art

To begin with, when one speaks of knowledge in connection with a work of art the reference may be to:

a. The making of a work of art, as when a poem or a concerto is created. One can ask what an artist has to know in order to make a work of art. Plato, in Book X of the *Republic*, thought that with a good eye for superficial resemblances the artist could dispense with profound knowledge of the subjects he was "imitating." Some novelists, on the other hand, claim that they must acquire a first-hand knowledge of the people and events they write about. Shakespeare is credited with a profound knowledge of human nature. Cézanne is often credited with "knowing" that nature's forms are combinations of the cube, sphere, and cylinder.

There is, then, some difference of opinion as to the importance of the artist's knowledge about what he is presenting or representing in a work of art. Surely Plato was right in his contention that one can make an image of a bed without knowing how to make the bed itself but, on the other hand, the ability to make a bed or the knowledge of human nature does not guarantee the ability to make images of these objects. Where the work of art does not claim to represent or present anything outside the artist's feelings or impressions, the problem of his knowledge *about* the content of the work of art, if I am not mistaken, becomes irrelevant, if not meaningless.

b. There is less controversy about the know-how of the artist. Some instances of modern poetry, painting, and drama to the contrary notwithstanding, artists *are* concerned with problems of technique. For one thing, their training, more often than not, has been involved with technique: of how to use the medium to achieve certain effects. Further, even with the greatest freedom in composition and painting, an artist develops his own way of being free, so that we do not readily mistake the painting of Marc Chagall for that of Jackson Pollock, the music of John Cage for that of Alban Berg, or the sculpture of

Moore for that of Brancusi. To the student of art these differences are readily evident and quite frequently are expressed as differences in technique. As for Croce's contention that the materialization of the aesthetic intuition is aesthetically of little importance, this did not convince even his fellow idealist, Bosanquet.[2]

No great mystery therefore shrouds these two kinds of knowledge in the arts. Knowing about one's subject and knowing how to use a technique are not peculiar to painters, poets, and composers. The carpenter, the stone mason, and the teacher also utilize these kinds of knowledge in the practice of their respective crafts. It is of some significance to note that controversies about the proper training of craftsmen usually revolve around the proper proportions of each of these kinds of knowledge in the curriculum. Some want more knowledge about life and reality and less technique, some stress technique with a minimum of knowledge, and some who wish to elevate a craft into a profession want more of both.

In art education the problem is complicated by the role of technical competence, or at least knowledge about technique, in appreciation. Does painting pictures help one to appreciate pictures one did not paint? Does the writing of poems pave the way for the appreciation of the poems to be studied in school? Since the meaning of "appreciation" is far from clear, it is not easy to answer this question. If appreciation includes admiration for the dexterity of the artist, then trying to produce art helps us to admire those who can do well what we ourselves botch. If appreciation includes just and informed criticism, then knowing, for example, how tempera and fresco paintings are produced, will inhibit judgments not appropriate to these types of painting. Knowing something about how atonal music is written promotes patience with sounds that sometimes cause anguish. Perhaps know-how serves appreciation by making it easier for the appreciator to get into the proper posture for perceiving whatever it is the work of art presents.

c. Another kind of knowledge about the arts is so clearly knowledge in the conventional sense of the term that it will be sufficient at this point merely to make note of it. Historical knowledge about works of art comprises the history of artists, accounts of developments of the arts and of individual art objects.

I am distinguishing here historical knowledge *about* art from art criticism and philosophy of art, even though one can hardly carry on the latter without some knowledge of the former. Nevertheless, one can imagine some historian undertaking to trace the origins of a poem or a set of poems without having any particular interest in the nature of poetry or an appraisal of it. Indeed, such a

---

[2]Benedetto Croce, *The Breviary of Aesthetic* (Houston, Texas: Rice Institute Pamphlets, 1915), II, 4, or Douglar Ainslie (trans.), *The Essence of Aesthetics* (London: W. Heinemann, 1921). Bernard Bosanquet, "Croce's Aesthetic," *Mind*, XXIX (1920), 212-215, and *Three Lectures on Aesthetic* (London: Macmillan, 1915), Ch. 2.

historian could write an acceptable Ph.D. thesis as the result of such an enterprise. By recording and sorting all the things that had been said about his particular objects of inquiry he could, without holding a theory or an opinion of his own, become an authority of sorts.

In art, as in other fields, a sound knowledge of history is the best defense against narrowness and foolishness. For it is silly to praise an artist only to discover that he did not produce the works attributed to him or that they were produced by his apprentice. Judgments about style and influence should also be solidly rooted in fact so far as the facts can be ascertained. Further, historical adequacy empowers the critic and philosopher to make appropriate comparisons and contrasts with regard to styles and periods that, in turn, sharpen discrimination and judgment.

Accordingly, the history of art exhibits a knowledge structure no different from the history of anything else. Nor does it present any peculiar pedagogical difficulty. Like other historical materials it runs the risk of either being on the dull side so far as the ordinary pupil is concerned or inaccurately exciting. The pedagogical problem lies rather in the relation between historical knowledge about art and the aesthetic experience of art.

d. Knowledge about the content which the artist presents, knowing how to present it, and knowledge about artists and works of art are important and necessary for the production and appreciation of art. Nevertheless, if this were the whole story, we would not as philosophers or as educators be interested in it. Everything that has been said so far about art could be said about the making and appreciating of coins, or stamps, or rocking chairs. If fine art had remained solidly integrated with the handicrafts, as it probably once was, the problem of knowledge in the arts would not arise.

It does arise because in our culture a work of art is created or presumed to be created for a distinctive purpose, and once created it acquires a being of its own with a special value of its own. That special value may lie in the delight it affords, the interest it commands, and, possibly, in the price it can bring. In some cases, however, the value is attributed to a work of art because it allegedly "says" something or expresses something that has to do with life at its most important level. Consider for example the following statement:

Music "expresses in a concentrated way the shocks and instabilities, the conflicts and resolutions, that are the dramatic changes enacted upon the more enduring background of nature and human life. The tension and the struggle has its gathering of energy, its discharges, its attacks and defenses, its mighty warrings and its peaceful meetings, its resistances and its resolutions, and out of these things music weaves its web."[3]

---

[3]John Dewey, *Art as Experience* (New York: Minton, Balch & Co., 1934), p. 236. (See p. 195 for a lyric passage on art as revealing reality as unity of all things.)

Or when Paul Tillich says that "All arts create symbols for a level of reality which cannot be reached in other ways."[4]

Such terms as "significant form," "expressiveness," and "communication" indicate that a work of art is making some cognitive claim; that not only is it an object in its own right, but that it also discloses, reveals, or illuminates something special. The nature of this something and the mode of its disclosure constitute an intriguing theoretical question about art and the locus of the mystery is the aesthetic experience. Somewhere in the artistic transaction the artist and the appreciator undergo an experience which is at the heart of both the making of a work of art and the appreciation of it. It is with the knowledge-structure of this aesthetic experience that one must sooner or later grapple.

Cognition in the Aesthetic Experience

Insofar as the aesthetic experience is a mode of cognition it belongs primarily to perception. On philosophical grounds, Kant argued that unless the sensa are in some Gestalt or pattern they will not be perceived, and unless sensa clusters are interpreted by a categorial schema as being this kind of thing or that, or meaning this or that kind of object, the sensa will not be understood. In this sense the aesthetic experience is no different from any other perception. If it differs from other types of perception, it is in the way the sensory content, its relational schema, and its categorical structures are interpreted.

a. The sensory elements in scientific and practical perception are used as clues to achieving knowledge and action, respectively. The redness of a rose, for example, helps to identify the type of rose we are dealing with or to decide whether or not we shall choose it for the flower arrangement on the table. But only insofar as the redness is attended to for the sake of perceiving it as redness does redness figure in aesthetic perception. Thus it is that in some works of art the attention-compelling qualities of the sounds, textures, or colors are its most notable features. In perception whose goal is primarily knowledge or prosperous action, on the contrary, the particular quality of the sensory elements is not important in its own right. Black figures on a white dial and white figures on a black dial are equally good, if they give the same information with the same ease.

b. With regard to the relational elements by virtue of which the sensa are intuited as a pattern, one can say with Kant that space and time are forms of sensuous intuition in aesthetic perception as in other types. Certainly it is difficult to imagine images apart from spatial and temporal frameworks. The primary difference lies in the fact that formal properties are important in works

---

[4]Paul Tillich, *Systematic Theology* (Chicago: Univ. of Chicago Press, 1951), I, 42.

of art not only as means to heightening perceptual effects, but also as perceptually interesting on their own account.

c. Scientific and practical perception interpret their sensa by use of categories that organize them for knowledge or for use. The chief goal of the interpretation is to relate the object or the cluster of sensa to other objects in some predictable fashion or as a means to some end. The interpretive phase of aesthetic perception, however, has ground rules of its own. First of all, whatever is perceived must be perceived as being located in the object. It cannot be perceived as located in one's memory or in some organ of sense within the body. Second, the interpretation always entails a displacement of modality. Sometimes this means that an auditory stimulus is interpreted as having visual or kinaesthetic qualities, as when a melody is described as jerky or bright. More often, however, the displacement is from secondary qualities of color, sound, and shape to tertiary ones such as are connoted by the adjectives cheerful, exciting, angry, sublime, sad, melancholy, etc. George Santayana regarded this form of displacement as distinctive of aesthetic perception, saying that it must always be a perception of value, never a mere noting of characteristics.[5]

Why certain patterns of sound and color have come to symbolize emotional states is a matter for anthropological and psychological inquiry. The fact is that they do even for untutored persons and that, therefore, they are expressive.

That the expression is not achieved by a proposition or set of propositions does not invalidate the claim of a work of art to be a source of information. The artist, says Dewey, has to think in terms of qualities. "To think effectively in terms of relations of qualities is as severe a demand upon thought as to think in terms of symbols, verbal and mathematical."[6]

The word ouch is not a sentence and, therefore, strictly speaking, not a statement, but that one can infer information about the utterer would not be denied.[7] How does a sound such as "ouch" become a source of information? By furnishing the hearer with a minor premise to the following syllogism:

All persons crying "ouch" are suffering pain;

This person is saying "ouch";

This person is suffering pain.

The major premise is a generalization from experience with pain in our culture.

Or a picture of a storm at sea becomes a source of information insofar as the

---

[5]George Santayana, *The Sense of Beauty* (New York: Scribner, 1896). For further and similar distinctions among modes of perception, see Iredell Jenkins, *Art and the Human Enterprise* (Cambridge, Mass.: Harvard Univ. Press, 1958), pp. 23-24, and Virgil C. Aldrich, "Chess Not Without the Queen," *Proceedings and Addresses of the American Philosophical Association*, 1957-1958.

[6]*Ibid.*, p. 46, 73, and David W. Ecker, "The Artistic Process as Qualitative Problem Solving," *The Journal of Aesthetics and Art Criticism*, XXI:3 (Spring, 1963), 283-290.

[7]That nondiscursive symbols can be cognitive is the burden of Susanne K. Langer's *Philosophy in a New Key* (Cambridge, Mass.: Harvard Univ. Press, 1942). This book has been especially influential with music educators, if frequency of quotation is any indication of influence.

picture resembles or purports to resemble storms in general or some storm in particular. Loud rolls on the drums are clues to thunderclaps in musical compositions because they resemble the sounds of thunder.

We can also glean information from expressions that by convention are clues or signals to the recipient. Thus the expression "How do you do?" in a greeting is not a genuine inquiry but rather a hint that the greeter is still a friend, or at least not in the advanced stages of hostility.

There is little doubt that works of art convey meanings by these uses of signs, but it is generally agreed that these instances are not what the controversy is about. The trouble is that in art the expressive elements or their totality must convey more than a literal resemblance and do more than trigger a random or conventional association. Further, the aesthetic response must not be the organic reflex to pain, but the apprehension of a logical expression of pain. The picture is asked to present a symbol that in color *looks* painful and in music *sounds* painful; it must locate pain where it cannot, in common sense, ever be found.

The work of art is expected to stimulate the perception of a meaning that, according to Iredell Jenkins, sharpens our insight into the actual character of things. If so, the actual character must be conveyed by the work of art and, since the thing is not in the work of art literally, it must be there as the form of the actual thing. And since this form is not the concept of the thing and not the literal imitation of it, it must be a metaphorical image, i.e., the representation of feelings, emotions, insights, and even ideas as sounds, colors, shapes, and motions.

How this can happen is still a matter of much theorizing. Virtually every aesthetic theory has some hypothesis as to why a poetic line, a colored shape, a gesture in a dance can symbolize in a way that is neither a literal reference, on the one hand, nor a more or less logically reconstructible association of ideas, on the other.

The fact that so many theories—that of Freud, Bergson, Reed, Jung, Cassirer, Langer, among many others—keep returning to myth, ritual, and legend as the source of the power of artistic symbolism leads one to conjecture that it is in the interpretive phase of perceptual experience that we shall probably find the significant difference from other modes of perception.

According to Kant, the interpretive phase of experience is structured by two systems of a priori operation. First, time and space as the forms of intuition organize sensa into some schematic design, and second, organization is affected by the categories of identity, exclusion, causality, and the like. To qualify as experience at all, sensory stimuli must first pass these two gatekeepers and *put on* their perceptible and intelligible costumes, so to speak.[8]

---

[8]*Critique of Pure Reason*, Transcendental Analytic, First Division. Also see D. W. Gotshalk, *Art and the Social Order* (Chicago: Univ. of Chicago Press, 1947), 17-20.

Leaving aside the question of the a priorism of these interpretive operations, it seems as if in aesthetic experience the forms of sensuous intuition may apply as they do in ordinary perception, but instead of the intellectual categories by which the sensa are organized conceptually, we now use imaginative schemata, and these, according to the theories referred to above, are the root metaphors to be found in myth, rite, legend, and dreams. Presumably all members of the race, either by nature or nurture, have available archetypal images by virtue of which the artist can speak to them through the images he creates.

If it is asked why so archaic a mode of communication survives, the answer might be that there is no way even now of speaking precisely and conceptually about the subjective realm of life. This realm is incorrigibly telelogical and can be understood only in dramatic terms — of agents and opponents, beginnings, climaxes, and resolutions. If this theory makes sense, then we can understand why in the aesthetic perception we cognize (interpret) not by recognizing a class to which our specimen belongs or by bringing into consciousness an idea associated in our previous experience with it. Rather, we cognize by recognizing in the image before us the very meaning that excited some racial ancestor to perceive it as something of unusual significance.

This hypothesis has some other consequences that it might be proper to mention without extensive discussion. One is that it helps to explain why response to art is, in one sense, universal and, in another, highly differential. Just being alive and living in a culture guarantee that the individual will be stirred by the metaphors of art. Fire will excite him, the moon mystify him, and the swelling of the tides fill him with awe. Art, using culture images of heroes and dragons, great adventures and escapes, will stir him even in childhood. Great rapes, battles with giants, struggles with angels, transformations of men into animals and trees need no sophisticated percipients in order to function in the aesthetic experience.

On the other hand, T. S. Eliot's *The Waste Land* or Dante's *Divine Comedy* are not for untutored readers. The great myths by being used in art become elaborated and refined, so that knowledge of these works is presupposed in many of their successors. For example, in line 408 of *The Waste Land* we read: "Or in memories draped by the beneficent spider."

As an image this stands on its own feet, yet in a note Eliot remarks anent this line: "Cf. Webster, *The White Devil*, V, vi: '. . . they'll remarry/Ere the worm pierce your winding-sheet, ere the spider/Make a thin curtain for your epitaphs.' " Here is a familiar case of an image being used again and again not only because spider webs suggest curtain making but also because poets read poetry.

Relevant to aesthetic education is the fact that when artists presuppose familiarity on the part of the percipient with certain root metaphors, their art is likely to become unsuitable for a generation that no longer has this familiarity. Thus poetry and other works of art that depend on the root imagery of Latin words, as in the case of Milton, or on familiarity with the Bible or Greek mythology are robbed of much of their impact if this background is missing. Hence the copious footnotes and glosses needed to teach Shakespeare, Milton, and perhaps even the literature of the last century as well.[9]

To summarize: the ground rules for qualifying as a genuine aesthetic experience are that it be predominantly an instance of perception rather than discursive reasoning or memory, that whatever is expressed be expressed in a symbol that embodies or presents the meaning rather than merely refers to it, and that the satisfaction or interest aroused by it shall be traceable to its sensory, formal, and expressive properties.

These requirements are reminiscent of the classical conditions for knowledge. Aristotle argued that certainty presupposed the *formal* identity of the object and the knower and explicated the psychological and epistemological apparatus that would account for such an identity. While modern theories of knowledge are chary of such demands and are willing to settle for far less than certainty in knowing, the ideal seems to linger on in theories of aesthetic experience. In the work of art par excellence reality is captured in an image and this form being identical with, or at least analogically identical with, certain life forms unites the perceiver imaginatively with the aesthetic object conveyed by the work of art. It may be profitable to explore this parallel a little further.

The meaning of knowledge, it seems to me, still entails some direct grasping of the object either in perception or by means of concepts or both. All other modes of knowing are approximations to the ideal situation in which the mind and the object are one. It is certainty that makes probability probable.

From the first, however, it has been clear that there is no certain way of knowing that the mind has achieved this unity except when it confined itself to juggling concepts it had itself constructed and defined. In matters of fact, however, the fallibility of sensory processes, while it did not rule out the possibility of certainty, cast a shadow on claims to certainty that no theory has ever dispelled.

To get around the difficulties imposed by the fallibility of sense, a superior faculty of intellectual intuition was proposed that would directly apprehend the essences of things and their relations. Not infrequently, as in Plato and Descartes, the condition for the illumination of the mind and the real was a state of purified receptivity. For Plato this meant a long period of training and discipline in the lesser forms of knowing and in the control of the passions. In Descartes systematic doubting until all possible subjective distortions are peeled away prepares for the moment of certainty. Bacon sought to exorcise idols of various kinds including those imposed by the peculiarities of one's

---

[9]On the role of myth, metaphor, rite, and language in art, cf., Langer, *op. cit.*, chs. 6, 7, 9. Also S. K. Langer (trans.), Ernst Cassirer, *Language and Myth* (New York: Harper, 1946). For a good sampling of selections from Freud, Jung, Bergson, Christopher Caudwell, and Nietzche, see Melvin Rader, *A Modern Book of Esthetics* (3rd ed.; New York: Holt, Rinehart and Winston, 1960).

culture. In all of these theories the moment of truth or illumination is not only a kind of knowing, but also a state of being that is supposed to provide a criterion by which to judge the claims of all subsequent "revelations." To the confirmed skeptic, however, "self-evidence" has always meant "no evidence."

The subjective determinants in cognition were regarded as inimical to knowledge not because they were in the person, but rather because they were peculiar to the person and therefore a threat to the claim of true statements to be universal. Subjective factors interpose themselves between the mind and the object and distort it. The skeptical, albeit optimistic, conclusion has therefore been drawn (a) that no freedom from distortion can be complete or (b) that distortions are all that we can have and (c) that truth can safely be defined as the distortions destined to be agreed upon by all competent observers. Whether the competent observer is one who finally gets rid of the distortions or the one with the right set of distortions is left open or dismissed as a fruitless question.

Nevertheless, the removal of distortions remains important in the cognitive and educative enterprise. Scientific method is one way of standardizing distortion or discounting it, and something of the same sort but on a different plane is suggested as a condition for creativity by Abraham Maslow. In his study of peak experiences, Maslow notes that they exhibit such characteristics as giving up the past and future, loss of ego, loss of self-consciousness, lessening of defenses and inhibitions, acceptance, strong aesthetic perception instead of abstraction, and trust *versus* trying and controlling.[10] These conditions of creativity resemble the conditions for achieving nondiscursive knowledge in that they mark the removal of the distorting conditions of self and culture.

There are then similarities between the creative attitude, the ground rules for the aesthetic experience, and an ideal of knowledge in which formal identity between the knower and the known is achieved. In all three, there is an emphasis on getting the slate ready to receive the message from the object, on letting the real have its way with the mind. This does not prove that the aesthetic experience is cognitive, but rather suggests that the descriptions given of the aesthetic experience, both in appreciation and creation, have a structural affinity with the classical paradigm for knowing. If this argues for anything, it is for tolerance of the belief that at the heart of the deepest kind of knowing is revelation or a display of the real.

Perception for the Sake of Perception

What has already been said about aesthetic perception indicates that it differs from perception controlled by the needs of action and that which is controlled by the need for knowledge. It is now a familiar story that our perception is selective, especially when guided by some active interest. The tailor perceives

---

[10]"The Creative Attitude," *The Structurist*, III (1963), 4-10.

a person in terms of his clothing, and a football coach perceives people in terms of strenuous feats on the gridiron. Action and interests based on action suck from the object those clues that are most relevant to action. The estimative sense, in the words of Aristotle, makes a judgment of this kind, and Henri Bergson, among others, argued that perception was eminently a practical faculty, suited primarily as a cognitive guide for action rather than metaphysical truth.

Perception for the sake of science, on the other hand, seeks clues in the object that will betray its inner properties, that is, those properties by virtue of which it can be classified and related to other objects and activities. The practical user of salt, for example, is interested in its appearance and taste; the scientist, in those properties that relate salt to other substances, a function for which taste and appearance are not of major significance.

The scientific function of perception has diminished in importance as the properties of objects most useful for understanding their behavior ceased to be accessible to ordinary perception. In scientific knowing, perception is still indispensable but it functions more as a check on the presence or absence of marks on dials and scopes than as a direct access to the structure of the object itself. Discursive reflection, that is, the whole complex of hypothetico-deductive reasoning with observation as a check, is the accepted pattern of reliable knowing rather than the unity of the mind and the object.

As differentiated from these two modes of perception, aesthetic experience has as its primary purpose the clarification and intensification of perception, rather than prosperous action or scientific knowledge. Aesthetic perception is complete rather than selective; reflexive rather than transitive. Gotshalk defined the work of art as an object of intrinsic interest to perception.[11] Whatever other goals it may and often does serve, a work of art must be interesting to perceive, although not necessarily delightful to perceive. This definition has the virtue of including objects or aspects of objects that on extra-aesthetic grounds are gruesome and revolting, and which can be found in many great works of art.

Before proceeding to the further analysis of the aesthetic object and the factors that make it interesting to perception, it may be in order to ask why pure perception or perception as such should be a goal of human endeavor. Why should we be interested in perceiving objects just for the sake of perceiving them?

One possible answer is that pure perception is an acquired taste. On this view, the original interest of man was action, and the perceptual awareness of objects served a survival function. After appearance was no longer useful to guide action it could be regarded simply as an appearance. Hence, on this view, children are absorbed in the sheer appearances of objects because as yet they

---

[11]*Op. cit., passim.*

do not know how to exploit perceptual clues practically. Later, as action becomes the dominant concern, the aesthetic interest lapses and has to be recovered by effort and training.

Some doubt on this hypothesis as a complete explanation is thrown by (a) the universal impulse to adorn useful objects and (b) the inveterate tendency of peoples in all cultures to stylize life into musical, pictorial, and linguistic sketches. These activities are indulged in even when no use or improvement of use can be found to explain them.

It seems more plausible to conjecture that first of all, clear perception, like clear thinking and like efficient movement, is enjoyed for its own sake. When the vision is blurred or hearing impaired, recovery of clear vision and hearing gives a pleasure that is as indubitable as it is indescribable. That sense organs constantly adjust themselves for clearer perception, and our unceasing search for instruments to extend perception, are ample witness to an inherent, perhaps innate, tendency.[12] In the second place, the interest and satisfaction attendant upon perceiving a field are augmented when the field is structured so as to engage the activities of the perceiver more extensively and more intensively. It therefore makes sense to contrive this enhancement of interest and satisfaction.

As an example of the foregoing thesis, suppose we begin with the activities of walking, running, and movements of the hands and torso as observed in ordinary life. Suppose we observe our neighbor walking briskly down the street of a weekday morning. The walk has a certain rhythm and pace, but our perception of it is likely to be no more than a registration of clues for inferences about what our neighbor is up to. We surmise that he is on his way to the office or the bus. Suppose now that our neighbor suddenly breaks into a little hop, skip, and jump routine. Our interest perks up immediately, forcing strange hypotheses into our minds as to what might be the cause of this unusual behavior. The walking has become expressive of something: joy, excitement, or nervousness. In any event, we now watch the scene more intently. As we do, suppose our neighbor wheels about to face us and begins a fairly simple tap dance. At this juncture we either call the police, or we become absorbed in the dance itself. The practical and intellectual attitudes will then have begun to turn into the aesthetic attitude. Our interest is in perceiving the field and the motions within it.

If, however, the neighbor continues the tapping indefinitely, our interest flags. The field has been explored; there is no further surprise to be anticipated, no further excitement. But suppose he varies the routine; suppose the rhythms

---

[12]Cf. Emil W. Menzel, Jr., and Richard K. Davenport, Jr., "Preference for Clear vs. Distorted Viewing in the Chimpanzee," *Science*, CXXXIV:3489, 1531, and R. S. Woodworth, *Dynamics of Behavior* (New York: Holt, 1958), p. 192.

become more complicated; suppose out of nowhere music sounds with a rhythm synchronized to the dancing; suppose a female dancer appears and joins our neighbor in his act. Suppose now instead of the drab ordinary street clothing, the dancers acquire brilliant costumes and that the simple music swells to a multi-instrumented orchestra. By this time our practical concerns with our neighbor will probably have been completely submerged in our aesthetic interest. Instead of one sense many of our senses are functioning at a high rate of intensity; instead of monotony there is variation of a pattern, there is contrast of pace, male and female, light and heavy, tension and release, a building up of climax and resolution. Before our eyes, so to speak, an ordinary piece of pedestrianism has been turned into a work of art, that is, into a field designed for perceiving and for not much of anything else.

Why do two dancers in synchronization interest us more than one? Why does the matching of the dancing gesture with a musical equivalent interest us more than either separately? Why do costume, setting intensify the interest? For one thing, each complication engages more of us; in other words, we are more "*inter esse*" within the field, not physically but imaginatively. The field becomes vivid, highlighted, red-lettered, and we too feel more alive, freer from the restrictions and distortions of ordinary life, freer to be ourselves because we have lost ourselves in the object and have, in a special sense, become one with it. However, there seems to be still another dimension of involvement. How interesting an object for perception will be depends on which nerve of life it touches. The little tap dance stirs a life rhythm, but no matter how it is complicated, varied, and dressed up, it still remains a delightfully refreshing but not a profound experience. Should the rhythm become more violent, our interest will increase, but delight gives way to a disturbed excitement. If on the stage Salome waves her grisly props, our perception acquires a depth of life involvement in comparison with which the tap dance is trivial and shallow.

If the dance is a caricature (a sketch) of war, of death, of love, of tragedy, of triumph, our perceiving becomes serious in the sense that we are beholding an expression that is also trying to be a statement about something so important, so close to the big issues in human life, perhaps so dangerous, so revolting that we have not yet formulated language to state it clearly. Perhaps as Jung, Freud, and others have conjectured, these works of art portray impulses and instincts that man would just as soon forget he had.

I have not taken the trouble, as one could, to argue that free activity of any kind is a source of delight. Perceiving and imagining as sheer activities disporting themselves for their own sake and freed from the stresses of need and duty are genuine values that need no justification, although indirectly the amount of such freedom a civilization permits is a good measure of its worth. This is so because this freedom for an adult population is a luxury that only substantial control over nature can make possible. As for duty, there is no little truth in Santayana's observation that morality is concerned primarily with preventing suffering and evil rather than with positive values.[13] If this is so, the more control a society has over natural and social evil, the less need is there to rely upon duty and conscience to prevent them.

But to return to our problem: is this knowledge? Is it verifiable knowledge? We must answer that in this sense it is not knowledge. The dance is not a set of propositions but a set of percepts organized into a total individual perceptual field. The components — however one decides to divide the field — do not have univocal meanings with interchangeable synonyms. The referents, if any, are themselves so vague, so amorphous, so indeterminate that some have never been named, much less defined.

If we are to call the deliverances of a work of art knowledge, it must be on a quite different conception of knowledge. It is no good to insist that a work of art refers to itself, for that is precisely what we do not mean by knowledge. It must refer to that which it displays and which is not completely identical with it. I have tried to indicate what this referent might be, namely, the import of reality for life on a scale running from the trivial to the profound. Since such an import is not a physical object there can be no question of public verification.

Nevertheless, the claim is often made that works of art display universals in a particular percept. The serenity of the ideal Greek character is supposed to be displayed in classic Greek sculpture and the grandeur of the creative powers of man and God in Beethoven's Ninth Symphony. This claim is not so mysterious as it sometimes sounds. Abstract qualities such as kindness, cruelty, and excitement can be symbolized pictorially much as a good carica- turist can in a few lines capture the essentials of a building, a fact, or even a mood. The rhythms and motions of nature and of life can likewise be captured in images, and there is then a truth expressed about them that is verified as all caricatures are, viz., by recognizing a structural resemblance. Thus twenty-five different caricatures of Winston Churchill could be "true" of Churchill. In this sense a caricature of Sir Winston could be said to capture *his* essence. And if his essence is to be blunt, aggressive, and lofty the artist may capture these qualities also and, if so, convey information not only about Churchill but about the bluntness, aggressiveness, and loftiness of the human spirit as well.

Art Theory and Art Criticism

The problem of the structure of knowledge in the arts involves not only the cognitive status of (a) what the work of art itself says or is supposed to say but also (b) what critics and theorists say about art. In one sense (a) collapses into (b) because works of art say nothing about themselves; only critics and theorists talk about what the work of art says. On the other hand, (b) the truth

---

[13]*Loc. cit.*

of what the critics and theorists say the work of art says depends on the truth of their theory about cognitive deliverances of works of art. If, for example, the work of art says nothing, then the critic who purports to interpret what it says is either a dupe or a fraud. In either case one would be wise to protect children from them and perhaps art as well.

On the other hand, even if an art work says nothing or nothing that can be stated intelligibly, it still may be possible for critics and theorists to say many things about art that are intelligible and which may help the individual to enhance the aesthetic experience.

Art criticism involves explication of the work of art and appraisal of it. Neither activity would be possible if some analysis of the work were not possible; if it were not possible for the critic to point to certain identifiable features of the work of art. Rational appraisal would be impossible if there could be no statement of rules and principles that works of art exemplified, or failed to exemplify, or exemplified in varying degrees. In addition, critical discourse is useless if it is so private and esoteric that others cannot understand it. Although some works of criticism themselves approach the status of works of art, most of them are discourses about works of art. These discourses are composed of (a) statements descriptive of the contents and structure of the work, (b) statements asserting the conformity of the work to a rule or principle, or (c) statements indicating possibilities that the artist might have realized but did not.

The content of critical discourse will be more apparent if the kinds of description and appraisal that can be made are sorted out. This analysis also indicates the way in which knowledge about works of art can be organized for instruction, because to learn to appreciate art is to learn to perceive and appraise it as a cultivated critic does.

Any work of art in any medium can be examined and evaluated with respect to the following factors: (a) the sensuous materials, (b) the manipulation (technique), (c) the formal design, (d) the expressiveness or significance, (e) the general function of being interesting to perception, and (f) the extra-aesthetic functions that it is designed or happens to serve.

For example, the colors in a painting may be brilliant or subdued, the sonorities in a piece of music can be pleasant or unpleasant. Different colors, sounds, textures, gestures are more or less attention-compelling, more or less pleasant, more or less interesting. Different media employ different materials and knowing how to handle these materials is part of the technical equipment of the artist. These sensuous materials are never found without some rudimentary form and therefore they carry some expressiveness. Even the syllables "zig" and "zag" do.

The important point, however, is that discriminations among the sensory qualities can be made and assertions about them can within reasonable limits be verified. Educationally, moreover, such discriminations can be learned and improved by learning; even pigs have been trained to distinguish among different pitches. The case with regard to techniques needs even less argument. For centuries men have learned "how" from masters, and there is no great difficulty in ascertaining how well they have learned.

The problem in formal design is more complicated but in principle no different. The principles of form, for example, harmony, balance, centrality, and development, can be specified by such devices as recurrence, similarity, gradation, variation, modulation, symmetry, contrast, opposition, equilibrium, rhythm, measure, dominance, climax, hierarchy, and progression.[14] These refer to qualities in the work of art that can be identified. Certain patterns of formal arrangement become conventional and traditional, e.g., the sonnet form, rondo, terza rima, passacaglia, triangle, oval, etc. These properties of the work of art can be noted, discussed, and judged, and one can learn to do so under tuition and improve one's performance by experience and practice.

With expressiveness we enter upon less firm ground for the reasons already discussed in relation to the nature of the aesthetic experience. In addition, one must consider that not all works of art are conspicuously expressive. A decorative design for a wall paper may not be. Some works of art play down expressiveness except as it issues from the formal properties of the work, although romantic works are less restrained in this matter. Some expressions are of the trivial, and some are of the profound aspects of life. This difference has been used to differentiate excellence in art from greatness.[15] So although every work of art, indeed every component of such a work, has some expressiveness, just as every component has sensory content and form, the charm or power of a work of art to command interest for perception may lie in, primarily, the formal qualities, or the sensory ones, or even in technical brilliance rather than in the overtones and undertones of human import.

On the other hand, in a painting such as Grant Wood's *American Gothic* it is the expression of an idea that attracts and holds our attention and makes us want to explore it further with the eye of the head and of the mind. Its form and sensory quality contribute to the expressiveness but in themselves are not especially interesting.

Next, there is the judgment about the general effectiveness of the work of art in capturing and holding perceptual interest, whatever the means and devices employed in doing so. Does the work expand under close scrutiny? Can it withstand repeated scrutiny? While such judgments are, to a large extent, based on subjective impressions, and while the range of difference in judgments of this type is wide, nevertheless, that this kind of judgment is not simply a register of purely subjective preference is proved by the fact that with experi-

---

[14]Gotshalk, *op. cit.*, 114ff.

[15]Cf. Leonard B. Meyer, "Some Remarks on Value and Greatness in Music," *The Journal of Aesthetics and Art Criticism*, XVII:4 (June, 1959), 486-500.

ence and study the critic can dissociate his own immediate preference from his estimate of the potentialities of the object for the preferences of others.

The judgments of these potentialities can also be based on systematic analysis of the sensory elements, the formal components, and expressiveness. By comparing a given work of art with others of its kind, a judgment of potentiality is founded. Long experience also reveals discrepancies between expectations and performance, or strokes of genius where none had been suspected. To repeat, these judgments can be explicated and defended in terms that others with comparable experience can understand.

Finally, an intelligible judgment is possible about whether or not, or to what extent, a work of art fulfills whatever extra-aesthetic functions it may claim. To what extent does a monument express the purpose for which it is erected? To what extent does the marching band arouse the spirit of the football fans? To what extent does the form of a ritual intensify the meaning of a wedding or a funeral? How does the architecture of a school building enhance the educational significance of the goings on within it? How does the shape of a boat affect its motion through the water? How well does a novel or an epic exhibit the value schema of an age so that it can be used educationally as a value exemplar? Whenever an extra-aesthetic claim of this sort is made for a work of art, the critic should be able to make some sort of defensible judgment. However, the number of variables in this kind of situation is large, and only rarely do works of art clearly enhance or detract from their extra-aesthetic functions. But of course we are speaking here of judgments made prior to the judgments of history. Given time, the judgments converge because the doubtful cases tend to drop from the competition.

In review then, it would seem that if our analysis is plausible it is possible to make the following intelligible and defensible judgments about a work with respect to: (a) the sensory elements, (b) the formal elements, (c) the expressive elements, (d) technical competence, (e) the general perceptual interest, and (f) the extra-aesthetic functionality. In addition to these six judgments it is possible to examine and judge the way in which items (a-d) contribute or are related to each other and to items (e) and (f). This adds up to quite a number of possible critical judgments about a work of art.[16]

Some of these judgments are instances of subsumption. "This is a sonnet" may be concluded from the definition of a sonnet plus an examination of a given poem to see whether it conforms to the definition. There is no lack of definitions of periods, styles, and techniques in the arts. The characteristics and generalizations on which definitions of styles and periods are based present difficulties but are not essentially different in kind from those facing other classificatory definitions. Some aestheticians are not optimistic of ever getting a set of necessary and sufficient characteristics that would define the nature of art

---

[16]For a somewhat different calculus, see Gotshalk, *op. cit.*, 183ff.

itself,[17] but again art is not the only complex human activity that is difficult to capture in a set of precise concepts, especially if one is serious about finding something like a real definition.

Nor does artistic criticism suffer from peculiar difficulties when it comes to the formulation and application of rules. The rules for composing sonnets are based on the definition of a sonnet which, in turn, was taken from the characteristics of certain poems accepted as typical sonnets. Once the choice of the example was made, the rules of sonnet-making could be formulated. The same procedures resulted in rules for the proportions of various types of buildings or the canons for the proportions of the human body, as in Vitruvius. Given the ideal case, the logic of the rules and principles of art presents no peculiar difficulty.

The difficulties come not from doubts about procedures but rather in the choice of the typical or ideal examples. There is much to be said for the contention that in any period the feature that is used to characterize art represents something that critics or artists feel has been neglected.[18] In a period in which formal considerations have been ignored in favor of the expressive elements, the accent of the reformers is likely to be on form. The ideal objects to be used as exemplars for defining art tend to be chosen accordingly. Transitional works appear and finally the new trend becomes established. During this transitional period there is much talk of freedom from the rules. However, it is a truism that this is merely a struggle for a different set of rules. In any event, neither critics nor philosophers of art are forced into silence during these unstable periods.

Educationally, the important point is that there are definitions, rules, and procedures in art that can be identified, pointed to and stated. This means that there can be systematic instruction in or, at least, about art, and that it need not be confined to apprentice training in art production.

Some Educational Issues

The impact of this discussion on the problems of art education can be gauged by taking up briefly the following questions:

1. Can the modes of analysis developed by art critics and philosophers of art be translated into curricular contents and teaching procedures?

I believe it has been shown that within the total domain of art there are many sectors—history, classifications of all kinds, analyses of art objects in many schema and on many dimensions—that can be taught. They qualify as knowledge in the conventional senses of that word. The question is not so much

---

[17]Morris Weitz, "The Role of Theory in Aesthetics," *The Journal of Aesthetics and Art Criticism*, XV (1956), 27-35, and Paul Ziff, "The Task of Defining a Work of Art," *Philosophical Review*, LXII (1953), 58-78.

[18]Weitz, *op. cit.*

whether this kind of material can be taught, but rather whether the teaching of it will promote or hinder the aesthetic development of the pupil. By the aesthetic development of the pupil is ordinarily meant (a) the improvement of taste, (b) the improvement of the standards by which taste is justified, and (c) the increase of the quantity and quality of subjective enjoyment or satisfaction with aesthetic objects.

Clearly, the word improvement implies choice among alternatives according to some value scale. About the only way to avoid this conclusion is to argue that quantity — or intensity — of subjective enjoyment is the only relevant criterion. Whatever the theoretical difficulties involved in such a forthright hedonistic standard of aesthetic value, there still remains the relevant question: if John enjoys hillbilly music as much or more than Paul enjoys chamber music, should something be taught to John so that he too will prefer chamber music?

If it could be shown that John could be no more happy with chamber music than with hillbilly ditties, or if it could be shown that he would be no more happy with any other music than he is with hillbilly songs, there would be no point to aesthetic education as far as John's musical training is concerned on the ground that one might increase his pleasure thereby. Short of this condition, however, there remains the possibility of using the kind of knowledge and analyses mentioned above to maximize the recipient's pleasure. Even if, conceivably, teaching the pupil to discriminate tonal and rhythm patterns more finely leads him to prefer hillbilly music to string quartets, on sheer hedonistic grounds, the teaching would be successful and justified.

This way of looking at art education is not to be dismissed as an academic gambit. Especially in a period when rules are ill-defined there is a strong tendency to throw up one's hands and reduce aesthetic education to the refinement of those discriminations that maximize vividness of perception, regardless of other critical considerations and norms.

2. On what grounds can a school justify shaping aesthetic preferences on standards other than psychological hedonism?

A case for changing taste in a given direction can be argued on the following grounds: (a) that it will increase the well-being or happiness (not merely the momentary pleasure) of the individual and/or (b) that it will increase the well-being of the social order on which the well-being and happiness of the individual are predicted or dependent.

The first claim has to be based upon testimony of individuals, and unless some observers are more qualified than others, the testimony will be inconclusive. In the counting of noses, a pig satisfied counts for as much as Socrates unsatisfied unless Socrates' qualifications make his judgments count for more than one. But what could give him this superiority? Knowledge, experience, and a set of standards for life that are, to some extent, independent of the object to be judged. These standards are grounded in a theory about the good, about reality, and about knowledge itself, i.e., by a complete philosophical system. In other words, if the quality of pleasure is to be taken into account, pleasure is no longer the crucial criterion. Once knowledge and experience are admitted as criteria for well-being or even pleasure itself, connoisseurship or expertise becomes the only practicable standard for the school.

I say practicable for two reasons. One is that theoretically there is no way of certifying experts and connoisseurs that will remove the disagreement among them. The other is that when we propose to operate our culture rationally, we mean that of two or more doubtful opinions, assertions, and hypotheses, that which is based on study and experience is to be preferred. As between judgments based on other grounds or no grounds at all, no rational choice is possible. The case in the arts is no different from that in any other department of instruction.

The justification of art education by the social welfare argument rests on whether art can serve an extra-aesthetic purpose and whether, if it can, it should do so. Part of the answer to the first query depends on the cognitive potential of works of art. If a work of art tells us something important about life, then insofar as this knowledge can be used apart from the aesthetic experience in which it was achieved, it acquires a social value. If works of art can develop certain aspects of personality needed for social justice or stability, not necessarily as sources of knowledge but simply as causes for the formation of attitudes or alternations of habits, then again art can be said to have extra-aesthetic social values.

The intimate relation of art to religion indicates in a more general way how and why art is used for extra-aesthetic purposes. A wedding, funeral, or birth acquires added significance if accented by rituals that employ music, costume, and stylized gestures. Artistic means can be used to capture attention and to rivet it to the event under scrutiny. In Dewey's terms, art converts the conglomerate of actions into *an* experience, framed and outlined, with a beginning, middle, and end. It makes the event vivid for perception and paves the way for intensified feeling and involvement. Much of what we call civilization consists of sublimating biological activities by imagining them as significant beyond their biological utility. Eating is transmuted by imagination which is then objectified by art into dining. Similarly, sex gratification is transmuted into more than coitus, fighting into more than mutual destruction, and human society into more than mutual aid.

There is little question that art has been used for extra-artistic purposes and that such purposes have often been the causes or occasions for the production of great works of art. The only methodological stricture seems to be that in making judgments about a work of art the aesthetic and extra-aesthetic criteria be kept separate and distinct.

The chief problem is a moral one. Should artists be used as instruments of social policy at all? Or should they be so used only if such use does not impair their aesthetic integrity? The schools face the same questions.

Let us somewhat arbitrarily answer the moral question by deciding that in principle artistic autonomy is more important socially than any specific nonartistic use that can be made of it. Without going into detail, an argument could be made that without such autonomy not only will art suffer, but also that its usefulness as a social instrument will deteriorate.

If we make this kind of decision, then the school would seem to be directed to promote that autonomy wherever possible and to give it priority in cases of conflict. This would mean that aesthetic education is not to be justified solely by its social consequences or other nonaesthetic consequences.

It would mean that literature would not be selected and taught *primarily* to inculcate democratic values or to develop character of one kind or another. On the other hand, given restrictions of time, the school may be wise to choose literature for the curriculum that is not only good art but also an aesthetic presentation of a value system important in the understanding and appreciation of our culture. Of course, if theory precludes the work of art from "saying" anything of this sort, this principle of selection would have no meaning.[19]

The other consideration that enters into the decision to foster aesthetic education for its extra-aesthetic consequences is that popular art is already being used to shape the values of the people. Because this kind of art can function with virtually no formal instruction in art, it can easily be used as an instrument of social control. Government, industry, and other power complexes can become the taste-makers by control of the mass media.

The serious artist makes a claim that insofar as his art does make pronouncements about value they are dictated by his aesthetic perception alone and not by parochial interests that have become vested within him. In this sense, he makes a claim to serve truth and can act as a corrective to art that is not so directed and motivated. I do not know how to evaluate this claim except that in any given era it might be shown that the serious artist has felt what events later confirmed; that dislocations between the individual and his society are often sensed by the artist without his even being consciously aware of what was disturbing him. I take it that this was what the quotation from William Carlos Williams meant to convey.

If at least some of the propositions in art theory and criticism have cognitive status, then art education could be the means for safeguarding the body politic from itself. Just as science is society's defense against distortions of intellect by prejudice and special interests, so high cultivation in art is society's defense against undisciplined feeling swayed by parochial interests and limited experience. If art does make some connection with reality, i.e., with the import of life, then art education at a high level is as essential to individual development and

---

[19]One need not accept Leo Tolstoy's dictum that only art which communicated an affirmation of the ultimate values of an age is good art in order to justify the use of this criterion in the selection of items for the school's curriculum in aesthetic appreciation. However, if no art or no good art can in principle communicate such an affirmation, then the criterion is meaningless.

social health as is science or industry. The distortions and aberrations of subjective experience, i.e., the life of feeling, are as dangerous as aberrations in knowledge of physical reality, perhaps more so.

Summary

It is now time to pull together the numerous threads that have been introduced to this discourse.

The structure of knowledge in the arts leads us to inquire, first of all, whether anything that qualifies as knowledge is to be found in the arts.

To answer this question it was necessary to distinguish between what the work of art itself had to say, what the artist and appreciator had to know in their respective activities, and what could intelligently be said about works of art. Does a work of art say anything? If so, can it claim to be knowledge? Are the competences needed to make or appreciate works of art classifiable as knowledge, and if so, of what kind? Are theories about what the work of art is supposed to accomplish classifiable as knowledge? Are judgments made by art critics classifiable or warrantable as knowledge?

I believe that aside from the question as to what the work of art itself says, the problems are not of special difficulty. I believe that one can identify and classify the types of knowledge involved in knowing about the content of a work of art, the know-how of technique, and the judgments about the work of art. Certainly, there is no insuperable difficulty in classifying the cognitive activity involved in making historical statements about art and artists, about periods, styles, and developments. Judgments about the sensuous materials of the work of art, its technique, its formal properties, and its extra-aesthetic function can be made in propositional form and reasons given for them that can be understood and, in some sense, checked by those who are competent to do so.

The sticky points all have to do with the expressive function of the work of art itself and the judgments that are based upon it. With regard to the work of art itself, there is, I take it, no serious argument that holds that a painting or a concerto makes explicitly conceptual, descriptive statements about reality. Works of art are not constructed out of concepts whose purpose is to symbolize referents outside of themselves in a nonambiguous way. There is no lexicon or syntax of the images that constitute art. In short, it is exceedingly hard to construe works of art as *statements* of meaning. But as objects of perception they can and often do express a meaning by making an image of some feeling or idea or some combination of them.

I have argued that such expressions, while not statements, and therefore not assertions, are, nevertheless, clues from which inferences that are assertions can be made. Thus, while Beethoven's Ninth Symphony is not a set of statements about the exaltation of creation, the sounds are images of that complex of mood, idea, feeling, and action. Hearing it, one could infer that this is what creation feels like and that it is all very impressive and important. From the clues in some works of art one can make immediate inferences about the nature of love, of death, of war, of ideals, of every divagation of human experience, actual and possible. In this sense the work of art can be full of information for lack of which, if we do not die, yet we are immeasurably poorer and more ignorant.

However, works of art can express little or much, the trivial as well as the profound, and in many instances what they express is secondary to the stimulation of rich and full perception that they afford. This intrinsic value of the aesthetic experience in one way simplifies the problem of justifying aesthetic education because none is needed, but in order of social importance means are higher than ends. Unless art has extra-aesthetic values it will encounter hard going in the competition for financial and curricular support.

It has been suggested that art education can make a case for itself if (a) one can defend the theory that it makes connection with reality in some unique way and is revelatory of it, (b) if one can defend the theory that one work of art is better than another, i.e., if there are intelligible standards, (c) that serious or fine art provides experience that is better than popular art or no art at all, (d) that art education, including the various knowledge forms it contains, can make a difference in preferences, and (e) finally, that such education can be protected from abuse in the form of political manipulation or social engineering.

Perhaps the safest and most modest claim that one ought to make for art education is that it helps to develop the perceptual habits of the person in that peculiar mode we have called aesthetic. To paraphrase Jenkins, from this aesthetic perspective, we exploit things in terms of their particularity by transforming them into images, which by virtue of art sharpen our insight into the actual characters of things, rather than enlarge our conception of relations among things, or bind them to our purposes.[20]

---

[20]*Op. cit.*, pp. 37 ff.

The Logic of Teaching in the Arts

B. OTHANEL SMITH

It is the purpose of this essay to examine the logic of teaching in the domain of valuation and in the area of appreciation in the arts. In the course of exploring this aspect of teaching, we shall deal briefly with the meaning of "teaching." It is hoped that the use of the word "logic" in connection with "teaching" will not alarm anyone. True, logic has seldom been a fashionable subject, and many teachers will doubt its usefulness. But any teacher who tries to lead a class through the lines of reasoning upon which a conclusion rests will sense instantly the logical aspects of his enterprise and the necessity of understanding them.

Meaning of "Teaching"

Almost everything we have come to know about teaching—or what we think we know about it—has been drawn by speculation from philosophy and psychology, salted with a bit of practical wisdom. We have not typically gone into the classroom to find out from actual observation what teaching is. Consequently, when we read in the books about problem-teaching, lecture-teaching, question-answer teaching, project teaching, individualized teaching, or any other of the so-called methods of teaching, we are reading about what an author thinks the teacher ought to do according to the teaching of philosophy

From the *Teachers College Record*, Vol. LXIII, No. 3 (1961), pp. 176-83. Reprinted by permission of the author and the *Teachers College Record*.

and psychology. The author does not tell us what a teacher actually does when he teaches. Yet how can we prescribe how the teacher should teach unless we can describe teaching as an observable and modifiable form of behavior?

To most of us, it seems obvious that matters of fact are determined by observation. But we have been slow to follow this maxim in our study of teaching, preferring to go along with the ancient Greeks, who believed in thinking rather than looking. Aristotle held that women have fewer teeth than men. He was married twice, but it never occurred to him to peer into his wives' mouths to test his belief. Of course, Aristotle was a genius in anybody's book, but his mistakes about nature and women only underline the fact that there is no substitute for observation when you want to know facts. If we want to know what teaching is, the place to begin is in the classroom. Teaching is describable in terms of what teachers actually do rather than what we think they ought to do. At least, it seems reasonable to hold that teachers do teach and that what they do when they teach is what constitutes teaching.

In a recent study currently in progress,[1] we made intensive observations of the behavior of teachers in the classroom to find out what they do when they teach. These observations are made from a special point of view—that of the logic of teaching. It is an important angle from which to look at teaching, no less important for the teacher of art or music or literature than for other teachers.

To study teaching as it actually goes on in the classroom, one must have a record of the teacher's performance. Of course, the most complete record would consist of films and sound recordings. But to get such a full account of teaching is very expensive. Instead, we have made tape recordings of classroom discussion, supplemented by notes taken on the spot by an observer. We have tape-recorded about 125 class periods in various academic subjects in grades nine through twelve.

From an analysis of these recordings, we conclude that teachers generally do two sorts of things: (1) They show how to do something, and (2) they say or tell something. The saying or telling is much the greater part of what the teacher does. We might, of course, have surmised that teaching consists in these two things from what we know about our language. The words "teach" and "show" have a common Teutonic origin. If this were not so, we would still assume the close association between teaching and showing from what we know about early man. Although the origins of teaching are lost in man's obscure beginnings, it is easy to conjecture that it first took the form of showing the young how to do simple hand work and other physical tasks.

It may be further surmised that as language grew and the experience of the race became stored in the language, teaching took on the form of saying and

---

[1]The analysis reported herein was made pursuant to a contract with the U.S. Office of Education, Department of Health, Education, and Welfare.

telling. Certain things, such as the deeds of heroes long dead, ideas about the spirits and gods, and explanations of events, could not be shown. They could only be talked about; thus, teaching came to include a form of talking.

Thus showing and saying or telling make up what we call teaching. No one can teach anything to anybody without either showing him something or saying something to him. Of course, the words "showing," "telling," and "saying" are vague and ambiguous. But they are clear enough for present purposes if we remember that we are using "showing" in the sense of showing *how* rather than in the sense of merely displaying or exhibiting, and that we are using "saying" or "telling" to mean narrating and relating as well as stating that such and such is the case, as it is the case that this is a beautiful day or that cats prowl.

Language of Teaching

Whether or not showing or saying is predominant in a teacher's behavior depends to a large extent upon what he is teaching. The teaching of history and literature, for example, depends primarily upon words, that is, upon talking about something or upon verbal exchanges between teacher and students. We cannot teach history by showing students how to "do" history. One does not learn how to do history as he learns to do sums in arithmetic or to mix paints. He learns history in the sense of learning what is said about the past, he learns to talk about the past. And the same can be said of the teaching and learning of literature. On the other hand, the teaching of typing, for example, leans heavily upon acts of showing. Although a teacher may tell a student how to type, it is often more effective to show him how to do it. Obviously, teaching the history and appreciation of art is like the teaching of history and literature. It is largely a verbal activity; it cannot be carried on without the use of language. But the teaching of art in the sense of teaching how to make art objects requires showing how as well as telling how.

To understand teaching in terms of verbal behavior, it must be kept in mind that talking is itself a form of doing or acting. This point can hardly be overemphasized, since we are so much accustomed to associating verbal behavior with passivity. We have been told that if the teacher does all the talking, no learning is going on at all. This view has been pounded into our heads for almost fifty years in spite of the obvious fact that no one ever taught anybody anything without talking.

What are some of the actions that a teacher uses language to perform? There are at least three sorts: logical actions, directive actions, and admonitory actions. These actions are readily observed in the verbal behavior of teachers at work in the classroom. We shall not go into the details of how the analysis of these behaviors was made. Suffice it to say that classroom discourse, taped and transcribed, was analyzed into units which we call episodes. An episode consists of a verbal exchange between a teacher and one or more students. The episode typically opens with a question asked either by the student or by the teacher. The exchange usually ends in some form of reinforcing comment by the teacher, either in such expressions as "okay" or "all right" or in the simple repetition, with approval, of what the student said. Between the opening and the close is the body of the episode, and which may involve a number of verbal exchanges.

Here is the simplest form of an episode. The teacher asks, "Who was Woodrow Wilson?" A student says, "He was the twenty-eighth president of the United States." The teacher says, "All right." But an episode may also be very complex, involving a large number of exchanges between teacher and students and among the students themselves. Our tape transcriptions were analyzed into some 3,300 episodes, which we could classify into categories of logic.

Let us indicate a little more clearly what we mean by a logical category by giving an example of a simple episode and then showing the various standpoints from which it can be viewed for purposes of classification. Suppose a teacher asks, "What is a noun?" A student replies, "A noun is the name of a place or thing," and the teacher says, "Okay!" If we ask about the effect of this verbal exchange upon the student—Does it upset him emotionally? Does it motivate him to learn about nouns?—we are asking a psychological question. If we ask whether or not the definition of a noun given by the student is acceptable by authorities in the field of English, we are asking a content question. But if we ask whether or not the definition, as given by the student, meets the logical criteria for being a definition, then the question is a logical one. Any episode which can be evaluated by the rules of logic falls into what we call logical categories.

Verbal Actions

Our studies show that the logical actions which teachers perform, or which they require their students to perform, are varied and complex. By analyzing the verbal behavior of the classroom, we have found twelve types of logical actions: defining, describing, designating, stating, reporting, substituting, valuating, opining, classifying, comparing and contrasting, conditional inferring, and explaining. We have also identified a non-logical category which we call "classroom management." We cannot say for sure that these logical actions are typical of all teaching, but we do think that subsequent investigations would bear out the claim that these actions are found in the classroom discourse of all subjects and grades.

It is reasonable to suppose, therefore, that teaching will be improved when teachers learn to perform these logical actions more effectively. About 75 per cent of classroom discourse is concerned with the manipulation of subject matter. Because the manipulation of content nearly always involves logical operations, to improve the way these operations are handled and performed in the classroom is to improve teaching. Thus, a direct way to improve teaching is to increase the teacher's ability to deal with and perform these logical actions, to improve his way of dealing with logical aspects of classroom discourse.

The other two forms of verbal action previously mentioned, directive and admonitory actions, are, naturally, very important aspects of teaching performance. And they are, of course, non-logical actions. The teacher uses words to direct the student in certain activities. Instead of showing the student how something is done (for example, instead of actually performing such overt acts as placing the hands properly on the keyboard of a typewriter), the teacher may tell the student to do thus-and-so. Verbal actions of this sort frequently occur in the teaching of skills, especially those involving overt action, such as the skills entailed by painting or performance on a musical instrument.

It is important to note that directive verbal behavior is effective only when the acts which students are to perform are repetitive. Repetitive acts can be diagnosed, and the individual performing them may thus be informed of his mistakes. Whatever can be repeated forms a pattern, and errors show up as deviations from the pattern. For example, there are patterns for typing, dancing, and for producing certain effects in color and sound. Directive actions help the student learn to perform within the patterns of such activities. But when the acts of the student are creative rather than repetitive, directive teaching behavior is irrelevant. No person can tell another how to be creative.

Admonitory action involves the teacher's approval or disapproval. He advises and enjoins. He tells students that their work is good or that they could have done better. All these are verbal actions, although the teacher may also use gestures and other natural expressions like frowns or smiles. But in admonishing the student with "John, you had better quiet down," he hardly expects the student to remember his words. He is concerned with the emotional impact of his words rather than with any knowledge they may convey.

Valuation and Appreciation

What has this analysis of teaching to do with the teaching of art? After all, it stresses the logical aspects of teaching and emphasizes the role of language. And one may naturally ask what bearing have logic and language on art. The answer is that they have much to do with the teaching of art because they bear directly upon the teaching of appreciation.

To appreciate is to recognize the worth of something, to value it highly, to appraise or estimate its worth. Appreciation is not the same thing as enjoyment. To enjoy is to like something, to feel the pleasure of it, to respond to it positively. If one enjoys a work of art, he likes it. Or he may appreciate it but not enjoy it. It would be self-contradictory to say, "I enjoy Matisse's 'White Plumes,' but I do not like it." At least, if someone were to say this, we would be entitled to ask him for some special explanation. On the other hand, it would not be self-contradictory to say, "I appreciate 'White Plumes,' but I do not like it." For the meaning of "appreciation" does not include the meaning of "liking." Neither would it be contradictory to say, "I enjoy 'White Plumes,' but I do not appreciate it," although we are not likely to hear anyone talk this way.

We can say, then, that appreciation has logical dimensions, whereas enjoyment is a psychological matter and has no logical aspects at all. Suppose I were to say, "I appreciate Matisse's 'White Plumes.'" It would be sensible for you to ask for evidence, for you to demand of me the facts and rules by which I decided upon the value of "White Plumes" as a work of art. If I fail to present such evidence, you may rightly doubt that I appreciate the painting. You may think with good reason that I was putting up a front. For appreciation involves judgments or conclusions; judgments and conclusions are logical matters, requiring evidence for their support. And I have produced no evidence to support my claim to appreciation.

But suppose you were to say, "I enjoy 'White Plumes.'" Then it would be odd for me to ask you for evidence that you enjoy it. Enjoyment is a psychological process or state, not something that rests upon proof. Your statement that you enjoy something is not a conclusion or judgment, but a report of how you feel about something. You may say, were I to question you, that you enjoy the painting even though I seem to doubt that you do. And you may go on to say that if I watch you when you are looking at the painting, I will see that you are enjoying it. But if such observations do not convince me, you can still maintain that you do like Matisse's "White Plumes." It would be somewhat like my trying to convince you that you do not have a headache when in fact your head is aching terribly.

Logically speaking, appreciating a work of art is comparable to deciding upon the desirability of a course of action, upon the truth of a statement or upon the moral rightness of conduct. To appreciate a work of art is to make a decision about it—to decide, for example, whether or not it is beautiful or original, whether it belongs to this school or that, or whether it expresses some significant aspect of culture. In short, to appreciate a work of art is not to describe it in any way, but to render a judgment about it.

Appreciation is thus logically oriented. To teach one how to handle appreciation questions is necessarily to be involved in performing certain logical operations—defining, valuing, explaining. These operations make up about 25 per cent of teaching performance in general. And it is reasonable to suppose that they comprise a considerable part of teaching in the domain of appreciation.

The Appreciative Decision

The role of logic in dealing with questions of appreciation underscores the kinship between art teaching and teaching in other fields. It is often assumed that teaching students to appreciate art is unlike teaching in other subjects, and some people say it is not really teaching at all, that appreciation is caught, not taught. These are both mistaken notions. Teaching students how to handle questions of appreciation is not essentially different from teaching them how to deal with questions of valuation in any field of learning. When teaching in the domain of valuation is performed thoroughly, it involves three things: a set of criteria or rules or standards for judging, a set of facts, and a judgment of how well the facts satisfy the criteria or standards. These same requirements hold for teaching in the domain of art appreciation because appreciation is a form of valuation.

Let us give some examples of valuation questions to show more concretely that appreciation questions are the same sort of thing:

1. In a study of *Cry the Beloved Country,* the teacher asks, "Is the law just that says that a man should be hanged who accidentally kills another man because he's frightened while robbing the man's house?"
2. In a history class, the teacher asks, "Do you think it's a safe assumption that Jackson would decide today, as he did a hundred and thirty years ago, on the same issue?"
3. In another class, a boy asks: "These magazines about true stories—Are those things really true?"
4. In an art class, a student asks, "Is it fair for an artist to use his medium to promote a point of view?"
5. In a literature class, the teacher asks, "Do you think it's true that one can arrange for another's happiness?"
6. In a physics class, the teacher asks, "Is friction good or bad?"

Such questions ask the student to decide something—to decide whether or not an assumption is safe, a statement is true, a law is just, an artist is fair, friction is good.

To make such decisions wisely requires a consideration of both facts and criteria. But all too often, when the student makes a decision in these cases, the teacher either accepts or rejects it without regard for the facts and criteria involved. This practice of disregarding facts and criteria is probably the chief defect of teaching in the domain of valuation. For example, here is an episode that is typical of the way value questions are handled in class:

Student: These magazines about true stories—Are those things really true?
Teacher: Well, I don't know whether that's a magazine or whether these articles are true.
Student: Well—it is—people send in their stories.
Teacher: Yes.

The point of this verbal exchange hinges on the uses of the word "true" and the ways of deciding the truth-value of a statement. But this fact is not recognized by the teacher, or else he chooses not to deal with it. As a result, the value question is passed over, and in consequence, the students fail to learn the difference between facts and criteria of judgment, and they also miss the experience of thinking through a value question to a justifiable judgment.

Questions of Criteria

A more appropriate way of dealing with the student's question of "Are these stories really true?" is to raise the further question of what is meant by "true." The student held that whatever a person writes from his own experience is true, and he concluded from this that what is printed in the true-story magazines is true because it is written from personal experience. Now, the teacher could have helped the class analyze logically the student's conclusion about the truth of the stories. He could have called attention to fact that the word "true" is a value term, that whether a statement is true or not is, in the final analysis, a matter of decision rather than a matter of fact, and that we use criteria to decide whether a statement is either true or false.

Specifically, the teacher could have helped the class see that the student's criterion of "true" was "Whatever a person writes from his own experience is true." This criterion could then have been put in the context of other criteria, and the basis of decision would have been profitably broadened. He could have suggested that some individuals hold the criterion that whatever is revealed is true, that others insist that whatever is intuited is true, that still others maintain that any statement which accords with observations is true, etc. Unless these various criteria are recognized by the students, the value question is dealt with at a very superficial level.

Once the diversity of possible criteria is recognized, differences of opinion will arise as to which criterion can best be used in the particular case. Until these differences are somewhat reconciled, there is no common ground for deciding the question of whether or not what is said in the stories is "true." Hence, the first thing to do when dealing with value questions in the classroom is to help the students to uncover the criteria which are being used and to select from among possible criteria those which are useful in answering relevant questions of value.

The next step is to examine the situation to see whether or not the facts of the case meet the criteria. Let us suppose, for purposes of illustration, that the student's criterion — that anything a person writes from his own experience is true — is an acceptable one. The factual question now to be faced is whether or not the stories in the true-story magazines are based upon personal experience. If they are, then by this criterion the stories are true. If it can be shown that these stories are not based upon personal experiences, then by the *same* criterion they are false. If one cannot find out what the stories are based upon, then their truth is indeterminate and one has to say that he does not know whether they are true or not.

These, then, are the phases involved in handling value questions in the classroom: first, identify and decide upon the criteria or standards of judgment; second, examine the situation to see whether or not the observed facts meet the criteria; and finally, in terms of the criteria and facts, decide upon the value of the object in question.

Valuation in the arts follows the same pattern. In dealing with value questions, the art teacher must be concerned with the facts and the criteria. If he deals with the facts alone, he may expand the student's enjoyment of art without necessarily increasing his appreciation of it. He may help the student analyze a painting by raising factual questions. For example, he may ask whether or not it is painted with brush strokes that follow the form; he may ask whether the painting consists mainly of floating squares of color, or he may ask whether nearby objects are diminished and the more remote ones increased in size. Then he may go on to ask about the effects accomplished by these various techniques. These are all factual questions, and a discussion of them may help the student understand a painting and thereby expand the range of things he may enjoy. But discussion of such questions does not lead to appreciation unless it is coupled with a discussion or analysis of some set of criteria by which value decisions are ultimately made.

Standards of Taste

At this point, however, the teacher may be (and usually understandably is) faced by a bewildering number of criteria. He will be faced by those which the students propose, and, in addition, by traditional value criteria inherited from previous periods in the history of art and aesthetic taste. For example, in times past, beauty in art was associated with beauty of the subject. Hence the skillful representation of a beautiful subject was—by this criterion—the essence of a beautiful painting. At another time, nobility of subject matter was held to be essential to beauty in art. Hence, if art was to imitate nature, it had to imitate nature in its ideal form. Then, as everyone knows, there came a revolt against content. Form, pure form, and not subject matter became the criterion of artistic beauty; a work of art was beautiful to the extent that its subject matter was refined away and pure design remained. Then some individuals came to hold that art is beautiful to the extent that its form consists in soft and flowing lines and subtle curves, whereas others stressed sharp lines and angles. Still other persons tended to associate beauty with a work of art which aroused the emotions. Of course, as any art teacher knows, this is a pitifully short list of standards of taste. But it will serve our purpose here.

What is a teacher to do when faced with such a congeries of criteria? For one thing, it is well for him to help the student see that criteria for deciding the aesthetic value of art shift from time to time, from one school of art to another, from one cultural phase to another. In this respect, the art teacher's task is no different from that of a teacher in any other subject in which attempts are made to deal with value questions. It is characteristic of value questions that the criteria by which they are settled are constantly in flux and beset with controversy.

For another thing, the teacher can direct the students to an examination of the various criteria themselves and to choosing those to be used in making their judgments. It is important here for the students to understand that when they decide upon criteria, they are by this choice determining what facts about the work of art are relevant and worth considering. They are also deciding at the same time the justification they will give for their judgment of the work of art in question. If the students are asked why they think the particular work is beautiful or good, they can answer logically only by reference to the criteria they have chosen and the facts observed about the work of art itself. In other words, questions which ask for explanations in art are answered by the same logic as similar questions in mathematics, English, social studies, and science.

In suggesting the handling of art appreciation in terms of logic, what we are saying is open to the objection that we are calling for a return to the old academic tradition in art—substituting understanding for intuition, reason for imagination, facts and rules for happiness and pleasure, logic for feeling. This objection is ill founded. There is not the slightest evidence that the use of logic in teaching impedes the intuitive or imaginative processes. Nor are the feelings neutralized by the performance of logical operations. It is true, however, that the use of reason and logic increases neither the intuitive nor the imaginative abilities. Indeed, we do not know how to develop these abilities through instruction or, for that matter, in any other way. The significance of what we have been suggesting boils down to the question of what we wish to accomplish by instruction in art appreciation. If we want students to be disciplined in the processes of making value judgments, to be skilled in the handling of value questions, to be alert to the pitfalls of reasoning and prudent in making decisions and taking actions, and to be perceptive of the deeper aspects of art, then a renewed emphasis upon the logical aspects of teaching in the arts, as well as in other subjects, seems clearly called for.

Research as the Verification of Aesthetics

EDMUND B. FELDMAN

It is too easy to hurl the epithet "mystificateur" at the old-fashioned humanist or the new-fashioned existentialist who questions the usefulness or validity of research in art education. More than likely this critic does not question research as an enterprise but the lack of aesthetic sophistication on the part of the entrepreneur. If we grant that some persons are too fond of their subjective judgments and *a priori* assertions about art and art teaching, nevertheless their reservations about the usefulness of research findings about aesthetic phenomena and art teaching practices may be soundly based. Fundamentally, I suppose, the sceptic wonders whether aesthetic judgments can be adapted to statistical usage (if seventy-five youngsters say they "like" "The Blue Boy," does this in any serious sense mean anything?). And then, suspecting that organismic responses can be reliably anticipated, he fears that successful research will somehow curtail artistic freedom. I am sure that today even uneducated persons recognize a connection between successful research in the social sciences and the ability to control large-scale human behavior. So the position of the sceptic is an ambivalent one: It involves fundamental disbelief in the claims of research and genuine fear that they may be sound.

Therefore, to allay the fears of the sceptic and to overcome the charge that

From *Studies in Art Education,* Vol. I, No. 1 (1959), pp. 19-25. Reprinted by permission of the author and *Studies in Art Education.*

research does not come to grips with the authentic character of human involvement in artistic affairs, I should like to suggest an agenda for research. It will deal with a relationship between the speculative realm of aesthetics and the practical realm of art education. Particularly, I want to deal with art education as the discipline directly concerned with the "verification" of propositions in aesthetics.

Research in Aesthetics and Research in Art Education

By research in aesthetics I mean investigation of an empirical character into the general circumstances surrounding the creation, understanding, and uses of art. By research in art education I mean empirical investigation of the teaching practices which result in the creation and understanding of art. Now, one does not know what research will uncover, and hence art educational research may incidentally add to our knowledge of the personality traits of artists, teachers, children, adolescents, and adults. But I think the important distinction between the two areas of research is that art educational research is always concerned about personality or creativity or adaptability or stimulation in connection with the production and use of the class of things we call art objects. One must not lose sight of the object. Investigation of behavior is properly undertaken when it is behavior which demonstrably leads to artistic production or experience.

Secondly, art educational research is concerned with the differentia of aesthetic response in a *context of teaching*. This is not said in order to delimit research artificially but in recognition of the fact that to be useful to teachers, research must consider the unique features of their situation. The aesthetician may be interested in how membership in a cultural group affects the content of aesthetic experience; the art educational researcher is interested in how teaching can *change* the content of aesthetic experience. This leads us to the observation that all educational research has some kind of systematic change in practice as its ultimate goal, while aesthetic investigation is more disinterested: aesthetics is content to increase its knowledge about artistic phenomena.

We have learned from other areas of pure or disinterested research that increased knowledge leads to increased power to make systematic changes. Hence the knowledge gained from aesthetic investigation is at our disposal in art education for the purpose of instituting systematic changes in teaching. Our researchers would be prudent, it seems to me, to investigate the impact of aesthetic propositions upon the production, use and understanding of art. Thus they would begin at a more sophisticated level of inquiry, one which is closer to the practice of art teaching. They should ask the questions which the artistically concerned person asks rather than the questions which the behaviorist psychologist asks because he possesses the tools to answer them.

The interest in systematic change which I attribute to art educational research suggests that we have a normative as opposed to a descriptive discipline. To practice a normative profession means to have an image of health or excellence or proper functioning. In other words, it means the practitioner has a bias in favor of his own view of excellence. This bias creates the possibility that art education research can be "interesting." That is, research is designed to fortify particular preconceptions about what artistic learning and production ought to be. In a vigorous research climate, therefore, the multiplication of biases will minimize the danger that artistic behavior may be controlled.

I should like to illustrate the difference between the normative interest of the art educator and the disinterested inquiry of the aesthetician. Suppose the aesthetician discovers that persons with a high school education and a certain income level and occupational status tend to prefer French Provincial furniture in their bedrooms and "art moderne" in their kitchens. He may relate this knowledge to a wide variety of apparently unrelated characteristics which persons in this group share: their social and political behavior, their attitudes about child rearing, their opinions of space research, the time they spend on gardening, etc. The aesthetician's investigation is undertaken on the basis of an intuition that some factor or set of factors *causes* these attitudes and traits to occur together. When he has identified these factors and formed a generalization about them, he has made his contribution. The art educator wonders what use can be made of this generalization and this constellation of traits in teaching. He must design a research experiment which confirms the operational validity of this knowledge in a context other than the one in which it was originally acquired. Then further, he must design research which shows how the relationships under scrutiny *can be changed*. This is the creative element in art educational research which involves the investigator's own set of values and priorities. Furthermore, this is the operation which I regard as the verification of a proposition in aesthetics. One cannot say that a generalization in aesthetics is valid, from *our* standpoint, until it has been put to work, so to speak, in an educational context.

Unconscious Aesthetic Assumptions

We may regard verification in this sense as a process — not of "finding true" — but of "making true" certain propositions in aesthetics. However, propositions in aesthetics are not usually understood or stated in a form which admits of verification in the classical sense. But aesthetic propositions continue to be made in the literature implicitly, they are taught or tacitly assumed in teacher education, and they are shared at many levels of awareness by pupils, parents, and administrators. These propositions may be regarded as unconscious aesthetic assumptions. Certainly teachers and artists and laymen hold such assumptions about creative ability, "beauty", critical standards, evaluative procedures, the relation between form and content, originality, and so on. Just as people hold ethical views they have never examined but which nevertheless inform their behavior, unconscious assumptions of an aesthetic character inform art teaching. It is not in the nature of art educational research, at least as currently conceived, to examine these unconscious aesthetic assumptions. This is probably because research itself has an unconscious bias in favor of the kinds of mensuration practiced in the physical sciences and tends to disbelieve in the existence of categories proposed by gestaltist or psychoanalytic psychologies. Perhaps it will be possible for art education research based on behaviorist models to make progress in this difficult area without resorting to the introspective methods it disdains. In any event, a means should be devised for accounting for the difference between theory and practice in art education, one which gathers information by a more sophisticated method than the circulation of questionnaires.

If art educational research sees the role of verification for itself, one can anticipate several fortunate outcomes. (1) The field of aesthetics, afflicted with a heavy metaphysical burden, will see its relation to life more clearly. It will be reconceived as a discipline which does more than speculate about art after the fact, but which has an impact upon the creation, teaching, and consumption of art. We may regard the present visible body of formal statements in aesthetics as a superstructure which is somehow related to a vaster, invisible, inchoate body of aesthetic assumption which is much more influential in the disposition of artistic affairs. Does it not seem reasonable that research should identify and bring to light the influences which in fact govern art instruction? (2) The persons and institutions charged with a responsibility to educate art teachers will gain a more accurate idea of what is being learned about art and carried into art teaching. At present one can only observe an embarassing discrepancy between the goals of teacher education programs and the actual performance of teachers in classrooms. (3) The discipline of art education itself will enter into an organic relation with aesthetics which does not now obtain. Currently, in our field, we teach a Philosophy of Art Education which is neither Aesthetics nor Methods of Art Education, but which draws upon both. I believe we *have* a philosophy of art education and an obligation to teach it to our students because the material in aesthetics has not been properly brought to bear upon its natural consequences in life. We have been obliged, in other words, to undertake on an unsystematic basis, the synthesis of materials from art education and aesthetics in the education of art teachers.

Some Existential Considerations

It can be argued that the creation of art does not depend upon knowledge of aesthetic principles. The artist does not need to know about aesthetics and some persons feel he should always remain innocent of aesthetics. Perhaps only mediocre works of art and a very thin kind of experience result from artistic activity which is consciously guided by art theory. The artist, child or adult, finds himself creating because he has to. Or, placed in a situation where there are materials, and guided and stimulated by a skilled teacher, he produces art objects inevitably. The teacher of art, for a variety of reasons, finds himself in a situation where he gives and receives, and one of the consequences of his being in that situation is that the other persons create art products. Art is an incidental result of their encounter. That is, for the students it is incidental. We cannot avoid the suspicion that for the teacher it is at least a partly intended result. The presence of some kind of motive on the part of the teacher before he *encounters* his pupils means that he functions both within and *outside of* the existential dialogue with his pupils. And to be outside of the dialogue, to have a motive in advance of and above teaching, even to have a *plan,* means having a theory on the basis of which action will be taken.

I recognize that the plan or theory is not the complete basis of what takes place in the teaching encounter. One revises a plan, or even discards it. The ground of one's action is shifted in the course of acting upon it. This is to say that one chooses among many alternative plans of action while teaching. Perhaps the excellent teacher possesses the ability to change his instruction so that he can respond authentically to the realities of the teaching encounter. In a sense, the plan is not real, but the teaching encounter and its qualities *are* real.

Consequently, it would seem that there are events taking place at the heart of teaching which it is exceedingly difficult for research to deal with. But this is only if we conceive of research as a purely external activity, an essentialistic activity which seeks to discover the *name* of the thing which teaching and learning is. I do not myself believe that the "mysteries" at the heart of teaching must necessarily remain inaccessible to research.

Now we may attempt to formulate a conception of verification through art educational research which takes into consideration this view of art teaching.

(1) All plans, motives, goals for the teaching of art take their origin from aesthetics. These are either formally understood or unconsciously assumed. In the first instance, therefore, the objective of research is to discover the aesthetic basis which one way or another informs the teaching or learning under scrutiny.

(2) Having identified the formal principle which underlies an artistic event, i.e., the principle of which the event is an illustration, the researcher attempts to invoke the same principle in other artistic events. Here research tries to find out if it has a theoretical instrument which not only explains, accounts for, an artistic phenomenon, but also will *cause* the phenomenon in the future. Thus far, we are working on an essentialistic basis.

(3) The theoretical instrument is brought into the teaching situation to discover how it responds to the contingencies of the pupil-teacher interaction. Thus far, the instrument has been dependent for its security upon the success the researcher has in predicting its operation in a number of instances. The

instrument exists because the researcher surveys his data and says it exists, and furthermore, asserts that it will continue to exist. But each time that a teacher and pupil meet, each of them knows that he is involved in a unique instance and each of them experiences the uniqueness of the event. Hence the verification, the "making true" of an aesthetic principle, consists of an account of the qualities of an event as seen from without and reported from within when a particular principle now used as a practical instrument is introduced in teaching.

The problem of art educational research as opposed to other kinds of scientific research is to find a procedure which is responsive to the individual's acute sense of contingency in aesthetic situations. This contingency is related to the freedom which teachers and pupils think or believe they have. Art seems to be the evidence of their freedom. I hope research will find a way to incorporate the unique qualities and events within artistic situations into its scientific endeavor.

II

THE PROBLEM OF DEFINITION

Introduction

In as much as the student who comes upon these readings may not have done any work in formal logic, this section is introduced by a discussion by Max Black devoted to eludicating the logic of definition. A careful study of Black's chapter should enable the reader to appreciate better why disputes originate in discourse about art and why confusion and ambiguity can often be traced to talking at cross purposes. Confusion in the use of language can be reduced, Black points out, if attention is paid to distinguishing different kinds of defintions and to understanding the rules for good definitions. The explanations of the terms class, subclass, genus, species, and differentia, moreover, should help render other essays in this section more manageable.

Definition

MAX BLACK

*The light of human minds is perspicuous words, but by
exact definitions first* snuffed *and* purged *from ambiguity.*
— Hobbes.

1. The Occasions of Definition

Language is a complex social instrument. We learn to use it, in childhood and
throughout adult life, by imitation, practice, and deliberate instruction.

For many purposes, imitation and practice are good enough; we learn to
make ourselves understood by watching others and trying to do likewise. And
this normally requires little conscious thought. A variety of situations arise,
however, in which a deliberate and conscious attempt to explain the meanings
of words must be made. The examples that follow illustrate some of the
purposes thereby served.

Introduction of new terms. A flight instructor must be able to refer to the
various parts of an airplane. If he left his students to discover the meaning of
"aileron," and the other technical terms, by trial and error, their studies would
end in crashes. It is easier and safer to *state explicitly* that an aileron is a
"lateral-control flap at the rear of the airplane's wingtips." An intelligent
hearer, to whom the words used in the explanation are familiar, will *immedi-*

From Max Black, *Critical Thinking* (2nd ed.; Englewood Cliffs, N. J.: Prentice-Hall, Inc., 1952),
pp. 203-24. © 1952. Reprinted by permission of Prentice-Hall, Inc., Englewood Cliffs, N. J., and the
author.

ately know how to identify an aileron. Most technical terms, words introduced to serve a special purpose, need to be accompanied by deliberate instruction in their use.

Removal of ambiguity. Two men are talking about "socialism." The first claims that "socialism is here already," since the Federal Government controls prices, wages, and the production of goods. The other retorts that socialism is a "logical absurdity": "Imagine anybody sharing a toothbrush with millions of fellow Americans."

Disputes of this kind, in which the contenders are talking about *different matters symbolized by the same word,* are all too common. It is noteworthy that *no disagreement concerning matters of fact may be involved;* for both men may agree about the extent of the control exercised by the Federal Government, and also about the impossibility of sharing all personal belongings. If the dispute nevertheless continues with unabated fury, it may be because the disputants insist on using the crucial term "socialism" in different senses. By "socialism" one man understands federal control of economic activity; the other, the common use of personal property.

When people talk "at cross purposes" in this way, the normal assumption (that others use words as we do) breaks down, and no "meeting of minds" is possible. The cure for such failure in communication is *definition* of the key terms in the argument....

Extension of meaning. When Marshal Pétain was on trial for treason, an important duty of the French court was to determine what meaning "treason" was to have *in that context.* Treason is generally understood to be breach of allegiance to the sovereign power of a state, but the lawmakers had not considered a case in which the head of a state himself gave aid and comfort to the enemy invader. The unusual circumstances made it necessary to give explicit definition of the crucial term. (For this reason, some of the chief witnesses were asked to explain their own conception of "treason.")

Similar situations constantly arise, and not only in legal practice. For our ideas must be applied in a constantly changing environment; a conscientious thinker must be prepared to stretch the meanings of the central terms of his thinking.

In the ancient cities of Greece, "democracy" meant a form of government in which a privileged minority (the "citizens") participated as a body in the conduct of civic affairs. As this type of democracy is unfeasible in a nation like our own with millions of citizens, we require some extension of meaning. Anybody who wants to preserve the values of ancient democracy will be led to ask such questions as: Is democracy compatible with minority rule? With *representative* institutions? Should it apply to economic as well as political matters? The answers adopted will provide the material for a *definition* of "democracy" in the contemporary context.

2. The Meaning of "Definition"

In the variety of situations illustrated above, we have seen that it is desirable to give explicit instruction in the use of words. We shall say that an explanation of the use of a word (or other sign) is a **definition.**

"Definition" is to be understood as having "process-product" variation in meaning according to circumstances.... It may mean either the activity of explaining how a word is to be used or the outcome of that activity—usually a certain *statement*. (We are, of course, explaining how *we* shall use the term "Definition," and thereby establishing an "individual" or "contextual" meaning of the term. But in so doing we are remaining close to some important "dictionary" meanings of the term.)

Definition of WORDS, not things. A dictionary has the entry, "*fox:* Red-furred sharp-snouted bushy-tailed quadruped." This may be contrasted with "Foxes are swift runners." The first statement (A), unlike the second (B), is not intended to make an assertion *only about foxes.*

In order to see this we need only to consider how the two assertions could be tested. To establish the truth of B, we must observe *foxes,* or use the testimony of others who are in a position to do this; moreover, this is *all* we need to do. One way of establishing the truth of A would be to wait for opportunities of hearing people say "That's a fox!" checking in each such case whether the speaker did indicate a quadruped that was bushy-tailed, and so on. If this procedure were followed, we should, as in the first case, observe foxes; but we should also observe people using *the word* "fox"; and A could not be tested *without* direct or indirect reference to such linguistic behavior. To look at foxes alone in order to test the definition would be as futile as looking at the planet Mars through a powerful telescope to see if the word "Mars" were inscribed on it. The reason we must pay attention to linguistic behavior in testing A is that the connection between *being a "fox"* and *having red fur* (or the other characteristics mentioned in the definition) is artificial or man-made. For this reason, also, the definition, A, unlike the second statement, can also be established without attention to foxes at all—as by asking sufficiently competent speakers of English what *they mean* when using the word.

In short a definition (in our sense) is always an assertion about a word, though it may also be an assertion about non-verbal things. It is to be carefully contrasted with statements in which *no* reference is made to words.

Standard forms for definition. As a reminder of the important point that definitions mention words, the definition examined might be written in the form:

The *word* 'fox' means a red-furred sharp-snouted bushy-tailed quadruped.

It is useful to have technical terms for referring to the different parts of such a definition. The word 'fox' is called the **definiendum** (from the Latin, meaning:

"that which is to be defined"), and the phrase "a red-furred sharp-snouted bushy-tailed quadruped" is called the **definiens** (Latin: "that which does the defining").

Thus a standard form of definition will be

"x" MEANS Y

where appropriate words are to be inserted at the places held open by the letters 'X' and 'Y'.

In a useful variation, the definiendum is presented as equivalent to another set of words that can be substituted for it. Thus "pleonasm" may be defined as follows:

"Pleonasm" *means the same as* "redundancy of expression."

The general form for this type of definition will be:

"x" MEANS THE SAME AS "Y"

3. The Relativity of Definition

Definition is a process in which the use of a word (or other sign) is explained *by somebody* and *for somebody*. As it "takes two to make a quarrel," so it takes *at least three* to make a genuine definition (the explanation and those who give and receive it). Definition, therefore, is more like a hand-shake than a sneeze: It is a social transaction.

The social transaction we call "definition" has as its purpose that the person to whom the definition is addressed shall be able to use the definiendum in the manner intended by the person supplying the definition. In order to be "good," a definition must achieve its purpose by causing the person to whom it is addressed to learn to use the definiendum in the way intended. A "good" definition is one that is good for the receiver of the definition. For the same reason, "good" medical treatment must cure the patient who receives it. The test of the medicine is its capacity to heal; the test of a definition is its capacity to enlighten *the person addressed*. A "good" definition that is not good *for somebody* is as much of an absurdity as a "comfortable" chair that makes nobody comfortable.

Important consequences follow from these simple considerations. First, it is plain that *different persons may need different definitions* (just as different patients may need different medical treatment even for the same disease).

A definition, as we have seen, uses words to explain the definiendum. In order to be adequate for the particular person addressed, the words used must be intelligible to him. And any definition that is understood is so far "good." A child has been heard to define "pepper" as "that sneezy stuff Mummy puts on my potatoes when she forgets." That might be good enough for a child, but it would not satisfy an analytical chemist. Yet a definition of "salt" as "sodium chloride with an admixture of impurities in amount not greater than one per cent of the total mass," while satisfactory for the purposes of the chemist, would be quite useless to the child.

By the **relativity of definition** we shall understand the principle that a definition ought to be formulated in a manner intelligible and useful to the particular hearer addressed. A "good" definition will be one that is both intelligible and *effective* in teaching its recipient the particular use intended.

Relativity of definition does not eliminate all uniformity of definition. Though men are diverse, and accordingly need diverse definitions, they are also similar and can often profit from the same definitions. This accounts for the usefulness of dictionaries, which are compilations of definitions *roughly* adequate for all who speak a certain language.

The truth of definitions. Consider, first, a case where a speaker invents a *new term* for his own use. His definition then has the form:

> By 'S' *I* shall mean (such and such)

or alternatively:

> By 'S' *let us* mean (such and such).

In this case, the definition clearly expresses a resolution (first form) or a proposal (second form). *A definition of this kind can be neither true nor false.* We can *accept* or *reject* it (on the grounds of its fitness for the purpose in hand), but to call it false would be as absurd as to call "Let us go for a walk" a lie. We shall call this kind a **stipulated** definition.

In sharp contrast is the case in which a speaker intends to give a definition conforming to some customary or contextual usage. The definition then takes the form:

> Such and such speakers when using 'S' *customarily mean* (such-and-such)

or else:

> When 'S' occurred *in this particular context* it meant (such-and-such).

This time the definition purports to be *true,* for it is not a proposal or resolution, but a report *about* the usage of the definiendum.

We shall call the latter types of definition **reported** definitions, of which "customary" or "dictionary" definitions will be a special case. All reported definitions are either true or false. (Thus the definition "In the English language, 'cow' means an inefficient admiral" is *false*.) Dictionaries are collections of reported definitions.

When occasion arises to give definitions of words *already in use,* there is seldom a clear-cut choice between adopting a stipulated or a reported definition. On the one hand it is important that we shall, so far as possible, choose *our* meanings of the words we use. But when handling words already used in relatively stable ways, to ignore the pre-existing meanings is to promote ambiguity and confusion. (It would be unwise to stipulate that "cow" should mean an inefficient admiral, so long as the same word continued to be used in the more familiar meaning.)

Freedom to assign meanings by means of a stipulated definition is therefore restricted by the definiteness of previous usage of the definiendum. When a word has relatively definite and precise customary uses (as in the case of "camera," say) there is almost no freedom to stipulate. When a word is used loosely (as in the case of "education"), freedom to stipulate is correspondingly greater. The art of definition consists in part in striking the right balance between the need to *make* our own signs (by assigning meaning to them) and the obligation to respect the meanings of signs already in use.

4. Rules of Definition

Most writers on logic follow an ancient tradition in providing a list of rules for good definitions. No doubt such rules are of use, or they would not continue to be given. Yet in view of what has already been said concerning the variety of purposes served by definition, and the need for adapting definitions to the background and needs of the hearer, infallible *recipes* for definition are not to be expected. Making a definition is like baking a cake; the artist's skill (whether he is a lexicographer or a cook) consists of making the best use of the materials available, and no one can learn how to do this by merely reading about the skills required. Nevertheless, there are some general maxims, which even the most skillful cooks do well to remember, and there are general hints on procedure in framing definitions that can help to forestall some common blunders.

1. *The definition should be adequate for the purpose it is to serve.*

This first rule is intended to help the reader clarify his purposes before attempting his own definitions or criticizing those of others. It is useful to ask such questions as "Am I trying to indicate the connotation of this word (or merely describing a part of its denotation)?" "Am I examining a stipulated or a reported definition?" and so on.

2. *The definition should be intelligible to the person addressed.*

The reasons for this rule have already been discussed under the heading of "relativity of definition." Among the most important implications are the following two:

2a: *The definiens should not contain any words that are as unintelligible (to the reader) as the definiendum.*

Since the definiens is intended to explain the use or meaning of the definiendum, it will not achieve its end unless composed of words that he understands relatively well. (Thus the definition " 'Dracocephalum' means the Dragonhead flower" will work only for a person who already knows how to recognize a Dragonhead.) Successful application of this rule requires accurate knowledge of the background of the person addressed. In situations where such knowledge is unobtainable (as when a writer addresses an unseen audience), it is necessary to rely on somewhat vague notions of the relative simplicity and familarity of language. Nobody would regard the following as a satisfactory definition:

> "Net: a reticulated texture with small interstices."

For it is impossible to imagine somebody familiar with the meaning of the pretentious definiens who would not know already how to use the word "net." (Dr. Johnson, who included this definition in his famous dictionary, was of course perpetrating a mild joke upon his readers.)

2b: *The definiens should not contain any part of the definiendum.*

To define a demon as one having demoniacal powers will not help the person addressed. For "demoniacal" means the same as "demon-like," and a person in doubt about the meaning of "demon" will certainly be equally in the dark as to the meaning of the words offered as substitutes. Such definitions are commonly called **circular.**

Circularity of definition is not always as obvious as in the illustration used. Consider, for instance, the facetious definition of a lady as "a woman in whose presence every man behaves like a gentleman." If this were intended as a serious clarification, it might be objected that the notion of a "gentleman" is as obscure as that of a "lady." (We might say that a lady is nothing but a "female gentleman.") The definition is guilty of circularity, even though the word "lady" does not occur *explicitly* in the definiens.

Hidden circularity, of this more subtle kind, is common in prolonged argument, in which chains of definitions occur. Thus, a writer may define peace as "the absence of war." This should put us on our guard immediately, since "peace" and "war" are correlative or polar words. If the writer elsewhere defines "war" without using the term "peace," his definition will survive our criticism. It may be found, however, that he defines war, in effect, as "a breach of a state of peace." Inserting this in the definiens of the original definition, we obtain " 'peace' means the absence of a breach of a state of peace" — which is clearly circular.

3. *The definiens and definiendum should be equivalent, i.e., should be substitutes for each other in every context.*

This rule is usually separated into two parts:

3a: *The definiendum should not be wider than the definiens.*

3b: *The definiendum should not be narrower than the definiens.*

The second of these rules is broken by the definition of a house as "a structure consisting of walls and a roof, used for human shelter"—for the definiens applies to theaters and cinemas as well as to houses. The first is broken by the definition of a house as "a brick structure used by humans as a permanent living place"—since houses may also be constructed of wood or other materials.

Gross breaches of these rules can usually be detected quite easily. But the rules establish a standard of perfection that is rarely achieved, except in the artificially constructed technical languages of the sciences. Consider the definition of "parapet" as "low wall at edge of balcony, roof, etc., or along sides of bridge, etc." (Quoted from a dictionary.) This is about as good a definition for most purposes as we can expect to find. Let us next examine whether definiens and definiendum are here equivalent. A story might contain the sentence "the steeplejack climbed on the parapet of the tower." Insertion of the definiens in place of the definiendum gives us the sentence "The steeplejack climbed on to the low wall at the edge of a balcony, roof, etc., or along the sides of a bridge, etc.,—of the tower." This is, of course, nonsense. The point is that even the satisfactory dictionary definition of "parapet" describes the different kinds of substitution to be made for the definiendum in various contexts, and does *not* provide a single phrase that can always be substituted for it. This is the best to be expected in most cases. (The attempt to substitute definiens for definiendum is usually illuminating, however, and often reveals unsuspected inadequacies in the definition.)

As a special case of the rule of equivalence of definiens and definiendum, we have the rule:

3c: *The definiens should not be expressed in metaphorical or figurative language.*

In a newspaper competition for a definition of "Loyalty," a prizewinning entry ran: "Loyalty is the flame of the lamp of friendship." Such a "definition" (if it deserves the name) can make no pretense at providing a definiens equivalent to the definiendum. The chief objection to this specimen is that the metaphorical expression ("flame of the lamp of friendship") fails to explain the use of the definiendum. (Imagine yourself trying to teach a foreigner the meaning of the word "Loyalty" by using *this* definiens.) And this weakness is characteristic of the use of metaphors or other "figures of speech." (Very likely, however, the competition was not searching for definitions in our sense of the term.)

4. *The definition should be an explanation of the meaning of the definiendum, not a statement only about the things mentioned by the definendum.*

This follows at once from our conception of definition as explanation of the meaning of words (or other signs). (See the discussion on page 67.)

It is not always easy to see clearly the difference between a statement about the *sign* S and a statement about the things referred to or *mentioned by* S.

Consider, for instance, one dictionary's definition of "steel" as "kinds of malleable alloy of iron and carbon *largely used as material for tools and weapons.*" The first part satisfies the demands of the rule, for it is true that nothing would be *called* "steel" (according to the customary convention) unless it were a kind of malleable alloy of iron and carbon. But the same is not true of the rest of the definition. Steel *is* largely used as material for tools and weapons, but it would still be *called* "steel" even if it were not. Suppose aluminum and plastics were eventually to displace steel as a constructional material; we should then no doubt say "steel is no longer used as a material for tools and weapons," and this would be an intelligible and self-consistent assertion. But if "steel" *meant* "material used for tools and weapons," the statement in question would be a *self-contradiction.* (Similarly, "This is a camera, but not designed for photography" is a self-contradiction, because "camera" *means* "apparatus for photography.")

Our discussion leads to the following test for determining whether the rule is obeyed. Suppose the definition to be inspected has the form "S is P." We examine whether "something is S but *not* P" is a self-contradiction. If it is, the rule has been observed. But if the statement is false without being self-contradictory, the rule has been broken. In the latter case, the original statement "S is P" expressed a *fact* about the referent of "S," not an explanation of the meaning of "S."

5. Division and Classification

Definitions conforming to our general specifications may take many forms. Among the most commonly useful are those in which the definiens determines the *connotation* of the definiendum. (All our examples have been of this kind, and some writers on logic refuse to apply the term "definition" to any other type of explanation of meaning.)

When giving a "connotative" definition (as we might call it), it is often convenient to follow a procedure know as **division.** This may be illustrated by a well-known indoor game, in which one player has to determine an object chosen by his friends during his absence from the room. The rules are that the single player may ask any questions, with the understanding that the only answers permissible are "Yes," "No," or, in cases where either reply would mislead, "Can't answer." (The player may not make more than two guesses at the solution.)

Here is a typical dialogue, as it might ensue under the direction of a skilful player: "Is it alive? *No.* Is it manufactured? *Yes.* Can it move around? *Yes.* Under its own power? *No.* Does it move above ground? *Yes.* In the air? *No.* On the ground? *Yes.* Does it sometimes contain people? *Yes.* Does it usually contain furniture? *Yes.* Is it a trailer? *Yes.* Any special trailer? *No.*" At this point the single player announces the correct answer as "a trailer." (The problem was an easy one: Good players are able to locate notions as elaborate as *the thoughts that Nero had while Rome was burning.*)

The speed and directness with which the correct answer ("a trailer") was reached was the result of following a systematic procedure. The first question used a *division* of all possible objects into the two classes of living and non-living things. The hidden object having been located in the class of non-living things, a further question located it among the *manufactured* things (in that class). The first two steps can therefore be shown in a diagram in this way:

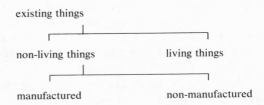

The remaining steps clearly follow the same pattern. In short, the expert player "narrows" down his search by successive division and subdivision of classes. (A poor player, however, asks questions at random, or fails to choose questions whose answers will appreciably reduce the field of search.)

The remaining steps will appear, diagrammatically, as:

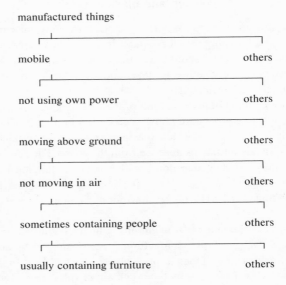

From this diagram we are now able to obtain a *definition* of "trailer," as "something inanimate, manufactured, mobile, not using its own power, on the ground, sometimes containing people, and usually containing furniture." This type of definition, in which the connotation of a term is given by progressive subdivision of a class, is known as **definition by division.**

For practical purposes, a definition of this type will usually contain fewer steps of division, and will begin with some class less inclusive than that of "all possible things." Thus, if one had occasion to explain to an English visitor the meaning of the word "trailer," and, taking a somewhat different route of definition, arrive at "a vehicle, drawn behind an automobile, and used as a place in which to live."

It is customary to refer to various aspects of the process of division by the words, "genus," "species," and "differentia." When a class is divided into subclasses, each of the latter is said to be a **species** of the larger class: Thus, white men are a species of men. Whenever A is a species of B, we say B is a **genus** of A: Thus, men are a genus of white men. It will be noticed that each class used in a process of definition by division (except the first and last) is both a genus *and* a species. Thus, in the example used, the class of manufactured non-living things is a genus of the class of mobile manufactured non-living things and a species of the class of non-living things. (Each class is included in larger classes and contains smaller classes.)

The property used in making a division of a class is known as the **differentia.** In dividing the class of triangles into the two species, equilateral triangles and non-equilateral triangles, the differentia is the property *having all its sides equal;* in dividing humans into men and women, the differentia is the property *being of the male sex.* (The traditional name for definition by division is definition *per genus et differentiam* — definition by means of a genus and differentiating property.)

Division as a means of classifying THINGS. The process of successive subdivision of classes, used in definition by division, is also widely useful as a means of organizing collections of *things.*

In this country, for instance, the F.B.I. organizes its collection of fingerprints according to the following system:

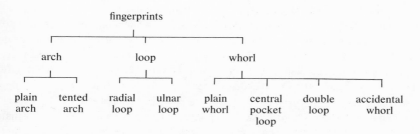

The terms used refer to certain distinguishable patterns in the prints: Thus in the "arch" pattern the lines run straight across the print; in the "loop" pattern they turn around and change their direction; in the "whorl" pattern, some of the lines make a complete circuit (the *full* directions are very complicated, however). It will be noticed that in this instance the first genus (the class of fingerprints) is divided into *more than two* species; it is usually convenient to allow this variation of our original pattern at any stage of the division.

Once the differentiae of the system of divisions are clearly understood, the division can be used in two ways. From it could be derived (stipulated) *definitions* of "plain arch," "tented arch," and the other terms used. But the same scheme can also be used as a way of sorting the fingerprints themselves into separate classes. When we are mainly concerned with sorting a given group of things into classes, we refer to the process of sorting as **classification.** But division and classification result in essentially the same end-product, a system of names for an orderly arrangement of classes and sub-classes.

Characteristics of satisfactory classification. It is sometimes recommended that a classification have the following features:

a. The basis of the classification will be made clear at each stage (*i.e.*, the differentiae used will be clearly described).
b. The division will be exhaustive at each stage (*i.e.*, all the members of the class being divided will occur in some one of the sub-classes). This is often achieved by having an Etcetera class, an "Omnium Gatherum," into which are dumped the objects that fit into no other category.
c. A class will always be divided into non-overlapping sub-classes. (This is to ensure that each object to which the classification applies will go into a unique compartment.)

(The number of stages of division, and the number of species allowed at each stage will be determined by the purpose of the classification. Among the most common purposes are the presentation of data, as in statistical tables; the arrangement of collections in accessible fashion, as in a filing cabinet or library; the grouping of objects into classes that show regular properties, as in scientific classification.)

These are, however, counsels of perfection. In practice, it is usually impossible to make the basis of classification fully explicit, and the principles on which a classification is based gradually change in the course of time.

In chemistry, for instance, a major classification of substances is into the two classes of "inorganic" and "organic." As the names suggest, the differentia originally used in making this division was the place or origin of the substance. For it was then believed that certain complex substances were produced *only* by living organisms. With the discovery that urea and other "organic" substances could be synthesized in the laboratory, the original basis of classification no longer seemed important. Nowadays, a chemist would probably say that the distinction between organic and inorganic substances depended on the fact that the former are complex compounds of carbon. But since certain compounds of carbon are still called "inorganic" the basis of the distinction is not clear, *even though the distinction still has importance.* The two classes of "organic" and "inorganic" substances shade into one another instead of being divided by a clear-cut boundary.

The difficulties of classification are well illustrated by the procedures used for classifying fingerprints, to which reference has already been made. The problem of classification is here much simpler than that encountered in the sciences. The F.B.I. is not trying to discover scientific laws *about* fingerprints; it is content to have some system by means of which any given fingerprint can be allocated to an appropriate category without excessive labor. But the great variability of fingerprint designs makes the division between these three main classes (and the smaller classes into which they are divided) one of degree rather than kind. It becomes necessary to give very precise and detailed instructions for locating a print in the right class. And even so, it is necessary to provide one class (that of "accidental whorls") in which are placed "those exceedingly unusual patterns that may not be placed by definition into any other classes." Those using the classification are also recommended to place very doubtful patterns in two categories (*e.g.,* to treat a pattern both as a loop and a tented arch.)*

The difficulties of classification illustrated in the analysis of fingerprints are a sufficient explanation of the extreme care given in all the advanced sciences to questions of classification and naming. And they illustrate once again the great importance that the right choice of names can have in assisting effective thinking.

6. Criticism of Specimen Definitions

We shall end this chapter with some brief comments on a representative selection of the types of definition often met in practice. (As usual, the reader is advised to do his own criticizing before reading the discussion provided.)

a. *Gilbertian: Of the humorously topsy-turvy kind characteristic of Gilbert and Sullivan opera (a G. situation).*

This dictionary entry is circular in appearance only. For a person might well be familiar with the name "Gilbert and Sullivan," without knowing the meaning of "Gilbertian." The definiens offered combines a statement of the connotation ("of the humorously topsy-turvy kind") with a description of specimens. The definiens is vague, but so is the definiendum. A satisfactory definition.

---

*Those interested can find more details in the pamphlet entitled "Classification of fingerprints," issued by the F.B.I.

b. A writer classifies education as "Specialized education; education for culture; and *charismatic education*" and goes on to explain the latter in a footnote as follows: "We must keep the unfamiliar term, as no other word quite so clearly conveys the idea. 'Conversional' is too clumsy, and 'inspirational' has been spoilt for any precise use. 'Education by infusion of grace' perhaps best conveys the idea to those reared in a Christian tradition." (F. Clarke, *Education and Social Change,* page 12. London: Sheldon Press, 1940.)

Here we have a technical term introduced that is not contained in standard English dictionaries and is not common in discussions of education. We might have supposed, then, that the writer would make a special attempt to tell us how he was using the term (which plays a very important part in his later argument). But it is not enough to be told that it is roughly equivalent to "conversional," and we are left guessing about several important details of the connotation. It would be especially important to know whether "charismatic" education is identical with what is commonly called "religious" education. The use of the phrase "education by infusion of grace" *suggests* a religious connotation, but does not explicitly identify "charismatic" and "religious." The definition is ambiguous and must be judged unsatisfactory.

c. *"A politician is a man who sits on the fence with his ear to the ground."* (Popular saying.)

This "definition" is of course a quip or an epigram rather than a sober attempt to explain the meaning of the word "politician." The humor of the remark depends on the malicious suggestion that indecision and lack of initiative are *defining* characteristics of a politician. It may be compared with "An expert is an ordinary man a long way from home" or similar remarks in which a terse comment is presented in the disguise of a defintion.

d. "War is by *definition* nothing more than wholesale and organized murder."

The writer has obligingly told us that he is presenting a definition (or part of a definition). If he had left out the words "by definition," it would have been difficult to know whether he was offering a definition of "war" or a statement *about war*. We are clearly being offered a *customary* definition of "war." If the writer were to say "I propose to mean by 'war' . . ." his remarks would have little interest unless he went on to show that his stipulated definition agreed with customary usage. The short way with this definition would be to apply the test of equivalence . . . and to argue that the ordinary person would *not* understand by "Germany went into wholesale and organized murder" the same as he would by "Germany went to war." But this type of criticism would overlook the writer's object. He is probably quite aware of the fact that "war" does not *literally mean* "wholesale and organized murder." But war does *resemble* murder on the grand scale. And what he is saying is *"This* aspect of war is the important one — all the rest, the uniforms and the conventions of warfare — are so many unimportant incidentals." And by using the highly emotive word "murder" he is conveying his own abhorrence of war, and influencing us to have similar attitudes. This important example, therefore, illustrates a type of definition in which a part of the connotation of the word (or what is alleged to be part of the connotation) is selected as being especially important, in an attempt to influence the attitudes of the hearer.

e. "Prejudice is a biased attitude of mind."

This definition was given by a student who was asked to give a brief definition of "prejudice," and is quoted in G. C. Field's *Prejudice and Impartiality.** As Professor Field points out, the idea of predjudice is "familiar and frequently used by us all." The definition must therefore be regarded as an attempt to clarify the meaning of a term already in use. Now "bias" means almost exactly the same as "prejudice"; so, if we want to *analyze* the meaning of "prejudice," it will hardly help us to be told that it involves bias. The definition must be rejected as circular.

f. "Prejudice is the influence on our thinking of any feeling, impulse, or motive which is not relevant to the immediate purpose of this thinking."

This is Professor Field's own definition of "prejudice," (page 9 in the same book) reached at the end of a detailed and careful discussion. As it stands, the definition is open to the objection of obscurity, since it contains the phrase "relevant to the immediate purpose" (of thinking). But the author has previously explained that "the immediate purpose" of thinking is "to arrive at a true conclusion, to find out something, to attain some piece of knowledge." According to him, any "feeling, impulse, or motive" is not "relevant" to this immediate purpose of thinking if it directs us away from it. The first objection is, therefore, removed.

A second objection might be that the definiens is too wide. If I am suffering from intense toothache, my feelings may make me so impatient of argument as to lead me to make a snap judgment about a question I am forced to consider. My feeling of toothache is then "irrelevant" to the "immediate purpose of thinking." But it would seem rather odd to say that the toothache *prejudices* me. The fact is that Professor Field has somewhat extended the common use of "prejudice" (which is more commonly used to mean approximately the same as

*London: Methuen & Co., 1932. Page 3.

"the holding of an opinion concerning a question not determined by the evidence"). But he does this for the purpose of emphasizing the importance of the notion of *relevance to the purpose of thinking* (as he explains in the course of his discussion). This may be regarded as a legitimate procedure.

Summary

When it is necessary to introduce new terms, remove an ambiguity, or extend the meaning of some word (or other sign), deliberate instruction in the use of signs is required. An explanation of the meaning of a sign is called a *definition*. (The word may be used in both "product-" and "process-" senses.) Any statement that is a definition, as here understood, *mentions* the word defined; it is to be contrasted with statements in which the word is used, but not mentioned. The standard forms adopted for definitions are *"X" means Y* and *"X" means the same as "Y."* The word (or other sign designed) is called the *definiendum,* the phrase by which its meaning is located the *definiens.*

Definition is a social transaction involving at least three factors — the explanation, and the persons by whom it is given and received. Satisfactory definitions must be adapted to the needs of the particular person addressed (the principle of *relativity of definition*).

A definition may take the form of a resolution or proposal that a word shall have a certain meaning (*stipulated* definition); or may record the way in which a word is already used in a language or some special context (*reported* definition). A stipulated definition will be neither true nor false; a reported definition must be one or the other. Freedom to stipulate meanings varies with the definiteness of the definiendum's previous usage: The more stable the pre-existing meaning of the sign, the less freedom to stipulate.

The rules of good definition specify that the definition shall be adequate for the purposes intended; shall be intelligible to the person addressed; shall not be circular; shall have a definiens neither wider nor narrower than the definiendum; shall not use metaphorical or figurative language; and shall mention, not use, the definiendum.

One of the most common types of definition is that in which the definiendum's connotation is located by successive division and sub-division of some initial class (*definition by division*). The sub-classes into which a given class is divided are known as its *species,* and it is known as their *genus.* The property that determines the division of the genus is known as the *differentia.*

A similar procedure may be used to sort *things* into a number of distinct classes and is then known as *classification.* In classification, the aim is to have non-overlapping species that together exhaust their genus, and are determined by precise and definite differentiae. But in practice this ideal can seldom be attained.

Introduction

The Work of Art

Recent philosophizing has resulted in a variety of writings that cast considerable light on the problem of defining art. Several of these essays ask whether it is profitable to try and discover the "essence" of art, that is, a set of necessary and sufficient properties the recognition of which enables one to know that a given object is in fact a work of art. Art, it is suggested, may be too complex a phenomenon for definitions of it to be formulated in this fashion. Hence, in "The Role of Theory in Aesthetics," Morris Weitz asserts that thinkers have been mistaken in their attempts to discover the essential elements of art. To treat the idea of art in this manner, says Weitz, is to view it as a closed concept, whereas the concept of art is more correctly conceived as having an open texture. This means that the definition of art will always be a function of changing conditions and influences. As stated in the Preface, whether a given X is experienced as a work of art, or a good one, requires a decision on our part, and the question should not be handled as if it were merely factual.

But Weitz does not deplore the failure to discover the essence of art. On the contrary, the absence of such certainty generates worthwhile debates over artistic excellence which teach us what to look for, how to look, and why it is important to look in certain ways. Consequently some familiarity with philosophical inquiries into the nature of art is needed for devising teaching and learning strategies in art education. Quite probably a variety of definitions are required to render justice to the many facets and complexities of works of art. The various definitions formulated by thinkers, then, are at once tools of analysis, canons of criticism, and methods of teaching.

Weitz's discussion, however, should not be interpreted to mean that all uses of the expression "work of art" are reasonable ones. Thus in "The Task of Defining a Work of Art" Paul Ziff attempts to specify the conditions under which the expression "work of art" is reasonably employed. In doing so, Ziff presents a model of analysis rich in pedagogical significance.

Ziff's approach starts with a clear-cut or characteristic case of a work of art: for example, Poussin's *The Rape of the Sabine Women*. Next he proceeds to borderline or controversial cases in order to indicate just what is implied in justifying a definition of art. Again, it is emphasized that the adjudication of disputes about art differs from cases involving ordinary objects, and that noting a set of necessary and sufficient properties is not the only method of giving definitions. Ziff's central point is that decisions as to a given X's status as a work of art are reached on the basis of similarities to characteristic examples. There are, of course, no rules for establishing a condition of sufficient similarity. Revolutions in art are thus seen as involving shifts in the application of the expression "work of art," with progressives tending to use the expression in novel ways and conservatives tending to employ it more conventionally. The conservative, however, is not always unreasonable in his use of the term. He merely places greater weight on some aspect, say, representation, and hence ascribes to art a different function and purpose. Finally, debates over the meaning of "work of art" are not merely verbal or linguistic since the designation of an object as a work of art has tangible social consequences. Ziff's analysis is peculiarly relevant to transitional periods in the history of art, such as our own, when art is undergoing redefinition.

The next selection, an excerpt from Israel Scheffler's "Definitions in Education," is included for the analogy it affords between definitions in art and definitions in education. Scheffler's contribution also provides an interesting sample of how philosophy of art can be used to illuminate problems in philosophy of education.

In a section of his discussion of definitions not reprinted here, Scheffler distinguishes three kinds of general, as opposed to technical, definitions. First are *stipulative* definitions (inventive and noninventive forms), which are made without reference to the predefinitional or prior usage of a term. Stipulative definitions are adopted mainly for purposes of economy and efficiency of discourse in a given context and involve legislation of conventions as well as a certain arbitrary choice in the assignment of meaning. By contrast, the second category, *descriptive* definitions, are explanatory in intent and attempt to mirror prior usage accurately. Third are *programmatic* definitions, which are like stipulative definitions in not being bound by prior usage, and like descriptive ones in raising questions that go beyond those of economy and convenience. Unlike both previous categories, however — and this is the important point — programmatic definitions always raise moral and practical issues. They contain proposals or prescriptions which are asserted with a view to influencing the practical conduct of schooling.

Definitions in education, Scheffler points out, rarely conform to one of the foregoing types. Rather, they frequently constitute overlaps between stipulative and programmatic or descriptive and programmatic definitions. For example, the definition "art is significant form" is not only a definition in terms of prior usage, that is, a descriptive definition; it may also be interpreted to suggest a program of action for art instruction. The prescription would be: In art instruction stress the significance of the formal relations in works of art. Needless to say, there are other definitions of art, all equally accurate with respect to predefinitional usage. Now it has often been the practice first to adopt a definition of art and then to justify the practical program of art education that the definition seemed to imply by appealing to the accuracy of the definition. But this line of reasoning is fallacious. Any definition of art that consists of an overlap of two kinds of definitions must be subjected to two separate and independent evaluations, and the established accuracy of the definition's descriptive aspects has no bearing on the desirability of the definition's programmatic aspects. In fact, the moral and practical evaluation of a proposed program of art instruction should precede decisions concerning the accuracy of proposed definitions.

In "Problems of Art," John Hospers provides a brief and useful summary of the major issues encountered in defining art. Noting that definitions of art are invariably persuasive, he indicates some neutral or nonnormative usages of the term art. His threefold classification of the aspects of works of art — material, formal, and associational — also serves as a convenient context in which to discuss the formalist *v.* the associationist controversy in aesthetic theory. Formalists, it is pointed out, maintain that only the material and formal aspects of art are important, while associationists insist that all three aspects, especially the associative, are indispensable. Once again, disagreement does not remain at a verbal level since it has practical consequences for schooling. For example, the development of aesthetic perception is sometimes stated as an objective of art instruction. But is the perception of associational properties in works of art — human qualities, emotions, ideas, values, etc. — genuinely aesthetic perception? Or is aesthetic perception restricted to noting sensory and formal elements in art objects? The question that arises is: To which aspects of art do we properly apply the term aesthetic? The next section tries to clarify the issues involved in this perplexing problem. All that is necessary to indicate here is that the associative use of knowledge is one of the fundamental applications made of learning, particularly in the study of the arts,[1] and that the view taken of the formalist *v.* the associationist controversy in art instruction may have considerable influence on how students experience not only works of art but the whole world of sensible things.

---

[1]For a helpful discussion of the uses of learning, see Harry S. Broudy, B. Othanel Smith, and Joe R. Burnett, *Democracy and Excellence in American Secondary Education* (Chicago: Rand McNally & Co., 1964), pp. 46-48.

The Role of Theory in Aesthetics*

MORRIS WEITZ

Theory has been central in aesthetics and is still the preoccupation of the philosophy of art. Its main avowed concern remains the determination of the nature of art which can be formulated into a definition of it. It construes definition as the statement of the necessary and sufficient properties of what is being defined, where the statement purports to be a true or false claim about the essence of art, what characterizes and distinguishes it from everything else. Each of the great theories of art—Formalism, Voluntarism, Emotionalism, Intellectualism, Intuitionism, Organicism—converges on the attempt to state the defining properties of art. Each claims that it is the true theory because it has formulated correctly into a real definition the nature of art; and that the others are false because they have left out some necessary or sufficient property. Many theorists contend that their enterprise is no mere intellectual exercise but an absolute necessity for any understanding of art and our proper evaluation of it. Unless we know what art is, they say, what are its necessary and sufficient properties, we cannot begin to respond to it adequately or to say why one work is good or better than another. Aesthetic theory, thus, is important not only in itself but for the foundations of both appreciation and criticism. Philosophers, critics, and even artists who have written on art, agree that what is primary in aesthetics is a theory about the nature of art.

From *The Journal of Aesthetics and Art Criticism,* Vol. XV, No. 1 (1956), pp. 27-35. Reprinted by permission of the author and *The Journal of Aesthetics and Art Criticism.*
*One of the Matchette Foundation prize essays for 1955 (Editor).

Is aesthetic theory, in the sense of a true definition or set of necessary and sufficient properties of art, possible? If nothing else does, the history of aesthetics itself should give one enormous pause here. For, in spite of the many theories, we seem no nearer our goal today than we were in Plato's time. Each age, each art-movement, each philosophy of art, tries over and over again to establish the stated ideal only to be succeeded by a new or revised theory, rooted, at least in part, in the repudiation of preceding ones. Even today, almost everyone interested in aesthetic matters is still deeply wedded to the hope that the correct theory of art is forthcoming. We need only examine the numerous new books on art in which new definitions are proffered; or, in our own country especially, the basic textbooks and anthologies to recognize how strong the priority of a theory of art is.

In this essay I want to plead for the rejection of this problem. I want to show that theory—in the requisite classical sense—is *never* forthcoming in aesthetics, and that we would do much better as philosophers to supplant the question, "What is the nature of art?," by other questions, the answers to which will provide us with all the understanding of the arts there can be. I want to show that the inadequacies of the theories are not primarily occasioned by any legitimate difficulty such e.g., as the vast complexity of art, which might be corrected by further probing and research. Their basic inadequacies reside instead in a fundamental misconception of art. Aesthetic theory—all of it—is wrong in principle in thinking that a correct theory is possible because it radically misconstrues the logic of the concept of art. Its main contention that "art" is amenable to real or any kind of true definition is false. Its attempt to discover the necessary and sufficient properties of art is logically misbegotten for the very simple reason that such a set and, consequently, such a formula about it, is never forthcoming. Art, as the logic of the concept shows, has no set of necessary and sufficient properties, hence a theory of it is logically impossible and not merely factually difficult. Aesthetic theory tries to define what cannot be defined in its requisite sense. But in recommending the repudiation of aesthetic theory I shall not argue from this, as too many others have done, that its logical confusions render it meaningless or worthless. On the contrary, I wish to reassess its role and its contribution primarily in order to show that it is of the greatest importance to our understanding of the arts.

Let us now survey briefly some of the more famous extant aesthetic theories in order to see if they do incorporate correct and adequate statements about the nature of art. In each of these there is the assumption that it is the true enumeration of the defining properties of art, with the implication that previous theories have stressed wrong definitions. Thus, to begin with, consider a famous version of Formalist theory, that propounded by Bell and Fry. It is true that they speak mostly of painting in their writings but both assert that what they find in that art can be generalized for what is "art" in the others as well.

The essence of painting, they maintain, are the plastic elements in relation. Its defining property is significant form, i.e., certain combinations of lines, colors, shapes, volumes—everything on the canvas except the representational elements—which evoke a unique response to such combinations. Painting is definable as plastic organization. The nature of art, what it *really* is, so their theory goes, is a unique combination of certain elements (the specifiable plastic ones) in their relations. Anything which is art is an instance of significant form; and anything which is not art has no such form.

To this the Emotionalist replies that the truly essential property of art has been left out. Tolstoy, Ducasse, or any of the advocates of this theory, find that the requisite defining property is not significant form but rather the expression of emotion in some sensuous public medium. Without projection of emotion into some piece of stone or words or sounds, etc., there can be no art. Art is really such embodiment. It is this that uniquely characterizes art, and any true, real definition of it, contained in some adequate theory of art, must so state it.

The Intuitionist disclaims both emotion and form as defining properties. In Croce's version, for example, art is identified not with some physical, public object but with a specific creative, cognitive and spiritual act. Art is really a first stage of knowledge in which certain human beings (artists) bring their images and intuitions into lyrical clarification or expression. As such, it is an awareness, non-conceptual in character, of the unique individuality of things; and since it exists below the level of conceptualization or action, it is without scientific or moral content. Croce singles out as the defining essence of art this first stage of spiritual life and advances its identification with art as a philosophically true theory or definition.

The Organicist says to all of this that art is really a class of organic wholes consisting of distinguishable, albeit inseparable, elements in their causally efficacious relations which are presented in some sensuous medium. In A. C. Bradley, in piece-meal versions of it in literary criticism, or in my own generalized adaptation of it in my *Philosophy of the Arts,* what is claimed is that anything which is a work of art is in its nature a unique complex of interrelated parts—in painting, for example, lines, colors, volumes, subjects, etc., all interacting upon one another on a paint surface of some sort. Certainly, at one time at least it seemed to me that this organic theory constituted the one true and real definition of art.

My final example is the most interesting of all, logically speaking. This is the Voluntarist theory of Parker. In his writings on art, Parker persistently calls into question the traditional simple-minded definitions of aesthetics. "The assumption underlying every philosophy of art is the existence of some common nature present in all the arts."[1] "All the so popular brief definitions of

---

[1]D. Parker, "The Nature of Art," reprinted in E. Vivas and M. Krieger, *The Problems of Aesthetics*, (N. Y., 1953), p. 90.

art — 'significant form,' 'expression,' 'intuition,' 'objectified pleasure' — are fallacious, either because, while true of art, they are also true of much that is not art, and hence fail to differentiate art from other things; or else because they neglect some essential aspect of art."[2] But instead of inveighing against the attempt at definition of art itself, Parker insists that what is needed is a complex definition rather than a simple one. "The defintion of art must therefore be in terms of a complex of characteristics. Failure to recognize this has been the fault of all the well-known definitions."[3] His own version of Voluntarism is the theory that art is essentially three things: embodiment of wishes and desires imaginatively satisfied, language, which characterizes the public medium of art, and harmony, which unifies the language with the layers of imaginative projections. Thus, for Parker, it is a true definition to say of art that it is ". . . the provision of satisfaction through the imagination, social significance, and harmony. I am claiming that nothing except works of art possesses all three of these marks."[4]

Now, all of these sample theories are inadequate in many different ways. Each purports to be a complete statement about the defining features of all works of art and yet each of them leaves out something which the others take to be central. Some are circular, e.g., the Bell-Fry theory of art as significant form which is defined in part in terms of our response to significant form. Some of them, in their search for necessary and sufficient properties, emphasize too few properties, like (again) the Bell-Fry definition which leaves out subject-representation in painting, or the Croce theory which omits inclusion of the very important feature of the public, physical character, say, of architecture. Others are too general and cover objects that are not art as well as works of art. Organicism is surely such a view since it can be applied to *any* causal unity in the natural world as well as to art.[5] Still others rest on dubious principles, e.g., Parker's claim that art embodies imaginative satisfactions, rather than real ones; or Croce's assertion that there is non-conceptual knowledge. Consequently, even if art has one set of necessary and sufficient properties, none of the theories we have noted or, for that matter, no aesthetic theory yet proposed, has enumerated that set to the satisfaction of all concerned.

Then there is a different sort of difficulty. As real definitions, these theories are supposed to be factual reports on art. If they are, may we not ask, Are they empirical and open to verification or falsification? For example, what would confirm or disconfirm the theory that art is significant form or embodiment of emotion or creative synthesis of images? There does not even seem to be a hint of the kind of evidence which might be forthcoming to test these theories; and indeed one wonders if they are perhaps honorific definitions of "art," that is,

---

[2]*Ibid*, pp. 93-94.
[3]*Ibid*, p. 94.
[4]*Ibid*, p. 104.
[5]See M. Macdonald's review of my *Philosophy of the Arts, Mind*, Oct., 1951, pp. 561-564, for a brilliant discussion of this objection to the Organic theory.

proposed redefinitions in terms of some *chosen* conditions for applying the concept of art, and not true or false reports on the essential properties of art at all.

But all these criticisms of traditional aesthetic theories — that they are circular, incomplete, untestable, pseudo-factual, disguised proposals to change the meaning of concepts — have been made before. My intention is to go beyond these to make a much more fundamental criticism, namely, that aesthetic theory is a logically vain attempt to define what cannot be defined, to state the necessary and sufficient properties of that which has no necessary and sufficient properties, to conceive the concept of art as closed when its very use reveals and demands its openness.

The problem with which we must begin is not "What is art?," but "What sort of concept is 'art'?" Indeed, the root problem of philosophy itself is to explain the relation between the employment of certain kinds of concepts and the conditions under which they can be correctly applied. If I may paraphrase Wittgenstein, we must not ask, What is the nature of any philosophical x?, or even, according to the semanticist, What does "x" mean?, a transformation that leads to the disastrous interpretation of "art" as a name for some specifiable class of objects; but rather, What is the use or employment of "x"? What does "x" do in the language? This, I take it, is the initial question, the begin-all if not the end-all of any philosophical problem and solution. Thus, in aesthetics, our first problem is the elucidation of the actual employment of the concept of art, to give a logical description of the actual functioning of the concept, including a description of the conditions under which we correctly use it or its correlates.

My model in this type of logical description or philosophy derives from Wittgenstein. It is also he who, in his refutation of philosophical theorizing in the sense of constructing definitions of philosophical entities, has furnished contemporary aesthetics with a starting point for any future progress. In his new work, *Philosophical Investigations,*[6] Wittgenstein raises as an illustrative question, What is a game? The traditional philosophical, theoretical answer would be in terms of some exhaustive set of properties common to all games. To this Wittgenstein says, let us consider what we call "games": "I mean board-games, card-games, ball-games, Olympic games, and so on. What is common to them all? — Don't say: 'there *must* be something common, or they would not be called "games"' but *look and see* whether there is anything common to all. — For if you look at them you will not see something that is common to *all,* but similarities, relationships, and a whole series of them at that . . ."

---

[6]L. Wittgenstein, *Philosophical Investigations,* (Oxford, 1953), tr. by E. Anscombe; see esp. Part I, Sections 65-75. All quotations are from these sections.

Card games are like board games in some respects but not in others. Not all games are amusing, nor is there always winning or losing or competition. Some games resemble others in some respects—that is all. What we find are no necessary and sufficient properties, only "a complicated network of similarities overlapping and crisscrossing," such that we can say of games that they form a family with family resemblances and no common trait. If one asks what a game is, we pick out sample games, describe these, and add, "This and *similar things* are called 'games'." This is all we need to say and indeed all any of us knows about games. Knowing what a game is is not knowing some real definition or theory but being able to recognize and explain games and to decide which among imaginary and new examples would or would not be called "games."

The problem of the nature of art is like that of the nature of games, at least in these respects: If we actually look and see what it is that we call "art," we will also find no common properties—only strands of similarities. Knowing what art is is not apprehending some manifest or latent essence but being able to recognize, describe, and explain those things we call "art" in virtue of these similarities.

But the basic resemblance between these concepts is their open texture. In elucidating them, certain (paradigm) cases can be given, about which there can be no question as to their being correctly described as "art" or "game," but no exhaustive set of cases can be given. I can list some cases and some conditions under which I can apply correctly the concept of art but I cannot list all of them, for the all-important reason that unforeseeable or novel conditions are always forthcoming or envisageable.

A concept is open if its conditions of application are emendable and corrigible; i.e., if a situation or case can be imagined or secured which would call for some sort of *decision* on our part to extend the use of the concept to cover this, or to close the concept and invent a new one to deal with the new case and its new property. If necessary and sufficient conditions for the application of a concept can be stated, the concept is a closed one. But this can happen only in logic or mathematics where concepts are constructed and completely defined. It cannot occur with empirically-descriptive and normative concepts unless we arbitrarily close them by stipulating the ranges of their uses.

I can illustrate this open character of "art" best by examples drawn from its sub-concepts. Consider questions like "Is Dos Passos' *U. S. A.* a novel?," "Is V. Woolf's *To the Lighthouse* a novel?," "Is Joyce's *Finnegan's Wake* a novel?" On the traditional view, these are construed as factual problems to be answered yes or no in accordance with the presence or absence of defining properties. But certainly this is not how any of these questions is answered. Once it arises, as it has many times in the development of the novel from Richardson to Joyce (e.g., "Is Gide's *The School for Wives* a novel or a diary?"), what is at stake is no factual analysis concerning necessary and sufficient properties but a decision as to whether the work under examination is similar in certain respects to other works, already called "novels," and consequently warrants the extension of the concept to cover the new case. The new work is narrative, fictional, contains character delineation and dialogue but (say) it has no regular time-sequence in the plot or is interspersed with actual newspaper reports. It is like recognized novels, A, B, C . . . , in some respects but not like them in others. But then neither were B and C like A in some respects when it was decided to extend the concept applied to A to B and C. Because work N + 1 (the brand new work) is like A, B, C . . . N in certain respects — has strands of similarity to them — the concept is extended and a new phase of the novel engendered. "Is N 1 a novel?," then, is no factual, but rather a decision problem, where the verdict turns on whether or not we enlarge our set of conditions for applying the concept.

What is true of the novel is, I think, true of every sub-concept of art: "tragedy," "comedy," "painting," "opera," etc., of "art" itself. No "Is X a novel, painting, opera, work of art, etc.?" question allows of a definitive answer in the sense of a factual yes or no report. "Is this *collage* a painting or not?" does not rest on any set of necessary and sufficient properties of painting but on whether we decide — as we did! — to extend "painting" to cover this case.

"Art," itself, is an open concept. New conditions (cases) have constantly arisen and will undoubtedly constantly arise; new art forms, new movements will emerge, which will demand decisions on the part of those interested, usually professional critics, as to whether the concept should be extended or not. Aestheticians may lay down similarity conditions but never necessary and sufficient ones for the correct application of the concept. With "art" its conditions of application can never be exhaustively enumerated since new cases can always be envisaged or created by artists, or even nature, which would call for a decision on someone's part to extend or to close the old or to invent a new concept. (E.g., "It's not a sculpture, it's a mobile.")

What I am arguing, then, is that the very expansive, adventurous character of art, its ever-present changes and novel creations, makes it logically impossible to ensure any set of defining properties. We can, of course, choose to close the concept. But to do this with "art" or "tragedy" or "portraiture," etc., is ludicrous since it forecloses on the very conditions of creativity in the arts.

Of course there are legitimate and serviceable closed concepts in art. But these are always those whose boundaries of conditions have been drawn for a *special* purpose. Consider the difference, for example, between "tragedy" and "(extant) Greek tragedy." The first is open and must remain so to allow for the possibility of new conditions, e.g., a play in which the hero is not noble or fallen or in which there is no hero but other elements that are like those of plays we already call "tragedy." The second is closed. The plays it can be applied to, the conditions under which it can be correctly used are all in, once the boundary, "Greek," is drawn. Here the critic can work out a theory or real definition in which he lists the common properties at least of the extant Greek tragedies.

Aristotle's definition, false as it is as a theory of all the plays of Aeschylus, Sophocles, and Euripides, since it does not cover some of them,[7] properly called "tragedies," can be interpreted as a real (albeit incorrect) definition of this closed concept; although it can also be, as it unfortunately has been, conceived as a purported real definition of "tragedy," in which case it suffers from the logical mistake of trying to define what cannot be defined – of trying to squeeze what is an open concept into an honorific formula for a closed concept.

What is supremely important, if the critic is not to become muddled, is to get absolutely clear about the way in which he conceives his concepts; otherwise he goes from the problem of trying to define "tragedy," etc., to an arbitrary closing of the concept in terms of certain preferred conditions or characteristics which he sums up in some linguistic recommendation that he mistakenly thinks is a real definition of the open concept. Thus, many critics and aestheticians ask, "What is tragedy?," choose a class of samples for which they may give a true account of its common properties, and then go on to construe this account of the chosen closed class as a true definition or theory of the whole open class of tragedy. This, I think, is the logical mechanism of most of the so-called theories of the sub-concepts of art: "tragedy," "comedy," "novel," etc. In effect, this whole procedure, subtly deceptive as it is, amounts to a transformation of correct criteria for *recognizing* members of certain legitimately closed classes of works of art into recommended criteria for *evaluating* any putative member of the class.

The primary task of aesthetics is not to seek a theory but to elucidate the concept of art. Specifically, it is to describe the conditions under which we employ the concept correctly. Definition, reconstruction, patterns of analysis are out of place here since they distort and add nothing to our understanding of art. What, then, is the logic of "X is a work of art"?

As we actually use the concept, "Art" is both descriptive (like "chair") and evaluative (like "good"); i.e., we sometimes say, "This is a work of art," to describe something and we sometimes say it to evaluate something. Neither use surprises anyone.

What, first, is the logic of "X is a work of art," when it is a descriptive utterance? What are the conditions under which we would be making such an utterance correctly? There are no necessary and sufficient conditions but there are the strands of similarity conditions, i.e., bundles of properties, none of which need be present but most of which are, when we describe things as works of art. I shall call these the "criteria of recognition" of works of art. All of these have served as the defining criteria of the individual traditional theories of art; so we are already familiar with them. Thus, mostly, when we describe something as a work of art, we do so under the conditions of there being present

---

[7] See H. D. F. Kitto, *Greek Tragedy*, (London, 1939), on this point.

some sort of artifact, made by human skill, ingenuity, and imagination, which embodies in its sensuous, public medium — stone, wood, sounds, words, etc. — certain distinguishable elements and relations. Special theorists would add conditions like satisfaction of wishes, objectification or expression of emotion, some act of empathy, and so on; but these latter conditions seem to be quite adventitious, present to some but not to other spectators when things are described as works of art. "X is a work of art and contains *no* emotion, expression, act of empathy, satisfaction, etc.," is perfectly good sense and may frequently be true. "X is a work of art and . . . was made by no one," or . . . "exists only in the mind and not in any publicly observable thing," or . . . "was made by accident when he spilled the paint on the canvas," in each case of which a normal condition is denied, are also sensible and capable of being true in certain circumstances. None of the criteria of recognition is a defining one, either necessary or sufficient, because we can sometimes assert of something that it is a work of art and go on to deny any one of these conditions, even the one which has traditionally been taken to be basic, namely, that of being an artifact: Consider, "This piece of driftwood is a lovely piece of sculpture." Thus, to say of anything that it is a work of art is to commit oneself to the presence of *some* of these conditions. One would scarcely describe X as a work of art if X were not an artifact, or a collection of elements sensuously presented in a medium, or a product of human skill, and so on. If none of the conditions were present, if there were no criteria present for recognizing something as a work of art, we would not describe it as one. But, even so, no one of these or any collection of them is either necessary or sufficient.

The elucidation of the descriptive use of "Art" creates little difficulty. But the elucidation of the evaluative use does. For many, especially theorists, "This is a work of art" does more than describe; it also praises. Its conditions of utterance, therefore, include certain preferred properties or characteristics of art. I shall call these "criteria of evaluation." Consider a typical example of this evaluative use, the view according to which to say of something that it is a work of art is to imply that it is a *successful* harmonization of elements. Many of the honorific definitions of art and its sub-concepts are of this form. What is at stake here is that "Art" is construed as an evaluative term which is either identified with its criterion or justified in terms of it. "Art" is defined in terms of its evaluative property, e.g., successful harmonization. On such a view, to say "X is a work of art" is (1) to say something which is taken *to mean* "X is a successful harmonization" (e.g., "Art *is* significant form") or (2) to say something praise-worthy *on the basis* of its successful harmonization. Theorists are never clear whether it is (1) or (2) which is being put forward. Most of them, concerned as they are with this evaluative use, formulate (2), i.e., that feature of art that *makes* it art in the praise-sense, and then go on to state (1), i.e., the definition of "Art" in terms of its art-making feature. And this is clearly to confuse the conditions under which we say something evaluatively with the meaning of what we say. "This is a work of art," said evaluatively, cannot mean "This is a successful harmonization of elements" — except by stipulation — but at most is said in virtue of the art-making property, which is taken as a (the) criterion of "Art," when "Art" is employed to assess. "This is a work of art," used evaluatively, serves to praise and not to affirm the reason why it is said.

The evaluative use of "Art," although distinct from the conditions of its use, relates in a very intimate way to these conditions. For, in every instance of "This is a work of art" (used to praise), what happens is that the criterion of evaluation (e.g., successful harmonization) for the employment of the concept of art is converted into a criterion of recognition. This is why, on its evaluative use, "This is a work of art" implies "This has P," where "P" is some chosen art-making property. Thus, if one chooses to employ "Art" evaluatively, as many do, so that "This is a work of art and not (aesthetically) good" makes no sense, he uses "Art" in such a way that he refuses to *call* anything a work of art unless it embodies his criterion of excellence.

There is nothing wrong with the evaluative use; in fact, there is good reason for using "Art" to praise. But what cannot be maintained is that theories of the evaluative use of "Art" are true and real definitions of the necessary and sufficient properties of art. Instead they are honorific definitions, pure and simple, in which "Art" has been redefined in terms of chosen criteria.

But what makes them — these honorific definitions — so supremely valuable is not their disguised linguistic recommendations; rather it is the *debates* over the reasons for changing the criteria of the concept of art which are built into the definitions. In each of the great theories of art, whether correctly understood as honorific definitions or incorrectly accepted as real definitions, what is of the utmost importance are the reasons proffered in the argument for the respective theory, that is, the reasons given for the chosen or preferred criterion of excellence and evaluation. It is this perennial debate over these criteria of evaluation which makes the history of aesthetic theory the important study it is. The value of each of the theories resides in its attempt to state and to justify certain criteria which are either neglected or distorted by previous theories. Look at the Bell-Fry theory again. Of course, "Art is significant form" cannot be accepted as a true, real definition of art; and most certainly it actually functions in their aesthetics as a redefinition of art in terms of the chosen condition of significant form. But what gives it its aesthetic importance is what lies behind the formula: In an age in which literary and representational elements have become paramount in painting, *return* to the plastic ones since these are indigenous to painting. Thus, the role of the theory is not to define anything but to use the definitional form, almost epigrammatically, to pin-point a crucial recommendation to turn our attention once again to the plastic elements in painting.

Once we, as philosophers, understand this distinction between the formula and what lies behind it, it behooves us to deal generously with the traditional theories of art; because incorporated in every one of them is a debate over and argument for emphasizing or centering upon some particular feature of art which has been neglected or perverted. If we take the aesthetic theories literally, as we have seen, they all fail; but if we reconstrue them, in terms of their function and point, as serious and argued-for recommendations to concentrate on certain criteria of excellence in art, we shall see that aesthetic theory is far from worthless. Indeed, it becomes as central as anything in aesthetics, in our understanding of art, for it teaches us what to look for and how to look at it in art. What is central and must be articulated in all the theories are their debates over the reasons for excellence in art — debates over emotional depth, profound truths, natural beauty, exactitude, freshness of treatment, and so on, as criteria of evaluation — the whole of which converges on the perennial problem of what makes a work of art good. To understand the role of aesthetic theory is not to conceive it as definition, logically doomed to failure, but to read it as summaries of seriously made recommendations to attend in certain ways to certain features of art.

The Task of Defining a Work of Art

PAUL ZIFF

I

One of the foremost problems of aesthetics has been to provide a definition (or an analysis, or an explication, or an elucidation) of the notion of a work of art. The solutions given by aestheticians to this problem have often been violently opposed to one another; e.g., contrast Tolstoi's answer with that of his predecessors. There is no doubt that the problem is a difficult one. But what I should like to consider here is just why it is so difficult. In this way I hope to make clear what is involved in such a definition and what an aesthetician must do, whether he knows it or not, to justify his definition of a work of art.

II

Suppose a child does not understand what a book is, is merely puzzled by people speaking about books. One of the many means at hand to help him grasp the use of that word "book" would be simply to show him a book. But one would not help or try to help him by picking out a pocket book, or a diary with blank pages, or a loose-leaf note book. What is wanted here is a perhaps fat book, but not too fat, with a hard cover, perhaps a gold-lettered leather-bound

From *The Philosophical Review,* Vol. LXII (1953). Reprinted by permission of the author and *The Philosophical Review.*

book. If someone doesn't know but wants to know what a table is, to learn the use of the word "table," it would not do to begin by showing him an esoteric table with ninety-six legs, only six inches high. Again one would take a good solid oak table with a modest number of legs, an ordinary, everyday sort of table, not a cabinet maker's nightmare. If we begin with a clear-cut case, one no one would ordinarily be tempted to dispute, we can then shift to the less clear-cut, the disputed, cases. A clear-cut case is a place to start from.

What would a clear-cut case of a work of art be? One is inclined to say a painting like Poussin's "The Rape of the Sabine Women," or Da Vinci's "Mona Lisa," or Rembrandt's "Night Watch," would do here, that no one would want to object. But suppose someone were to say, "No, none of these are works of art." If, when we pointed to an ordinary everyday sort of table, someone were to object, "No, that's not a table," we could and should say he was clearly confused, in one way or another. Maybe he imagined we had not pointed at the table, that we had pointed at a chair; or we might suppose that he supposed the word "table" was only and always applied to multiplication tables; and so forth. Perhaps cultivated confusion at a sophisticated level, but nothing else but confusion, could be the root of a dispute over our clear-cut example of a table; but a refusal to call the Poussin, or the Da Vinci, or even the Rembrandt a work of art, need not be the blossom of a merely blooming confusion. For it is in fact possible to dispute whether any particular painting is a work of art or not, and people do dispute such questions, in a way that it is not in fact possible to dispute whether any particular object is a table or not.

And this is to say simply that there are and can be no such clear-cut cases of works of art in quite the same sense as there can be such clear-cut cases of tables, chairs, and so forth. That this is so stems partly from the fact that there are many uses of the phrase "work of art" in a way in which there are very few uses of the word "table." (For even though the word "table" does have many diverse uses, e.g., one can speak of multiplication tables, dinner tables, table lands, etc., there are very few uses of the word "table" in connection with those ordinary everyday objects that one customarily sits at and eats off of, i.e., tables. But in this sense, there are many distinct and different and even "competing" uses of the phrase "work of art.") And it also stems partly from the fact that among these many uses of the phrase "work of art," some are aptly described as laudatory or eulogistic. The many reasons why this is so will, I trust, become clear in the course of this discussion. For the time being, even though the examples of works of art which I have cited might not or need not be accepted by everyone, they are the clearest cases available, and as such they provide a useful base for our explorations.

In selecting a clear-cut example of a carpenter's hammer, one could choose a hammer with a handle exactly twelve and three-quarters inches long. Perhaps the title of the book we pointed to, the leather-bound book with gold lettering, was *Anna Karenina*. But in describing or talking about the example of a hammer to a child who did not grasp the use of the word, one would not say, "The handle of the hammer is exactly twelve and three-quarters inches long." Instead, one would be much more apt to say, "The handle of the hammer is about a foot long," or something of that sort. In the kind of case we have envisaged, the former statement would, at best, be altogether misleading. Whether a description is liable to mislead depends roughly on why it is wanted. In describing the clear-cut case of a hammer, when we want to help someone understand how the word "hammer" is used, we mention those facts about the object that make it, in fact, such a clear-cut case. That is why we would not say, "The handle of the hammer is exactly twelve and three quarters inches long." This really does not matter; it does not affect and is entirely irrelevant to the status of the example as a clear-cut case. But the fact that the handle is about a foot long is really relevant here. Similarly, we would not mention the particular title of the book, which we were using as a clear-cut case; but the fact that it had a title would be relevant.

Suppose we point to Poussin's "The Rape of the Sabine Women" as our clearest available case of a work of art. We could describe it by saying, first, that it is a painting. Secondly, it was made, and what is more, made deliberately and self-consciously with obvious skill and care, by Nicolas Poussin. Thirdly, the painter intended it to be looked at and appreciated, where it could be contemplated and admired. In short, he intended it to be treated in a way very much like the way that works of art are customarily treated. In saying this I do not wish to suggest that Poussin intended his work to be exhibited in a museum gallery. I do not know, but I would suppose the painting was intended to be hung in some chateau, or something of that sort. So perhaps in this respect the painting is not treated in the way intended by the painter. But there is good reason to believe that the painter did intend the painting to be displayed in an appropriate manner, to be treated with care, and to be preserved for as long as possible. And there is good reason to believe that Poussin did intend the painting to be contemplated, studied, observed, admired, criticized, and discussed by some people, if not by just any people. Fourthly, the painting is or was exhibited in a museum gallery where people do contemplate, study, observe, admire, criticize, and discuss it. What I wish to refer to here by speaking of contemplating, studying, and observing a painting, is simply what we may do when we are concerned with a painting like this. For example, when we look at this painting by Poussin, we may attend to its sensuous features, to its "look and feel." Thus we attend to the play of light and color, to dissonances, contrasts, and harmonies of hues, values, and intensities. We notice patterns and pigmentation, textures, decorations, and embellishments. We may also attend to the structure, design, composition, and organization of the work. Thus we look for unity, and we also look for variety, for balance and movement. We attend to the formal interrelations and cross connections in the work, to its underlying structure. We are concerned with both two-dimensional and three-dimensional movements, the balance and opposition, thrust and recoil, of spaces and volumes. We attend to the sequences, overlaps, and rhythms of line, form, and color. We may also attend to the expressive, significant, and symbolic aspects of the work. Thus we attend to the subject matter, to the scene depicted, and to the interrelations between the formal structure and the scene portrayed. We attend to the emotional character of the presented forms, and so forth. This is, very roughly, what I have in mind when I speak of contemplating, studying, and observing this Poussin painting. (Lest there be any misunderstanding, let me say explicitly that I am not saying that when ordinary people either contemplate or study or observe or attend to or look at or in any way concern themselves with this Poussin painting, they do in fact always attend to or concern themselves with all of the aspects of the painting that I have here mentioned. This is plainly untrue. But it is true that some people, when they look at this painting, are concerned with some of its many aspects that I have mentioned, while other people concern themselves with other of its aspects. And it is true, certainly, that all of these aspects of the painting are attended to at one time or another, and occasionally even all by one very unordinary person at one time.) Fifthly, this work is a representational painting with a definite subject matter; it depicts a certain mythological scene. Sixthly, the painting has an elaborate and certainly complex formal structure. Finally, the painting is a good painting. And this is to say simply that the Poussin painting is worth contemplating, studying, and observing in the way I have ever so roughly described.

It must be clear that whether the Poussin painting does or does not in fact fit the description that I have given is totally irrelevant to what I am saying. For example, it is at least within the nebulous realm of possibility that I am much mistaken in saying it is a good painting. It is even more than merely possible that I have been misinformed about Poussin's intentions. And maybe I have made other mistakes as well. But whether this is so or not does not in the least matter, for I am not trying to show that the Poussin painting is in fact a work of art. Rather I am trying to clarify what may be meant by saying that the Poussin painting is a work of art. What is important here is this: Because I believe the Poussin painting does fit the description I have given, I believe that it is, and I have chosen it as, one of the clearest available cases of a work of art. Our concern here is only with the description and not with whether the description fits the particular case. Each of the various facts mentioned in the foregoing description are characteristic of a work of art; it is these characteristics that concern us.

In order to make clear what the difficulties are in formulating and justifying a defintion of a work of art, in the following section I shall present what I take to be an adequate definition based on the preceding account of the Poussin painting. However, I shall not here attempt to show that the definition is in fact adequate.

III

All of the characteristics mentioned in the preceding description of the Poussin painting together constitute a set of characteristics. Several characteristics taken together constitute a set of characteristics if and only if all of the characteristics mentioned are relevant in determining whether something is or is not a work of art and if they are the only characteristics that are so relevant. Anything possessing all of these characteristics can then be said to be a characteristic case. Consequently, if the Poussin painting does in fact fit the description given above, it is such a characteristic case.

The set of characteristics given provides us with a set of sufficient conditions for something's being a work of art. Anything clearly satisfying these conditions can be said to be a work of art in exactly the same sense of the phrase "work of art" in which the Poussin painting can be said to be a work of art. It is important to notice that I said "clearly satisfying these conditions." The word "clearly" is crucial here. There is a temptation to say that the preceding description of the Poussin painting provides nothing more than a rough schema of what could be said about the work. This is not quite true, but it is a way of emphasizing the truth that there is a great deal of latitude in the various details of the description given. For example, one of the facts mentioned about the Poussin painting was that it is a representational work. Suppose we now consider a statue of Praxiteles: are we to say that it is representational? Someone might say that a statue cannot be representational in quite the same sense in which a painting can be. On the other hand, it could be claimed that both a statue and a painting can be said to be representational, in the very same sense of the word, but that they are merely different species of representative works. Again, someone might say that a sculptor does not make a statue in quite the same sense in which a painter makes his painting. And again it could be said that there is no difference in sense but only a difference in species. And this kind of question can be raised in connection with each of the characteristics mentioned.

I take it that we are inclined to speak of a difference in sense when we are impressed by, or wish to stress, dissimilarities. But when we are impressed by, or wish to stress, similarities, we are then inclined to speak of a mere difference in species. Now by speaking of a case that "clearly" satisfies the conditions given above, I mean to refer to a case in which there is no inclination to speak of a shift in sense with respect to any of the characteristics listed. Unless this point is attended to, it might mistakenly seem that we do not have a set of sufficient conditions, for one can conjure up some curious cases.

Suppose an object were found, satisfying the conditions given above, but with this one eccentricity: the scene depicted, and consequently the formal structure as well, changed periodically, without being changed. Imagine an object fitting the description, but having the peculiarity that, without being moved, it moved occasionally about the room. Thus in a way these odd objects behave somewhat like living organisms. One could be somewhat reluctant to call these things works of art. It would indeed be difficult to know what to say. Shall we say that our set of characteristics does not, therefore, provide a set of sufficient conditions? For we have not mentioned the fact that the object is a stable object, that it does not change or move about periodically of its own accord. This would be a mistake. We should be uncertain whether these odd objects were works of art solely because we should be uncertain whether they did in fact fit the description which we have given. It would be queer to say of an object that it was a painting and that it periodically moved about the room of its own accord. It would be equally queer to say of an object that it was a painting depicting a certain scene and that the scene periodically changed of its own accord. For facts like these cast a doubt on whether the object is a painting in the sense of the word "painting" originally intended, and on whether the painting depicts a scene in the sense of the phrase "depicts a scene" originally intended. But if an object does clearly satisfy the conditions stated, there can be no doubt but that it can be said to be a work of art in the very same sense of the phrase "work of art" in which the Poussin painting can be said to be a work of art.

Although the above set of characteristics provides a set of sufficient conditions, it does not provide a set of necessary and sufficient conditions. No one of the characteristics listed is necessarily a characteristic of a work of art. But a definition in terms of necessary and sufficient conditions is merely one kind of definition, one way of describing the use of a word or phrase. Another kind of definition, and the kind we are here concerned with, is one in terms of various subsets of a set of characteristics, or, in less exotic language, in terms of similarities to what I have called a characteristic case, a case in which an entire set of characteristics is exemplified.[1] The following examples should serve to clarify what is meant by speaking of similarities to a characteristic case.

Suppose we have a naturally formed stone object that has the shape of a woman reclining. Indeed, it looks as though some sculptor has fashioned it, though we know that this is not the case. What is more, it is worth contemplating, studying, and observing in a way analogous to the way described in connection with the Poussin painting. Further suppose that people do in fact contemplate, study, and observe it, that it is displayed in a museum, and so forth. In virtue of its similarities to the characteristic case, this object can be said to be a work of art. The points of similarity between this object and the Poussin painting constitute a particular subset of the set of characteristics

---

[1] Let me note that I am deeply indebted to Professor Max Black, both through his published papers and from discussions with him, for many of the ideas in this paper. In particular, I have, I trust, here profited from his account of a definition in terms of overlapping and interacting criteria; cf. "The Definition of Scientific Method," *Science and Civilization*, ed. by R. C. Stauffer (Madison, University of Wisconsin Press, 1949).

listed above. Imagine this sort of case: we have a nonrepresentational painting, deliberately made by an artist, who intended it to be exhibited and displayed, and who wanted people to contemplate, study, and observe it. But in fact the painting is not worth contemplating, studying, and observing. What is more, no one does bother with it at all. It is not exhibited, displayed, and so forth; rather it is buried away in some cellar. This too, in virtue of its similarities to the characteristic case, can be said to be a work of art. Again, the points of similarity between this work and the characteristic case constitute another subset of the set of characteristics given above.

In each of the preceding examples, when it was said that the object was a work of art in virtue of its similarities to the characteristic case, it was implicitly assumed that the similarities noted were sufficient to warrant the claim that the objects were works of art. No rule can be given to determine what is or is not a sufficient degree of similarity to warrant such a claim. If for one reason or another the dissimilarities become impressive (and what impresses one need not impress another), one is then reluctant to call the object a work of art. For example, a Greek vase is, in many ways, similar to a New England bean pot. Both are artifacts; both were made to serve domestic purposes; neither was intended to stand in a museum; and so forth. Nonetheless, a Greek vase is a work of art while a New England bean pot is not. To see that this is so, consider those points of similarity between a Greek vase and the Poussin painting that are also points of dissimilarity between a Greek vase and a New England bean pot. We do not, in fact, treat a New England bean pot in a way similar to the way we treat the Poussin painting; whereas we do, in fact, treat a Greek vase in a way quite similar to the way we treat the Poussin painting. We set up Greek vases on pedestals; we do display and exhibit them in museums and galleries, and what is more, it is worth while to do so. We do not in fact contemplate, study, observe, admire, criticize, and discuss bean pots in a way that we do Greek vases or in the way we do the Poussin painting; furthermore, it seems most unlikely that it would be worth while to do so. Unlike bean pots, and like the Poussin painting, many Greek vases are representational. One is inclined to speak, and one does speak, of the formal structure of a Greek vase in a way similar to the way one speaks of the formal structure of the Poussin painting. We do not, in fact, speak of the formal structure of a bean pot, nor is there usually any inclination to do so. Now if one starts, as it were, from the Poussin painting and then shifts to the Greek vase, one begins to feel the strain. For a Greek vase was not (or so we are supposing) intended to be treated in a way similar to the way the Poussin painting is treated. It was designed to fulfill a specific utilitarian function. Many Greek vases are not representational. They were not, in the time of the Greeks (or so we are supposing), set up on pedestals. They were not displayed and exhibited in museums and galleries. They were not contemplated, studied, observed, admired, criticized, and discussed in a way similar to the way in which the Poussin painting is. One begins to feel the strain in speaking of a Greek vase as a work of art. Now if one tries to speak of a bean pot as a work of art, the strain becomes too great. We have reached a breaking point, and one is inclined to say things like, "A bean pot *cannot* be classed as a work of art." It is only a matter of degree.

Finally, neither a poem, nor a novel, nor a musical composition can be said to be a work of art in the same sense of the phrase in which a painting or a statue or a vase can be said to be a work of art. For such things as poems, novels, musical compositions, possess none of the characteristics listed in our set of characteristics. E.g., a poem is not exhibited or displayed; one does not contemplate, study, and observe a poem; a poem is not representational; and so forth. And even though a poem may seem to possess some of the characteristics listed, for one can and does speak of a good poem, the dissimilarities between what is meant in speaking of a good poem and what is meant in speaking of a good painting are sufficiently impressive to warrant our saying it is a different sense of the word "good." All of this, however, does not show that one cannot reasonably use the phrase "work of art" to refer to poems, novels, musical compositions, as well as to paintings. If one wished to describe a use of the phrase "work of art" in which there is such a systematic shift in sense, one could do so in terms of several sets of characteristics. One would take a clear-cut case of a poem and obtain a set of characteristics, then a clear-cut case of a novel and obtain another set, and so forth. Then something would be a work of art, in this use of the phrase, if it possessed some subset of the set of characteristics pertaining to paintings, or some subset of the set of characteristics pertaining to poems, and so forth. This may seem an extremely complex way of using the phrase "work of art." but it is actually often used in somewhat this way by critics who speak of the "art of painting," the "art of poetry," and so forth. Such a "blanket" use of the phrase may be warranted by the fact, if it is a fact, that each set of characteristics is analogous in composition to every other set; e.g., the analogue of contemplating a painting is reading a poem, the analogue of a good painting is a good poem, the analogue of display is publish, and so forth.

There is no need to elaborate this definition any further for the purposes of this discussion. The preceding account is sufficiently explicit to stir up and bring to the surface all the important difficulties that must be noted here.

IV

The definition just given provides a rough description of only one use of the phrase "work of art." But this phrase is and has been used in many ways. So long as art remains what it has always been, something changing and varied, so long as there are artistic revolutions, the phrase "work of art," or some equivalent locution, will continue to be used in many ways. For when such revolutions occur, there is inevitably a shift in some uses of the phrase "work of art." Some understanding of the nature of the disputes that occur over what is and what is not a work of art during such periods of artistic revolution is essential to an understanding of what an aesthetician is doing in offering some one, and only one, definition of a work of art.

When nonrepresentational and abstract painting first attracted attention in the early part of this century, many people complained bitterly that the nonrepresentational and abstract works were not works of art. Thus one critic wrote: "The farce will end when people look at Post-Impressionist pictures as Mr. Sargent looked at those shown in London, 'absolutely skeptical as to their having any claim whatever to being works of art.' "[2] Other critics insisted, with equal vehemence, that the Post-Impressionist paintings most certainly were works of art. If one looks with an impartial eye at these disputes between the traditional and the modern critics, one thing is quite clear. In many cases the parties to the disputes were using the phrase "work of art" in more or less different ways. Indeed, the modern critics, the defenders of the new works, were introducing a more or less novel use of the phrase. To see that this is so, it is necessary to attend to some of the typical complaints that were voiced against modern art by the traditional critics.

In a review of the first exhibition of modern art in America, Mr. Kenyon Cox claimed that

the real meaning of this Cubist movement is nothing else than the total destruction of the art of painting—that art of which the dictionary definition is "the art of representing, by means of figures and colors applied on a surface, objects presented to the eye or to the imagination." ... Now the total destruction of painting as a representative art is a thing which a lover of painting could hardly envisage with entire equanimity, yet one may admit that such a thing might take place and yet an art remain that should have its own value. A Turkish rug or a tile from the Alhambra is nearly without representative purpose, but it has intrinsic beauty and some conceivable use. The important question is what it is proposed to substitute for this art of painting which the world has cherished since there were men definitely differentiated from beasts. Having abolished the representation of nature and all forms of recognized and traditional decoration; what will the "modernists" give us instead?[3]

It is often erroneously supposed that traditional critics held representation to be a necessary characteristic of a work of art. This is not true. Such critics did maintain that it was a relevant characteristic, but few insisted it was necessary in that without representation there could be no work of art. What is true is that traditional critics weighted this characteristic enormously, so that it was of paramount importance in determining whether a given work was or was not a work of art. In their reaction against this view, some of the modern critics have

---

[2]Royal Cortissoz, "The Post-Impressionist Illusion," *Three Papers on "Modernist Art,,*(New York, Amer. Acad. of Arts and Letters, 1924), p. 42. Reprinted from *Century Magazine*, April, 1913.
[3]"The 'Modern' Spirit in Art," *op. cit.*, pp. 6-8. Reprinted from *Harper's Weekly*, March 15, 1913.

apparently gone to the extreme of suggesting that representation is wholly irrelevant to art.[4] In this respect, our definition would be apt to satisfy neither a conservative traditional critic nor an extreme modern critic. The shift in the notion of a work of art that was brought about through the modern developments was, with respect to the question of representation, primarily a shift in emphasis, and only secondarily a shift with respect to necessary conditions. The point is that representation was of paramount importance in virtue of the fact that "accurate" representation played the role of a necessary condition in determining what was and was not a good painting. This leads us to another point of difference between the traditional and modern critics.

I am inclined to suppose both traditional and modern critics would accept the seventh characteristic listed in our definition, viz., that the work be a good one, as a relevant characteristic of a work of art. (Whether they considered it to be a necessary characteristic is a difficult question that need not concern us here.) But it is fairly obvious that what the traditional critics meant in speaking of a good painting or a good drawing was somewhat different from what the modern critics meant. For example, Mr. Royal Cortissoz, in reviewing the first exhibition of modern art in America, severely criticized Van Gogh's drawing.

The laws of perspective are strained. Landscape and other natural forms are set awry. So simple an object as a jug containing some flowers is drawn with the uncouthness of the immature, even childish, executant. From the point of view of the Post-Impressionist prophet, all this may be referred to inventive genius beating out a new artistic language. I submit that it is explained rather by incompetence suffused with egotism.[5]

Somewhat later in his review, while discussing Matisse's drawing, Mr. Cortissoz stated that

whatever his ability may be, it is swamped in the contortions of his misshapen figures. The fact is that real genius in these matters will out. Degas, who has been all his life a disciple of Ingres, uses a magic of draftmanship akin to that of his idol, though the style and spirit of his work are wholly his own.[6]

It is, I take it, fairly clear that Mr. Cortissoz' notion of a good drawing, of a good painting, would today be objected to. For he, together with most traditional critics, apparently held that a necessary condition (though not, of course, a sufficient condition as is sometimes naïvely supposed) for a drawing to be considered a good drawing is that the perspective be "true," the form "realistic," and so forth. Few if any critics today would subscribe to this view.

Perhaps the clearest indication of the fact that the modern critics were using

---

[4]Cf. Clive Bell, *Art*, pp. 28-30, where such a view is, or seems to be, suggested.
[5]*Op. cit.,* p. 31.
[6]*Ibid.,* pp. 36-37.

the phrase "work of art" in a more or less novel way is to be found in the oft-repeated charge that the new works had broken with tradition. For in claiming that there had been such a break, the traditional critics can be taken as claiming that the degree of similarity between the new works and those accepted in the tradition as works of art was insufficient to warrant the claim that the new works were works of art. The dissimilarities were felt to be overwhelming; the gap was held to be too great to bridge. The modern critics, of course, denied that there had been any such rupture, at least not with the tradition as they saw it; rather they insisted that tradition had been reasonably extended and developed. They repudiated the charge of a complete break by exhuming and pointing to the works of such people as El Greco to justify the modern use of distortion, just as somewhat later the Surrealists were to exhume the works of Acrimboldo and Bosch in an effort to make their own fantasies more palatable to the public. It is for this reason, among others, that the works of Matisse have so often been compared with Egyptian portraits, Japanese prints, and so forth, while the similarities between Picasso's work and practically everything in any tradition have been set forth exhaustively. Whether modern art did in fact break with European tradition is not a point that need concern us. But the fact that the tradition was at least extended cannot be denied and is here relevant. For this is merely another way of saying that there was some shift in the notion of a work of art. Let it be quite clear that I am not claiming to have here *shown* that the modern critics were introducing a somewhat novel use of the phrase "work of art." To show that such was the case, it would be necessary to present a great deal more evidence than I have done. But everything about the disputes between the traditional and the modern critics certainly suggests that the modern critics were in fact using the phrase "work of art" in a somewhat novel way. And if the likelihood of this is granted, that is sufficient for the purposes of this discussion.

Once it is realized that the modern critics were most likely using the phrase "work of art" in a somewhat novel way, there is, or is apt to be, a temptation to say that the disputes between the traditional and the modern critics were merely verbal. For one may be inclined to say that in a modern critic's use of the phrase, the new works were in fact works of art, while in a traditional critic's use, they were not. But this is a temptation which we must certainly resist. Even though it may be true that the new works were works of art in a modern critic's use of the phrase, and were not works of art in a traditional critic's use, it would be quite absurd to think that, therefore, the disputes were merely verbal. The disputes, in part, arose from conflicting decisions over the way to use the phrase "work of art," but such decisions were not and certainly need not be thought arbitrary. Decisions may not be true or false, but they can be reasonable or unreasonable, wise or unwise. In effect, the traditional critics maintained that their decision to use the phrase "work of art" in a traditional way was the most reasonable one, and consequently their use of the phrase was the most reasonable use; the modern critics made exactly the same claim in favor of their own somewhat radical use of the phrase. Sometimes these claims were made explicitly; at other times, such a claim is implicit in the criticism, favorable or unfavorable, given to the new works. To understand what is involved in such a claim and what is meant by speaking of a "reasonable use" of a word or phrase, it is necessary to see why it may be important to use a word or phrase in one way rather than another, and what there is that may be worth arguing about.

V

There is no sense in speaking of a "reasonable use" of a word or phrase *in vacuo*. What is or is not a reasonable use depends on the particular context in which the question is raised, on the kind of considerations involved, and so forth. For example, if you want to be understood, you are well advised to use your words in some ordinary and familiar way; but if being understood is not at issue, this advice is not to the point. Not being understood may be one consequence of using a word or phrase in a particular way, but there may be other consequences, and consequences of a different kind. For example, it is, I suppose, no part of the meaning or the use of the phrase "excessive speed" that if a driver of a vehicle involved in an accident is held to have been driving at an excessive speed, he is likely to suffer certain penalties under the law. But even though this may be said to be no part of the use of the phrase, it is nevertheless an important fact which a jurist must keep in mind when attempting to specify the use of the phrase in a court of law. It would be unwise, for example, to lay down a ruling that would constitute a precedent for taking excessive speed to be any speed over posted limits. For a man may drive at a speed greater than the posted limit in an attempt to avoid an impending accident. It would be unreasonable to penalize him for making the attempt if it happened that even so he was unable to avoid the accident.

What I am saying is that once the legal consequences and implications of declaring a person to have been driving at an excessive speed are relatively fixed, we can then, in the light of these consequences and on the basis of certain moral and legal notions concerning the purposes to be accomplished by means of these consequences, say what is or is not a reasonable defintion and a reasonable use of the phrase "excessive speed" in a court of law. (One can, of course, reverse this process and argue that once the notion of excessive speed is fairly well fixed in the sense indicated above, it is unreasonable to penalize a man merely for driving at an excessive speed. Thus someone could argue that his use of the phrase in the sense indicated above was reasonable, the consequences that are likely to occur in the course of using the phrase unreasonable. In a sense, the use of the phrase and the significant legal consequences likely to occur in the course of using the phrase each provide a standpoint for criticism.

We can criticize either the use of the phrase in terms of the fairly fixed legal consequences or the legal consequences in terms of the fairly fixed use.)

To ask "What are the consequences and implications of something's being considered a work of art?" is to ask an equivocal question to which there can be no univocal answer. We must first know in what context we are to suppose the phrase "work of art" is being used. (Just so one can speak of the consequences of using the phrase "excessive speed" in one way or another only when the context is specified. In a court of law the use of such a phrase may have significant consequences which, in some other context, simply are not forthcoming.) In the context where critical disputes are carried on, there are in fact many significant consequences arising from the fact that a certain type of work is considered a work of art. For disputes between critics are not private affairs. They are carried on in a social context, and they are significant only when set in the framework provided by such a context.

It is, I suppose, no part of the meaning or the use of the phrase "work of art" that if a certain type of work is considered a work of art, works of this type will eventually find their way into a public museum. Nonetheless, public funds will, in fact, be spent on these works. The public will be advised to see and study such works. Books will be written and read about them, and so on. These are in fact some of the present characteristic social consequences of something's being considered a work of art in Western society. The social consequences and implications of something's being considered a work of art have varied in time, and no doubt they will continue to do so. For they are merely an aspect of the particular role art plays in a particular society, and as the character of the society changes, the role of art in the society may also change, together with the characteristic social consequences and implications of something's being considered a work of art in that society. Now although the traditional and the modern critics almost certainly disagreed about the specific characteristics of a work of art, they agreed both in their desires and in their expectations with regard to the characteristic social consequences and implications of something's being considered a work of art. Their agreement in this respect lent substance to their disputes over the use of the phrase "work of art." Indeed, the traditional critics explicitly and with great vehemence maintained that the Post-Impressionist works ought not to be placed in museums; that the public funds ought not to be spent on them; that the public would be ill-advised to spend its time looking at them or reading books about them; and so forth. All of this the modern critics explicitly and emphatically denied. (And this is one obvious reason why it would be quite absurd to call such disputes merely verbal.) Now to determine whether a certain type of work ought or ought not to be placed in a museum, purchased with public funds, and so on, it is necessary to consider what purposes it is to serve when once it has been purchased, when public funds have been spent on it, and so on. And this is to say that in order to determine what is or is not a reasonable use of the phrase "work of art," it is necessary to consider not only the characteristic social consequences and implications of something's being considered a work of art, but also the purposes to be accomplished by means of these consequences—i.e., the various functions of a work of art in society. The role that the functions of a work of art play in determining whether a particular use of the phrase "work of art" is reasonable or not, may be clarified by the following example.

Consider the second characteristic mentioned in our definition of a work of art, viz., that the work be made, deliberately and self-consciously with obvious skill and care, by some person. The traditional view would be that this is a necessary characteristic of a work of art. E.g., in *Art as Experience,* Dewey writes:

Suppose, for the sake of illustration, that a finely wrought object, one whose texture and proportions are highly pleasing in perception, has been believed to be a product of some primitive people. Then there is discovered evidence that proves it to be an accidental product. As an external thing, it is now precisely what it was before. Yet at once it ceases to be a work of art and becomes a natural "curiosity." It now belongs in a museum of natural history, not in a museum of art.[7]

I am very much inclined to object to Dewey's use of the phrase "work of art," but it is most unlikely that such an objection can be made directly on the grounds that his use of the phrase is unreasonable. To see why this is so, it is necessary to see precisely what is at issue here. This may appear to be a relatively trivial point, one hardly worth disputing over; for there may in fact be fairly few natural objects that one is inclined to exhibit and display. What is and what is not excluded from a museum is in this case, however, of only secondary importance. The exclusion of a natural object from a museum of art is primarily of interest when viewed as symptomatic of a particular orientation toward the works that are in fact displayed in a museum. If one adopts a view similar to that of Dewey, there is a tendency to treat the work of art primarily as a "manifestation" of the artistic activity engaged in by the person who produced the object. One is then tempted to look through the work of art to the artist's "experiences," "feelings," and so forth. Furthermore, one is tempted to say that this "revealing" aspect of the work is essential to its functions as a work of art. Now the relevance of the artist's "experiences" to an appreciation of his work is an extremely complex problem which I shall not even attempt to consider here. But I mention these points in order to stress the fact that such considerations as these are relevant in attempting to determine whether the fact that the object was made by a person is or is not a necessary condition for its being a work of art. To claim that Dewey's traditional use of the phrase "work of art" is unreasonable would, in effect, be to claim that the mere fact that an

[7]Page 48.

object is an artifact does not suffice to show that it is thereby incapable of satisfactorily fulfilling the various functions of a work of art. But since such a claim would be made on the basis of a particular view of these functions, Dewey's use of the phrase ought properly to be considered in relation to his own view of what these functions are or ought to be.

There is no doubt but that the explicit disagreements between the traditional and the modern critics stemmed from more or less divergent conceptions of what the functions of a work of art are or ought to be in our society. In writing of the first exhibition of Post-Impressionist works in England, Roger Fry pointed out that the new movement in art "implied a reconsideration of the very purpose and aim as well as methods of pictorial and plastic art."[8] He characterized the purpose of the new art by saying it was devoted to "the direct expression of feeling" and to the making of "images which by the clearness of their logical structure, and by their closely knit unity of texture, shall appeal to our disinterested and contemplative imagination with something of the same vividness as the things of actual life appeal to our practical activities."[9]

What Mr. Fry says here is, of course, quite vague, but he was dealing with an extraordinarily difficult topic. Vague or not, he is quite right in suggesting that modern works serve somewhat different purposes from the accepted works that has preceded them, no matter how difficult it may be to say precisely wherein the difference lies. To consider but one aspect of this enormously complicated question, a traditional view of a function of a work of art was that it was to constitute an object of Beauty, which would inspire, profit, and delight the beholder. Now "Beauty" is not a term likely to be applied to a host of modern works, e.g., to one like Picasso's "Guernica." "Guernica" is no doubt a magnificent, powerful, superbly conceived and executed work, but it is not a thing of "Beauty." It is true that there are many paintings in European tradition to which one would be equally reluctant to apply the term "Beauty," e.g., Grünewald's "Crucifixion" in the Isenheim altarpiece, but it is also true that the obvious religious purpose of the Isenheim altarpiece is something more or less alien to modern art. That modern works do in fact serve somewhat different purposes from the accepted works that had preceded them is perhaps best signalized by the technical innovations introduced and employed by the modern artists. The extent of these innovations must not be underestimated.

It is true that the modern use of distortion has its analogue in El Greco's work among others, but it is also true that El Greco's work was practically ignored until the twentieth century. And of course even his work appears naturalistic in contrast with a work like "Les Demoiselles d'Avignon." To feel the full impact of the modern innovations in the use of color, it is merely necessary to see a work by Miro hung in a gallery alongside works done before

---

[8]*Vision and Design* (Pelican Books, 1937), p. 194.
[9]*Ibid.*, p. 195.

1850. Again one may admit that e.g., Poussin employed intense hues, and Giotto's work must have been quite brilliant at one time; but it is impossible to ignore the fact that many modern painters such as Miro and Matisse employ huge flat masses of color in an altogether new way, a way that is simply incompatible with and wholly alien to the spatial character of a Poussin painting. These and many other such technical innovations all herald the fact that modern paintings are devoted to somewhat different purposes and aims from those of the works that had preceded them. For the widespread adoption of new methods of working in art has, in fact, always been correlative to a more or less radical variation in the purposes and aims of art. (Just so the technical innovations of the monodic revolution in music at the beginning of the seventeenth century, the development of the so-called *stile moderno* or *seconda prattica* with its use of the thorough bass, the introduction of the recitative, and so forth, were the technical correlates of the development of secular music. Indeed, in the eyes of the modern critics of the period, the *stile antico* was seen as the sacred style appropriate to church music.)

Whether the traditional critics' disapproval of the purposes and aims of the new works stemmed from a failure to understand fully what these purposes and aims were, or whether this disapproval was based on a full understanding, is a purely historical question that need not concern us here. That they did disapprove is beyond question, for they voiced this disapproval in no uncertain terms; e.g., in concluding his review of the first exhibition of modern art in America, Mr. Cox adjured his readers to remember that

it is for you that art is created, and judge honestly for yourselves whether this which calls itself art is useful to you or to the world. You are not infallible, but, in the main, your instincts are right, and, after all, you are the final judges. If your stomach revolts against this rubbish it is because it is not fit for human food.[10]

Most aestheticians today, I believe, would say the modern critics were right in contending that the Post-Impressionist paintings were works of art. Indeed, few people now dare to question the status of modern art as art, and those who do are at once labeled "Philistines" and "reactionaries." But if we say the modern critics were right — and I do not presume to question the matter here — if we say their decision to use the phrase "work of art" in a somewhat new way was a wise one and their use of the phrase was the most reasonable, we must not rashly assume that the traditional critics' use of the phrase "work of art" could be held to be unreasonable when examined on the basis of the traditional critic's own view of what the functions, purposes, and aims of a work of art are or ought to be. On the contrary, it is most likely that when so considered, their use of the phrase would prove to be quite reasonable. Thus an objection to their use of the phrase would most likely have to be made, and no doubt could be

[10]*Op. cit.*, p. 18.

made, in terms of a prior objection to their view of what the functions of a work of art are or ought to be. (For one can reasonably dispute over the question of what the functions of a work of art are or ought to be just as one can reasonably dispute over what is or is not a reasonable use of the phrase "work of art.") In accepting the modern critics' decision, we are, in effect, accepting something of their view of what the present functions, purposes, and aims of a work of art are or ought to be in our society.

What then is an aesthetician doing when he offers some one and only one definition of a work of art? It should be clear that he is not describing the actual use of the phrase. As I have tried to indicate above, this phrase is and has been used in many ways. No one definition can mirror this manifold and varying usage. Instead, an aesthetician is describing one, perhaps new, use of the phrase "work of art," which he either implicitly or explicitly claims to be the most reasonable use of the phrase in the light of the characteristic social consequences and implications of something's being considered a work of art, and on the basis of what the functions, purposes, and aims of a work of art are or ought to be in our society. What these purposes and aims are or ought to be is a matter of here and now. For as the character of society changes, as new methods of working are developed, these purposes and aims will also change. With the development of new means there will be new ends that can be served, and with the appearance of new ends, new means will have to be developed to serve them. Art neither repeats itself nor stands still; it cannot if it is to remain art. An attempt to provide a definition and a justification of a definition of a work of art is, as Collingwood has stated, not "an attempt to investigate and expound eternal verities concerning the nature of an eternal object called Art"; rather it is an attempt to provide "the solution of certain problems arising out of the situation in which artists find themselves here and now."[11] An aesthetician is not and certainly ought not to be expected to be a seer foreseeing the future of art. He is not an oracle, though he may choose to speak like one. As new and different kinds of works are created, as the character of society changes and the role of art in society varies, as it has so often done throughout history, it may and most likely will be necessary to revise our definition of a work of art.

---

[11]*The Principles of Art*, p. vi.

Definitions in Education and Art

ISRAEL SCHEFFLER

*　　*　　*

Definitions of terms in education are, to be sure, not generally embedded in as precise a network of practical rules as are legal definitions, but, in combination with broad and informal (though socially fundamental) principles of action, they often serve nevertheless as vehicles for debating new programs of education, new views of method, aims, or content. We have already seen one example in the case of the term 'curriculum.' Definitions in education thus may be said to resemble definitions in art which, though of no legal significance, also serve frequently to express changing conceptions of the artist's task.[13] For example, definitions of artistic innovators often extend the use of the term 'work of art' to new sorts of objects; the counter definitions of conservatives withhold the term from these same objects. Both sets of definitions are, furthermore, often consonant with artistic tradition, that is, they are in conformity with prior usage. The dispute can thus not be taken, in such cases, to be a matter of the meaning of terms alone. Rather, it is a question of divergent artistic programs, conveyed by opposing programmatic definitions that are also descriptively accurate. An attempt to define a work of art is not, in the words of Collingwood, "an attempt to investigate and expound eternal verities concern-

From Scheffler, Israel, *The Language of Education,* 1960. Reprinted by permission of the author and Charles C. Thomas, Publisher, Springfield, Illinois.
[13]For the points made in this paragraph, I am indebted to Ziff, P.: The task of defining a work of art, *The Philosophical Review*, 62:58, (January) 1953.

ing the nature of an eternal object called Art," but rather to give "the solution of certain problems arising out of the situation in which artists find themselves here and now."[14]

Education, like art, literature, and other phases of social life, has changing styles and problems in response to changing conditions. These conditions require decisions governing our practical orientation to them. Such decisions may be embodied in revision of our principles of action or our definitions of relevant terms or both. In the making of new definitions for such purposes, there is no special insight into meanings that tells us how revisions and extensions are to be made. Not an inspection of the uniquely real meanings of terms (if this were possible) is here relevant, but an investigation in the light of our commitments, of the practical alternatives open to us as well as of alternative ways of putting desired decisions into effect.

The way in which this point is often overlooked in professional writings on education may be illustrated by the following description of a new program for secondary schooling:

The curriculum was organized around four sorts of activities, story projects, hand projects, play projects, and excursion projects; opportunity was provided for continuing evaluation of activities, and such evaluation was directed by pupils. The organization of this school program proceeded naturally from the belief that the fundamental meaning of the concept of education is to help boys and girls to active participation in the world around them.

The issue is here put in terms of fundamental meanings. But, in fact, what is at stake? Clear cases of the concept 'education' as embodied in usage prior to the advent of modern innovations did not include cases where play and excursions as well as pupils' continuing evaluation characterized the educational program. But some of the clear cases, like the present example, did involve special institutions, overall direction by adults, evaluation of achievement, and so forth. The present educational innovation, as a matter of fact, is both sufficiently like and sufficiently unlike clear past instances to constitute a borderline case.

To propose an educational reform along the lines of the above passage is to say that such a procedure ought to be tried under the aegis of the schools. The proposal may thus be said to assimilate the borderline case to the past clear cases, leaving intact all those principles of action formulating our positive orientation to educational endeavor. The stated definition tries to do just that by, in effect, dwelling on the resemblances, i.e., on the common aim to help boys and girls to active participation in the world around them. It would, however, be easy to concoct alternative definitions that built on the differences,

---

[14]Collingwood, R. G.: *The Principles of Art.* Oxford at the Clarendon Press, 1938, p. vi, quoted in Ziff, Op. cit.

segregating the new reform from previous clear cases of 'education.' The issue, in short, is one of practice, and needs evaluation in terms of our preferences and commitments as well as in terms of expected effects. What is to be done with respect to this proposed educational reform is thus our practical responsibility and cannot be decided by inspection of the concept of 'education.'

Let us now consider a final example of a somewhat more abstract sort. In educational discussions, it is often said that a definition of 'man' provides directions for curriculum making and for evaluation of methods of schooling.[15] It is, indeed, true that the way in which we organize our educational efforts and operate our schools is conditioned by prevalent definitions of human nature. It is not, as we have seen, that practical educational consequences are derivable from accurate definitions taken in isolation but rather that they may be conveyed by such definitions in contexts where relevant principles of action are taken for granted. The conclusion often drawn in educational theory is that we must first decide what the correct definition of 'man' is, and that then practical educational consequences will only need to be inferred by us through the application of pure logic.

This picture is, however, wrong not only in postulating a simple deductive implication between definitions of human nature and practical educational consequences, but also in failing to take account of the several points noted above regarding definitions that are both descriptive and programmatic. There are an indefinite number of alternative definitions of 'man,' indefinitely many ways of dimensionalizing his structure and capacities, all equally accurate. To choose one such dimensionalization on the basis of its accuracy and to proceed to read off curricular counterparts to each dimension, as is often done, is to beg the whole question. One basis of choice of a definition for educational purposes must be a consideration of the very consequences for educational practice to be expected as a result of adoption of such a definition. The programmatic character of such a definition means that it requires evaluation with respect to the program conveyed. Indeed, such evaluation may even lead us to adopt a non-inventive stipulation that clearly violates prior usage; it surely may lead us to differentiate between equally accurate descriptive definitions that convey different programs. It is just because definitions of the latter sort are programmatic that their adoption should follow rather than precede a moral and practical evaluation of the programs they convey. Inspection of meanings cannot substitute for such an evaluation.

An analogous point holds for the transfer of definitions from science to education, a transfer whose dangers we have already intimated. We remarked that the scientific definitions are continuous with the theories and evidence

---

[15]In this connection see, for example, Ducasse, C. J.: What can philosophy contribute to educational theory?, *Harvard Educational Review*, 28:285, (Fall) 1958. Ducasse asks what the several dimensions of man's nature are, as a preliminary to determining the chief dimensions of education, which (as he says) "correspond, of course, to those of man's nature."

in their respective domains, and that they may therefore best be treated apart. They cannot be fitted into our stipulative, descriptive, and programmatic categories without serious distortion. They are to be judged, roughly, by their contribution to the adequacy of their respective scientific networks in accounting for the facts. It follows that, to take a scientific definition for programmatic use is not to avoid the need for evaluation of the program such use conveys. The scientific adequacy of a definition is no more a sign of the practical worthwhileness of such a program than accuracy with respect to prior usage.

Finally, note must be taken of the converse truth. Just as, if a definition is accurate it does not automatically follow that its associated program is worthwhile, so if a definition is inaccurate, it does not automatically follow that its program is not worthwhile. We have already seen, in the case of non-inventive stipulative definitions that are also programmatic, the possibility of a worthwhile program conveyed by a descriptively inaccurate formula. Nevertheless, writers occasionally do argue, invalidly, that their definitions are accurate, since their programs are worthwhile, and they provoke the equally invalid rejoinder that their programs cannot be worthwhile since their definitions are inaccurate. The issue thus set up needs cutting through rather than intensified partisanship. It needs to be recognized, in short, that the same definitional formula on a given occasion may be both descriptive and programmatic, and that it thus requires double evaluation.

Problems of Art

JOHN HOSPERS

*   *   *

The term "art." "Art" is a term of which definitions are almost inevitably persuasive. . . . The word "art" has a favorable emotive meaning—at least to those
who practice the arts and talk about them—and thus anyone who has cherished
ideals on the subject will want to use the word "art" to denote whatever kind of
product he venerates most highly. Semantically, this makes the situation
extremely confused though of course it is quite understandable. Thus, at one
extreme, Tolstoy said that whatever works of art, so-called, did not express
simple and profound emotions which could communicate themselves easily to
all mankind and thus promote the brotherhood of man, were "false art"; and at
the other extreme, Clive Bell has said that art has nothing to do with the life of
humanity, that in approaching it one should leave all memories of life behind
and view it as a realm of pure form, and that any work which fails to satisfy this
approach is "not really art." Both of these, needless to say, are persuasive
definitions of "art," "false art" being whatever does not live up to the writer's
stipulative definition of the term "art."

As opposed to these persuasive definitions, there are fairly neutral ways in
which the word "art" is used. (1) In its broadest descriptive sense, art is
opposed to nature: a work of art is anything which exists as a result of human

From John Hospers, *An Introduction to Philosophical Analysis.* © 1953, by permission of Prentice-
Hall, Inc., Englewood Cliffs, New Jersey, and the author.

effort and contrivance (perhaps that of animals as well), as opposed to "nature as we find it." It may have no esthetic interest at all, yet it is a work of art in this broad sense. Bonfires, tractors, paintings, cities, and piles of garbage are all works of art in this sense.

(2) In a somewhat narrower sense, the arts are the "cultural subject-matters": thus, we speak of a Bachelor of Arts degree, and the arts here include all the natural sciences, history, philosophy, and all the subjects for which a candidate for the B. A. would ordinarily get credit. It excludes those subjects specifically designed for certain professions, such as stenography, medicine, engineering, and the like.

(3) In a narrower sense still, the arts include only works in those media which produce *esthetic* effects, for example, *every* painting is a work of art, regardless of its merit. (In a eulogistic or persuasive sense, only those paintings which fulfill certain criteria, whether Tolstoy's or Bell's or somebody else's, are works of art.)

Even here there is a distinction, albeit a vague one. There are the *fine* arts and the *practical* arts. The practical arts have some practical end in view, some function to fulfil in the business of daily life regardless of their esthetic value: for example, weaving, costume design, engraving, woodworking, glass making, and most architecture. Since each of these arts is capable of considerable esthetic effect, however, it is usual to call them "art" even in the esthetic sense we are now considering; while at the same time they are distinguished from the "fine arts," which fulfil no practical end but are cultivated primarily or entirely for purposes of esthetic appreciation: for example, music, literature, sculpture, painting.

The fine arts are usually classified according to their respective media: (1) Visual arts — or the arts of space. (2) Auditory art — music in its various forms. Here what is apprehended is not a group of simultaneously existing objects or colors and shapes in space, but a temporal succession of sounds. Many differences arise in the analysis of these arts because of a difference in their medium. (3) Symbolic arts: literature. The medium here is words and their meanings. The words alone are not sufficient: when uttered aloud, they are merely sounds (not even musical sounds), and when seen on paper, they are mere ink-marks, capable of esthetic contemplation as objects of graphic art (such as penmanship and typography) but hardly as literature. The beauty of the printed ink-marks makes no difference to the merit of the poem (although it may make the poem more enjoyable to read), but that of the marks on the canvas makes all the difference to the painting. (4) Arts of theatre. These employ no new medium but combine two or more of the other three. Drama combines the visual (stage design) with literature (the dialogue), opera combines all three, ballet combines the visual with music, and so on.

Many problems and distinctions arise when one begins to think and talk about the arts. Only a few of them can be listed here.

1. *Aspects of works of art.* Many writers employ a threefold division of the aspects of works of art: material (also called sensuous or surface), formal, and associational. Without attempting strict definitions, let us attempt very briefly to characterize them. (There are, of course, other possible divisions.)

(1) *The material aspect.* "When we find delight in the surface texture of an object, in hearing the sheer volume or the quality of a sound, or in noting the saturation or hue of some color,"[11] we are responding to the material aspect. For example, a considerable part of our enjoyment from sculpture lies in the material — whether it be wood, stone, brass, marble, ivory, jade, or clay — from which the object is made. The esthetic enjoyment derived from jewels is chiefly of this kind. It is the most elementary and the most readily enjoyed of the types of esthetic value.

(2) *The formal aspect* is the one to which we respond in the contemplation of *relations* among the various elements in a work of art. Our enjoyment of a melody is principally the enjoyment of the relationships of tones to each other; single tones produce but little esthetic effect. Most paintings are highly complex structures of lines, colors, and masses, from whose mutual relations perhaps the chief esthetic satisfaction in visual art is to be drawn. This kind of esthetic value is not as easily appreciated as the others, but in the opinion of most of those who have studied the arts over a long period of time, it is the most enduring source of esthetic satisfaction once the appreciation of it has been developed.

(3) *The associational aspect* is different from both of the other kinds in that an appreciation of it is not an appreciation of something perceived in the work of art, but of something *conveyed by* it. Here we enjoy something that is not in the perceived object — something read into the work rather than directly perceived in it. The recognition of a figure in a painting as a representation of Louis XIV, for example, is associational, unlike the esthetic effect to be derived from the relations of line and color. Whenever we say "The music is *triumphant*," "The painting is religious in its feeling," "This play expresses the idea that man is a contemptible little animal," and the like, we are responding associationally.

The principal dispute in this region of the philosophy of art has to do with the comparative importance of these sources of esthetic response. Specifically, the dispute is between the formalists (who admit only the first two, with emphasis upon the second) and the associationists (who admit all three, with emphasis upon the third). The associationists hold that the chief esthetic value to be derived from works of art is the appreciation of the emotions expressed, the objects represented, and the ideas conveyed. The formalists hold that the enjoyment of these things is "not really esthetic" at all, and that the distinctively esthetic values are apprehended only when we derive our satisfaction from the

---

[11]Hunter Mead, *An Introduction to Esthetics* (New York: The Ronald Press, 1952), p. 84.

intricate relationships of line and color, tones and harmonies, rhythms and cadences, in a work of art. Whereas the associationist might say of the first movement of Mozart's G Minor Symphony (No. 40) that it begins with a sprightly theme, gay and bouncing yet tinged with melancholy, as if the composer's joy were tempered with grief . . ., the formalist would find his satisfaction in the comtemplation of the interweaving of the various themes and variations in the total structure of the movement:

I. *Exposition*	II. *Development*	III. *Recapitulation*
a1, a1	d1	a1, a1
a2	d2	a2 (extended)
bridge passage	d3	bridge passage
b1, b1	returning passage	b1, b1
b2		b2
bridge passage		bridge passage
c1, c1		c1, c1
c2		c2
c3		coda

The associationist would be interested primarily in the general mood evoked by a landscape painting, a hint of melancholy perhaps, a tinge of autumn in the air, the effect of the waning afternoon sunlight on the reeds and water; the formalist meanwhile would derive his principal enjoyment of the painting from viewing it as an interplay of forms—the curve of the hill here matching (but not exactly) the curve of a cloud there, the rhythm of certain color-patterns progressing from one end of the painting to another until stopped by a massive form just at the edge, the total balance (satisfying yet not perfectly symmetrical), the size and shape of the space here between these two forms in relation to other sizes and shapes of spaces between other forms in the painting, and so on.

To some it seems that these two sources of satisfaction necessarily impede and conflict with each other[12]—that a tension is set up between them so great that if the one is there we cannot easily concentrate upon the other. To others it seems that the two are not in opposition at all[13]—rather, that one must study them separately for a time and then "fuse" them together, and that the ultimate in esthetic experience occurs not in enjoying the formal aspect alone, nor yet the associational aspect alone, but in the two together, so closely related that in our response to the work of art we are not aware of them as distinct entities at all: the two are transformed as in a chemical compound rather than a mere mixture.

There are many controversies connected with this basic issue into which we

---

[12]See, for example, Roger Fry, *Transformations* (London: Chatto & Windus, 1926).
[13]See, for example, L. A. Reid, *A Study in Esthetics* (New York: Macmillan, 1931).

cannot enter here. Let us only stop to ask very briefly a few typical questions:

First, do the two kinds of appreciation conflict? This seems surely to be a question about what different observers of art feel—a question in descriptive psychology. Briefly, the answer would seem to be something as unexciting as this: "Some people can enjoy the two together and some can't."

Second, which source of esthetic satisfaction is more important? Here again the question is not clear. Does it mean "Which affords a more intense esthetic experience?" (and in this case, to whom does it afford it?) or perhaps "Which is the more lasting in its esthetic effects upon the observer?" Like so many questions, this one must be made more specific before it can be answered intelligibly at all.

Third, is the controversy between formalists and associationists a verbal one? The formalist says that the appreciation of the associational aspect of art is "not truly esthetic"; is he doing more than refusing to use the word "esthetic" to apply to something for which other people *do* use the word? Insofar as he is doing this, the controversy is surely a verbal one. But it is not therefore trivial; for by doing this he is calling attention to a source of satisfaction which is very likely to go unappreciated, one which, perhaps far more than most people are aware, is or can be so different from anything that the associative aspect of art can give that the two should not be put under the same heading by being given the same name. . . .

2. *The function of art.* Some say that the function of art is to provide esthetic experiences (whether by means of all, or only some, of the sources just listed). Others say that the function of art is *not merely* to provide esthetic experiences but also (1) to evoke emotions (other than esthetic emotions),[14] or (2) to represent objects and situations from life, or (3) to wield a moral influence upon individuals or upon society, in favor of some particular code of ethics or some social or economic theory.

Many volumes have been written defending and attacking these different views of the function of art. We cannot go into the matter further here; let us only stop to ask ourselves, What kind of a dispute is this? If the function of a thing is what it actually does, then the answer seems to be that works of art do all of these things—some doing more of one and some more of another. But the dispute would usually be interpreted as being one about what works of art *ought* to do. Thus interpreted, the answer depends upon our answer to the general question about the meaning of judgments involving the word "ought"—and whether the word "ought" is here being used in a moral sense or in some other sense.

---

[14]It is more usual to say "*express* emotions." But the word "express" is very misleading. More often than not the phrase "expression of emotions" stands for a process which takes place in the *artist,* not the audience. Here we are concerned, however, with the effect of works of art on the audience, and so for the sake of clarity we speak of *evoking* emotions. These emotions may or may not be of the same kind as those which the artist has expressed.

Or the issue may be represented as being one about the "purpose," or the "true purpose," of art. But, as we saw earlier . . . a purpose implies someone to have the purpose. In this case, the answer would have to be given in terms of what purpose the artist had in creating this particular work of art. Thus interpreted, there can hardly be a single answer to the question. Different artists have different purposes in mind, and some of them probably create as if by divine inspiration without any conscious purpose in mind at all.

3. Perhaps the most fruitful and challenging kind of enterprise in the philosophy of art lies in the detailed analysis of meaning—the meanings of terms used specifically in the arts, terms which are incessantly used in discussion but not often clarified. One such term, "beautiful," we have already considered in some detail. But there are others which, from the point of view of both the artist and the student of art, count at least as heavily: "style," "technique," "meaning," "form," "content," "expression," "classic," "romantic," "realistic," "naturalistic," and so forth. Many confusions and misapprehensions can result, even in a comparatively simple discussion of the arts, if such terms as these are not clarified. Consider, for example, the term "form":[15] people say "I don't care about the form, I only care about what it says," "If the subject-matter of a poem is not what makes it a good poem, it must be the form," and so on. But the term "form" is an elusive one. Sometimes by "form" we mean shape: we say that two pennies have the same form although they have different "matter." Sometimes we mean a species or class: thus, we speak of two compositions as both being in the sonata *form*. Sometimes we have reference to a mode of arrangement of things as opposed to the things that are so arranged: thus, three rhyming lines of poetry could be put in the orders ABC, ACB, BAC, BCA, CAB, or CBA, though the lines thus ordered are the same in each case. Sometimes we refer to the "how" as opposed to the "what": we take the underlying idea or theme of a work of art to be the content (the what), and the way in which it is expressed by the artist (the how) is called the form. Here is an example of how confusions can arise: a person is convinced that it is not the theme which an artist selects for treatment, but rather how he treats this theme, that determines the merit of a work of art: the how and not the what, the form and not the matter. He then feels himself committed to the view that only the form (in *another* sense of the word, though he is unaware of this) of a work of art is important (primarily the arrangement of its lines and colors) and that the other elements such as we have called the "associative" are of no relevance at all. This conclusion, of course, is unwarranted; the mood the artist has created in his painting has just as much to do with his treatment of the theme as does the formal arrangement of its elements. But, through confusion in the use of the viciously ambiguous term "form," he may not know this.

---

[15]See, for example, L. A. Reid, *A Study in Esthetics,* Chapter 7; Morris Weitz. *Philosophy of the Arts,* Chapter 3.

Introduction

The Meaning of "Aesthetic"

The next four selections set forth some of the uses of "aesthetic" to be found in discussions of art and aesthetic experience and analyze some important components of aesthetic experience itself. Together with Broudy's interpretation in Section One, these essays should enable the teacher and student to build a perspective on this problem.

In "What Makes a Situation Aesthetic?" J. O. Urmson attempts to explicate what distinguishes aesthetic thrills, satisfactions, disgusts, etc., from other experiences such as moral, personal, intellectual, and economic ones. When, in other words, is a person in the aesthetic field? It is noteworthy that instead of beginning with responses to complex works of art, Urmson starts with our reaction to a large variety of ordinary things, holding that there are no special objects or emotions which are exclusively aesthetic, though objects and emotions are, of course, constituents in the aesthetic field. Urmson concludes that deciding whether someone's appreciation is aesthetic requires inspection of the reasons supplied for specific appraisals. When this is done, it is found that the grounds given are often "the way the object looks (shape and color), the way it sounds, smells, tastes, or feels." Then there are those more complex occasions when we are interested in something beyond mere color and shape, or simple sensible qualities. This occurs when an object looks, say, "strong" or "triumphant" — qualities which, Urmson claims, are nonaesthetically desirable.

Urmson's contribution is representative of a look at the meaning of aesthetic from the point of view of recent linguistic investigations. But it is testimony to the achievement of John Dewey that his philosophy of art still figures prominently in contemporary discussions of aesthetic problems. It is difficult, however, to abstract from Dewey's writings a concise statement of his aesthetic theory. For this reason, an analysis of Dewey's aesthetics by D. W. Gotshalk is included as the next selection.

Gotshalk acknowledges the debt owed by contemporary philosophy to Dewey for his pioneering effort in clearing the air and regaining the primitive relevance of philosophical thinking to the problems of men. Yet the adequacy for present-day issues of a philosophy which moved in the biosocial context of the individual and his interactions with an environment is a matter of dispute. The questions of survival and evolution in a biotic sense may be regarded as solved, while problems concerning distinctively human ends, about which Dewey's thinking was rather incomplete, oppress us all the more heavily. In

"On Dewey's Aesthetics," Gotshalk contends that Dewey, despite his uneasiness about any kind of mere speculation, did advance a short distance beyond the line separating Darwinian from uniquely human contexts. And what is more important, Dewey made this step, perhaps quite unintentionally, in his work on aesthetics.

Although Dewey never saw himself as a system-builder, he seems to have felt that his work lacked completeness unless it provided a place for the aesthetic. Gotshalk indicates that Dewey met the challenge rather late in his career in *Art as Experience* by "depicting aesthetic experience...as pure experience or as the highest fulfillment of that adjustment between striving organism and social setting which is the shared aim of all live creatures." Yet this very attempt to locate the aesthetic securely within the texture of life involved Dewey in certain difficulties which can be resolved, claims Gotshalk, only by acknowledging the *special* character and status of art, something that Dewey's egalitarian temperament was loath to admit.

Gotshalk points out that Dewey conceives the aesthetic as (a) an element in *any* experience which has attained wholeness. Yet Dewey also describes (b) a *specifically aesthetic* experience — in most cases the result of confrontation with works of art — which must meet two criteria not required of ordinary experience: immediacy and intuitive grasp of the quality of the whole. This distinction between two types of experience, then, may be taken as a sign of Dewey's awareness of the unique character of beholding works of art.

Another difficulty arises in Dewey's definition of the work of art. For Dewey, the physical entity created by the artist is merely the product of art. The *work* of art comes into being only through the creative and imaginative interaction between the percipient and the product of art. In other words, the object that leaves the hands of the artist is only potential which achieves actuality within the strictly private experience of the beholder through a creative process of perception. This means there are as many "works of art" as there are distinctive instances of perception. More importantly, it also means that discourse about art is impossible since two persons cannot be talking about the same work of art. This, however, completely contradicts the crucial role assigned to communication and the appropriation of meaning through shared activities which is evident throughout Dewey's general philosophy. The alternatives, it would seem, are either to deny the importance of communication or, as Gotshalk suggests, to admit that a work of art is not only a physical object, but a *special* kind of object. It is an object possessing expressive as well as formal and functional dimensions which can be discovered through an act of perception that is informed and properly disciplined and not merely creative in a general, unrestricted way.

In Gotshalk's view, *Art as Experience* contains many valid and valuable insights into the nature of art and aesthetic experience. But most of all it provides proof that art is a good in its own right which should not be subordinated to or subsumed under something beyond itself. Art is a good, says

Gotshalk, because it "gives us a form of self-awareness (a mirror) not to be found in mere life, contributing thereby to a unique dimension of man's being."

The type of human activity which eventuates in works of art has understandably attracted much attention and speculation, and attempts have abounded to discover *the* creative process, that is, a universally valid pattern exhibited by any activity designated as artistic. Monroe C. Beardsley in "On the Creation of Art" sets himself the problem of (a) refuting theories that seek to extract a generally applicable pattern from creative activity; (b) setting forth generalizations that *can* be made about the work of the artist; and (c) pointing out the relationship between the process and the product of art.

Beardsley explicates two widely held accounts of creative activity: what he calls the Propulsive and the Finalistic theories. According to the Propulsive Theory, the agent controlling the artistic process comes into existence prior to the onset of activity and guides and directs everything that follows. The most popular form of the Propulsion explanation is the notion of "art as expression." This means that the artist begins with some vaguely felt emotion which expresses and clarifies itself progressively as the work of art develops. The difficulty here, says Beardsley, is formulating standards of judgment. Since the emotion or idea that gave rise to the work was at first unclear and chaotic, there would be no way of deciding whether and to what extent the finished product expresses this original feeling.

One version of the Finalistic theory is the designation of the creative process as "qualitative problem-solving."[1] In this view, creation is controlled by a previsioned goal, while the process leading to that goal consists of a series of problems and solutions. The difficulty with this notion, according to Beardsley, lies in calling *problems,* that is sets of means-ends relationships, what actually are *tasks* involving regional qualities and the perceptual conditions on which they depend. A *problem* arises out of some real conflict and demands a determinate solution, while the main question confronting the artist is what to do next. The perceptual conditions which the artist manipulates in order to achieve regional qualities are not properly understood, claims Beardsley, as means employed toward a predetermined end.

While denying that the creative process follows a set formula, Beardsley nonetheless isolates certain features common to artistic endeavors. First of all, the work of the artist is purposive in some sense; it is leading somewhere. Although the artist may not have any clear notion of the goal, he does know what directions *not* to take.

Secondly, each process that results in a work of art generates its own

---

[1]Beardsley has perhaps incorrectly interpreted the theory of art he chooses for criticism as an example of the Finalistic Theory. However, the wisdom of retaining the language of means-ends and problem solving to describe the artistic process has been questioned not only by Beardsley. In this connection, see Justus Buchler. *The Concept of Method* (New York: Columbia University Press, 1961), Chapter XI; and Paul J. Olscamp, "Some Remarks about the Nature of Aesthetic Perception and Appreciation," *The Journal of Aesthetics and Art Criticism,* Vol. XXIV, No. 2 (Winter 1965), p. 253.

momentum and direction. The control is not a single factor imposed externally; rather it evolves *during* a process in which each stage is determined by the conditions of and the possibilities permitted by the unfinished work.

Thirdly, three general stages can be discerned in artistic work: incept, development, and completion. The incept may be provided by any idea or occurrence in the artist's life. While it does sustain some relation to the finished product, it is not at all clear whether it remains dominant throughout the development. The development itself is carried forward through an interplay between preconscious and conscious activities. The preconscious phases are those of invention and inspiration, but their psychological conditions are not as yet well understood. During the conscious phases, inspired inventions are either selected or rejected according to how they are perceived in relationship. This, in other words, is criticism continually brought to bear on the evolving work. Completion confronts the artist with the dual problem of deciding when *he* has finished, that is, when he has done all he can for the work, and when the *work* is finished.

And yet, Beardsley claims, understanding the creative process makes no difference in our relationship to the work of art. Indeed, were we to permit our appreciation of the work to be influenced by the process, we would be victims of a variant of the Intentional Fallacy, which Beardsley has criticized elsewhere. Beardsley concludes that the locus of creativity, rather than residing in the genetic process, is found in the work itself as it lives in the experience of the beholder. This claim, however, does not make inquiry into the artist's mode of operation irrelevant. The creative process is interesting in itself, for undeniably something very special takes place. Moreover, it exhibits to us one more aspect of man the maker—the maker, that is, of self-creative objects which we call works of art.[2]

In "Visual Metaphors of Value in Art," E. H. Gombrich investigates the peculiar capacity of artistic experience to embody or express certain of man's higher values. Metaphors in general are made possible by the propensity of the human mind to find equivalences for the most disparate phenomena and to substitute one for another. Qualities may be transferred from one sensory experience to another and converge in synaesthetic metaphors which are quite common in everyday parlance. We speak, for instance, of "loud colors," a "velvety tone," or a "clean fight." By a similar process of convergence and transference, visual qualities may be experienced as equivalences of moral values. This is particularly evident in art criticism where value metaphors such as "vulgar," "dignified," or "meretricious" abound. In fact, Gombrich maintains that in our living experience aesthetic values always find resonance in other areas of value, and there are probably very few people who have never experienced great art in terms of moral values. This assertion is supported by a

---

[2]It would be an interesting assignment to study Beardsley's conclusion in this matter in relation to Gotshalk's critique of Dewey's conception of the work of art.

consideration of the emergence and development of certain value metaphors in the history of art.

In medieval religious art, for example, the sparkle and costliness of gold provided a universal and unsophisticated value metaphor that afforded an apprehension of the supernatural in terms of the sensual. During the Renaissance, however, a process of sophistication commenced which led the cultured individual to abhor immediate gratification of the senses through outward splendor. The civilized person now prized dignity, restraint, decorum, in short, the control of the passions. The artistic metaphor for this new cultural value was found not so much in what art emphasized than in what it expressly rejected. "Pure," "unadorned," and "noble simplicity" became terms of critical acclaim. In both art and society, renunciation, domination of impulses, nobility, and the Good converged into the highest form of value.

One further contribution of the Renaissance was to bestow upon art an autonomous value. This independent value of art in turn became an "area of metaphor" during the Victorian era. "Art," as denoting something to be prized in its own right, was equated with economic success and expressed metaphorically through ornament. In other words, the Victorians revelled in ornament because it "stood for" art and all that it implied. Against this background, the twentieth century initiated the second revolution of sophistication; it rejected Victorian ornament—now labeled "tasteless ostentation" or "vulgar gratification"—in favor of the "clean line." Today, says Gombrich, we instinctively prefer what is suggestive of the rational, the hygenic, the streamlined, and we draw our metaphors chiefly from the world of engineering. Again, then, a process of denial and rejection has created new, supposedly higher, values and their equivalent metaphorical expressions in art. But this second revolution of sophistication has also liberated areas formerly under an aesthetic ban, and we are now permitted to enjoy medieval and other primitive forms of art as "pleasantly naive."

The ability of art to create value metaphors has been rendered problematic by contemporary developments. The process of sophistication through renunciation has gathered momentum, and negation follows upon negation with increasing rapidity. Now a great work of art, says Gombrich, is characterized not merely by negation and denial, but by the discipline and control of powerful impulses and emotions. In much of modern art, however, the emphasis on negative aspects, that is, on the absence of illustration, representation, sentiment, is pushing the work of art ever closer to the work of taste. Furthermore, specialization and the break-up of an unquestioned community of standards frustrate the formation of universal metaphors.[3]

---

[3]For additional comments on the subject of symbols and metaphors, see E. H. Gombrich, "The Use of Art for the Study of Symbols," *American Psychologist,* Vol. XX, No. 1 (January 1965), pp. 34-50. For a recommendation regarding the proper use of the term symbol in aesthetics, see L. A. Reid, "Susanne Langer and Beyond," *British Journal of Aesthetics,* Vol. V, No. 4 (October 1965), pp. 357-67.

What Makes a Situation Aesthetic?

J. O. URMSON

Philosophers have hoed over the plot of aesthetics often enough, but the plants that they have raised thereby are pitifully weak and straggling objects. The time has therefore not yet come for tidying up some corner of the plot; it needs digging over afresh in the hope that some sturdier and more durable produce may arise, even if its health be rather rude. I therefore make no excuse for reopening what seems to me to be the central problem of aesthetics: I hope that by a somewhat new approach I may succeed in making a contribution, if but a small one, towards its solution.

We may refer to a person as, in a given situation, getting an aesthetic thrill or aesthetic satisfaction from something, or of his finding something aesthetically tolerable, or aesthetically dissatisfying, or even aesthetically hateful. In a suitable context the adjective 'aesthetic' and the adverb 'aesthetically' may well be superfluous, but it is sometimes necessary to introduce one of these words in order to make it clear that when we refer, say, to a person's satisfaction we are not thinking of moral satisfaction, economic satisfaction, personal satisfaction, intellectual satisfaction, or any satisfaction other than aesthetic satisfaction. If we merely know that someone gained satisfaction

From Joseph Margolis (ed.), *Philosophy Looks at the Arts* (New York: Charles Scribner's Sons, 1962), pp. 13-26. This essay was originally published in the *Proceedings of the Aristotelian Society*, Supplementary Volume XXXI (1957), pp. 75-92. Reprinted by permission of the author and the Aristotelian Society.

from a play we do not know for sure that we are in the aesthetic field. Thus a play may give me moral satisfaction because I think it likely to have improving effects on the audience; economic satisfaction because it is playing to full houses and I am financing it; personal satisfaction because I wrote it and it is highly praised by the critics; intellectual satisfaction because it solves a number of difficult technical problems of the theatre very cleverly. But the question will still be open whether I found the play aesthetically satisfying. Though these various types of satisfaction are not mutually exclusive, it is clear that when we call a satisfaction aesthetic the purpose must be to mark it off from the other types.

The philosophical task to be tackled in this paper is therefore this: to make explicit what it is that distinguishes aesthetic thrills, satisfactions, toleration, disgust, etc., from thrills, satisfactions, etc., that would properly be called moral, intellectual, economic, etc. I put the question in this form because I think that it is tempting to consider the aesthetic as an isolated matter and within the field of the aesthetic to concentrate unduly upon the most sublime and intense of our experiences; but I am convinced that it is important to ensure that our account of the aesthetic should be as applicable to toleration as to our most significant experiences and should make it clear that in characterizing a reaction or a judgment as aesthetic the point is to distinguish it from other reactions and judgments that are moral, economic, and so on. Only thus can we hope to bring out the full forces of the term 'aesthetic.'

This is not intended to be a problem especially about the appreciation of works of art. No doubt many of our most intense aesthetic satisfactions are derived from plays, poems, musical works, pictures and other works of art. But to me it seems obvious that we also derive aesthetic satisfaction from artifacts that are not primarily works of art, from scenery, from natural objects and even from formal logic; it is at least reasonable also to allow an aesthetic satisfaction to the connoisseur of wines and to the gourmet. I shall therefore assume that there is no special set of objects which are the sole and proper objects of aesthetic reactions and judgments, and which are never the objects of an economic, intellectual, moral, religious or personal reaction or judgment. We may judge a power-station aesthetically and find economic satisfaction in a work of art that we own. We may take it, then, that we are not exclusively concerned with the philosophy of art, and that whatever the criteria of the aesthetic may be they cannot be found by trying to delimit a special class of objects.

If the aesthetic cannot be identified by its being directed to a special class of objects, it might be more plausibly suggested that the criteria of the aesthetic are to be sought by looking for some special features of objects which are attended to when our reaction or judgment is aesthetic; beauty and ugliness have often been adduced as the features in question. Alternatively it has often been suggested that aesthetic reactions and judgments contain or refer to some unique constituent of the emotions of the observer, either a special "aesthetic emotion" or an "aesthetic tinge" of some other emotion. I think that most commonly theories elicited by our problem have been variations on one or other of these two themes, a variation on the first theme being called an objectivist theory and a variation on the second being called subjectivist. I propose to give some reasons in this paper for finding both these theories unsatisfactory as answers to our problem, even if neither is wholly false as a mere assertion; in their place, I shall suggest that the correct answer is to be given in terms of the explanation of the reaction or the grounds of the judgment. I shall make some tentative remarks about what sort of grounds for a judgment make that judgment aesthetic, but cannot even begin the systematic treatment of the subject.

Let us revert to an illustration already casually used, and suppose that we observe a man in the audience at a play who is obviously beaming with delight and satisfaction. If I now maintain that his delight is purely economic, what have I to do in order to establish this contention? If the question at issue were whether he was delighted or merely contented it would no doubt be necessary to ascertain fairly accurately his emotional state; but if it be agreed that he is delighted and the only issue is whether his delight is properly to be called economic, it is surely clear that phenomenological study of his emotions is not necessary. If, however, we find him to be the impresario, and he agrees that the complete explanation of his delight is that there is a full house and the reaction of the audience indicates a long run, what more could possibly be needed to justify us in describing his delight as economic? It seems hard to dispute that in the case of economic delight, satisfaction, disappointment and the like the criterion of the reaction's being economic lies in the nature of the explanation of the reaction. Similarly it would be beyond dispute that a man's delight was wholly personal if it were conceded that its explanation was entirely the fact that his daughter was acquitting herself well in her first part as a leading lady; again his delight will be moral if wholly explained by the belief that the play will have a good effect on the conduct of the audience. It would, I suggest, be very surprising if the way of establishing that delight, satisfaction and other reactions were aesthetic turned out to be quite different from the way in which we establish them to be moral, personal, economic, intellectual, etc. Nor would it be surprising merely as a novelty; it would be logically disturbing to find that one had suddenly to depart from a single *fundamentum divisionis*, which had sufficed for all the other types, when one came to the aesthetic.

We must now note a further point about the logical relation between the concepts of the moral, the aesthetic, the economic, the intellectual, and the personal, as applied to reactions, both because it is of some logical interest and because a misunderstanding of it has led to some silly theories. *Triangular, square* and *pentagonal,* as applied to surfaces, are clearly species of a single genus and as such are mutually exclusive; there is a single *fundamentum divisionis* which is the number of sides that the rectilinear surface has. The same applies, *mutatis mutandis,* to *bachelor, married* and *widowed* as applied to men. On the other hand *triangular, red* and *large* are three logically unconnected predicates of surfaces, and *bachelor, bald* and *wealthy* are similarly unconnected predicates of men. What then are we to say about the predicates *moral, economic* and *aesthetic* as applied to, say, satisfactions? Clearly they are not technically species of a genus for they are not mutually exclusive as are species of a single genus; I may be simultaneously satisfied by a single object aesthetically, morally and economically, just as well as a man may be simultaneously bald, wealthy and a widower. But on the other hand to ask whether a satisfaction is moral or aesthetic makes as good sense as to ask whether a surface is square or triangular, whereas only in a very odd context can one ask whether a man is bald or a widower; furthermore, if a satisfaction is wholly moral it is not at all aesthetic, whereas being wholly bald does not prevent a man from being a widower. Thus moral, aesthetic and economic satisfactions seem neither to be logically disconnected nor to be true species of a genus.

Aesthetic and moral satisfactions thus seem to be related as are business and sporting associates. A man may be both a business and a sporting associate, yet the point of calling a man a business associate is to distinguish his status from that of a sporting or other type of associate, as it does not distinguish him from, say, an associate first met at Yarmouth. In the same way, to call a satisfaction aesthetic has the point of distinguishing its status from that of being a moral or economic satisfaction, though a satisfaction may be both aesthetic and moral. It surely follows that the criteria for a reaction's being aesthetic cannot be wholly unrelated to the criteria for its being moral or economic — they must be connected in such a way that we can see how being wholly one excludes being also another and yet how a single reaction can be both moral and aesthetic.

If we find the criterion for distinguishing aesthetic from kindred reactions in the nature of the explanation of the reaction we can readily account for this logical situation. To say that a satisfaction is wholly aesthetic, for example, will be to say that the explanation or grounds of the satisfaction are wholly of one sort, which will necessitate that the satisfaction cannot rest also on moral grounds; on the other hand there is clearly nothing to prevent our satisfaction from being multiply-grounded and thus simultaneously aesthetic and moral, aesthetic and economic, and so on.

But if we were to accept different kinds of criteria of the aesthetic, the moral and the economic we should be in difficulties here. Thus if a philosopher were to hold (and some apparently do) that a moral judgment is one that asserts an object to have a certain character and an aesthetic judgment to be one that announces or expresses the special emotional state of the speaker he would be maintaining views which, however plausible when consistently adhered to in isolation, are poor bed-fellows. For one would expect a wholly moral judgment, interpreted as ascribing a moral character, to deny implicitly the presence of a special aesthetic or special economic character; similarly a wholly aesthetic judgment, interpreted as expressing a special aesthetic emotion, should deny implicitly the presence of a special moral or economic emotion. Consistency is required here.

So much for the logical point of being clear on the relation between the aesthetic, the moral, the economic, etc. Unclarity on the point can lead to other less philosophical confusions. Thus the belief that moral considerations are relevant to a thing's aesthetic rank seems to stem from an awareness that appreciation may be simultaneously based on aesthetic and moral considerations coupled with a blindness to the fact that to call an appreciation aesthetic has as part of its point the effect of ruling out the moral as irrelevant. At the opposite extreme those who rage at any moral comment on a work of art are so conscious that the moral is irrelevant to the aesthetic that they suppose some error in allowing one's general satisfaction to have both a moral and an aesthetic component.

I have illustrated sufficiently the dangers of considering aesthetic reactions and judgments in abstraction from moral, economic and other kindred reactions and judgments. Similarly we must not concentrate on aesthetic delight and neglect other aesthetic reactions. The view that delight is aesthetic when that emotion has some special aesthetic tinge is not unplausible in isolation; we can no doubt bring aesthetic disgust under the same theory easily enough. But what if I am asked for an aesthetic judgment on what seems to me a very ordinary building and I reply truthfully that I find it merely tolerable? Am I reporting an emotion of toleration which has an aesthetic tinge, or perhaps an absolute tinge with no emotion to be tinged? But if I be taken to report merely the absence of any emotion or tinge by what criterion can we say that I am making an aesthetic judgment at all? It is surely important that we should be able to distinguish an aesthetic judgment of toleration from merely refraining from any aesthetic judgment at all; to regard a thing with mere aesthetic toleration is quite different from not considering it in an aesthetic light at all.

Thus the view that what distinguishes the aesthetic reaction and judgment is the presence of a special emotion or a special emotional tinge has already proved unsatisfactory on two counts. First, we have seen that we require a similar type of criterion of the aesthetic, the moral, the intellectual and the economic reaction, whereas the emotional criterion is very unplausible in some of these cases. Secondly, we have seen that however plausible with regard to strong emotional reactions, the emotional view is most unplausible when we consider such cool aesthetic reactions as that of bare toleration. Even if these difficulties were overcome, it is perhaps worth noticing that on this view a single reaction which involved, say, simultaneous economic, moral, aesthetic and intellectual satisfaction might well be required to involve an emotion having a quite kaleidoscopic variety of tinges.

But apart from these more logical points it is surely clear that when we experience emotions that we should wish to call aesthetic they are often very different from each other. Thus Tovey (*Essays in Musical Analysis,* Vol. I, p. 200) speaks of a theme "which gives Mozart's most inimitable sense of physical well-being" precisely because most of even the most delightful musical themes are so different in emotional effect. Or again, is it so clear that aesthetic emotions are different in kind from others? Tovey, we have seen, compares a Mozart theme to a quite non-aesthetic delight, and Housman can be adduced as a still more striking, since unwilling, witness. Enumerating three types of "symptoms" of poetical delight in his lecture, *The Name and Nature of Poetry,* he says: "One of these symptoms was described in connection with another object by Eliphaz the Temanite: 'A spirit passed before my face; the hair of my flesh stood up'"; another he describes by using Keats' words about his feelings for Fanny Brawne, "Everything that reminds me of her goes through me like a spear"; the third, he says, "consists in a constriction of the throat and a precipitation of water to the eyes," an experience which is surely common to many emotional situations, and not confined to the aesthetic.

The objection to the view that what distinguishes the aesthetic judgment or reaction from others is that it alone involves the recognition or awareness of beauty and ugliness, if offered as a solution to our problem, is rather different. As a minor objection it is worth pointing out that we should hesitate to call many things for which we have a great aesthetic admiration "beautiful," that 'beautiful' is a relatively specialized word of aesthetic appraisal, though this will inevitably elicit the answer that here 'beauty' is being used with a wider meaning than is currently assigned to it. But granted that 'beauty' and 'ugliness' are being used with a wide enough significance, the trouble with this answer to our problem is not that it is false but that it is futile. Of course if I admire a thing aesthetically I must be aware of its beauty, or of its charm, or of its prettiness or some other "aesthetic characteristic"; this is true in the same way as it is platitudinously true that moral admiration must involve awareness of a thing's moral goodness or rectitude or of some other "moral characteristic." But the trouble is that we have no independent way of telling whether we are aware of beauty or ugliness on the one hand or rightness or wrongness on the other; to know this we must know whether our admiration is aesthetic or moral, or, more accurately, to try to discover whether our admiration is aesthetic or moral and to try to discover whether we are aware of beauty or rightness are not two distinct inquiries but a single inquiry described in two ways neither of which is more luminous than the other. To identify the aesthetic judgment by the aesthetic characters of which it involves awareness is therefore not helpful.

Let me now set out more generally and completely the view that I wish to urge. The terms 'good,' 'bad' and 'indifferent' are, I take it, among the widest terms of appraisal that we possess, and we do appraise things on the basis of criteria, criteria to be formulated in terms of the "natural" features of the things appraised. But usually we wish at any time to appraise a thing only from a restricted point of view. We may, for instance, wish to appraise a career from the restricted point of view of its worth as a means to earning a livelihood; to do so we restrict our attention to a special set of the criteria of a good career, all others being for the purpose irrelevant. I wish to suggest that the moral, the aesthetic, the economic, the intellectual, the religious and other special appraisals should all be understood as being appraisals distinguished by their concentration on some special sub-set of criteria of value. To say that something is good as a means is not to say that it is good in some special sense distinct from that of "good as an end" but to appraise it from a special point of view; similarly to judge a thing aesthetically good or first-rate is not to call it good in a sense different from that in which we call a thing morally good, but to judge it in the light of a different sub-set of criteria. We may if we wish to choose to invent a special meaning for 'beautiful' in which it becomes shorthand for 'good from the aesthetic point of view,' but that is only a dubious convenience of no theoretical significance. The central task of the philosopher of aesthetics is, I take it, to clarify the principles on which we select the special set of criteria of value that are properly to be counted as relevant to aesthetic judgment or appraisal. We may recognize an aesthetic reaction by its being due to features of the thing contemplated that are relevant criteria of the aesthetic judgment, and the aesthetic judgment is one founded on a special sub-set of the criteria of value of a certain sort of thing.

It may justly be said that so far I have done little more than to assert this view dogmatically, though I should wish to claim that I have given it some *a priori* probability by showing that it is a view which will enable us to deal with some of the difficulties that other views cannot surmount. Certainly I have as yet done nothing to indicate on what principles the criteria of value relevant to the aesthetic judgment are selected.

This lacuna can only be properly filled by field-work, and then only filled completely by a full-scale work on aesthetics. By doing field-work I mean studying examples of people actually trying to decide whether a certain judgment is or is not aesthetic and observing how they most convincingly argue the matter. Unfortunately to do this on an elaborate scale in one paper of a symposium is hardly possible; I can but ask you to believe that this paper has been written only after a considerable amount of such work, and produce one or two examples of it to show more clearly what I have in mind.

In his more philosophical moments A. E. Housman tried to account for the peculiar nature of the aesthetic in terms of emotional, and even physical, reactions; but here is an example of what he has to say at a more literary and less philosophical level: "Again, there existed in the last century a great body of Wordsworthians, as they were called. It is now much smaller; but true appreciation of Wordsworth's poetry has not diminished in proportion: I suspect that it has much increased. The Wordsworthians, as Matthew Arnold told them, were apt to praise their poet for the wrong things. They were most attracted by what may be called his philosophy; they accepted his belief in the morality of the universe and the tendency of events to good; they were even willing to entertain his conception of nature as a living and sentient and benignant being; a conception as purely mythological as the Dryads and the Naiads. To that thrilling utterance which pierces the heart and brings tears to the eyes of thousands who care nothing for his opinions and beliefs they were not noticeably sensitive; and however justly they admired the depth of his insight into human nature and the nobility of his moral ideas, these things, with which his poetry was in close and harmonious alliance, are distinct from poetry itself.''

It does not matter whether we agree with Housman about Wordsworth; but I do hope that all will agree that this is the right sort of way to set about showing that an appreciation is not aesthetic. Clearly Housman does not deny that what the nineteenth century admired in Wordsworth was admirable; but he says that if your admiration of Wordsworth is based on certain grounds (the philosophical truth and moral loftiness of the content of the poetry) it is not aesthetic admiration, whereas if it is based on what Housman calls the "thrilling utterance," by which the surrounding paragraphs abundantly show him to mean the sound, rhythm and imagery of the words used, then it is aesthetic admiration. Whether Housman is right about Wordsworth or not, whether he has selected the most important criteria of poetical merit or not, this is the type of argument to be expected in a competent discussion; but to have argued the case by adducing the claim that Wordsworthians tended to concentrate rather on traits other than beauty would in fact have been to have restated the case rather than to have argued it. Moreover, if some Wordsworthian had maintained that Wordsworth's pantheism did bring tears to his eyes it would clearly have made no difference to the argument; it is concentration on the utterance, rather than having tears in your eyes, that makes you truly appreciative of the poetry.

Housman's *The Name and Nature of Poetry* is a mine of similar examples. Though he says in a theoretical moment: "I am convinced that most readers, when they think that they are admiring poetry, are deceived by inability to analyze their sensations, and that they are really admiring, not the poetry of the passage before them, but something else in it, which they like better than poetry," in fact all the concrete examples are in accordance with my theory and not his own. Thus the later seventeenth century writers are said by Housman to have but rarely true poetic merit not on the basis of any analysis of sensations but because, for example, they aimed to startle by novelty and amuse by ingenuity whereas their verse is inharmonious.

If, then, Housman's practice is sound it vindicates my view and stultifies his; nor is the obvious fact that we would not rate highly poetry that did not move us, relevant to the question how we are to distinguish a high aesthetic rating from another type of high rating. If field work and reflection in general vindicate my contention as do these examples from Housman I cannot see what else can be relevant; but I freely own that it is the cumulative weight of a large collection of examples from a variety of fields that is necessary, and these I have not supplied; nor could we ever attain a strict proof.

But all this being granted we are still only on the periphery of our subject and the most difficult question remains to be dealt with. It is comparatively easy to see that there must be general principles of selection of evaluative criteria which determine whether our evaluation is to be counted as aesthetic, moral, intellectual or of some other kind; nor is it at all difficult to give examples of what anyone, who is prepared to accept this way of looking at the matter, can easily recognize as being a criterion falling under one or another principle. It would be a very odd person who denied that the sound of the words of a poem was one of the criteria of the aesthetic merit of a poem, or who maintained that being scientifically accurate and up to date was another; similarly it is clear that the honesty of a policy is a criterion of its moral goodness whereas, even if honesty is the best policy, honesty is not a direct criterion of economic merit. But it is by no means so easy to formulate these general principles.

This difficulty is by no means peculiar to aesthetics. Part of the general view of which the aesthetic doctrine given here is a fragment is that what determines whether a judgment is moral is what reasons are relevant to it; but everyone knows the difficulty of answering the question what makes a judgment a moral judgment. (In my terminology Kant's answer would be that the reasons must refer to the rationality or otherwise of consistently acting in a certain way.) Certainly it would be over-optimistic to expect to find very precise principles; probably there will be some overlap of criteria between the various spheres of evaluation in anybody's practice; certainly there are some overt border-line disputes whether this or that criterion is relevant to, say, aesthetic evaluation.

I think, however, that there is one peculiar difficulty in trying to find the principle, however vague, that determines what sort of reasons are relevant to a judgment if it is to be counted as aesthetic. When we think of giving reasons for an aesthetic judgment we tend at once to call to mind what we would give as reasons for our appreciation of some very complex works of art; rightly considering, for example, that the plays of Shakespeare are things intended especially for consideration from the aesthetic point of view (I believe that a work of art can most usefully be considered as an artifact primarily intended for aesthetic consideration), we tend to think that we can most usefully tackle our problem by examining what would be relevant to an appreciation of, say, *Hamlet,* merely leaving aside obvious irrelevancies like cost of production. But this is most unfortunate, because, dealing with things intended primarily for aesthetic appreciation, we are inclined to treat as relevant to aesthetic appreciation very much more than we would in the case of things not so officially dedicated to aesthetic purposes; for practical purposes it would be pedantic to do otherwise. Moreover it is obviously very difficult to get straight our grounds for appreciating anything so complex. I am inclined to think that if *Hamlet* were rewritten to give the essential plot and characterization in the jargon of the professional psychologist there could still be a lot to admire that we at present mention in our aesthetic appreciations, but we would no longer regard it as aesthetic appreciation but rather an intellectual appreciation of psychological penetration and the like.

For these and other reasons, it seems to me hopeless to start an inquiry into the nature of aesthetic grounds by concentrating our attention on great and complex works of art. Among the other reasons is that in evaluating great works of art the reasons proximately given will almost inevitably already be at a high level of generality and themselves evaluative — we will refer to masterly style, subtle characterization, inevitability of the action and so on. If we are to have any hope of success we must first set our sights less high and commence with the simplest cases of aesthetic appreciation; in this paper, at least, I shall try to look no further.

If we examine, then, some very simple cases of aesthetic evaluation it seems to me that the grounds given are frequently the way the object appraised looks (shape and color), the way it sounds, smells, tastes or feels. I may value a rose bush because it is hardy, prolific, disease-resistant and the like, but if I value the rose aesthetically the most obviously relevant grounds will be the way it smells; the same grounds may be a basis for aesthetic dislike. Though I might, for example, attempt to describe the shape to make you understand what I see in it these grounds seem to me to be really basic; if I admire a rose because of its scent and you then ask me why I admire its scent I should not in a normal context know what you want. These grounds are also those that we should expect to be basic in aesthetics from an etymological point of view, and while one can prove nothing philosophically from etymologies, etymological support is not to be despised. Things, then, may have sensible qualities which affect us favorably or unfavorably with no ulterior grounds. Surely there is no need to illustrate further these most simple cases of aesthetic evaluation.

But there are some slightly more sophisticated cases which need closer inspection. I have in mind occasions when we admire a building not only for its color and shape but because it looks strong or spacious, or admire a horse because it looks swift as well as for its gleaming coat. These looks are not sensible qualities in the simple way in which color and shape are. It is clear that in this sort of context to look strong or spacious or swift is not to seem very likely to be strong or spacious or swift. I might condemn a building for looking top-heavy when I knew very well that it was built on principles and with materials which insured effectively that it would not be top-heavy. It is no doubt a plausible speculation that if a building looks top-heavy in the sense relevant to aesthetics it would probably seem really to be top-heavy in the untutored eyes; but if an architect, who knows technically that a building is not top-heavy, judges it to look top-heavy when he considers it aesthetically he is in no way estimating the chances of its being blown over.

We are now considering the facts which, exclusively emphasized, lead to the functional view of aesthetics. The element of truth in that view I take to be that if a thing looks to have a characteristic which is a desirable one from another point of view, its looking so is a proper ground of aesthetic appreciation. What makes the appreciation aesthetic is that it is concerned with a thing's looking somehow without concern for whether it really is like that; beauty we may say, to emphasize the point, is not even skin-deep.

We have, then, isolated two types of aesthetic criteria, both of which are cases of looking (sounding, etc.) somehow; in the simpler type it is the sensible qualities, in the narrowest sense, that are revelant; in the slightly more complex type it is looking to possess some quality which is non-aesthetically desirable that matters. We like our motor-cars in attractive tones and we like them to look fast (which does not involve peering under the bonnet); we like, perhaps, the timbre of a bird's note and we like it also for its cheerful or nobly mournful character, but would not be pleased if it sounded irritable or querulous; the smell of a flower may be seductive in itself but it will be still better if it is, say, a clean smell. Both these elementary types of criteria go hand in hand and are constantly employed.

The most obvious criticism of these suggestions is not that they are wrong but that they are incapable of extension to the more complicated situations in which we appraise a work of art. I cannot try now to deal with this sort of objection in any full way. But I should like to make two small points. First, I would repeat my suggestion that we are inclined to allow in non-aesthetic criteria "by courtesy" when we are evaluating a work of art, so that we may even include intellectual merit. Secondly, the fact that such things as intellectual understanding are essential to an aesthetic appreciation of a work of art does not in itself establish the criticism. If for example we enjoy listening to a fugue it is likely that a part of our appreciation will be intellectual; no doubt intellectual understanding of what is going on is also necessary to aesthetic appreciation; but the fact that I cannot enjoy the sound of a theme being continually employed, sometimes inverted or in augmentation or in diminution, unless I have the theoretical training to recognize this, does not prevent my aesthetic appreciation from being of the sound. I am still appreciating the way a thing sounds or looks even when my intellect must be employed if I am to be aware of the fact that the thing does look or sound this way.

There remain many difficulties; above all the notion of "looking in a certain way," especially in such cases as when we say something looks strong or swift, needs more elaboration. But to carry out this task is beyond the scope of this paper. Apart from a short appendix, I shall now close with a brief summary, a summary of a paper which is intended to do no more than to distinguish the aesthetic judgment and reaction from others and perhaps to indicate the best way in which to proceed to the further problems of the philosophy of aesthetics.

Summary

1. The problem raised is how an aesthetic judgment, reaction or evaluation is to be distinguished from others.

2. We should expect to find a criterion which allows us to distinguish the aesthetic, the moral, the economic, the intellectual and other evaluations by a single *fundamentum divisionis*.

3. All evaluations are made on the basis of criteria for the merit of the kind of thing in question.

4. An aesthetic evaluation is one which is made on the basis of a selection from the total body of relevant criteria of merit.

5. In at least the simpler cases of aesthetic evaluation the relevant criteria appear to be those which are concerned with the way the object in question looks or presents itself to the other senses.

6. It is impossible to distinguish the aesthetic by a special object, by a special characteristic attended to, or by a special emotion.

Appendix

It may appear to some that too little importance has been accorded to the emotions in this paper. To avoid misunderstanding I will mention one or two ways in which I recognize the importance of considering the emotions in aesthetics.

First, I recognize that we would be very little interested in the aesthetic aspect of things but for their emotional effect upon us.

Secondly, I acknowledge that if we experience an emotional thrill when we look at a picture or hear a piece of music we do not normally have to examine our grounds and reasons to know that we are reacting aesthetically in a favorable way. But I do want to maintain that it is the nature of the grounds that makes our appreciation aesthetic and that if on an examination of our grounds we find, as sometimes happens, that our reasons are appropriate rather to moral evaluation or are erotic, or what you will, we will, if we are honest, recognize that our reaction was not after all aesthetic. Of course we have trained ourselves to a great extent to approach pictures and music from the aesthetic angle so that we shall not in general be mistaken if we rely on an unanalyzed impression.

Thirdly, there are a great number of terms that we use in aesthetic evaluation—*pleasant, moving, pretty, beautiful, impressive, admirable* and *exciting* among others. I do not know what makes one more appropriate than another in a given context; partly, perhaps, they are more or less laudatory, or are based on a still more restricted selection of criteria than a mere judgment of goodness or badness; but I suspect that the choice of word is at least in part determined by the precise character of the emotion experienced.

For these and other reasons I do not wish to belittle the importance of the emotions in the philosophy of aesthetics; but I do wish to deny most emphatically that the aesthetic field can be distinguished from others by an attempt to analyze the emotions involved therein: and that is all that the thesis of this paper requires.[1]

---

[1][Mr. Urmson wishes to add the following note—Ed.]: "Though I would still approach the problems discussed in this paper in much the same way, I would now dissent from its positive contentions in some important ways. In particular I would now wish to say that when we judge a thing as of a kind we do so by criteria which are specially applicable to that kind whereas when we judge something from the economic point of view ('economically it is a good thing'), from the aesthetic point of view, from the butcher's, baker's, candlestick-maker's point of view, we are not judging it as of a kind at all but by criteria appropriate to the particular point of view, in the light of which anything can be judged, of whatever kind it may be. Thus I can judge that a certain concrete-mixer is of high (or low) aesthetic merit—by the criterion appropriate to the aesthetic point of view—even if being of aesthetic merit is not in any way a criterion of a good concrete-mixer. My confusion arose in part from the fact that for many things, such as dining room tables, being good from the aesthetic point of view is a criterion for being good of a kind."

On Dewey's Aesthetics

D. W. GOTSHALK

Art as Experience is a wide-ranging work, discussing every philosophical question about the fine arts that the author appeared to believe to be relevant to his day. Thirty years later it seems a curious amalgam of the illuminating and the confusing, introducing a great deal of common sense into the treatment of some topics and some esoteric twists into the discussion of other topics, and as a whole advancing Dewey's philosophy in a direction in which it still seems to fall short of what is now needed. In this essay I shall consider (I) Dewey's theory of aesthetic experience and (II) his theory of the work of fine art as stated in *Art as Experience*. Then I shall discuss (III) the relation of the aesthetics in this book to Dewey's general philosophy and to a philosophical need of our day.

I

According to one strain in *Art as Experience,* the aesthetic exists whenever wholeness enters into experience. An experience must develop naturally and have a culmination, an ending as well as a middle and a beginning. But whenever it completes a pattern of fulfillment it rises to aesthetic stature.

From *The Journal of Aesthetics and Art Criticism*, Vol. XXIII, No. 1 (Fall, 1964), pp. 131-38. Reprinted by permission of the author and *The Journal of Aesthetics and Art Criticism*.

The enemies of the esthetic are neither the practical nor the intellectual. They are the humdrum; slackness of loose ends; submission to convention in practice and intellectual procedure. Rigid abstinence, coerced submission, tightness on one side and dissipation, incoherence and aimless indulgence on the other, are deviations in opposite direction from the unity of an experience.[1]

On this view, the aesthetic exists in *an* experience, or "when the material experienced runs its course to fulfillment."[2] Thus, scientific and intellectual activities, political ventures and moral actions all attain aesthetic stature when they are brought to successful completeness, and achieve an integration of means and ends, parts and whole, in a well-articulated organic unity.

In contrast to this view of the aesthetic, which identifies it with the complete and the consummatory, Dewey gives a much more restricted view in which the *material* element of experience makes a difference—mere unity, even consummatory unity, is not enough. "It cannot be asserted too strongly that what is not immediate is not esthetic" and the immediacy of aesthetic experience is also described as "an esthetic necessity."[3] The unity of *an* experience must not only be there, but it must be incorporated in properties immediately experienced and having an immediate intrinsic quality of their own. If we are dealing with materials having no intrinsic quality, such as "signs or symbols"[4] and we look through them to their abstract meanings and operate with these abstractions, our experience may have unity, we may bring our thought to a consummation, a conclusion, a resolution of perplexity, but the unity will not be the aesthetic unity and our experience will be intellectual, not aesthetic. Moreover, not only must the aesthetic be incorporated in the immediate and be a pervading quality running through the immediate, but there must also be a seizure or grasp of the unique quality of the whole before there is an aesthetic experience. This is particularly true in the aesthetic experience of works of art.

Not only must this quality be in all "parts" but it can only be felt, that is, immediately experienced. I am not trying to describe it, for it cannot be described nor even be *specifically* pointed at—since whatever is specified in a work of art is one of *its* differentiations. . . "Intuition" has been used by philosophers to designate many things . . . But the penetrating quality that runs through all the parts of a work of art and binds them into an individualized whole can only be emotionally "intuited." The different elements and specific qualities of a work of art blend and fuse in a way which physical things cannot emulate. This fusion is the felt presence of the same qualitative unity in all of them. "Parts" are discriminated, not intuited. But without the intuited enveloping quality, parts are external to one another and mechanically related.[5]

---

[1]*Art as Experience* (New York, 1934); now in a Capricorn paperback (New York, 1958), p. 40. Quotations are from paperback edition.
[2]*Ibid.*, p. 35.
[3]*Ibid.*, p. 119.
[4]*Ibid.*, p. 38.
[5]*Ibid.*, p. 192. Italics in text.

In sum, the aesthetic exists not merely where there is unity in an experience, and where this unity is incorporated in immediate qualities but where there is a certain kind of act — an intuition, a seizure of the individual quality or pervading tonality, of the immediate object and all that it incorporates. When one attains to this kind of encompassing feel of the total entity, an unanalytic and in this sense unintellectual grasp of this totality in its immediacy, one might be said to have an aesthetic experience.

It cannot be said that Dewey himself is clearly aware of these two very different views of the aesthetic in his theory. He moves in and out of them noiselessly, as if they were the same, now emphasizing one, now the other. Generally speaking, he emphasizes the first view — the aesthetic is the integrated or unified — when he wishes to argue against the compartmentalizing of experience, and to develop the theme that all life may have aesthetic quality: scientific, moral, political, and similar activities. He emphasizes the second view — the aesthetic is the qualitative immediate as intuitively grasped — when he wishes to describe the fine arts in a vivid and distinctive manner. Dewey seems torn between the recognition that fine art is different and an egalitarian horror of anything different, and he adjusts his sights to one view or the other, and gives a changed meaning to the concept of the aesthetic according to the situation or context in which he is operating.

Apart from this comment, I would like to make one additional observation on these two views of the aesthetic in *Art as Experience*.

The aesthetic in both senses used by Dewey is a normative, not a descriptive, term. By this I mean that the aesthetic experience in the sense of any experience that is self-enclosed and complete, with its own end and means in it, moving rhythmically to a consummation that rounds it off into a live organic whole, and the aesthetic experience as an intuition or seizure of the pervading individual quality of an object in its sensuous immediacy, are both concepts delineating ideal tendencies in experience, and setting up paradigms for experience, rather than transcripts of the usual way experience ordinarily is in any area. The aesthetic, as used by Dewey, is, as he says of beauty, "properly an emotional term,"[6] or, more accurately, the name for an ideal, and Dewey's theory of the aesthetic experience is one more variant of the traditional view that the aesthetic is the experience of beauty or the aesthetic ideal.

This seems a too restricted view of aesthetic experience. The broken and fragmentary, objects and experiences without organic unity or a discernible pervading quality, the distorted and ugly, and things generally that do not lead necessarily to an agreeable or consummatory or mystical response, are thereby excluded from aesthetic experience, as if one should not be permitted to taste these as well as the beauties. The difficulty here is not particularly Dewey's, nor confined to aesthetics. We recognize that ordinary moral experience is the

---

[6]*Ibid.*, p. 129.

experience of good *and* evil, but when we define moral experience we tend to do so in terms of some ideal, the fulfillment of a law, a goal, a concept of the good. The experience of evil is thereby excluded by definition from moral experience, whereas in actual conduct it is probably more included than the experience of good or of the ideal. But, be this as it may, a concept of the aesthetic experience wider than either of the two that Dewey offers would seem to be called for.

II

In regard to Dewey's view of the work of fine art, the chief point I wish to discuss is not any ambiguity or variation in meaning of Dewey's theory but what seems to be Dewey's central conception of this work. This conception is already hinted at darkly on the first page of *Art as Experience*. Here Dewey distinguishes between a product of art and a work of art. The product of art is the physical and external entity turned out by the artist—the statue in the square, the painting on the wall, the poem on paper. The work of art "is what the product does with and in experience."[7]

> The *product* of art—temple, painting, statue, poem—is not the *work* of art. The work takes place when a human being cooperates with the product so that the outcome is an experience that is enjoyed because of its liberating and ordered properties.[8]

A kind of creative collaboration is required for the existence of a work of art. The artist and the spectator each must make a contribution. "The painting as a picture is *itself* a *total effect* brought about by the interaction of external and organic causes."[9] Accordingly, a work of art is perpetually new, created by each individual experiencer. "A new poem is created by everyone who reads poetically."[10] No merely passive attitude—a look of recognition—but a creative participation is the role of the art spectator, and the work of art is the end product of this creative participation, the brand-new experience supervening upon the product of the artist.

This is a curious and certainly unconventional view of a work of art, since people ordinarily think that a work of art is the work of the artist—the temple, painting, statue, poem which Dewey mentions. One is tempted to speculate why Dewey held this view. One factor seems to be "fear of the pedestal." If art is considered solely the activity of a special kind of being called artists, and works of art special products, art objects might rightly be set apart, considered fit only for esoteric inspection, and separated from life in museums. Art should

---

[7]*Ibid.*, p. 3.
[8]*Ibid.*, p. 214. Italics in text.
[9]*Ibid.*, p. 250. Italics in text.
[10]*Ibid.*, p. 108.

be of the texture of life and nourished by life, and to secure this Dewey conceives works of art as requiring not only artists but also live spectator participation. A second factor behind Dewey's conception might have been the belief that the ordinary view could cut works of art off in another way from continuous connection with experience. An object of art in being produced is presumably being experienced by the producer. But if that is all of the experience needed for it to exist as a full-fledged work of art, presumably it could spend a very long part of its immortal life hidden away outside experience yet be truly and fully a work of art. This would of course run strongly counter to the main theme and message of Dewey that art is experience.

But whatever the reasons for Dewey's conception of the work of art, this view has some very odd consequences. For one thing it means that there is strictly no one work of art, such as painting X, a painting by Matisse, but an indefinitely large number of Xs, as indefinitely large a number as people who view X aesthetically. Of course, there is the canvas on the wall, one canvas, but this is not the work of art, only an external, physical object, presumably a fit object for study by a physicist. The real painting is what a spectator does with this object or the aesthetic result he achieves from it, and since each person is different and in true appreciation puts the whole of himself into his activity, the real work of art will be something different in each case, and something fundamentally different, since in an organic whole each organ modifies the entire whole. Obviously, then, when two people — art critics or philosophers or others — talk about the painting X as a work of art, they will not be talking about the same thing. Nor can what they say be rightfully intended to apply to what the other knows as painting X. Each will be sealed off in his own private aesthetic world, and discussion, communication, sharing, cooperation, and all the other fine things Dewey wished to emphasize as essential to high-grade human experience, will break down here, since on this level a common basis in a common *work of art* on which they might rest is non-existent.

A further logical consequence of Dewey's view of the work of art is that it also allows for an extra access of caprice and sentimentality in the artistic transaction. If this transaction is not complete until the spectator has been creatively active, why may not the spectator introduce his own special whims and feelings into the end result? To be sure, the physical product of art does set up limits: it might be difficult to dream a lugubrious sentimental romance into the first movement of Beethoven's *Fifth Symphony*. Still, on the theory before us, strictly speaking, is it impossible? After all, if the work of art is a collaboration, why may not the spectator in putting the final touches on the work re-arrange everything according to his own wishes? The original artist was a free creator. Why should not the final artist be equally privileged? In sum, if the work of art is after all what its originator *and* his collaborator create, why should not the collaborator create, why should not the collaborator emboss the original product with all of the peculiar fancy and feeling of his own being, and bring about a quite marked transformation in the direction of refinement or grossness, delicacy or sentimentality, or anything else of which he is capable?

The fact seems to be that Dewey here, as in so many other places, has gotten hold of a genuine and even commonplace truth, but, in the interest of promoting some large and worthy cause—democracy, intelligent mass participation, making everything live for everybody, bringing everything into the arena of useful and serviceable experience—has twisted this truth into almost unrecognizable shape by following out certain associations that seem to point in the direction he wished to promote. When Dewey says,

> A work of art no matter how old and classic is actually, not just potentially, a work of art only when it lives in some individualized experience. As a piece of parchment, of marble, of canvas, it remains (subject to the ravages of time) self-identical throughout the ages. But as a work of art, it is recreated every time it is aesthetically experienced.[11]

he is saying or implying several important and true things, and specifically two. He is saying or implying that a work of art is intended for human consumption (if only the artist's own consumption) and that an active process (here called by Dewey recreation) is required to consume it properly. But neither of these quite correct views is incompatible with the view that a work of art is the product he gives us to appreciate, that *for us* it becomes actually what it is as a work of art only when we appreciate it properly, and that proper appreciation is not remaking the work of art but apprehending what it actually is as made. What Dewey has done, in order to get everyone into the act on an equal footing, is to make what is usually called the actual work of art a pure potential, which it actually is only before it is created by the artist. Then he has assumed that the consumer by appreciation actualizes it. What seems to be the case, is that the actual work of art is actual enough (subject to the ravages of time) if the artist has created it. But, as created, it is only potentially an object of appreciative experience for the potential consumer, and becomes for him not an actuality but an actually appreciated actuality when he actually consumes it.

This is hardly the place to enter into a more detailed criticism of Dewey's view of the work of fine art, but perhaps one further point might be suggested. Dewey's reference to the product of art as external and physical is presumably meant to further his own view that the work of art is primarily human and psychological, i.e., primarily a matter of *live* experience. But it tends also, I think, to set thought off in the wrong direction. The actual product of art or the work of the artist is external and physical of course—that is, it has a material dimension. But as it comes from the artist, it also has a formal and expressive and functional dimension, and these dimensions are part of its public being, and they can be discovered in the public product of art by properly oriented

---

[11]*Ibid.*, p. 108.

attention. There is no need to regard the public product of the artist as merely material or physical and external, in the manner of Croce. I have argued this point at length elsewhere[12] and will not repeat the argument here. I shall only remark on the irony of Dewey's position. Presumably, Dewey's aim was to interpret art so that it was not an esoteric affair but a widely shared and commonly enjoyed transaction. But instead of insisting on the complex *public* differences between a merely physical object and a physical entity transformed in its being by the imaginatively guided technical processes of an artist, which would give him a broad public basis for interpreting art in a public and socially sharable way, Dewey considers this transformed physical entity (the product of art) as itself merely another physical and external object to be contrasted with the work of art itself. As a result, he makes the crucial difference between the physical and the artistic to lie in the seclusive and esoteric and private experiences of individual percipients. This is idealism come home to roost with a vengeance.

III

Despite these difficulties in Dewey's theories of the aesthetic experience and the work of fine art, *Art as Experience* on page after page sets forth truths about the arts and the experience of art that are elementary and basic to a philosophical knowledge of these subjects. The chapters on Expression, Form, and the Substance of the Arts are rich in ideas collected from many sources and stated in a simple authoritative manner. If Dewey's style is not always elegant, sometimes clumsy, and even bleary, his matter usually reaches down to bedrock essentials and spreads firmly over a very wide acreage. I myself have been especially impressed by Dewey's strong sense of the continuity between art and other human activities, and the need he felt to strengthen this bond and to make art count for more in the total life of peoples. In this connection, where the arts are considered in relation to their full human context, it might not be inappropriate to consider Dewey's aesthetics itself in its own fuller philosophical context, and to make a comment on a bearing of his aesthetics upon a broader philosophical problem of our day.

Although his background was Hegelian and idealistic, and although his philosophy seems everywhere to underline the oneness and inclusiveness of experience, Dewey always insisted with some emphasis that in philosophy he was not a system-builder. He believed that philosophy should always follow the promptings of the subject under study, and adjust itself with whatever sacrifices of consistency were needed to the demands of the evidence in each case. This particularistic approach seemed to him to make system-building an unpromising project, and those who have looked *a priori* upon *Art as Experi-*

---

[12]My *Art and the Social Order* (Chicago, 1947, 1951); (N. Y., 1962), Part II.

ence as a pure-blooded example of the aesthetics of pragmatism and part of a larger system, such as Pepper[13] and Croce,[14] seemed to Dewey to have missed the point and spirit — the experimentalism — of his whole outlook. Nevertheless, there seems to have been an organizing principle in Dewey's thought, even if this thought had no *a priori* organization. Perhaps this can be summed up as well as in any other way by saying that Dewey was a reconstructor or reformer. Change was not only the substance of life. To change was the mission of thought and life, education was an instrument of change, and intelligence was "a continuously reconstructive agency."[15]

This theme admits of many forms. But characteristically in Dewey it tended to occur in a bio-social form. The human individual is customarily described as a live creature, a biotic being born into a family within a larger social environment which shapes his mind in its early existence. This live creature seeks health and growth, and adjusts to its environment to gain these. And the environment encourages many adjustments useful to these ends and shapes many habits in useful ways. But the environment perpetually needs reconstruction to make the creature's ends more abundantly realizable. It tends to set up fixed patterns of being and action, many of them suitable for a time perhaps but, in a changing world, inevitably obstructive or harmful to the growing creature. It is here that natural science and democracy and an evolutionary philosophy enter as among the latest and most effective instruments of human growth. Natural science provides a new and powerful method for transforming the environment from a passive or obstructive object into a usable servant of human wants, and democracy provides a conception of the members of the human race as equal partners in a struggle for natural ends common to all men and open to all alike. To urge these ideas and the changes in individual and society implied by these ideas is perhaps the deepest theme of Dewey's evolutionary philosophy, stated in very crude and simplified terms.

Into such an undertaking one might be properly puzzled to know how art and aesthetic experience could possibly fit. Art and aesthetic experience are reputed to deal with ethereal and unwordly things which exist apart from the hard practical struggle of social life and individual adjustment. This puzzle of the place of art and aesthetic experience in a bio-social context is indeed the very challenge that Dewey sets himself to meet in *Art as Experience*. He meets the challenge by depicting aesthetic experience, and especially the experience of fine art, as pure experience or as the highest fulfillment of that adjustment between striving organism and social setting which is the shared aim of all live creatures. He writes,

---

[13]S. C. Pepper, "Some Questions on Dewey's Estetics," *The Philosophy of John Dewey* (Evanston and Chicago, 1939), pp. 371 ff.
[14]B. Croce, "Dewey's Aesthetics and Theory of Knowledge," *JAAC*, XI (1952), 1-7.
[15]John Dewey, *The Philosophy of John Dewey*, p. 45.

Experience is the result, the sign, and the reward of that interaction of organism and environment which, when it is carried to the full, is a transformation of interaction into participation and communication,[16]

and he says later,

esthetic experience is experience in its integrity. Had not the term "pure" been . . . so often employed to suggest that there is something alloyed, impure, in the very nature of experience and to denote something beyond experience, we might say that esthetic experience is pure experience. For it is experience freed from the forces that impede and confuse its development as experience; freed, that is, from factors that subordinate an experience as it is directly had to something beyond itself.[17]

"Esthetic experience" he also writes, "is imagination" and

the conscious adjustment of the new and the old *is* imagination. Interaction of a living being with an environment is found in vegetative and animal life. But the experience enacted is human and conscious only as that which is given here and now is extended by meanings and values drawn from what is absent in fact and present only imaginatively.[18]

In a peculiarly high degree this elevation of experience to an imaginative wholeness is what happens in the creation and experience of fine art.

There seems little doubt that in this view of art and experience Dewey has got hold of a conception of the greatest interest and relevance. However, it is a question today whether the whole bio-social approach within which Dewey operated is adequate, and whether even its best results may not have to be recast. Natural science, democracy, and the philosophy of evolutionary change during Dewey's first hundred years brought mankind great gains. But they also brought great turmoil and apprehension, and every large stride forward in service to human growth has been matched by an equally large stride forward in the technology of human extinction. There still seems something radically wrong in a civilization that has employed these means, and what seems wrong and not altogether absent in Dewey is, I think, a certain confusion and incompleteness about ends.

In saying this, I do not mean such confusion and incompleteness as we have illustrated in Dewey's conceptions of the ends of aesthetic experience and of the work of fine art. Such technical difficulties can be found in the thought of any major philosopher. The problem is much broader and consists of a kind of approved indefiniteness about specifically human ends, as if our bio-social evolutionary nature had set the goals and all that was needed was to supply the particular and pertinent ideas and the physical and corporative machinery to reach these goals. I believe this is distinctly not the case. Indeed, the ends set

[16]*Op. cit.,* p. 22.
[17]*Op. cit.,* p. 274.
[18]*Op. cit.,* p. 272.

man by his bio-social evolutionary nature—the ends of life and survival and growth of creature and kin in competition with other animate creatures—are now already attained in principle. Generally, man has won the Darwinian struggle and, at this moment on our planet at least, he is "top dog" in the animate kingdom, and evolution is now in his hands, not he in its. Thus, the distinctive human problems now are not so much survival and evolution and growth in a biotic sense, but the ends of human life in its own sense. The problem is to spell out, precisely and clearly, the *unique* ends within human existence itself, and Dewey's recognition of aesthetic experience as pure experience, or as experience whole and complete and not subordinate to something beyond itself but good in its own right, is perhaps his best effort to reach out beyond a Darwinian context to the unique human context wherein man is an end in his own right.

In Dewey's psychology, however, there are in the main only two major levels, the biological and the social, and what is commonly referred to by the term *mind* consists of biological impulse modified by social learning. This is to omit a level of human existence where indeed men are most human and from which what is human in man's animal and social nature largely derives. This is the level of self-consciousness where man becomes aware of himself as man and as an autonomous individual. The most crude and immature forms of this self-consciousness are in diffidence, estrangement, guilt-feelings, loneliness, withdrawal, uncertainty, self-doubt, and all of those introverted and anxious types of states of mind that certain existentialists recently have made so much of and that Dewey tended to regard merely as obstructions to action to be put aside as swiftly as possible. But to regard this introspective aspect of experience merely as a practical impediment and to overlook its more profound implications for philosophy is, I think, to miss one of the simplest lessons of our common humanity. Still, the highest forms of this self-consciousness are not in abnormal states, nor in the picturesque ontic or fact-states of dread and care and the like that existentialists delineate. The highest forms are in the detached understanding of human aims, and particularly in the clarification of the distinctive aims of major human undertakings. And these are its highest forms because they provide the great perspectives within which what is characteristically and preeminently human in our life as an autonomous phenomenon can be discerned with a minimum of incompleteness, bias, and fragmentation.

The detachment required for such broad perspectives, and the aloofness, always seemed to make Dewey uneasy. He felt more at home closer to the "go" of things, and amid things happening. Here, in re-forming events portending immediate meanings or consequences, he found the real problems of men, and the biotic or bio-social approach served perfectly to frame these problems of men. In this context, however, all forms of behavior—philosophical and scientific thinking being behavior—become types of more or less intelligent adaptation, means to ends, and the whole distinctive level of human life, wherein man and his characteristic efforts are ends in their own right, fades away, and only in the rather late recognition of the aesthetic as the internally complete and satisfying does Dewey begin to make some restitution of what has thus been swept away.

We might say, then, of Dewey's philosophy that in taking its main stand on the bio-social level, it brings us to the threshold of a distinctively human understanding, but it goes only the shortest distance over the threshold. This demand for human understanding is now more than ever upon us. As never before in history, the human race has become one large interconnected body of peoples and has discovered in itself a homogeneity and a heterogeneity never before felt so vividly on so large a scale. In this situation, a great growth in self-awareness through analytic clarification of distinctive human aims and ends in all areas is one of the most obvious and outstanding necessities. Dewey himself, I believe, gives us a beginning toward this. In his aesthetics, as in other parts of his philosophy, there is an instructive exploration of fundamentals that cannot be ignored. But one must gather these fundamentals into a more complex and consistent and unique focus to provide what is now required. For Dewey, it has been said, "art makes life better, but it does not make something better than life."[19] Well, in a sense this is obviously true, but in a sense it is also false. For art does make something better than life. It gives us a form of self-awareness (a mirror) not to be found in mere life, contributing thereby to a unique dimension of man's being. It is to explore this unique dimension of self-awareness on all its sides, articulating the distinctive purposive structures of human activities in all these areas, placing the human being not merely in a bio-social context but in a reflectively human context, that seems the great philosophical task now before us. Dewey, as I have suggested, moved into this area of detached self-scrutiny with considerable uneasiness, fearing the cloud-castles of purely dialectical and linguistic invention and preferring the more earthy orientation of natural science and practical life. This pioneering effort cleared the air of many snares and delusions, and regained a primitive relevance for philosophical thinking. But it left the great unique areas of human effort only partially explored with considerable fog over what had been explored, setting up thereby in a very puzzling but challenging manner one of the great philosophical tasks that now seems most relevant.

---

[19]Edna A. Shearer, "Dewey's Esthetic Theory," *J. of Philosophy*, XXXII (1935), 664.

On the Creation of Art

MONROE C. BEARDSLEY

From the times of Homer and Hesiod, creative artists have wondered about the source of their power to summon into existence things hitherto unseen and even unthought. In our day, it has begun to seem feasible to solve this problem with something like conclusiveness. Yet much of its mystery remains.

A number of distinct questions are involved here, only one of which I shall take up. For example, I shall not inquire why the artist creates in the first place — what obscure impulses compel him to make shapes or melodies, to dance or tell stories. This question has been given two sorts of answer. The first is in terms of conscious motives (the artist wants fame, money, love, power, etc.) — and here it seems pretty evident that there must be a vast variety of true answers, depending on the artist, the work at hand, and even the time of day or night. The second is in terms of unconscious needs and drives — and this I am not competent to pursue. Again, I shall not inquire how the creative process begins — what evokes the first stroke of the brush, the first words of the poem. In the creation of every work, no doubt something does come first, perhaps a single little fragment, perhaps a rush of ideas. This initial element of what later becomes the work has been referred to by various metaphors, some of them misleading, as we shall see — *germ, cell, seed, nucleus;* I will call it the *inceptive element,* or, for short, *incept.* The incept of the work may simply pop into the

From *The Journal of Aesthetics and Art Criticism,* Vol. XXIII, No. 3 (Spring 1965), pp. 291-304. Reprinted by permission of the author and *The Journal of Aesthetics and Art Criticism.*

artist's mind — like Mozart's melodies or Housman's verses — or it may come from external sources, accidentally, like the notes struck by a cat on the keyboard or the pattern made by mud in the gutter. When it does come from within, it no doubt has preconscious causal conditions, though to trace them would surely be a difficult undertaking.

What I mean by the creative process is that stretch of mental and physical activity between the incept and the final touch — between the thought "I may be on to something here" and the thought "It is finished." My problem is about what goes on in this interval — how the work of art itself comes into existence and takes on its character through the stages or phases of this process.

I

Many students of art have assumed, or expected to find, that there is such a thing as *the* process of art creation — that is, a pattern universally or characteristically discoverable whenever substantial works of art are produced. They would allow, of course, for many differences between one creative process and another, depending on the artist's habits and temperament, the medium in which he moves, and the demands of the particular work in progress. But they argue that beneath these differences there is what we might call the *normal creative pattern,* and that to understand this pattern would contribute much to our understanding of the finished product.

Nor is it unreasonable to suppose that there is such a creative pattern to be isolated and described. First, it might be said, the common character of works of art in all media — whatever it is that enables us to class them together — presents a prima-facie case for a creative pattern. For things that are alike may well have been produced in a similar way. Second, there is the analogy with aesthetic experience. For if there is a pattern of appreciation common to the arts, then why should there not be a pattern of creation, which would, in a sense, be its inverse? Third, there is the analogy with other kinds of creative activity. Dewey's classic description of the process of inquiry, or problem-solving, remains the standard one, though it has been refined and extended since its first appearance in *How We Think.* Practical and scientific problems differ considerably among themselves, just as works of art do, and if there is a common pattern of thought provoked by the former, there may be a common pattern of activity required for the latter.

It is true that the theory of a common character of the arts and the theory of a special aesthetic experience have been questioned in recent years.[1] I appreci-

---

[1] The former by Paul Ziff and Morris Weitz, whose views I have discussed in "Art and the Definitions of the Arts," *JAAC,* XX (1961), 175-87; the latter by George Dickie, in "Is Psychology Relevant to Aesthetics?" *Philosophical Review,* LXXI (1962), 285-302, and more fully in "The Phantom Aesthetic Experience," forthcoming.

ate the force of the objections, which I won't go into here, but, like many others, I am not ready to abandon either of the theories. In any case, of course, the three arguments I have mentioned above are not conclusive; they are but suggestive analogies. If there is a common creative pattern, then it can be discovered only by direct study of creative processes. And we might expect to find three main sources of evidence: the artist, the psychologist, and the philosopher.

Our first inclination, of course, is to turn to the creative artist himself, for he ought to know, if anyone does, what is going on in his mind during that mysterious interval between the first pin-fall or brick-fall of an idea and the final laying down of pen or brush. And it is true that much of our best and most useful information about creative processes does come from artists. The trouble is that, for reasons of their own, they are often inclined to the most whimsical and bizarre statements, and seem to enjoy being deliberately misleading. For example, Christian Zervos tells us that Picasso once said to him:

> I take a walk in the forest of Fontainbleau. There I get an indigestion of greenness. I must empty this sensation into a picture. Green dominates it. The painter paints as if in urgent need to discharge himself of his sensations and his visions.[2]

But this is a most curious description of the creative process. If the painter suffers from a surfeit of green, does he avoid looking at green any more for a while? No, he goes to his studio, squeezes out the green pigment, and proceeds to cover a canvas with it. This is like drinking grapefruit juice to cure an acid stomach. To make the indigestion theory of artistic creation plausible, the green-surfeited painter would surely go off to paint a *red* painting—red being the chromatic analogue of sodium bicarbonate.

We have had, by the way, many other metaphorical models of the creative process or the mind during creation—though perhaps none more colorful than Picasso's heartburn. The famous treatise of John Livingston Lowes, *The Road to Xanadu,* is full of them—the "hooked atoms" jumbled about, the "deep well" of the unconscious into which the poet dips, the imagination as "loom." Once we read of Shelley's "fading coal." Now it is the digital computer that furnishes the most tempting figure.

Or consider a famous statement by Henry James, in his preface to *The Spoils of Poynton.*[3] He begins by saying that the "germ" of his novel, as he called it, lay in a story told at a dinner party in London. James dilates upon "the sublime economy of art," which starts with such a "prick of inoculation," when the virus is communicated, and then goes on to build a work out of itself. The lady who told the story began by mentioning a woman at odds with her son over the furniture in an old house bequeathed to the son by his father. James remarks

[2]Brewster Ghiselin, ed., *The Creative Process: A Symposium* (U. of California, 1952), p. 51.
[3]Henry James, *The Art of the Novel*, ed. R. P. Blackmur (N. Y., 1934), pp. 119-24.

"There had been but ten words, yet I had recognized in them, as in a flash, all the possibilities of the little drama of my *Spoils,* which glimmered then and there into life." James says he didn't want to hear any more of the story, because the germ was complete in itself; the seed had been "transplanted to richer soil." This claim has often been repeated and taken as a text. But if we look in his *Notebooks,* where he tells a good deal about the process of writing *The Spoils of Poynton,* we find that in fact, on the day after the party (December 24, 1893), James wrote down not only the germ but the whole story, as it was told him, and that in fact many other germs came into the picture before very long, as well.[4]

Probably the greatest contributions made by creative artists to the solution of our problem are not their own theories about what they do, but the records they leave us in the form of sketches and early drafts. We cherish, for example, the notebooks of Beethoven, the sketches and studies in which Picasso worked out his ideas for *Guernica,* and the rich materials contributed to the special collection at the University of Buffalo by living poets who are willing to allow scholars to study their methods of work, their ventures, erasures, substitutions, corrections, and revisions. I shall have occasion to make use of these materials later.

As for the psychologists, despite the considerable effort (or at least speculation) that has gone into the study of the artist's unconscious, not much is available by way of well-established conclusions about the way the poet's or painter's mind is actually working when he is on the job.[5] Some of the most interesting contributions have been made by gestalt psychologists, for example, Rudolf Arnheim, in his psychological study of some materials in the Buffalo collection, and in his recent study of *Guernica.*[6]

Among the most valuable of the psychological investigations are those undertaken nearly thirty years ago by Catharine Patrick.[7] She first secured a group of 55 poets (with 58 "non-poets" as a suitable control group), and, after putting them at ease, confronted them with a certain picture and made them write a poem about it. She asked them to talk aloud as they thought, and took down their words in shorthand. Then she went to the painters, and, tit for tat, presented them with a part of a poem by Milton, which they were to illustrate in some way — while again, she took down their vocal musings, and also kept note

---

[4]*Notebooks,* Ed. F. O. Matthiessen and Kenneth Murdock (N. Y., 1947), pp. 136-137. For further stages in the development of this novel (tentatively entitled *The House Beautiful*) see the references on p. 138. (This information was kindly given to me by Professor S. P. Rosenbaum of Indiana University.)

[5]Douglas Morgan, "Creativity Today," *JAAC,* XII (1953), 1-24; and Stuart E. Golann, "Psychological Study of Creativity," *Psychological Bulletin,* LX (1963), 548-565.

[6]*Poets at Work* (N. Y., 1948), by various authors, and *Picasso's Guernica: the Genesis of a Painting* (U. of California, 1962).

[7]*Creative Thought in Poets, Archives of Pschology,* No. 178 (1935): "Creative Thought in Artists," *J. of Psychology,* IV (1937), 35-73.

of what they were drawing, as time passed. Every encounter was carefully timed. And the results were supplemented by questionnaires.

These interviews resulted in a good deal of very interesting material. Professor Patrick set out to determine whether the typical process of artistic creation passes through the four stages classically distinguished by Graham Wallas in his book on *The Art of Thought*—the stages of preparation, incubation, inspiration, and elaboration. And she concluded that these stages can indeed be distinguished. But the most remarkable feature of her material, it seems to me, is precisely the opposite. All four of these activities are mixed together; they are constantly (or alternately) going on throughout the whole process.

When we turn to the philosophers, we find a few who have tried to bring together into something of a general theory the insights of artists and psychologists. They, too, of course, have their own occupational hazards, or professional vices, and are too readily drawn away from contact with actual works of art into theorizing about what might ideally be true. For one who has a metaphysical axe to grind, it is easy enough to find a congenial formula to describe the creative process. Depending on the angle of approach, the artist will be said to be converting sensations into intuitions, receiving divine inspiration, reshuffling the atoms of immediate experience, embodying the ideal in sensuous form, working out the consequences of an initial postulate, or affirming the authenticity of existence. But I am looking for less ambitious theories than these.

II

Philosophic reflection on the available empirical data has given us two widely-held accounts of the creative process. When we consider any artistic work of major proportions, whose creation we know something about, we are often struck by the gap between the final achievement and its humble incept. Clearly, the process between can be said to have moved in a desirable direction. Now in the usual case, although lucky accidents may make an important contribution, this process appears to be at least partly controlled. The problem for the aesthetician is, then: What is the nature of this control?

The earliest people who raised this question—Homer, Hesiod, and Pindar— were inclined to give it a supernatural answer, attributing their own feats to the intervention of the Muses. And the theory of divine inspiration, often in a pantheistic version, remains with us. But if we insist upon a naturalistic theory of artistic creation, we find two main ones. And these are distinguished in a way familiar to other branches of philosophy.

According to what I shall call the Propulsive Theory, the controlling agent is something that exists prior to the creative process, and presides over it throughout. According to the Finalistic Theory, the controlling agent is the final goal toward which the process aims. No doubt the two theories run into each other in the minds of some philosophers, and perhaps we need not strain to keep them wholly distinct. But even if there are not two theories, there are at least two errors — and this is what I am most concerned to note.

The theory of art as expression is probably the most popular form of the Propulsive Theory of the creative process. And I shall take R. G. Collingwood as representative of expressionism at its best.

When a man is said to express emotion, what is being said about him comes to this. At first, he is conscious of having an emotion, but not conscious of what this emotion is. All he is conscious of is a perturbation or excitement, which he feels going on within him, but of whose nature he is ignorant.[8]

Before the emotion is expressed, the artist is oppressed by it; he works so his mind will become "lightened and eased" (p. 110). His aim is to make his emotion clear to himself (pp. 111, 114) — indeed, to discover what the emotion is (p. 111). Thus Collingwood postulates a single emotion that preserves its identity throughout the process of creation — if the work is to be genuine — and determines the main course of that process.

The first difficulty with this theory is that no principle of identity can be provided for this emotion.

If artists only find out what their emotions are in the course of finding out how to express them, they cannot begin the work of expression by deciding what emotion to express (p. 117).

Well said. But, on the other hand, after the artist has expressed his emotion, and come to experience it clearly, how does he know it is the same emotion he started with? He cannot compare them, since the other was unknown to him. How does he know that the emotion he feels now is not a new and different emotion — an emotion that is perhaps felt as the *effect* of the finished work, rather than as its cause? As far as I can see, Collingwood has no answer to this. And, moreover, in order to preserve his theory he has to say some rather surprising things. For example,

No artist, therefore, so far as he is an artist proper, can set out to write a comedy, a tragedy, an elegy, or the like. So far as he is an artist proper, he is just as likely to write any one of these as any other (p. 116).

I am sure that statement would have startled Sophocles or Shakespeare — not to mention Racine and Molière. According to Collingwood, the genuine artist says, "I feel an emotion coming on; no telling what it is until I write something (or paint it, or compose it); how will I know what I've felt until I see what I've

---

[8]R. G. Collingwood, *The Principles of Art* (Oxford, 1938), p. 109. See also Alan Donagan, *The Later Philosophy of R. G. Collingwood* (Oxford, 1962), ch. 5, §3.

done?" If he insists from the start on writing a tragedy, he will be forcing his emotion into some channel, and the result cannot be art.

The whole concept of *clarifying* an emotion is itself very obscure. I have a suspicion that when Bruckner finished one of his enormous symphonies, his emotions were no more clear to him than they were at the start. At least, they are no more clear to me. They are big emotions; anyone can see that. But clarity is hardly the word for them. On the other hand, nothing could be more clear than the special quality of the opening of Mozart's *G Minor Symphony;* but what reason do we have for thinking that Mozart's composition of this symphony began with some obscure or indescribable emotion, rather than with the subject of the first four bars? And what about artists who have spent years on a single work—are we to say that the very same emotion was there throughout, striving to clarify itself?

An interesting and well-worked-out version of the Finalistic or goal-directed theory of art creation has recently been presented by David Ecker.[9] He describes the creative process as "qualitative problem-solving," borrowing the concept from John Dewey. The stages of the process, he says, consist of a series of problems and solutions: if I use this cool green here I can get this plane to recede; "this jagged shape contrasts sharply with those open volumes" (p. 285), etc. Now he makes it clear that the problems posed are within the work itself: "Artistic problem solving takes place in the artist's medium" (p. 285). The problem need not be verbally formulated (p. 286), and various logical terms that might be applied to the process (such as "verification" and "hypothesis") are "grossly misleading" (p. 288). But the process is to be analyzed in terms of the categories of means and end; the choices involved, and the general direction, are controlled by the previsioned goal. (It is plain that Ecker's account would be strongly repudiated by Collingwood; according to Ecker, the poet *must* begin by intending to write a tragedy, or comedy, or something—for otherwise he has no problem to solve.) Ecker quotes a very illuminating passage from the sculptor Henry Moore:

... I sometimes begin a drawing with no preconceived problem to solve, with only the desire to use pencil on paper, and make lines, tones and shapes with no conscious aim; but as my mind takes in what is so produced a point arrives where some idea becomes conscious and crystallizes, and then a control and ordering begins to take place.

Or sometimes I start with a set subject; or to solve, in a block of stone of known dimensions, a sculptural problem I've given myself, and then consciously attempt to build an ordered relationship of forms ....[10]

The first part of this statement is very clear, and restricts one side of Ecker's theory. There may be, says Moore, no "preconceived problem to solve"—the

---

[9]"The Artistic Process as Qualitative Problem Solving," *JAAC*, XXI (1963), 283-290.
[10]Ghiselin, *op. cit.*, p. 77.

only problem, if there is any, arises after the occurrence of the incept, the first lines of the drawing. The "control and ordering" begins with the elements of the work itself. The second part of the statement can be understood, it seems to me, in a similar way. Sometimes, says Moore, he starts with a subject — say, he is to make a reclining figure. Or a set of outside dimensions, within which to work. But basically this is the same sort of thing; the incept can be some lines randomly drawn on paper, or the subject, or the block of untouched marble, with its own particular size and shape.

The trouble appears when this is called a *problem*. What is the problem? It might be: "How can I make a good drawing using these lines I've already drawn?" Or "How can I make a good sculpture of a reclining figure?" Or "How can I make a good sculpture out of this block of marble?" But these are queer things to call *problems:* they are really *tasks,* the terms of which are voluntarily accepted by the artist. The main question involved in each of them is simply: "What do I do next?" A problem arises out of a conflict of some kind — a goad that the sculptor does not require. And it calls for a specific and determinate solution or set of solutions — which is not what the sculptor achieves.

Elsewhere I have stated my objections to the end-means terminology in art.[11] Actually, when Ecker gives his examples of ends and means, it is clear that he is not really talking about these at all, but about the relation between what I call regional qualities and their perceptual conditions. The cool green is not a means to the receding plane; it is one of the localized features of the visual design that help to make the plane recede. The recession of the plane, to put it another way, is a comparatively large-scale property of the work, which depends (in part) upon a comparatively small-scale property, the cool green. Now, if we ask which the artist first intended and has as an "end-in-view," it is tempting to say, with Ecker, that the artist

arranges qualitative *means* such as lines, colors, planes, and textures, to achieve his qualitative *end,* which we might name "cubist," "impressionist," or "expressionist" (p. 287).

But Ecker has already conceded that the end-in-view may be "some intended order" as well as a "pervasive quality" (p. 286). It may often be the case that what the artist is consciously after is a certain arrangement of lines, colors, planes, and textures, and the resulting regional quality is unexpected. It is odd to speak of the color as a "means" when it is chosen for no ulterior motive.

The error here is a subtle one, but a very crucial one in talking about art. It consists in jumping from the fact that regional qualities depend upon their perceptual conditions to the conclusion that the former are therefore always

---

[11]*Aesthetics: Problems in the Philosophy of Criticism* (N. Y., 1958), pp. 78-80.

ends-in-view and the latter means, in the process of creation. Perhaps no great harm would usually be done, but this way of speaking leads to an impasse, which is fully exhibited in a sentence quoted from John Dewey by Ecker:

The doing or making is artistic when the perceived result is of such a nature that *its* qualities *as perceived* have controlled the question of production.[12]

Take the finished painting; note its quality. Now suppose we have photographs of various stages of the work, taken at daily or hourly intervals, let us say, while the painter was working. None of these, of course, has the *specific* quality of the finished painting. But Dewey says this quality was all along controlling the artist's work. Since the quality did not exist until the painting was finished, it could only have been in the artist's mind. Does that mean that from the earliest stages of a painting, from the incept onward, the painter has definitely in mind some regional quality that he is trying to bring into existence on the canvas? It is conceivable that this is sometimes the case, but most of the experience of artists goes against it: it would be remarkable if the exact regional quality of the final painting were that plain to the painter from the start.

Now, Dewey's statement can be interpreted in a somewhat more plausible way, if we introduce the notion of degrees of intensity for these regional qualities. The final painting, let us say, is characterized by a firm semi-geometrical solidity and rigidity, with decisive lines and interlocking forms. We look at the first tentative strokes put down by the painter, in the earliest photograph, and we see that somehow, dimly but unmistakably, this final quality is foreshadowed in the early draft — a touch of it is already there, though nothing like the way it is there at the end. So the process of creation lying between these stages could be described, at least in part, as one in which a regional quality hit upon early in the game is gradually intensified with the complication of new lines and colors. So in this sense, it could be that the final quality has been at work throughout — not as a foreseen goal to which the process is heading teleologically, but as a present quality whose immediately perceivable value suggests to the painter that it would be even more valuable if there were, so to speak, more of it.

There is no doubt that something like this does often happen. Sometimes, we can see in the earliest stages of a great work that the quality we value so highly in the finished product has begun to emerge. But this is not always the case, by any means. Sometimes the quality that appears most definitely at the start turns out not to be fruitful; the artist's attempt to intensify it leads to radical formal rearrangements that end by destroying the original quality and substituting a very different one. The melody that was first tried out as a quick rondo theme becomes the subject of a slow movement — almost unrecognizably altered. The

---

[12]*Art as Experience* (N. Y., 1934), p. 48.

poem that started out as a few ironic lines about a current political issue transforms itself, almost against the poet's will, into a moving meditation on the human condition. Nor is such a process—contrary to what Dewey implies—any the less artistic because not the same, but different, qualities have been active in generating the process at different stages.

Vincent Tomas has effectively criticized the finalistic view that artistic creation is "a paradigm of purposive activity."[13] There is a sense of "heading somewhere," though without a given goal in terms of which success or failure can be defined as it can when the torpedo is launched towards a target. Yet, paradoxically, "the artist *can* say that certain directions are not right." And Tomas' solution, sound so far as it goes, is to emphasize the critical ingredient in creation. His theory is that creation is a self-correcting process, in which the artist constantly redirects its aims. Tomas does not show in detail how the artist does this. But I believe he is right, and I will try to develop and defend this theory.

III

The real nature of the artist's control over the creative process will elude anyone who looks for a single guiding factor, whether a need or an end. It is internal to the process itself. I do not plan to argue for a single creative pattern, but to show how, in the absence of any such general pattern, each individual process that eventuates in a work of art *generates* its own direction and momentum. For the crucial controlling power at every point is the particular stage or condition of the unfinished work itself, the possibilities it presents, and the developments it permits. There are three things to discuss here, and I will say something about each—the incept, the development, and the completion of the work.

The first control over the artistic process is set up by the incept itself. And I want to emphasize, as I have said before, that the incept may be any sort of thing: the first sentence of a story or the last, a simple plot situation, a character, theme, scene, figure of speech, or tone or style. Paul Valéry has told us, instructively:

My poem *Le Cimètiere marin* began in me by a rhythm, that of a French line . . . of ten syllables, divided into four and six. I had as yet no idea with which to fill out this form. Gradually a few hovering words settled in it, little by little determining the subject, and my labor (a very long labor) was before me.[14]

---

[13]"Creativity in Art," *Philosophical Review*, LXVII (1958), 1-155; "A Note on Creation in Art," *Journal of Philosophy*, LIX (1962), 464-69. The former is reprinted in Tomas, ed., *Creativity in the Arts* (Englewood Cliffs, N. J., 1964).

[14]"Poetry and Abstract Thought," *The Art of Poetry*, trans. Denise Folliot (N.Y., 1961), p. 80.

Elsewhere, Valéry adds that his playing around with possibilities of this rhythm led to a certain kind of stanza, then —

Between the stanzas, contrasts or correspondences would be set up. This last condition soon required the potential poem to be a monologue of "self," in which the simplest and most enduring themes of my affective and intellectual life, as they had imposed themselves upon my adolescence, associated with the sea and the light of a particular spot on the Mediterranean coast, were called up, woven together, opposed . . . . All this led to the theme of death and suggested the theme of pure thought.[15]

This is exactly opposite to the usual idea that the poet must begin with his theme, or thesis, and that he characteristically then devises a suitable subject or set of images, and finally settles on the appropriate stanzaic form and meter. Now, I'll have to confess at this point that I am wide open to one kind of skeptical criticism. Considering that this particular poem is one of the most obscure poems in the French language, it might be said, we can draw no general conclusions from Valéry's method of composing it — what can you expect from a poet who begins with rhythms and ends with themes? Still, Valéry's account shows there is no one, privileged, order in which a poem has to get written. And even in the composition of more conventional poems, many different items (including metrical patterns) actually come first. Stephen Spender, for example, tells us in an essay that one of his poems began with a vision of the sea, and that another time, the words "A language of flesh and roses" came into his head as the incept of a possible poem while he was standing in the corridor of a train looking at a landscape of pits and pitheads — though at the time he was writing his essay, the words had not yet grown into an actual poem.[16] From a famous essay by Allen Tate, we gather that two elements of his "Ode to the Confederate Dead" were present from the start — the idea he calls *solipsism* and the idea of the dead — though it took ten years to fuse them together.[17] And according to Muriel Rukeyser, her poem "Orpheus" began with a sudden terrifying image of disintegration that came to her as she walked along a crowded street in New York.[18]

One of the most important questions about the role of the incept in the creative process is this: Does it exercise a pervasive influence throughout? If the Propulsive Theory is correct, one would expect to find the incept dominating the whole process, for whatever appears first would presumably be closely related to the original emotion. On second thought, I am not sure this really follows; it is hard to say what can be predicted from Collingwood's unknown and unknowable emotion. Again, if the Finalistic Theory is correct, one would

---

[15]"Concerning '*Le Cimetière marin,*' " *ibid.*, p. 148.
[16]"The Making of a Poem," *Partisan Review*, XIII (1946), 294-308 (also in Tomas, *op. cit.*).
[17]"Narcissus as Narcissus," *On the Limits of Poetry* (N. Y., 1948).
[18]Frank Barron, *Creativity and Psychological Health* (Princeton, 1963), p. 229n. For examples of fiction incepts see Malcolm Cowley, ed., *Writers at Work* (N. Y., 1959), esp. pp. 7-8.

also expect the incept to dominate, for it would presumably embody the original problem or goal which directs the process to the end.

Now, one thing is evident: once an element is chosen, it sets up demands and suggestions as to what may come next, and also places limits upon it. Draw a single line on a piece of paper. If you do not think what you have there is worth much attention, the question is what you can do next to improve upon it. You can balance it, cross or oppose it by other lines, thicken and emphasize it, transform it into a more complex line or a shape, etc. Or, of course, you can erase it — but then you are rejecting it as an incept, and putting an end to that particular creative process. That every stage of the process powerfully affects the succeeding stage is plain; but our present question is whether the first stage is somehow dominant over all. Artists have spoken rather differently about this. For instance, Picasso once said that "Basically a picture doesn't change, that the first 'vision' remains almost intact, in spite of appearances."[19] But he also said that a picture cannot be thought out ahead of time, and "changes as one's thoughts change." The sketches for *Guernica* do have a notable continuity despite all the changes. The bull and the horse were there in the first sketch, and a woman appeared in one of the later sketches done the same day.

Another example is provided by Beethoven's long series of sketches for the spacious melody that he used for the variations in the slow movement of his string quartet in E flat, *Op. 127*. These have been studied by Victor Zuckerkandl.[20] When they are placed side by side, they illustrate the force of the incept very clearly. The first full bar of the final melody, with its stepwise motion upward from A flat to F, is there almost complete from the very first sketch, though with a slightly different rhythm; and the rest of the story is a struggle, resumed from time to time over a long period, to find an adequate continuation and completion of that incept. Beethoven tries various ways of carrying on the melody, and abandons them; he tries the initial bar in the key of C, in duple tempo, with turns and rhythmic alterations, to see if it can be made to move into the long flowing line that the incept seems to call for. The whole keeps changing its regional character as it grows, yet some of its outstanding final qualities can be described as intensifications of qualities that were there in the first sketch. But this is by no means true of all of Beethoven's work; Allen Forte, a careful student of the piano sonata, *Op. 109,* has remarked that "in many instances one can hardly recognize the final version from the initial sketches."[21]

---

[19]Arnheim, *op. cit.*, p. 30.

[20]I am referring to a lecture given in the spring of 1963 at Swarthmore College.

[21]*The Compositional Matrix* (Baldwin, N. Y., Music Teachers National Association Monographs, 1961), p. 4. Cf. Ernst Krenek's analysis of the sketches for the false entry of the subject in the *Eroica:* "The Problem of Creative Thinking in Music," in *The Nature of Creative Thinking*, a symposium published for the Industrial Research Institute, Inc. (New York U. 1952), pp. 54-57.

Indeed, an incept that initiates a successful creative process may become almost lost in it. Of course there must be some continuity from incept to final work, otherwise we could not say that the incept was the start of that particular work. But there is a wide range of deviation from the straight line of development. An ingredient that has one quality as it first appears to the artist may later find a context that alters its quality completely. Dostoyevsky's novel *The Idiot* is an interesting case in point. We have a large collection of manuscript notes and drafts to tell us the agonizing story of Dostoyevsky's working out of that novel. In the very early stages, the Idiot (as he is called from the beginning) is

described as a powerful, proud, and passionate individual. There is something Byronic about him, and he resembles those criminal, self-willed creations Valkovski and Svidrigailov. He is sensual, performs extravagant actions, and perhaps his most marked trait is egoism.[22]

Could anything be farther from the Idiot of the final novel? For two months, through eight detailed plans for the novel, Dostoyevsky worked toward the deadline for the first installment (published January 1868). As the plans succeed each other, we see certain characters take on the Christlike characters of Prince Myshkin as we now have him, and we see the Idiot developing a double nature that prepares the way, in the eighth plan, for his reversal of personality. Even so, the novel was still significantly changing between the first installment and the later ones.

Once the work is under way, with a tentative commitment to some incept, the creative process is kept going by tensions between what has been done and what might have been done. At each stage there must be a perception of deficiencies in what now exists, plus the sense of unrealized possibilities of improvement. The motivating force, as Tomas says, is a negative critical judgment. And this same point has been made by Valéry. To understand poetry, he remarks, we must study

word combinations, not so much through the conformity of the meanings of these groups to an idea or thought that one thinks should be *expressed,* as, on the contrary through their effects once they are formed, from which one chooses.[23]

In other words, as the poet moves from stage to stage, it is not that he is looking to see whether he is saying what he already meant, but that he is looking to see

---

[22]Ernest J. Simmons, *Dostoyevsky* (Oxford U., 1950), p. 202. See his whole book for very illuminating accounts of Dostoyevsky's creative processes.

[23]"A Poet's Notebook," *op cit.*, p. 178. Compare John Dryden's dedication of *The Rival Ladies* (in Ghiselin, *op cit.*, p. 77): "When the fancy was yet in its first work, moving the sleeping images of things toward the light, there to be distinguished, and then either chosen or rejected by the judgment."

whether he wants to mean what he is saying. Thus, according to Valéry, "Every true poet is necessarily a first rate critic"—not necessarily of others' work, but of his own.[24]

Each time the artist—whether poet, or painter, or composer—takes a step, he adds something to what is already there (A), and makes another and different object (B). If he judges B worse than A, he must go back. If B is better than A, the question is whether it is good enough to stand alone as a work of art. If not, the question is whether B can be transformed into still another and better object, C. If this is impossible, if every attempt to improve it only makes it worse, then the whole project is left unfinished, for it is unfinishable.

One of the most puzzling questions about the creative process is how the artist knows when to stop. If the Propulsion Theory is correct, the answer is that he stops when his original impulse has exhausted itself. If the Finalistic Theory is correct, then the artist compares his work at every stage with the intact memory of his original vision of his goal, and when they match the work is done. But without these theories, it becomes more difficult to explain what it means to come to an end of a creative process.[25]

There are really two questions here: how the artist knows when *he* is finished, and how he knows when the *work* is finished. The first question is no doubt the easier. The artist comes to a point when he can no longer think of any way to improve his work. This becomes more and more difficult as the work progresses. In the early stages, lines and colors, stanzas and melodic fragments, can be added quite freely to see whether they can be assimilated. But in the later stages, as the work becomes more complex, the effect of every addition or alteration is more serious; a wrong line or color, a wrong word or melodic figure, can throw the whole thing badly off. Of course, the artist can never be certain he has done all he can. Happy is the painter, who can say, with Matisse,

Then a moment comes when every part has found its definite relationship and from then on it would be impossible for me to add a stroke to my picture without having to paint it all over again.[26]

Many a painter has been notorious for a never-say-die determination to hang on to his paintings in the hope that he will think of a way of bettering them— unless extreme poverty or a wily dealer induces him to part with them. (Valéry,

---

[24]"Poetry and Abstract Thought," *ibid.*, p. 76. This is echoed by Richard Wilbur on *The Nature of Creative Thinking*, p. 59, and by Ben Shahn, in *The Shape of Content* (see selection in Tomas, *op. cit.*, p. 20).

[25]I. A. Richards, "How Does a Poem Know When It is Finished?" in Daniel Lerner, ed., *Parts and Wholes* (N. Y., 1963).

[26]"Notes of a Painter," in Eliseo Vivas and Murray Krieger, eds., *The Problems of Aesthetics* (N. Y., 1953), p. 259.

by the way, says he wouldn't have published "*Le Cimètiere marin*" when he did, had it not been snatched from him. "Nothing is more decisive than the mind of an editor of a review," he remarks—though perhaps he could have put up more of a fight.)[27]

The artist generally knows, then, pretty well whether *he* is finished—but that is not the same as saying that the *work* is finished. For when the artist has done all he can, the question remains whether the work has enough to it, whether it is worthy of standing by itself, as an object of aesthetic enjoyment. If he judges so, the artist says it is done. If he judges not, the artist says it is unfinished. And of course the threshold of contentment varies enormously from artist to artist.

These points are illustrated by the famous puzzle of Schubert's unfinished symphony. Unlike most great unfinished works, it was not cut short by death (Schubert had six more years to live), but simply abandoned by the composer after he had completed two magnificent movements. Hans Gál has proposed an interesting solution.[28] Schubert began a scherzo in B minor, which would have been the third movement. In the manuscript, the parts are at first quite fully indicated, then they drop out, as the composer loses interest, and the movement trails off in the trio. The trouble is that the opening subject is one of startling emptiness and dullness—and yet it is a compulsive theme, hard to get away from once it is started, especially if the scherzo must be in the conventional key. "Those obtrusive four bars," as Gál calls them, get a grip on the composer; he cannot shake them off, or, apparently, find a way of starting anew so long as every time he picks up the manuscript they stare him in the face. If we agree with Gál's hypothesis, the scherzo is a formidable example of a composition that cannot be well finished—even by a master. It must have required a powerful force indeed to make a composer leave off a symphony so excellently begun.[29]

In one respect, the foregoing account diverges from a remark by Rudolf Arnheim in his study of Picasso's *Guernica*. Arnheim speaks of the creative process as being "goal-directed throughout"[30]—a view I challenged earlier. And summing up the whole process, he says,

A germinal idea, precise in its general tenor but unsettled in its aspects, acquired its final character by being tested against a variety of possible visual realizations. When at the end, the artist was willing to rest his case on what his eyes and hands had arrived at, he had become able to see what he meant.[31]

---

[27]*Op cit.*, p. 144.

[28]"The Riddle of Schubert's Unfinished Symphony," *The Music Review*, II (1941), 63-67.

[29]It is harder to understand what distractions led Mozart to abandon the more than 100 unfinished compositions (not counting the *Requiem*) that his widow preserved for us. See Erich Hertzmann, "Mozart's Creative Process," *Musical Quarterly*, XLIII (1957), 187-200.

[30]*Op. cit.* p. 134.

[31]*Op. cit.*, p. 135.

I would not put such stress upon the words, if these two sentences had not been so exact and eloquent up to the final clause. But the words "become able to see what he meant" seem to imply that what Picasso ended with was an expression, an explication, an embodiment, a realization, or whatever, of what was already in his mind at the start. Better, I think, to say that he had become able to mean something much better than he was able to mean a few months before, and that what he now was able to mean—that is, to make—was enough.

To draw together these remarks and examples, perhaps we can decide how far to generalize. Though there are no universal *stages* of the creative process, there are two clearly marked *phases,* which constantly alternate throughout. They involve an interplay between conscious and preconscious activities. There is the *inventive* phase, traditionally called *inspiration,* in which new ideas are formed in the preconscious and appear in consciousness. And there is the *selective* phase, which is nothing more than criticism, in which the conscious chooses or rejects the new idea after perceiving its relationships to what has already tentatively been adopted.

The problem of what goes on in the preconscious is apparently still unsolved. We would like to know how it is that a composer, having sung two bars to himself, suddenly thinks of a way to continue it—or that a painter, having outlined a figure, thinks of certain colors that might be added—or that a poet may look at a line he has just written and think of possible substitute words. To take a few examples from R. P. Blackmur,[32] suppose the poet has written "breathless tiptoeing," and it occurs to him that "flowering tiptoeing" might be better; or suppose he has written "chance deepening to choice" and substitutes "chance flowering to choice." Whether the new words are better than the old is the question to be decided by his conscious mind; but why one set of words rather than another comes to consciousness is the more mysterious question.

The psychological dispute seems to be formulable this way: to what extent are the preconscious processes associative; to what extent do they involve closure or strengthening of gestalts?[33] As far as I can make out both of these processes seem necessary to account for what the preconscious presents to the conscious. If, for example, "flowering" replaces "deepening" because of some meaningful connection of this figure with other images earlier in the poem, then we can say that the unconscious has found some degree of closure. On the other hand, the substitution may have only a very remote relationship to other words already set down, but it may serve to break down an existing gestalt, to introduce a more unstable cluster of meanings, which may lead to a more inclusive synthesis later. In this case, the word *flowering* would be described as due to free—or at least freer—association. It seems evident, in any case, that

---

[32]*Poets at Work*, p. 48.
[33]This is the point at issue, for example, between Lawrence S. Kubie, *Neurotic Distortion of the Creative Process* (U. of Kansas, 1948), esp. pp. 53-61, and Arnheim, *Picasso's Guernica,* p. 70.

unless the preconscious can produce both kinds of ideas—those that close a gestalt and those that break one—poems could not get composed, nor could paintings or musical works.

IV

It is no doubt high time to face up to the question that is bound to arise after all these reflections and speculations about the creative process: what is the point of them? Or, in other words: what difference does it make to our relationship with the arts that we understand the creative process in one way or another? And here my answer is brief and unequivocal. It makes no difference at all. I think it is interesting in itself to know, if we can, how the artist's mind works, but I do not see that this has any bearing upon the value of what he produces. For that value is independent of the manner of production, even of whether the work was produced by an animal or by a computer or by a volcano or by a falling slopbucket.[34]

This statement would be vigorously repudiated by some who have studied the creative process: they claim that their studies throw light on the "meaning" and "beauty" of poems, to use the words of Donald Stauffer, writing on "Genesis, or the Poet as Maker."[35] If we knew, says Stauffer, the genesis of a poem by Housman, it would "enable us to interpret this particular work with more precision." But his method puts the enterprise in none too favorable a light, it seems to me. Digging through the early stages of the composition of Marianne Moore's poem, "The Four Songs," he finds a typescript in which the poem is entitled "Poet to Lover (Admitting Limitations)." Moreover, he turns up other titles that the poet considered and rejected: "Poet to Plain-Reader," "Poet to Ordinary Man," and, oddly, "Asphodel." (This poem has as many titles as the White Knight's song "Asitting on a Gate.") All these titles, says Mr. Stauffer, "should prove of value in interpreting the complete poem,"[36] and he proceeds to put them to use. But think of the implications. The poet discards the titles, and the genetic interpreter plucks them out of the wastebasket and uses them as though they had not been discarded. This is a pretty high-handed way to treat Marianne Moore. The logic of the situation is clear. Either the title of a poem makes a difference to the way it is read, or it does not. If not, then knowing the discarded titles has no effect on our interpretation. If so, then each title makes a slightly different poem, and Mr. Stauffer is simply refusing to read the poem that Miss Moore wanted us to read. Granted that her choice does not have to be final; some of the titles she threw away could conceivably be better

---

[34]For a decisive argument along this line, see John Hospers, "The Concept of Artistic Expression," *Proceedings of the Aristotelian Society*, LV (1955), 313-344.
[35]In *Poets at Work*, p. 43.
[36]*Ibid.*, p. 63.

than the one she kept. (After all, remember the time she was commissioned to suggest names for a brand-new car that the Ford Motor Company was planning to bring out. She came out with some lovely ones, but in the end they called it the Edsel.) But if you do not accept her title, then at least do not pretend that you are interpreting her final poem.

The informed observer will, of course, detect in these genetic maneuvers a particularly persuasive form of that vulgar error which William Wimsatt, Jr. and I stigmatized some years ago as the Intentional Fallacy. I do not know whether it is in good taste for me to rake over these old coals, but whenever a fallacy gets to be so old-fashioned and so familiar as this one, it is always heartening to find new instances of it, so that you know you are not beating a dead horse—even if he is not exactly the picture of health. What we attacked under a single name (intentionalism) were in fact two closely related forms of unsound argument: that which attributes a certain meaning to a work on the ground that the artist intended the work to have that meaning, and that which appraises the work at a certain value on the ground that it does or does not fulfill the artist's intention. If we took to interpreting poems in terms of what they were like before they were finished, we would be turning the whole creative process upside down, by refusing to consider the final product on its own terms. Let this method become popular, and you can expect poets, painters, and musicians to keep their wastebaskets emptied, by burning their early sketches just as soon as possible.

Is this our final conclusion, then—that questions about creativity are irrelevant to questions about actual works of art? Somehow it does not seem enough. From the beginning of thought about art, though in many different forms, the creativity of art has been noted and pondered. Associationists, intuitionists, romantics, and idealists have offered explanations. In the making of such works, something very special seems to be happening; something fresh is added to the world; something like a miracle occurs. All this is true. There is such a thing as creativity in art, and it is a very important thing. What I want to say is that the true locus of creativity is not the genetic process prior to the work but the work itself as it lives in the experience of the beholder. Let me explain—all too briefly and puzzlingly, no doubt—what I mean.

To begin with, what is a melody? It is, as we all know, a gestalt, something distinct from the notes that make it up, yet dependent upon them for its existence. And it has its own quality, which cannot be a quality of any particular note or little set of notes. Recall that melody from Beethoven's E flat Quartet—grave, serene, soaring, affirmative, yet in a way resigned. Now when we hear a melody, however simple, we hear two levels of things at once: the individual notes and the regionally qualified melody that emerges from them. We hear the melody being born out of the elements that sustain it; or we hear the elements, the tones and intervals, coming together in an order that calls into existence an entity distinct from them, and superior to them. In the experience of a melody, creation occurs before our very ears. And the more intense the created qualities, the more complex the sets of cooperating elements, the tighter their mutual relations, the more fully we can participate in that basic aesthetic experience.

I need not argue in detail that the same holds for works of fine art. The essential feature of such a work — I am tempted to say, but recognizing that I am likely to sound dogmatic — the essential feature is not merely that certain visual elements (lines, shapes, colors) are assembled together, but that as we concentrate on their natures and relations, we become aware, suddenly or gradually, of what they add up to as a whole. For what they add up to is not an addition at all, but the projection of a new pattern, a new quality of grace or power.

When we consider a poem in this perspective, we see again that the important creativity is in the operation of the work itself. The sound-qualities, such as meter and rhyme-patterns, are one sort of emergent; more importantly, the interactions and interinanimations of words, in figurative or unusual language, create hitherto unmeant meanings; and more importantly, the objects and events of the poem mysteriously are made to accumulate symbolic reverberations, by which they seem to have a significance far beyond themselves. And this takes place in the act of reading; the excitement of seeing it happen is precisely the peculiar excitement of reading poetry.

The British literary critic, L. C. Knights, has made some comments that seem to me very similar to what I want to say, in a special issue of *The Times Literary Supplement,* on "The Critical Moment."[37] His example is from Wordsworth's famous sonnet,

Dull would he be of soul, who could pass by
A sight so touching in its majesty.

That is a strange combination of ideas — "touching" and "majesty." Knights says this:

The peculiar pleasure of that last line — though the pleasure is independent of conscious recognition of the source — comes from the movement of mind by which we bring together in one apprehension 'touching' and 'majesty': feelings and attitudes springing from our experience of what is young and vulnerable, that we should like to protect, fuse with our sense of things towards which we feel awe, in respect of which it is we who are young, inexperienced or powerless.

The "movement of mind" of which he speaks, in bringing these two opposed feelings into a fusion, through the words of the poem, is an act of creation, for out of that fusion comes a new, complex, vital feeling that has elements of both and yet is reducible to neither. So, says Knights, the creative use of words

---

[37]July 26, 1963, p. 569.

"energizes" the mind — "new powers of vision and apprehension come into being."

It may seem that this way of looking at artistic creativity demeans the artist by making not him, but the work itself, the creative thing. But I do not think so. I do not forget that man is the maker — of nearly all the great works we have, or are likely to have. But the finest qualities of a work of art cannot be imposed on it directly and by fiat; the artist can, after all, only manipulate the elements of the medium so that *they* will make the quality emerge. He can only create a solemn melody by finding a sequence of notes that will have that quality. The powers he works with are, in the end, not his own but those of nature. And the miracle he makes is a miracle that celebrates the creative potentialities inherent in nature itself. But when in this way the artist makes plain to us over and over the marvellous richness of nature's potentialities, he also presents us with a model of man's hope for control over nature, and over himself. Artistic creation is nothing more than the production of a self-creative object. It is in our intelligent use of what we are given to work with, both in the laws of the universe and in the psychological propensities of man, that we show our mastery, and our worthiness to inhabit the earth. In this broad sense, we are all elected, or perhaps condemned, to be artists. And what keeps us going in the roughest times is the reminder that not all the forms and qualities and meanings that are to emerge in the fullness of time have already appeared under the sun — that we do not know the limits of what the universe can provide or of what can be accomplished with its materials.

Visual Metaphors of Value in Art

E. H. GOMBRICH

I. Code and Metaphor

This paper is concerned with the peculiar way or ways in which artistic experiences have come for many of us to stand for, embody, or express some of the highest values, including moral values.[1]

As I shall be concerned mainly with the way colours and contours have been handled, in the historical past, to evoke a sense of these values, my subject may be described as 'visual metaphors of value'. This use of the term 'metaphor' may be in need of some preliminary justification. If we take the classical, Aristotelian, definition of metaphor, the term can apply only to a figure of speech: "When Homer says that Achilles 'Leapt on his foes like a lion' it is a

From E. H. Gombrich, *Meditations on a Hobby Horse* (London: Phaidon Press Ltd., 1963). This paper was first published in Lyman Bryson, and others (eds.), *Symbols and Values, an Initial Study. XIIIth Symposium of the Conference on Science, Philosophy, and Religion in Relation to the Democratic Way of Life* (New York: Harper and Brothers, 1954). Reprinted by permission of the author and Phaidon Press.
[1]I should like to thank Professor Hoxie N. Fairchild and Professor G. Bing (The Warburg Institute, University of London) for valuable criticism. I do not know whether such revisions as I have been able to make (including the addition of Section VI) will remove all the differences of opinion, but I hope they will somewhat clarify my meaning without upsetting the tentative and provisional framework of the hypothesis which is here offered for discussion.

simile; but when he says 'he leapt, a lion, on his foes' it is a metaphor."[2] This is a distinction which must, of necessity, disappear in the realm of the visual arts. Thus we may say that when Thorwaldsen designed his once famous memorial for the Swiss guards who were killed during the French Revolution, the 'Lion of Lucerne', he wanted to convey in visual terms 'they died like lions' or 'they died, lions'. We are used to saying in such a context that the lion is a *symbol* of courage, but there are reasons to prefer the term 'metaphor'.[3] The organizers of this Conference have asked us to leave symbols that function as pure signs out of consideration. Yet this is precisely what the word 'symbol' has frequently come to mean in art.[4] It is traditionally employed for the distinctive 'emblems' or 'attributes' by which gods, saints, or personifications are distinguished. These symbols are signs which form something like a code laid down by tradition[5]. The attributes of divinities and personifications were recorded and explained in special manuals. Most frequently such attributes are derived from the residue of an illustrative context—Jupiter carries the thunderbolt, because he is recognizable as the thunderer, St. Catherine the wheel because it is her distinctive instrument of martyrdom, and Charity children who provide a minimum opportunity for exercising her special virtue. In contrast to this use of images as labels, the lion—to remain with our example—is not a code-sign. The image of a lion can be used in different contexts, precisely as can any linguistic or visual image, to convey very different ideas. The only thing these ideas usually have in common is that they are derived from such traditional lore about the lion as is crystallized in bestiaries and fable. It is this lore which defines what may be called the area of metaphor. Which of these qualities we decide to use, however, depends largely on our wish and whim. In one context we may want to convey the idea of nobility traditionally associated with the King of Beasts, in another its ferocity, in a third, maybe, some ludicrous aspect as illustrated in the story of the lion fearing the crowing of the cock. Each of these qualities, as the old writers on symbolism well knew, can be isolated and 'transferred' to another object: *'Leo propter aliquam similitudinem significat Christum, et diabolum'*, as St. Thomas Aquinas puts it.[6] Returning to Thor-

---

[2] *Cf.* W. Bedell Stanford, *Greek Metaphor,* Basil Blackwell, Oxford, 1936, p. 25. This work also contains a stimulating discussion of recent theories of metaphor.

[3] The relation between metaphor and visual symbol is discussed by Fr. Vischer, 'Das Symbol', in *Philosophische Aufsätze, Eduard Zeller gewidmet, Leipzig, 1887,* a paper that directed the attention of Aby Warburg, founder of the Warburg Institute in London, to this complex of questions.

[4] A brief survey of the history of this distinction is to be found in K. Bühler, *Sprachtheorie,* Gustav Fischer, Jena, 1934, pp. 185-86.

[5] A distinction between 'codes' and 'symbols' is proposed by A. Kaplan and Ernst Kris in 'Esthetic Ambiguity', Ernst Kris, *Psychoanalytic Explorations in Art,* New York, 1952.

[6] For the connection between 'metaphor' and 'visual emblem', *cf.* Mario Praz, *'Studies in Seventeenth-Century Imagery', Studies of the Warburg Institute,* London, 1939, 3, p. 55. For the quotation from St. Thomas (*Quaestiones Quodlibetales,* VII, art, XIV, ad. 4) and its application to problems of visual symbolism, my article on 'Botticelli's Mythologies', *Journal of the Warburg and Courtauld Institutes,* 1945, VIII, p. 37, note 2.

waldsen therefore, we are entitled to say: this is not a code-symbol of the type 'the lion in art means courage'. Rather should we say, 'because of its alleged courage the lion lends itself to being used as a symbol (or metaphor) for heroes'.

It seems important in our context to insist from the outset on this distinction, because the temptation to regard all symbols as codes can be overcome only by being made conscious. The belief that symbols or images can be said to 'have' a meaning (or at the most a polarity of meanings) constantly reappears in different forms.[7] Its latest version is to be found in the writings of C. G. Jung, where it is often implied that certain images are endowed with an intrinsic and constant significance. It is easy to see how this conviction might arise. Freud's discovery of dream symbolism, and the recurrence of similar symbols in folklore and myth, suggested to some interpreters that our unconscious really does use a fixed code for the transmission of its secret desires. If that were so we could speak of meanings 'belonging' to symbols. Once unriddled in any context we would have, as it were, a dictionary meaning, valid for any other context. But the evidence also bears a different interpretation.[8] When anthropologists say 'upright poles are phallic symbols', they may be regarded as using a shorthand label for the longer but more nearly accurate formulation, 'upright poles lend themselves so well to use as phallic symbols that their use for this (conscious or unconscious) purpose is exceedingly widespread'.

In what follows, then, I shall not be concerned with the fixed or conventional visual code-symbols of value, such as they exist in religious ritual, but with visual qualities that lend themselves to symbolic use. A simple example of what I shall call a visual metaphor is the use of the colour red in certain cultural contexts. Red, being the colour of flames and of blood, offers itself as a metaphor for anything that is strident or violent. It is no accident, therefore, that it was selected as the code sign for 'stop' in our traffic code and as a label of revolutionary parties in politics. But though both these applications are grounded on simple biological facts, the colour red itself has no fixed 'meaning'. A future historian or anthropologist, for instance, who wanted to interpret the significance of the label 'red' in politics would get no guidance from his knowledge of our traffic code. Should the colour that denotes 'stop' not stand for the 'conservatives' and green for the go-ahead progressives? And how should he interpret the meaning of the red hat of the cardinal or the Red Cross?

---

[7]For an older version of this belief *cf*. my article, 'Icones Symbolicae', *Journal of the Warburg and Courtauld Institutes,* 1948, XI. The philosophical implications of a belief in an 'inherent meaning' of symbols or words are placed in their historical perspective by K. R. Popper, *The Open Society and its Enemies,* Routledge & Kegan Paul, Ltd., London, 1945, chapter II, section 2.

[8]*Cf.* H. Hartmann, Ernst Kris, and R. M. Loewenstein, 'Some Psychoanalytic Comments on Culture and Personality' in *Psychoanalysis and Culture,* edited by G. B. Wilbur and W. Muensterberger, International Universities Press, Inc., New York, 1951.

II. Metaphor and Substitution

The possibility of metaphor springs from the infinite elasticity of the human mind; it testifies to its capacity to perceive and assimilate new experiences as modifications of earlier ones, of finding equivalences in the most disparate phenomena and of substituting one for another. Without this constant process of substitution neither language nor art, nor indeed civilized life would be possible. Psychoanalysis has made us familiar with the wide range of substitution which enables man to find gratification in goals far removed from his original biological needs. It has shown us, for instance, how the child's attitude toward its mother may be applied and reapplied in changing circumstances to new objects of love. The term 'transference', used by psychoanalysts to describe this process, happens to mean exactly the same as the Greek word *'metapherein'*. In a recent paper[9] I have attempted to show that even an apparently rational artistic process such as visual representation may have its roots in such 'transference' of attitudes from objects of desire to suitable substitutes. The hobby horse is the equivalent of the 'real' horse because it can (metaphorically) be ridden.

It is against this background that we must see our present problem of how, in art, a visual quality may be experienced as the equivalent of a moral value. The metaphors of daily speech may provide a convenient starting point for the study of these equivalences, particularly those which 'transfer' qualities from one sensory experience to another. These so-called synaesthetic metaphors[10] which make us speak of a 'velvet tone', a 'black bass', a 'loud colour', etc., are specially interesting for us, because here no conscious transfer takes place. Somehow in the centre of our minds the qualities of blackness and of a bass voice converge and meet. Similarly, we speak of a loud colour not because we consciously relate a quality of sounds to a visual impression, but because the colour 'strikes us that way', as another vivid metaphor puts it. Now this convergence is inseparable from the experience of values; in fact, biological values constantly lend themselves as ready metaphors for other values. Warmth, sweetness, and light provide us with early and intense experience of gratification, and so we speak of a warm friendship, a sweet child, a shining deed. But other experiences also come into play. Economic value provides the metaphor for 'value' in general. This may be why we start our letters 'Dear Sir'. Social values of the past have faded into metaphors that make us speak of a 'noble' gesture. Values impressed by early education get transferred and applied in figures of speech, such as a 'clean fight', and so on. In all these instances we again have something like synaesthesia. The friendship is *expe-*

---

[9]'Meditations on a Hobby Horse' reprinted in [the volume of that name].
[10]Stanford, *op. cit.*, pp. 47 ff.

rienced as 'warm', it 'warms our heart'. If this unity of experience is not merely a matter of words,[11] it allows us to draw two rather useful conclusions. One concerns the 'diagnostic' value of aesthetic vocabulary. As long as criticism has existed, critics have used metaphors to express their approval or disapproval. They have branded colour combinations as 'vulgar' or exalted forms as 'dignified', have praised the 'honesty' of one artist's palette and rejected the 'meretricious' effects of others. Perhaps these terms in their aggregate tell us more about the aesthetic experience than is usually allowed? For this is the other conclusion that may suggest itself—writers on aesthetics have been at work so long telling us what art is *not*, they have been so anxious to rid art of any heteronomous values, that they have created a rather forbidding void in the centre. The synesthesia of values crystallized in our linguistic habits shows, I believe, that this void is artificial. The vexed question, whether or not aesthetic values may be said to exist 'independently', need not concern us here. What matters is that in our living experience they always find resonance in other areas of value. There was once a historical reason for protesting against a confusion of values in criticism, most of all against a facile confusion of art and morality, but now when this danger no longer exists we should again acknowledge the fact that there are few people who never experience great art in terms of moral values. It will be the principal aim of this paper to suggest the direction in which we should look for an explanation of this fact.

III. Gold as a Symbol

The love of light, surely, reaches deep into our biological nature, and so does the attraction of glitter. What wonder that this elementary reaction provided mankind with its basic symbol of value? For what else is gold but the glittering, sunlike metal that never ages or fades? Or what else are jewels but gaily sparkling stones which do not break? There was a time—and it is not so very far back—when riches, economic wealth, could thus feast the eye, when the miser could enjoy the sparkle of his hoard, instead of having to admire balance sheets. The fact that wealth can no longer be seen, that it no longer provides direct visual gratification, belongs with the many dissociations of value from immediate experience which are the price we pay for our complex civilization. There are many documents from the past which testify to the appeal of what

---

[11]The theory of facial expression first propounded by Piderit in 1859 (*cf.* K. Bühler, *Ausdruckstheorie,* Gustav Fischer, Jena, 1933), according to which reactions to taste (sweet, bitter, etc.) provide us with the elements of mimic expression, suggests that this unity reaches back to a stage of development when impressions are not yet differentiated and sorted out. Here, too, as with perception, it might be claimed that the most generalized global reaction is not a stage of 'abstraction', but the most primitive way of apprehending the world—a state of affairs which Aristotle's description of the metaphor as the outcome of analysis and transfer of qualities tends to obscure, (*cf.* K. Bühler, *Sprachtheorie,* Gustav Fischer, Jena, 1934, p. 346) and to which a purely associationist psychology cannot do justice.

might be called mutually reinforcing metaphors of value, sparkle and costliness, and one such document introduces us into the heart of our problem.

In the twelfth century, Abbot Suger of St. Denis wrote a famous account of his renovation of the Church of his Abbey (the first Gothic building) and of the treasures he dedicated to it. In a famous passage of this record he describes how the sight of a precious reliquary studded with gems 'carries his mind from the material to the spiritual world', *anagogico more*. The philosophical background of this passage has been fully elucidated by Suger's latest editor, Professor Erwin Panofsky.[12] He has shown how Suger regards his treasure in terms of the mysticism of light ascribed to the Neoplatonist Dionysius the Areopagite, whose memory was specially cultivated in Suger's Abbey. It was here that Suger could find a developed doctrine of religious symbolism which makes light the visible manifestation of the divine. Panofsky suggests, moreover, that the sight of the gleaming gems induced in the Abbot something like a religious trance; but in our context it is relevant that this trance could never have been induced by tinsel. Only because the Abbot had been overawed in his devotions by the awareness of the tremendous values here embodied, and only because his philosophy sanctioned an apprehension of the supernatural in terms of sensuous symbols, could the glitter do its work as a metaphor for the realm of light. Here, as always, seeing cannot be separated from knowing.

Suger's account is exceptional only through the clarity of his analysis. The use of the precious and the gleaming as a metaphor for the divine is, of course, almost universal in religious art.[13]

In his book *Symbolism and Belief,* Professor E. Bevan has enumerated some of these basic metaphors which have served mankind for the visualization of the 'higher' powers. Height itself is one of them, and indeed the author makes the point that we cannot escape this spatial metaphor whether we use the words 'superior value', 'exalted', 'excellent', 'transcendent', or countless others.[14] In art, as in life, the co-ordinates of light-dark, high-low, are frequently joined by physical beauty *versus* ugliness, using the terms not in any abstruse sense, but simply denoting desirable health and vigour as opposed to deformity and decay. The power of these metaphors is exemplified in countless elaborate allegorical pictures in which a host of beautiful personifications hurl crowds of ugly symbolic monsters from exalted regions of radiant light into an abyss of darkness. These pictures exemplify the most universal and unsophisticated type of visual metaphor of value in which the fair stands for the good, the healthy for the friendly, the radiant for the holy. Though the philosophy of

---

[12]*Abbot Suger on the Abbey Church of St. Denis and its Art Treasures,* edited, translated, and annotated by Erwin Panofsky, Princeton University Press, Princeton, 1946, pp. 21 and 64.

[13]J. Bodonyi, '*Entstehung und Bedeutung des Goldgrundes in der Spätantiken Bildkomposition*', *Archeologia Ertesitoe,* 1932-1933, XLVI, and my review in *Kritische Berichte zur Kunstgeschichtlichen Literatur,* 1935.

[14]Edwyn Bevan, *Symbolism and Belief,* Allen & Unwin, London, 1938, pp. 28 f.

Plato has given some kind of metaphysical sanction to this idea of the equivalence of the beautiful with the divine, this symbolism is really rather too obvious to be particularly interesting. In fact, art has long since conquered regions of metaphor far beyond such simple identification.

IV. Noble Simplicity

When in the fifteenth century, Leone Battista Alberti discussed the decoration suitable for places of worship, he considered the use of gold only to reject it. Quoting the authority of Plato and of Cicero he advocated the use of plain white, as he was convinced that the divine powers loved purity best in life and art.[15] At first sight it might seem as if Alberti had only exchanged one visual metaphor, that of sparkle, for another, that of 'purity'. But if we study his advice in the context of humanist culture, we see that there is an important difference between Suger's immediate experience of divine radiance in the splendour of his reliquaries and Alberti's love of purity. The difference lies precisely in the fact that Alberti rejects the gratification of outward splendour in favour of something more 'dignified'. He values the white wall not only for what it is, but for what it is *not*. The terms 'pure' and 'unadorned' themselves imply this element of negation. Art now stands in a cultural context in which an expectation aroused and denied can by itself become expressive of values.

Of course this negation is only meaningful when it demonstrates a renunciation in favour of 'higher' values. In the non-conformist meeting house the rejection of glitter and colour is done in the name of a pure religion, and the aesthetic factor is pushed to the very fringe of experience. The austere simplicity of a shack may sometimes impress us, but it is not what Alberti had in mind; for the Renaissance was confident that such renunciation could be directed to higher values *within* the realm of art. This marks the beginning of a thorough process of sophistication that, for good or ill, has divorced the art of Western civilization from a simple appeal to the senses. Not that Renaissance writers despised gold, but that they were everywhere anxious to prove that art itself creates a value that can 'trump' gold. Alberti elsewhere tries to make this clear to his readers by explaining that a leaden statue by Phidias would be worth more than its weight in gold.[16] And it was the pride of the Renaissance artist that his art created higher values than the mere surface attractions of sparkle.

A strange historical misunderstanding has created the prejudice that the art of the Renaissance glorified the splendours of visual gratification against the austere spiritualism of the Middle Ages. The contemporaries of this great revolution saw it in very different terms. The very first appraisal of the import

---

[15]L. B. Alberti, *De Re Aedificatoria*, book VII, chapter 7.
[16]L. B. Alberti, *Della Pittura*, book II.

of Giotto's 'revival' of art, contained in Boccaccio's *Decamerone* less than a generation after the master's death, is quite unambiguous on this score. Boccaccio celebrates Giotto as the painter who

had brought back to light that art that had been buried for centuries under the errors of those *who painted rather to delight the eyes of the ignorant than to please the intellect of the wise.*[17]

This contrast between a low kind of art that appeals to the eyes of the simpleminded and a 'higher' form that can be appreciated only by the cultured, becomes a commonplace of criticism in the sixteenth and seventeenth centuries. It is amusingly illustrated in Vasari's *Lives of the Painters*[18] where we read the anecdote of Sixtus IV, who promised a special prize to the artist who would acquit himself best out of the team of four employed in the Sistine Chapel. While the true masters, Botticelli, Perugino, and Ghirlandajo, gave of their best, the fourth, Cosimo Rosselli, knew that he was 'poor in invention and weak in design'. Much to the amusement of his colleagues he plastered his fresco with gaudy colours, ultramarine and gold, to cover up its shortcomings. In the end the laugh was his, for the Pope, who knew nothing about art, not only awarded the tyro the prize, but even insisted on the others giving their frescoes a generous sprinkling of gold.

The taste that is here ridiculed is the 'vulgar' taste of the Philistine, and it only adds spice to Vasari's story that this Philistine is the Pope himself, who thus proves himself inferior in culture to the artists he employs. There is no need to add further examples. For in the strict hierarchic society of the sixteenth and seventeenth centuries the contrast between the 'vulgar' and the 'noble' becomes one of the principal preoccupations of the critics. Not that they recognized this contrast for a metaphor. On the contrary. Their belief was that certain forms or modes are 'really' vulgar, because they please the low, while others are inherently noble, because only a developed taste can appreciate them. Their examples of what constitutes 'decorum' always point in the same direction. There is always a strong negative element in what constitutes 'good taste'. It presupposes a mind not easily swayed by the appeal of immediate gratification which would be a lure to the 'vulgar'. Thus loud colours, provocative dress, expletive speech, are all a 'breach of decorum' and 'in bad taste'.

This equation between 'taste' and 'manners' is of course deeply rooted in the traditions of our culture. In his fascinating book on the process of civilization, Norbert Elias[19] has demonstrated in some detail how the gratification of our appetites becomes subject to increasing social restraints which can be traced in

---

[17]G. Boccaccio, *Decamerone, Giornata, VI Novella,* 5.
[18]Life of Cosimo Rosselli.
[19]N. Elias. *Über den Prozess der Zivilisation,* Haus zum Falken, Basel, 1939.

the varying social codes. In this sphere we have no difficulty in understanding why the values of taste and manners were equated with the pyramid of hierarchical power, the 'noble' at the top and the 'vulgar' at the base. It is an historical fact that social taboos usually spread from the top downward. The nobleman ate daintily while the villain still gulped his food. Though, in point of fact, the aristocracy—like Vasari's Pope—did not always show a similar sophistication in matters of art, the metaphor of the noble was derived from this basic stratification. Of course ideally the restraint of the 'noble' is not only one of behaviour. Whatever the reality may have been like, it is first and foremost conceived as a moral restraint, a control of the passions, a domination of impulse. This applies to Roman '*gravitas*' no less than to knightly '*mesure*' or '*courtoisie*'—and when Nietzsche, in his hysterical praise of the 'noble', singles out 'the slow gesture, the slow glance'[20] as a physiognomic characteristic of his admired aristocrat, he still characterizes the person of strong self-control who is not impelled by spontaneous appetites to look or move.

If this analysis of a critical metaphor is correct, we gain, perhaps, a first glimpse into the process by which art itself can become to us a symbol of moral value. In the co-ordinate system erected by our culture, renunciation of gratification, nobility, and the Good converge and become one. To test this impression gained from historical material, the historian can do no better than to resort to introspection.[21]

V. Clean Lines

The conditions for such an introspective test are not too inauspicious. For in the past few decades we have gone through a revolution of 'taste' which has much in common with the process of 'sophistication' characterized in the preceding section. If the Renaissance (to put it schematically) rejected glitter for 'nobility', the twentieth century has rejected ornament for the sake of 'clean outlines'. Everybody familiar with the catchwords under which this battle was and is still being waged will recognize that here, too, social and moral issues seem inextricably intertwined with questions of aesthetic value. Perhaps, however, we have now acquired sufficient distance to see the contending parties with some detachment. Why did the Victorians revel in ornament? The quickest schematic answer would be to say that ornament had come to 'stand for' Art. In the complex give and take of our aesthetic reactions this is hardly a surprising development. In the Renaissance art had acquired an 'autonomous' value, divorced (as we have seen) from preciousness and brightness. What is

---

[20]*Der Wille zur Macht*, Aphorism 943.
[21]I need hardly say that this introspection is guided by theoretical expectations, derived, in my case, from the thought and the writings of Ernst Kris, whose *Psychoanalytic Exploration in Art* contain several models in which the idea of an 'optimum distance' is developed.

more natural than that this value, in its turn, became an 'area of metaphor'? To praise a landscape the eighteenth century called it 'picturesque' — associated with things seen in pictures.[22] To make a pair of scissors praiseworthy the Victorian designer shaped it on the pattern of Gothic tracery, to let it partake of the aura of value that surrounded the relics of the 'Age of Faith'. In itself this use of ornament is not new in the nineteenth century. All fashion in ornament — and who could draw the line between style and fashion? — rests on such associations. The Florentine burgher of the Renaissance who adorned his house with a porch '*all' antica*', wanted thereby to transform it into a likeness of an ancient temple, to proclaim his allegiance to the values of the noble Romans. In the dim distant past, of course, ornament had had a more direct power.[23] To the primitive artist who turned the handle of a vessel into a snake, or its spout into a beak, the handle became a snake and the spout a beak, partaking, thereby, of the magic force inherent in them. Even here, we might say, metaphor is at work: the table 'legs' end in protective claws and thus the table is made 'one' with the guardian animal. But, however that may be, by the time we reach the Victorians, ornament has become the metaphor of Art, and of Art as the symbol or visible token of wealth. The Victorian interior with its aspidistras and tigerskins, its velvet curtains and 'ornaments' on the mantle-piece, its furniture covered with ornamental allusions to the art of all respected ages, is really shaped in the likeness of an aristocratic museum in which the spoils of centuries display the owner's 'connoisseurship'. Suddenly all this is victimized by sophistication and falls under the taboo of 'tasteless ostentation'. We were asked to tear down the heavy curtains and enlarge the windows to let light and air into the 'stuffy' rooms, to sweep away the knick-knack which only 'collects dust', to knock down the 'false' stucco ornament, and to remove the useless excrescences from our furniture in favour of 'clean', functional lines. There may have been some rational impulse behind this revolution. Possibly Pasteur's discovery of germs and the dangers lurking in unsweepable corners had something to do with its beginnings. But whatever it may have been that set the ball rolling, introspection shows, I submit, that concern for hygiene is really not the whole story. Much of modern design which we instinctively prefer is not so much more 'hygienic' in an objective sense as *suggestive* of cleanliness and rational living. If the Victorians took their visual metaphors from the museum, we take ours from the operating theatre and the factory. If primitive man turned his table into a metaphor of a protecting animal and the Renaissance burgher his palace into a metaphor of a Roman temple, we are asked to see our house as a 'machine to live in'. The machine itself, of course, or rather the world of engineering, has become an area of metaphor on which we

---

[22]*Cf.* Christopher Hussey, *The Picturesque*, Putnam, London, 1927.
[23]E. Loewy, '*Ursprünge der bildenden Kunst*', *Almanach der Akademie der Wissenschaften in Wien*, 1930.

constantly draw. The 'streamline' contour is employed metaphorically where no rapid airstream will ever cause friction, to suggest or 'express' efficiency. Similarly, hygiene, cleanliness, purity, have become areas of metaphor that cause us to wrap our wares in cellophane and turn our rooms into chromium-plated offices. And, just as with the change to 'decorum' in the Renaissance, the revolution is felt to have strong social overtones. The main objection against the Victorian interior is that it is 'vulgar', by which is meant that it allows a too easy, childish gratification in the gaudy and 'cheap'. Books on 'good' and 'bad' design hint openly that to prefer one lampstand to another is a sign of social inferiority. Meanwhile, of course, the tide has already turned. In the sphere of art the 'organic' forms of a Henry Moore appeal more to the really 'advanced' groups than the 'constructivist' purity of Mondrian or Pevsner. In design Victorian 'atrocities' have acquired the distinction of being 'amusing'—which must be taken to mean that they have receded far enough into the background no longer to be dangerous.

For this, above all, introspection seems to show—that our rejection of Victorian ornament and all that went with it, was not just a matter of aesthetic preference. What strikes us as 'vulgar' in art or design does not merely leave us indifferent, it gives us positive displeasure to the point of making us 'feel sick'. Our creation of new visual metaphors for the 'chaste and pure' finds its necessary counterpart in a strong aversion to such forms as strike us as meretricious and indecent. The very disgust we feel at the 'cheap', the 'gaudy', the 'sloppy', proves our strong emotional involvement. Nor is the nature of this involvement hard to guess. We react as if we resisted seduction, and this is suggested too by the metaphors we use. We speak of a painting as 'pretty-pretty', to imply that such primitive gratification as it offers is not for the grown-up mind. We call it 'chocolate boxy' to describe its inartistic invitation to self-indulgence. Everywhere our reaction suggests that we have come to equate such indulgence with other childish gratifications we have learned to control. We find the 'cheap' work 'too sweet', 'cloying', 'mushy', and 'bulgy', with an obvious erotic overtone. There is some evidence that it is only works that have more recently fallen under the taboo of sophistication which have this effect on us. Forms of the more distant past may strike us sometimes as poor but rarely as 'vile'. The use of gold which so shocked Renaissance writers as a sign of childish vulgarity now impresses us as pleasantly naive. We feel we can afford some indulgence in this simple pleasure. We are close to a sophistication of the second degree which welcomes the 'primitive' as a value, providing a metaphor for all that is strong, direct, forthright, and 'unsophisticated'. The art of the past has often had to lend itself to this symbolic use.[24]

If the results of this brief excursion into introspection can be generalized, our

---

[24]*Cf.* Meyer Schapiro in his review of Arthur Upham Pope's 'Survey of Persian Art', *The Art Bulletin*, March, 1941, p. 85.

attitude to certain elements of artistic expression follows indeed a curve similar to that of our attitude to other forms of gratification. The findings of Elias would seem to apply here no less than in other fields of 'good behaviour'.[25] The process of civilization advances what he calls *die Peinlichkeitsgrenze*, the threshold of what is felt to be embarrassing, but frees other areas which are felt to be completely under control. The reaction of the 'Philistines' to the sophisticated regressions of modern art suggests that these, too, are experienced as a threat against which the mind must mobilize its defences. Both the 'highbrow' and the 'lowbrow' experiences moral worth in some works of art and rejects others as 'indecent' — and both may have more subjective right to their attitudes than we are sometimes inclined to concede.

VI. Impulse and Restraint

The result of the two preceding sections might be summarized by saying that in the context of our culture art not only embodies those natural metaphors which have so frequently attracted the attention of aestheticians — violent colours for violent emotions — but also their negation, and that it is very often through such negation, restraint, or renunciation, that art creates new metaphors of 'higher' values. But before we proceed to generalize on these findings certain difficulties have to be overcome. One concerns the relation of 'art' to 'taste'. Not that the two can ever be quite nearly separated, or that it would be a fruitful undertaking to 'define' their limits. But even without committing ourselves to a verbal definition, we all know what is meant when we say that 'good taste' is often satisfied by rather poor art, provided that it remains on its best behaviour. We may even feel intuitively (if we are romantically inclined), that 'taste' may, at times, stand in opposition to art and suffocate its vitality. These dangers of the ideal of 'noble simplicity' were well brought out at the very time of its greatest vogue during the 'Age of Taste' by none other than Sir Joshua Reynolds, P.R.A., in a passage that deserves full quotation:

When simplicity, instead of being a corrector, seems to set up for herself; that is, when an artist seems to value himself solely upon this quality; such an ostentatious display of simplicity becomes then as disagreeable and nauseous as any other kind of affectation. He is, however, in this case, likely to sit down contented with his own work; for though he finds the world looks at it with indifference or dislike, as being destitute of every quality that can recreate or give pleasure to the mind, yet he consoles himself that it has simplicity, a beauty too pure and chaste to be relished by vulgar minds.

---

[25]*Loc. cit.* The value of Elias's findings seems to me to lie in the fact that he allows us to dispense with the assumption of a biological evolution in historical times such as seems postulated by A. Ehrenzweig, *Psycho-Analysis of Artistic Vision and Hearing,* London, 1953, for here the methodological warnings formulated by K. R. Popper, *The Poverty of Historicism,* London, 1957, apply.

It is in art as in morals; no character would inspire us with an enthusiastic admiration of his virtue, if that virtue consisted only in an absence of vice. . . .[26]

We might elaborate the moral simile, offered us by Reynolds himself, and suggest that conformity is not virtue; that where there are no passions to be controlled restraint is not experienced as a value. Something analogous is no doubt experienced in the face of those artistic negations or renunciations that are the present object of our attention. Not that it must always be possible to distinguish the 'noble simplicity' of the true work of art from its less noble isotope, the 'work of taste'. In architecture, for instance, opinions on this point are apt to vary considerably — witness the diverse estimate of the stature of the Renaissance architect, L. B. Alberti, the very master we selected for his doctrine of the 'purity' of white unadorned walls. But by and large we have the feeling that we are able to distinguish mere absence of emotion from control of emotion, and that the great work of art is marked by an intensity of impulse, matched and dominated by an even greater intensity of discipline.

We are here touching upon a problem of physiognomic understanding that was the lifelong preoccupation of Ludwig Klages, who, unfortunately, marred the value of his intuitive insights by his Bergsonian irrationalism and his hatred of rational argument. Klages's starting point was graphology. He was anxious to show that the same trait or absence of traits in the handwriting of individuals acquired a different meaning if we experienced them as due to the weakness of drives or the strength of resistance. He introduced the idea of the '*Formniveau*', the intuitively perceived level of performance that allows us to sense that presence of 'life' that may pulse through the most disciplined of scripts.[27] The type of duality he apparently had in mind is expressed in less metaphysical form, in terms of 'heart' and 'head', in the following description by a performing musician of a great fellow musician at work:

We in the orchestra are on closer terms with the conductor than anyone else, and are in an unassailable position to judge whether he is making music from his heart or from his head. Let it be well and truly understood that in Toscanini the two are in perfect balance. All his music-making springs from his inmost being, though his mind directs his heart, as every member of the orchestra is made aware in the first five minutes of his rehearsal. He is completely caught up in the music, and every line of his face shows the depth and intensity of his feeling. And it pours forth from him. The fact that he is master of his power does not mean that he is dishonest with himself, but that all power on earth, to be effective, has to be in control. Look at him in the act of building up a climax. He asks more and more until the orchestra's breath and strength are almost used up, and then from his reserves he gives forth still more of himself, until the most vital point of all is

---

[26]Sir Joshua Reynolds, *Fifteen Discourses,* Everyman Edition, J. M. Dent & Sons Ltd., London, 1928, p. 135.
[27]L. Klages, *Ausdrucksbewegung und Gestaltungskraft,* J. A. Barth, Leipzig, 1923.

reached. He never allows his forces to expand themselves to waste, nor does he ever overpaint a phrase.

His crowning glory is the presentation of a work with such divine simplicity that it suddenly appears in a new and fresh light – yet, incredibly, only as the composer left it.[28]

The phenomenon here characterized in such pleasantly untechnical language would probably be called 'ego control' by the psycho-analyst. It is a quality that is particularly well exemplified in the art of the musical performer with its temptations and the possibility of rational checks. When we are told, for instance, that Toscanini 'never overpaints a phrase' we understand that he never yields to the allurement of a moment, as minor performers do, that he renounces the 'cheap effects' that may provide immediate gratification but disrupt the architecture of the whole, and that the gain from this austerity in the presence of intense emotion is that 'divine simplicity' that becomes a musical metaphor of highest values.

Perhaps a little more can even be extracted from this example. For the performer stands half way between the creator and the public and somehow partakes of the problem of both. Only recently Paul Hindemith has stressed his belief in the Augustinian doctrine of music as an image of moral order which is attained by the listener through his active collaboration in the act of musical creation.[29] Again he describes an appeal to ego-control *versus* a mere indulgence in the pleasures of sound, the passive surrender he attributes to Boethius's theory of music. We here gain a hint of the hierarchy of values within music which has its parallel in the other arts. The design of the whole dominates over the surface attractions of the parts, just because it presupposes a higher degree of control on the part of the creator and the beholder or listener. The noble renunciation in art is renunciation of part effects for the sake of submission to the larger structure. But not every withholding of gratification is experienced as a metaphor of nobility. There is something like a depraved sophistication, a playing with the *'raffinement'* of colour or sound, that teases and surprises but seems to use negation as a spice rather than as a sacrifice to higher values. Only the sternest moralist would deny these effects their place in art, but ancient academic doctrine which relegated them to a lower plane may have had some psychological justification behind it.

VII. Is Beauty Truth?

There is no more famous and no more moving record of what we have called the 'confluence of values' than Keats's 'Ode On a Grecian Urn'. It was this (real or imagined) work of art, of course, that inspired the much quoted and

[28]Bernard Shore, *The Orchestra Speaks,* Longmans Green & Company, London, 1938, p. 182.
[29]Paul Hindemith, *A Composer's World,* Harvard University Press, Cambridge, Massachusetts, 1952.

much abused utterance, 'Beauty is truth, truth beauty'. Are we to see more in this than a mere exclamation of ecstatic enjoyment? If we read the poem with our present preoccupations in mind, we may be struck by its imagery of gratification withheld, of passion unfulfilled. The very first line introduces this motif:

> Thou still unravish'd bride of quietness,

and the poem soon rises to that paean of renunciation

> Heard melodies are sweet, but those unheard
> Are sweeter; . . .
> Bold Lover, never, never canst thou kiss,
> Though winning near the goal — . . .
> More happy love! more happy, happy love!
> For ever warm and still to be enjoy'd
> For ever panting, and for ever young;
> All breathing human passion far above,
> That leaves a heart high-sorrowful and cloy'd, . . .

Is it because it is a *'cold'* pastoral, stilled and remote, that the urn acquires the dignity of a universal symbol? One may be tempted to think so. For beyond the general neo-platonic faith in the truth of the artist's vision such as it is expressed in Keats's letters,[30] the idea that the realm of beauty can be entered by man only at the price of renunciation plays an important part in eighteenth-century aesthetics. Thus Schiller's speculations turned upon the contrast between the enslavement of our animal nature and the freedom of aesthetic contemplation.

> *Wollt ihr schon auf Erden Göttern gleichen,*
> *Frei sein in des Todes Reichen*
> *Brechet nicht von seines Gartens Frucht!*[31]

But whatever the exact roots and implications of Keats's exclamation there remains the fact that great art has given to many the feeling that they are in the presence of 'truth'. Usually discussions of that point turn on the conviction that all great art is 'truthful' because it is 'sincere' and 'honest' — just as bad art is often branded as the opposite. No investigation of the moral aspects of art can shirk this important issue. What we want to know is how we should interpret this intuition that the great work of art is 'sincere'.

In this section I shall try to explain why this favourite term of the critics should no less be considered a metaphor than the terms of 'nobility' or 'purity'

---

[30]*The Letters of John Keats,* edited by J. B. Forman, Oxford University Press, Oxford, 1947, p. 67f.
[31]*Das Ideal und das Leben;* for the philosophical background see also Schiller's essay, *Über das Pathetische,* which is of great interest in our present context.

—and, conversely, as in the previous examples, why this metaphor still describes some kind of psychological reality. The temptation to take the metaphor literally is even greater here than in previous instances. We are assured that the artist is sincere and truthful if and only if he expresses what he 'really feels'. But the difficulties in the way of this naive version of expressionism have often been pointed out. Nobody would seriously maintain that a musician who writes a sonata must wait for a sad mood to write the adagio and has to postpone the writing of the 'scherzo' till he feels gay.[32] And even if he did, who would ever know and thank him for it? What right have we to inquire after an artist's private feelings? And how can we know that what strikes us as 'false sentiment' did not express an actual experience of a truly sentimental soul?

Obviously we have here a confusion of various meanings of the term 'expression'. In everyday usage the term 'expression' refers most frequently to the manifestation of feelings through gesture, inflection, or facial expression. But even here we must be wary of confusion. Blushing is a sign of embarrassment, frowning is a sign of anger. Both indicate the presence of certain emotions much as the proverbial smoke indicates the presence of fire. But there is a difference between these forms of 'expression'. Blushing is a symptom of embarrassment—and as such largely outside our control. A blush, therefore, cannot, be dishonest. Frowning is a symptom of anger, but it so happens that we can also frown intentionally. We can frown at will to communicate the fact that we are angry. The frown as an 'expression' of anger can become the equivalent of a verbal communication. It becomes a shorthand formula which the teacher or actor can use for the statement (true or false), 'Now I am annoyed'. When we speak of 'expression' in daily life, we lump symbol and symptom together. We have our reasons for doing so. For the living expression of social intercourse is made up of both types of sign. Convention has taught us to control and canalize the symptoms of our emotions, to let them conform to certain symbolic standards.[33] It is only in extreme situations that the average grown-up allows genuine symptoms to overwhelm his conscious control or that he feels driven to employ symbols of feelings which are in no way symptomatic of his state of mind.

When critics of the pre-Romantic age spoke of 'expression' in art, it was always the 'symbolic' sense they had in mind. They discussed the expression of figures *in* the picture, the anguish of Laocoon, the fury of Herod, they analysed the means a poet or musician has at his disposal to 'paint the affects'—as the eighteenth century put it—and noted the vocabulary which the various arts have developed for this purpose. Translated into the terminology of this essay they would say that the major key lends itself to the musician as a symbol or

---

[32]For this criticism *cf.* P. Hindemith, *loc. cit.,* pp. 35 f.
[33]*Cf.* Ernst Kris, 'Laughter as an Expressive Process', *loc. cit.,* pp. 127 ff.

metaphor of gaiety, that a stormy sky in the background of a massacre can be used as a metaphor of passionate grief. To them, in other words, art was not 'expression' but made use of 'expressions', developed and held in readiness by tradition or 'style'.

As long as the term 'expression' was thus confined to the symbols used by the artist, the question of his own 'sincerity' did not arise. It was only with the advent of Romanticism that this term became one of the favourite epithets of critics, and this shift of emphasis is connected with the increasing belief in the function of art as communication of emotions. The work of art as such, in other words, was valued as a symptom of the artist's state of mind, as an 'expression of personality', and this, at once, raised the issue of the genuine *versus* the false expression.

But have we really a right to equate artistic truth with truthful communication? Does the idea that the morality of great art rests on a coincidence of symbol and symptom not rather hide than reveal the complex relationship between the artist and his work?[34] It is true that Horace advises the poet 'You must feel pain yourself if you want me to cry', but such advice no less than Wordsworth's contrasting recollection 'in tranquillity' should be considered technical hints rather than moral injunctions. The artist's private feelings at the moment of production clearly do not enter here, and as to his personality—we have long learned to see the immense complexity that shields behind this simple word. We could hardly ever recognize an artist whom we knew only through his work. So how far is his personality 'expressed' in it?

And yet the feeling of 'sincerity' we have in the face of certain masterpieces cannot be disputed, any more than of 'nobility', 'purity', or 'discipline'. The suspicion arises that they are all metaphors pointing to a similar centre. When we find a teacher's frown 'expressive', we are not concerned (unless we are the pupils) whether his rage is 'real' or only 'put on'. We rather mean that it is convincing, because it is not merely a symbol in isolation (that would strike us as false), but that it is co-ordinated with other symbols of anger, a scornful voice, a tight lip, and set in the proper curve of rising anger. It is possible that most people will perform more convincingly if they talk themselves into real anger, but surely it is not this that would make it more moral. And so we are led to the conclusion that once more it is the submission of the part to the whole, the element of control, of bridled emotion rather than of disconnected symptoms, that is responsible for this intuition of 'honesty', and that may make art analogous to a moral experience.

---

[34]Somewhat similar distinctions between symbol and symptom are made by R. G. Collingwood, *The Principles of Art*, Oxford University Press, Oxford, 1938, but I cannot quite share the author's conclusions. The most stimulating discussion of the problem of personal expression, as far as poetry is concerned, may be found in the exchange of letters by E. M. W. Tillyard and C. S. Lewis, *The Personal Heresy*, Oxford University Press, Oxford, 1939.

This suspicion that the feeling of 'truth' or 'sincerity' in art is due to the synesthesia of values, is strengthened if we look into the reasons why certain types of paintings are so often charged with the corresponding sin of 'insincerity' and 'false sentiment'. A scrutiny of critical literature would probably reveal that such charges refer more often than not to what we called symbols rather than symptoms; to the swooning saints of Bolognese seventeenth-century painters, the coquettish maidens of Greuze, or the theatrical pathos of Doré. In our present context we are not concerned with the question whether these works ought to be valued or not—they are anyhow coming into their own among the sophisticated—but simply how we should interpret this charge of dishonesty. It could be substantiated only if it could be maintained that Reni wanted to claim the Saint's emotion as his own. But there can be no question of that. Reni did not want to 'express' piety, he wanted to use 'an expression of piety', as he understood it, for a picture of a saint, and so the criterion of honesty *versus* dishonesty really does not apply.

It is not hard to guess, on the other hand, why so many people feel compelled to use this handy metaphor of opprobrium against such pictures. They are the victims of the same 'process of civilization' which imposed its taboo on gold and ornament. The scope of emotion we are permitted to show in society has much contracted even since Victorian days. We have tried to reduce both symptom and symbol to the minimum needed to secure contact among really sensitized people. Works of art which display symbols running counter to these taboos 'get under our skin', they 'make us sick'. We suspect them of wanting to seduce us to a forbidden form of exhibitionism and we evade them by throwing doubt on their sincerity. As we do not want to cry, we turn the dictum of Horace against them and maintain that they never felt pain—as if they had claimed that they did. Here, too, the aversion to expressive symbols (which Romanticism led them to confuse with symptoms) has driven the taste of the sophisticated continuously backward in time to more primitive and archaic art which did not assail their nerves with easily interpretable expression. The primitives could not offend by an unseemly display of obvious emotions. Their admirers tried to run away from expression and landed ever deeper in expressionism. Perhaps it tickled their pride to fancy themselves able to penetrate through the impenetrable mask of an Aztec idol and to detect expression where the 'vulgar' would see only ugliness and rigour. Perhaps in trying to gauge the expressive value not of faces and gestures but of lines, colours, and patterns, they felt permitted to indulge in the experience of emotion without trespassing on the taboo of 'false sentiment'. There is, of course, a valuable side to this revolution of taste. It lies in the recognition that art yields emotional satisfaction only at the price of renunciation. But unless the critic gains some insight into the mechanisms here at work, the metaphors he uses can also do harm, and a good deal of such harm, I submit, has in fact been done by the identification of art with symptomatic expression.

VIII. Hopes and Dangers

The symbol has been recognized as a force of social control and cohesion ever since Carlyle, in the turbulent pages of the *Sartor Resartus*, spoke of the 'Poet and inspired Maker; who, Prometheus-like, can shape new Symbols, and bring new fire from Heaven to fix it there', and execrated the 'tatters and rags of superannuated worn-out symbols . . . dropping off everywhere, to hoodwink, to halter, to tether you . . .'[35] It is not long ago that A. N. Whitehead elaborated his words, reminding us that 'Those societies which cannot combine reverence for their symbols with freedom of revision, must ultimately decay either from anarchy, or from the slow atrophy of a life stifled by useless shadows.'[36]

As we move away from the hierarchical society of the past, problems of symbols and values become, in fact, more acute. We have seen how strongly this type of society imprinted its fame of preference on the terms in which art was conceived. The 'noble' and the 'vulgar', the 'high' and the 'low', the 'dignified' and the 'common', are today not much more than pale, fading metaphors for what were once tangible realities. We need not mourn their passing away in order to realize that here an area of metaphor is passing out of our consciousness which, for centuries if not longer, gave man a symbol of value, however crude. It did even more—it provided a bait or reward for the 'process of civilization' itself. Ever since the Renaissance, perhaps indeed since the Courts of Love, 'courtoisie', culture, urbanity, were rewarded by a rise in the social scale. The development of a taste ready to forego immediate gratification for 'higher' satisfactions was among the accomplishments so rewarded. We are used to looking down on snobbery, the pretence of culture for the sake of social advancement,[37] but what begins as pretence often becomes genuine—at least in a second generation. Snobbery in this wider sense may have been one of the most powerful engines in keeping culture going. It provided the social pressure that induced people to learn the stock of symbols or common images called 'general culture'; it put a price on self-restraint. When Molière's M. Jourdain wants to leave his bourgeois state behind to become a *gentilhomme*, he calls in the Masters of Music, of Dancing, of Fencing, and of 'Philosophy'. We may laugh with Molière or we may feel somewhat embarrassed at his snobbery, but the fact remains that hierarchical society exacted a high entrance fee—a remodelling of the whole person to certain standards. Today these mechanisms are still at work, but they are relaxing their grip. Specialization threatens the community of areas of metaphor, liberalization of society the unquestioning community of standards. What are the chances that

---

[35]*Loc. cit.*, 'Of Symbols'. The whole chapter deserves the attention of students of the subject.
[36]Alfred North Whitehead, *Symbolism, Its Meaning and Effect*, Cambridge University Press, Cambridge, 1928.
[37]For a brief but telling analysis of snobbery, *cf.* George Boas, *A Primer for Critics*, The John Hopkins Press, Baltimore, 1937.

art may provide the symbols of value which society seems in danger of losing?

If our analysis has been correct, such chances exist, but there is little room for easy optimism. For art is not the 'universal language' that could link classes and civilizations. The reason is that it does not rely on a universal area of metaphor common to all mankind. Even where it does not make use of a 'code', even where it does not allude to specific lore, it relies for its effect on the complex interplay of attraction *and* repulsion, gratification and renunciation for the sake of 'higher' values. If we have come a little nearer to understanding how this balance can serve for those who are attuned to its particular kind of equilibrium, as a metaphor of the 'good' in all its converging forms, we have also learned how much of this response depends upon factors beyond easy control. It is regulated from the centre of our being; it is intimately linked with the degree of our emotional maturity and the level of our culture. In psycho-analytic terminology these are matters which largely depend upon the strength of our ego and the state of its defences and are thus not easily adjusted by courses on 'art appreciation' alone.

There are tendencies discernible in our modern world which seem to hold out hope. The means of mass communication, so often execrated as spreaders of vulgarity, seem to have 'conditioned' a much wider audience than ever before to the true understanding of music: partly no doubt, as their sponsors claim, by familiarizing many listeners with classical masterpieces, but partly also, one may suspect, by providing such a cloying surfeit of easy gratification contained in popular 'hits', that the values of subtler harmonies became desirable and understandable to an increasing number of listeners. Perhaps the gaudy colours of advertisements may help in a similar way to create a response to the restraint of great art.

Against these positive factors, however, we must set the negative conclusions that might be drawn from some of our observations. The Beauty of the 'Grecian Urn' becomes Truth because of what may be called its 'plenitude of values' held in miraculous equilibrium — passion and denial, 'hot pursuit' in the 'cold pastoral'. The danger from the emergence of new values, that constantly threatens art, is precisely the danger to this equilibrium. It is a danger well illustrated in the satirical remark on 'simplicity' quoted above from Reynolds,[38] and it is a danger that constantly increases with what I have called the process of sophistication. This process implies, as I have tried to show, that a work of art comes to stand in a context where it is valued as much for what it rejects and negates as for what it is. In modern art these negations and negations of negations have reached a bewildering complexity and the social taboo of the

---

[38]Some equally devasting remarks on certain idols of modern criticism can be found in Sir Donald Tovey, *A Musician Talks*, I. *The Integrity of Music,* Oxford University Press, London, 1942, especially pp. 38-39, where the intellectual respect for such compositional devices as 'inversion' is held up to healthy ridicule.

'cheap' and 'vulgar' falls with capricious speed on one aspect of art after the other—releasing areas only just condemned to be patronized or enjoyed. Of course these negations and releases have their genuine function, they correspond to a real shift in balance experienced by the artists and their friends. But the danger is that an increasing emphasis on the negative aspects—the *absence* of illustration, representation, imitation, sentiment, contrivance—may push the work of art ever closer to the work of taste; which is clearly the opposite effect of the one desired. It is a danger still increased by the catchwords of our time, in which the static social values of 'noble' *versus* 'vulgar' are replaced by the 'dynamic' values of 'progressive' *versus* 'backward'. In this battle of ideologies the poorest work can do service as a badge to proclaim the value of 'progress' or 'traditionalism'—in fact, the poor work can perhaps proclaim this value louder because it need not concern itself with that equilibrium of values which alone makes art into a worthy symbol of our highest values.

The critic who would attempt to prescribe to the artist what to do, or leave undone, in order to create symbols of value, would invite ridicule. The abortive art of Nazi Germany and of Soviet Russia stands as a warning against such presumption. Yet the critic has his share of responsibility in these matters. Art is not just 'the expression of the age'[39]: it is the work of people who have to find approval if they want to live. The catchwords of value which the critic discerns in the drift of social trends and to which he, in turn, gives currency, ring in the ear of the creative artist and often guide his preferences or impose taboos. It is all the more important for him to be aware that his metaphors *are* metaphors, but that they spring from that living centre where the 'good', the 'clean', the 'noble', the 'true', the 'healthy', the 'natural', the 'sincere', the 'decent', are but the facets of one untranslatable experience of a plenitude of values that speaks to the whole man—as great art has always done.

---

[39]The emptiness of this claim has been shown up by George Boas, *Wingless Pegasus,* The John Hopkins Press, Baltimore, 1950, Appendix I.

III

THE PROBLEM OF EXPLANATION

Introduction

During the past three decades the concept of explanation has been intensively analyzed, especially in the disciplines of history and science. This work has stimulated philosophers in education to inquire into the meaning of explanation in a variety of educational contexts. What, then, is the meaning of "explanation?" What are the different forms explanation may take? Can art be explained or only described? If the latter, then what is the difference between an explanation and a description? Or between an explanation and an interpretation? Since explaining is one of the most important operations performed by teachers and students, this section is devoted to gaining a perspective on this task.

In "Explanation," Leonard F. Swift asserts "explanations occur whenever attention moves beyond the offering of information or the execution of performance to matters of meaning, relationships, causes, factors, and reasons." The meaning of explanation, moreover, always depends on the context in which an explanation is demanded and on what is set to be explained. Further, explanations are typically called for whenever things are a source of perplexity. Among the many kinds of explanation that can be discerned, Swift differentiates two broad groups: relational and nonrelational usages. The latter are distinguished by basically linguistic considerations while the former call attention to both linguistic and logical processes; that is, in addition to problems of meaning the logical relations among statements are also significant. Subsumed under nonrelational explanation are what Swift calls explanation-as-definition, explanation-as-description, and explanation-as-classification. Relational explanation, on the other hand, comprises genetic, causal, and teleological explanations.

Swift's essay, in brief, is a plea for paying more attention to the patterns of explanation and their uses in the planning of teaching and learning episodes, and it is hoped that teachers will find ways to translate his examples into analogous situations in the teaching of art. A start can perhaps be made by substituting, say, Amiens Cathedral in Swift's example "Explain the organization of the United Nations." How many different explanations of Amiens Cathedral are possible in view of Swift's analysis?

Explanation

LEONARD F. SWIFT

Many terms commonly used in educational theory and practice have been the themes of extended discussions — "needs," "interests," and "problem," for example. Other terms have figured much less obtrusively in educational theory, though they occur frequently at the applied level of actual classroom instruction. One such term is "explanation." Theorists both offer and call for explanations, and teachers in the discourse of instruction employ the terms "explanation" and "explain" with considerate frequency. The terms appear in several kinds of educational contexts, but not always with the same meaning. It is with different meanings of "explanation" that this essay will be concerned.

Some of these meanings appear in the course of broad philosophical discussion and analysis as well as in the processes of instruction. For example, outside the common classroom situations which call for explanations of one kind or another, there are questions which ask: What is the appropriate form of an explanation? Is explanation in history or in biology different from explanation in other fields of inquiry? Does science really explain, or does it merely describe?

In addition, there are claims about different types of explanation along with an array of terminology for talking about them. There are, for instance, such

From B. Othanel Smith and Robert H. Ennis (eds.), *Language and Concepts in Education* (Chicago: Rand McNally & Company, 1961), pp. 179-94. Reprinted by permission of the author and Rand McNally & Company.

expressions as "causal explanation," "historical explanation," "teleological explanation," "genetic explanation," and "dispositional explanation." These terms and the claims associated with them appear in connection with inquiry in different fields when attention shifts from a particular explanation to the grounds of the explanation and the quality of its support.[1] All of these terms and meanings of explanation will not be considered with equal emphasis, but the essay will sort out some of them as exhibited in classroom discourse and will attend to some criteria related to extending understanding of the grounds of explanation.

In classroom discourse the verbal situations or contexts for evoking explanations occur nearly every day. The elements of these contexts are often sets of assertions in the form of particular factual statements. In a history class the statements may name some events or states of affairs; individuals and their stated positions and decisions; public and private agencies and groups; policies, viewpoints, and activities; trends and developments; or other human and institutional phenomena. In other kinds of ordinary subject matter, the statements may name physical and biological phenomena, properties of geometric figures, or characteristics of elements of language and of works of literature. On some occasions, in addition to descriptive material, there may be a series of performances, such as the translation of a passage from one language to another, the punctuation of a paragraph, or the demonstration of a geometrical proof.

Given these instructional contexts with either assertions or performances as the raw material, explanations occur whenever attention moves beyond the offering of information or the execution of performance to matters of meaning, relationships, causes, factors, and reasons. In instruction the explanations are usually invited by such directives as "Explain why a candle is extinguished when covered by a glass," "Explain the action of the compass needle," "Explain the stock-market crash," "Explain why plants need sunshine," "Explain the sentence 'Lend me your ears.' "

By examining the ordinarily expected responses to such directives it is possible to notice more clearly some different uses of "explanation." In these responses at least two broad groups of usages are discernible, called for convenience the "relational" and the "non-relational" usages of explanation. They are distinguished by virtue of the presence of different sets of logical and linguistic processes. The non-relational usages in general call for attention to processes that are largely linguistic, whereas the relational usages invoke attention both to linguistic and to logical matters.

---

[1] Richard B. Braithwaite, *Scientific Explanation* (Cambridge, Eng.: Cambridge University Press, 1953); Herbert Feigl and May Brodbeck, eds., *Readings in the Philosophy of Science* (New York: Appleton-Century-Crofts, Ind., 1953); Patrick Gardiner, *The Nature of Historical Explanation* (London: Oxford University Press, 1952); D. L. Miller, "The Meaning of Explanation," *Psychological Review*, LIII (July, 1946), 241-46; *Theory and Practice in Historical Study* (Social Science Research Council Bulletin 54; New York: Social Science Research Council, 1946).

1. Non-Relational Usages

Of the non-relational usages, one appears in an expected response to the question "Explain the sentence 'Lend me your ears.'" The answer takes the form of a series of utterances stating the meaning of that sentence in more familiar and non-metaphorical language. Ordinarily in such an explanation there are no reasons offered in the form of generalizations about public speakers in mass groups in moments of social crisis. Nor is there a series of deductive inferences from propositions about Elizabethan playwrights. Instead, the process is a kind of translation from one type of language into another. The kind of understanding involved is not understanding of relationships expressed in statements of general principles, but understanding of meaning — a linguistic understanding dealing with a figure of speech.

Similar usage of explanation occurs in other subject matter, in the study of foreign languages as well as in science, social studies, and mathematics, when some term, expression, sentence, or passage is to be expressed in familiar words. In effect, this usage ("Explain the sentence. . . .") corresponds to "Give the meaning of. . . ." It is more precisely an "interpretation" — a term convenient for naming a linguistic process as distinct from the logical process of deduction. In other cases where the topic is concerned with a particular term (e.g., "Explain the term. . . ."), the usage of "explain" is equivalent to "define," and the process called for is the making of a definition.

From an instructional point of view this usage of "explain" may not be especially demanding, but it generates no great ambiguity or confusion. The presence of a term, a sentence, or a passage in the phraseology of the question asked is ordinarily a satisfactory indicator of the procedure to be followed. If clarity of meaning is an acceptable objective, the interpretation and the definition usages of "explain" are appropriate in ordinary classroom speech, and they do not inevitably lead to difficulty. On the other hand, the chief limitation may be that if questioning regularly stops with interpretation or definition, opportunities for extending understanding by dealing with other forms of explanation are overlooked, with a consequent loss of attention to significant processes of thinking and reasoning.

A second form of non-relational explanation arises from such questions as "Explain how to bisect an angle," "Explain how to locate a biography," or "Explain the organization of the United Nations." For the United Nations item one appropriate response would name the branches — the new Security Council, the General Assembly, the Secretariat — and give a description of the function of these branches. When this is done with factual accuracy the explanation is judged to have been performed. With this usage, "explanation" is the equivalent of "description." The expected response is a series of statements naming certain movements and operations, cataloguing information, or naming and describing the characteristics of especially constituted groups. The process involves a series of utterances related not by deduction but by classification with reference to categories drawn from the topic named in the question.

As with explanation in the sense of interpretation, there need not be ambiguity or confusion with respect to the process to be followed. The student who responds to "Explain how to bisect an angle" does not ordinarily present a proof of why a line drawn in a specified manner from the apex of an angle divides the angle into two equal parts. Rather, he describes a set of operations verbally and illustrates the description by performance. The presence of the expression naming the matter to be explained is usually a reliable clue to the procedure, and the expression "explain how" serves as further evidence. The possibility of confusion between explanation and description is thus avoided by means of the elements of the question.

Such a process of explanation-as-description is an appropriate part of instruction and in fact is often a necessary step in establishing the context for explanations of the relational type. But again, if questioning ceases with merely the "describe" usage of explanation, opportunities for extending understanding are neglected, and an occasion that might become fruitful for broadening knowledge of linguistic and logical processes fails to materialize.

2. Relational Usages

From another standpoint, however, a directive of the form "Explain the organization of the United Nations" does involve ambiguity. It can be interpreted descriptively in the manner indicated above as a non-relational type of explanation. But it may also be interpreted according to relational usages, that is, in a sense of accounting for, or of giving reasons for. These usages can be confused to the extent that one line of response may be offered when another is expected. For example, the original question "Explain the organization of the United Nations" might be viewed as the equivalent of "Why was the United Nations organized?" Responses along this line can take several forms according to the usage attached to the term "explain." A response can be a chronological or genetic explanation, a causal explanation, or a teleological explanation, that is, an explanation involving purposes.

The chronological or genetic response would contain a report of a highly selected series of composite events prior to the formation of the United Nations, such as earlier attempts at international organization, the activities of the League of Nations, and the events and conferences during World War II. Here the original question about the United Nations would be construed as "What developments led up to the organization of the United Nations?" If accepted as satisfactory, the explanation would thus refer to a narration of some selection of prior events.

On the other hand, for a causal explanation the question would be construed as "What causes or factors brought about the organization of the United

Nations?" A causal explanation customarily would categorize selected information by any one of such systems as political, economic, and social causes; internal and external (domestic and foreign) causes; primary and secondary causes; or underlying and immediate causes.

Still another usage would construe the formation of the United Nations not as an event, but as a set of decisions. This usage has been called "teleological," not in the nineteenth-century deterministic sense of events themselves somehow tending toward a fixed state, but in the sense that human beings make decisions in light of purposes or aims to be achieved. According to this usage, the question might be viewed as "For what reasons was the United Nations organized?"

The immediately foregoing usages of "explanation" may involve recurring breakdowns in classroom communication unless steps are taken to specify the meaning to be attached to "explain." However, procedures for avoiding the breakdown by sorting out the various lines of response can frequently be detected in classroom situations. These procedures may occur in the form of trace questions ("Trace the events or developments leading up to . . . ."); in the form of cause questions ("What were the causes of . . .?"); and in the form of reason or purpose questions ("What are the reasons for . . .?"). All of these kinds of explanation are commonly taken as pointing to some significant aspect of understanding, depending on the nature of the topic under consideration.

3. Scientific Explanation

There remains another usage of "explanation" that involves greater concern for the grounds of the particular explanations that are offered. Called "scientific explanation," it is a usage that is relational in that the processes are not only linguistic, but they are also concerned with reasoning. The procedures involve attention both to the kinds of statements in a particular explanation and to the relationships between them.

Instances of scientific explanation appear in connection with a *why* kind of question. A historical event is described, a phenomenon is encountered, and the question arises, "Why did this occur?" or "What brought this about?" The why question may assume a variety of linguistic forms, but at the heart of the matter is the attempt to account for the event or phenomenon by offering reasons or factors or influences. For this usage of explanation the relationships and the statements that are related can be seen in an instance from ordinary experience.

Take the common question "Why did the car tire go flat?" and a possible response or reason "There's a nail sticking in the groove of the tread." Here, an ordinary experience, the explanation is in the form of a "reason." The understanding or acceptance by the hearer of this reason-explanation rests on his familiarity with a general proposition, the generalization that tires with nails in them usually lose air. The generalization expresses a relationship between situations like the presence of nails in the walls of containers of compressed air and the level of air pressure in the containers. Since routine experience has familiarized practically everyone with this generalization, the reason is accepted, and the generalization is used as a basis for action in the form of looking for the nail and repairing the puncture. In this usage "explanation" refers to a set of logically related statements: first, a generalization of some kind; second, a recognition on the basis of evidence that the situation at hand is an instance of that generalization; and third, the usually tacitly accepted or obvious conclusion of a statement that describes the event to be explained. The first part—the generalization—is: Tires that have nails in them generally lose air. In this case the generalization is supported by common knowledge based on ordinary experience in a culture that often rides on air. The second part—recognition that the case at hand is an instance of that generalization (that there is in fact a nail in the tire)—is supported by evidence from direct observation. The third part—the conclusion—is a statement: The tire is flat. It is usually omitted from ordinary conversation or tacitly recognized by a gesture or exclamation of dismay, depending on the temperament of the car owner.

Although this structure is detectable, the matter to be explained as an item of ordinary experience is not a new and hitherto unaccounted for phenomenon from the perspective of the accumulated knowledge of a field of inquiry. For this reason the logical structure of the explanation is not called into issue, although it may be on other occasions. The focus of attention lies rather in the content of statements about existing conditions. The concern is to locate what in another manner of speaking (the Aristotelian manner) is called the "efficient cause."

When other concerns arise, as in the designing of teaching procedures, a recognition of the structure of scientific explanation enables the designer to see several different patterns with ensuing alternatives for teaching procedures. The pattern of scientific explanation is triadic, with three legs, like the old-fashioned milking stool or the tripod for an engineer's transit. Here the elements have been shown in the logical form of (1) generalization, (2) evidential statement, and (3) conclusion.

This pattern of scientific explanation and the statements comprising it are clearly distinct from the pattern established by the chronological sequence. The chronological sequence is composed of a series of statements describing a time-order of such events as the tire inflation, the nail piercing the tire wall, the air escaping, and the driver's noticing the flat tire. The logical form of the scientific explanation is also distinct from the pattern established by the psychological problem-solving sequence. In the problem-solving sequence the pattern involves these elements: first, the observation of a flat tire and the associated concern or dismay; second, an inference about the probable presence of a puncture as a source of the difficulty; third, the use of this inference as a hypothesis that there must be a nail somewhere; next, a test in the form of a search for the nail; and finally, a solution in the form of removal of the nail and repair of the tire. Logical form, chronological form, and problem-solving form thus represent different schema for viewing the matter. The first emphasizes analysis and understanding of relationships of statements. The second involves narrative and emphasizes time sequence. The third emphasizes action toward a new state of affairs.

An instance of scientific explanation in a more rigorous form is given by Hempel and Oppenheim.[2] In this context the structure of scientific explanation is again evident, along with criteria for the elements that make up that structure. The phenomenon to be explained—the explicandum—is the action of a mercury thermometer thrust into hot water.

A mercury thermometer is rapidly immersed in hot water; there occurs a temporary drop of the mercury column, which is then followed by a swift rise. How is this phenomenon to be explained? [Or, as the question might occur in classroom instruction, why did this happen?] The increase in temperature affects at first only the glass tube of the thermometer; it expands and thus provides a larger space for the mercury inside, whose surface therefore drops. As soon as by heat conduction the rise in temperature reaches the mercury, however, the latter expands, and as its coefficient of expansion is considerably larger than that of glass, a rise of the mercury results.

This account consists of statements of two kinds, according to Hempel and Oppenheim: "Statements of one kind express certain general laws; in our case these include the laws of the thermic expansion of mercury and of glass, and a statement about the small thermic conductivity of glass." These statements have the same function as the generalization about nails in tires in the less rigorously analyzed instance of the flat tire. Statements of the other kind "indicate certain conditions which are realized prior to or at the same time as, the phenomenon to be explained." Hempel and Oppenheim refer to them as "antecedent conditions." In the illustration the antecedent conditions include, among others, the fact that the thermometer consists of a glass tube which is partly filled with mercury and which is immersed in hot water. These antecedent conditions correspond in the case of the flat tire to statements about the structure of the tire, the air pressure, and the presence of the nail. "The two sets of statements, if adequately and completely formulated, explain the phenomenon under consideration. They entail the consequence that the mercury will first drop, then rise. Thus the event under discussion is explained by subsuming it under general laws, i.e., by showing that it occurred in accordance with those laws, by virtue of the realization of certain antecedent conditions."

[2]Carl G. Hempel and Paul Oppenheim, "Logic of Explanation," *Readings in the Philosophy of Science,* Herbert Feigl and May Brodbeck, eds. (New York: Appleton-Century-Crofts, Inc., 1953), pp. 319-52.

4. Criteria of Scientific Explanation

The structure of the explanation which Hempel and Oppenheim delineate is broadly similar to the more ordinary instance of the tire, but it is more complete in that the authors describe more of the law-statements and statements of antecedent conditions. With these instances in mind, it is possible to notice several of the criteria for the adequacy of an explanation in the sense of scientific explanation. Some of these criteria are logical and some are empirical — empirical in the sense of material or observable truth.

A first criterion has to do with internal consistency. The criterion of consistency may be seen by regarding the form of the explanation as a chain of reasoning, a chain in which the generalization statement is one premise, the evidential or subsuming statement of antecedent conditions is another premise, and the description of the event to be explained is a conclusion. This chain of reasoning must be as logically tight as possible. The reasoning should not run afoul of any of the logical fallacies, and any particular explanation would be deemed inadequate to the extent that it displayed such fallacies. In skeletal form the reasoning would appear something like this when stated as hypothetical or if-then reasoning: If any inner-tube tire is punctured, it ordinarily deflates; this tire is an inner-tube tire and it has been punctured; hence, this tire is deflated.

It is conceivable, of course, that in many instances of explanation there will be more than one such chain of reasoning. Often the phenomenon to be explained can be analyzed in several parts, as in the case of the thermometer. The mercury first falls slightly, then rises. An analogous case in tire inflation, of course, would occur if the tire were inflated to an excessively high pressure so that the tube split and then suddenly went flat. In the more complex cases, there will be several lines of reasoning, just as there are several lines of supporting ropes to the masts of ships or to radio and TV transmitter towers. For each line the criterion of logical consistency would be applicable.

A second criterion of adequacy is the presence of law-statements or generalizations. These are statements of a considerable degree of generality so that many instances of one kind of phenomena are brought together in one term of the generalization and related to many instances of another kind of phenomena brought together in the other term of the generalization. Instances of the application of heat to mercury are related to instances of the expansion of mercury. With such phenomena the relation has sufficient regularity and precision to be assigned the status of a law of thermic expansion. With other phenomena it may not be possible to state the relation with such precision nor to deduce the law from still broader statements. Thermic expansion, for example, can be deduced from statements about molecular action. In the less rigorous cases the expression "generalization" or "law-like statement" or "statement of greater or less probability" may be more fitting than the expression "law."

But aside from the question of the probability status, the generalization should be broad enough to avoid being trivial. It should not be so limited as to have no explanatory power or to offer no ground for action if the case is concerned with changing states of affiars. A trivial explanation in the tire instance would perhaps be the following: To the question "Why is the tire flat?" the answer might be "Because there isn't any air in it." Another example would be the retort to the question "Why are you pushing your car?" — "Because it won't go." In social studies the question "Why did the colonists migrate?" might be answered trivially, "Because they wanted to go to some other location." In this sense a trivial explanation offers as a statement in its premises merely another version of the conclusion, and thus is logically circular. To go to some other location in effect means to migrate. For a tire to be flat means not to have any air in it. In such explanations the logical requirement is infringed by virtue of the fallacy of circularity.

In other cases it may be that the triviality of an explanation lies not in circularity, but in the degree of familiarity, and that an explanation or reason which is trivial to one person may not be trivial to someone else who is reaching a new individual level of understanding. In these cases assessment of triviality turns not on the logical matter of fallacy, but on the psychological matter of the level of understanding of the parties to the explanation process. In any case, for a scientific explanation the criterion of breadth depends on the nature of the question and the kind of inquiry in which the explanation question arises. In general, the presence of some more or less rigorous generalizations with considerable breadth of explanatory power is a vital element.

It is in this latter connection that explanation in classroom situations is frequently remiss. In social studies, for example, those who make explanations — text authors, teachers, students, and often the original investigators — fail to recognize the role of generalizations and neglect to attempt to formulate them. Teachers, often unaware of the role of generalizations, do not encourage students to use them. Instead, in much instruction teachers accept a list of reasons which constitute only one of the elements of scientific explanation. In the neglect, opportunities to cultivate both appreciation for deduction and for the nature of generalization in a legitimate manner are continuously lost from processes of instruction.

A third criterion of the elements of a formal explanation is an empirical one. The generalizations must be testable by procedures which follow recognized canons of inquiry. This empirical criterion is applicable to those matters which are themselves social events or physical phenomena. For those matters to be explained which are non-empirical — a rule or a principle, for example — the premises need to be grounded on some other foundation, such as consistency within the system of which they are a part. But in the case of physical events like the tire going flat or the thermometer changing, empirical testing procedures are available. In the instance of the tire, the generalization about nail punctures and flat tires is obviously at a level easily tested by direct observation. The laws about thermic expansion are also testable, although presumably in a laboratory context. In the case of economic or political generalizations, testability may be less rigorous and will usually require inquiry in a broader arena of space and time, such as the arena of national histories.

A case in point from the realm of economic activity is Gresham's law — the generalization loosely expressed to the effect that bad money drives good money out of circulation. This so-called law is ordinarily used to account for some aspects of events related to monetary or currency inflation, such as the hoarding of the more reliable forms of coinage. For this law the accumulation and the weighing of evidence comprise the testing process, and this process requires examination of a series of instances of monetary inflation or of purposeful currency depreciation, such as the reduction of the amount of silver in the standard coinage. The series of instances may include the monetary practices of European kings who called in some denominations of coins, melted them down, and reissued them with a lower proportion of silver. The instances also might include cases of currency depreciation in the American revolutionary era, as well as the printed money inflation in Austria and Germany after the First World War. Such similar instances serve as a basis for examining what has occurred at times when both good and bad money have been in circulation and where there has been some kind of change in the nature of the circulating medium.

Investigations of this scope may not often take place in social studies classes. Sometimes, in American history texts at least, the generalization about good and bad money is stated, and it is usually accepted as part of the given nature of economic activity. But the generalization remains open to scrutiny on the basis of evidence, whether or not in a customary subject matter it actually gets examined.

In the political realm the arena for the collection of evidence might be less extensive, depending on the phenomena to be explained. For example, the recent defeat of proportional representation in a municipal election in Cincinnati was explained by some commentators, in part, by reference to the strength of the county Republican organization, which was opposed to the proportional system of representation. For this event the generalization would be: If in any local election one party is thoroughly organized, compared to the other, the position of the less organized party is usually defeated. The explanation would continue with the statement of antecedent conditions that in the Cincinnati election the county Republican group, compared to the pro-PR group, was in fact thoroughly organized with an active and complete roster of ward and precinct officials and captains, and that it was opposed to proportional representation. The conclusion would be: Hence, proportional representation was defeated.

The test of the generalization about election success and party organization would rest on the study of a series of municipal elections with instances of thorough party organization and of election success and failure. The test would thus take into account both positive and negative evidence and so conform more closely to recognized standards of inquiry. It would also conform to appropriate sampling procedure. Such an inquiry in the field of American municipal government may not actually have been performed by political scientists, but certainly the generalization about careful organization is a well-known maxim of practical politics.

Another point to notice about the nature of the generalizations employed, especially in social studies, is that they are not the loose, didactic kind of claim to the effect that history shows this or history shows that. They are, instead, carefully examined or examinable propositions within a delimited context of similar instances and with terms which can be precisely defined. The term "thorough party organization," for example, can be defined by counting wards and precincts, stating a proportion of ward and precinct officials to available positions, and noting the level of activity of getting voters registered and to the polls. Further, the generalizations are not the sweeping, so-called laws of civilization or decay in which inclusiveness of phenomena and looseness of definition of terms are so great that the generalizations may make interesting speculative literature but defy examination by careful weighing of positive and negative evidence.

A fourth criterion of the adequacy of an explanation pertinent to the world of events and physical phenomena is the obvious one of empirical truth. The weight of evidence concerning the explanatory generalizations must support them. It must be the case that thorough party organization *is* associated with election success, or that bad money *does* drive good money out of circulation. Also, the statement of antecedent conditions must be true. The total array of evidence must support the report that these conditions do prevail, whether the evidence is from direct observation, as in watching activities of precinct captains, or whether it is documentary and a summary of statistical data, as in the case of reports about the nature of the money in circulation.

5. Relational Explanation in Historical Study

With the pattern of formal explanation in mind, and with recognition of the criteria for the selection and relationship of those elements, it is useful to note one or two other examples of explanation drawn from historical study. Common questions in history courses are, "Why was there a war between the North and South?" or "Why did some North American colonies revolt against England?" or "Why was there a revolution in France against the Old Regime?" For questions like these the generalizations can be expressed also in the form of if-then statements. For the Civil War question, the statement would be in this form: If nations exhibit *A, B, C* characteristics, then there is usually a civil war. In this case, the characteristics according to historical scholarship would include such variables as the kind of governmental structure, a kind of economic and property structure, a geographical and political configuration usually called sectionalism, and a set of ideological beliefs. The explanation in prose form would consist, first, of an assertion of some such complex generalization as a whole, or in separate statements, and evidence from civil wars in general in the context of modern nations to indicate the soundness of the generalization. Second, the explanation would consist of assertions with supporting evidence that these variables in a particular configuration did exist in the United States at a particular time. Third, it would consist of the conclusion that therefore there was a war between the North and the South.

In the case of the French Revolution the explanation would include a generalization of this kind: If monarchies exhibit D, E, F features, there is usually a revolution. Second, there would be evidence to show that the French Old Regime did exhibit these characteristics; and third, there would be the conclusion about the occurrence of the conflict. An adequate explanation thus can be seen as a kind of "explanation sketch," to use a term suggested by Hempel[3] in another discussion of explanation. These sketches may be relatively brief (not more than two or three sentences) when the topic is not judged to be important enough to explore in detail. For other topics the explanation sketches may be considerably longer.

In this connection, notice that explanations may be carried on at different levels of generality and inclusiveness. A particular observable phenomenon may be explained in terms of low-level laws, as the rise of the mercury is explained by the law of expansion. The law of expansion in turn may be explained by a broader or higher level law about the relationship of molecular activity and heat. The breadth or level of this explanation or the inclusiveness of the propositions in the explanation depends again on the context of the inquiry and on the kind of questions raised in initiating the explanation.

In much historical material there are several levels and contexts intermixed. When historical inquiry is directed toward particular figures — political party leaders, presidents, kings, prime ministers, diplomats, generals, administrators — the accounts are at the biographical level. When the biography is detailed and extensive, the explanatory generalizations, either explicit or implicit, may be from the area of psychology. Often individual actions are explained in terms of purpose or intent. Jefferson's purchase of Louisiana is usually explained by saying that his purpose or intent was to secure certain objectives. If the pattern of scientific explanation is to be followed carefully, however, the generalizations in these individual psychological explanations would take this form: If

---

[3]Carl G. Hempel, "The Function of General Laws in History," *Readings in Philosophical Analysis,* Herbert Feigl and Wilfrid Sellars, eds. (New York: Appleton-Century-Crofts, Inc., 1949), pp. 510-14.

persons of *A, B, C* characteristics are in situations of *D, E, F* kind, they commonly act in *P, Q, R* fashion. The "*A, B, C* characteristics" refers to the beliefs, attitudes, and information of the individual. The "*D, E, F* kind of situations" refers to the configuation of the state of affairs with which the individuals are dealing. The "*P, Q, R* fashion" refers to the performances associated with such individuals in such situations. Thus Lincoln, with a given temperament and confronted with certain situations, customarily told humorous stories, or on other matters selected the policies that led to preservation of the federal union.

At another level explanation may be dealing with groups of people rather than with individuals — Puritans, apprentices, colonial merchants, industrial managers, frontier trappers, European migrants, selected ethnic groups in one or another section of the country. At this level the generalizations are often drawn from the area of social psychology. At still another level the explanation may be dealing with broad states of affairs and complexes of events, such as structures of government, monetary systems, and systems of production. With each level the context of the explanatory generalizations will be of a different order, and the generalizations will be drawn from different social science disciplines — political science, economics, sociology, social psychology, or geography. It is through assumption or explicit statement of different levels of generalizations and from explanatory generalizations drawn from different disciplines that historical inquiry yields different historical interpretations and different historical syntheses, such as the frontier synthesis, the economic interpretation, and the constitutional interpretation in American history.

The usage of "explanation" as scientific explanation or the usage of "explanation" as an explanation sketch involving explicit generalizations is undoubtedly different from the pattern usually encountered in classroom instruction or in ordinary teaching materials. The commonly encountered form is a kind of truncated or incomplete form. Classroom explanations usually call for lists of reasons or causes, and texts commonly offer such lists. In some cases, as in social studies where certain events have customarily received more attention — the colonization movement, the American Revolution, most wars, and some economic movements, in American history courses at least — the lists of reasons are fairly elaborate. In most cases, however, the reasons are only partial statements of antecedent conditions — statements to the effect that such and such conditions did in fact exist. These explanations are truncated in the sense that the generalizations (political, economic, social, or psychological) are usually omitted. The content of the reasons may be detailed in description, and it even may be absorbing narrative, but it is not related as evidence for a conclusion about the occurrence of an event, since the other premise or set of premises — the generalizations — are missing.

Occasionally, too, the explanation offered or expected is in the form of a recital of a series of events. This is often the case with accounts of affairs in the decade before the American Revolution. The various acts and policies of the successive British ministries are presented in chronological order. This recital of events is similar to the chronological account of the tire going flat. It is simply a listing of occurrences. A recital of events may clearly have a legitimate place in instruction as one step toward a kind of factual knowledge, but it is often taken as *the* explanation instead of being viewed more accurately as one usage of explanation. It is perhaps this confusion of chronological explanation with scientific explanation that leads to the common fallacy of *post hoc ergo propter hoc* — that an event *B* which occurs after an event *A* is the result of *A* or is accounted for by *A*. Students accustomed only to explanations by chronology have little equipment available to help them examine the weaknesses in *post hoc* explanations. They are habituated only to searching in the arena of earlier events for the explanations for later events, and they are not accustomed to the additional search for assumed generalizations about relations of political, economic, and sociological phenomena. They are accustomed to accepting explanations as "reasons for," rather than to examining and reflecting about explanations as chains of reasoning based on assumed generalizations about some aspect of the total social order. "Explanation" solely as a chronology or list of reasons thus creates an instructional situation which stops short of a more careful analysis and which ignores the danger of running aground on fallacious reasoning.

There are, then, several usages of "explanation" embedded in instructional activities and materials, one of which when viewed in its complete pattern is referred to as "scientific explanation." If, along with other usages when they are appropriate to immediate instructional purposes, scientific explanation is taken into consideration, there are a number of implications for instructional design. Some of them are cautionary. For example, not all instances of this usage of explanation will be occasions for focus on the logical structure or even on the generalizations which are assumed. Some generalizations may not be worth special attention in instruction. Instead, they may be accepted as given or as items of common-sense familiarity. If the question arises, "Why did people migrate in large numbers to California in 1848-49?" it can be met in the incomplete form by the answer, "Because gold was discovered there." The generalization that people will flock to areas where valuable minerals are newly discovered, or simply that many people are attracted by prospective riches, is probably not a new insight into social phenomena for most students. Here, the process of detecting and formulating it as a generalization is not worth the time.

On the other hand, if explanations in general are to be improved in teaching and in inquiry, both their content and their structure will be objects of attention, and instruction associated with explanations will be designed in part to show several things: the nature of generalizations as distinct from particulars and from over-generalizations; the role of generalizations as premises in explanations which in a more complete pattern are one form of logical reasoning; the kinds of errors that can creep into an explanation, as indicated by both the logical and empirical criteria; the processes for testing the statements that comprise the explanation; and the procedures for defining terms to eliminate shifts of meaning in the explanation.

In brief, employment of the various usages of explanation, including scientific explanation, offers broader opportunities for developing understanding in a particular discipline as well as for developing knowledge and skill in the use of significant tools for rigorous thinking and for careful inquiry.

Introduction

Explanation and Art History

Just as a response to the question "What is art?" can influence curricular decisions, so answers to questions concerning the nature of art history can affect the ways in which art-historical knowledge functions in art instruction.

One of the classic delineations of art history is Erwin Panofsky's "The History of Art as a Humanistic Discipline." In calling the history of art a humanistic rather than a scientific discipline, Panofsky is concerned to distinguish the object and method of investigation of the humanist from the object and method of inquiry of the natural scientist. Science, it is asserted, transforms the variety of natural phenomena into a cosmos of nature, whereas the humanities transform the variety of human records into a cosmos of culture. In the latter process, writes Panofsky, the art historian as humanist manifests a special quality of synthetic intuition that involves re-creating the artistic intentions to which monuments or works of art bear witness. It is this re-creating of artistic intentions that requires the art historian to assume a distinctive attitude toward his materials.

But Panofsky is also quick to point out the similarities between the methods of the humanist and the scientist. In the methods of each, for example, investigation begins with observation. The selection of an object of investigation, moreover, is governed by a guiding hypothesis, that is, a general theory on the part of the scientist and a general historical conception on the part of the humanist. Furthermore, whatever is brought to light during investigation must be interpreted within the boundaries set by the field of inquiry. The rendering of "intelligibility" also entails arts of description, classification, interpretation, and explanation, including judgments about the "truth" or "correctness" of the guiding theory or historical conception. Finally, conclusions in both domains are reported in appropriate language to communities of experts for confirmation or disconfirmation.

That the art historian needs a working definition of art is also stressed by Panofsky. What is art? Art is a man-made object demanding to be experienced aesthetically. It follows that the art historian's task is to make explicit the multifarious aspects—formal, social, personal—that give rise to the unique aesthetic demands works of art make on beholders.

If teachers and students are sometimes bewildered by, and occasionally even hostile toward, the explanations of art historians, it is perhaps because the methodology of art history is not sufficiently understood. There are an unusually large number of things an art historian must get right before he can report his conclusions. For example, in another important essay Panofsky has indicated that explanation may proceed at three levels.[1] First is pre-iconographical description which entails enumeration of motifs, or pure forms having primary or natural meanings. Prerequisite for correct pre-iconographical description are wide practical experience and expert knowledge of the history of style. The second discipline in the repertory of art-historical method is iconographical analysis, which combines motifs into images, allegories, and stories. In addition to the kind of knowledge required in pre-iconographical description, the art historian at this level must possess cultivated familiarity with literary sources and the history of types. Third, and most important, is the discipline of iconological interpretation which determines the intrinsic meaning of a work of art. Building upon correct pre-iconographical description and iconographical analysis, explanation at this level sees a work of art as a symptom of a situation in the history of culture and ideas, as a distillation through the personality of the artist of the underlying principles and attitudes of an age or nation. Once again, for such interpretation the art historian must be endowed with what was previously called synthetic intuition, and, furthermore, must have a firm grasp of the history of cultural symptoms. The journey from the lower to the higher and more encompassing planes of art-historical explanation may be long and arduous and fraught with innumerable details and complexities, but it is characteristic of the ground rules of art-historical scholarship that travelers must present evidence of having made the trip.

One of the chief problems with iconological method has been the difficulty involved in knowing when a particular element of a work is represented in its own right and when it is a symbol of something else. Consequently, iconology has been accused of imparting more symbolic meaning to a work than was intended by the artist.[2] This obstacle can only be circumvented, it is emphasized, by scrupulous attention to secondary sources so as to ascertain the ideas, symbols, and trends with which the artist can reasonably be assumed to have been familiar and which were congenial to his personality and style.

It would be misleading, however, to give the impression that iconography and iconology have always been the mainsprings of methodology in art history. The character of art-historical scholarship has varied depending on the assumptions thinkers have brought to their work and on the nature of the works of

---

[1]Erwin Panofsky, "Iconography and Iconology: An Introduction to the Study of Renaissance Art," *Meaning in the Visual Arts* (New York: Doubleday Anchor Books, 1955).
[2]For a summary of Panofsky's views and a brief criticism of iconological method, see Jan Bialostocki, "Iconography and Iconology," *Encyclopedia of World Art*, Vol. VII (New York: McGraw-Hill Book Co., Inc., 1963), columns 769-85.

art investigated. Thus Walter Abell in "Toward a Unified Field in Critical Studies" shows that theories about art reflect roughly the same kinds of evolutionary tendencies that art reveals. These major critical traditions are conveniently summarized by Abell as iconography, biographical criticism, historical determinism, aesthetic materialism, aesthetic teleology, and pure visibility. All of these traditions, says Abell, are important for understanding the character of art. His specific concern, however, is to find a basis for unifying different viewpoints into an encompassing system that does justice to individual theories while denying the claim of any single theory to comprehensiveness.

A psycho-historical theory of culture is Abell's contribution. This theory explains art in connection with the transformation of social pressures which are taken as the ultimate determinants of human feeling. This symbolic transformation occurs, it is claimed, through the working of an obscure tension-imagery process within the psyche. The study of art, therefore, must proceed at the foundation level of depth history, at the transformative level of depth psychology, and at the level of criticism of varied forms of cultural expressions. Whatever the difficulties in Abell's theory, his observation that the situation in art history resembles that in astronomy before the discoveries of Kepler helps us to understand the need to incorporate the factual data of art history into broader explanatory generalizations.

The problem of explanation is treated explicitly by Thomas Munro in "Levels of Explanation in the History of Art." Throughout these editor's comments the terms explanation and interpretation have been used interchangeably, as indeed they are by art historians themselves. But in studies devoted to the concept of explanation, efforts are often made to restrict the use of explanation to models which exhibit a deductive structure, or as Swift points out, models which display the pattern of scientific explanation. In such models, the thing to be explained is a logically necessary consequence of the explanatory premises. Munro says we can think of explanation in the ordinary sense of making something clear, that is, in the sense of reaching an understanding of the cause or origin of something, and in a more rigorous sense of showing how universal laws explain causal relations or descriptive connections. Rigorous explanations of this latter sort are extremely difficult, if not impossible, to achieve in historical scholarship. But Munro argues that we can get along with partial, limited explanations which assert that in light of current knowledge, events of character G *tend* to occur regularly in conjunction with conditions, say, D, E, F. In explanations of this type, says Munro, the most we can hope for are empirical correlations of the kind that show, for example, that a complicative evolutionary tendency of culture in general will ordinarily produce a complicative evolutionary tendency in art. The rules for formulating partial explanations demand the necessary proximity of elements purporting to explain something, evidence that such elements were in fact operative in antecedents, and consideration of differential as well as common factors affecting the work of artists.

As for the meaning of evolution in the arts, Munro favors a pluralistic hypothesis or a moderate flexible determinism. That is to say, the character of art is influenced "by the increasing practical value, intellectual interest, and aesthetic satisfaction of growing mentally and building more culturally elaborate forms."

Sociological explanation of art, says Arnold Hauser in "The Scope and Limitations of a Sociology of Art," makes claim to scientific status despite the fact that no general laws can be formulated to explain the causal relations between art forms and socioeconomic forms.[3] Hauser's notion of sociological explanation then is a form of what Munro calls partial or limited explanation. Hauser's leading principle is that "everything in history is the achievement of individuals; individuals always find themselves in a certain definite situation in time and place; their behavior is the product both of their own inborn capacities and of the situation."

What specifically is involved in sociological accounts of art? For Hauser this implies an approach to style criticism that relies upon the grasping of typical relationships which enable one to infer causes of stylistic change. Not style as such, then, but style *and* social change, or the form and dynamics of style, are the central concern of investigation. Only psychological and sociological explanations are adequate for this purpose, claims Hauser, for understanding requires relating the work of art to psychic and collective aspirations. Some products of medieval art, for instance, are best explained not only in connection with the tenets of Scholastic philosophy, which certain works have been purported to express, but also in relation to the medieval system of feudalism, the credo of chivalry, the development of new urban centers and classes, and advancing technology, not to mention the new organizations of work in the monasteries and masons' lodges and guilds.[4]

In brief, sociological method seeks to give answers to "why" questions: Why at different times in history should artists decide to express themselves in optical rather than tactile modes? with recessional rather than planar spatial organizations? with more or less visual complexity? Finally, Hauser points out, strictly sociological explanation does not aim to account for individual genius. It merely requires, on the one hand, the recognition that spiritual human endeavor is in tension with material conditions of living and, on the other, that this tension is partly a product of social forces. Much in other words can be said about the efforts of artists and the nature of art without destroying art's special character. The social aspects of art have been neglected too long in art instruction, and it is hoped that Hauser's essay, along with others in this

---

[3]Arnold Hauser, *The Philosophy of Art History* (New York: Alfred A. Knopf, Inc., 1959), p. 272.
[4]*Ibid.*, p. 260.

section, will encourage teachers and students to seek understanding of the broader contextual setting in which works of art are made and appreciated.

It is seen that the concept of "style" figures prominently in the investigations of art historians. Indeed, the concept of style currently provides the basic structure for the history of art. Among the several definitions one of the most interesting is James S. Ackerman's notion in "Style" that style is "a class of related solutions to a problem — or responses to a challenge — that may be said to begin whenever artists begin to pursue a problem or react to a challenge that differs significantly from those posed by the prevailing style or styles." Using the image of style as a means of establishing orderly relationships among works of art, Ackerman attributes stylistic innovation to the tension between stability and change, a condition to which the artist must perforce submit. Avoiding deterministic biological metaphors, or images of cyclical evolution, Ackerman sets forth a contextual approach to the study of art in which perspectives on style formation are gained *within* the process itself. In this view, works of art are seen not as tending successively *toward* the solution of a given problem but rather as a succession of steps *away from* one or more original solutions of a problem. Change in style, that is to say, is explained as the manifestation of the artist's creativity and imagination and not exclusively of social and historical forces.

Ackerman's essay prompts several interesting pedagogical questions. In selecting exemplars of art for serious study in the schools, for example, should only what Ackerman calls "destiny fulfilling" works be approved? Or are some "destiny denying" works candidates for study? Furthermore, is it desirable, in consideration of built-in value judgments, to retain the language of "High" or "Classic" for the cultural periods and styles included in the preparation of instructional units? Would not furthermore transitional periods be peculiarly relevant for study inasmuch as during such periods the process of rejecting, retaining, and forming new elements of style is most discernible? Of course, answers to these questions, and others that could be raised, will depend on how teachers interpret the objectives of art instruction. For example, in an age when aesthetic responsibility is becoming a form of genuine freedom and individuality, the image of the artist expressing *his* freedom and imagination by retaining or rejecting elements of style during a period undergoing change may be pedagogically relevant. On the other hand, if it is the *work of art*, and not the *artist*, that is taken to be the source of greater educational value, then art history will be put to different uses. And there is much to be said for this latter point of view. This issue, of course, is simply another instance of the "process *v*. product" argument in art education.[5]

---

[5]Also at issue are senses of "artistic expression." For a helpful discussion of artistic expression as process, communication, evocation, and properties, see John Hospers, "The Concept of Artistic Expression," *Proceedings of the Aristotelian Society,* Vol. LV (1954-55), pp. 313-44. Reprinted with some changes in Morris Weitz (ed.), *Problems in Aesthetics* (New York: The Macmillan Co., 1959), pp. 193-217.

The History of Art as a
Humanistic Discipline

ERWIN PANOFSKY

I

Nine days before his death Immanuel Kant was visited by his physician. Old, ill and nearly blind, he rose from his chair and stood trembling with weakness and muttering unintelligible words. Finally his faithful companion realized that he would not sit down again until the visitor had taken a seat. This he did, and Kant then permitted himself to be helped to his chair and, after having regained some of his strength, said, "Das Gefühl für Humanität hat mich noch nicht verlassen"—"The sense of humanity has not yet left me"[1] The two men were moved almost to tears. For, though the word *Humanität* had come, in the eighteenth century, to mean little more than politeness or civility, it had, for Kant, a much deeper significance, which the circumstances of the moment served to emphasize: man's proud and tragic consciousness of self-approved and self-imposed principles, contrasting with his utter subjection to illness, decay and all that is implied in the word "mortality."

Historically the word *humanitas* has had two clearly distinguishable mean-

From *Meaning in the Visual Arts* by Erwin Panofsky. Copyright © 1955 by Erwin Panofsky. Reprinted by permission of the author and Doubleday & Company, Inc.
[1]E. A. C. Wasianski, *Immanuel Kant in seinen letzten Lebensjahren (Ueber Immanuel Kant*, 1804, Vol. III), reprinted in *Immanuel Kant, Sein Leben in Darstellungen von Zeitgenossen*, Deutsche Bibliothek, Berlin, 1912, p. 298.

ings, the first arising from a contrast between man and what is less than man; the second, between man and what is more. In the first case *humanitas* means a value, in the second a limitation.

The concept of *humanitas* as a value was formulated in the circle around the younger Scipio, with Cicero as its belated, yet most explicit spokesman. It meant the quality which distinguishes man, not only from animals, but also, and even more so, from him who belongs to the species *homo* without deserving the name of *homo humanus;* from the barbarian or vulgarian who lacks *pietas* and παιδεία—that is, respect for moral values and that gracious blend of learning and urbanity which we can only circumscribe by the discredited word "culture."

In the Middle Ages this concept was displaced by the consideration of humanity as being opposed to divinity rather than to animality or barbarism. The qualities commonly associated with it were therefore those of frailty and transience: *humanitas fragilis, humanitas caduca.*

Thus the Renaissance conception of *humanitas* had a twofold aspect from the outset. The new interest in the human being was based both on a revival of the classical antithesis between *humanitas* and *barbaritas,* or *feritas,* and on a survival of the mediaeval antithesis between *humanitas* and *divinitas.* When Marsilio Ficino defines man as a "rational soul participating in the intellect of God, but operating in a body," he defines him as the one being that is both autonomous and finite. And Pico's famous "speech," "On the Dignity of Man," is anything but a document of paganism. Pico says that God placed man in the center of the universe so that he might be conscious of where he stands, and therefore free to decide "where to turn." He does not say that man *is* the center of the universe, not even in the sense of the classical phrase, "man the measure of all things."

It is from this ambivalent conception of *humanitas* that humanism was born. It is not so much a movement as an attitude which can be defined as the conviction of the dignity of man, based on both the insistence on human values (rationality and freedom) and the acceptance of human limitations (fallibility and frailty); from this two postulates result—responsibility and tolerance.

Small wonder that this attitude has been attacked from two opposite camps whose common aversion to the ideas of responsibility and tolerance has recently aligned them in a united front. Entrenched in one of these camps are those who deny human values: the determinists, whether they believe in divine, physical or social predestination, the authoritarians, and those "insectolatrists" who profess the all-importance of the hive, whether the hive be called group, class, nation or race. In the other camp are those who deny human limitations in favor of some sort of intellectual or political libertinism, such as aestheticists, vitalists, intuitionists and hero-worshipers. From the point of view of determinism, the humanist is either a lost soul or an ideologist. From the point of view of authoritarianism, he is either a heretic or a revolutionary (or a counter-revolutionary). From the point of view of "insectolatry," he is a useless individualist. And from the point of view of libertinism he is a timid bourgeois.

Erasmus of Rotterdam, the humanist *par excellence,* is a typical case in point. The church suspected and ultimately rejected the writings of this man who had said: "Perhaps the spirit of Christ is more largely diffused than we think, and there are many in the commmunity of saints who are not in our calendar." The adventurer Ulrich von Hutten despised his ironical scepticism and his unheroic love of tranquillity. And Luther, who insisted that "no man has power to think anything good or evil, but everything occurs in him by absolute necessity," was incensed by a belief which manifested itself in the famous phrase: "What is the use of man as a totality [that is, of man endowed with both a body and a soul], if God would work in him as a sculptor works in clay, and might just as well work in stone?"[2]

II

The humanist, then, rejects authority. But he respects tradition. Not only does he respect it, he looks upon it as upon something real and objective which has to be studied and, if necessary, reinstated: *"nos vetera instauramus, nova non prodimus,"* as Erasmus puts it.

The Middle Ages accepted and developed rather than studied and restored the heritage of the past. They copied classical works of art and used Aristotle and Ovid much as they copied and used the works of contemporaries. They made no attempt to interpret them from an archaeological, philological or "critical," in short, from an historical, point of view. For, if human existence could be thought of as a means rather than an end, how much less could the records of human activity be considered as values in themselves.[3]

---

[2]For the quotations from Luther and Erasmus of Rotterdam see the excellent monograph *Humanitas Erasmiana* by R. Pfeiffer, Studien der Bibliothek Warburg, XXII, 1931. It is significant that Erasmus and Luther rejected judicial or fatalistic astrology for totally different reasons: Erasmus refused to believe that human destiny depends on the unalterable movements of the celestial bodies, because such a belief would amount to a denial of human free will and responsibility; Luther, because it would amount to a restriction of the omnipotence of God. Luther therefore believed in the significance of *terata,* such as eight-footed calves, etc., which God can cause to appear at irregular intervals.
[3]Some historians seem to be unable to recognize continuities and distinctions at the same time. It is undeniable that humanism, and the entire Renaissance movement, did not spring forth like Athena from the head of Zeus. But the fact that Lupus of Ferrières emended classical texts, that Hildebert of Lavardin had a strong feeling for the ruins of Rome, that the French and English scholars of the twelfth century revived classical philosophy and mythology, and that Marbod of Rennes wrote a fine pastoral poem on his small country estate, does not mean that their outlook was identical with that of Petrarch, let alone of Ficino or Erasmus. No mediaeval man could see the civilization of antiquity as a phenomenon complete in itself and historically detached from the contemporary world; as far as I know, mediaeval Latin has no equivalent to the humanistic *"antiquitas"* or *"sacrosancta vetustas."* And just as it was impossible for the Middle Ages to elaborate a system of perspective based on the realization of a fixed distance between the eye and the object, so it was equally impossible for this

In mediaeval scholasticism there is, therefore; no basic distinction between natural science and what we call the humanities, *studia humaniora,* to quote again an Erasmian phrase. The practice of both, so far as it was carried on at all, remained within the framework of what was called philosophy. From the humanistic point of view, however, it became reasonable, and even inevitable, to distinguish, within the realm of creation, between the sphere of *nature* and the sphere of *culture,* and to define the former with reference to the latter, *i.e.* nature as the whole world accessible to the senses, except for the *records left by man.*

Man is indeed the only animal to leave records behind him, for he is the only animal whose products "recall to mind" an idea distinct from their material existence. Other animals use signs and contrive structures, but they use signs without "perceiving the relation of signification,"[4] and they contrive structures without perceiving the relation of construction.

To perceive the relation of signification is to separate the idea of the concept to be expressed from the means of expression. And to perceive the relation of construction is to separate the idea of the function to be fulfilled from the means of fulfilling it. A dog announces the approach of a stranger by a bark quite different from that by which he makes known his wish to go out. But he will not use this particular bark to convey the idea that a stranger *has* called during the absence of his master. Much less will an animal, even if it were physically able to do so, as apes indubitably are, ever attempt to represent anything in a picture. Beavers build dams. But they are unable, so far as we know, to separate the very complicated actions involved from a premeditated *plan* which might be laid down in a drawing instead of being materialized in logs and stones.

Man's signs and structures are records because, or rather in so far as, they express ideas separated from, yet realized by, the processes of signaling and building. These records have therefore the quality of emerging from the stream of time, and it is precisely in this respect that they are studied by the humanist. He is, fundamentally, an historian.

The scientist, too, deals with human records, namely with the works of his predecessors. But he deals with them not as something to be investigated, but as something which helps him to investigate. In other words, he is interested in records not in so far as they emerge from the stream of time, but in so far as they are absorbed in it. If a modern scientist reads Newton or Leonardo da Vinci in the original, he does so not as a scientist, but as a man interested in the

---

period to evolve an idea of historical disciplines based on the realization of a fixed distance between the present and the classical past. See E. Panofsky and F. Saxl, "Classical Mythology in Mediaeval Art," *Studies of the Metropolitan Museum,* IV, 2, 1933, pp. 228 ff., particularly pp. 263 ff., and recently the interesting article by W. S. Heckscher, "Relics of Pagan Antiquity in Mediaeval Settings," *Journal of the Warburg Institute,* I, 1937, pp. 204 ff.

[4]See J. Maritain, "Sign and Symbol," *Journal of the Warburg Institute,* I, 1937, pp. 1 ff.

history of science and therefore of human civilization in general. In other words, he does it as a *humanist*, for whom the works of Newton or Leonardo da Vinci have an autonomous meaning and a lasting value. From the humanistic point of view, human records do not age.

Thus, while science endeavors to transform the chaotic variety of natural phenomena into what may be called a cosmos of nature, the humanities endeavor to transform the chaotic variety of human records into what may be called a cosmos of culture.

There are, in spite of all the differences in subject and procedure, some very striking analogies between the methodical problems to be coped with by the scientist, on the one hand, and by the humanist, on the other.[5]

In both cases the process of investigation seems to begin with observation. But both the observer of a natural phenomenon and the examiner of a record are not only confined to the limits of their range of vision and to the available material; in directing their attention to *certain* objects they obey, knowingly or not, a principle of pre-selection dictated by a theory in the case of the scientist and by a general historical conception in the case of the humanist. It may be true that "nothing is in the mind except what was in the senses"; but it is at least equally true that much is in the senses without ever penetrating into the mind. We are chiefly affected by that which we allow to affect us; and just as natural science involuntarily selects what it calls the phenomena, the humanities involuntarily select what they call the historical facts. Thus the humanities have gradually widened their cultural cosmos and in some measure have shifted the accents of their interests. Even he who instinctively sympathizes with the simple definition of the humanities as "Latin and Greek" and considers this definition as essentially valid as long as we use such ideas and expressions as, for instance, "idea" and "expression" — even he has to admit that it has become a trifle narrow.

Furthermore, the world of the humanities is determined by a cultural theory of relativity, comparable to that of the physicists; and since the cosmos of culture is so much smaller than the cosmos of nature, cultural relativity prevails within terrestrial dimensions, and was observed at a much earlier date.

Every historical concept is obviously based on the categories of space and time. The records, and what they imply, have to be dated and located. But it turns out that these two acts are in reality two aspects of one. If I date a picture about 1400, this statement would be meaningless if I could not indicate *where* it could have been produced at that date; conversely, if I ascribe a picture to the Florentine school, I must be able to tell *when* it could have been produced in

---

[5]See E. Wind, *Das Experiment und die Metaphysik,* Tübingen, 1934, and *idem,* "Some Points of Contact between History and Natural Science," *Philosophy and History, Essays presented to Ernst Cassirer,* Oxford, 1936, pp. 255 ff. (with a very instructive discussion of the relationship between phenomena, instruments and the observer, on the one hand, and historical facts, documents and the historian, on the other).

that school. The cosmos of culture, like the cosmos of nature, is a spatio-temporal structure. The year 1400 means something different in Venice from what it means in Florence, to say nothing of Augsburg, or Russia, or Constantinople. Two historical phenomena are simultaneous, or have a determinable temporal relation to each other, only in so far as they can be related within one "frame of reference," in the absence of which the very concept of simultaneity would be as meaningless in history as it would be in physics. If we knew by some concatenation of circumstances that a certain negro sculpture had been executed in 1510, it would be meaningless to say that it was "contemporaneous" with Michelangelo's Sistine ceiling.[6]

Finally, the succession of steps by which the material is organized into a natural or cultural cosmos is analogous, and the same is true of the methodical problems implied by this process. The first step is, as has already been mentioned, the observation of natural phenomena and the examination of human records. Then the records have to be "decoded" and interpreted, as must the "messages from nature" received by the observer. Finally the results have to be classified and coordinated into a coherent system that "makes sense."

Now we have seen that even the selection of the material *for* observation and examination is predetermined, to some extent, by a theory, or by a general historical conception. This is even more evident in the procedure itself, as every step made towards the system that "makes sense" presupposes not only the preceding but also the succeeding ones.

When the scientist observes a phenomenon he uses *instruments* which are themselves subject to the laws of nature which he wants to explore. When the humanist examines a record he uses *documents* which are themselves produced in the course of the process which he wants to investigate.

Let us suppose that I find in the archives of a small town in the Rhineland a contract dated 1471, and complemented by records of payments, by which the local painter "Johannes *qui et* Frost" was commissioned to execute for the church of St. James in that town an altarpiece with the Nativity in the center and Saints Peter and Paul on the wings; and let us further suppose that I find in the Church of St. James an altarpiece corresponding to this contract. That would be a case of documentation as good and simple as we could possibly hope to encounter, much better and simpler than if we had to deal with an "indirect" source such as a letter, or a description in a chronicle, biography, diary, or poem. Yet several questions would present themselves.

The document may be an original, a copy or a forgery. If it is a copy, it may be a faulty one, and even if it is an original, some of the data may be wrong. The altarpiece in turn may be the one referred to in the contract; but it is equally possible that the original monument was destroyed during the iconoclastic riots

---

[6]See, *e.g.,* E. Panofsky, "Ueber die Reihenfolge der vier Meister von Reims" (Appendix), *Jahrbuch für Kunstwissenschaft,* II, 1927, pp. 77 ff.

of 1535 and was replaced by an altarpiece showing the same subjects, but executed around 1550 by a painter from Antwerp.

To arrive at any degree of certainty we would have to "check" the document against other documents of similar date and provenance, and the altarpiece against other paintings executed in the Rhineland around 1470. But here two difficulties arise.

First, "checking" is obviously impossible without our knowing what to "check"; we would have to single out certain features or criteria such as some forms of script, or some technical terms used in the contract, or some formal or iconographic peculiarities manifested in the altarpiece. But since we cannot analyze what we do not understand, our examination turns out to presuppose decoding and interpretation.

Secondly, the material against which we check our problematic case is in itself no better authenticated than the problematic case in hand. Taken individually, any other signed and dated monument is just as doubtful as the altarpiece ordered from "Johannes *qui et* Frost" in 1471. (It is self-evident that a signature on a picture can be, and often is, just as unreliable as a document connected with a picture.) It is only on the basis of a whole group or class of data that we can decide whether our altarpiece was stylistically and iconographically "possible" in the Rhineland around 1470. But classification obviously presupposes the idea of a whole to which the classes belong—in other words, the general historical conception which we try to build up from our individual cases.

However we may look at it, the beginning of our investigation always seems to presuppose the end, and the documents which should explain the monuments are just as enigmatical as the monuments themselves. It is quite possible that a technical term in our contract is a ἅπαξ λεγόμενον which can only be explained by this one altarpiece; and what an artist has said about his own works must always be interpreted in the light of the works themselves. We are apparently faced with a hopeless vicious circle. Actually it is what the philosophers call an "organic situation."[7] Two legs without a body cannot walk, and a body without legs cannot walk either, yet a man can walk. It is true that the individual monuments and documents can only be examined, interpreted and classified in the light of a general historical concept, while at the same time this general historical concept can only be built up on individual monuments and documents; just as the understanding of natural phenomena and the use of scientific instruments depends on a general physical theory and vice versa. Yet this situation is by no means a permanent deadlock. Every discovery of an unknown historical fact, and every new interpretation of a known one, will either "fit in" with the prevalent general conception, and thereby corroborate and enrich it, or else it will entail a subtle, or even a fundamental change in the

---

[7]I am indebted for this term to Professor T. M. Greene.

prevalent general conception, and thereby throw new light on all that has been known before. In both cases the "system that makes sense" operates as a consistent yet elastic organism, comparable to a living animal as opposed to its single limbs; and what is true of the relationship between monuments, documents and a general historical concept in the humanities is evidently equally true of the relationship between phenomena, instruments and theory in the natural sciences.

III

I have referred to the altarpiece of 1471 as a "monument" and to the contract as a "document"; that is to say, I have considered the altarpiece as the object of investigation, or "primary material," and the contract as an instrument of investigation, or "secondary material." In doing this I have spoken as an art historian. For a palaeographer or an historian of law, the contract would be the "monument," or "primary material," and both may use pictures for documentation.

Unless a scholar is exclusively interested in what is called "events" (in which case he would consider all the available records as "secondary material" by means of which he might reconstruct the "events"), everyone's "monuments" are everyone else's "documents," and vice versa. In practical work we are even compelled actually to annex "monuments" rightfully belonging to our colleagues. Many a work of art has been interpreted by a philologist or by an historian of medicine; and many a text has been interpreted, and could only have been interpreted, by an historian of art.

An art historian, then, is a humanist whose "primary material" consists of those records which have come down to us in the form of works of art. But what is a work of art?

A work of art is not always created exclusively for the purpose of being enjoyed, or, to use a more scholarly expression, of being experienced aesthetically. Poussin's statement that "la fin de l'art est la délectation" was quite a revolutionary one,[8] for earlier writers had always insisted that art, however enjoyable, was also, in some manner, useful. But a work of art always *has* aesthetic significance (not to be confused with aesthetic value): whether or not it serves some practical purpose, and whether it is good or bad, it demands to be experienced aesthetically.

---

[8]A. Blunt, "Poussin's Notes on Painting," *Journal of the Warburg Institute,* I, 1937, pp. 344 ff., claims (p. 349) that Poussin's "La fin de l'art est la délectation" was more or less "mediaeval," because "the theory of *delectatio* as the sign by which beauty is recognized is the key of all St. Bonaventura's aesthetic, and it may well be from there, probably by means of some populariser, that Poussin drew the definition." However, even if the wording of Poussin's phrase was influenced by a mediaeval source, there is a great difference between the statement that *delectatio* is a *distinctive quality* of everything *beautiful,* whether man-made or natural, and the statement that *delectatio* is the *end ("fin") of art.*

It is possible to experience every object, natural or man-made, aesthetically. We do this, to express it as simply as possible, when we just look at it (or listen to it) without relating it, intellectually or emotionally, to anything outside of itself. When a man looks at a tree from the point of view of a carpenter, he will associate it with the various uses to which he might put the wood; and when he looks at it from the point of view of an ornithologist he will associate it with the birds that might nest in it. When a man at a horse race watches the animal on which he has put his money, he will associate its performance with his desire that it may win. Only he who simply and wholly abandons himself to the object of his perception will experience it aesthetically.[9]

Now, when confronted with a natural object, it is an exclusively personal matter whether or not we choose to experience it aesthetically. A man-made object, however, either demands or does not demand to be so experienced, for it has what the scholastics call an "intention." Should I choose, as I might well do, to experience the redness of a traffic light aesthetically, instead of associating it with the idea of stepping on my brakes, I should act against the "intention" of the traffic light.

Those man-made objects which do not demand to be experienced aesthetically, are commonly called "practical," and may be divided into two classes: vehicles of communication, and tools or apparatuses. A vehicle of communication is "intended" to transmit a concept. A tool or apparatus is "intended" to fulfil a function (which function, in turn, may be the production or transmission of communications, as is the case with a typewriter or with the previously mentioned traffic light).

Most of the objects which do demand to be experienced aesthetically, that is to say, works of art, also belong in one of these two classes. A poem or an historical painting is, in a sense, a vehicle of communication; the Pantheon and the Milan candlesticks are, in a sense, apparatuses; and Michelangelo's tombs of Lorenzo and Giuliano de'Medici are, in a sense, both. But I have to say "in a sense," because there is this difference: in the case of what might be called a "mere vehicle of communication" and a "mere apparatus," the intention is definitely fixed on the idea of the work, namely, on the meaning to be transmitted, or on the function to be fulfilled. In the case of a work of art, the interest in the idea is balanced, and may even be eclipsed, by an interest in form.

However, the element of "form" is present in every object without exception, for every object consists of matter and form; and there is no way of determining with scientific precision to what extent, in a given case, this element of form bears the emphasis. Therefore one cannot, and should not,

[9]See M. Geiger, "Beiträge zur Phänomenologie des aesthetischen Genusses," *Jahrbuch für Philosophie,* I, Part 2, 1922, pp. 567 ff. Furthermore, E. Wind, *Aesthetischer und kunstwissenschaftlicher Gegenstand,* Diss. phil. Hamburg, 1923, partly reprinted as "Zur Systematik der künstlerischen Probleme," *Zeitschrift für Aesthetik und allgemeine Kunstwissenschaft,* XVIII, 1925, pp. 438 ff.

attempt to define the precise moment at which a vehicle of communication or an apparatus begins to be a work of art. If I write to a friend to ask him to dinner, my letter is primarily a communication. But the more I shift the emphasis to the form of my script, the more nearly does it become a work of calligraphy; and the more I emphasize the form of my language (I could even go so far as to invite him by a sonnet), the more nearly does it become a work of literature or poetry.

Where the sphere of practical objects ends, and that of "art" begins, depends, then, on the "intention" of the creators. This "intention" cannot be absolutely determined. In the first place, "intentions" are, *per se*, incapable of being defined with scientific precision. In the second place, the "intentions" of those who produce objects are conditioned by the standards of their period and environment. Classical taste demanded that private letters, legal speeches and the shields of heroes should be "artistic" (with the possible result of what might be called fake beauty), while modern taste demands that architecture and ashtrays should be "functional" (with the possible result of what might be called fake efficiency).[10] Finally our estimate of those "intentions" is inevitably influenced by our own attitude which in turn depends on our individual experiences as well as on our historical situation. We have all seen with our own eyes the transference of spoons and fetishes of African tribes from the museums of ethnology into art exhibitions.

One thing, however, is certain: the more the proportion of emphasis on "idea" and "form" approaches a state of equilibrium, the more eloquently will the work reveal what is called "content." Content, as opposed to subject matter, may be described in the words of Peirce as that which a work betrays but does not parade. It is the basic attitude of a nation, a period, a class, a religious or

---

[10] "Functionalism" means, strictly speaking, not the introduction of a new aesthetic principle, but a narrower delimitation of the aesthetic sphere. When we prefer the modern steel helmet to the shield of Achilles, or feel that the "intention" of a legal speech should be definitely focused on the subject matter and should not be shifted to the form ("more matter with less *art*," as Queen Gertrude rightly puts it), we merely demand that arms and legal speeches should not be treated as works of art, that is, aesthetically, but as practical objects, that is, technically. However, we have come to think of "functionalism" as a postulate instead of an interdict. The Classical and Renaissance civilizations, in the belief that a merely useful thing could not be "beautiful" ("non può essere bellezza e utilità," as Leonardo da Vinci puts it; see J. P. Richter, *The Literary Works of Leonardo da Vinci*, London, 1883, nr. 1445) are characterized by a tendency to extend the aesthetic attitude to such creations as are "naturally" practical; we have extended the technical attitude to such creations as are "naturally" artistic. This, too, is an infringement, and, in the case of "streamlining," art has taken its revenge. "Streamlining" was, originally, a genuine functional principle based on the results of scientific research on air resistance. Its legitimate sphere was therefore the field of fast-moving vehicles and of structures exposed to wind pressure of an extraordinary intensity. But when this special and truly technical device came to be interpreted as a general and aesthetic principle expressing the twentieth century ideal of "efficiency" ("streamline your mind!"), and was applied to arm chairs and cocktail shakers, it was felt that the original scientific streamline had to be "beautified"; and it was finally retransferred to where it rightfully belongs in a thoroughly non-functional form. As a result, we now less often have houses and furniture functionalized by engineers, than automobiles and railroad trains de-functionalized by designers.

philosophical persuasion—all this unconsciously qualified by one personality, and condensed into one work. It is obvious that such an involuntary revelation will be obscured in proportion as either one of the two elements, idea or form, is voluntarily emphasized or suppressed. A spinning machine is perhaps the most impressive manifestation of a functional idea, and an "abstract" painting is perhaps the most expressive manifestation of pure form, but both have a minimum of content.

IV

In defining a work of art as a "man-made object demanding to be experienced aesthetically" we encounter for the first time a basic difference between the humanities and natural science. The scientist, dealing as he does with natural phenomena, can at once proceed to analyze them. The humanist, dealing as he does with human actions and creations, has to engage in a mental process of a synthetic and subjective character: he has mentally to re-enact the actions and to re-create the creations. It is in fact by this process that the real objects of the humanities come into being. For it is obvious that historians of philosophy or sculpture are concerned with books and statues not in so far as these books and sculptures exist materially, but, in so far as they have a meaning. And it is equally obvious that this meaning can only be apprehended by re-producing, and thereby, quite literally, "realizing," the thoughts that are expressed in the books and the artistic conceptions that manifest themselves in the statues.

Thus the art historian subjects his "material" to a rational archaeological analysis at times as meticulously exact, comprehensive and involved as any physical or astronomical research. But he constitutes his "material" by means of an intuitive aesthetic re-creation,[11] including the perception and appraisal of

---

[11]However, when speaking of "re-creation" it is important to emphasize the prefix "re." Works of art are both manifestations of artistic "intentions" and natural objects, sometimes difficult to isolate from their physical surroundings and always subject to the physical processes of aging. Thus, in experiencing a work of art aesthetically we perform two entirely different acts which, however, psychologically merge with each other into one *Erlebnis:* We build up our aesthetic object both by re-creating the work of art according to the "intention" of its maker, and by freely creating a set of aesthetic values comparable to those with which we endow a tree or a sunset. When abandoning ourselves to the impression of the weathered sculptures of Chartres, we cannot help enjoying their lovely mellowness and patina as an aesthetic value; but this value, which implies both the sensual pleasure in a peculiar play of light and color and the more sentimental delight in "age" and "genuineness," has nothing to do with the objective, or artistic, value with which the sculptures were invested by their makers. From the point of view of the Gothic stone-carvers the processes of aging were not merely irrelevant but positively undesirable: they tried to protect their statues by a coat of color which, had it been preserved in its original freshness, would probably spoil a good deal of our aesthetic enjoyment. As a private person, the art historian is entirely justified in not destroying the psychological unity of *Alters-und-Echtheits-Erlebnis* and *Kunst-Erlebnis.* But as a "professional man" he has to separate, as far as possible, the re-creative experience of the intentional values imparted to the statue by the artist from the creative experience of the accidental values imparted to a piece of aged stone by the action of nature. And this separation is often not as easy as it might seem.

"quality," just as any "ordinary" person does when he or she looks at a picture or listens to a symphony.

How, then, is it possible to build up art history as a respectable scholarly discipline, if its very objects come into being by an irrational and subjective process?

This question cannot be answered, of course, by referring to the scientific methods which have been, or may be, introduced into art history. Devices such as chemical analysis of materials, X-rays, ultra-violet rays, infra-red rays and macrophotography are very helpful, but their use has nothing to do with the basic methodical problem. A statement to the effect that the pigments used in an allegedly mediaeval miniature were not invented before the nineteenth century may settle an art-historical question, but it is not an art-historical statement. Based as it is on chemical analysis plus the history of chemistry, it refers to the miniature not *qua* work of art but *qua* physical object, and may just as well refer to a forged will. The use of X-rays, macrophotographs, etc., on the other hand, is methodically not different from the use of spectacles or of a magnifying glass. These devices enable the art historian to see more than he could see without them, but *what* he sees has to be interpreted "stylistically," like that which he perceives with the naked eye.

The real answer lies in the fact that intuitive aesthetic re-creation and archaeological research are interconnected so as to form, again, what we have called an "organic situation." It is not true that the art historian first constitutes his object by means of re-creative synthesis and then begins his archaeological investigation—as though first buying a ticket and then boarding a train. In reality the two processes do not succeed each other, they interpenetrate; not only does the re-creative synthesis serve as a basis for the archaeological investigation, the archaeological investigation in turn serves as a basis for the re-creative process; both mutually qualify and rectify one another.

Anyone confronted with a work of art, whether aesthetically re-creating or rationally investigating it, is affected by its three constituents: materialized form, idea (that is, in the plastic arts, subject matter) and content. The pseudo-impressionistic theory according to which "form and color tell us of form and color, that is all," is simply not true. It is the unity of those three elements which is realized in the aesthetic experience, and all of them enter into what is called aesthetic enjoyment of art.

The re-creative experience of a work of art depends, therefore, not only on the natural sensitivity and the visual training of the spectator, but also on his cultural equipment. There is no such thing as an entirely "naïve" beholder. The "naïve" beholder of the Middle Ages had a good deal to learn, and something to forget before he could appreciate classical statuary and architecture, and the "naïve" beholder of the post-Renaissance period had a good deal to forget, and something to learn, before he could appreciate mediaeval, to say nothing of primitive, art. Thus the "naïve" beholder not only enjoys but also, unconsciously, appraises and interprets the work of art; and no one can blame him if he does this without caring whether his appraisal and interpretation are right or wrong, and without realizing that his own cultural equipment, such as it is, actually contributes to the object of his experience.

The "naïve" beholder differs from the art historian in that the latter is conscious of the situation. He *knows* that his cultural equipment, such as it is, would not be in harmony with that of people in another land and of a different period. He tries, therefore, to make adjustments by learning as much as he possibly can of the circumstances under which the objects of his studies were created. Not only will he collect and verify all the available factual information as to medium, condition, age, authorship, destination, etc., but he will also compare the work with others of its class, and will examine such writings as reflect the aesthetic standards of its country and age, in order to achieve a more "objective" appraisal of its quality. He will read old books on theology or mythology in order to identify its subject matter, and he will further try to determine its historical locus, and to separate the individual contribution of its maker from that of forerunners and contemporaries. He will study the formal principles which control the rendering of the visible world, or, in architecture, the handling of what may be called the structural features, and thus build up a history of "motifs." He will observe the interplay between the influences of literary sources and the effect of self-dependent representational traditions, in order to establish a history of iconographic formulae or "types." And he will do his best to familiarize himself with the social, religious and philosophical attitudes of other periods and countries, in order to correct his own subjective feeling for content.[12] But when he does all this, his aesthetic perception as such will change accordingly, and will more and more adapt itself to the original "intention" of the works. Thus what the art historian, as opposed to the "naïve" art lover, does, is not to erect a rational superstructure on an irrational foundation, but to develop his re-creative experiences so as to conform with the results of his archaeological research, while continually checking the results of his archaeological research against the evidence of his re-creative experiences.[13]

---

[12]For the technical terms used in this paragraph, see The Introduction to E. Panofsky, *Studies in Iconology* [New York: Harper & Row, 1962].

[13]The same applies, of course, to the history of literature and of other forms of artistic expression. According to Dionysius Thrax (*Ars Grammatica*, ed. P. Uhlig, XXX, 1883, pp. 5 ff.; quoted in Gilbert Murray, *Religio Grammatici, The Religion of a Man of Letters*, Boston and New York, 1918, p. 15), Γραμματική (history of literature, as we would say) is an ἐμπειρία (knowledge based on experience) of that which has been said by the poets and prose-writers. He divides it into six parts all of which can be paralled in art-history:

1) ἀνάγνωσις ἐντριβὴς κατὰ προσῳδίαν (expert reading aloud according to prosody): this is, in fact, the synthetic aesthetic re-creation of a work of literature and is comparable to the visual "realization" of a work of art.

2) ἐξήγησις κατὰ τοὺς ἐνυπάρχοντας ποιητικοὺς τρόπους (explanation of such figures of speech as may occur): this would be comparable to the history of iconographic formulae or "types."

Leonardo da Vinci has said: "Two weaknesses leaning against one another add up to one strength."[14] The halves of an arch cannot even stand upright; the whole arch supports a weight. Similarly, archaeological research is blind and empty without aesthetic re-creation, and aesthetic re-creation is irrational and often misguided without archaeological research. But, "leaning against one another," these two can support the "system that makes sense," that is, an historical synopsis.

As I have said before, no one can be blamed for enjoying works of art "naïvely" — for appraising and interpreting them according to his lights and not caring any further. But the humanist will look with suspicion upon what might be called "appreciationism." He who teaches innocent people to understand art without bothering about classical languages, boresome historical methods and dusty old documents, deprives *naïveté* of its charm without correcting its errors.

"Appreciationism" is not to be confused with "connoisseurship" and "art theory." The connoisseur is the collector, museum curator or expert who deliberately limits his contribution to scholarship to identifying works of art with respect to date, provenance and authorship, and to evaluating them with respect to quality and condition. The difference between him and the art historian is not so much a matter of principle as a matter of emphasis and explicitness, comparable to the difference between a diagnostician and a researcher in medicine. The connoisseur tends to emphasize the re-creative

---

3) γλωσσῶν τε καὶ ἱστοριῶν πρόχειρος ἀπόδοσις (offhand rendering of obsolete words and themes): identification of iconographic subject matter.

4) ἐτυμολογίας εὕρησις (discovery of etymologies): derivation of "motifs."

5) ἀναλογίας ἐκλολισμος (explanation of grammatical forms): analysis of compositional structure.

6) κρίσις ποιημάτων, ὃ δὴ κάλλιστόν ἐστι πάντων τῶν ἐν τῇ τέχνῃ (literary criticism, which is the most beautiful part of that which is comprised by Γραμματική): critical appraisal of works of art.

The expression "critical appraisal of works of art" raises an interesting question. If the history of art admits a scale of values, just as the history of literature of political history admit degrees of excellence or "greatness," how can we justify the fact that the methods here expounded do not seem to allow for a differentiation between first, second and third rate works of art? Now, a scale of values is partly a matter of personal reactions and partly a matter of tradition. Both these standards, of which the second is the comparatively more objective one, have continually to be revised, and every investigation, however specialized, contributes to this process. But just for this reason the art historian cannot make an a priori distinction between his approach to a "masterpiece" and his approach to a "mediocre" or "inferior" work of art — just as a student of classical literature cannot investigate the tragedies by Sophocles in any other manner than the tragedies by Seneca. It is true that the methods of art history, *qua* methods, will prove as effective when applied to Dürer's *Melencolia* as when applied to an anonymous and rather unimportant woodcut. But when a "masterpiece" is compared and connected with as many "less important" works of art as turn out, in the course of the investigation, to be comparable and connectable with it, the originality of its invention, the superiority of its composition and technique, and whatever other features make it "great," will automatically become evident — not in spite but because of the fact that the whole group of materials has been subjected to one and the same method of analysis and interpretation.

[14]*Il codice atlantico di Leonardo da Vinci nella Biblioteca Ambrosiana di Milano*, ed. G. Piumati, Milan, 1894-1903, fol. 244 v.

aspect of the complex process which I have tried to describe, and considers the building up of an historical conception as secondary; the art historian in the narrower, or academic, sense is inclined to reverse these accents. But the simple diagnosis "cancer," if correct, implies everything which the researcher could tell us about cancer, and therefore claims to be verifiable by subsequent scientific analysis; similarly the simple diagnosis "Rembrandt around 1650," if correct, implies everything which the historian of art could tell us about the formal values of the picture, about the interpretation of the subject, about the way it reflects the cultural attitude of seventeenth century Holland, and about the way it expresses Rembrandt's personality; and this diagnosis, too, claims to live up to the criticism of the art historian in the narrower sense. The connoisseur might thus be defined as a laconic art historian, and the art historian as a loquacious connoisseur. In point of fact the best representatives of both types have enormously contributed to what they themselves do not consider their proper business.[15]

Art theory, on the other hand—as opposed to the philosophy of art or aesthetics—is to art history as poetics and rhetoric are to the history of literature.

Because of the fact that the objects of art history come into being by a process of re-creative aesthetic synthesis, the art historian finds himself in a peculiar difficulty when trying to characterize what might be called the stylistic structure of the works with which he is concerned. Since he has to describe these works, not as physical bodies or as substitutes for physical bodies, but as objects of an inward experience, it would be useless—even if it were possible—to express shapes, colors, and features of construction in terms of geometrical formulae, wave-lengths and statical equations, or to describe the postures of a human figure by way of anatomical analysis. On the other hand, since the inward experience of the art historian is not a free and subjective one, but has been outlined for him by the purposeful activities of an artist, he must not limit himself to describing his personal impressions of the work of art as a poet might describe his impressions of a landscape or of the song of a nightingale.

The objects of art history, then, can only be characterized in a terminology which is as re-constructive as the experience of the art historian is re-creative: it must describe the stylistic peculiarities, neither as measurable or otherwise determinable data, nor as stimuli of subjective reactions, but as that which bears witness to artistic "intentions." Now "intentions" can only be formulated in terms of alternatives: a situation has to be supposed in which the maker of the work had more than one possibility of procedure, that is to say, in which

---

[15]See M. J. Friedländer, *Der Kenner,* Berlin, 1919, and E. Wind, *Aesthetischer und Kunstwissenschaftlicher Gegenstand, loc. cit.* Friedländer justly states that a good art historian is, or at least develops into, a *Kenner wider Willen.* Conversely, a good connoisseur might be called an art historian *malgré lui.*

he found himself confronted with a problem of choice between various modes of emphasis. Thus it appears that the terms used by the art historian interpret the stylistic peculiarities of the works as specific solutions of generic "artistic problems." This is not only the case with our modern terminology, but even with such expressions as *rilievo, sfumato,* etc., found in sixteenth-century writing.

When we call a figure in an Italian Renaissance picture "plastic," while describing a figure in a Chinese painting as "having volume but no mass" (owing to the absence of "modelling"), we interpret these figures as two different solutions of a problem which might be formulated as "volumetric units (bodies) *vs.* illimited expanse (space)." When we distinguish between a use of line as "contour" and, to quote Balzac, a use of line as "le moyen par lequel l'homme se rend compte de l'effet de la lumière sur les objets," we refer to the same problem, while placing special emphasis upon another one: "line *vs.* areas of color." Upon reflection it will turn out that there is a limited number of such primary problems, interrelated with each other, which on the one hand beget an infinity of secondary and tertiary ones, and on the other hand can be ultimately derived from one basic antithesis: differentiation *vs.* continuity.[16]

To formulate and to systematize the "artistic problems"—which are of course not limited to the sphere of purely formal values, but include the "stylistic structure" of subject matter and content as well—and thus to build up a system of *"Kunstwissenschaftliche Grundbegriffe"* is the objective of art theory and not of art history. But here we encounter, for the third time, what we have called an "organic situation." The art historian, as we have seen, cannot describe the objects of his re-creative experience without re-constructing artistic intentions in terms which imply generic theoretical concepts. In doing this, he will, consciously or unconsciously, contribute to the development of art theory which, without historical exemplification, would remain a meager scheme of abstract universals. The art theorist, on the other hand, whether he approaches the subject from the standpoint of Kant's *Critique,* of neo-scholastic epistemology, or of *Gestaltpsychologie,*[17] cannot build up a system of generic concepts without referring to works of art which have come into being under specific historical conditions; but in doing this he will, consciously or unconsciously, contribute to the development of art history which, without theoretical orientation, would remain a congeries of unformulated particulars.

When we call the connoisseur a laconic art historian and the art historian a loquacious connoisseur, the relation between the art historian and the art

[16]See E. Panofsky, "Ueber das Verhältnis der Kunstgeschichte zur Kunsttheorie," *Zeitschrift für Aesthetik und allgemeine Kunstwissenschaft,* XVIII, 1925, pp. 129 ff., and E. Wind, "Zur Systematik der künstlerischen Probleme," *ibid.,* pp. 438 ff.
[17]Cf. H. Sedlmayr, "Zu einer strengen Kunstwissenschaft," *Kunstwissenschaftliche Forschungen,* I, 1931, pp. 7 ff.

theorist may be compared to that between two neighbors who have the right of shooting over the same district, while one of them owns the gun and the other all the ammunition. Both parties would be well advised if they realized this condition of their partnership. It has rightly been said that theory, if not received at the door of an empirical discipline, comes in through the chimney like a ghost and upsets the furniture. But it is no less true that history, if not received at the door of a theoretical discipline dealing with the same set of phenomena, creeps into the cellar like a horde of mice and undermines the groundwork.

V

It may be taken for granted that art history deserves to be counted among the humanities. But what is the use of the humanities as such? Admittedly they are not practical, and admittedly they concern themselves with the past. Why, it may be asked, should we engage in impractical investigations, and why should we be interested in the past?

The answer to the first question is: because we are interested in reality. Both the humanities and the natural sciences, as well as mathematics and philosophy, have the impractical outlook of what the ancients called *vita contemplativa* as opposed to *vita activa*. But is the contemplative life less real or, to be more precise, is its contribution to what we call reality, less important than that of the active life?

The man who takes a paper dollar in exchange for twenty-five pounds of apples commits an act of faith, and subjects himself to a theoretical doctrine, as did the mediaeval man who paid for indulgence. The man who is run over by an automobile is run over by mathematics, physics and chemistry. For he who leads the contemplative life cannot help influencing the active, just as he cannot prevent the active life from influencing his thought. Philosophical and psychological theories, historical doctrines and all sorts of speculations and discoveries have changed, and keep changing, the lives of countless millions. Even he who merely transmits knowledge or learning participates, in his modest way, in the process of shaping reality—of which fact the enemies of humanism are perhaps more keenly aware than its friends.[18] It is impossible to conceive of our

---

[18]In a letter to the *New Statesman and Nation*, XIII, 1937, June 19, a Mr. Pat Sloan defends the dismissal of professors and teachers in Soviet Russia by stating that "a professor who advocates an antiquated pre-scientific philosophy as against a scientific one may be as powerful a reactionary force as a soldier in an army of intervention." And it turns out that by "advocating" he means also the mere transmission of what he calls "pre-scientific" philosophy, for he continues as follows: "How many minds in Britain today are kept from ever establishing contact with Marxism by the simple process of loading them to capacity with the works of Plato and other philosophers? These works play not a neutral, but an anti-Marxist rôle in such circumstances, and Marxists recognize this fact." Needless to say, the works of "Plato and other philosophers" also play an anti-Fascist rôle "in such circumstances," and Fascists, too, "recognize this fact."

world in terms of action alone. Only in God is there a "Coincidence of Act and Thought" as the scholastics put it. Our reality can only be understood as an interpenetration of these two.

But even so, why should we be interested in the past? The answer is the same: because we are interested in reality. There is nothing less real than the present. An hour ago, this lecture belonged to the future. In four minutes, it will belong to the past. When I said that the man who is run over by an automobile is run over by mathematics, physics and chemistry, I could just as well have said that he is run over by Euclid, Archimedes and Lavoisier.

To grasp reality we have to detach ourselves from the present. Philosophy and mathematics do this by building systems in a medium which is by definition not subject to time. Natural science and the humanities do it by creating those spatio-temporal structures which I have called the "cosmos of nature" and the "cosmos of culture." And here we touch upon what is perhaps the most fundamental difference between the humanities and the natural sciences. Natural science observes the time-bound processes of nature and tries to apprehend the timeless laws according to which they unfold. Physical observation is only possible where something "happens," that is, where a change occurs or is made to occur by way of experiment. And it is these changes which are finally symbolized by mathematical formulae. The humanities, on the other hand, are not faced by the task of arresting what otherwise would slip away, but of enlivening what otherwise would remain dead. Instead of dealing with temporal phenomena, and causing time to stop, they penetrate into a region where time has stopped of its own accord, and try to re-activate it. Gazing as they do at those frozen, stationary records of which I have said that they "emerge from the stream of time," the humanities endeavor to capture the processes in the course of which those records were produced and became what they are.[19]

In thus endowing static records with dynamic life, instead of reducing transitory events to static laws, the humanities do not conflict with, but complement, the natural sciences. In fact these two presuppose and *demand* each other. Science — here understood in the true sense of the term, namely, as a serene and self-dependent pursuit of knowledge, not as something subservient to "practical" ends — and the humanities are sisters, brought forth as they are by that movement which has rightly been called the discovery (or, in a larger

---

[19]For the humanities it is not a romantic ideal but a methodological necessity to "enliven" the past. They can express the fact that the records A, B and C are "connected" with each other only in statements to the effect that the man who produced the record A must have been acquainted with the records B and C, or with records of the type B and C, or with a record X which was in turn the source of B and C, or that he must have been acquainted with B while the maker of B must have been acquainted with C, etc. It is just as inevitable for the humanities to think and to express themselves in terms of "influences," "lines of evolution," etc., as it is for the natural sciences to think and to express themselves in terms of mathematical equations.

historical perspective, rediscovery) of both the world and man. And as they were born and reborn together, they will also die and be resurrected together if destiny so wills. If the anthropocratic civilization of the Renaissance is headed, as it seems to be, for a "Middle Ages in reverse" — a satanocracy as opposed to the mediaeval theocracy — not only the humanities but also the natural sciences, as we know them, will disappear, and nothing will be left but what serves the dictates of the sub-human. But even this will not mean the end of humanism. Prometheus could be bound and tortured, but the fire lit by his torch could not be extinguished.

A subtle difference exists in Latin between *scientia* and *eruditio,* and in English between knowledge and learning. *Scientia* and knowledge, denoting a mental possession rather than a mental process, can be identified with the natural sciences; *eruditio* and learning, denoting a process rather than a possession, with the humanities. The ideal aim of science would seem to be something like mastery, that of the humanities something like wisdom.

Marsilio Ficino wrote to the son of Poggio Bracciolini: "History is necessary, not only to make life agreeable, but also to endow it with a moral significance. What is mortal in itself, achieves immortality through history; what is absent becomes present; old things are rejuvenated; and young men soon equal the maturity of old ones. If a man of seventy is considered wise because of his experience, how much wiser he whose life fills a span of a thousand or three thousand years! For indeed, a man may be said to have *lived* as many millennia as are embraced by the span of his knowledge of history."[20]

---

[20]Marsilio Ficino, Letter to Giacomo Bracciolini (*Marsilii Ficini Opera omnia,* Leyden, 1676, 1, p. 658): "res ipsa [*scil.,* historia] est ad vitam non modo oblectandam, verumtamen moribus instituendam summopere necessaria. Si quidem per se mortalia sunt, immortalitatem ab historia consequuntur, quae absentia, per eam praesentia fiunt, vetera iuvenescunt, iuvenes cito maturitatem senis adaequant. Ac si senex septuaginta annorum ob ipsarum rerum experientiam prudens habetur, quanto prudentior, qui annorum mille, et trium milium implet aetatem! Tot vero annorum milia vixisse quisque videtur quot annorum acta didicit ab historia."

Toward A Unified Field in Critical Studies

WALTER ABELL

The approach to universality and definitiveness achieved by the historical side of our historico-critical development, has by no means characterized its critical side. Here our knowledge is still in a formative and fermentive state. Any effort to grasp the field as a whole confronts us with a bewildering intricacy of schools and counter-schools, of oppositions and conflicts, of multiple problems rather than unifying solutions.

An iconographer like Mâle will tell us that medieval art is a "closed world" to us unless we learn to decipher the obscure "hieroglyphics of its subject-matter."[1] Exactly opposite assertions come to us from critics imbued with the concept of "pure visibility." They insist that subject matter is "irrelevant" to artistic significance and that we should concentrate our attention on the "plastic form" inherent to visual creations as such. One recurrent point of view urges that to understand art and artist we must, in Taine's words, "comprehend the general social and intellectual condition of the time to which they belong. Herein is to be found the final explanation; herein resides the primitive cause

Reprinted by permission of the publishers from Walter Abell, *The Collective Dream in Art*, Cambridge, Mass: Harvard University Press, Copyright, 1957, by the President and Fellows of Harvard College.
[1]See his *Religious Art in France, XIII Century*, pp. vii-viii.

determining all that follows it."[2] We have had earlier occasion to quote Lionello Venturi as a spokesman of the opposite view that "the consideration of art as a document in the life of peoples" is to be classed among the "deviations from the criticism of art," and that "the only reality of art is the personality of the artist, as it is manifested in his works of art."[3]

Other mutually conflicting points of view could be indicated. The reader desiring a comprehensive survey of the intricacies of recent critical thought can turn to the later chapters in such summaries as Bernard Bosanquet's *History of Aesthetic* (1892), Lionello Venturi's *History of Art Criticism* (1936), and Gilbert and Kuhn's *History of Aesthetics* (1939).

It is doubtful whether the ferment of ideas just suggested can be reduced to any single systematic framework which would be satisfactory to everybody. After considerable effort to obtain perspective on the field as a whole, however, the author has concluded that it can fairly well be charted under six headings: six approaches or points of view, six directions of attention and emphasis, each of which may be said to constitute a tradition within the totality of recent efforts to interpret art. These six main critical traditions, together with some outstanding representatives of each of them are as follows:

(1) *Iconography.* Emphasis on subject matter and its natural or literary sources as a basis for understanding art. Active during the Middle Ages in a preoccupation with sacred texts, the iconographical approach expanded during the Renaissance to include the direct imitation of nature among the objectives of art and keys to its subject matter. It has since reverted mainly to concern with literary sources, especially the forgotten ones associated with past forms of art. Characteristic recent contributions to this tradition have been made by Emile Mâle, Erwin Panofsky, and Edgar Wind.

(2) *Biographical Criticism.* Emphasis on the creative personality as the chief basis for understanding art. Exponents of this point of view have been chiefly concerned with the life and work of individual artists. The tradition extends from the Renaissance, when Vasari and others wrote their *Lives,* to the present day. Under the influence of psychoanalysis, its sphere of inquiry has been extended in the twentieth century to include the unconscious depths of the creative personality—an extension illustrated by Freud's *Leonardo Da Vinci.*

(3) *Historical Determinism.* Emphasis on civilization and environment as the conditioning sources of art forms. This point of view was presented by John Winckelmann in the eighteenth century, by Hippolyte Taine in the nineteenth. E. Viollet-Le-Duc, Henry Adams, and others have thought in more restricted ranges of historical reference. A marginal, ethically centered variation of the tradition occurs in the work of Ruskin, Tolstoy, and others who stress the

---

[2]Hippolyte Taine, *Lectures on Art, First Series,* translated by J. Durand (New York: Henry Holt, 1875), p. 30.
[3]Venturi, *History of Art Criticism,* pp. 309 and 301.

moral effect which art should have on society, as distinguished from the historical effect which society has upon art.

(4) *"Esthetic materialism."* Emphasis on material, technique, and function as the chief factors determining art forms. Most frequently applied to architecture and the useful crafts, but has been proposed for all the arts. Lessing advanced the thesis in his *Laocoon* (1766). A century later Gottfried Semper formulated it into a system in *Der Stil in den Technischen und Tektonischen Kunsten* (Style in the Crafts and Structural Arts; 1863). Viollet-Le-Duc employed this point of view as well as the preceding one. One of the earlier statements of it by an American was Charles Herbert Moore's *Gothic Architecture* (1899).

(5) *"Esthetic teleology."* Art forms explained as the outcome of a psychological "will to art" associated with epochs or races. Enunciated at the beginning of the twentieth century by Alois Riegl as an incidental critical aspect of a historical work: *Spatromische Kunstindustrie* (Late Roman Industrial Arts). Adopted as the basis for a "psychology of style" by Wilhelm Worringer in his *Abstraction and Empathy* and *Form Problems of Gothic*.

(6) *Pure Visibility.* Works of art explained in terms of the formal significance resulting from the organization of lines, colors, and other plastic elements. Employed as a means of descriptive classification by Heinrich Wölfflin in his *Principles of Art History*. Indicated as the chief basis of esthetic values by many recent critics, among others Roger Fry, Clive Bell, and Albert C. Barnes.

In the foregoing outline we have listed the six approaches chronologically, following the approximate order of their historical emergence in works which still play an active part in our critical literature. In this order they seem indistinctly to reveal the same sequence which we discussed earlier in connection with the evolution of artistic styles and of related influences during the same centuries. One of the earliest concepts of creative motivation is the medieval one of divine inspiration, which corresponds with the religious emphasis in medieval life and art; one of the latest of such concepts is that of pure visibility, which corresponds with recent abstraction. Between these temporal extremes we can find other correspondences, such as that between the individualism of the Renaissance, its artistic expression in such forms as portraiture, and its critical expression in emphasizing individual genius as the source of what is artistically important.

From our point of view it is not surprising that theories about art should reveal evolutionary directions corresponding to those followed by art itself. Not only are the theorists dependent upon the work of the artists; the artists are influenced by an intellectual climate which includes the work of the theorists and both, in the measure of their creative capacity, are responding to common cultural directives.

Dialectically, the six traditions have tended to group themselves into three pairs of thesis and antithesis. Iconographical interpretations have been op-

posed by formal ones, individualistic by social ones, mechanistic by teleological ones. In the heat of debate, which is usually intensified by the clash of
personalities, it has frequently seemed to the champions of each point of view
that the difference between their position and that of their opponents was one
of truth as opposed to error. Reflective wisdom suggests that any point of view
maintained by a number of serious thinkers over a period of time has *something*
to recommend it; that each of the six traditions, therefore, may be accepted as
embodying *a* truth, or *an aspect* of truth, and that if *the* truth can be reached at
all, it presumably lies in the direction of a synthesis capable of resolving the
oppositions between the various traditions into a larger unity.

If we turn our attention to possible bases for such a unity, organic relations
between the six traditions begin to suggest themselves. In the first place, as
indicated by Diagram 11, they would seem to fall into two groups: one
concerned with the inherent attributes of art, the other with forces which
motivate the creation of art. In the first group are the traditions devoted
primarily to the subject matter, the form, the material, the technique, and the
physical functions of works of art. In the second group are those devoted to
creative motivation as ascribed respectively to the individual artist, to races,
and to historical states of civilization.

ASPECTS OF ART INVOLVED	CRITICAL TRADITIONS
Intrinsic attributes of art	Iconography and other studies in subject matter
	Pure visibility emphasizing form
	Esthetic materialism emphasizing material, technique, and function
Motivation of art	Biographical studies emphasizing personality of the artist
	Esthetic teleology emphasizing will to art resident in races
	Historical determinism emphasizing influence of civilization and environment

Diagram 11. An organic classification of recent critical traditions.

The three approaches gathered in our first group, though they have occasioned more than one internecine feud, are in no sense incompatible with each
other. Each deals with, and illuminates, certain aspects of the work of art. In
studying a fully integrated work of art like a Gothic cathedral, where all aspects

237

are merged, we might follow each approach in turn to our enlightenment. Through the iconographic approach we could penetrate the mysterious world of religious imagery presented by the sculpture and stained glass of the building itself, and by the painting of its altarpieces and other accessories. The visibility approach would quicken our perceptions of design, focusing our attention upon the proportions of mass and space, the rhythmic flow of lines, the harmonies of color, the repetition and endless variation of motifs such as that presented by the pointed arch. The material approach would show us the dependence of the whole fabric upon the physical properties of stone and glass, upon the physical forces of weight and thrust, and the marvelous adaptation of pier, arch, and buttress to their functions as members of the structural organism. From this same material approach we could also, if we wished (thinking back to Lessing), learn some of the reasons why the same religious subject receives different formations in the portals, the windows, and the altarpieces; differences due in part to the respective natures of carved stone, of stained glass, and of painted surfaces.

It is obvious that each of these approaches contributes something to the observer's understanding of, and responsiveness to, the work of art; obvious, therefore, that all have their value for the study of art. The limitations that may be ascribed to them are not those of insignificance or error but of partiality. If and when any of them has revealed such limitations, it has done so either in regarding itself as a self-sufficient basis for the interpretation of art, or in opposing other approaches. Truth for each would seem to lie in recognizing itself as a component aspect of a larger whole, and in maintaining positive relationships toward other approaches in the interests of that larger whole. Such an attitude would promote integration on two levels. It would liberate the three approaches of our first group from their respective limitations and their mutual conflicts, harmonizing them within the balanced totality of the group. And it would open the way for recognition of organic connections between the first group as a whole and the factors comprising our second group.

The author's earlier work, *Representation and Form,* was an effort in the first of these directions. Its point of departure was the recent opposition between the pure-visibility tradition and that which has ascribed significance to subject matter. Its outcome was the proposal of a basis of synthesis within which, from the esthetic point of view, the two could be integrated with each other. This was a step toward a unitary conception of the work of art, but the unity which it conceived was one of surface factors, or what we are here calling the "intrinsic attributes" of art objects. It did not extend the inquiry to the forces of motivation or inspiration upon which both the formal and the representational characteristics of works of art are ultimately dependent. Hence it might be compared to a study of the manifest imagery of dreams that did not raise the question of what latent motivation had inspired the manifest imagery. Its depth limitation in this respect is shared by all studies that confine their fields of reference to the factors dealt with by the traditions of our first group. This brings us to the second and wider basis of integration suggested above: the relationship between the traditions listed in our first and our second groups which is, in principle, the relationship between resulting effects and their motivating causes.

Iconographical, formal, and functional studies, when pursued in isolation, have not concerned themselves directly with questions of creative motivation, but each approach has tended to assume motives reflecting its own preoccupations. Iconography has attached so much importance to "influences" that it might seem to imply that the historic works of art were created for the purpose of being influenced — an idea so preposterous that no one seriously entertains it. More reasonable, as a motive related to iconography, would be the assumption that the creative purpose lay in representing the subject matter of the work studied. Functionalism, for its part, has tacitly assumed that the aim of art was to achieve fitness to material and structural demands; formalism, that its aim was to achieve finely organized perceptual relationships.

In each case we may accept the statement as involving a partial motivation: the immediate motivation for a component aspect of the total work. But reflection should make clear that in no case alone, nor in all together, do these statements involve an adequate motivation for art as a whole. If we say in so many words that the purpose of building the Gothic cathedrals was to allow architects to pose and solve problems of thrust and counter-thrust, the proposition joins the ranks of the preposterous. That the purpose was to represent subject matter for its own sake is hardly less so. The subjects were considered important for their power to express something external to themselves — religion — and if we extend our frame of reference to include religion, then we have left our first group of concerns, strictly speaking, and connected the subject matter intrinsic to the first group with one of the forces of civilization included in the second.

The remaining alternative, that the artist creates in order to achieve esthetic form, corresponds so well with the conscious aspect of his own creative experience, and also with our enjoyment of formal beauty, that we might seem justified in accepting it as an ultimate motivation. That it can hardly be so, however, is suggested by various considerations. In the case of artistic undertakings as vast as those of the cathedrals, the pleasures of perceiving harmony and proportion would hardly seem a sufficient incentive to inspire whole communities to spend immense sums of wealth and effort over generations of time. And even in the case of small individually executed works such as easel paintings, for which esthetic form may seem a sufficient justification, the student of depth psychology can hardly accept the conscious formal experience as independent of presumed unconscious motivants.

Subject, form, and structure, it appears, are means to more inclusive and elusive ends, not ends in themselves. They are agencies for fulfilling motivation, not types of motivation. The realization of this fact has led various thinkers to proceed upon the assumptions, or to formulate the theories comprising our second group of traditions: those ascribing the motivation of art to the impulse and capacity of the individual artist, to a racial will to art, and to the historical energies of a state of civilization. Before scanning these traditions, we might note that the Middle Ages had previously proposed a motivation for art which has faded out of more recent thought but which, like all things past, is no doubt destined to reappear in modified and perhaps more analytical form in the future.

There was in medieval consciousness no realization that art had a history, no sense of it as a reflection of human cultures, no emphasis upon individuals as its creators. Like the rest of the universe it was explained and justified as a revelation of the glory of God. A monk, Theophilus, wrote a treatise on art in the twelfth century. He discusses techniques and formal concerns, but presents them as recipes serving a purpose, not as purposes in themselves. The purpose was to manifest divinity through the adornment of places of worship. In accomplishing that purpose, Theophilus tells the artist, "you have in some way exposed to the eyes of the faithful the Paradise of God. . . You have succeeded in letting the Creator be praised in creation and in showing God to be admirable in his work."[4]

The Renaissance, still unaware of historical and cultural determinism, but highly aware of a new individualistic detachment from the body social, proposed the first of our extant ideas of motive: the genius of the individual artist. At the time of its Renaissance inception, this individualistic motivation was "still trailing clouds of glory." As we read one of its early literary embodiments, Vasari's *Lives,* we are continually made aware of genius as the special gift of God. Giotto accomplishes his artistic revolution "by the favour of Heaven." Leonardo's superiority is such as "manifestly to prove that he has been specially endowed by the hand of God himself, and has not obtained his pre-eminence by human teaching, or the power of man."[5] Vasari seems but to paraphrase himself in ascribing the genius of Raphael, of Michelangelo, and other great artists to the same divine source. There was in this conception a recognition that genius, though embodied in individuals, is not individually self-contained or self-explanatory, but the external source here ascribed to it was not destined to remain convincing for subsequent Western thought. The greatness of the great man was gradually detached from religious affiliations and was explained in terms of superior intellectual and esthetic endowment or, with the advent of psychoanalysis, in terms of impulse generated by the individual unconscious.

---

[4]Venturi, *History of Art Criticism,* p. 70.
[5]Giorgio Vasari, *Lives.* My two quotations are taken respectively from I, 48, and II, 370.

Biographical criticism had special value for the development of the philosophy of art in that it was an instrument of correlation and synthesis. Instead of
confining attention exclusively to objects of art, it called for observation of the
relations between certain objects of art and a human being. In thus recognizing
a tie between art and life, it introduced a correlative approach which, if pursued
to its logical conclusion, was bound eventually to lead beyond the individual.
Although the purely biographical approach was long considered, and by
biographers is sometimes still accepted, as a sufficient basis for the discussion
of an artist's work, it contains ingredients for its own dissolution into larger
circles of human experience.

The individual, as we have more than once had occasion to observe, does not
exist alone but in society. The study of his life and art inevitably leads to some
degree of consideration for the given society in general and for the particular
members of it with whom the individual was most closely associated. Leonardo
da Vinci may, in Vasari's eyes, have derived his genius from God and have
owed nothing "to the power of man," but he did not study with God; he studied
with Verrocchio. Accordingly, having explained the divine source of the artist's
genius on the first page of his *Life* of Leonardo, Vasari arrives on the second
page at the youthful aspirant's apprenticeship to the older master, and by page
three is relating Leonardo to social enterprises full of the techno-economic
concerns of the epoch such as "the formation of a canal from Pisa to Florence."[6]

Thus, while the theoretical assumption as to the motivating source of art
might remain centered in the psychology of the individual, the practice of
biographical criticism inevitably demanded a larger frame of reference. Recognition of this fact led many writers subsequent to the Renaissance to entitle
their works, not the "Life," but the "Life and Times" of the given artist.
Through the "times," the way was open for a consideration of historical and
social factors in their relationship to art.

In the biographical tradition, historical factors remained a background
against which the individual stood out in vigorous highlight. By the eighteenth
century another tradition was arising to reverse the emphasis. Synchronizing
with the emergence of Western historical consciousness, aware for the first
time of such inclusive entities as the whole rise and fall of Greek civilization,
this tradition gave its chief thought to the saga of societies, the epic march of
civilizations. Seen in such panoramic perspective the individual shrank to the
role of a participant, albeit perhaps a leading participant, in the historical
destiny of his epoch, and even his epoch receded into place as one of the
phases of a cycle of civilization. This point of view in general we are calling

---

[6]Vasari, *Lives,* II, 372.

historical determinism (the biographical one might be called personal determinism). Actually historical and social factors are so numerous and complex that they permit of many intellectual analyses, with the result that the tradition concerned with them is a complex of several different formulations or subtraditions.

The two most important of these in the literature of art are listed last in our table of traditions (Diagram 11). They are historical determinism proper and what, for purposes of distinction, may be called racial determinism. We have noted in an earlier and more general context that a third variant, economic determinism, can be considered as a restricted form of historical determinism. Historical determinism proper received its first major exposition in *The History of Ancient Art* by John Winckelmann (1764). Winckelmann ascribed the progress and superiority of art among the Greeks "partly to the influence of climate, partly to their constitution and government, and the habits of thinking which originated therefrom, and, in equal degree also, to respect for the artist, and the use and application of art."[7] "Being consecrated to the gods, and devoted only to the holiest and best purposes of the land," the artist's "work was made to conform to the lofty ideas of the whole nation." All these conditioning factors — geographical, political, religious, and others — are elaborated in Winckelmann's discussion.

What the eighteenth century thus conceived with reference to its absorption in Classical antiquity, the nineteenth applied to its new enthusiasm for the Western Middle Ages. Writers like Viollet-le-Duc and, later and within narrower limits, Henry Adams, studied medieval art in relation to its historical background. Supported by an intervening century of growth in both historical and critical consciousness, Viollet-le-Duc related Gothic art to a remarkably extensive and remarkably solid frame of reference. His exposition of the functional aspects of Gothic architecture, such as the evolution of its structural organism, remains basic today, and his conception of the conditioning forces to which architectural structure must adapt itself extends from "the nature of the materials" to "the climate" and "the historical conditions of epoch."[8] His discussion of the historical background of Gothic art refers to the new expansive force of Western life after the eleventh century, the emergence of the free cities, and many of the other historical circumstances adduced in our chapter on Gothic history.

Winckelmann and Viollet-Le-Duc had both related their concepts of historical determinism to the study of one selected type of art: in the first case, primarily Greek art, with marginal references to other ancient national styles;

[7]John Winckelmann, *The History of Ancient Art,* translated by G. H. Lodge (Boston: Osgood, 1872). Our two consecutive quotations are taken respectively from II, 4 and 21.
[8]E. Viollet-Le-Duc, *Dictionnaire Raisonné de l'Architecture Française du XIe au XVIe Siecle* (Paris: Morel, 1882), I, 116.

in the second case, French medieval art. The first writer to separate historical determinism from a single context and propose it as a theory having the validity of a general principle, applicable to all historical contexts, appears to have been Hippolyte Taine (1828-1893). Relating his observations to the art of Greece, of medieval Europe, of Renaissance Italy, and of the seventeenth-century Low Countries, with references to other areas and periods, and also in the light of extensive studies in English, Spanish, and other literatures, Taine proposed a motivation sequence in four principal terms. These terms, elaborated in their author's *Philosophy of Art,*[9] are as follows.

(1) A "general situation" involving such realities as a "state of wealth or poverty, a particular form of society, a certain species of religious faith," gives rise (2) to "corresponding needs, aptitudes, and sentiments." This reigning mentality finds its most complete embodiment in (3) a "representative man" — the youthful Greek athlete, the medieval monk — who becomes the culture hero of the period and the primary subject of its art. The artists then strive to express the character of this representative man in (4) "sounds, forms, colors, or language giving this character sensuous form, or which comport with the tendencies and faculties comprising it."

It will be observed that the first, second, and fourth terms of the above sequence — general situation, resulting sentiments, and their artistic expressions — closely parallel the psycho-historical sequence of historical circumstances, psychic state, and cultural expressions. Taine's theory, much more solid and penetrating in his development than it may sound in our summary, is probably the most complete formulation of the principle of historical determinism to be found in the literature specifically devoted to art.

The last of our six main critical traditions, which we have referred to as "racial determinism," emerged somewhat obliquely from the esthetic teleology of Riegl. The latter had enunciated a "will to art" — *kunstwollen* — as the basic factor in the motivation of works of art. The principle was important not only because it related art to obscure psychological impulse, but because it provided a corrective to the widespread tendency to judge one form of art in terms of another. Riegl was himself chiefly occupied with the decorative arts of the declining Roman world; arts which, in relation to the High Classical standards of preceding periods, had frequently been condemned as decadent. Riegl maintained that these arts owed their nature, not to negative inability to fulfill the artistic aims of previous periods, but to a positive fulfillment of the intent, the artistic will, of their own period. Every period, he said, has its own will impulse or "will" as a motivation for its art. Consequently, that art can be judged only by the degree to which it fulfills its own will. To judge it by

---

[9]Included in Taine, *Lectures on Art, First Series.* My quoted references are taken from the summary which Taine gives in chapter IX, pp. 157-161.

comparison with other types of art that owed their nature to other intentions is to misjudge and to fail to understand it.[10]

The will to art as Riegl conceives it has much in common with the second term in Taine's motivating sequence: the "needs, aptitudes, and sentiments" corresponding to a particular historical situation. Riegl himself leaves the nature of the artistic will vague and its source largely undetermined. As Gilbert and Kuhn have put it, "Riegl's 'will to art' leaves us in doubt as to whether we have to do with a psychological hypothesis or a rudimentary metaphysics."[11] Riegl's most direct successor, Wilhelm Worringer, ostensibly decided for the psychological alternative by making the "will" concept the basis of a "psychology of style." In Worringer's general statements of theory, both psychological and historical determinants are given due consideration. The changes in the will to art as it passes from period to period are recognized as standing in orderly relationship to "the variations that take place in the constitution of the mind and soul of mankind," and these variations in turn are governed by the "fundamental process of the whole historical evolution of mankind: the checkered, fateful process of man's adjustment to the outer world."[12]

In practice, Worringer abandons both psychology and history. He makes no use of the findings of scientific psychology of any school, and little if any reference to the political, economic, or other circumstances of historical epochs. His "psychical categories" turn out, in Spenglerian fashion, to be "timeless racial phenomena" associated with the supposedly unchanging natures of primitive man, of Classical man, of Oriental man, and of Gothic man. We are thus left with race as the ultimate determinant of art in Worringer's system. Teutonic racial stock becomes "the *conditio sine qua non* of the Gothic."[13] Its artistic expression is not limited to Gothic proper of the high Middle Ages "but through the centuries manifests itself continually in ever new disguises" as a "latent Gothic." This "latent Gothic" characterizes all Western European art from the bronze age to the present day.

Such a theory provides no means of explaining the differences which Western European or other art undergoes in its passage through successive phases of its history, but it does call attention to a certain continuing element which, in Worringer's terms, is conceived as the result of racial determinism. The precarious equilibrium of the concept of race is amusingly illustrated by the fact that to the German, Worringer, Teutonic stock is the indispensable racial source of Gothic art, whereas the Frenchman, Viollet-Le-Duc, attributes

---

[10]Riegl gives a general statement of his will-to-art theory on pp. 8-11 in *Spätromische Kunstindustrie,* Vienna edition (Wien. Osterr: Staatstruckerei, 1927).

[11]Gilbert and Kuhn, *History of Aesthetics* (Bloomington: Indiana University Press, 1953), p. 547.

[12]Wilhelm Worringer, *Form Problems of Gothic* (New York: Steckert, 1920), pp. 25-26.

[13]Worringer, *Form Problems of Gothic,* p. 45 and again p. 146.

Gothic achievements to the genius of the Gallo-Roman peoples occupying the basins of the Seine, the Loire, and the Somme.[14]

In summary, our second group of traditions may be said to indicate the personality of the individual artist, the genius of the race to which he belongs, and the historical and environmental conditions which that race is experiencing, as three alternative bases for the motivation of art. Here again the three proposals are in no sense incompatible with each other. An individual artist emerges from some racial stock and the stock to which he belongs undergoes the conditioning circumstances of historical evolution. Each of these levels of life and experience might well be expected to play some part in the motivation of art.

We have now briefly reviewed all six of the traditions in terms of which I have been attempting to analyze our inheritance of critical thought within the field of art. Although these traditions have by no means existed in ideal harmony with each other, we can see from the foregoing discussion that they are capable of ideal interrelationships. They mutually complete rather than contradict, each other. The traditions of historical and racial determinism emphasize the ultimate sources of collective human experience. The biographical tradition emphasizes the individual artist who emerges from this collective background and becomes an organ of expression for it. The traditions of subject, form, and function emphasize characteristic instrumentalities employed by the artist, or submitted to by him, in fashioning specific works of art. Thus grouped, our six traditions may be conceived as component aspects of an organic totality, providing together our most comprehensive perspective on the interpretation of art. It is no doubt because each contributes knowledge and insight essential to the completeness of the totality that all have survived as living critical traditions.

But if each tradition envisages some aspect of the artistic totality, and if all are capable of organic interconnections, we should also observe that the several traditions differ greatly in their relative inclusiveness. The iconographic, formal, and functional ones, when pursued within the limits of their own disciplines, are relatively narrow, each confining itself to one component aspect of works of art. The biographical tradition provides a beginning of synthesis by bringing all the aspects of the work of an artist into relationship with his creative personality. The racial tradition offers a broader synthesis, for theoretically at least, it can consider all the factors just indicated plus their relationship to the race to which the artist belongs. The historical tradition reaches a maximum synthesis, including all the foregoing factors as seen in relationship to the environment and the historical condition of the race or society involved.

---

[14]Viollet-Le-Duc, *Dictionnaire Raisonné*, I, 144-145.

With the foregoing summary in mind, we are now in position to compare the psycho-historical theory with the background of art studies against which it must take its place. Three observations emerge from such a comparison. First, our theory is most nearly identified with the specific tradition which we have called historical determinism. Its direct critical antecedents are to be found in the work of writers like Winckelmann, Viollet-Le-Duc, and Taine. In varying lesser degrees it overlaps with the theories of all thinkers who have stressed connections between art and society: with those of Ruskin and Tolstoy, though it does not involve their ethical emphasis; with those of Coomaraswamy, though it does not involve his metaphysical emphasis.

CRITICAL TRADITIONS	PSYCHO-HISTORICAL EQUIVALENTS
Iconographical concern with religious and other subject matter	Varied aspects of cultural tension imagery
Pure visibility concern with form	
Materialist concern with material, technique, function	
Biographical emphasis on individual creative personality	Individual artist as immediate formulator of cultural tension imagery
Teleological emphasis on will to art in Riegl's original general sense	Creative potential of a collective psychic state
Racial determinants	Historical circumstances emerging from the interplay of human groups and their environments
Historical and environmental determinants	

Diagram 12. Correlation of factors emphasized by six critical traditions with equivalent elements of psycho-historical theory.

Second, like its predecessors in the tradition of historical determinism, it involves the maximum range of analytical and interpretive interrelationships. Its concern extends from the specific characteristics of works of art through states of individual and cultural mentality to historical and geographical preconditions. Within this extended range of observation, it includes elements equivalent to all those emphasized by the several other traditions. It therefore provides a medium of synthesis within which these other traditions can be unified with each other or, since they will presumably persist as specializations, can at least be seen in relationship to an encompassing whole. The basis of equivalence between the specialities and our psycho-historical frame of reference may be indicated in another table.

In their more philosophical moments, when detached from the narrower problems of their specific disciplines, the representatives of the several traditions are usually aware of extensions which connect their field with others in a larger whole. As an example, we may cite the essay in which Erwin Panofsky has summarized his views on the aims and methods of iconography. Beginning with a definition of iconography as "that branch of the history of art which concerns itself with the subject matter or meaning of works of art, as opposed to their form,"[15] Dr. Panofsky subdivides the realm of meaning into three strata. First, and largely "pre-iconographical," is the meaning of natural subject matter which can be interpreted in terms of practical experience with everyday objects and events. Second, and constituting the main field for "iconographical analysis in the narrower sense of the word," is the "conventional subject matter constituting the world of images, stories, and allegories" which can be interpreted only through a "knowledge of literary sources." Third, calling for "iconographical interpretation in a deeper sense," is the world of " 'symbolical' values" "conditioned by personal psychology and 'Weltanschauung.' " On this third and deepest level, the interpretation of the meaning of a work of art must envisage the "History of cultural symptoms or 'symbols' in general (insight into the manner in which, under varying historical conditions, essential tendencies of the human mind were expressed by specific themes and concepts)."

It is evident that on Panofsky's third stratum, where iconography extends its borders to encompass the "essential tendencies of the human mind" as affected by "varying historical conditions," the iconographer recognizes connections between the subject matter of art and the entire frame of reference involved in the psycho-historical theory. But this third stratum is more in the nature of an ideal horizon for iconography than a territory which it has occupied and developed. In practice iconographers have rarely turned to psychologists for any accurate analysis of mental tendencies, and have seldom related their material to the intricacies of historical circumstance. Their efforts have largely been confined to "iconographical analysis in the narrower sense of the word"; in short, to a study of possible connections between artistic subject matter and literary sources. Hence the need for the correlation of iconography with other traditions in a more extended frame of reference such as that provided by the psycho-historical theory. In varying degrees, the same can be said of the other traditions we have been reviewing.

A third relationship between the psycho-historical theory and its background of critical traditions remains to be mentioned. If we synthesize those traditions in the manner suggested by our last table, we obtain a frame of reference sufficiently inclusive for a full interpretation of art but in certain respects not sufficiently intensive. Of the total range from historical backgrounds through

---

[15]Erwin Panofsky, *Studies in Iconology* (New York: Oxford University Press, 1939), p. 3. My remaining quotations are taken from the synoptic table, pp. 14-15.

psychological states to their artistic manifestations, only the latter have been exhaustively studied by our critical writers. All that can be known about the structure, function, and representational significance of objects of art has been, or is being, made available to us by these writers in ample measure. When they deal with the biographies of artists, that subject also is likely to be well covered. But their broader allusions to general history and to psychology rarely if ever possess an equivalent depth.

History, it is true, received serious attention from the more penetrating historical determinists like Winckelmann and Viollet-Le-Duc. In emphasizing the importance of a study of general history for an understanding of art, we are following in their footsteps, but we can do so with the hope of progress in a number of respects. Funds of historical knowledge and gains in historical perspective that were not available in the eighteenth and nineteenth centuries are at our disposition today. The recent interplay between history and other social sciences like anthropology has helped to close the mental gap between conceptions of the dead past and the living present. The increasing diffusion of depth concepts permits us to recognize as historical effects what earlier determinists often mistook for historical causes. Consequently we can pursue the search for causes on a deeper level.

A greater deficiency of our critical heritage as a basis for interpreting art lies in its relation to psychology. Although the spokesmen of more than one critical tradition have acknowledged the importance of this subject, pointing in its direction with such gracious phrases as "the essential tendencies of the human mind" and "the variations that take place in the constitution of the mind and soul of mankind"; and although Worringer has described his findings as a "psychology of style," the fact remains none of our major critical writers has attempted to come to grips with the intricacies of detailed study of psychology and the further intricacies of an attempt to apply the results of that study to an understanding of art.

In view of the limitations—or let us say in view of the need for further development—of our critical heritage with regard to history and to psychology, our final observation concerning the relation of the psycho-historical theory to its critical antecedents carries us back full circle to the general correlational studies with which this volume began. To achieve a frame of reference fully adequate for the interpretation of art, we need not only to synthesize our critical inheritance as such, but also to bring it into more active interplay with the growing volumes of historico-social knowledge and of psychological knowledge. This, as our earlier chapters have emphasized, the psycho-historical theory attempts to do. What we have been saying about critical studies is, so to speak, an enlarged detail of our more general reference to the humanities in Part I. By reintegrating this detail with the discussion of psychological studies and of historical studies that was there advanced, we return to the total psycho-historical concept on which the present volume is based.

II

It would be tempting, perhaps desirable, to extend our discussion of implications to the more remote realms of the philosophy of art and of esthetics. The psycho-historical theory is itself a philosophy of culture and therefore invites comparison with other such philosophies. Since the humanities in general comprise one of its component terms, it must also carry implications with regard both to esthetic experience and to the formulation of esthetic theories. These subjects, however, are so complex, sometimes so remote from artistic actuality, and in part so dependent upon long-range cyclic considerations, that only passing reference to them will be made at the present time.

Without attempting any extensive comparison of the various efforts that have been made to arrive at a philosophy of the arts, we may note that one of the systems most recently proposed by a philosopher seems to be essentially in harmony with our own. This is the system presented by Susanne Langer in her books, *Philosophy in a New Key* and *Feeling and Form: a Theory of Art*. In emphasizing the importance of "symbolic transformation," in defining art as "the creation of forms symbolic of human feelings,"[16] Dr. Langer worked her way from philosophic sources to a position which we in turn have reached on the basis of quite different sources.

What our sources can perhaps assist us in contributing is a greater integration of the concept of symbolic transformation with the actualities of cultural life. It is not clear to the present writer that *Feeling and Form* offers very concrete indication as to *what,* beyond the vague concept of "feeling," is being transformed or *by what process* it is being transformed. And the results of the transformation appear to be rather distantly viewed as types, without detailed study of any art as found in any specific cultural epoch or of the historical developments undergone by any art during a considerable span of its cultural evolution.

The psycho-historical point of view, while following the same general line of thought with regard to the principle of symbolic transformation, attempts to graft that principle as fully as possible with actuality at each of the three main levels in our conception of it. In our view it is, in the last analysis, the social pressures of history that are being transformed, they being the ultimate determinants of human feeling at any given time and place. It is the obscure working of the tension-imagery process within the psyche by which the transformation is affected. And it is in the arts, philosophy, and religion, observed in the organic order of their historic unfolding, that the results of the transformation appear to us. Hence a continuing and deepening study of the subject cannot remain within the scope of the principle, but must pursue the intensive studies at the foundation level of depth history, at the transforma-

---

[16]Susanne K. Langer, *Feeling and Form: a Theory of Art* (New York: Charles Scribner's Sons, 1953), p. 40.

tional level of depth psychology, and at the manifest level of the history and criticism of the varied forms of cultural expression.

Turning now to cast a glance in the direction of esthetics, we should give the estheticians credit for one accomplishment that has been lacking in most of the disciplines previously considered: that is a serious study of psychology as a means of increasing our understanding of the arts. The progress recently made in this direction can probably best be followed by referring to the files of the *Journal of Aesthetics and Art Criticism*.[17] But if the esthetician has frequently been strong with respect to psychology, he has not infrequently been weak with respect to artistic and historical actuality. His studies, like those in the philosophy of art, have usually been conducted on a plane of such generality that works of art are seen as conceptual types rather than as concrete specimens related to each other in sequences of historical change. Esthetics would gain much if it could achieve an integration with the history of the arts comparable to its present close relations with psychology.

With regard to specific esthetic points of view, it is obvious that the psycho-historical theory aligns itself with relativistic rather than with absolute conceptions of the subject. Neither esthetic experience nor the intellectual analysis of it can be exceptions to principles which, in our view, affect culture as a whole. They must therefore be conditioned by, and subject to change with, the changing interrelationships between mediums of expression, collective psychic states, and historical circumstances. Their orientation will shift from period to period as part of the same drift of cultural symbolism that modifies the forms of art.

Within the mobile of conditioning relationships, there will be a number of inner systems: the powerful dynamism of the passing period, the slow movement of cultural tradition through the whole cycle of a given civilization, and the general range of responses that operates—or can be assumed to operate—for humanity as a whole. This last relativism to human constitution would seem to be the nearest we can come to any absolute determination of beauty, but it would also seem to be the least effective in determining the artist's ideals for, or the observer's reactions to, specific forms of art or specific aspects of nature.

In fact we might go so far as to assert that the permanence of the human constitution, if assumed to imply a corresponding permanence of esthetic reactions, involves an illusion. We might call it the "illusion of esthetic fixity" and compare it to the illusion of cosmic fixity which makes us feel that the earth is standing still, when in fact it is spinning on its axis and rotating around a sun that is itself in motion—all at terrific velocities.

The illusion of esthetic fixity results from a failure to discriminate between our biological potentials and their actualization through culture. If, because all

---

[17]Published by the American Society for Aesthetics, under the editorship of Thomas Munro. This journal is issuing its thirteenth volume during 1955-56.

men have eyes, we are led to the assumption that therefore they see alike, we are forgetting the indications of the social sciences that what they see is largely a result of their socialization. To an anatomist the eyes of our grandfathers and of ourselves would be of the same type, but most of our grandfathers could not "see" the beauty in the paintings of Cézanne and most of us can see it. The difference of seeing is cultural, not constitutional. Correspondingly, every change of cultural context will produce some equivalent change of perception and of esthetic response.

The conception of esthetic experience as a focus of changing relationships involves implications for all the aspects of the subject. Some of these implications can be suggested by a brief reference to "esthetic types"—the beautiful, the sublime, the humorous, the grotesque, and others. Traditional studies of these types are largely confined to what we may call the "descriptive" level: that is to say their main concern is to describe the characteristics of each type as observable in certain examples from nature and from art.[18] Accepting the description as accurate, psycho-historical thinking identifies it with the manifest cultural surface and, here as elsewhere, calls for a study of the motivating depths.

If we search the classic discussions of the esthetic types for motivations, only one is likely to appear. That consists in the perceptions, responses, and impulses of the individual artist or observer. Thus in contrasting different effects produced by different artists in treating the theme of the Laocoön, Louis Flaccus asks why "tragedy and pathos are so arrestingly present" in some of the examples and yet "are all but absent in El Greco's painting. If Michelangelo had painted the picture they would have been there. The reason must lie in personal preferences and attitudes."[19]

The esthetic types are in fact identified by Flaccus with "a personal bent ... Sublimity marks the genius of Aeschylus; Sappho, Catullus, and Keats are voices of beauty; Whitman's poetry naturally falls within the characteristic; Tennyson is idyllic; and Byron is picturesque. There is sensuous beauty in Titian, tragedy in Michelangelo, grace in Praxiteles, pathos in Scopas, rough strength in Van Gogh, idyllic charm in Watteau, decorative appeal in Botticelli and in Gauguin."[20]

Our whole frame of reference would indicate that while the personal bent of the artist or observer will play a part in any esthetic situation it will, so to speak, float upon the double current of a cultural context which is in historical motion. Our earlier study of the grotesque can here be recalled as an indication that this esthetic type owed its vitality in Gothic times to forces which, far from stopping with individual aptitude, involved the whole destiny of Gothic

---

[18]See Flaccus, *The Spirit and Substance of Art,* part IV, "The Aesthetic Types" (New York: Crofts, 1926), pp. 225-337.
[19]*Ibid.,* p. 226.
[20]*Ibid.*

society. Our study also indicated that the grotesque, which may appear static as a descriptive type, was in constant change from the largely terrible to the largely humorous when it was observed as a cultural actuality.

If we extend our study of the types in evolutionary directions, integrating the description of them with their history as an aspect of the history of the arts, a further relation appears. The various types do not all occur miscellaneously with equal force at the same time, and they do not occur in haphazard order. The historical relationship between the sublime in Masaccio and the beautiful in Raphael appears to be the same as that between the sublime in Phidias and the beautiful in Praxiteles. In other words, the emergence of esthetic dispositions and their maximum expressions in art, as well as their maximum effulgence upon nature, appears to be controlled by historical laws. There is in every historical situation a high potential for certain types, a low potential for others, and the changing sequence of potentials apparently follows an equivalent cyclic pattern in different civilizations.

To summarize the general attitude toward esthetic problems that would accord with psycho-historical thinking, we might say that this attitude would not only be relativistic, but would also be dynamic, socially conscious, and historically conscious. It would be dynamic in relating all esthetic considerations to motivating forces that must be explored within the realm of cultural dynamics. It would be socially conscious in conceiving individual motivations as emergent from collective ones. It would be historically conscious in recognizing that collective motivations follow evolutionary courses and that therefore esthetic sensitivities, like works of art, present problems of historical order.

III

In concluding the attempt of the last two chapters to review the present state of studies in the history and criticism of art, and in the philosophy of art and esthetics, one is tempted to make a comparison which would have been appropriate at a number of points along the way. It is a comparison that has a bearing upon our conception of cultural orbits and was in fact implied by an earlier allusion to planetary orbits; a comparison that bears also upon the relation of short-range to long-range studies in the history of art, and upon the relation of the factual data of art history to the theoretical constructions of the philosophy of art and of esthetics. It is the comparison that can be drawn between our recent studies in the arts and the condition of astronomy at the end of the sixteenth century. To make clear the interest of this comparison, let us recall the situation that had developed in the astronomical studies of that time.

Earlier developments culminating in the assiduous observations of Tycho Brahe on the changing positions of the planets, had resulted in the accumulation of larger and larger funds of astronomical data. Most of these data, however, had not as yet been integrated and illuminated by the discovery of the general laws of which they were particular outcomes.

Meanwhile, in Kepler, the age had produced an astronomer gifted with unusual powers of generalization but one who was not himself an exhaustive observer. Much of Kepler's earlier effort was wasted in developing hypothetical systems that were inadequate because not based on sufficiently detailed data. Some of these systems were published in the *Prodromus of Cosmographical Dissertations* (1596). When Kepler asked his older colleagues, Galileo and Brahe, for an opinion of this volume, "The former praised the ingenuity and good faith which it displayed; and Tycho, though he requested him to try to adapt something of the same nature to the Tychonic system, saw the speculative character of his mind, and advised him 'to lay a solid foundation for his views by actual observation, and then, by ascending from these, to strive to reach the cause of things.' "[21]

The highest results of the whole scientific development could, in fact, only be achieved if speculative genius was brought to bear upon a large accumulation of accurate data. Kepler eventually realized this and thenceforth burned with eagerness to gain possession of Brahe's observations and to use them as a basis for higher calculations of a general order. This fruitful union of opposites became possible in 1601 when, as assistant to Brahe, Kepler was given access to the latter's observations on the movements of Mars. With these observations to guide and correct his speculations, Kepler was eventually able to work out his epoch-making laws of planetary motion. Fact and concept merged as two aspects of a single statement of observed reality. "The great performance in the sky" became more wonderful, not less so, because man had found the key to "the artful structure of the movements," and was able to recognize organized relations behind what had previously appeared as unrelated facts or discrepancies.

In our field of the study of the arts, we seem to have reached a stage of development much like that which prevailed in astronomy before Kepler's culminating discoveries. The vast funds of detail accumulated by our art historians, like Brahe's observations, are still largely on a factual plane, but their extent and variety suggest that it should be possible to achieve broader generalizations on the basis of them.

Generalizing effort is not lacking on the part of our philosophers and estheticians, but all too often it suffers from the same limitation as Kepler's early efforts: the dominance of conceptual or speculative principles over observation. One feels that the theorist in these fields might well heed Brahe's advice "to lay a solid foundation for his views by actual observation" before attempting to formulate general principles.

---

[21]David Brewster, *Martyrs of Science* (London: Chatto and Windus, 1895), p. 196.

But with such a wealth of accurate historical observation available to us, and with a large amount of speculative talent being exercised, it seems that if the latter could be brought squarely into line with the former, the time should be ripe for discoveries of a higher order. Perhaps we could reach the position in which speculation and fact would coalesce with each other to emerge as demonstrable laws. Who knows, for instance, but that long-range historical studies pursued into the realm of cultural orbits may not one day culminate in the discovery of laws of cultural motion more momentous in their bearing on human life than are the laws of planetary motion?

Levels of Explanation in the
History of Art

THOMAS MUNRO

1. Explanation and Description.
Partial Explanation

A mature, inquiring mind is not content to observe events without trying to understand their causes and effects. Since Francis Bacon, the quest for causal explanation in science has been increasingly linked with that for means of control. When the course of events appears to affect us for good or ill, to satisfy or frustrate our desires, we wonder how it could be redirected so as to satisfy us more completely. Long before Bacon, the study of history was undertaken for the purpose (among others) of helping man to act more wisely in the light of past experience; especially through understanding the causes of past trouble and how to avoid it in future. Even when control is remote or impossible, thoughtful observers like to find some plausible explanation for great events like the fall of Rome or important processes like evolution.

Since Hume, most philosophers have recognized that what we commonly regard as causal explanation is, fundamentally, an inference from observed associations among events in human experience. We cannot know with certainty the essential nature of causation in ultimate reality. But, for all practical and many theoretical purposes, people are usually satisfied with more superfi-

From Thomas Munro, *Evolution in the Arts* (Cleveland: Cleveland Museum of Art, 1963), pp. 420-25, 445-52. Reprinted by permission of the author and the Cleveland Museum of Art.

cial, partial explanations on the empirical level, in terms of observed relations among phenomena.

Several kinds of explanation and of causal relation are distinguished in philosophy and science. They differ somewhat in relation to the kinds of thing for which an explanation is sought; also in relation to the context of inquiry and the special interests of the inquirer. Some of the things to be explained are particular events such as the assassination of Julius Caesar. In art history, one may ask what caused a change of style: e.g., El Greco's increasing distortions of anatomy. Was it due to astigmatism (as some academic critics used to say) or to his early, Byzantine influence, or to the intense religiosity of Spain, or to the fact that this style seemed the next step ahead after Tintoretto's mannerism? Or to a combination of many different factors?

In the philosophy of art history, we are not concerned so much with the explanation of particular cases as with that of general processes and trends; also with general methods of explanation and theories of causation. This chapter deals with the problem of explaining evolution in art and with the chief proposed answers to it.

Evolution has been regarded in the past, not only as something to be explained, but as a way of explaining other things, including art. Spencer's "universal law" of evolution was advanced as an explanation of development in every field. Darwin's "natural selection" was accepted as explaining a great variety of biological phenomena, such as fossils, protective coloring in animals, and similarities in structure and function among apes and men. In criticism of this view, Thomas Huxley remarked that evolution is not an explanation of the cosmic process, but merely a generalized statement of the method and results of that process. It is certainly not a complete explanation; it does not explain what power or powers originated, directed, and still direct the evolutionary process. Huxley's dictum implies a sharp distinction between explanation and description; that no matter how full the description, the process cannot be "explained" in terms of "how" alone; explanation demands an answer to the question "Why? By what controlling power?" This distinction gave a welcome loophole, in Victorian Europe, for the reintroduction of religious faith, which claimed to answer the "why?"; also for naturalism and agnosticism, as in Spencer's doctrine of the Unknowable.

Huxley's distinction has also been applied to the problem of explaining evolution itself, in both the organic and cultural fields. If it is no explanation at all to tell *how* things happen, if we cannot show why or by what ultimate agency evolution proceeds, then (it is said) we cannot explain evolution at all, but only describe it.

Some distinction along these lines is valid and useful. We have followed it so far in trying only to show *that* evolution in art has occurred, and some of the principal *ways* in which it has occurred — e.g., through processes of cultural descent, accumulation, complication, and simplification. This main thesis, that evolution in art occurs in certain ways, can be discussed and supported without introducing any theory whatever about the *cause* of evolution. Discussing it so has enabled us to avoid many distracting issues along the way. However, to avoid them entirely would be to content oneself with the mere shell of a theory, and to ignore some of the most interesting, controversial aspects of the discussion.

We have summarized the leading theories up to date and touched occasionally on causal issues in the last few chapters. Without offering any radically new solution, the remaining chapters will briefly weigh and interrelate those theories which seem to retain some vitality at the present time. No single theory of cause will be found sufficient. There seem to be elements of truth in several and they are not completely exclusive. For the present a moderate pluralism, in which many hypotheses are weighed, seems the only reasonable course in the philosophy of history.

The explanation of historical events encounters special difficulties, many of which we have considered in previous chapters. Unlike the artificially controlled situations in a clinic or chemical laboratory, historical situations do not repeat themselves exactly enough to permit the formulation of precise descriptive laws, in terms of which a particular effect can be explained or predicted with assurance. It is impossible to observe past historical events directly; what happened and what led up to them must be inferred from fragmentary, often unreliable evidence. It is impossible to experiment with human behavior in the large on any extensive scale. Experiments are tried, as with a new system of government or a new style of art; but hardly ever under standardized conditions, permitting objective analysis of causes and effects in comparison with a control group. The enormous complexity and diversity in cultural events make it hard to discern exact recurrences within them. Cultural phenomena seem to be constantly changing their behavior. Unknown and unexpected variables constantly upset our predictions. In view of the lack of adequate "covering laws," some theorists have argued that the only complete explanation of a given event would be the full description of all previous events, which is of course impossible. Philosophers have often warned us that an event or condition is not fully explained or evaluated merely by tracing its genesis, especially through a single sequence of events leading up to the present one.[1]

The sharp dichotomy between description and explanation is still being used as a means of attacking evolutionism in the cultural field. As such, it is largely a revival of the old, extreme type of historicism, which tried to make a sharp

---

[1] For critiques of the "genetic method" in historicism, by Sidney Hook and others, see J. H. Randall, *Nature and Historical Experience* (Columbia U. Press, New York, 1958), pp. 64 f.; also Patrick Gardiner, *Theories of History*.

distinction between history and science. Since historical events are unique, it argues, there can be no laws of history; hence no explanation and no prediction. Evolution is attacked on the ground that it can neither explain anything nor be explained itself.

Although containing the usual elements of truth, this argument again goes too far. So sharp a dichotomy between description and explanation, like that between history and science, is excessive and unwarranted. It is agreed that *complete, certain, ultimate* explanations are now impossible in history as they are in science and philosophy. But *partial, tentative, empirical* ones are not. They are more difficult in theories of history than in the exact sciences, and must be accordingly modest in their claims. With this due caution, explanatory hypotheses are as possible in regard to cultural history, including that of art, as elsewhere in the empirical sciences. They can be gradually tested out against empirical data and strengthened, weakened, or corrected. A true but partial explanation is better than none if it is not mistaken for the whole, the necessary and sufficient explanation; if it does not give us a false, distorted picture of the whole sequence of events.

What is explanation? To what extent does it require a demonstration of causal relationship? As usual, there are different meanings and opinions. In the ordinary sense, "to explain" is "to make plain or clear to oneself; to reach an understanding, as of a cause or origin." (Webster). Any way of helping toward an understanding may qualify as explanation in this popular sense. Sometimes the emphasis is on cause or origin, sometimes on interpretation of a term or idea, sometimes on a statement of motive or purpose, and so on. The *Philosophical Dictionary* (1942) likewise defines "explanation" in a general sense as "the process, art, means or method of making a fact or a statement intelligible; . . . the result or expression of what is made intelligible." This may be the meaning attributed to a thing or a genetic description of it.

There is also a much more rigorous, exacting concept of explanation in logic and the mathematical and physical sciences. Webster states it as "to demonstrate (a phenomenon) as determinable from known conditions and stimuli or deducible from accepted premises." According to the *Philosophical Dictionary,* explanation in a technical sense is "the method of showing discursively that a phenomenon or a group of phenomena obeys a law, by means of causal relations or descriptive connections." There are three kinds of causal explanation, according to this authority: genetic (in terms of the direct, immediate conditions producing a phenomenon), descriptive (material elements of the phenomenon), and teleological (the end intended or to be attained). Explanation does not need to emphasize cause, for it can be "the search for generalizations whose variables are functionally related so that the value of any one variable is calculable from the value of the others, whether or not causal relations are noticeable or ultimately involved. . . . "

There has recently been much discussion of the nature of explanation in writing history; especially as to whether it can approach that of the natural sciences in being based on general laws. In opposition to those who would separate history and science as radically different, Carl G. Hempel in a much-quoted paper (1942) has argued "that general laws have quite analogous functions in history and in the natural sciences, that they form an indispensable instrument of historical research, and that they even constitute the common basis of various procedures which are often considered as characteristic of the social in contradistinction to the natural sciences." He defines a general law as "a statement of universal conditional form which is capable of being confirmed or disconfirmed by suitable empirical findings." It is about the same as a "universal hypothesis" and asserts a regularity of the following type: "in every case where an event of a specific kind C occurs at a certain place and time, an event of a specified kind E will occur at a place and time which is related in a specified manner to the place and time of the occurrence of the first event." Such hypotheses are used, says Hempel, in historical explanation and prediction; they imply that whenever events of the kind described in the first group occur, an event of the kind to be explained will take place. There is no difference in this respect, he continues, between history and the natural sciences; "both can give an account of their subject-matter only in terms of general concepts, and history can 'grasp the unique individuality' of its objects of study no more and no less than can physics or chemistry."

Patrick Gardiner (1959, p. 270) mentions some objections to this theory: especially that attempts to state the "laws" presupposed in historical explanation have often been vague and unspecific, or else so highly determinate and particularized as not to qualify as laws. W. H. Walsh, in an essay on " 'Meaning' in History," (Gardiner, p. 303), goes farther in charging that "Despite everything that has been said on the subject in the last 200 years, no one has yet produced a reputable example of an historical law." (Comte's, Marx's, and Toynbee's attempts do not qualify, he thinks.) Even those who advance such laws seem unsure of the circumstances in which they can be expected to apply. Hempel himself points out that many of the explanations offered in history are based on "probability hypotheses" rather than on universal, deterministic laws. They are therefore "explanation sketches" rather than complete explanations; that is, vague indications of the laws and conditions which would be relevant. They need "filling out" to become full-fledged explanations.

We need not, perhaps, regret too much the lack of universal laws in historiology, for they would not, in themselves, give complete understanding of events which exemplify them. As Gardiner remarks, it is part of the task of an explanation to make something intelligible, and this is seldom if ever achieved "merely by showing that it is the sort of thing which can always be expected to happen under certain types of circumstance. (1959, p. 270; *cf.* W. Dray, *Laws and Explanation in History.* Oxford, 1957). This limitation applies, however, to almost all kinds of attempted explanation. They show mainly that the event or idea in question is part of some larger type or causal tendency; that it fits into some larger complex of interacting factors. This always leaves us with the question, "how and why did this larger state of affairs come to be so in the first place?"

Since it is unrealistic to hope for exact historical laws at present, it seems advisable to get along with something less ambitious. We can accept as a partial explanation anything which seems to promise greater understanding; to make the fact in question more intelligible. Lacking universal laws, we can try to develop a number of "probability hypotheses"; not necessarily of a formal, mathematical sort, but as rough, informal generalizations, subject to correction in the light of more careful research.

Such generalizations can be stated cautiously as apparent *tendencies* under certain conditions. One can say that A often *tends,* under conditions B and C, to be followed by D. This implies that, in the light of observation up to date, A seems to exert an influence in the direction of D, or to be otherwise positively correlated with D. The influence may be slight or strong, steady or occasional, dependent on few or many contributing factors. It is said that a people whose conditions of life are too easy, with few enemies, ample food and temperate climate, tends to become lazy and luxury-loving. Long concentration of wealth in the hands of a well-entrenched aristocracy with traditions of refined enjoyment seems to favor development of the arts of decoration, entertainment, and ritual, as in the Japan of the *Tale of Genji.* But how strong and regular these tendencies are cannot be stated without much comparative study. "Necessity is the mother of invention" is a half-truth at the most; it is true only under certain conditions, with certain cooperating causes—e.g., when people have the desire, initiative, courage, basic knowledge, and skill to invent what they need. But it has enough truth to be a partial explanation in many cases and in the general development of technology. If not a full-fledged hypothesis, it is at least a start toward one. "History repeats itself" is a partial truth; "history does not repeat itself" is also partly true.

Many of the generalizations advanced as laws by such philosophers as Comte, Marx, and Spencer, and later branded as false, contain an element of truth or probability. They describe types of sequence in events which happen often though not always. They deserve empirical testing rather than wholesale acceptance or rejection. The same can be said of the theory that successive discoveries of new sources of energy have led in the past to deep, far-reaching cultural changes and developments, amounting to new stages in cultural evolution.[2] This can be restated as a causal hypothesis to the effect that major

---

[2]Hoebel, p. 619. *Cf.* L. A. White, "Energy and the Evolution of Culture," *American Anthropologist,* Vol. 45 (1943), 335-356.

increases in the control of energy tend to produce more highly evolved cultural stages. But, as often happens, the influence is reciprocal: such discoveries are also the result of a higher cultural development, as in scientific technology. Whether continued evolution will result is problematic: the discovery of nuclear power may lead to annihilation or genetic weakening.

Hypotheses and partial explanations of history are not limited to explicit theories of cause, although most of them contain some causal implications. Some of them take the form of describing persistent and recurrent processes in history, modes and mechanisms by which historic change occurs. If it is true that art and culture evolve, this knowledge helps increase our understanding of history although it is not a complete explanation. Any knowledge of how the major processes of history are interrelated is explanatory in a broad sense of that term. It would help us understand both history and evolution to know that evolution is (or is not) one phase in a larger cyclical pattern. It helps explain evolution to know that it contains several widespread processes, such as natural selection and cultural diffusion. These are modes and mechanisms by which evolution proceeds. They can also be regarded as contributing causes of evolution. Sometimes they operate and seem to have great influence; at other times not. Like the behavior of electrons and protons in the atom, such a mode is usually not directly observable to the casual eye. Though conceived as phenomenal and not an exact picture of ultimate reality, it has to be inferred from sense-evidence by refined and complex techniques. It operates on a deeper level than ordinary sense-experience reveals. The modes thus discovered, such as the chemical elements and their behavior, are much fewer in number and more regular in operation than the profusion of sensory phenomena as seen in ordinary experience. What seem to the casual observer as utterly diverse, remote phenomena, such as the perfume of a tropical flower and the bones of a fossil reptile, are shown to be instances of the same basic process operating along somewhat different lines under different conditions. Thus discovering the hidden analogies and recurrent patterns beneath phenomena, reducing apparent chaos and diversity to relative order and simplicity, partly satisfies the understanding. This is true especially when, as in the case of natural selection, the causal principle can be used as a tool for prediction and control.

The process of natural selection is one of the ways in which evolution operates, another being artificial selection as in animal breeding. The concept of natural selection helps explain evolution by showing how the latter works. Natural selection does not always coincide with evolution, however. As we have seen, it sometimes favors devolution, when simpler types are fitter for survival. Evolution and natural selection are somewhat distinct processes, which coincide on the whole. The knowledge of both helps to explain a multitude of still smaller processes, by showing in detail how these work;

especially by showing the intermediate steps and obscure mechanisms involved. The theory of evolution as a total process postulates a development from the extremely simple and indefinite to the extremely complex and definite (as in man, culture, and art). But, until Darwin, its obscure, intermediate steps had not been understood; therefore the whole process seemed unlikely. Darwin's description of natural selection was further filled in and corrected by the descriptions of mutation and Mendelian inheritance. These help explain how genetic change occurs. The other phase of natural selection, that of environmental influence, has been clarified by accounts of many changes, such as the drying of the swamps which had favored reptilian life. Geology, biochemistry, botany, ecology, anthropology, and other sciences contribute their shares to filling in the total picture. Science and historiography cooperate in building up a systematic description of the cosmic process, including man's role in it, as seen from our limited viewpoint with our limited powers. Science emphasizes the recurrences, history the uniquenesses; but both deal with both. Thus to describe the cosmic process more and more fully is to explain it more fully, though with no expectation of completeness or complete objectivity.

As we increase our understanding of the cosmic process, we automatically increase our power to predict the future; never certainly, but tentatively as in weather forecasting. From the fact that the earth has spun around the sun so long, we cannot be completely sure that it will do so tomorrow, but it is safe to assume so for all practical and many theoretical purposes. The same is true of evolution in life, culture, and art, with this difference: the process itself being so diverse and inconstant, so often arrested or reversed, we cannot be nearly so sure that it will continue. Its past length and persistence in certain areas give considerable ground for expecting that it will. But so many more variables enter the picture than in astronomy that we cannot, with present knowledge, predict specific lines of artistic evolution with any assurance. There is no good reason to suppose, however, that reliable prediction cannot be gradually increased along these lines as we learn more about the causal factors and persistent tendencies involved. This has occurred in meteorology and economics. Increased knowledge will also, theoretically, give increased powers of control, but society may decide not to use them to the full.

The question will always remain of why or how there came to be an evolutionary process in the first place. Any specific answer to it extends the story backward in time, with the possibility of an infinite regression of such questions and answers. In trying to explain what started the process or makes it continue as it does, we enter a path along which science can take us but a little way. Beyond it, we enter the realms of metaphysics and of fantasy.

* * *

9. Empirical Explanations, General and Particular

Scientists and historians in the cultural field now spend little time debating metaphysical explanations, even those which are frankly empirical or naturalistic. They mention such concepts as teleology and determinism chiefly to reject or exclude them from scientific discussion as too speculative and unverifiable. Some times they charge their adversaries with making metaphysical assumptions, without realizing that they themselves are making different ones. But there is a conscious effort to restrict discussion to verifiable hypotheses, especially those susceptible to quantitative demonstrations. Scientists try accordingly to avoid all theorizing on first principles, ultimate causes, and general concepts of reality; to deal only with observable recurrences in phenomena and proximate causes (in the sense opposed to "ultimate"). The sequence of events and proximate causes can be traced back indefinitely — perhaps for billions of years, to the formation of the oldest galaxies — without raising metaphysical questions as to how there came to be any formation at all, or anything to form. Matter, space, and time can be indefinitely described and explained in purely empirical terms without raising epistemological questions about their relation to underlying reality or the *Ding an sich*. Evolution can be described and partially explained in terms of modes and mechanisms, pervasive trends and processes like complication and diffusion, without asking what originated these patterns in phenomena or what propels them along whatever paths they take.

A partial explanation of this sort may take the form of an assertion that events or conditions of type A tend to cause events or conditions of type B. It may be based on empirical observation or made arbitrarily, as a hypothesis to be tested in later observation. It may be comparatively broad in scope, as in the Marxist theory that socio-economic changes tend to produce changes in artistic style, or more specific, as in saying that modern formalistic art "expresses" (i.e., is caused by) the decadence of capitalistic civilization. Such a generalization implies an attempted explanation of historical events of the type specified: e.g., of the formalistic trend in post-impressionist and abstract European paintings in the twentieth century. It also implies a prediction that capitalistic decadence will tend in future to produce such art. It suggests a means of control, through social revolution. Negatively, it implies that decadent capitalism does not usually produce other kinds of art (e.g., realistic) and that formalism does not usually occur in other socio-economic situations (e.g., communistic). Such a generalization, if accepted as true, would be taken as a partial explanation of any particular case of formalism in modern art. It will not, of course, be accepted by science as true or probable without a considerable amount of evidence.

To explain a particular event in art more and more fully, one should in the first place analyze the event or effect objectively and carefully. In what ways and to what extent is this work or style of art "formalistic"? In the second place, one should know as fully as possible the various sequences of related events which preceded and accompanied it. Third, one should link these up with well-supported generalizations as to the usual causal relations between such variables. Something of this sort is done in the medical diagnosis of a disease. To explain and perhaps control it, one tries to fit it into the context of relevant general knowledge about such symptoms or effects. The general knowledge lies at hand in technological manuals, classified so as to offer tentative explanations for various sets of effects under various circumstances. The diagnostician must be on the watch for unexpected variables which may have produced an unusual sequence of events.

Are we asking too much? Is it impossible to explain historical events to this extent? Yes, say the extreme historicists, for there can be no laws or valid generalizations about unique events and no predictions on the basis of past experience. We have rejected this extreme view. Certainly there are no absolute laws, no exact recurrences, and no certain predictions; but there can be rough approximations to these, and they have some theoretical as well as practical validity. All culture, all accumulation of wisdom, is a process of learning by past experience, of oneself and others. We could not learn by experience if life and history did not constantly repeat themselves in some ways. Every event is the joint result of many different factors, some known or discoverable and others not. There are always unpredictable variables, but not always enough to prevent things from taking their usual course. Thus we come to expect certain outcomes with more and more reliability in fields where much analysis of contributing causes has been done, as in medicine and meteorology. We predict with more and more accuracy and plan more successfully as a result. We have learned in democracy that putting great power in the hands of a military leader, not subject to popular election, runs the risk of dictatorship. We have learned that when an artist's livelihood depends on the approval of officials, he is apt to produce in ways which will please them. We also see occasional exceptions to these rules.

The limitations of historical explanation are shared to some extent by all sciences. Except perhaps for formal logic and pure mathematics, whose grounds of demonstration are still controversial, all the sciences are definitely based on empirical observation. They describe, not ultimate reality, not what must be by the very nature of things, but what has been observed in human experience or directly inferred from it. The "laws" and principles of causation they imply describe certain observed recurrences within a certain realm of phenomena which have apparently persisted for a long time and will probably, but not necessarily, continue to do so. The physical, biological, social, psychological, and cultural sciences offer no fundamental explanations, but only describe how things are happening, have happened, and will probably happen in their respective realms. They explain particular instances in part by showing how these fit into larger processes and recurrent sequences within the phenomenal world, including that of inner experience.

Phenomena in the social, psychological, and cultural sciences (including aesthetics) are much more variable than those in the physical sciences and therefore harder to describe in laws of uniform recurrence. Statistical correlations and estimates of frequency and probability are usually the most they can achieve. Accordingly, they cannot explain a particular event or type of phenomenon—e.g., the occurrence of artistic genius or of Shakespeare in particular—as neatly as astronomy can explain an eclipse. It is not an example of one, great, regular process or the result of similar, interacting forces like the simultaneous movements of several planets. It is the result of many diverse, irregular processes and influences, such as those of biological heredity, physical environment, psychological and cultural environment, all at a certain moment of history. Their multiplicity, diversity, variability, and inaccessibility to observation reduce the explanatory power of science in such a case to a minimum. As the sciences learn more about the various causal factors involved, they increase the possibility of fuller understanding. But this will require cooperation between the sciences, in describing the relative strength and specific interaction of factors.

The difficulty of explaining particular events does not imply that history or cultural evolution in general is completely inexplicable. The behavior of large numbers of cases and long-range trends is often understood and predicted, as in actuarial statistics. One may not be able to tell which individuals will die from a certain cause in a certain year, but one can predict fairly well how many individuals of different types will do so. One can tell whether certain causal factors (e.g., tuberculosis and automobile accidents) are increasing proportionately. Rises and falls in some of the factors affecting artistic ability are fairly obvious, such as the decrease in ecclesiastical influence on education and art, the shift of patronage to secular agencies, the decline in influence of academic rules of art production, the increase in worldwide diffusion of styles. In so large a process as the evolution of art, many minor, local, temporary, individual factors cancel out and leave fewer types of causal factor to be considered as widespread, long-range influences on the total flow of events.

To explain an event in terms of an unbroken "chain of causes" leading up to it is nearer the truth than one which admits of intervening miracles, magic transformations, creations *ex nihilo,* events without causes, or events without effects. But it is still oversimplified in reducing causation to a single line.[8] Every

---

[8]The article on "Causality," in the *Dictionary of Philosophy* (1942, p. 47), begins by defining it as "a relation between events, processes, or entities in the same time series, such that when one occurs, the other necessarily follows (sufficient conditions)." Other varieties of causal relation listed are nec-

effect has many joint causes, simultaneous and successive, along with factors in its history which have worked in a contrary or neutral way. Every cause contributes to many joint effects, branching out indefinitely and uncertainly into the future. No end can be assigned, except arbitrarily, to the dense fabric of interacting factors which branch out forward, backward, and sidewise into space-time from any given event.

Some of those leading up to the event are always more powerful than others, more unusual and therefore striking in this context, or suddenly active while the rest remain constant. It is usually easy to list a number of factors which seem to have contributed to the event in question. The difficulty is to estimate their relative strength or to be sure one has listed all the important ones.

Some of the things to be explained in history are singular events, such as a sudden, violent death. Any such event has innumerable contributing causes: In crime detection the main explanation sought is an account of who or what killed the person, how and for what motive; also, perhaps, whether the killer was psychologically responsible for his act and planned it in advance. A criminologist or sociologist might be interested more in the type or phenomenon of which this was an instance. What causes such homicides? What has caused a recent increase or decrease? One might try to explain this in terms of widespread socio-economic trends; e.g., by showing a general correlation between crimes of violence and unemployment. Such correlations, if established, would be thought to help explain a particular case: e.g., if the killer had been unemployed, and had been raised in a slum environment. A psychologist might also say that man's innate, universal, aggressive impulses were basically responsible, though aided by the occasional breakdown of moral, socializing institutions.

The detective story and other types of mystery story illustrate in literary form some of the chief problems of historical explanation. A's body is found, let us say, with a wound easily explained as the immediate cause of death and as made by a bullet. "Who fired it and from what motive?" are the main problems. Other observable phenomena point to various characters as possible killers, and perhaps confirm that they have contributed somewhat to the death. But the act of X in firing the shot is singled out among all contributing factors as *the* important cause. Its role was most active and decisive, precipitating a sudden, drastic change in the total situation. In this it may be like the straw that breaks the camel's back or the final vote that breaks the tied election, having no more influence (except by temporal order) than many other like events.

For dramatic purposes, it is quite justifiable to emphasize the conspicuous,

---

essary, sufficient, and contributory condition. "Multiple causality" is said to involve several causes which are severally contributory and jointly sufficient. Causality, the article continues, has been said to occur between processes, parts of one process, changing parts of a whole, objects, events, ideas, or something of one and something of another of these types. When one is said to follow causally this may mean that it must succeed but can not be contemporaneous with or prior to the other.

precipitating causes. Hence they feature largely in the biographies of artists, as well as in plays and novels. But for purposes of deeper understanding and control this may be misleading. However explosive, they are never the whole cause; the situation may have been such that some other spark would have touched it off before long, as when two hostile armies stand glaring at each other.

From a metaphysical standpoint, in relation to the cosmos as a whole, it may be true that every event is the joint result of an infinite number of interacting factors, reaching outward infinitely far in space and backward in time. At least, one can draw no sharp line in retrospect, as to where the chain of predisposing causes started. But from the practical standpoint of human affairs, one must stop at a reasonable distance from the event to be explained. Granting the broad, enveloping power of cosmic structure over each of its manifestations, one must arbitrarily limit the explanation to those previous events and condi-tions which seem fairly closely concerned. They will be (a) fairly *near* to the result in space and time (or connected with it by a bridge of events, as in the influence of an ancient manuscript, just discovered, on a modern writer). (b) There must be some evidence to show them *actually* operative on the anteced-ents of the event in question. Thus if Beethoven's late style is the problem, one may take account of his age, increasing deafness, illnesses, and emotional disappointments. These are known to have affected his personality, attitude toward life, and musical expression.[9] (c) One must look for *differential* factors as well as those equally affecting many other artists of his time; factors which may throw some light on ways in which he and his works were more or less unique. The opportunity to take lessons from Mozart was more unusual than that of hearing his music.

It is a partial explanation to show that a trait in the artist's work is connected with his personality or mood at a certain time. But one must guard against implying that any one such correlate is the whole cause. One must guard against overstressing any one type of cause, such as the physiological, emo-tional, or economic. The artistic traditions inherited at successive periods of the artist's life must be, if possible, related to his personal tendencies to react to them in certain ways: rejecting some elements, accepting and altering others.

A partial explanation, based on incomplete knowledge of previous events and causes, may be worse than none at all. It may be so misleading as to give a false interpretation of the whole, with disastrous consequences. As in Othello's misinterpretation of the handkerchief, many clues may point to the wrong person and strengthen false hypotheses until a single fact is known, which makes them fall into place along a different causal pattern.

Analogous problems and partial solutions can be found in relation to any

---

[9]*Cf.* J. W. N. Sullivan, *Beethoven: His Spiritual Development* (Knopf, New York, 1927), pp. 79, 243. The late quartet in A minor is here explained in part as "connected with a serious illness."

single artistic event. Mention has been made of Picasso's painting, the *Demoiselles d'Avignon*. In explaining it, some historians would stress previous influences in the visual arts, such as the discovery of African Negro sculpture by Paris artists and the general trend away from realistic representation. Some would stress individual, psychological factors such as a "regressive," "primitivistic" impulse in the painter toward symbols of savage aggression.

Where did Mallarmé get the idea for "The Afternoon of a Faun"? Was it from a picture by Boucher of a pair of nymphs like those in the poem? For such questions of past causation, one must analyze evidence internal and external to the work of art. Nuances in a picture can show, by their similarity to known works of the master, whether they are probably by the same hand. If not, could they be due to a change in his style? If so, is there any discrepancy in style, material, or technique which shows he could not have painted it?

Certain types of cause or antecedent may seem expecially important in the light of present interests. Thus an heir to property or title traces back his ancestry with special concern on the male side through each generation, sometimes forgetting that those on the maternal side were equally his progenitors. Sometimes a certain type of factor attracts, attention once or twice by conspicuous association with some important artistic effect. Genius runs in one family; insanity in another; both in a third. Tradition says that genius is born, not made. Some theorists jump to the conclusion that it is hereditary; others that it is allied with insanity. Still others, more cautious, treat both as mere hypotheses, to be tested out in a wide sampling of biographies of artists. From the days of Galton and Lombroso to the present such research has gone on sporadically, with no very positive conclusion. For every case where genius runs in a family, there are others in isolation, arising from the most undistinguished parentage. Then one turns to environment for an explanation. In the Bach family, was it perhaps the musical atmosphere, the pressure to follow in one's elders' footsteps, that was chiefly responsible? What of the Bruegel, Tiepolo, Scarlatti, Dumas, and other artistic successions? Is there any special type of family environment, of school and neighborhood environment, of class and social structure, persistently favorable to artistic genius? So runs the search for possible lines of explanation; each a hypothesis to be tested empirically. So far no psychological or social type seems to provide a very high correlation with genius in general or with any particular kind of art.[10]

Meanwhile, another approach to the causation of individual and social creativeness in art goes on in the educational process. When conducted experimentally, education becomes the greatest of all possible laboratories for psychosocial technology, in the arts and elsewhere. During the twentieth century the experimental attitude has been especially active in art education on

---

[10]On psychological studies of artists' biographies and related subjects, see Munro, "Methods in the Psychology of Art," in *Art Education: its Philosophy and Psychology* (New York, 1956), pp. 179 ff.

the lower grades of school, with the aid of other institutions such as the art museum. Dedicated to the aim of stimulating and fostering creativeness in children of all racial and socio-economic groups, it assumes as a hypothesis that proper educational methods can achieve this aim. In other words, it assumes that education is or can be one factor in the production of artistic ability. Probable as this seems in general, no one kind of artistic education has yet proved its superiority in that respect. Freedom of expression, ample equipment, every conceivable encouragement, have so far produced many incidental values including widespread competence and cultivated taste, but so far little outstanding genius. In the most baffling way, genius insists on arising in the most unlikely places and often after what seem to be the worst possible methods of education.

10. What Causes Evolution in Art?
A Pluralistic Hypothesis

Assuming that evolution has occurred and is still occurring in the arts, in the sense defined above, how can it be explained in causal terms? We have just seen that no complete or theoretically satisfying answer is possible. One may take one's pick of the existing metaphysical theories of the ultimate cause or prime mover of all events, as material or spiritual. Such an answer, if true, explains everything in a general way and nothing in a specific way.

By showing the operation of certain more specific principles or processes, such as natural selection, immanent determinism, socio-economic determinism, cultural diffusion, and independent invention, we begin to give a somewhat clearer conception of "how it happened." But even these are still very general concepts, and do not take us much closer to an understanding of specific styles or style trends. Each is infinitely variable in itself as to specific content and details of operation. Their interrelations and relative influence — e.g., that of diffusion as compared with independent invention — are still in dispute and our present information does not warrant any definite answer.

If we begin at the empirical end, rather than with general hypotheses, we must specialize on the particular data of some one time and place, or else be overwhelmed by the diversity of phenomena. At the present stage of historical theory, there is no continuous bridge between the very particular and the very general. Conflicting philosophies of art history, would-be scientific hypotheses, swim in suspense above the infinite variety of events, waiting for some place to put their feet down.

As to the immanent phase, let us assume that there is some hereditary, endogenous drive in the human species toward development, mental and social growth with complication; but that this drive is often weak and easily deflected or reversed by outer pressures.

As to the environmental phase, let us assume that physical and social environments interact in the process of cultural selection, which is somewhat analogous to natural selection in the organic world. This would imply that cultural products, including works and styles of art, tend to vary in each generation; that environments determine which shall survive and which die out; also how the surviving types shall adapt themselves to different conditions.

The facts show a long-range, over-all tendency of art to complication, and many complex types survive. Not all complex types survive, and some simple ones do. (The facts are similar in regard to organic evolution.) When the more complex types of art survive, it may be because they help the groups which make and use such art to gain security, prosperity, and power. Or it may be because they succeed in winning and holding the favor of influential groups through successive generations for aesthetic or other reasons. This they can do only through satisfying some innate, potential desire in man.

Amplifying this hypothesis a little, we may suppose that man developed as an organic species through natural selection, with an innate physical equipment capable of and inclined toward complex cultural development in general. He was predisposed to experimenting, learning, and transmitting cultural achievements; to producing and enjoying what later evolved into art. He was, on the whole, predisposed to wanting to improve and develop his cultural possessions along more complex lines, though with important exceptions and regressions. This predisposition was perhaps, from the biological viewpoint, a freak or hypertrophy, innately developed far beyond the requirements of physical survival; but, having it, man has felt at times impelled to use it constructively. Hence the term *homo faber*. This was not his only predisposition, obviously; he is also predisposed to fight, seize, and destroy; but on the whole the constructive side has made considerable headway. The impulse to construct and enjoy complex cultural products and activities, including art, did not become fully conscious, rational, and explicit until a fairly advanced stage of civilization. On the earlier stages, it was less conscious and less differentiated from primary needs and satisfactions. Man's ancestors took the road of competing for survival and power through intelligence, practical ingenuity, symbolic learning, and culture. In the long process, man found that many complex activities and products were not only useful but aesthetically satisfying. The arts developed out of primitive culture in more and more specialized ways, as man developed stronger tastes for aesthetic satisfactions, whether combined with utilitarian devices or apart from them.

Thus the complicative, evolutionary tendency of art was an integral part of the complicative tendency of culture in general. It did not need or have a separate motivation or a distinctive set of causes. It was carried along through early cultural stages by the same motives which impelled the evolution of culture as a whole; by the increasing practical value, intellectual interest, and aesthetic satisfaction of growing mentally and building more elaborate cultural forms. Only in urban civilizations such as the Greek was the process of artistic complication explicitly recognized and evaluated. Then it was sometimes denounced, as by Plato; but by that time its momentum had become too strong to be stopped. It appealed to popular taste if not to philosophers, and this helped to accelerate it. However, strong resistances to cultural complication developed in certain branches of ancient civilization, including utilitarian technology and art. Hence the evolution of art remained slow and irregular. Not until the late eighteenth and nineteenth centuries was it recognized as a large-scale process and approved as desirable by leading philosophers and scientists.

11. Summary

To demonstrate the fact of evolution in the arts, it is not strictly necessary to offer any explanation of *why* it happens or what makes it happen. Attempts at fundamental explanation of historical events and cultural phenomena encounter serious difficulties. The theory of evolution can be stated simply as a description of observable types and tendencies in phenomena, without reference to what causes them. However, a thorough discussion should include some attention to both. The foregoing chapter compares the implications and the strong and weak points of several past attempts.

Complete, certain, ultimate explanations of the universe and human history are impossible. Partial, tentative, empirical ones are not. Historical events vary so much that no exact "covering law" has been found. To show the sequence of events leading up to a certain phenomenon, or the larger processes of which it is a part, is not a complete explanation, but it may be useful and enlightening. The theory of evolution, if true, can provide a partial explanation of artistic phenomena to the extent of showing some of their antecedents and causal relations.

Attempts at historical explanation are on various levels of depth. Those of empirical science are more far-reaching and reliable than those of naïve guesswork. Those of metaphysics try to reach the deepest level, but are speculative or fanciful. They apply the main traditional world-views in postulating a natural or supernatural, material or spiritual first cause and present directive force. All such theories leave much unanswered.

Determinism and indeterminism, parallelism and diffusionism, can all be interpreted in extreme or moderate ways. They can lean toward naturalism or supernaturalism. Determinism can stress the role of environment or that of heredity. The position taken here is one of moderate, pluralistic, flexible determinism. It is naturalistic and empirical as opposed to metaphysical idealism. .

Analogies among the arts of unconnected peoples seem to point to some amount of inherent determinism, but not of compelling strength. Persistence and change of direction in the processes of art are both causally related to basic human traits as well as to environmental factors. Art and life often veer toward one extreme type or another, then move to correct the balance.

Much empirical study is needed to discover partial correlations, positive or negative, between various types and trends in art and those in other fields of phenomena. A wide range of variables, both hereditary and environmental, must be examined. Observed correlations can be used as partial, tentative explanations of particular events.

The Scope and Limitations of a
Sociology of Art

ARNOLD HAUSER

A work of art is a challenge; we do not explain it, we adjust ourselves to it. In interpreting it, we draw upon our own aims and endeavors, inform it with a meaning that has its origin in our own ways of life and thought. In a word, any art that really affects us becomes to that extent modern art.

Works of art however are like unattainable heights. We do not go straight toward them, but circle round them. Each generation sees them from a different point of view and with a fresh eye; nor is it to be assumed that a later point of view is more apt than an earlier one. Each aspect comes into sight in its own time, which cannot be anticipated or prolonged; and yet its significance is not lost, for the meaning that a work assumes for a later generation is the result of the whole range of previous interpretations.

We are now living in the day of the sociological interpretation of cultural achievements. This day will not last for ever, and it will not have the last word. It opens up new aspects, achieves new and surprising insights; and yet this point of view evidently has its own limitations and inadequacies. At best perhaps, before its day is over, we may be able to anticipate some of the future criticisms and become aware of its insufficiencies without forgoing the insights that have been and may be gained within these limits.

From Arnold Hauser, *The Philosophy of Art History* (New York: Alfred A. Knopf, 1959), pp. 3-17. Reprinted by permission of Alfred A. Knopf and the author.

There are still people who do not feel quite happy when spiritual phenomena, or, as they prefer to call them, the higher spiritual values, are in any way brought into connection with the struggle for existence, class conflict, competition, prestige, and the like. To deal with them fully would take us too far from our subject; here we can only remark that requiring the spiritual to be preserved from all contact with the material frequently turns out to be a way of defending a position of privilege.

Far more worthy of consideration are those who resist a sociological interpretation of spiritual achievements from a conviction that any significant structure, and above all a work of art, is an independent entity, a closed and complete system in itself, the elements of which are to be entirely explained in terms of interdependence, without any recourse to circumstances of its origin or to its influence. For a work of art undoubtedly has an inner logic of its own, and its particular quality is most clearly seen in the internal structural relations of the various levels of organization and the various motifs distinguishable in it. It is further indisputable that consideration of genetic relationships, that is, of the stages by which the artist moved from one idea or motif to another, not merely introduces a different emphasis, but is also likely to blind us to internal connections and alter the values upon which the aesthetic effect of the work depends. The factors that are most important in the actual production of the work are not equally important in giving it artistic value and effectiveness. Again, the practical aims of the artist, that is, the extraneous purposes that the work of art may be intended to serve, are not always in accord with the inner aesthetic structure that the work reveals. But the exponents of the theory of "art for art's sake" — and that is what is at issue here — are not content with asserting that a work of art is a microcosm and exerts a sovereign power over men; they maintain that any reference to actualities beyond the work must irretrievably destroy its aesthetic illusion. That may be correct, and yet this illusion is not all, to produce it is not the exclusive or the most important aim of artistic endeavor. Even if it be true that we have to loosen our hold upon reality to a certain extent in order to fall under the spell of art, it is no less true that all genuine art leads us by a detour, which may be longer or shorter, back to reality in the end. Great art gives us an interpretation of life which enables us to cope more successfully with the chaotic state of things and to wring from life a better, that is, a more convincing and more reliable, meaning.

The purely formal laws of art are not essentially different from the rules of a game. However complicated, subtle, and ingenious such rules may be, they have little significance in themselves, that is to say, apart from the purpose of winning the game. Considered as mere movements, the maneuvers of football players are unintelligible and, in the long run, boring. For a time one can find a certain pleasure in their speed and suppleness — but how meaningless are these qualities compared with those noted by the expert observer who understands the object of all this running, jumping, and pushing. If we do not know or even want to know the aims that the artist was pursuing through his work—his aims to inform, to convince, to influence people—then we do not get much farther in understanding his art than the ignorant spectator who judges the football simply by the beauty of the players' movements. A work of art is a communication; although it is perfectly true that the successful transmission of this requires an outward form at once effective, attractive, faultless, it is no less true that this form is insignificant apart from the message it communicates.

The work of art has been compared to the opening of a window upon the world. Now, a window can claim the whole of our attention or none. One may, it is said, contemplate the view without concerning oneself in the very least with the quality, structure, or color of the window-pane. By this analogy, the work of art can be described as a mere vehicle for experiences, a transparent window-pane, or a sort of eye-glasses not noticed by the wearer and employed simply as means to an end. But just as one can concentrate one's attention upon the window-pane and the structure of its glass without taking note of the view beyond, so, it is said, one can treat the work of art as an independent, "opaque" formal structure, complete in itself and in isolation, as it were, from anything external to it.[1] No doubt one can stare at the window-pane as long as one likes; still, a window is made to look out of.

Culture serves to protect society. Spiritual creations, traditions, conventions, and institutions are but ways and means of social organization. Religion, philosophy, science, and art all have their place in the struggle to preserve society. To confine oneself to art, it is first of all a tool of magic, a means of ensuring the livelihood of the primitive horde of hunters. Then it becomes an instrument of animistic religion, used to influence good and bad spirits in the interest of the community. Gradually this is transformed into a magnification of the almighty gods and their earthly representatives, by hymn and panegyric, through statues of gods and kings. Finally, in the form of more or less open propaganda, it is employed in the interests of a close group, a clique, a political party, a social class.[2] Only here and there, in times of relative security or of social estrangement of the artists, it withdraws from the world and makes a show of indifference to practical aims, professing to exist for its own sake and for the sake of beauty.[3] But even then it performs an important social function by providing men with a means of expressing their power and their "conspicuous leisure."[4] Indeed, it achieves much more than that, promoting the interests of a certain social stratum by the mere portrayal and implicit acknowledgment of its moral and aesthetic standards of value. The artist, whose whole livelihood, with all his hopes and prospects, depends upon such a social group,

---

[1]José Ortega y Gasset: *La Deshumanización del Arte* (1925), p. 19.
[2]Cf. Arnold Hauser: *The Social History of Art* (1951), I, 23-103.
[3]Ibid., I, 91-4; II, 684, 731-4, 780, 786.
[4]Thorstein Veblen: *The Theory of the Leisure Class* (1899), p. 36.

becomes quite unintentionally and unconsciously the mouthpiece of his customers and patrons.

The discovery of the propaganda value of cultural creations, and of art in particular, was made early in human history and exploited to the full, whereas thousands of years passed before man was ready to acknowledge the ideological character of art in terms of an explicit theory, to express the idea that art pursues practical aims either consciously or unconsciously, is either open or veiled propaganda. The philosophers of the French, and even of the Greek enlightenment, discovered the relativity of cultural standards, and doubts regarding the objectivity and ideality of human valuations were expressed again and again in the course of the centuries; Marx, however, was the first to formulate explicitly the conception that spiritual values are political weapons. He taught that every spiritual creation, every scientific notion, every portrayal of reality derives from a certain particular aspect of truth, viewed from a perspective of social interest, and is accordingly restricted and distorted. But Marx neglected to note that we wage a continual war against such distorting tendencies in our thought, that in spite of the inevitable partialities of our mental outlook, we do possess the power of examining our own thought critically, and so correcting to a certain extent the one-sidedness and error of our views. Every honest attempt to discover the truth and depict things faithfully is a struggle against one's own subjectivity and partiality, one's individual and class interests; one can seek to become aware of these as a source of error, while realizing that they can never be finally excluded. Engels understood this process of pulling oneself out of the mud by one's own bootstraps when he spoke of the "triumph of realism" in Balzac.[5] But no doubt such correcting of our ideological falsification of the truth operates within the limits of what is thinkable and imaginable from our place in the world, not in a vacuum of abstract freedom. And the fact that there are such limits of objectivity is the ultimate and decisive justification for a sociology of culture; they stop up the last loophole by which we might hope to escape from the influence of social causation.

Apart from its external limitations, the sociology of art also has internal limitations. All art is socially conditioned, but not everything in art is definable in sociological terms. Above all, artistic excellence is not so definable; it has no sociological equivalent. The same social conditions can give rise to valuable or to utterly valueless works, and such works have nothing in common but tendencies more or less irrelevant from the artistic point of view. All that sociology can do is to account in terms of its actual origin for the outlook on life manifested in a work of art, whereas for an appreciation of its quality everything depends upon the creative handling and the mutual relations of the elements

---

[5]Letter to Miss Harkness, April 1888, in Karl Marx & Friedrich Engels: *Literature and Art* (1947), pp. 42-3.

expressing that outlook. Such elements may assume the most diverse aesthetic quality, and again the qualitative criteria may be the same in spite of great diversity of outlook. It is no more than an idle dream, a residue of the ideal of *kalokagathia,* to suppose that social justice and artistic worth in any way coincide, that one can draw any conclusions with regard to the aesthetic success or failure of a work from the social conditions under which it has been produced. The great alliance envisaged by nineteenth-century liberalism between political progress and genuine art, between democratic and artistic feeling, between the interests of humanity in general and universally valid rules of art was a fantasy without any basis in fact. Even the alleged connection between truth of art and truth in politics, the identification of naturalism with socialism, which was from the beginning a basic thesis of socialistic art theory and still is part of its creed, is very dubious.[6] It might be very satisfying to know that social injustice and political oppression were punished with spiritual sterility, but this is not always the case. There have indeed been periods such as that of the Second Empire, in which the predominance of a not very sympathetic social type was characterized by bad taste and lack of originality in art; but along with that inferior art much valuable work was being produced as well. Along with Octave Feuillet there was Gustave Flaubert, along with the Bouguereaus and Baudrys, artists of the rank of Delacroix and Courbet. It may, however, be significant that from the social and political point of view Delacroix was no closer to Courbet than to Bouguereau, that the common artistic aims of these two artists did not rest upon any sort of political solidarity.

Still, on the whole one may say that in the Second Empire the *arriviste* bourgeoisie got the artists it deserved. But what is one to say about epochs such as those of the Ancient Orient or the Middle Ages, in which a most severe despotism or a most intolerant spiritual dictatorship, far from preventing the production of the greatest art, created conditions of life under which the artist did not seem to suffer in the least, certainly no more than he now fancies himself to suffer under the compulsions of even a very liberal form of government? Does not this show that the preconditions of quality in art lie beyond the alternatives of political freedom or unfreedom, and that such quality is not to be compassed by sociological methods?

And what of examples that seem to suggest a contrary view: Greek classical art, which had scarcely any connection with the common people and only the very slightest connection with democracy? Or the "democracy" of the Italian Renaissance, which was anything but a democracy in reality? Or cases from our own day which show the attitude of the masses to art?

It is reported that some time ago an English firm published a book of reproductions of paintings of the most various sorts — good and bad, examples

---

[6]Hauser, op. cit., II, 775.

of popular and of more refined taste, devotional pictures, illustrations of anecdotes, and genuine pictorial creations all jumbled up together. The purchasers of the book were requested to indicate the pictures they preferred. The result was that, although as book-buyers the persons questioned were more or less cultivated, and although eighty per cent of the reproductions fell within the category of "good art," thus loading the scales in its favor, not one of the first six pictures getting the most votes belonged to this category.[7]

If we took this kind of response to signify that the great public is definitely opposed to the better sort of art and prefers the worse, we could at any rate formulate a sociological law establishing a relation—though an inverse relation—between aesthetic quality and popularity; but there is no trace of any consistent attitude to aesthetic quality in this case. Undoubtedly there is always a certain tension between quality and popularity, at times—as now with modern art—an open conflict. Art that is worth anything is addressed to those who have attained a certain cultural level, not to the "natural man" of Rousseau; understanding of it depends upon certain educational preconditions, and its popularity is inevitably limited. Uneducated people, on the other hand, do not positively favor bad art over good; they judge success by quite other than aesthetic criteria. They react, not to what is artistically good or bad, but to features that have a reassuring or a disturbing effect upon their course of life; they are ready to accept what is artistically valuable provided that it supplies vital value for them by portraying their wishes, their fantasies, their daydreams, provided that it calms their anxieties and increases their sense of security. One must not, however, forget that the strange, the unaccustomed, the difficult has, merely as such, a disquieting effect upon an uneducated public.

Thus sociology fails to explain the connections between artistic quality and popularity; and to questions about the material conditions of the creation of works of art it gives answers that are not altogether satisfying. For sociology is subject to certain limitations common to all those disciplines, notably psychology, which employ the genetic method to deal with cultural forms, limitations arising out of that method. It is in fact likely to lose sight, from time to time, of the work of art as such and to consider it a record of something more important than the work itself. And just as the factors psychologically decisive in the creative process are not always identical with the artistically most important factors in the work, so also the sociologically most significant features of a work or of a school are not always the ones that are aesthetically relevant. From a sociological point of view a second-rate or third-rate artist may occupy a key position in a particular artistic movement. The social history of art does not replace or invalidate art history, or vice versa; each starts from a different set of facts and values. When the social history of art is judged by the standards of art history, the facts begin to seem distorted. To counter this

---

[7] I have been unable to obtain further information about the work in question.

impression, one may point out that even art history adopts standards different from those of simple art criticism, and again from those of immediate aesthetic experience, that there is often a decided tension between historical and aesthetic values. The sociological view of art is to be rejected only if it claims to be the sole legitimate point of view, and if it confuses the sociological importance of a work with aesthetic value.

Apart from this shifting of emphasis, which, though it may confuse is easily compensated for, the sociology of art has in common with other disciplines employing the genetic method a further inadequacy in the eyes of the art-lover: it claims to derive special and unique characteristics of works of art from that which is of quite another order, from something general and artistically indifferent. The worst example of this sort of trespassing is seen in any attempt to show that artistic quality or artistic talent is dependent upon economic conditions. It would be too cheap a retort merely to assert that only a few dogmatic simpletons have proposed to derive spiritual forms directly from economic facts, that the formation of ideologies is a long, complicated, gradual process, far different from that envisaged by vulgar materialism. Complicated, full of interruptions and contradictions the way may be that leads from certain social conditions to the creation of spiritual values, as for instance from Dutch ·middle-class capitalism to the works of Rembrandt; still, in the end one has to decide whether or not such conditions are relevant. One can put off the decision, conceal one's position, talk of dualism and dialectic, reciprocity and mutual dependence of spirit and matter; but after all one is either an idealist or a realist, and has to face the question of whether genius falls from heaven or fashions itself here on earth.

However one may decide this ultimate question, the translation of economic conditions into ideologies remains a process that can never be completely clarified; at some point or other, it involves a gap or leap. But we should not suppose that only the transition from material conditions to the spiritual involves us in a leap of this sort; all transition from one spiritual form to another, change of style and fashion, collapse of an old tradition and rise of a new, influence of one artist on another, or even a single artist's turns of direction—all these changes are equally discontinuous and inexplicable. Seen from without, every change looks abrupt and remains, strictly speaking, unintelligible. Continuous gradual change is something of which we have only a subjective, inner experience; it cannot be reconstructed from objective data.

The leap from the material to the spiritual is immeasurable, and yet we make this leap within the sphere of social life, even within the sphere of economics. The most primitive economy is a humanly organized economy, not a natural condition; nature once left behind, we do not anywhere encounter the merely material; we may think we are talking about material conditions, but the leap into the realm of spiritual conceptions has already occurred. The distance between natural occurrences and the most primitive economy is thus in a way greater than that from primitive economy to the highest flights of the human spirit, although every stretch of the way is broken by abysses.

One of the most obvious shortcomings of the sociology of art, as of all genetic explanation of spiritual structures, derives from the endeavor to analyze into simple elements an object whose very nature consists in its complexity. No doubt scientific explanation involves simplification, analysis of the complex into such components as occur in other complexes also. Outside the field of art this procedure does not destroy anything really of the essence of the object, but when applied to art, it eliminates the object as presented in its completeness, the only way in which it can be properly presented. If one eliminates or purposely neglects the complexity of the work of art, interweaving motifs, ambiguity of symbols, polyphony of voices, mutual dependence of form and content, unanalyzable fluctuations of cadence and emphasis, then the best of what art offers us is gone. Still, sociology is not alone in incurring this sort of loss, for all scientific treatment of art has to pay for knowledge gained by destroying the immediate, ultimately irretrievable, aesthetic experience. In even the most sensitive and understanding historical analyses of art, that original direct experience has been lost. All this is, of course, no excuse for the special shortcomings to which the sociologist is prone, nor does it liberate him from the duty of correcting the defects of his point of view as best he may, or at least of being aware of them.

The work of art is not only a source of complex personal experience, but also has another kind of complexity, being a nodal point of several different causal lines. It is the outcome of at least three different types of conditions: psychological, sociological and stylistic. As a psychological being, the individual retains not merely the freedom of choosing among the various possibilities permitted by social causation; he is also always creating for himself new possibilities in no way prescribed by his society, even though they may be restricted by the social conditions under which he lives. The creative individual invents new forms of expression, does not find them ready-made. What he takes for granted is of a negative rather than positive character: it is the totality of what cannot be thought, felt, expressed, or understood at that particular historical moment. Undoubtedly, such "blind spots" of an epoch can be established only subsequently; our actual state of affairs always has an anarchical look, as if the individual could do with it just what he fancies. Subsequently one comes to see a social law that has moulded the individual choices in accordance with a unitary trend. In a similar way a stylistic line gradually comes to be recognized, along which particular modes of expression which have seemed to be freely selected fall into place. Indeed, stylistic trends, even more than sociological, have definitely the appearance of being objective regularities that impose themselves upon the individual choices; viewed retrospectively, the individuals seem to be little more than carriers of these anonymous stylistic trends.

But the history of style cannot do away with either psychological or sociological causation. It will never be possible to explain by purely formal, stylistic considerations why a line of artistic development breaks off at a certain point and gives place to a completely different one instead of going on to further progress and expansion — in short, why a change occurred just when it did. The "climax" of a line of development cannot be foretold on the basis of formal criteria; revolution occurs when a certain style is no longer adapted to expressing the spirit of the time, something that depends on psychological and sociological conditions. Change of style, no doubt, occurs in a direction determined from within; but there are always a number of possible directions, and in any case the "maturity" of choice is never fixed in advance or secure from the unforeseeable. Among the circumstances governing the occurrence of the change, social conditions are probably pre-eminent; but it would be a mistake to suppose that social conditions produce the forms in terms by which the artistic revolution expresses itself; these forms are just as much the product of psychological and stylistic as of sociological factors. When one considers social causation, psychology appears as a sort of incipient, abortive sociology; when one regards the psychological motivation, sociology looks like a refusal to trace events to their ultimate origins in the make-up of the human soul. From the stylistic point of view, both psychology and sociology make the same mistake: they derive what is special to art from motives of a heterogenous character, explain artistic forms in terms of something that has nothing to do with "form." Only in descriptive analysis is the uniqueness and complexity of the work of art preserved; it is inevitably destroyed by attempts at pragmatic explanation, whether genetic or teleological. In this respect psychology and art history are on the same footing as sociology.

The inadequacy, however, that we often find in the sociologist's view of art is not simply the result of the method of research which sociology shares with psychology and art history. It is also owing to the rather undeveloped language applied by the sociologist to the subtly differentiated world of art, a language vastly inferior to the far more refined and appropriate language of the psychologist and the art historian. The concepts with which the sociologist works are woefully inadequate for dealing with the wealth and subtlety of artistic production. Categories such as "courtly," "bourgeois," "capitalistic," "urban," "conservative," and "liberal" are too narrow and schematic and also too rigid to do justice to the special character of a work of art. Each category comprehends such a variety of artistic views and aims that it does not tell us much that is really relevant. What do we really know about the artistic problems with which Michelangelo had to wrestle, about the individuality of his means and methods, when we have noted merely that he was contemporary with the formulae of the Council of Trent, the new political realism, the birth of modern capitalism and absolutism? When we know all this, we perhaps understand better his restless spirit, the turn that his art took in the direction of mannerism, possibly even in some measure the astounding inarticulateness of his last works. His greatness and the incomparable quality of his aims are no more explained this way than Rembrandt's genius is to be explained by the economic and social conditions that were at once the foundation of his artistic career and his undoing. Here we come up against the definite limits of sociological inquiry.

But if there are such limits, do they really matter? If sociology is unable to penetrate to the ultimate secret of the art of a Rembrandt, are we to dispense entirely with what it can tell us? For example, are we to refuse to probe into the social preconditions of his art, and so of the stylistic pecularities that distinguish it from the art of the contemporary Flemish painters, notably Rubens? That would be to ignore the only means of throwing light upon the otherwise unintelligible fact that two such different types of art as Flemish baroque and Dutch naturalism arose almost simultaneously, in direct geographical contact with one another, on the basis of similar cultural traditions and a long political experience in common, but under markedly different economic and social conditions. Certainly, we have here no explanation of Rubens's greatness or the mystery of Rembrandt. But then, what genetic explanation of this stylistic difference is there other than the sociological one that Rubens produced his works in a courtly-aristocratic society, Rembrandt his in a bourgeois world, with its inclination to inwardness? That Rubens, unlike Rembrandt, went to Italy and absorbed the spirit of Italian baroque is rather a symptom than an explanation in itself. Mannerism was in fashion at the turn of the century in the northern provinces as in the southern, and at first Protestant tendencies were to be found in the South just as much as in the North. But in Flanders, in consequence of the Spanish rule, there was an ostentatious court, an aristocracy accustomed to appear in public, a magnificient Church — all things that did not exist in the sober, protestant Holland that repelled the Spaniards. There, on the contrary, we find a bourgeois capitalism, liberal and without much feeling for prestige, and so ready to let its artists work according to their own fancies, and starve as they pleased. Rembrandt and Rubens are unique and incomparable; not so their styles and their fates. The various turns and changes that we detect in the course of their artistic development and the story of their lives are by no means without parallel, and do not incline us to attribute the difference of type in their art simply to individual disposition and personal genius.

Sociology possesses no philosopher's stone, does not work miracles or solve all problems. Still, it is more than just one departmental discipline among many. As was theology in the Middle Ages, philosophy in the seventeenth century, and economics in the eighteenth, it is a focal discipline in our day, one upon which the entire world-view of the age centers. To recognize the claims of sociology is to decide in favor of a rational ordering of life and for a struggle against prejudices. The idea upon which this cardinal position of sociology is founded is the discovery of the ideological character of thought, a discovery made in several different guises, during the past hundred years, in Nietzsche's and Freud's exposures of self-deception no less than in Marx's historical materialism. To get clear about oneself, to become conscious of the presuppositions of one's own character, thought, and will is the requirement upon which all these different thinkers insist. Sociology endeavors to probe into the preconditions of thought and will which derive from a man's social position. Objections made to such research are mostly due to the fact that correct estimation of these social connections is not a purely theoretical matter; men are inclined to admit them or deny them on ideological grounds. Many of those who will not hear of sociology exaggerate its deficiencies in order that they need not become conscious of their prejudices. Others resist sociological interpretation of everything in the spiritual realm, not wishing to give up the fiction of a timeless validity of thought and a meta-historical destiny for man. Those on the other hand who accept sociology as simply one means toward more perfect knowledge have no reason to minimize either its undeniable limitations or the extent of its unexplored possibilities.

Style

JAMES S. ACKERMAN

Art historians are especially preoccupied with defining the nature and behavior of style.[1] For history to be written at all we must find in what we study factors that at once are consistent enough to be distinguishable and changeable enough to have a "story." In political-social history these factors are sometimes institutions, sometimes persons or groups — units that retain their identity over a span of time or shift of locale, yet change and develop as they react to their environment and its changes.

In the study of the arts, works — not institutions or people — are the primary data; in them we must find certain characteristics that are more or less stable, in the sense that they appear in other products of the same artist(s), era or locale, and flexible, in the sense that they change according to a definable pattern when observed in instances chosen from sufficiently extensive spans of time or of geographical distance. A distinguishable ensemble of such characteristics we call a style.

From James S. Ackerman and Rhys Carpenter, *Art and Archaeology.* © 1963, by permission of Prentice-Hall Inc., Englewood Cliffs, New Jersey, and the author.
[1]Since this chapter appeared as "A Theory of Style" in the *Journal of Aesthetics and Art Criticism,* XX (1962), 227-37, I have taken the opportunity to make some changes prompted by the cordial and penetrating criticisms of Herbert Blau, Donald Egbert, Walter Hipple, Timothy Kitao, Thomas Parkinson, and Leo Steinberg.

We use the concept of style, then, as a way of characterizing relationships among works of art that were made at the same time and/or place, or by the same person or group. If we do not know where, when, or by whom works of art were produced, then the process may be inverted to allow hypotheses that works of the same style are from the same time, place, or person(s). In this second role, style is an indispensable historical tool; it is more essential to the history of art than to any other historical discipline.

Because works of art are preserved for reasons other than their historical or biographical significance, they often lose all extrinsic evidence of their historical position, so that no record survives of the artist(s), era, or locale that produced them. Without such evidence — coordinates of time and space — it is impossible to plot the graphs of consistency and change that are a prerequisite for the writing of history. But isolated fragments of evidence may be extended into a credible historic account by conclusions based on style; one signed work may be sufficient to construct the whole production of an artist, one dated work to associate a type of art with an epoch.

Style thus provides a structure for the history of art. Other structures are possible (e.g., the biography of artists), but that of style is the most comprehensive, since it is the only one that can be built with minimal external documentation on the evidence of works of art alone. Because our image of style is not discovered but created by abstracting certain features from works of art for the purpose of assisting historical and critical activity, it is meaningless to ask, as we usually do, "What is style?" The relevant question is rather "What definition of style provides the most useful structure for the history of art?"

I suggested that the concept of style is a means of establishing *relationships* among individual works of art. In this it resembles the concepts of society and culture, which are based on similar definitions of relationships; anthropologists also use the word *style* to designate a complex of behavior patterns within a society. There is no objective correlative for our image of a style; we may observe and define certain traits or characteristics in a single work of art, but we cannot call them traits of Rembrant's style, Gothic style, or Tuscan style without summoning our experience of other works by Rembrandt, or the "Gothic period" (which is itself a historian's invention), or from Tuscany. A particular work of art therefore may represent or exemplify characteristics of a style in the way that a person may represent a society, but to say that it has a style, as we often do, is not illuminating. The word *style* defines a certain currency — distinguishable in the work (or in some portion of the work) of an artist, a place, or a time — and it is inefficient to use it also to define the unique traits of single works of art; uniqueness and currency are incompatible. The virtue of the concept of style is that by defining *relationships* it makes various kinds of order out of what otherwise would be a vast continuum of self-sufficient products.

In using an image of style to establish orderly relationships among works of art, we follow the path of the artist, who — by accepting or altering certain features of the arts around him — establishes a relationship that is the predominant factor in the formation of his individual style. For the artist and for his audience, style is a protection against chaos; it serves the same purpose as do cultural patterns and institutions in society. A class of works of art of any kind — pyramids, portraits of rulers, still lifes — is orderly and distinguishable because it is necessary to human beings not only to express themselves within established patterns, but to experience the world around them in accordance with such patterns; our perceptual mechanisms cause us to interpret what we see in terms of what we know and expect. The factor of stability in style can be traced to a sort of inertia; presumably, if natural inclinations were undisturbed by imagination, ambition and other desires, society and language would remain fixed and art would have a history of more or less competent copies of the work of some Daedalic demigod. But we are mercifully favored with passions that struggle with — though they never quite overcome — that inertia, and these contribute the flexible factor in style.

The artist submits to this tension between stability and change, between the reproduction of existing forms and the invention of new ones, by necessity, not by choice. Unlike a machine, he cannot reproduce without inventing, for when change is not prompted by inventiveness it is prompted by boredom. So art has never been static; when it is not vital, it actively degenerates. Conversely, the artist cannot invent without reproducing; in order to make a meaningful innovation he must be able to concentrate his forces upon the few aspects of his work where circumstances favor fresh departures; for the rest, he relies on the support of his tradition and of his environment. An artist cannot invent himself out of his time and, if he could, he would succeed only in making his work incomprehensible by abandoning the framework in which it might be understood.

The relationship of stability and change varies according to the pace and degree of individualization of a culture; in recent art a powerful factor of flexibility causes radical shifts of style in the course of a generation, while in ancient Egypt stability predominated to the point that barely perceptible innovations were sufficient to secure the vitality of a style for three millennia.

In the tradition of modern Western criticism, the forces that make for change in art have been praised more warmly than those that make for stability. Since the Romantic period the military hero has been admired more for his adventurousness than for his caution, and the artist-hero more for his innovations than for his ability to sustain tradition. This preference exemplifies a "progressive" view of art opposed, presumably, to a conservative view that would favor the forces of stability. Neither is really relevant to criticism. Change and stability simply are primeval forces in style and cannot be invested with value except in terms of some preconceived image of man's destiny.

If the characteristics of the work of art that contribute to a definition of style must exhibit some stability and flexibility, then all of its possible characteristics cannot contribute in equal measure. Conventions of form and of symbolism yield the richest harvest of traits by which to distinguish style. I mean by conventions an accepted vocabulary of elements—a scale of color, an architectural order, an attribute of a god or a saint—and a syntax by which these elements are composed into a still life, a temple, or a frieze. We get an image of the style of an individual by observing the interaction of his private conventions and the public conventions of his time and place. Since conventions, like language, are the basic vehicle for the communication of meaning, society aids the artist in promoting their stability and in controlling the rate, the degree, and even the nature of their change. Religious symbolism, for example, is determined by religious establishments as well as by artists, and other less utilitarian conventions, such as those of landscape painting or of recent abstract art, are sustained, if not formulated, by the needs of an economically powerful class.

Other inherent characteristics help less in determining style; aspects of the work of art as a material object change so little in the course of history that they might appear almost anywhere at any time. So to say that a painting is done on wood, that a statue weighs three hundred pounds, or that a building is thirty feet high is to make a statement that, for all its precision, conveys little of style.

Technique, or the process by which matter is given form, is a more sensitive gauge of style than the strictly material aspect of the work of art, but less sensitive than the conventional character. To say that a temple is constructed of doweled ashlar blocks and that its trussed roof rests on lintels supported by columns is to reveal more of its style than to say that it is built of marble, wood, and iron; but it does not distinguish a Greek temple from a Roman or Neoclassic one.

Yet technique may be a fundamental stylistic determinant; this occurs because usually it is not merely a means, but serves important formal or symbolic functions. In Gothic architecture the ribbed vault, which represents a substantial advance in engineering, is not just a device for achieving an expressive form; it is itself an expressive form, whereas in the skyscraper design of the last generation, the aim to "reveal" the skeletal steel frame in the exterior design had a symbolic motivation. (The skeleton, in fact, had to be covered for fire protection; its reflection in the facade design, often achieved artificially, symbolized "honesty.") Gothic and early twentieth century architects were uncommonly interested in structure, and their interest promoted an extraordinary flexibility in technique. Structural change in Gothic architecture was so rapid and so rational that it can be traced systematically in a succession of cathedrals started within the same generation; vaulting or buttressing methods alone are sufficient to provide a key to chronology. By contrast, the technical change in other great phases of European architecture—from 550 to

350 B.C. or from A.D. 1450 to 1650—was negligible, almost an insignificant component of style.

One of the most stubborn and challenging problems of art history is to explain the motivations and behavior of change in style. While this involves concentration on flexible factors, we could not separate one style from another, or speak of a style, without first defining it in terms of stable factors. We create classes such as Impressionism, Baroque art, or Picasso's Blue Period on the assumption that a certain complex of elements common to a group of works is sufficiently stable, distinct, and relevant to justify characterizing it as a style. In a similar way, political historians distinguish "periods" within the constant flux of human action—the Middle Ages, the Reformation, or the Colonial Era—in terms of what they believe to be cohesive and significant social events. This definition of a style in terms of its stable factors is a hypothesis (and one that we must challenge constantly) that makes it possible to study change. While style usually can be defined in reference to a more or less fixed block of historical time, the study of its processes of change requires reference to the succession of events within that block.

For most of the five hundred years of modern art history the patterns of change have been described in biological metaphors. Vasari, the most scholarly historian of the Renaissance, believed that style, "like human bodies, has a birth, a growth, an aging and a death." The scheme survived into the last century, when it got refinements from Darwin and his colleagues and when terms such as *the evolution* (or *life*) *of style* entered our vocabulary.[2] Most of Vasari's followers before 1850 were interested chiefly in the art of two epochs —antiquity and the Renaissance—which were susceptible to being fit into the biological life cycle, and even those who turned from Classicism toward the Gothic found that the formula still could be used. Toward the end of the last century, scientific scholarship and the broadening of taste encouraged a more specific and less normative model of evolution from an archaic to a classic to a baroque phase. There remained, however, a bias in favor of the classic; the Parthenon, Amiens, and Raphael were thought to be peaks of the cycle (as expressed in the terms *High Gothic; High Renaissance*) toward which earlier artists aspired and from which later artists retreated.

At the turn of the century, Alois Riegl, who supported his theory of style with studies of nonclassical phases (late Roman, early Baroque art), was influential in persuading colleagues to grant equality to all phases. He promoted a principle that typifies art history in this century, that the best solution to an

---

[2]Historians of the last century who adopted evolutionary metaphors generally misapplied them in support of deterministic theories of history (aided by some evolutionists who also were teleologists and "vitalists"). But modern evolutionary theory discourages all such efforts, and indeed offers the most convincing support for the nondeterminist kind of interpretation I am proposing here. See, e.g., George G. Simpson, *The Meaning of Evolution* (Yale, 1949, 1960).

artistic problem is the one that best fulfills the artist's aim. But this relativism in the sphere of value was accompanied by determinism in explaining the dynamics of style; in place of the biological metaphor, Riegl put cycles of evolution from an early "haptic" to a later "optic" phase. At the same time, Heinrich Wölfflin offered a still more influential theory of preordained evolution from classical to baroque form in terms of polar formal categories: closed-open, linear-painterly, etc. As compared to the biological tradition, which had the disadvantage of being applicable to only three of the major styles of Western art, that of Riegl and Wölfflin describes more universal patterns of style, though eras remain—among them Carolingian and nineteenth century art—that give little support to their systems. In the past half century no new theories of style have taken root; in this country none were even proposed until quite recently.[3] This is not due so much to satisfaction with earlier theories as to the rise of a narrow scientism that has made philosophical speculation suspect. Although we cannot work without a theory of style, and although we continue to speak of classical, baroque, or painterly forms, we have allowed the systems that give meaning to these terms to slip into the unconscious, where they operate without the benefit of our control, as a barrier against new perceptions.

All of the major theories of style have been determinist in the sense that they define a preordained pattern of "evolution": the earlier phase of a style is *destined* to move toward the later. This is to say that at any stage in the process some force other than the will of artists must be at work directing invention toward the goal that ultimately is to be achieved. Twentieth century scholars do not grant a priority of value to any phase of the evolution, but a value concept lurks in the shadows; if it is the destiny of styles to evolve as they did, then those works of art that promoted that evolution are destiny-fulfilling and those that did not are destiny-denying. The implication that the former are superior cannot be avoided. So, in our handbooks of the history of styles it appears that the chief function of any work of art is to contribute toward the works that follow it in a sequence; and the greater the contribution the more "significant" the work. The history of art has been fashioned into another version of the materialist success story.[4]

It is easy to understand how historians studying Greek, Gothic, or Renaissance art first formulated a biological model and later a more sophisticated theory of an innate dynamics of style; in those periods the sequence of works is

---

[3]See Vincent Scully, "The Nature of the Classical in Art," *Yale French Studies,* XIX/XX (1957), 107 ff.; J. S. Ackerman, "Art History and the Problems of Criticism," *Daedalus* (Winter 1960), pp. 253 ff. (reprinted in *The Visual Arts Today,* ed. Gyorgy Kepes [Wesleyan U.P., 1960]); Lincoln Rothschild, *Style in Art* (Yoseloff, 1960); and George Kubler, *The Shape of Time* (Yale, 1962).
[4]See Meyer Schapiro's classic survey and critique of style theory in *Anthropology Today,* ed. A. L. Kroeber (U. of Chicago, 1953), pp. 287-312; reprinted in *Aesthetics Today,* ed, Morris Philipson (Meridian, 1961), pp. 81-113. My earlier statement on this subject, "Art History and the Problems of Criticism" (see note 3), was criticized by Thomas Munro in the *Journal of Aesthetics and Art Criticism,* XIX (1961), 414f.

so evident, the number of "unsuccessful" productions so few, that it appears almost inevitable that the Temple of Hera at Olympia should have led ultimately to the Parthenon, or the portal sculpture of the façade of Chartres to that of Rheims and finally to that by Claude Sluter. The process is orderly; it is similar in ancient Greece and late medieval Europe, which otherwise are dissimilar civilizations, and finally it is so much like biological growth that we are tempted almost irresistibly to define it as natural or necessary. At the least it would seem that the designer of Olympia and the sculptors of Chartres were making the first steps toward the goal that was gained by their successors.

But the account of a sequence of increasingly successful solutions to a problem contains a concealed germ of determinism. It introduces a trap into which historians habitually fall, as a result of the benefits of hindsight. When we review the surviving evidence of a process in the past we can see the effects as well as the causes of any event within the process. We can, for example, designate a work from a later moment as a "classic" solution and judge any earlier work according to what it contributed or failed to contribute to that solution. Or, with Wölfflin, we can praise—or cite as especially significant—solutions in the classic phase that contributed most to the making of the baroque phase.

We cannot erase our image of the totality of a style process in the past, but this need not discourage us from trying to interpret a work of art in terms of its proper context rather than its effects by gaining perspectives *within* the process at points short of its termination. At any one of these points we shall find an artist making a statue or designing a cathedral. He, too, is aware of works preceding his, and of works being made by his contemporaries, and these constitute an important source in the formation of his style. Given our habits of hindsight, it is necessary to add that he is not aware of the works that will follow his; he knows only past and present. He accepts and rejects aspects of what he finds in things about him and he adds something of his own. By his choice and by his contribution he moves a step—sometimes a leap—away from the past. Are we, then, justified in saying that he has moved toward the future?

In his terms the future is a void—how can he move toward it? If he dreams of its wonders, the dreams themselves, like his art, are creations of the present. He may happen to contribute to the future, but only by having concentrated primarily on the making of something intrinsically worthwhile in the present. If the sculptors at Chartres had visualized as the ultimate goal of their effort something like the Rheims figures, they surely would have carved something like the Rheims figures. Anyone who seeks to alter or to accelerate the change of style primarily in the hope of anticipating the future is likely to become, like the fashion designer, an expert in and purveyor of taste.[5]

---

[5]I received some warranted cirticism of my initial phrasing of this idea (article cited in note 3), which suggested that artists are not prophets, that they communicate present experience, not hope for the

What ultimately ·prevents an artist from controlling the future is the unpredictable behavior of his successors. His effect upon them is partly a matter of chance. It depends on his work being seen by someone and, if it is, on the receptivity of those who see it. Powerfully expressive works are more likely to be influential than weaker ones, but often they are rejected vigorously even by artists — not only when they are considered too radical (Michelangelo's late pietàs; William Blake's paintings) but even when they are considered not radical enough (Botticelli in 1505, Ingres in 1860).

These observations suggest a different approach to defining the process of change in style. What is called evolution in the arts should not be described as a succession of steps toward a solution to a given problem, but as a succession of steps away from one or more original statements of a problem. Each step, for the artist who takes it, is a probe that reaches to the limits of his imagination; he cannot consciously make a transition to a succeeding step, for if he visualizes something he regards as preferable to what he is doing, he presumably will proceed to do it, unless he is constrained in some way. So we cannot speak properly of a sequence of solutions to a given problem, since with each solution the nature of the problem changes.

We might visualize a style as a a great canvas on which generations of artists have painted. The earliest ones set out a composition; later ones keep some of it, rub some out, and add some of their own; the next do the same and so on. At any moment in the process there is a complete picture, but no indication of what it will look like after the succeeding artist has done his share. At the close of the process, when some artists have started on another picture, this one is abandoned. But the final image, although composed of contributions from every artist, cannot be said to represent the aims of the earlier ones, or to represent a solution to the problem posed by the first of them.

The pattern of style change, then, is not determined by any destiny or by a common goal, but by a succession of complex decisions as numerous as the works by which we have defined the style. We can detect a pattern or distinguish a common problem because each decision in turn, by its choice of elements that are to be retained or rejected, and by its innovations, gives to the whole a determinable configuration. The configuration may *appear* purposeful or predestined because each successive work retains something of those that precede it and because its innovations, though not anticipated in earlier works,

---

future. I should have seen that artists, like most of the rest of us, are eager to leave an imprint on the future, and that, unlike many of us, they may, if they are gifted and win an audience, be effective prophets. Many works of art, partciularly since the Renaissance, have been motivated in part by the artist's desire to change the world. In my eagerness to attack historical determinism I failed to point out that while the ability of a particular work of art to compel a following is not *necessarily* a sign of its greatness, it can be. Thus historians and critics are justified in pointing to the impact of masterpieces on future generations as material evidence of their stature, so long as they do not invert the argument to use the quantity of influence of a given work as a measure of its quality.

are coherently related to them. But what actually motivates the process is a constant incidence of probings into the unknown, not a sequence of steps toward the perfect solution.

So we return to an earlier observation that the pattern of change is a product of the tension in society and in the artist between the instinct for the stability and security of established schemes and the human capacity (resulting partly from biological and psychological differences) for creating something unique and individualized. Change is slow when the former is stronger, rapid when the latter prevails. As a rule, the factor of stability gets more support from society and its institutions, and the factor of change from the individual imagination; creative vision seldom is granted to groups. On the rare occasion when inspired patronage (Emperor Frederick II, Louis XIV) does more than the artist to motivate a style, the patron proves to be a creative individual who deserves to be called an artist. Given our background in the dialectic of German art history, it is necessary to emphasize that a nation, a religion, a *Zeitgeist,* is likely, except in its formative stage, to *resist rather than to promote* change in style. The idea that Germans, Roman Catholics, or Baroque Man embody a creative expressive will (I am recalling Riegl's "Kunstwollen") apart from the contributions of their artists I find incomprehensible and distasteful. If German art is German, it is not because any creative innovation in it has been produced by a mystical German Spirit, but because the nation and its artists show a tendency to keep certain kinds of innovation and to cast out other kinds. It is by this conservative, post facto, pressure that society affects art.

In proposing an alternative to current interpretations of patterns of change in style, I do not want to overrate the significance of chronological succession. To do so is to imply that each work necessarily is related more closely to its immediate predecessors than to others of an earlier stage of a style or in what we have defined as different styles. Indeed, the demands of society and the inclinations of artists make the innovations of the latest work by contemporaries in the same culture especially interesting, because they represent attempts to solve in a familiar language the kind of problem that is challenging at the moment. But the creative process is complex enough to be stimulated at many points; often the art of earlier times or of foreign places offers solutions to such problems, too — it even may suggest new problems, since its language is less familiar. So inspiration may came from far as well as from near; sometimes, especially in the formulation of a new problem, the distant past is actually closer than yesterday, as Roman art was closer than Gothic to the early Renaissance or primitive sculpture closer than Impressionism to some painters of the early 1900's.

In visualizing a style process, then, we must keep in mind that the individual innovations that give it pattern may be motivated as easily from outside as from within the style itself. Since the artist may experience and put to use in making a work of art anything in his environment, the historian must reconstruct as much of that environment as possible. Each work of art can be considered a repository of experiences entering from every direction in the artist's surroundings. That it owes a special debt to great predecessors in the same tradition, to the artist's teachers and colleagues, is no more than a plausible hypothesis; the role of these likely contributors must be weighed against that of all the works of art and other possible visual and non-visual stimuli available to the artist.

This contextual approach—establishing an open, as opposed to a closed, system—has been used by the best modern historians and need not be described in detail, but the absence of it in a majority of studies, particularly those devoted to the work of individual artists, causes the assumption of an internal "evolution" from one work to the next to gain precedence over a deep analysis of the genesis of each work in succession.

My primary aim is to explain change in style as the manifestation rather of the imagination of individual artists than of historical forces that guide the actions of men and nations. But if we attributed every aspect of change to the operation of individual free will, we should not be able to explain the crucial phenomenon that originally encouraged deterministic and evolutionary theories: that sequences in quite different cultures may reveal similar patterns of change. In Greek, Gothic, and Renaissance art there appears to be a phase of equilibrium (usually described as *classic*) preceded by a more formalized, and followed by a freer phase. The fact that this pattern cannot be found in every sequence (e.g., Roman, Carolingian, nineteenth century art) does not lessen our responsibility to explain it where it can be found, if it really is, as I believe, justified by the evidence of the monuments themselves. The problem is to discover an explanation of recurrent patterns that avoid on the one hand the tyranny of external historical forces or laws, and on the other hand the anarchy of mere chance.

Perhaps the clearest instance of a recurrent pattern in art is in the development of techniques from a stage of crudity and exploration to a stage of refinement. Sculptors, for example, may learn to carve with greater finesse or to cast more and more complex forms up to a point at which they attain—within the requirements of their style—a maximal potential for their body, tools, and materials. But technique does not always behave in this way; desire for progress in finesse occurs with variable intensity and even may be absent. Nor is it always possible, for some problems are solved at the start of a style, as when the Van Eycks, the first great painters to adopt oil glazes, achieved in their earliest surviving pictures a technical perfection that was never surpassed and rarely equalled.

There is no predetermined law of technical progress any more than there is a law of stylistic evolution. Even where we find techniques systematically refined to a point at which they reach their maximal potential, the succeeding steps cannot be predicted; at that point, artists may abandon the benefits of finesse

(Manet as against the Salon painters); maintain the level achieved (Renaissance sculpture after Donatello) or be unable to sustain a high level of performance (mosaics and stained glass after 1300).

But while technique need not progress in refinement, it often does progress, and where technical problems are similar in different styles, the pattern of the progress is similar. Figural stone sculpture in the round is found in many diverse cultures; the typical pattern of change begins with stiff, frontal, and blocky figures and passes on to more mobile and rounded ones. One reason for this is that the technique of carving stone with a metal instrument does not change fundamentally; in any epoch the beginner has difficulty in turning a block into a human figure without retaining a blocklike character. The stone and the chisel impose their own laws that the artist must obey, and this is true at the most refined as well as at the most primitive level; there is a limit to freedom, to the length an unsupported arm can be extended without breaking, to the amount that can be cut from the lower position of the block without weakening the superstructure. Such limits — together with the classical heritage — explain certain similarities between highly developed techniques in different eras (the figure in Hellenistic sculpture, Bernini, Canova).

We find another example of the pressures exerted on the artist by technique in the development of skeletal structure in Gothic architecture. The invention of the rib vault and the flying buttress made it possible to lighten vaults and walls, which had been uniformly massive in Romanesque building, by concentrating stresses in chosen points. The lightening process was barely noticeable in the first experiments with bulky members, but once conceived, it was continued to the limit of the structural strength of stone (and even beyond, as demonstrated by the collapse of the choir of Beauvais Cathedral). A similar development of skeletal structures occurred with the introduction of the steel frame in the last century, in that it encouraged a systematic development away from massiveness and a metamorphosis of the masonry wall into glass, as in Gothic architecture.

In discussing figural sculpture and skeletal structure I have implied that there is something about the posing of the technical problem that suggests the direction in which a succession of solutions is likely to move. But what that something is cannot be explained in terms of technique alone; it is also a matter of formal and symbolic aims. What impels an artist along the path toward finesse is not so much a love of skill for its own sake as the conception of forms that are beyond the reach of existing skills. In figural sculpture this conception often has something to do with imitation; the style is drawn from its blocky beginnings to freer and more rounded forms because the human body is freer and more rounded than a block. So long as each artist in turn is intrigued by the problem of mimesis the process is likely to continue along the scale from the blocky to the illusionistic. The aims seldom are so simple; in one sense archaic Greek figural sculptors followed such a path, but at the same time they became increasingly intrigued by a sophisticated linear refinement that was not illusion-istic; sculptors of the early fifth century B.C. had to reject that refinement vigorously in order to resume the mimetic process; but they in turn were drawn to idealization and generalization as well as to imitation of the human body.

The appeal of illusion best illustrates how the acceptance of a problem directs the artist, for he continually may adjust his art to conform to his perceptions of the world about him. The notebooks of Leonardo da Vinci are evidence of just this process of adjustment; nature is taken to be an objective goal toward which art can and should strive, and minute observations of it are systematically translated into the terms of painting. But the example of Gothic architecture proves how problems that cannot be solved by models in nature may still guide the process of solutions. The development of the skeletal structure was motivated, among other things, by a continuing desire to get more light. So long as this desire prevailed, the revision of forms was bound to be in the direction of substituting glass for stone—first, by concentrating stresses in the skeleton, and second by reducing the mass of the skeleton itself.

These observations do not modify my earlier strictures against predeter-mined patterns. The artist involved in such a process need not be striving toward a distant and unobtainable goal; he merely may be refining the solution of his predecessor. So the Gothic architect might say "At Soissons they managed to get more glass and thinner piers than at Paris but I shall do still better." He did not have the "classic" solution of Amiens in mind. The same psychology would apply even in cases where it might be said that there is only one correct solution, for example, the geometrical projection of a three-dimen-sional figure onto a two-dimensional plane in Renaissance painting.

One plausible explanation, then, for patterns of change in style is that where a certain problem posed at the start of a style continues to challenge artists over an extended span of time, and only where it suggests one type of solution rather than another, the process will show progressive refinement toward the prefer-red type of solution. When similar patterns are exhibited in different cultures, it is likely that the preferred type of solution is in some way similar. Refinement of this kind is neither inevitable nor necessarily desirable. The stability of Egyptian art is due to the fact that the solutions found at an early stage were considered optimal for centuries; by contrast, Roman and nineteenth century art tended to shift often from one problem to another. In short, the psychology of artistic production admits but does not demand systematic and recurrent patterns of change in style.

On what grounds may we establish the limits or extent of a style, and differentiate it from other styles? Sometimes the question is partially answered by social-historical phenomena, as in epochs when a new style is started abruptly to satisfy a new need (early Christian architecture) or terminated by disaster or acculturation (Aztec, Northwest Indian art); or when it is coextensive with a closed political or geographical unit (ancient Egypt). Most of Western art, however, from Greek antiquity to the present day is a great mega-style within which we attempt to find plausible subdivisions that help to clarify the historical process.

Style is not the only framework within which historical process can be studied in the arts. Classes of works exemplifying a particular technique or a formal or symbolic convention reveal processes that may span several styles (e.g., the history of the dome, of perspective, of landscape painting, of the iconography of the immaculate conception). Another kind of framework is formed by the entire body of work produced within an arbitrarily chosen span of time such as a decade, a century, or a political reign. But limits of this kind, which presume some special significance to mere contemporaneity, are less likely to prompt fresh perceptions than those suggested by criteria of style deduced from works of art themselves. The framework most highly favored by students of Renaissance and modern art — lifework of a single artist — is subject to similar deficiencies. It has the apparent advantage that its limits are inexorably fixed by mortality, and that it normally is coextensive with a consistent personal style that behaves as a minuscule echo of larger styles. But the presumption of consistency in human beings is unwarranted; the life span of an individual can be almost as insensitive a measure of style as any arbitrarily chosen segment of time. One artist or the artists of a century may adhere to a single style or shift from one style to another, and in our time such shifts are more the rule than the exception.

We distinguish one style from another by noting differences in the use of conventions, materials, and techniques. We do this by referring to an image of the norms of a style as a whole — style in the stable sense; but the image does not help to determine chronological or geographical limits. We can easily define generic differences between a Gothic and a Renaissance statue without being able to specify which statues are the first works of Renaissance sculpture.

We cannot find a specific moment at which one style gives way to another because the creative process involved in contributing to the formation of a new style is not of a different order from other creative acts. Both radical and conservative artists choose what they want to retain and what they want to reject from their tradition and contribute something of their own. When the balance favors retention, styles survive; when it favors rejection, they dissipate — though they may flourish, particularly in the provinces, long after desertion by the adherents of a new current. Since the extinction of one style is neither the prerequisite for nor, necessarily, the result of the initiation of another, old and new styles may exist side-by-side and mutually influence one another; and several new ones may coexist even in the same locale. (Paris of the early twentieth century harbored Cubism, Fauvism, Futurism, etc.)

A style, then, may be thought of as a class of related solutions to a problem —

or responses to a challenge — that may be said to begin whenever artists begin to pursue a problem or react to a challenge that differs significantly from those posed by the prevailing style or styles. It is easy to detect a "significant" difference when artists vigorously reject major features of a traditional style and consciously aim to eliminate them from their work (Carolingian and Renaissance architecture, most early twentieth century movements); but the distinction is quite unclear when the inventions of an artist who thinks of himself as a faithful bearer of tradition become the nucleus of a wholly new style, and one style flows into another without perceptible deflections. I think of Giotto and Duccio; they represent the flowering of the late Middle Ages and/or the origins of the Renaissance, according to the historian's needs — to his definition of what is significant.

If we accept, then, a theory of confluent, overlapping, and interacting styles in place of a cyclical-evolutionary theory, the problem of fixing limits becomes much less urgent. The cycles of traditional art history must have beginnings and ends and new cycles need to be started by somebody; but the limits of confluent styles such as Gothic-Renaissance or Renaissance-Baroque can be fixed wherever the problem at hand requires, since they admittedly have no objective reality.

So long as it matters a great deal when and by whom a new style is inititated, it is difficult to distinguish the innovator from the genius, for the premium tends to be placed rather on novelty than on quality. While the two are not necessarily antithetical, a theory that exaggerates the importance of the initiation of styles cannot admit a dispassionate examination of the relationship of novelty to quality. The great artist is often an innovator, but his genius does not consist so much in the innovations themselves as in his ability to make them expressive and forceful. Innovations can be made by anyone, and often minor artists have conceived novelties that gained significance and force only in the hands of their betters. It is useful to designate as the start of a style the work of a great master, but often he is only one, and not always the first, to employ the new elements that characterize the style. But by the power of his art he frames the innovations into problems or challenges that continue to absorb his successors for generations. These successors are expressing their respect, not for the novelty but for the quality and authority of certain works of art. Being artists and not chroniclers, they tend to be indifferent to the question of whether those works were the first of their kind.

By taking a neutral position with respect to innovation, we awaken our perceptions to the realm of qualities that distinguished artists evoke from traditional elements in their art. Equally important is the evaluation of "minor" and "unsuccessful" styles, which are forced into the background by cyclical or dialectic theories that allow only one "major development" at one time. Because Leonardo and Raphael were so effective around 1505, the powerful and original art of Botticelli and Piero di Cosimo at the same period has been relegated to obscurity. It is revealing that this art, at the close of the Florentine early Renaissance, should have suffered more from our historical biases than other comparable terminal expressions—the late Michelangelo, El Greco, Vermeer, Turner. I believe that the members of this second group, who had little following in their time (younger artists could not emulate or understand their achievements), were "successful" in modern times because our own art had trained us to appreciate them. A theory that properly accredits the so-called minor and terminal expressions by accentuating the complexity of the context of any work of art should promote a subtler and more penetrating criticism.

If our image of a style is formed about a succession of works that develops the potential of a given problem, then styles of a relatively modest extension make the most rewarding frame for study. Grand, epochal frames such as Renaissance and Baroque are too large to help in making critical distinctions; we cannot agree on defining their problem. Renaissance scholars generally recognize this difficulty, but the monolithic image of the Baroque still causes works of radically opposed styles (Bernini and de Hooch!) to be forced into a single category. At the opposite extreme, the channel of works by a single artist may be too constricted, for reasons that I have already stated.

The subdivision of large epochs into lesser spans (Early and High Renaissance, Mannerism) is a compromise—partly a hangover of the old biological metaphor—which confuses criteria of style (*Mannerism* is a style term) with vague chronological measures (*Early Renaissance* means c. 1400-1500 in Italy and something else in other countries). Categories that are created for the purpose of making distinctions of style should be built logically on criteria of style. Furthermore, since the selection of a style as the object of study inevitably involves a presumption of cohesiveness, it should follow and not precede the hypothesis that a certain group of works is closely integrated and clearly distinguished from other groups. If we assume the existence of a style at the start (a danger with pat concepts such as "classic" and "romantic" periods, etc.) we shall delude ourselves into crowding into it what does not belong.

In this chapter I have tried to define principles based as far as possible on the examination of the creative process, so that the individual work of art, and not the force of some vague destiny, might be seen as the prime mover of the historical process revealed by style. So I have interpreted the concept of a style and of its limits as a generalization that we form, by comparing individual works, into shapes that are convenient for historical and critical purposes. I hope that my image of confluent and concurrent styles, by avoiding the implication of a predetermined evolution and hierarchy of values, may admit a method that is sensitive to the actual causes and effects of works of art, and that it may encourage the interpretation of any creative act in terms of the total context in which it was performed.

Introduction

Explanation, Art Criticism, and Norms

"Criticism" is unquestionably one of the most troublesome terms encountered in discourse about art. It is sometimes used to refer to any critical statement, descriptive or evaluative, uttered about works of art, and at other times it is used to refer only to evaluative assertions. Moreover, the term has either positive or negative connotations depending on the meanings that have become attached to it in one's personal experience.

Monroe C. Beardsley places the practice of criticism in a median position between the work of art and the discipline of aesthetics conceived as philosophical inquiry. That is, just as criticism is concerned primarily with the properties of the work of art, so aesthetics is concerned with those principles that are involved in the clarification and confirmation of critical statements.

Beardsley distinguishes two types of critical statements: nonnormative descriptive and interpretive statements, and normative or evaluative statements. Evaluative statements, the principal emphasis of the selection reprinted here, may involve assertions about a work's cognitive, moral, or distinctively aesthetic value. Contained in statements about a work's aesthetic value, says Beardsley, we find genetic, affective, and objective reasons. Of these types of reason Beardsley takes objective reasons as the most relevant. Objective reasons typically single out characteristics of a work such as its unity, complexity, or intensity, or some combination of these qualities. That is to say, works of art tend to be aesthetically good or bad with respect to the character of their organization, the nature of their complexity, or their peculiar intensity. Beardsley acknowledges that the terminology of merits and defects has its difficulties, one being that a feature, say, complexity, which is a merit in one context may be a defect in another. Still, each art form exhibits certain standards of good and bad which Beardsley calls its Specific Canon. He then asserts that the Specific Canons of the various arts may be subsumed under a more general system of canons: the Canon of Unity, the Canon of Complexity, and the Canon of Intensity. It is claimed that these are three critical standards which can be appealed to meaningfully in the judgment of any aesthetic object, be it auditory, visual, or verbal.

It is clear that aesthetics should be of assistance not only to the critic but also to the teacher and student of art who often find themselves playing the role of critic in the classroom. Indeed, as Frank Sibley points out in "Aesthetic Concepts," criticism is a very common operation. The part of Sibley's essay not reprinted here is devoted to a discussion which attempts to clarify the logic of aesthetic terms. A term is peculiarly aesthetic, says Sibley, whenever its application requires the exercise of taste or perceptiveness. Many words, it is pointed out, function nonaesthetically depending on the way in which they are used. But whether terms are aesthetic in an exclusive or metaphorical sense, they require for their proper application entities which are visible, audible, or otherwise discernible. Aesthetic language, in other words, cannot exist apart from phenomena capable of being experienced nonaesthetically. Second, Sibley points out that aesthetic concepts are not condition-governed, that is, there are no nonaesthetic features of objects such that the presence of some set of them would logically justify the employment of the aesthetic term. Third, aesthetic concepts are not rule-governed; while we learn them from examples, such examples do not function in the manner of precedents from which rules and principles may be abstracted for use in new situations.

Aesthetic concepts are, of course, prominent in the language of the critic who, through certain kinds of verbal behavior, often attempts to persuade others to perceive in works of art qualities he has noticed. The fact that the critic is able to do this has often been a source of puzzlement. But Sibley finds it difficult to understand why, for what transpires between the critic explaining a work of art and the audience whose perception is enriched is an entirely natural process. The fact that the language of criticism is largely metaphorical or quasi-metaphorical does not make it uncommon; the ability to make metaphors, that is, comparisons between disparate kinds of objects and experiences, seems to be an attribute of normal human intelligence.[1] Furthermore, the capacity to discern aesthetic qualities is cultivated early in a person's life through contact with parents, friends, and teachers. When pointing out, for instance, the expressive qualities of a sunset or landscape formation, adults employ aesthetic language, and to the extent that they consciously promote the child's propensity for metaphor, they do just what the critic does. Accordingly, as there is no mystery about the critic's success in explaining qualities of art, there should be no serious difficulties standing in the way of a teacher's cultivating a more refined aesthetic sensibility.[2] Sibley's description of what the critic does will come as no revelation to the teacher of art. But that the teacher

---

[1] See Gombrich, "Visual Metaphors of Value in Art," this volume.

[2] I say "explaining qualities of art." This is, of course, a weak sense of explain. For a recent discussion of aesthetic explanation, see Frank Sibley, "Aesthetic and Nonaesthetic," *The Philosophical Review*, Vol. LXXIV, No. 2 (April 1965), p. 140.

and student function in ways similar to the art critic is perhaps an image which has not yet found its way into the classroom.[3]

It is also hoped that Sibley's remarks will stimulate more concern for the ways in which aesthetic concepts develop in the child. Experimental evidence suggests that young persons have the capacity for aesthetic appreciation and quite often use aesthetic terms in response to both nature and works of art.[4] But it would appear that they do not understand the aesthetic concepts they know and apply; they have not translated tacit into explicit knowledge.[5] At what point students should be encouraged to start intellectualizing this knowledge is not certain. However, the problem deserves systematic investigation.

In "Art Criticism," D. W. Gotshalk provides an illustration of how a philosophy of art implies a theory of criticism. Gotshalk defines criticism as the evaluation of objects created for aesthetic experience. It consists of three distinct phases: the *genetic* phase, that is, a study of the factors that shaped the work; the *immanent* phase, or a study of the major features of the work; and the *judgment* phase, which is the systematic application of a set of relevant standards to a work that is known genetically and immanently. In historical perspective, the three phases of criticism have received varied emphasis. But these critical traditions notwithstanding, the problem of relevant standards still persists.

---

[3]See Ralph A. Smith, "Images of Art Education," *Studies in Art Education,* Vol. VII, No. 1 (Autumn 1965).

[4]C. W. Valentine. *The Experimental Psychology of Beauty* (London: Methuen and Co., Ltd., 1962), pp. 110-18. The study of concept formation and attainment is, of course, currently enjoying great vogue, especially with respect to the development of mathematical and science concepts. However, one should proceed cautiously in generalizing findings from this literature to instructional contexts in art education. Consider, for example, the following sober conclusion of a recent survey. In *Concept Growth and the Education of the Child* (London: King, Thorne and Stace, Ltd., 1965), p. 198, J. G. Wallace writes: "It is a sad commentary on the effectiveness of our methods of enquiry that after some eighty years of psychological investigation and a discontinuous history of forty years of laboratory experiment, our fund of accepted knowledge on the subject of conceptualization comprises so little of consequence that it is hardly worth compiling."

[5]This is probably not an accurate way of stating matters. It derives from certain interpretations of Jean Piaget's notions of stages of development in the formal thought of the child. For example, George A. Miller in *Psychology: The Science of Mental Life* (New York: Harper and Row, 1962), p. 311, writes that "The final phase of intellectual development begins when the childs starts to describe or explain the principles and operations that he has previously learned in a tacit, unverbalized way. From about eight to twelve years the child's knowledge is largely organized in terms of concrete operations to be performed on concrete objects. In many situations the child obviously knows the rules for performing a task, since he can be consistently successful, yet at the same time he does not know them, since he cannot communicate them . . . . [The] situation can be rudely described by saying they know a great deal more than they understand. Adolescence, famous for its social crises and its emotional tempests, is also the period during which the tacit becomes explicit, when what is known becomes understood." As Piaget has said, the essential fact "is this fundamental social transition (and not physiological growth alone)." Quoted in Wallace (*op. cit.*), p. 205. Some suggestions, very tentative in nature, relating curriculum content to developmental phases described by Piaget may be found in Ralph A. Smith, "Patterns of Meaning in Aesthetic Education," *Council for Research in Music Education,* Bulletin #5 (Spring 1965), p. 7. Published by the Council, College of Education, University of Illinois.

Gotshalk devotes his attention to the development and application of such adequate standards. Each work of art should, ideally, have four terminal dimensions: materials, form, expression, and function, each of which can be judged apart from the others and can yield what is called a separate terminal value. In appraising terminal features, the critic asks the question: Do the materials, form, expression, and function of the work constitute satisfying aesthetic foci? By considering the relationships that each of the four terminal values sustains with the remaining three, a set of twelve interdimensional, or instrumental, criteria is derived. The appropriate question then becomes: Do the dimensions work together, augment and implement each other, harmonize, etc.?

To be sure, the application of these sixteen standards of criticism is not a simple matter. One difficulty lies in the complexity of most works of art, another in the language of criticism, and a third in the subjectivity of critics, especially their differences in outlook and temperament. These differences, says Gotshalk, can usually be overcome in the judgment of interdimensional competence. No matter how disparate their dispositions, two critics can usually agree on, or have the same objective impressions of, matters such as the appropriateness of a certain color to a certain expression. But in the judgment of terminal aesthetic adequacy, differences in temperament cannot always be reduced; a form that is strong and confident to one critic may never be anything but violent and aggressive to another. Yet this lack of agreement is troublesome only if we insist that art criticism should deliver universally valid verdicts. But art criticism, Gotshalk holds, is suggestive, not legislative. In this view, the work of the critic becomes an instrument of suggestion, indicating to others what an adequate appraisal of the stature of a work might be. So conceived, art criticism can be a very great aid to appreciation.

In "The Educative Function of Criticism," Jerome Stolnitz states as the function of criticism the improvement of aesthetic perception. Enriched awareness, says Stolnitz, can be fostered by any of five kinds of criticism: criticism by rules, contextual criticism, impressionistic criticism, psychological criticism, and intrinsic or New Criticism. Stolnitz cautions, however, that art criticism may also be distinctly antieducative. This happens whenever the critic forgets that criticism is no substitute for direct experience, or when he is more interested in scholarship than in the aesthetic response to art. Once again, the reader of a critical analysis must also bear in mind that a critique is a hypothesis, not a dogmatic verdict. Hence, any interpretation which is relevant and coherent, and which abets genuine aesthetic experience, must be respected. Obviously no one critical judgment can capture and distill the full range of aesthetic meanings in a good work of art.

The selections on criticism have thus far stressed qualitative judgments of individual works of art. Before moving on to the next selection, however, it is worth remarking that an important distinction obtains between verbal aesthetic criticism—the kind we usually identify as the proper province of the art critic—

and institutional aesthetic criticism, or what has been called "criticism in action."[6] The historical vicissitudes of a painting or sculpture provide us with an example of the latter. The preservation or neglect of works, such as overpainting or other alterations made to conform to new styles and standards, give valuable clues to the critical temper of an age even when no written evaluations of works of art have come down to us.

The relation between art history and criticism has never been too clear. Can art historians, for example, avoid making qualitative judgments of the works they explain? Are they as insensitive to the qualities of works of art as is sometimes supposed? On the other hand, of what use is history to the critic who, it is often said, may set his limitations for appraisal within the closed system of the work itself? The next two essays help to clarify the problems implicit in determining the "boundaries" of art criticism.

Central to disputes over the boundaries of art criticism is the concept of "artistic intention." Some would say, for example, that it is the task of the critic in his explanation to make reference to the intentions that guided the artist. This would involve inferences from the work to the nature and workings of the mind behind it. Or "intention," it is said, may refer to the work of art itself, for instance, to the kind of response it "intends" the beholder to make. In "Criticism and the Problem of Intention," Richard Kuhns realizes these and other difficulties with the concept of intention, but claims that intention can still be a useful category in criticism provided a new meaning is stipulated for it. Hence Kuhns proceeds to give what, recalling Scheffler's discussion of definitions, may be termed a noninventive stipulative and programmatic definition of intention. In so doing, Kuhns provides a model of what is involved in efforts to reconstruct the meaning of a term that has enjoyed conventional usage but for which a new meaning is to be prescribed.

Kuhns first seeks to clarify what characterizes a work of art as a perceptual object. The most frequently encountered explanatory term is that of form which, according to Kuhns, may be used in two senses, each of which will result in a different type of explanation. Form may refer to the kind of experience an art object affords, in which case the critic will attempt to discover and justify a peculiar function. Or, form may be employed in the sense of structure, which makes the critic's explanation one of the elements of the works and their relationships. It is evident that Kuhns prefers this latter type of explanation, for he considers the work of art in terms of its elements, their functional relations, and the value of the variables which are functionally related. The values assigned to these variables are determined by the artist's style which, in turn, organizes the elements in such a fashion as to sustain a constant focal effect. It is this focal effect of the work which Kuhns chooses to define as the work's *intention*.

---

[6]Rosario Assunto, "Criticism," *Encyclopedia of World Art*, Vol. IV (New York: McGraw-Hill Book Co., Inc., 1961), columns 114-18.

Kuhns has thus evolved a definition of intention that refers to nothing beyond the closed system constituting the work of art. A critic, says Kuhn, may legitimately confine his explanation to this closed system. However, the nature of the intention, or focal effect, of a particular work may make it desirable to expand the boundaries of relevance to include other factors. But once these boundaries are drawn, explanation must be restricted to the system thus defined.

A distinction between the art historian and the critic of art is often made by reference to the presumed greater objectivity of the former and the notorious subjectivity of the latter. But in "The Historian as Critic," James S. Ackerman tries to demonstrate that objectivity and subjectivity are not polar states of mind. In discourse about art, an "objective" statement is still a report on the personal response of a particular individual, and we are justified in calling it objective only to the extent that its meaning can be clearly communicated to and verified by a large number of other persons. Subjective statements, in this view, are merely those that are more difficult to transmit. Thus, objectivity and subjectivity are seen as the starting and terminal points of a spectrum of communicability.

Art criticism, claims Ackerman, can be said to extend over this entire spectrum. At the most objective end, the work of art is examined in terms of its physical properties and materials. Techniques, however, are already harder to objectify, and still farther along we find statements about the formal and symbolic conventions governing the work. Such conventions are explored by analytical methods, and here subjectivity enters more significantly because the critic must bring to his analysis a considerable fund of personal knowledge and experience. Synthesis lies at the far end of the spectrum of criticism; it evaluates the work as a unique experience by a process generally called subjective or intuitive. In this synthetic phase the superior critic crowns his empirical and analytical exposition with revealing insight, a task that requires sensitivity to the work as well as a capacity for turning visual experiences into a verbal account.

In contrast to the critic, says Ackerman, the art historian tends to restrict his attention to physical description and analysis of conventions. Furthermore, history is more concerned with reconstructing the context in which the work of art was produced, while criticism tends to articulate responses in relation to current modes of thought. But the spheres of activity of the critic and the historian are not mutually exclusive. In fact, Ackerman seems to recommend a superior alloy of the two, the critic-scholar.

Aesthetics and Criticism

MONROE C. BEARDSLEY

There would be no problems of aesthetics, in the sense in which I propose to mark out this field of study, if no one ever talked about works of art. So long as we enjoy a movie, a story, or a song, in silence — except perhaps for occasional grunts or groans, murmurs of annoyance or satisfaction — there is no call for philosophy. But as soon as we utter a statement about the work, various sorts of question can arise.

For example, a fine arts magazine's review of a showing by a British painter remarks upon the variety of shapes that appear in his paintings, including

perfectly overt numerals, thrown in for good measure. Sometimes these merely signify the date — although they are not for *that* reason included so boldly in Davie's design; but rather, because they are, very simply, such primary, such obvious *symbols*. They stand, in the composition, as symbols of symbols — and Davie is, like so many other important contemporary artists, more concerned to express the fact that his work comprises symbols than to make these symbols symbolize something specific. This is not strange: it is simply the outcome of possession by that profound sense of reality which the truly creative artist in any age is always assailed by. . . . To celebrate his perception of the reality of whatever it is he is perceiving — that is the artist's object in painting. There is therefore nothing esoteric in the undecipherable crypto-symbols which force their way past Alan Davie and onto his canvases.

From *Aesthetics: Problems in the Philosophy of Criticism,* by Monroe C. Beardsley, © 1958, by Harcourt, Brace & World, Inc. and reprinted with their permission and that of the author.

How can the numerals be "symbols," if they symbolize nothing "specific," and how can they be "crypto-symbols" if they are not "esoteric"? What *is* a symbol in a painting, and especially what are "symbols of symbols"? How are the painter's symbols connected with his "profound sense of reality," and what does the word "reality" mean in such a context? If this sense of reality, and the goal of "celebrating" the perception of it, are common to painters of all ages, how does it happen that the desire to be somehow symbolic without caring much *what* you symbolize is a peculiar characteristic of contemporary artists?

A reviewer in a literary magazine comments upon a new novel:

> When an American writer attempts to enter the mind of an alien culture it is important for his reader to know whether or not the writer is scrupulous. Is the novelist truly writing, as Hemingway might say, or is he merely seeking picturesque (and irrelevant) symbols for his own private fantasies?
>
> Now, in reading Robert Ramsey's admirable novel [*Fiesta*] about contemporary Mexico the reader need have no fears. Mr. Ramsey's novel is authentic. It is not about the author's own experience. It hews to Mexican experience, and the author's presence is sensed only as a conscience at work. This is a reassuring sort of presence.

Why is it important for the reader to know whether or not the writer is "scrupulous," and to be assured that the novel is "authentic"? Indeed, how can the reader (or reviewer) possibly find out? What does it mean to say that the novel contains a "conscience at work," and what is the evidence for this statement?

A record reviewer discusses the symphonies of Anton Bruckner:

> Bruckner is quite capable of stopping dead at the end of his first theme and then taking up his second without any polite or cajoling bridge passage whatever. He often uses long stretches of unison without harmonic trimmings, a process which strikes the confirmed Bruckner lover as extremely daring, but which sometimes sounds crude on first hearing. When Bruckner comes to the finish of a big, baroque movement he often hammers it home quite unabashedly with periods and exclamation points, and he is a great user of sequences in the building of his powerful climaxes. In a composer of less genius, these habits might seem either unsophisticated or arrogant. But they are part and parcel of Bruckner's musical personality, and their very lack of sophistication is closely related to the earnestness, the great honesty, and the painstaking effort to communicate noble and simple ideas that endear Bruckner to those who are well acquainted with his music.

What is meant by "harmonic trimmings," "baroque," "sequences"? Why should daring be considered a desirable thing in music? How can musical habits that the reviewer would apparently consider faults in other composers be transformed into merits by Bruckner's earnestness and honesty? And in what conceivable way can music without words be expected to "communicate noble and simple ideas"?

It would be easy to think of many other questions about these quotations, which are fairly rich in unclear terms and challengeable assumptions. They are not offered as Horrible Examples, and we need not consider at this point how far they are typical: that would be hard to decide, for discourse about art ranges from passages that embody the subtlest insight and finest judgment to passages that achieve a level of pretentious unintelligibility that would not be tolerated, much less praised as profound, in other fields. But the three passages above, and the questions about them, do exhibit some of the puzzles that may trouble a thoughtful reader. It is such puzzles that give rise to the subject of aesthetics.

Aesthetics and Criticism

Most of the statements in the passages just quoted are about objects called "works of art." For the present, we shall use the term in a rough sense that will have to be sharpened later.

Works of art fall into a number of readily distinguishable subclasses, and so, correspondingly, do the statements about them. Statements about literary works are called "literary criticism"; there is also music criticism, dance criticism, and so on. I will use the term "critical statement," very broadly, to refer to any statement about a work of art, that is, any statement about such objects as poems, paintings, plays, statues, symphonies. A critical statement is not necessarily critical in the sense of condemning the work — it need not be a value judgment at all — nor is it necessarily a statement made by a professional critic. "*Romeo and Juliet* is in five acts"; "Smetana's *String Quartet in E Minor* is autobiographical"; "Yves Tanguy's painting, *Mama, Papa Is Wounded!* (1927, Museum of Modern Art, New York) has a sinister air" — these are critical statements, whether true or false, and no matter who makes them. Thus critical statements are answers to questions like these: How does the representation of space in Van Gogh's *Night Café* (1888, Stephen C. Clark Collection, New York) contribute to its nightmarish quality? Are there defects in the orchestration of the finale of Schubert's *Symphony in C Major (No. 7)*? What metaphysical outlook is reflected in Shelley's *Adonais*:

The One remains, the many change and pass?

Is *The Cherry Orchard* a better play than *The Wild Duck*? Questions like these are for the critic, amateur or paid, to deal with.

When, however, we ask questions, not about works of art, but about what the critic *says* about works of art, that is, about his questions or his answers, then we are on another level of discourse. What can the word "autobiographical" mean when applied to music? By what method does a critic determine the metaphysical outlook of a poem? What would be a good reason for saying that one play is better, or worse, than another? Questions like these are questions of aesthetics.

As a field of study, aesthetics consists of a rather heterogeneous collection of problems: those that arise when we make a serious effort to say something true and warranted about a work of art. As a field of knowledge, aesthetics consists of those principles that are required for clarifying and confirming critical statements. Aesthetics can be thought of, then, as the philosophy of criticism, or *metacriticism.*

The aim of aesthetics may be clearer if we compare it briefly with two other fields of philosophy: ethics and philosophy of science. "It is wrong to kill," is a moral statement, true or false. Ethics, or at least one branch of ethics, undertakes the examination of moral statements. For example, we might ask, "What does the word 'wrong' mean?" or "How can we know that a certain kind of act is wrong?" These questions are about the meaning and proof of moral statements, but they are not themselves moral questions. Again, it is one task of the physical scientist to provide us with true theories about the properties of subatomic particles, electrons, protons, mesons, etc. But as philosophers we are interested in other questions: Do these particles really exist, independently of the human mind, or are they logical constructs? Does the inquiry into nature presuppose any metaphysical propositions, such as the principle of causality or induction? Can scientific method be applied to all of human behavior? These questions are about science itself; they are not physical, but philosophical, questions.

At a very fundamental level, of course, all the fields of philosophy, including ethics, philosophy of science, and aesthetics, converge upon certain very broad and very fundamental problems. And in the course of this book we shall encounter several problems that would take us, if we pursued them, into other branches of philosophy: metaphysics, theory of knowledge, theory of value. But there is nevertheless a reasonable justification for dividing up philosophical problems, if the fences are not raised too high. Whenever we think about anything, there are some very general principles of reasoning we take for granted, and it is the business of general logic to investigate these principles. But besides the problems involved in this investigation, there are special problems that arise when we try to think hard and well about, say, right and wrong, or about unobservable physical entities, or about history, or God, or sense experience—or works of art. And in this book we shall be concerned with the problems that are peculiar to reflection upon works of art.

If we conceive of aesthetics in this way, we can, in principle, make a clear separation between aesthetics and criticism. Studying ethics may not make you more moral than you were before, and studying philosophy of science certainly does not qualify you to be a scientist. So, too, studying aesthetics does not make you a critic, and still less a painter or a poet. Yet it is demonstrable that neither aesthetics nor criticism can be carried on independently of the other; though each has its own tasks, they depend upon each other.

In the first place, we can't do aesthetics until we have some critical statements to work on. In this book we shall have to make assertions about particular works of art, in order to raise questions about the criteria of their meaningfulness and the tests of their truth. Hence there will be discussion of particular arts, drawing upon what has been discovered by critics. But just because the arts themselves are so interesting, we must be careful not to lose sight of our main purpose, which is not primarily to increase our knowledge of the arts, but to improve our thinking about them. Thus if someone says that Bruckner was earnest and honest, and you don't agree, there is material here for a lively argument; he is one of the most controversial of composers. But the aesthetic problems involved are of a different order. Not: Was Bruckner honest? But: How do you *tell* whether a composer is honest or not? Is biographical evidence relevant here, or is the honesty audible in the music itself? And if we could prove that he was honest, would it have anything to do with the value of his symphonies?

Second, it is clear that, for the sake of reasonable criticism, these aesthetic questions must be asked. To be a good critic, it is not enough to accumulate a vast amount of information about, and a rich experience of, the art you are interested in: you must be able to organize those data in a fruitful way, and you must formulate them so that they can be understood. And this is where aesthetics comes in. Sooner or later, for example, in talking about almost any art, a word like "reality" is bound to crop up: Yes, in some sense, of course, painters are interested in reality. But in *what* sense? Two art critics who have known each other for years may develop such intellectual sympathy that when one speaks of a "profound sense of reality" in a painting, the other understands exactly what he means. Much more often, I am afraid, people think they understand what is meant when they really don't at all. And sometimes they don't really care whether they understand what is meant, if they have a vague feeling that something profound is being said. The critic himself may be more concerned to express the fact that his words are symbols "than to make these symbols symbolize something specific."

Thus "reality" may mean the surface appearances of things, the sense qualities that are open to immediate inspection: smells, tastes, textures. A "profound sense of reality" could then be a strong interest in sense appearance, a fascination with it, a desire to reproduce it. It is not at all clear that in this sense, however, "the truly creative artist in any age is always assailed by" it, or rather by the "possession" of it. This description fits the French impressionists, but not the medieval Gothic or Byzantine artist. Moreover, if the painter is interested in sheer sense appearance, why does that make him use symbols? Surely when the numeral 6 is recognized as symbolizing a number, the perceiver's attention is distracted from the sheer sense qualities of the numeral to the abstract entity that it signifies. Now, of course, "reality" has other important senses; it may mean, for example, a world behind the qualities immediately sensed: a supernatural world known not through sense experience but through intuition or pure reason. The Gothic and Byzantine artist is interested in reality in this sense, and such an interest would explain a painter's use of symbolism; but that is not the same as "to celebrate his perception of the reality of whatever it is he is perceiving."

This cluster of questions about the term "reality" will come up again in its appropriate place. I have dwelt on it here in order to show a little more fully what sort of inquiry we must be prepared to engage in. It is quite possible to be a good scientist without ever philosophizing about science, but the progress of science depends upon *someone's* pausing at some times to think deeply about its methods, the meaning of its basic terms, and even its role as a human enterprise among other enterprises. If the scientist himself does this, he is at that time asking philosophical questions; in the long run, the clearer scientists are about what they are doing, and why, and how, the better our science will be. Again, it is possible for a person to lead a morally blameless life without asking himself what is the nature of the ultimate good, or what is the basis of moral responsibility; but in the long run the clearer we are about what makes life worth living, the more successful we can be in pursuing it; and the sounder our conception of the correct way to decide what is right or wrong, the more rational our decisions are likely to be. In the same way, it is indispensable, in order to keep criticism from degenerating into sheer burbling, nonsensical jargon and maverick evaluations, that someone consider, and consider with care and persistence, the foundations of criticism. We must ask what presuppositions critics make about perception, about value, about knowledge, about reality, and we must examine these presuppositions to see whether they are justified. We must consider the meaning of their basic terms, and the logic of their arguments, and subject them to analysis and test. It is not up to the critic to justify his own assumptions, but he must believe that they *can* be justified or he would be dishonest to make them.

In the course of this book, then, we shall think of aesthetics as a distinctive philosophical inquiry: it is concerned with the nature and basis of criticism — in the broad sense of this term — just as criticism itself is concerned with works of art. Now it must be admitted that this way of staking out the boundaries of the field does not correspond exactly to that of all other aestheticians. Indeed, it is one of the inconveniences in this field that its scope is subject to so much difference of opinion. The chief difference is this: it is customary to include among the problems of aesthetics the nature of the creative process itself; what social and psychological conditions move the painter and poet, and how they go about their work. Now, I do not consider all the problems one can raise about art and artists as problems of aesthetics; I take as central the situation in which someone is confronted with a finished work, and is trying to understand it and to decide how good it is. He will encounter many problems, if he reflects with persistence on what he is doing, but probably he need not inquire into the psychology of artistic creation.

The question, What makes the artist create? is a psychological question, in my view, not a philosophical one. And it is, I think, useful to make a distinction between *psychological aesthetics,* which deals with questions about the causes and effects of works of art, and *philosophical aesthetics,* which deals with questions about the meaning and truth of critical statements. "Aesthetics" in this book is an abbreviation for "philosophical aesthetics." Nevertheless, we shall see that we cannot ignore psychology; its data and conclusions will bear upon ours at many points. For example, when we consider the logic of evaluation, we are led to ask about the nature of aesthetic experience, and this is a psychological question. Where the psychological data are as yet too sparse to answer the question decisively, we can at least analyze the question, and formulate it as clearly as possible, so that we can see what sort of psychological data would be required in order to answer it.

The Problems of Aesthetics

It would be possible to make out a case for saying that it is neither necessary nor desirable for people to talk about works of art. Such talk can be harmful. Some books about poetry are so interesting that they distract people from reading the poetry itself. Sometimes the remarks of critics, even bad and ignorant critics, have enough prestige-value to spread false conceptions of painting and music, so that people miss what is most precious in these arts because they go to them with the wrong expectations. For example, much that is put into the usual notes given out at symphony concerts would be better left unwritten, for it leads the audience to sentimentalize over the composer instead of listening attentively to the music.

But something can be said on the other side, too. There is considerable evidence that teachers of literature, fine arts, and music can help people increase the pleasure they get from poems, paintings, and concertos. Perception can be sharpened, and taste refined. Even some parts of the creative process can apparently be taught in fine arts and music schools, or at least usefully encouraged by instruction. The newspaper reader has reason to be grateful to the reviewer who warns him away from poor plays. And, quite apart from all these considerations, a work of art, like a rare plant, a pile of prehistoric bones, a revolution, or the human brain, is a phenomenon in our environment of some considerable interest in itself, about which we may legitimately feel a persistent curiosity. The great critics have wanted to know, pretty much for the sake of knowing, what makes a poem work, what general features distinguish good melodies from bad, what are the possible modes of visual representation.

In any case, people won't stop making statements about works of art. The question is not whether we shall talk, but whether we shall do it well or badly.

311

We must try not to talk too much or too soon, or trivially, or incorrectly, or irrelevantly, or misleadingly. If it is true, as I believe it is, that the arts have a place in the best human life—a question to which we shall return in the last chapter—then they are worth a good deal of effort. We cannot all be poets or composers, but we ought to take some pains to ensure that what we say about art helps, rather than hinders, the fulfillment of its purpose. And this is a continuing task. For new kinds of painting, new kinds of poetic speech, new sounds in music, are always coming into existence, and they provide the critic with new problems. Moreover, there are always plenty of silly, stupid, or vicious things being said about art, things that need clearing up and clearing away.

For example, a fourteen-foot bronze sculpture, representing a father, mother, son, and daughter, is set up in a new police facilities building in Los Angeles. The figures are attenuated, small-headed, faceless; they are said to symbolize the police-protected family. A City Councilman, speaking for a horrified group of citizens, calls it "probably the most scandalous satire and caricature of the American people that I have ever seen," and suggests that it be torn down and replaced by a realistic sculpture showing a policeman and policewoman apprehending a malefactor. The Hollywood Association of Artists urges that the group be composed of "easily recognizable figures" modeled from actual police personnel, and executed by an artist who has taken a loyalty oath. It can easily be seen that though this complex issue is partly political, there are also woven into it disagreements about the nature of sculpture, its values, and its place in the life of the community. If we could straighten out these disagreements, the conflict would at least become more manageable. There may not be, in these times, quite as pressing a need for sound ideas about works of art as for sound ideas about the great moral and political issues of the day. But to have a good philosophy of art is, after all, no inconsiderable part of having a good philosophy. And philosophy is our ultimate concern here.

The problems of aesthetics are opened up by the basic question that can be asked of any statement about a work of art, as, indeed, it can be asked about any statement whatsoever: What reason is there to believe that it is true? This question, as we shall see more fully later, leads to subordinate questions, e.g., What does the statement mean?

What sorts of thing do we want to say about works of art? I do not wish to raise here the question, What is the *function* of criticism?—whether it is more important, say, for critics to judge works of art, or promote and puff them, to act as a barker or as an entrepreneur between artist and public. The critic, if he has any use at all, may play several social roles, and at a late stage of our inquiry we shall be able to discuss these more effectively. Most critics, I suppose, would in the end justify their activity by the claim that it is auxiliary to appreciation, to the full or proper enjoyment of art, whether or not it assists artistic creation. In any case, whatever the critic may have in mind as an ultimate purpose, he tries to achieve that purpose by telling us something about the work, and it turns out that there are three basically different kinds of thing he can tell us, each of which raises aesthetic problems peculiar to itself.

First, we must distinguish between *normative* statements and *non-normative* statements about works of art. Normative statements are *critical evaluations*. You are evaluating a work of art when you say it is good or bad, ascribe to it beauty or ugliness, recommend it as an object to be sought after or avoided. I know no thoroughly satisfactory way of defining "normative statement," but for the present it will be sufficient to indicate the class in a rough way: critical evaluations are those that apply to works of art the words "good" or "beautiful," their negatives, or other predicates definable in terms of them.

The problems that arise in considering the meaning and logical justification of critical evaluations are the hardest problems we have to face, and they will be reserved for the last chapters of the book. This procedure is, I hope, a sign of circumspection rather than timidity; the task of dealing with them will be much easier if some other matters are taken up first. In this sector we encounter the most puzzling and unsatisfactory concepts. For example, we can approach the problems of critical evaluation by asking what sorts of reason people give for praising a work of art. One reason often given is that the work is *beautiful*: the *Sistine Madonna* (ca. 1515, Gallery, Dresden), Keats' *Eve of St. Agnes,* Fauré's *Requiem.* But suppose one person says it is beautiful and another says it is not; how can the question be settled, or, short of violence, *is* there any way of settling it? The first question is surely what is meant by "beauty," for perhaps the two disputants are using the term in different senses. Is beauty a quality of some sort, inherent in the object, or a tendency of the object to affect people in certain ways, or is there no such thing at all? Is beauty in literature the same as beauty in music? And what sort of evidence about the work is required to prove that it is beautiful? Is beauty common to all good works of art, or only to some? Some people think that a work of art can be great even if it is ugly; others think not. These are some of the puzzling questions raised by the word "beauty," and they await us later.

A second distinction should be made between two kinds of non-normative statement, those that *interpret* and those that simply *describe* works of art.

A *critical interpretation,* for the purposes of this book, is a statement that purports to declare the "meaning" of a work of art—this is not to be confused with the quite different sense in which, for example, a pianist is said to "interpret" a sonata in playing it a certain way. I use the term "meaning" for a semantical relation between the work itself and something outside the work. Suppose it is said that a tone poem contains a joyful affirmation of life, or that it "refers to" something in the life of the composer; or that a dance "represents" the awakening of young love; or that a bridge in a novel "symbolizes" or

313

"signifies" the crises of life; or that a modern office building "expresses" the functional efficiency of modern business. These statements are critical interpretations.

Though the act of interpreting a work is less complicated than the act of evaluating it, it is complicated enough, and raises its own set of problems. Consider, for example, the term "express." How do we determine whether a building "expresses" something? What, if anything, does this term imply about the experience of the architect in designing it, about the relation between the qualities of the building and the purposes it serves, and about the experience of the observer? What connection, if any, is there between the expressiveness of the building and its beauty as an architectural design?

But before these questions can be considered, we must deal, more briefly, with some problems that arise merely in describing the characteristics of works of art. Statements that inform us about the colors and shapes of a painting, or summarize the plot of a motion picture, or classify an operatic aria as being of the *A B A* form, are critical descriptions. The central problems in this sector of the field involve the concept of *form*. Probably no word occurs oftener in the language of criticism. It is opposed, in different contexts, to "expression," to "representation," to "content," to "matter," to "meaning." The possession of form is regarded sometimes as a distinguishing feature of works of art in general, and sometimes as a mark of artistic excellence within this class. But again: How is the term used? Which of its uses are worth preserving and which must be rejected as misleading? What is important to know about the form of a work of art, in whatever sense of "form" is adopted?[1]

---

[1] Some lively examples of critical puzzles and confusions that demand aesthetic examination (and will be examined later) are given by J. A. Passmore, "The Dreariness of Aestetics," *Mind*, N.S. LX (1951): 318-25, reprinted in William Elton, ed., *Aesthetics and Language*, New York: Philosophical Library, 1954, pp. 36-55.

Critical Evaluation

MONROE C. BEARDSLEY

The problems to which we now come have been put off as long as possible in the hope that a circumspect approach would make them more vulnerable. They are the problems that arise in evaluating, that is, in making normative statements about, aesthetic objects. In these last three chapters we shall inquire what, if anything, could be a good reason for asserting, or believing, critical value-judgments.

For example, the authors of an excellent book on Picasso have this to say about his epoch-making painting, *Les Demoiselles d'Avignon* (1907, Museum of Modern Art, New York):

The Young Ladies of Avignon, that great canvas which has been so frequently described and interpreted, is of prime importance in the sense of being the concrete outcome of an original vision, and because it points to a radical change in the aesthetic basis as well as the technical processes of painting. In itself the work does not bear very close scrutiny, for the drawing is hasty and the colour unpleasant, while the composition as a whole is confused and there is too much concern for effect and far too much gesticulation in the figures. . . . The truth is that this famous canvas was significant for what it anticipated rather than for what it acheived.[1]

From *Aesthetics: Problems in the Philosophy of Criticism,* by Monroe C. Beardsley, © 1958, by Harcourt, Brace & World, Inc., and reprinted with their permission, and that of the author.
[1]Frank Elgar and Robert Maillard, *Picasso,* trans. by Francis Scarfe, New York: Praeger, 1956, pp. 56-58.

Note first that they make a distinction between two ways of considering the painting: its significance as an event in the history of painting or in the development of Picasso's style, and its value "in itself," simply as an aesthetic object. Considered in the second way, they say, it is not a very good painting, and they give the following reasons: (1) "the drawing is hasty," (2) the color is "unpleasant," (3) "the composition... is confused," (4) "there is too much concern for effect," (5) there is "far too much gesticulation in the figures." Point 4 is not very clear, and perhaps points 4 and 5 are really one.

Several questions about this argument might occur to us at once. First, what is the critical judgment which these reasons are supposed to support? It is put in a rather casual way: "the work does not bear very close scrutiny." We cannot tell exactly what judgment this makes, but very probably it is at least a vague comparison: Picasso was later to paint better pictures in a style that developed out of the one in this painting, e.g., *Guernica* (1937, Museum of Modern Art, New York). Second, why is a "hasty" drawing necessarily a poor drawing? If "haste" refers simply to the amount of time the draughtsman took, then are there not excellent hasty drawings by Rembrandt, Paul Klee, and Picasso himself? Or does "haste" refer, not to the act of drawing, but to some characteristic of the drawing itself? Third, why is "unpleasant" color, "confused" composition, or considerable "gesticulation in the figures" necessarily a blemish in a painting? For example, could an admirer of the painting not reply that what is so interesting in the painting — its peculiar combination of ritualistic rigidity and dramatic tension — would not be there unless the figures were in those odd and melodramatic postures? For though the authors do not rate it among Picasso's greatest work, they surely mean to concede it some value, and indeed it is hard to see how it could have great historical importance if it were not good enough to show the possibilities of such a style.

The passage raises even more ultimate questions about the purpose of criticism itself. To what good end is this judgment of Picasso's painting made? Some critics hold that their business is just to describe and interpret, and thus help us to the fullest possible acquaintance with the complexities of an aesthetic object. Others hold that they should add a brief report of the degree of their own liking or disliking, and a prediction about the probable reactions of others — "I am no angler, but people who like fishing will enjoy this book." Other critics feel called upon to rate the work in some more objective way, absolutely or comparatively. Boswell says that in the long list of works, projected but never started, that Johnson gave to his friend Langton, there was the following:

A Table of the *Spectators, Tatlers,* and *Guardians,* distinguished by figures into six degrees of value, with notes, giving the reasons of preference or degradation.[2]

[2]*Life of Johnson,* Oxford Standard ed., New York: Oxford U., 1933, Vol. II, p. 619.

That would have been an interesting document, an example of judicial, or evaluative, criticism at its most extreme, grading aesthetic objects like meat, tobacco, or students. Whether such a project is even in principle feasible will be one of our later questions.

The normative problems are best approached with some caution. We shall begin by taking a survey of typical reasons that critics actually give, classifying them, and subjecting them to a preliminary logical examination, to see how far the problems can be clarified and simplified before we meet them head on.

Reasons and Judgments

An argument for a critical evaluation may be compressed into the following formula:

X is good
bad
better or worse than Y,
   because ...

Here X is an aesthetic object of any sort, poem or play, statue or sonata, and therefore the normative words, "good," "bad," "better," and "worse" are understood to be used in an aesthetic context. What follows the word "because" is a *reason* for the judgment. It is not necessarily a conclusive reason, in the sense that by itself it would warrant the conclusion, but it claims to be a relevant reason, in the sense that its truth has some bearing, along with other reasons, upon the conclusion. What sorts of reasons do critics give?

There are two groups of reasons that can be separated from the rest, and, tentatively at least, set aside as not of concern to us here. The first group consists of reasons that refer to the cognitive aspects of the work. Thus we find that the critical formula, above, is sometimes completed in such ways as these:

... it is profound.
... it has something important to say.
... it conveys a significant view of life.
... it gives insight into a universal human problem.

These statements praise X for making a contribution to our knowledge; let us say they are reasons for attributing a *cognitive value* to X. . . .

The second group of reasons is somewhat more heterogeneous:

... it is uplifting and inspiring.
... it is effective social criticism.
... it is morally edifying.
... it promotes desirable social and political ends.
... it is subversive.

317

These all seem to attribute — or in the last case, deny — *moral value* to *X* — if we count desirable social effects as moral. In what respects an aesthetic object may be morally valuable we have not yet inquired, but we shall, in Chapter XII. Meanwhile it seems legitimate to set aside this second group of reasons, too, and from this point on confine ourselves to those reasons that are neither cognitive nor moral.

We are left with a third large group of reasons that are peculiarly aesthetic, such as the reasons given for the judgment of *Les Demoiselles d'Avignon*. And these in turn divide into three subgroups, each of which we must examine rather carefully. There are the reasons that refer to features of the aesthetic object itself: the composition is "confused"; there is "too much gesticulation." Let us call these *Objective Reasons*. There are the reasons that refer to effects of the object upon the percipient: the color is "unpleasant," that is, gives displeasure. Let us call these *Affective Reasons*. There are the reasons that refer to the causes and conditions of the object, that is, to the artist or his materials: the drawing is "hasty," if this means it was done in haste; there was (in the painter's mind?) "too much concern for effect." Let us call these *Genetic Reasons*. It will be convenient to use the word "standard" to refer to anything that is appealed to in a critical reason. Thus when a critic gives "hasty drawing" as a reason for a negative evaluation, he is assuming that careful drawing is desirable, and I shall say he is using carefulness of drawing as a standard.

We must now discuss each of the three groups of reasons, but in reverse order.

Genetic and Affective Reasons

I call a reason Genetic if it refers to something existing before the work itself, to the manner in which it was produced, or its connection with antecedent objects and psychological states:

> . . . it fulfills (or fails to fulfill) the artist's intention.
> . . . it is an example of successful (or unsuccessful) expression.
> . . . it is skillful (or shows poor workmanship).
> . . . it is new and original (or trite).
> . . . it is sincere (or insincere).

I do not propose to discuss all of these reasons here, but I want to bring out some general points about them and show how I think they might be analyzed.[3] They raise many puzzling questions, of which the chief ones have to do with the concept of intention.

---

[3]Further comments are reserved for the Notes and Queries at end of chapter.

"André Gide's *The Immoralist* is a perfect novel, for in it he accomplished exactly what he set out to do." Or, "The first movement of Schubert's *Second Symphony in B Flat Major* is inferior to most of Mozart's first movements for in it Schubert failed to realize his intention." Such are the frequent idioms of intentionalistic evaluation. We have already . . . dealt with intention as a standard of description and interpretation, but new problems are raised by this normative role. The method of evaluation that it supports consists of two steps: (1) find what the creator intended the work to be, and (2) determine whether, or how far, the work falls short of the intention.

I want to show that these Genetic Reasons, and in particular the appeal to intention, cannot be good, that is, relevant and sound, reasons for critical evaluations. The heart of the argument against them can be summed up briefly, and it is, in my opinion, utterly conclusive. But the summary may require some supplementary comment to be convincing, for there are several disguises that the intentionalistic standard can assume, and several devices for confusing it with other, and more persuasive, standards. Essentially, however, the argument is this: (1) We can seldom know the intention with sufficient exactness, independently of the work itself, to compare the work with it and measure its success or failure. (2) Even when we can do so, the resulting judgment is not a judgment of the work, but only of the worker, which is quite a different thing.

The first point is evident. If we have no external evidence of the creator's intention, there is nothing we can compare the work with, and it cannot fail to be a complete success, however poor; or, more accurately, the words "success" and "failure" cannot strictly be applied to it. Of the intentions of Shakespeare, Vermeer, the Etruscan sculptors, the makers of the *Thousand and One Nights,* and the composers of old folk songs, we have no evidence at all outside the works they left us. If fulfillment of intention were the *only* test of value, then we could not evaluate these works at all, and we could have no way of knowing whether they are good.

But suppose we do have some external evidence; in by far the greatest number of cases, it must be much too skimpy to enable us to say with assurance that the work falls short of the intention. For notice in the first place how good the evidence would have to be. If a man tells us he is going bowling, we infer his intention, for we can assume that most bowlers have the same intention, namely to get as high a score as they can. This is a standardized task with a constant goal (namely, 300); it can be set over and over again and formulated adequately in words. So, too, an archer or a billiards player can point out his target precisely and unambiguously. But it is a far different matter for a poet to tell us in words, outside his poem, what exactly he had in mind for it to be. Moreover, a task like the bowler's is a restricted one, in the sense that it can be controlled throughout by a single intention. But the act of writing a concerto is one in which the intentions change and grow constantly; which intention, then, is it that the product is to be compared with, and how can even an articulate composer describe that intention in words exactly enough to make the comparison possible?

There still remains, it must be admitted, a small area within which some comparison is possible. A painter could say to us, as he selects his canvas and opens his paints, that the picture he is about to paint will be cheerful and gay, and he might fall short of this goal if he does not know how to arrange the local conditions—shapes and colors—so that they will have that regional quality. If he is a good painter, of course, he may well abandon his original aim in the middle, having hit on some other possibilities that interest him more. But it is conceivable that he should fail, and that we should discover it. Or, again, a writer could tell us that he intends one of his characters to be a figure of mystery, or of dignified sadness, or of nobility, and he may be unable to construct such characters and prevent them from falling into inconsistency or bathos. But, again, few creators have left us such specific records in their notes and memoirs. We do not know whether Schubert started out by conceiving a B flat symphony in the hope that it would be different in some important way from what it turned out to be. And if we say that it is not a success *because* it is not as good as we wish it to be, we are not saying that Schubert did intend something better, but that he ought to have done so.

The second point is quite independent of the first. If we could determine the success of Gide in fulfilling his intention—if, for example, we take his word that he was content with his novel, we are no further along toward an evaluation of that work, for the question immediately arises whether it was *worth* intending. Gide may have been satisfied, but that does not mean we must be; and, conversely, Mendelssohn was never satisfied with his "*Italian*" *Symphony in A Major* (*Op. 90*), but many listeners are. If someone performs a hard task, like constructing a ship in a bottle, we bestow praise on him for his competence or skill, and this we can do even if we privately think he was wasting his time. When we speak of a "skillful work," this is a judgment about the producer, and is logically irrelevant to the question whether the product is good or bad. So many words unfortunately conceal this distinction: consider, for example, the word "mistake." Suppose a critic notes in a painting some casual-looking lines or peculiar distortion of figures. He wants to know whether to praise them or not, and he asks whether they were a "mistake." Now if this means, "Were they intentional? Did the painter's hand slip?" the question is whether the painter was a bungler: in short, whether *he* deserves praise. But what the critic is probably interested in is another question: whether the line or the figure can be justified by what it contributes to, or detracts from, those features of the work that are valuable and desirable; for example, without the distortion, the figure would be less spiritual or less graceful. This is a separate question, for a bungler might by chance produce a good work, and a master might deliberately and with great pains draw a line that spoils his picture. It has been said that if Blake had made his woodcuts with more skill their most valuable qualities might have been weakened.

The plausible arguments in favor of the intentionalistic method yield to attack when we bear in mind the distinction between judging the creator and judging his creation, and when we keep to a clear sense of "intention"; it turns out that either the appeal to intention is irrelevant to evaluation or that the apparent appeal to intention is a covert appeal to some other standard that is not Genetic at all. Before we leave the Genetic Reasons, however, perhaps we should consider briefly one more standard that is really complex and subtle in its ramifications, namely, originality.

Originality in art is commonly regarded as a good thing; the question is why. Now, first of all, we must note that it is Genetic, in the strict sense: to say that an object is original is to say that when it was created it differed in some notable way from anything else that was known by its creator to exist at that time. In this strict sense, it is clear that originality has no bearing upon worth: it might be original and fine, or original and terrible. Caravaggio was one of the most original painters who ever lived—but that does not make him one of the greatest. But suppose we confine ourselves to good works of art—including Caravaggio's—and ask whether originality is not a ground for admiring them more than we would on other grounds. Even here, we can easily set up test cases to divorce originality from value. Suppose there are two of Haydn's symphonies very much alike, and we do not know which he wrote first; are we going to say that A becomes better when we decide that it was the earlier, but reverse our judgment when newly discovered band parts give priority to B?

It is the composer's originality that counts, not the music's. We admire, and justly, the originality of Haydn and Beethoven and Stravinsky and Bartok, providing they wrote not only originally but well. But this admiration is based on something like an economic ground, or on the general welfare. After certain sounds have come into the world—after eighty-three Haydn quartets and, at latest count, a hundred and seven symphonies—for all their incredible variety within a certain range, we bow to the law of diminishing returns. It is more of a contribution to our aesthetic resources, so to speak, if another composer will enlarge the range of chamber music and the symphony, with original innovations, rather than work within the same range. For this we praise him, but from such praise nothing follows about the goodness of the work, except that usually, of course, we would not think that his originality *deserved* praise unless the results were valuable enough to suggest that the original idea was worth following up.

I call a reason Affective if it refers to the psychological effects of the aesthetic object upon the percipient:

> ... it gives pleasure (or gives no pleasure).
> ... it is interesting (or dull and monotonous).
> ... it is exciting, moving, stirring, rousing.
> ... it has a powerful emotional impact.

The Affective method of critical evaluation consists in judging the work by its psychological effects, or probable psychological effects, upon the critic himself, or others. As will appear later, I do not consider such Affective Reasons irrelevant to the judgment of aesthetic objects in the way I consider the Genetic Reasons irrelevant. This is a rather long story, which has to be worked out in the following chapter. At this stage, I shall only claim that the Affective Reasons by themselves are inadequate, because they are uninformative in two important ways.

First, if someone asserts that he listened to the slow movement of Beethoven's *String Quartet in E Flat Major* (*Op. 127*), and that it gave him "pleasure," or advised us that it would give us pleasure, I think we would consider this remark a weak response to that momentous music. And yet it is true in some very broad and tepid sense that it does give pleasure, just as salted peanuts and a cool dive give pleasure. We are constrained, therefore, to ask what kind of pleasure it gives, and how that pleasure, if pleasure it must be called, differs from other pleasures and gets its peculiar quality precisely from those differences. And this line of inquiry would take us into the second point. For an Affective statement tells us the effect of the work, but it does not single out those features of the work on which the effect depends. We could still ask, in other words, *what* is pleasure-giving about that music that is absent from other music, and this line of inquiry would be parallel to the first, since it would lead us to discriminate this sort of pleasure from others that have different causes and objects.

The same two questions could be raised about the general notion that seems to be implicit in the other Affective Reasons: the work is good if it leads to a strong emotional response of some sort. How does the emotional response differ from the strong emotional responses produced by telegrams announcing deaths, close calls with a skidding car, the serious illness of a child, or getting married? Surely there is an important difference, which the emotional-response reason must take account of to be complete. And what in the aesthetic object causes the emotional response? Perhaps some intense regional quality on which our attention is focused in the experience. Indeed, some of these Affective terms ... are often really misleading synonyms for descriptive terms: they mean that the object has some regional quality to a fairly intense degree. And in that case, the reason is, of course, no longer Affective, but Objective.

I call a reason Objective if it refers to some characteristic—that is, some quality or internal relation, or set of qualities and relations—within the work itself, or to some meaning-relation between the work and the world. In short, where either descriptive statements or interpretive statements appear as reasons in critical arguments, they are to be considered as Objective reasons. The distinction may seem a little artificial here, for according to some theories certain types of interpretive statements, for example, "X represents Y," could be reformulated in such a way as to refer to effects of the work upon its percipients. But I put interpretations in with the Objective Reasons, though I do not assume that all the Objective Reasons that critics have ever given are good reasons.

Even if we confine ourselves now to Objective Reasons, we still have a very large variety, so it might naturally occur to us to wonder whether any further subdivisions can be made. I think when we take a wide survey of critical reasons, we can find room for most of them, with very little trouble, in three main groups. First, there are reasons that seem to bear upon the degree of *unity* or disunity of the work:

> ... it is well-organized (or disorganized).
> ... it is formally perfect (or imperfect).
> ... it has (or lacks) an inner logic or structure and style.

Second, there are those reasons that seem to bear upon the degree of *complexity* or simplicity of the work:

> ... it is developed on a large scale.
> ... it is rich in contrasts (or lacks variety and is repetitious).
> ... it is subtle and imaginative (or crude).

Third, there are those reasons that seem to bear upon the *intensity* or lack of intensity of human regional qualities in the work:

> ... it is full of vitality (or insipid).
> ... it is forceful and vivid (or weak and pale).
> ... it is beautiful (or ugly).
> ... it is tender, ironic, tragic, graceful, delicate, richly comic.

The first two groups of reasons do not seem to raise any difficulties that we have not already noticed in discussing the terms "unified" and "complex." It is obvious that critics very often explicitly advance the unity of a work as a reason for praising it, or assume that unity is a good thing; and I have never encountered the argument that a work was good because it was disorganized. I have read the following in *The New York Times* about the *Rhapsody in Blue:*

The humor, gusto and sentiment are all there. The work is not tightly organized by symphonic standards, but its very looseness of design adds to its charm.

I think this has to mean, not that it is better precisely because it is loosely organized, but that its peculiar qualities, its "humor, gusto and sentiment," would perhaps be weakened by a more highly organized form. If a critic said that a work is poor just because it is too unified, I think his context would show he meant that it is too simple (that is, too lacking in interesting complexities) or too cold (that is, too lacking in intense regional qualities).

It is perhaps less obvious that critics very often explicitly advance the complexity of a work as a reason for praising it, or assume that complexity is a good thing. Sometimes critical theorists talk as though complexity was invented by modern critics and was unknown to Homer, Virgil, and Horace. But when it is said that a simple lyric may be a fine poem, I think this is because it may yet have a high degree of unity and an intense quality. And, indeed, certain regional qualities can only be had in aesthetic objects that are relatively simple — see the Jensen *Composition*, PLATE I, and *Municipal Lodging*, PLATE III* — but in this case we do not praise them for their simplicity, but for their intensity.

The reasons in the third group are the most puzzling. There seems to be no doubt that there is such a class of actual reasons:

A: "This painting is good."
B: "Why?"
A: "Oh, it has such a sense of eternal calm and stillness about it."

I take "eternal calm and stillness" to refer to a pervasive regional quality here, as in other examples, and I (tentatively) understand "beautiful" in the same way, though this very special term will have to be discussed at greater length in the following chapter. But there is one difficulty that presents itself at once.

You could say — with what justification we shall later consider — that a good aesthetic object must have *some* marked quality, and not be a sheer nonentity or a zero. The quality does not matter — it can be sad or cheerful, graceful or rugged, soft or stern, provided it be *something*. But this may be too broad. We can think of works with uncontrolled horror or disgustingness — realistically painted corpses, Henry Miller's *Tropic of Cancer*, or the razor slicing the eye at the beginning of the surrealistic film, *The Andalousian Dog*. In these works we have intensity of quality, all right, but that does not make them good. It may be that certain qualities are simply not contemplatable for any time with normal human endurance, and that we must except these, if we can draw the line. Or it may be that it is not human regional qualities as such, but those we already value in human beings, that we accept as standards in critical evaluation. More likely, I think, it is that in certain works the intensity of the quality is achieved

---

*John Jensen, *Composition*, Robert M. Walker, Swarthmore, Pa.; and Käthe Kollwitz, *Municipal Lodging*, Solomon E. Asch, Swarthmore, Pa.

at too great a sacrifice of unity. This is perhaps what the critics meant by saying that in *Les Demoiselles d'Avignon* there is "too much concern for effect."

But again it might be argued that it is not just any human regional quality that is given as a ground of praise, for some qualities are cited as grounds of dispraise: pompousness, pretentiousness, ostentatious vulgarity; a work is bad *because* it is flashy, or labored, or sentimental. Now these terms are predicates, of course, but not all predicates refer to positive perceptual qualities. Where such characteristics as these are cited as grounds for dispraise, they can, I think, be analyzed as negative. Pompousness is the outward form of grandeur and greatness — it is a long symphony with enormous crescendos — combined with an inner emptiness, lack of vitality and richness. Sentimentality in a poem is not a sentiment, but a claim on the speaker's part to a feeling that he does not dramatize and present in the texture and objects of the poem. No doubt all these words are far too subtle to be disposed of so briefly, and no doubt their meaning varies; I leave many questions hanging in the air. But I suggest that so far as these characteristics are standards of (negative) critical evaluation, they refer not to intensity of quality, but to its absence, or to lack of unity or complexity: to slackness, faintness, flabbiness, the work's inability to live up to its own promises, declining power after a good start.

Merits and Defects

Now, suppose a critic supports a value judgment by pointing out some feature of the particular work in question: "Wordsworth's 'Ode: Intimations of Immortality' is less good that it would be if its theme were not so vague." The form of this declaration claims that this vagueness is a defect in this poem, just as one might say that the grandeur of its imagery is a merit in it. By "defect" and "merit" I mean features that detract from its value or contribute to it: they are defective, or "bad-making," and meritorious, or "good-making," features respectively. Similarly we might say that firmness without hardness is a good-making feature, and worminess a bad-making feature, of apples.

But this terminology of merits and defects raises an important question. Can a feature be a merit in one poem and a defect (or neither) in another? Or does calling the feature a merit in one poem entail, or presuppose, a general principle according to which it is meritorious wherever it occurs? Is grandeur of imagery always a merit and vagueness of theme always a defect? Now, notice in the first place that we are not asking for universal conditions of goodness and badness. A wormy apple may still be a good apple, if the worm's operations have been confined to a small sector, provided the apple has other qualities that are desirable in apples. The worm is a defect, but not a fatal one. So a poem, indeed the "Ode" itself, may be a great poem because of its good-making features even though it has some bad-making features. Thus if there is a general principle — stated as, "Vague themes are always defects in poetry," or, "Grand imagery is always a merit in poetry"—this principle does not mean that these features are either *necessary* or *sufficient* conditions of goodness in poetry, but only that, other things being equal, their presence makes it better or worse.

It does not seem that the contribution of each feature of an aesthetic object can be considered in an atomistic fashion. This is true of many things in life; mustard depends on frankfurters, as a baseball bat depends on a baseball, for its maximum value; it is not, so to speak, a good-making feature of a picnic unless both are present. But then there *is* a general principle connecting baseball bats and picnics, though it is not simple: In the presence of baseballs, baseball bats are fun-making features of picnics—assuming certain sorts of picnickers. And similarly we might hold that to claim brilliant imagery as a merit in one poem is to commit yourself to some general principle about the capacity of grand imagery to help along poems, at least poems in which certain other features are present. But to commit yourself to the existence of such a principle is, of course, not to be able to state it. The critic may have a hunch that in the "Ode" the grandeur of imagery is a good-making feature, but then it would become a critical question whether it is always such or whether its being such depends upon being associated with other features. If we know what we mean by "good," as I hope we shall later, then this question becomes an empirical one.

Similar remarks hold for the merits and defects that fine arts and music critics single out for attention. For example, deep space is a good thing in some paintings, while flat space is a good thing in others; different qualities depend for their intensity upon each other. Exactness in perspective and in the size-distance relations of figures is needed in a Piero della Francesca or in a Rembrandt etching, where the violation of it in one part of the work would introduce a disturbing disunity; but its violation in a Cézanne still life or in some works by Tintoretto and Toulouse-Lautrec is a merit because of the qualities that are obtained in this way. Sometimes the critic can see things at once, and with a confident perceptiveness. Yet an adequate justification for saying that any feature is a defect or a merit in any work would include an explanation in terms of some general principle about the value-contribution of that feature, alone or in combination with others.

A principle about defects and merits in one art we may call a *Specific Canon*. The next question is whether such Specific Canons can always be subsumed under *General Canons* that apply, not to poetry in particular, but to all the arts. Suppose, for example, a drama critic claims that it is a defect in a certain play that the action takes place over thirty years, and the story thus becomes diffuse. Now, again, he does not have to claim that the shorter the action of a play, the better it necessarily is; nor does he have to fall back on one of the neoclassic rules, such as that the action of a play should take no more than twenty-four hours; nor does he have to say that the best plays are always those whose action is the shortest possible, that is, exactly the same as the time of the play itself, such as Ben Jonson's *The Silent Woman,* Ibsen's *John Gabriel Borkman,* Tennessee Williams' *Cat on a Hot Tin Roof.* But he could perhaps claim, if his reason were questioned, that, other things being equal, the shorter the time of action, the more unified the play will tend to be; and the longer the time, the more it will tend to fall apart. This tendency may be, in some plays, counteracted by other unifying features, unfortunately lacking in the play in question. Now, this argument would subsume the long action-time as a defect under a Specific Canon — "A long action-time is a bad-making feature in a play that has a large number of characters, striking changes of scenery, and no symbolic carry-over from act to act." But the argument does more than this, for it subsumes this Specific Canon for the drama under a more General Canon, by claiming that the long action-time is a perceptual condition of disunity. The General Canon is, then, something like "Disunity is always a defect in aesthetic objects," or, in other words, "Disunity is a bad-making feature of aesthetic objects." And this is the same Canon that was appealed to when *Les Demoiselles d'Avignon* was said to have a "confused" composition.

The classification of Objective Reasons that we have made so far, then, shows that at least a very large variety of them can be subsumed under three General Canons: the Canon of Unity, the Canon of Complexity, the Canon of Intensity. In other words, the objective features of plays, poems, paintings, and musical compositions referred to in the Special Canons can, at least most of them, be conditionally justified as standards because they are, so to speak, unifying, complexifying, or intensifying features of the works in which they occur, either alone or in combination with other features.

Applying the General Canons

The next question is whether in fact *all* Objective Reasons can be subsumed under these three Canons. This is, no doubt, a very bold question, for considering the subtlety and flexibility of critical language and the waywardness of some critical thinking, it would be almost incredible if it turned out that all the Objective Reasons given by critics were subsumable under three headings — unless the headings were so vague or so general that they could cover every logical possibility. But let us see what we discover if we examine some cases of critical reasoning with our threefold classification in mind.

Cleanth Brooks, in his well-known essay on Tennyson's "Tears, Idle Tears," compares this poem with "Break, Break, Break," and explains why he judges it to be a much better poem.[4] The former, he says, is "very tightly organized," whereas the latter brings in an "irrelevant" reference to the "stately ships," and is "more confused." Here he is clearly appealing to the

---

[4]"The Motivation of Tennyson's Weeper," *The Well Wrought Urn,* 1947, New York: Reynal and Hitchcock, pp. 153-62.

327

Canon of Unity. He says that the latter "is also a much thinner poem," and is "coarser"; it avoids "the psychological exploration of the experience," whereas the former has "richness and depth" because of its "imaginative grasp of diverse materials." Here he is appealing to the Canon of Complexity; the first poem has more *to* it, both in range and in subtlety. He speaks of the "dramatic force" and of the "dramatic power" of "Tears, Idle Tears," and particularly praises the intensity of its final stanza, in contrast to "Break, Break, Break." And here he is appealing to the Canon of Intensity. Brooks raises the question whether the opening paradox of "idle tears" is a merit or a defect, but in the light of his discussion he concludes that it contributes valuably to the complexity of the poem rather than detracting from its unity.

Or, consider a comparison of Picasso's two versions of *The Three Musicians,* one in the Museum of Modern Art, New York (1921), the other in the Philadelphia Museum of Art (also 1921):

The first . . . is the most moving of these, as well as the most solid and the most soberly coloured. The figures of the three characters are laid out in broad rectangular planes, while their faces give the impression of primitive masks. Only the harlequin, in the centre, with his yellow-and-red-checked dress and the curves of his guitar, serves to add a touch of cheerfulness to this sombre, eerie, hieratic work, whose structure bears witness to profound thought and incomparable craftsmanship. The other version . . . is painted in a different spirit altogether. . . . But though the composition is more varied and the colouring pleasanter, while more emphasis is given to depth and the decorative intention is more obvious, this variant lacks the dignified grandeur of the New York picture. . . . More complex, and fresher in colour, this final version has neither the severity nor the stark economy of the other, which impresses by its dignified generosity of conception.[5]

The traces of intentionalism here can probably be converted into an Objective terminology: "economy," we saw . . . can mean variety of significance in line and shape, hence a kind of complexity; the "profound thought and incomparable craftsmanship" do not enter as Objective Reasons, but are (deserved) praise for Picasso. What do we have left? The two paintings are not compared with respect to unity at all; it is taken for granted that the composition in both is unified, and that this is one of the factors relevant to the high value attributed to both paintings. The paintings are compared with respect to complexity; it is a merit in the Philadelphia one that it is more complex, more varied, and richer in decorative detail, and that it has a depth lacking in the New York one. But this aspect is said to be over-balanced by the third comparison: the New York one has a certain difficult-to-describe regional quality, its "hieratic" sombreness, its "severity," its "dignified grandeur" which is far more intense than any regional quality present in the Philadelphia one; and this is claimed to be a considerable merit.

[5]Elgar and Maillard, *op. cit.,* pp. 104-06, 126-29.

It would be instructive to compare a number of passages dealing with music, say in the writings of Donald F. Tovey, though I have not found a single passage that combines such a variety of reasons as those just considered. We might examine his analysis of Mozart's *Linz Symphony in C Major* (K. 425), or of Mendelssohn's *"Italian" Symphony*. But perhaps this comparative passage will serve:

> Thus, Schubert is apt to weaken and lengthen his expositions by processes of discursive development where Beethoven would have had a crowd of terse new themes; while, on the other hand, Schubert's developments are apt indeed to develop some feature of one of his themes, but by turning it into a long lyric process which is repeated symmetrically. Dvořák is apt to be dangerously discursive at any point of his exposition, and frequently loses his way before he has begun his second group, while his developments often merely harp upon a single figure with a persistence not much more energetic or cumulative than that of the Dormouse that continued to say "twinkle, twinkle" in his sleep. But none of these matters can be settled by rule of thumb.[6]

Here phrases like "discursive development" and "loses his way" seem to bear upon the unity of the work; "a crowd of terse new themes" and "merely harp upon a single figure" seem to bear upon its complexity; "weaken," "lyric," "energetic or cumulative" seem to bear upon the intensity of its qualities. Tovey assumes that it is relevant to take these into account in considering the value of music, though of course he is not trying to make any final disposition of these masters.

The three Canons, then, support a large number of critical reasons. This is not due, I think, to their being vague, for they are not too vague to be testable and usable. . . . Nor is it due to some concealed ambiguity that makes the set really tautological, like saying every aesthetic object is either complex or not. For it is easy to invent reasons that fall outside these three Canons, such as the Genetic ones, or these:

> . . . it was printed in a syndicated newspaper column.
> . . . it deals with Japanese pearl-diving.
> . . . it was written by a Communist.

Only these don't happen to be good reasons. We can find other critical formulae that do not at first glance seem to be subsumable under the three Canons, for example:

> . . . it is sincere.
> . . . it has spontaneity.
> . . . it violates (or is faithful to) its medium.
> . . . it fully exploits (or fails to exploit) its medium.

---

[6]Donald F. Tovey, *Essays in Musical Analysis,* London: Oxford U., 1935, Vol. I, pp. 13-14.

With such formulas there may be a preliminary question concerning their intelligibility; indeed, we have glanced at some of these terms already. But I believe that on analysis they will be found either to fall outside the group of Objective Reasons into intentionalism or affectivism, or else to connect indirectly with the Canons.

Nor is the plausibility of this conclusion due to the fact that the Canons permit free-wheeling rationalizations. It might seem that you could justify practically anything as a good aesthetic object: surely it must have *something* in its favor that can be connected with one of the Canons. Now, there is truth in this objection, but I do not think it is deplorable. We have not yet raised the question whether it would be possible to *grade* aesthetic objects in terms of some scale; at this point we are only asking what a critic could sensibly talk about if he were asked to name the good things or the weaknesses in an aesthetic object, and we ought to encourage the critic, as well as ourselves, to be as open as possible to the variety of good things that can be found in art. The Canonic scheme is generous in this sense, even if its principles are few. But at the same time it remains true that in some aesthetic objects one can point out numerous defects, and serious, that is, pervasive, ones, whereas in others one can find only a few; and similarly with merits.

For example, a certain college library has a plaque that contains the following lines, by W. D. Foulke:

> How canst thou give thy life to sordid things
> While Milton's strains in rhythmic numbers roll,
> Or Shakespeare probes thy heart, or Homer sings,
> Or rapt Isaiah wakes thy slumbering soul?

You could spend quite a while pointing out how bad this is, and you would have a hard time finding things good about it. From the point of view of unity, it breaks down on an elementary level; the addressee is giving his life to sordid things while Shakespeare is probing his heart and Isaiah is waking him up. This mixture would be tolerable, if the diverse images did not, on reflection, show a profound looseness in conception, the various poets being thrown together by the word "while." From the point of view of complexity, the poem is utterly lacking in subtlety; it contains dead spaces like "Homer sings"; and none of the possible connotations of "sordid" or "probes" get taken up and developed, but they are canceled out by the other words. From the point of view of its human regional qualities, it is feeble and half-hearted, even as moral advice. And it has no rhythmic, syntactical, or verbal life. These things cannot be truly said of Wordsworth's "Ode."

To sum up, the three general critical standards, unity, complexity, and intensity, can be meaningfully appealed to in the judgment of aesthetic objects, whether auditory, visual, or verbal. Moreover, they are appealed to constantly by reputable critics. It seems to me that we can even go so far as to say that all their Objective reasons that have any logical relevance at all depend upon a direct or an indirect appeal to these three basic standards. This may be too sweeping a claim; at any rate, it is stated explicitly enough so that it can be attacked or defended. . . .

Aesthetic Concepts

FRANK SIBLEY

*   *   *

A great deal of work remains to be done on aesthetic concepts. In the remainder of this paper I shall offer some further suggestions which may help towards an understanding of them.

The realization that aesthetic concepts are governed only negatively by conditions is likely to give rise to puzzlement over how we manage to apply the words in our aesthetic vocabulary. If we are not following rules and there are no conditions to appeal to, how are we to know when they are applicable? One very natural way to counter this question is to point out that some other sorts of concepts also are not condition-governed. We do not apply simple color words by following rules or in accordance with principles. We see that the book is red by looking, just as we tell that the tea is sweet by tasting it. So too, it might be said, we just see (or fail to see) that things are delicate, balanced, and the like. This kind of comparison between the exercise of taste and the use of the five senses is indeed familiar; our use of the word "taste" itself shows that the comparison is age-old and very natural. Yet whatever the similarities, there are great dissimilarities too. A careful comparison cannot be attempted here though it would be valuable; but certain differences stand out, and writers who

From Joseph Margolis (ed.), *Philosophy Looks at the Arts* (New York: Charles Scribner's Sons, 1962), pp. 77-87. This article was originally published in *The Philosophical Review*, Vol. LXVIII (October, 1959), pp. 421-50. Reprinted by permission of the author and *The Philosophical Review*.

have emphasized that aesthetic judgments are not "mechanical" have some-times dwelt on and been puzzled by them.

In the first place, while our ability to discern aesthetic features is dependent upon our possession of good eyesight, hearing, and so on, people normally endowed with senses and understanding may nevertheless fail to discern them. "Those who listen to a concert, walk round a gallery, read a poem may have roughly similar sense perceptions, but some get a great deal more than others," Miss Macdonald says; but she adds that she is "puzzled by this feature 'in the object' which can be seen only by a specially qualified observer" and asks, "What is this 'something more'?"[10]

It is this difference between aesthetic and perceptual qualities which in part leads to the view that "works of art are esoteric objects . . . not simple objects of sense perception."[11] But there is no good reason for calling an object esoteric simply because we discern aesthetic qualities in it. The *objects* to which we apply aesthetic words are of the most diverse kinds and by no means esoteric: people and buildings, flowers and gardens, vases and furniture, as well as poems and music. Nor does there seem any good reason for calling the *qualities* themselves esoteric. It is true that someone with perfect eyes or ears might miss them, but we do after all say we *observe* or *notice* them ("Did you notice how very graceful she was?," "Did you observe the exquisite balance in all his pictures?"). In fact, they are very familiar indeed. We learn while quite young to use many aesthetic words, though they are, as one might expect from their dependence upon our ability to see, hear, distinguish colors, and the like, not the earliest words we learn; and our mastery and sophistication in using them develop along with the rest of our vocabulary. They are not rarities; some ranges of them are in regular use in everyday discourse.

The second notable difference between the exercise of taste and the use of the five senses lies in the way we support those judgments in which aesthetic concepts are employed. Although we use these concepts without rules or conditions, we do defend or support our judgments, and convince others of their rightness, by talking; "disputation about art is not futile," as Miss Macdonald says, for critics do "attempt a certain kind of explanation of works of art with the object of establishing correct judgments."[12] Thus even though this disputation does not consist in "deductive or inductive inference" or "reasoning," its occurrence is enough to show how very different these judgments are from those of a simple perceptual sort.

Now the critic's talk, it is clear, frequently consists in mentioning or pointing out the features, including easily discernible non-aesthetic ones, upon which

---

[10]Macdonald in Elton, *op. cit.,* pp. 114, 119. See also pp. 120, 122.
[11]Macdonald, *ibid.,* pp. 114, 120-123. She speaks of non-aesthetic properties here as "physical" or "observable" qualities, and distinguishes between "physical object" and "work of art."
[12]*Ibid.,* pp. 115-116; cf. also John Holloway, *Proceedings of the Aristotelian Society,* supplementary Vol. XXIII (1949), pp. 175-176.

the aesthetic qualities depend. But the puzzling question remains how, by mentioning these features, the critic is thereby justifying or supporting his judgments. To this question a number of recent writers have given an answer. Stuart Hampshire, for example, says that "One engages in aesthetic discussion for the sake of what one might see on the way ... if one has been brought to see what there is to be seen in the object, the purpose of discussion is achieved. ... The point is to bring people to see these features."[13] The critic's talk, that is, often serves to support his judgments in a special way; it helps us to *see* what he has seen, namely, the aesthetic qualities of the object. But even when it is agreed that this is one of the main things that critics do, puzzlement tends to break out again over *how* they do it. How is it that by talking about features of the work (largely non-aesthetic ones) we can manage to bring others to see what they had not seen? "What sort of endowment is this which *talking* can modify?. . . Discussion does not improve eyesight and hearing" (my italics).[14]

Yet of course we do succeed in applying aesthetic terms, and we frequently do succeed by talking (and pointing and gesturing in certain ways) in bringing others to see what we see. One begins to suspect that puzzlement over how we can possibly do this, and puzzlement over the "esoteric" character of aesthetic qualities too, arises from bearing in mind inappropriate philosophical models. When someone is unable to see that the book on the table is brown, we cannot get him to see that it is by talking; consequently it seems puzzling that we might get someone to see that the vase is graceful by talking. If we are to dispel this puzzlement and recognize aesthetic concepts and qualities for what they are, we must abandon unsuitable models and investigate how we actually employ these concepts. With so much interest in and agreement about *what* the critic does, one might expect descriptions of *how* he does it to have been given. But little has been said about this, and what has been said is unsatisfactory.

Miss Macdonald,[15] for example, subscribes to this view of the critic's task as presenting "what is not obvious to casual or uninstructed inspection," and she does ask the question "What sort of considerations are involved, *and how,* to justify a critical verdict?" (my italics). But she does not in fact go on to answer it. She addresses herself instead to the different, though related, question of the interpretation of art works. In complex works different critics claim, often justifiably, to discern different features; hence Miss Macdonald suggests that in critical discourse the critic is bringing us to see what he sees by offering new interpretations. But if the question is "what (the critic) does and how he does

---

[13]Stuart Hampshire in Elton, *op. cit.,* p. 165. Cf. also remarks in Elton by Isenberg (pp. 142, 145), Passmore (p. 38), in *Philosophy and Psycho-analysis* by John Wisdom (Oxford, 1953), pp. 223-224, and in Holloway, *op. cit.,* p. 175.

[14]Macdonald, *op. cit.,* pp. 119-120.

[15]*Ibid.,* see pp. 127, 122, 125, 115. Other writers also place the stress on interpretation, cf. Holloway, *op. cit.,* p. 173 ff.

it," he cannot be represented either wholly or even mainly as providing new interpretations. His task quite as often is simply to help us appreciate qualities which other critics have regularly found in the works he discusses. To put the stress upon *new* interpretations is to leave untouched the question how, by talking, he can help us to see *either* the newly appreciated aesthetic qualities *or* the old. In any case, besides complex poems or plays which may bear many interpretations, there are also relatively simple ones. There are also vases, buildings, and furniture, not to mention faces, sunsets, and scenery, about which no questions of "interpretation" arise but about which we talk in similar ways and make similar judgments. So the "puzzling" questions remain: how do we support these judgments and how do we bring others to see what we see?

Hampshire,[16] who likewise believes that the critic brings us "to see what there is to be seen in the object," does give some account of how the critic does this. "The greatest service of the critic" is to point out, isolate, and place in a frame of attention the "particular features of the particular object which *make* it ugly or beautiful"; for it is "difficult to see and hear all that there is to see and hear," and simply a prejudice to suppose that while "things really do have colors and shapes . . . there do not exist literally and objectively, concordances of colors and perceived rhythms and balances of shapes." However, these "extraordinary qualities" which the critic "may have seen (in the wider sense of 'see')" are "qualities which are of no direct practical interest." Consequently, to bring us to see them the critic employs "an unnatural use of words in description"; "the common vocabulary, being created for practical purposes, obstructs any disinterested perception of things"; and so these qualities "are normally described metaphorically by some transference of terms from the common vocabulary."

Much of what Hampshire says is right. But there is also something quite wrong in the view that the "common" vocabulary "obstructs" our aesthetic purposes, that it is "unnatural" to take it over and use it metaphorically, and that the critic "is under the necessity of building . . . a vocabulary *in opposition to the main tendency of his language*" (my italics). First, while we do often coin new metaphors in order to describe aesthetic qualities, we are by no means always under the necessity of wresting the "common vocabulary" from its "natural" uses to serve our purposes. There does exist, as I observed earlier, a large and accepted vocabulary of aesthetic terms some of which, whatever their metaphorical origins, are now not metaphors at all, others of which are at most quasi-metaphorical. Second, this view that our use of metaphor and quasi-metaphor for aesthetic purposes is unnatural or a makeshift into which we are forced by a language designed for other purposes misrepresents fundamentally the character of aesthetic qualities and aesthetic language. There is nothing unnatural about using words like "forceful," "dy-

---

[16]*Op. cit.*, pp. 165-168.

namic," or "tightly-knit" in criticism; they do their work perfectly and are exactly the words needed for the purposes they serve. We do not want or need to replace them by words which lack the metaphorical element. In using them to describe works of art, the very point is that we are noticing aesthetic qualities related to their literal or common meanings. If we possessed a quite different word from "dynamic," one we could use to point out an aesthetic quality unrelated to the common meaning of "dynamic," it could not be used to describe that quality which "dynamic" does serve to point out. Hampshire pictures "a colony of aesthetics, disengaged from practical needs and manipulations" and says that "descriptions of aesthetic qualities, which for us are metaphorical, might seem to them to have an altogether literal and familiar sense"; they might use "a more directly descriptive vocabulary." But if they had a new and "directly descriptive" vocabulary lacking the links with non-aesthetic properties and interests which our vocabulary possesses, they would have to remain silent about many of the aesthetic qualities we can describe; further, if they were more completely "disengaged from practical needs" and other non-aesthetic awarenesses and interests, they would perforce be blind to many aesthetic qualities we can appreciate. The links between aesthetic qualities and non-aesthetic ones are both obvious and vital. Aesthetic concepts, all of them, carry with them attachments and in one way or another are tethered to or parasitic upon non-aesthetic features. The fact that many aesthetic terms are metaphorical or quasi-metaphorical in no way means that common language is an ill-adapted tool with which we have to struggle. When someone writes as Hampshire does, one suspects again that critical language is being judged against other models. To use language which is frequently metaphorical might be strange for some *other* purpose or from the standpoint of doing something else, but for the purpose and from the standpoint of making aesthetic observations it is not. To say it is an unnatural use of language for doing *this* is to imply there is or could be for this purpose some other and "natural" use. But these *are* natural ways of talking about aesthetic matters.

To help understand what the critic does, then, how he supports his judgments and gets his audience to see what he sees, I shall attempt a brief description of the methods we use as critics.[17]

(1) We may simply mention or point out non-aesthetic features: "Notice these flecks of color, that dark mass there, those lines." By merely drawing attention to those easily discernible features which make the painting luminous or warm or dynamic, we often succeed in bringing someone to see these aesthetic qualities. We get him to see B by mentioning something different, A. Sometimes in doing this we are drawing attention to features which may have gone unnoticed by an untrained or insufficiently attentive eye or ear: "Just

---

[17]Holloway, *op. cit.,* pp. 173-174, lists some of these very briefly.

listen for the repeated figure in the left hand," "Did you notice the figure of Icarus in the Breughel? It is very small." Sometimes they are features which have been seen or heard but of which the significance or purpose has been missed in any of a variety of ways: "Notice how much darker he has made the central figure, how much brighter these colors are than the adjacent ones," "Of course, you've observed the ploughman in the foreground; but had you considered how he, like everyone else in the picture, is going about his business without noticing the fall of Icarus?" In mentioning features which may be discerned by anyone with normal eyes, ears, and intelligence, we are singling out what may serve as a kind of key to grasping or seeing something else (and the key may not be the same for each person).

(2) On the other hand we often simply mention the very qualities we want people to see. We point to a painting and say, "Notice how nervous and delicate the drawing is," or "See what energy and vitality it has." The use of the aesthetic term itself may do the trick; we say what the quality or character is, and people who had not seen it before see it.

(3) Most often, there is a linking of remarks about aesthetic and non-aesthetic features: "Have you noticed this line and that, and the points of bright color here and there . . . don't they give it vitality, energy?"

(4) We do, in addition, often make extensive and helpful use of similes and genuine metaphors: "It's as if there were small points of light burning," "as though he had thrown on the paint violently and in anger," "the light shimmers, the lines dance, everything is air, lightness and gaiety," "his canvasses are fires, they crackle, burn, and blaze, even at their most subdued always restlessly flickering, but often bursting into flame, great pyrotechnic displays," and so on.

(5) We make use of contrasts, comparisons, and reminiscences: "Suppose he had made that a lighter yellow, moved it to the right, how flat it would have been," "Don't you think it has something of the quality of a Rembrandt?", "Hasn't it the same serenity, peace, and quality of light of those summer evenings in Norfolk?" We use what keys we have to the known sensitivity, susceptibilities, and experience of our audience.

Critics and commentators may range, in their methods, from one extreme to the other, from painstaking concentration on points of detail, line and color, vowels and rhymes, to more or less flowery and luxuriant metaphor. Even the enthusiastic biographical sketch decorated with suitable epithet and metaphor may serve. What is best depends on both the audience and the work under discussion. But this would not be a complete sketch unless certain other notes were added.

(6) Repetition and reiteration often play an important role. When we are in front of a canvas we may come back time and again to the same points, drawing

attention to the same lines and shapes, repeating the same words, "swirling," "balance," "luminosity," or the same similes and metaphors, as if time and familiarity, looking harder, listening more carefully, paying closer attention may help. So again with variation; it often helps to talk round what we have said, to build up, supplement with more talk *of the same kind*. When someone misses the swirling quality, when one epithet or one metaphor does not work, we throw in related ones; we speak of its wild movement, how it twists and turns, writhes and whirls, as though, failing to score a direct hit, we may succeed with a barrage of near-synonyms.

(7) Finally, besides our verbal performances, the rest of our behavior is important. We accompany our talk with appropriate tones of voice, expression, nods, looks, and gestures. A critic may sometimes do more with a sweep of the arm than by talking. An appropriate gesture may make us see the violence in a painting or the character of a melodic line.

These ways of acting and talking are not significantly different whether we are dealing with a particular work, paragraph, or line, or speaking of an artist's work as a whole, or even drawing attention to a sunset or scenery. But even with the speaker doing all this, we may fail to see what he sees. There may be a point, though there need be no limit except that imposed by time and patience, at which he gives up and sets us (or himself) down as lacking in some way, defective in sensitivity. He may tell us to look or read again, or to read or look at other things and then come back again to this; he may suspect there are experiences in life we have missed. But these are the things he does. This is what succeeds if anything does; indeed it is all that can be done.

By realizing clearly that, whether we are dealing with art or scenery or people or natural objects, this is how we operate with aesthetic concepts, we may recognize this sphere of human activity for what it is. We operate with different kinds of concepts in different ways. If we want someone to agree that a color is red we may take it into a good light and ask him to look; if it is viridian we may fetch a color chart and make him compare; if we want him to agree that a figure is fourteen-sided we get him to count; and to bring him to agree that something is dilapidated or that someone is intelligent or lazy we may do other things, citing figures, reasoning and arguing about them, weighing and balancing. These are the methods appropriate to these various concepts. But the ways we get someone to see aesthetic qualities are different; they are of the kind I have described. With each kind of concept we can describe what we do and how we do it. But the methods suited to these other concepts will not do for aesthetic ones, or vice versa. We cannot prove by argument or by assembling a sufficiency of conditions that something is graceful; but this is no more puzzling than our inability to prove, by using the methods, metaphors, and gestures of the art critic, that it will be mate in ten moves. The questions raised admit of no answer beyond the sort of description I have given. To go on to ask, with puzzlement, how it is that *when* we do these things people come to see, is like asking how is it that, when we take the book into a good light, our companion agrees with us that it is red. There is no place for this kind of question or puzzlement. Aesthetic concepts are as natural, as little esoteric, as any others. It is against the background of different and philosophically more familiar models that they seem queer or puzzling.

I have described how people justify aesthetic judgments and bring others to see aesthetic qualities in things. I shall end by showing that the methods I have outlined are the ones natural for and characteristic of taste concepts from the start. When someone tries to make me see that a painting is delicate or balanced, I have some understanding of these terms already and know in a sense what I am looking for. But if there is puzzlement over how, by talking, he can bring me to see these qualities in this picture, there should be a corresponding puzzlement over how I learned to use aesthetic terms and discern aesthetic qualities in the first place. We may ask, therefore, how we learn to do these things; and this is to inquire (1) what natural potentialities and tendencies people have and (2) how we develop and take advantage of these capacities in training and teaching. Now for the second of these, there is no doubt that our ability to notice and respond to aesthetic qualities is cultivated and developed by our contacts with parents and teachers from quite an early age. What is interesting for my present purpose is that, while we are being taught in the presence of examples what grace, delicacy, and so on are, the methods used, the language and behavior, are of a piece with those of the critic as I have already described them.

To pursue these two questions, consider first those words like "dynamic," "melancholy," "balanced," "taut," or "gay" the aesthetic use of which is quasi-metaphorical. It has already been emphasized that we could not use them thus without some experience of situations where they are used literally. The present inquiry is how we shift from literal to aesthetic uses of them. For this it is required that there be certain abilities and tendencies to link experiences, to regard certain things as similar, and to see, explore, and be interested in these similarities. It is a feature of human intelligence and sensitivity that we do spontaneously do these things and that the tendency can be encouraged and developed. It is no more baffling that we should employ aesthetic terms of this sort than that we should make metaphors at all. Easy and smooth transitions by which we shift to the use of these aesthetic terms are not hard to find. We suggest to children that simple pieces of music are hurrying or running or skipping or dawdling, from there we move to lively, gay, jolly, happy, smiling, or sad, and, as their experiences and vocabulary broaden, to solemn, dynamic, or melancholy. But the child also discovers for himself many of these parallels and takes interest or delight in them. He is likely on his own to skip, march, clap, or laugh with the music, and without this natural tendency our training would get nowhere. Insofar, however, as we do take advantage of this tendency and help him by training, *we do just what the critic does*. We may merely need to persuade the child to pay attention, to look or listen; or we may simply *call* the music jolly. But we are also likely to use, as the critic does, reiteration, synonyms, parallels, contrasts, similes, metaphors, gestures, and other expressive behavior.

Of course the recognition of similarities and simple metaphorical extensions are not the only transitions to the aesthetic use of language. Others are made in different ways; for instance, by the kind of peripheral cases I mentioned earlier. When our admiration is for something as simple as the thinness of a glass or the smoothness of a fabric, it is not difficult to call attention to such things, evoke a similar delight, and introduce suitable aesthetic terms. These transitions are only the beginnings; it may often be questionable whether a term is yet being used aesthetically or not. Many of the terms I have mentioned may be used in ways which are not straightforwardly literal but of which we should hesitate to say that they demanded much yet by way of aesthetic sensitivity. We speak of warm and cool colors, and we may say of a brightly colored picture that at least it is gay and lively. When we have brought someone to make this sort of metaphorical extension of terms, he has made one of the transitional steps from which he may move on to uses which more obviously deserve to be called aesthetic and demand more aesthetic appreciation. When I said at the outset that aesthetic sensitivity was rarer than some other natural endowments, I was not denying that it varies in degree from the rudimentary to the refined. Most people learn easily to make the kinds of remarks I am now considering. But when someone can call bright canvasses gay and lively without being able to spot the one which is really vibrant, or can recognize the obvious outward vigor and energy of a student composition played *con fuoco* while failing to see that it lacks inner fire and drive, we do not regard his aesthetic sensitivity in these areas as particularly developed. However, once these transitions from common to aesthetic uses are begun in the more obvious cases, the domain of aesthetic concepts may broaden out, and they may become more subtle and even partly autonomous. The initial steps, however varied the metaphorical shifts and however varied the experiences upon which they are parasitic, are natural and easy.

Much the same is true when we turn to those words which have no standard non-aesthetic use, "lovely," "pretty," "dainty," "graceful," "elegant." We cannot say that these are learned by a metaphorical shift. But they still are linked to non-aesthetic features in many ways and the learning of them also is made possible by certain kinds of natural response, reaction, and ability. We learn them not so much by noticing similarities, but by our attention being caught and focussed in other ways. Certain phenomena which are outstanding or remarkable or unusual catch the eye or ear, seize our attention and interest, and move us to surprise, admiration, delight, fear, or distaste. Children begin by reacting in these ways to spectacular sunsets, woods in autumn, roses, dandelions, and other striking and colorful objects, and it is in these circumstances that we find ourselves introducing general aesthetic words to them, like "lovely," "pretty," and "ugly." It is not an accident that the first lessons in aesthetic appreciation consist in drawing the child's attention to roses rather than to grass; nor is it surprising that we remark to him on the autumn colors rather than on the subdued tints of winter. We all of us, not only children, pay aesthetic attention more readily and easily to such outstanding and easily noticeable things. We notice with pleasure early spring grass or the first snow, hills of notably marked and varied contours, scenery flecked with a great variety of color or dappled variously with sun and shadow. We are struck and impressed by great size or mass, as with mountains or cathedrals. We are similarly responsive to unusual precision or minuteness or remarkable feats of skill, as with complex and elaborate filigree, or intricate wood carving and fan-vaulting. It is at these times, taking advantage of these natural interests and admirations, that we first teach the simpler aesthetic words. People of moderate aesthetic sensitivity and sophistication continue to exhibit aesthetic interest mainly on such occasions and to use only the more general words ("pretty," "lovely," and the like). But these situations may serve as a beginning from which we extend our aesthetic interests to wider and less obvious fields, mastering as we go the more subtle and specific vocabulary of taste. The principles do not change; the basis for learning more specific terms like "graceful," "delicate," and "elegant" is also our interest in and admiration for various non-aesthetic natural properties ("She seems to move *effortlessly, as if* floating," "So very *thin* and *fragile,* as if a breeze might destroy it," "So *small* and yet so *intricate,*" "So *economical* and *perfectly adapted*").[18] And even with these aesthetic terms which are not metaphorical themselves ("graceful," "delicate," "elegant"), we rely in the same way upon the critic's methods, including comparison, illustration, and metaphor, to teach or make clear what they mean.

I have wished to emphasize in the latter part of this paper the natural basis of responses of various kinds without which aesthetic terms could not be learned. I have also outlined what some of the features are to which we naturally respond: similarities of various sorts, notable colors, shapes, scents, size, intricacy, and much else besides. Even the non-metaphorical aesthetic terms

---

[18]It is worth noticing that most of the words which in current usage are primarily or exclusively aesthetic terms had earlier non-aesthetic uses and gained their present use by some kind of metaphorical shift. Without reposing too great weight on these etymological facts, it can be seen that their history reflects connections with the responses, interests, and natural features I have mentioned as underlying the learning and use of aesthetic terms. These transitions suggest both the dependence of aesthetic upon other interests, and what some of these interests are. Connected with liking, delight, affection, regard, estimation, or choice — *beautiful, graceful, delicate, lovely, exquisite, elegant, dainty;* with fear or repulsion — *ugly;* with what notably catches the eye or attention — *garish, splendid, gaudy;* with what attracts by notable rarity, precision, skill, ingenuity, elaboration — *dainty, nice, pretty, exquisite;* with adaptation to function, suitability to ease of handling — *handsome.*

have significant links with all kinds of natural features by which our interest, wonder, admiration, delight, or distaste is aroused. But in particular I have wanted to urge that it should not strike us as puzzling that the critic supports his judgments and brings us to see aesthetic qualities by pointing out key features and talking about them in the way he does. It is by the very same methods that people helped us develop our aesthetic sense and master its vocabulary from the beginning. If we responded to those methods then, it is not surprising that we respond to the critic's discourse now. It would be surprising if, by using this language and behavior, people could *not* sometimes bring us to see the aesthetic qualities of things; for this would prove us lacking in one characteristically human kind of awareness and activity.

Art Criticism

D. W. GOTSHALK

I. The Phases of Art Criticism

A philosophy of art implies a general theory of art criticism. By stating what fine art is, a philosophy of art implies what criticism of art should be about, if it is to be art criticism. Nor are the implications of our philosophy along these lines difficult to see. The distinctive nature of fine art, we have said, is the creation of objects for aesthetic experience. It follows that criticism of art as art, or in its distinctive nature, should be an evaluation of the objects created by art as objects for aesthetic experience.

This general conception of art criticism conceives its major business as judgment or evaluation. But subordinate phases can be distinguished within the critical process. The chief of these are the genetic and the immanent.

The genetic phase of art criticism is a study of the factors that have shaped a work of art. In our chapter on the creative process we described these factors as subjective and objective. The subjective are psychological factors, such as sensitivity, imagination, personality, taste, aims, the value system, and the peculiar experiences of the artist. The objective are environmental factors, such as materials, physical milieu, traditional influences, social needs, and what is usually called the "cultural climate" of the creator. Accordingly, the genetic

From *Art and The Social Order,* by D. W. Gotshalk, Dover Publications, Inc., New York 14, N.Y. Reprinted by permission of the author and Dover Publications, Inc.

phase of art criticism would be the delineation of some or all of these factors with a view to an evaluation of the work of an individual creator or a period of art history.

Sometimes such psychological and environmental studies are made in abstraction from the aim of tying them in with a critical estimate of the works of an individual or period. This abstraction may be motivated by modesty, i.e., by a feeling that the task of tracing out the subjective and objective factors that go into the works of an artist or a group of artists is of sufficient magnitude to be an independent project. Or the abstraction may be motivated by a zeal to be "scientific" — i.e., to be descriptive and not normative. In any case the resulting studies are not, strictly speaking, art criticism at all. They are biography or history. Only when these studies are linked with some attempt to evaluate the aesthetic stature of the work of an individual or period do they move beyond biography and history into the province distinctive of art criticism.

The second, or immanent, phase of art criticism is a study of the major features within the work of art itself. We have described these features as four: materials, form, expression, and function. The immanent phase is, first of all, an effort at clarification and elucidation of these dimensions of the public object by description of some or all of their terminal or instrumental properties. In contrast to the genetic phase, the aim here is not so much to describe what has shaped a work — the background — as what is actually in the work — the foreground. The aim is sympathetic penetration and vivid adumbration of the actual intrinsic perceptual properties of the public object with a view to making an adequate critical judgment of the work under consideration. Some works are internally less intelligible than others; and often, when we come to learn what is actually in them, our critical opinions change radically. This is the great service to criticism of the immanent phase, providing, with the genetic, the documentary bases of the judgmental activity.

Sometimes, like the genetic phase, the immanent also is conducted in abstraction from evaluation. A book on opera tells us the stories of the operas. An article on a painter tells us the subjects of his paintings and the "manners" that he has employed in them. Such descriptions are not, strictly speaking, criticism at all but mere reporting. Only when they are tied in with, and are used to aid, an attempt to evaluate the work of an artist or of a group of artists are they more than reporting and properly a part of art criticism.

In a sense the judgmental activity of art criticism itself might be considered a phase — the third phase — of the critical process. In this sense the judgmental activity would be considered as the culmination and completion of the genetic and immanent phases. To know the genetic factors of a work of art or its immanent features, with a view to estimating their worth, is not yet to estimate this worth explicitly. An additional element is needed, viz., the application of a set of general standards. The genetic and immanent phases prepare the way for the judgmental. They characterize the background and foreground of a work in such a way that an informed estimate is possible and standards can be applied. But the standards must be applied and an estimate delivered. The judgmental phase of art criticism at its best is simply the systematic application of a set of relevant general standards to a work of art that is known genetically and immanently. The standards used, it should be emphasized, must be appropriate or relevant. They must enshrine value possibilities that works of art can actualize to some extent, since it is plainly futile to ask a work of art to do something impossible for it to do. But these standards are not genetic or immanent actualities. They are ideals, and the judgmental phase of art criticism is the explicit evaluation of the actualities of a work of art in the light of a canon or an appropriate set of relevant value possibilities or ideals.

Art criticism, then, might be described as embracing a genetic and immanent phase, but as aiming at an explicit appraisal of works of art for aesthetic perception, according to a canon or a set of relevant standards. The genetic and immanent phases of art criticism are subordinate and auxiliary to the judgmental phase, which is the essence of the process. In this sense art criticism is simply the fullest possible appraisal of works of art as aesthetic objects according to a set of appropriate standards. This, it is understood, is criticism of art-in-its-distinctive-nature, or art criticism as such, not criticism of art-in-its-total-nature or in all its ramifications and connections beyond the process of aesthetic perception.

II. Proposed Canon of Judgment

Since the essence of criticism is the evaluation of works of art as aesthetic objects according to an appropriate set of standards, the basic problem for a philosophical analysis of art criticism is to determine what the appropriate standards for art criticism are. What are the value possibilities that can be demanded of works of art because they are works of art? What is the total set of aesthetic values capable of realization by artistic creations?

In the four preceding chapters one of the main aims was to describe just such a set of value possibilities. We may summarize the results as follows: Each dimension of a work of art is capable of possessing terminal values, and, in relation to each of the other dimensions, it is capable of possessing instrumental values. Each dimension can itself be a focus of intrinsic perceptual interest, and each can be a means of implementing for intrinsic perception the quality of the other three dimensions. Accordingly, a work of art ideally is capable, at a minimum, of four terminal values and twelve instrumental values or of sixteen different aesthetic values, and any work of art is capable of being judged in at least sixteen different respects aesthetically.

Stated in this way, our proposed canon of art criticism may seem too complex and unwieldy for practical use or theoretical discussion. But the canon can be stated more simply. Primarily, the canon asks two major questions of a work of art: first, do the dimensions of the work of art, its materials, form, expression, and function, constitute intrinsically satisfying aesthetic foci? And, second, do these dimensions work together, augment and implement one another, co-operate to reveal and to reinforce the nature of one another? Do they harmonize, or are they discordant? These are the two leading questions for any comprehensive evaluation of a work of art, according to our theory.

Stated in this generalized way, these two questions involve certain subquestions integral to the judgmental process: e.g., the first question involves the subquestion as to what in particular might make the dimensions of works of art intrinsically satisfying aesthetic foci. Such subquestions will receive attention later, as occasion permits. But the two leading questions, as such, outline the scope and the main demands of a comprehensive evaluation of a work of art as art; and the aim of art criticism is simply to formulate the most precise possible answers to these questions, according to our theory.

III. Obstacles to the Application of the Proposed Canon

Even when the proper questions of art criticism are understood, there are certain obvious obstacles to formulating precise answers to them. At least three conditions must be fulfilled.

First, the critic must be able to encompass a work of art adequately, discerning all its major aspects and the relations between these aspects. This is a very difficult feat. A distinguished critic says regarding the form of a novel: "To grasp the shadowy and fantasmal form of a book, to hold it fast, to turn it over and survey it as leisure — that is the effort of a critic of books, and it is perpetually defeated. Nothing, no power, will keep a book steady and motionless before us, so that we may have time to examine its shape and design. As quickly as we read, it melts and shifts in the memory. . . . A cluster of impressions, some clear points emerging from a mist of uncertainty, that is all we can hope to possess, generally speaking, in the name of a book."[1] Nor is the form of the works of the so-called "static" arts always easy of apprehension or retention. Usually, this form is composed of a dense variety of elements, e.g., in a painting, of color, line, shape, mass, light, dark, texture; and, as a rule, the patterns of these elements can be grasped only by lengthy sequential perception. In the case of larger works, such as great buildings, the apprehension of form may take much more time and much more memory, with their concomitant uncertainties. And what is true of artistic form is often true of the other dimensions of the public object, which are frequently complex, and of the relations of form to these dimensions and of these dimensions to form and to

[1] Percy Lubbock, *The Craft of Fiction* (London: Jonathan Cape, Ltd., 1921), p. 1.

one another. Generally speaking, works of art spread before attention a vast and often elusive array of offerings requiring time, effort, patience, experience, knowledge, and capacity of a high order before one can even begin to encompass them adequately.

This objective complexity not only makes difficult the successful operation of such a canon of judgment as that proposed above but also helps to explain much of the apparent diversity and conflict in criticism. Usually, a few features of a work of art are ample to supply a theme for a critical discourse. And, as there is no important work of an artist without merits, so there is no important artist without defects. To revert to the novelists: "Fielding lacked at least one-half of all the 'finer feelings'; the structure of Goldsmith's one novel would shame a kindergarten; Jane Austen regarded the failure to possess an inherited income as placing a man outside the pale of humanity; Dickens had the sentimentality of a nursemaid; Theodore Dreiser cannot write the English language."[2] Accordingly, two able critics may give the most divergent judgments on the work of an artist without actually being inaccurate, irrelevant, unintelligible, or even biased beyond excusable limits. One critic may write at great length on the lively characterizations or skilful designs in the novels of Jane Austen. Another may write at equal length on the deficiencies of this novelist's social perspectives. Thanks to the complexity of works of art, each critic may be right and his criticism sound, although the critics may seem both to themselves and to others to be disagreeing about the artist completely.

Besides the objective complexity, there is a subjective complexity — the nature of the critic. This nature can also make the successful operation of the proposed canon difficult, since for its successful use the canon requires that a critic attain a very clear and comprehensive grasp of a work. Temporary conditions may interfere with this: inattention, ill-health, distractions, and pressures of various types. Equally interfering may be irrational sympathies or antipathies for the race, creed, nationality, or personality of the artist or biases induced by nonaesthetic factors, such as the commercial success, popularity, or partisan backing of a work. Below such obvious impediments are deeper obstacles — defects of sensitivity, feeling, imagination, knowledge, education, intellectual penetration, germane experience. Freedom from these defects is needed in a high degree if the proposed canon is to be applied properly. With a simple canon the necessary equipment of a critic may be simple, sometimes no more than willingness to open his mouth in public. But with a highly complex canon applied to a highly complex object, method and diligence must be combined in the critic with an equally complex power to see clearly and fully, before he is in a position to operate with the canon at all adequately.

Incidentally, much of the conflict, confusion, and divergence in art criticism

---

[2]J. W. Krutch "The Half-truth of the Whole Truth," *Nations,* CXLIV (January 2, 1937), 21.

can probably be traced more directly to this second obstacle than to the first. Particularly is this true of criticism of new works of art. Often critics do not know enough, have not sensitivity or imagination enough, or are not sufficiently free from powerful preconceptions and preferences simply to see new works in their actual nature, as a study of the critical pronouncements made upon the works of innumerable great artists when they first appeared eloquently reveals. Nor is this true merely of new works. Even in the criticism of the "classics," critics often reveal surprising deficiencies in orientation or imaginative grasp, or they ride favorite hobbyhorses at a fast clip. All this makes for conflict and diversity in criticism, as well as for poor criticism. The requirements for a good critic, especially in subjective equipment, are of a very high order, as will become increasingly clear as our discussion proceeds. And, as long as these requirements are not fulfilled in a reasonable degree, criticism will not only fail in its proper aims but be mired in interminable conflict.

A third obstacle to the successful application of the proposed canon is the language with which art criticism traditionally operates. By and large, it is a language of concealed comparatives. For example, a critic may describe the posturings in an opera as "exaggerated." What he means is that, in comparison with some implied standard—say, attitudes prevalent in twentieth-century Western life—the posturings are exaggerated. But in comparison with some other standard—say, attitudes prevalent in the eighteenth-century court life depicted in the opera—the posturings may be "realistic." In general, the language of ordinary criticism, both descriptive and evaluative, moves against a background of standards that the critic often leaves so shadowy that his language conveys no more than an emotion of approval or disapproval. The cure, of course, is constant overt comparison and constant specification, as far as this is possible, of the sense in which a term is applied. "A perfectly honest view of a very ordinary novel in the critic's own opinion, may make use of adjectives that are equally applicable to novels that the critic himself would rank enormously higher in the very aspects indicated. Constant overt comparison is required to other works of the same author or of other authors to indicate any precise meaning for the terms applied. It is this inadequacy of language to the needs of criticism that makes valuable criticism one of the more difficult literary arts. . . . . The critic's standards . . . . will function to communicate the character of specific works of art to others, only if these others have the same basis to relate them to, unless the critic by various means indicates with some precision his own peculiar qualitative scale, the indifference points at which the degrees of any quality attributed by him positively begin to apply. Except in the very few cases where our adjectives— like those for color and pitch—are systematized pretty fully, the available descriptive terms are so extremely indeterminate that their application alone would hardly differentiate in degrees at all, without explicit comparison. Criticism, as we have it, is too vague in its terminology to be taken very seriously as more than roughly descriptive on the one hand, and on the other as expressive of the critic's personal feelings, and this only to the degree in which his literary powers are adequately creative."[3]

IV. Possibilities of Universal Agreement

The common assumption regarding art criticism is that its aim is to produce statements about the aesthetic merits and demerits of works of art that are valid without exception for all informed and intelligent people. Everyone is quick to observe that in practice art critics never come very close to doing this. But the explanation is usually that art critics are jealous or biased or overopinionated or constitutionally quarrelsome or in some other way limited people. The belief that there is only one right verdict about a work of art and that the art critic should deliver it is usually not questioned fundamentally or seriously.

In a moment we shall question this belief, but, in the meantime, let us suppose it to be valid. And let us ask: If the three obstacles mentioned above were overcome—if the objective complexity of the work of art were surmounted, the complex subjective equipment necessary for a critic to see clearly as well as comprehensively were provided, and the impediments of the language of criticism were eliminated—and our proposed canon of criticism were permitted to operate without obstacle, would the result be statements about the aesthetic merits and demerits of works of art valid without exception for all informed and intelligent people? What are the possibilities of universal agreement? Since our canon has two parts, one concerned with terminal values and one with instrumental values, let us answer this question by considering these types of value, beginning with the terminal.

Suppose two persons are judging the terminal worth of the materials of a work of art, say, the colors of a painting. One person approves their intrinsic perceptual qualities, describing the colors as robust and powerful. The second person disapproves of the qualities, describing the colors as harsh and garish. Theoretically, both persons have applied the same general standard—terminal aesthetic adequacy of materials. But the result is two diverse and conflicting judgments. The judgmental phase, however, need not end here. Let us suppose that the first person is relatively inexperienced regarding colors and works of art, the second relatively experienced. By further clarification of the nature of colors through comparisons and elucidations and by increased experience of works of art, the first person may come to agree with the more experienced person. He may agree, now that he has seen, for example, the color realizations in the greatest paintings, that the colors of the painting mentioned above are

---

[3]D. W. Prall, *Aesthetic Analysis* (New York: Thomas Y. Crowell Co., 1936), pp. 201-2. Cf. L. Wittgenstein, *Philosophical Investigations* (New York: The Macmillan Co., 1953), I, par. 84.

comparatively harsh and garish—the judgment of the second person. In this sense nothing is more profitable than disputes about tastes and nothing diminishes the differences between the critical judgments of persons intelligently concerned with art more than a common understanding and experience and an education of sensitivity that can be fostered in the process of resolving disputes about tastes.

Nevertheless, disputes about terminal values may end not in complete agreement, as here, but in complete disagreement. Even with critics whose education, sensitivity, resources of language, and insight are very superior and roughly equal, this may be the case. Human beings are constructed differently as well as similarly, and there is a temperamental individuality in them that seems at present incapable of eradication. Some people are dominantly phlegmatic, some dominantly volatile; some are dominantly intense and quick, some dominantly slow and mild. And these bents of human nature, as well as the sheer power and resources to see and hear, will obviously affect terminal evaluations. Suppose that the two persons mentioned above had been of opposite temperaments, for example, hearty and fragile, and the painting in question a very brilliantly colored modern Mexican work. It is possible that, after the fullest examination of the color realizations of the greatest paintings, the first person might still hold that the colors of the painting are robust and powerful, while the second continued to hold that they are harsh and garish or to hold that they are robust and powerful and to be sickened by such robustness and power.

And what is true about the terminal values of materials may also be true about the terminal values of form, expression, and function. To one temperament the form of a work may be too sprawling and heavy, to another the same form may be of accommodating ease and grandeur. To one temperament the expressiveness of a work of art may be deep and profound, to another it may be too mystical or turgid. To one temperament a work of art may be a magnificient memorial, to another it may be overpretentious. Such disagreements in critical judgments seem ultimate, assuming them to arise not from education, environment, capacity for discernment, or similar factors but from the natural temperament that these factors release as well as modify. On this basis, if on no other, some ultimate diversity of critical judgments regarding terminal values of works of art seems theoretically inescapable in the application of our proposed sixteen-value canon, even when the three obstacles described above have been removed from the path of the critic.[4]

Besides the four terminal values, there are the twelve instrumental values.

---

[4]Of course, if biochemistry should ever be able in the future to produce human beings so that all were in all psychophysical respects absolutely alike, this position would become untenable. But, at present, this prospect seems improbable, not to mention slightly monstrous.

Do these entail an equally irreducible diversity of critical judgments? Is universal agreement possible here? I think that universal agreement is always theoretically possible here, for such judgments are not, in the strictest sense, matters of temperament at all. They have to do simply with interdimensional adequacy within the work of art. To be sure, art criticism here lacks mathematical precision. It cannot demonstrate in Euclidean fashion that the colors of a painting, for example, are appropriate to the expressiveness, that they fit and reinforce the expressiveness. Yet it can exclude from such judgments temperamental affinities either for the colors or for the expressiveness. A person may not be charmed either by the reds or by the melodrama of a Delacroix. Yet he may be capable of agreeing with another who is charmed by both that the reds are judicious and effective in augmenting and reinforcing the melodrama. The chief basis for judging interdimensional competence as such is not temperament but sensitivity to an artist's instrumental achievement and knowledge of what other artists in the same field have achieved. To be sure, two critics chosen at random may disagree in their interdimensional evaluations of a given work of art. But if both have sufficient sensitivity to discern accurately what is there and if both have wide and roughly equal knowledge of interdimensional achievements in the art in question, the disagreement is likely to be small, and even to vanish. In this sense disagreements about interdimensional competence seem even more capable of resolution by discussion than do disagreements about terminal values. Mathematically precise agreement, as I have said, is not possible. Art criticism by its language is limited to rough comparatives which are capable only of very crude and approximate mathematical correlates. But, given wide knowledge in an art and equal sensitivity to and experience of interdimensional achievement, given more generally the removal of the three obstacles mentioned above, very great agreement on instrumental values seems possible, and ultimate agreement is not an irrelevant ideal.

In view of this, it may be thought that the only worth-while art criticism is interdimensional or "technical" criticism. This conclusion is correct under two conditions: first, that the proper aim of art criticism is merely to make statements capable of winning universal agreement and, second, that interdimensional criticism exhausts the possibilities of making such statements in art criticism.

As to the second point, it is important to observe that terminal criticism by no means produces only conflict and diversity and that it harbors possibilities of much judgmental agreement. Temperaments differ, and, at some point in a wide and searching criticism of works of art, two critics of diverse temperaments will disagree. But temperaments have neutral zones. There are areas of value into which the mild and intense, the phlegmatic and volatile, enter without sharp conflict. Moreover, there is much more in the termini of works of art than temperamental appeals. A good artistic form, for example, as we have seen, synchronizes with the basic biophysical and attention structure of the human being and with the basic pattern of human aspiration and remembrance. It has a larger than temperamental appeal. Having different individual qualities, a specific good form by Giotto, it is true, may appeal more to a given temperament than a specific good form by Rubens, or vice-versa. But, because each form is finely constructed simply as form, it may make a definite appeal to the most diversely tempered critics and bring a deep terminal satisfaction to all. If, because of temperament, a critic who has felt the power of both still rates one form slightly higher than the other, his differences with a second critic on this score may be almost completely neutralized by the deeply universal appeal of both forms.

Something of this sort is also true about the other dimensions. The dimension of expression, for instance, frequently contains a vision of some phase of human life and experience that reflects the artist's value inclinations and realizations and personality operating on a certain "subject." In creations of the greatest artists, this vision may reveal very forcefully certain basic qualities of human feeling, character, and conduct — qualities that, for all their sketchiness and incompleteness and temperamental colorings, may yet convey stimulating insights into the actualities and possibilities of human life and the conditions of human good. Owing to temperament, different critics may differ in the exact degree of worth that they accord the insight of a Sophocles or a Shakespeare, a Mozart or a Beethoven. But certain works of these artists may seem to disclose so clearly the logic of certain human actions or the nature of certain human feelings that the differences of critics due to temperament may be minor and incidental notes in a largely unanimous approval.

In general, works of art at their best give us in their termini a refined and clarified perceptual "vision" or revelation of material properties and aesthetic and nonaesthetic functions, as well as of the existential structure of our world and the characteristics of action, things, and human beings. And this vision or revelation can be measured by its comparative perceptual refinement and clarity, i.e., by the comparative incisiveness, inclusiveness, and coherence for perceptions that the peculiar terminal realizations of the artist possess. Here, incidentally, is a set of criteria for the judgment of the termini of art, a set of substandards under the more inclusive standard of terminal adequacy, which answers the subquestion mentioned at the end of Section II of this chapter as to what in particular might make the dimensions of works of art intrinsically satisfying aesthetic foci. These substandards cannot be wholly freed from temperamental entanglements, since they involve measuring the degree of refinement and clarification of the *personal* realizations of artists which naturally will be rated differently by different temperaments. But such differences can become quite minor features in the judgment of termini in terms of their comparative depth, width, and consistency for perception and can lead to judgments that are, on the whole, free from radical disagreements arising from merely temperamental preferences.[5]

Thus, given a reasonable neutralization of the three obstacles mentioned above; given, in particular, critics who have the knowledge and the receptor competence, the breadth of view and the verbal skill, to overcome the main objective and subjective complexities and the more elementary linguistic difficulties confronting criticism, much agreement regarding the terminal values of works of art is also ideally possible. It seems right, therefore, to conclude that art criticism should not exclude terminal criticism and be confined solely to interdimensional criticism, even assuming that the proper aim of art criticism is to make value statements about works of art capable of winning universal agreement.

V. The Aim of Art Criticism

But are value statements commanding universal agreement the proper aim of art criticism? I wish to suggest a different view which retains what is possible in this commonly assumed belief but does not involve the frustration of criticism by temperament in the region of terminal values that this belief does when taken as stating the proper aim of art criticism.

This new view conceives the business of art criticism as that of pointing out, with what clarity the language of criticism permits, the stature of a work of art in the eyes of the critic in such a way that others can find out better what in an adequate perception its stature would be for them. The business of criticism is not to formulate value statements, all universally true as they stand, but to make value statements that, if not universally true, are translatable into the personal value language and understanding of others.

In this conception of art criticism the universal interdimensional and terminal value statements possible to criticism retain their position intact. But the status of temperament is different. The set of deep-seated and peculiar value attitudes constituting a critic's temperament becomes an instrument of suggestion instead of an instrument of decision regarding terminal values. Its business is not to determine the terminal values of works of art for others but to be a medium for the projection of judgments that will help others better to determine what these values are for themselves. Thus, under this conception not only can the universal truths that criticism can reach be preserved, but the universal service of criticism, curtailed under the other aim by temperament,

[5]Cf. S. C. Pepper, *Aesthetic Quality* (New York: Charles Scribner's Sons, 1937, 1938), chap. ix, and *The Basis of Criticism in the Arts* (Cambridge, Mass.: Harvard University Press, 1945), and Bertram Morris, *The Aesthetic Process* (Evanston: Northwestern University Press, 1943), pp. 180-81, on the substandards mentioned in this paragraph.

can be extended. Nothing a critic says need be wasted private talk, provided he sets it off so that others can translate his peculiar terminal enunciations into their own private perspectives. On this view the good critic is not only the judicious critic, able to discern the universal values of works of art, but also the suggestive critic, able by his projections to lead us to find the peculiar and unique terminal values that exist for us in works of art. He contributes to an articulation of our own individual experience of art, as well as to an articulation of the common thread that can run through all experience of art by his peculiarly suggestive judgments of the public object.

This view of the aim of the art critic and art criticism is recommended by a number of circumstances. The first has already been mentioned. The view enables criticism to retain what is possible in the commonly assumed aim and to circumvent the frustrations of criticism entailed by this aim in the region of terminal values. A second circumstance is probably even more important. This is the belief that the individual values of works of art — the temperamental colorings, the purely personal slant of artists — are as basic and precious in certain respects as the universal values and that, since such values will be judged somewhat differently by different temperaments according to whether the artist and judging percipient are temperamentally akin or not, criticism should not try to do more here than facilitate the judgments of diverse percipients. To deny the temperamental colorings in works of art is not possible. To deny their authentic value to percipients temperamentally harmonious with the temperament of the artist would be callow. Under such circumstances the best plan for criticism would seem to be to illumine these temperamental colorings in such a way that their value to diverse percipients is immediately clear or can be discovered and known with greater clarity. And this should be the aim of art criticism according to the view we have been stating.

Two other arguments also favor the view here set forth. First, art criticism is not open to many of the usual criticisms made of it, for example, that it is exhibitionism, that it is setting up one's self as a world norm, that it is an effort to inflict a critic's predilections on others, all of which statements are to some extent true so long as it is assumed that the aim of criticism in all areas is the enunciation of judgments universally binding as they stand. Second, art criticism can be of very great and genuine usefulness to appreciation, creation, and other activities. This last point is so important for understanding both our general position and certain views expressed in later chapters that it deserves extensive attention.

VI. Some Uses of Art Criticism

With the aim just described, the canon previously outlined, and a reasonable freedom from the three impediments already mentioned, art criticism, I believe, can, first of all, be of very great assistance to appreciation. By means of the standards of interdimensional competence and of universal terminal achievement, it can separate a vast quantity of inferior works from those more rich in universal values. So many so-called "works of art," from current escapist confections to the more sentimental and bombastic of traditional creations, possess merely a few piquant terminal features, usually in the dimension of expression. In interdimensional competence or solid workmanship they are usually weak, and in depth, width, and coherence of terminal achievement they are invariably deficient. Such works often provide agreeable illusions and pastime to persons who wear sufficiently heavy aesthetic blinkers. But just for that reason they can help to clog the paths of appreciation. In particular, they can overpower the popular mind and rear a high wall between the mass of men and man's superior artistic achievement. Good criticism can do an inestimable service here by ceaselessly reducing the size of this wall and by keeping alive in as many people as possible the sense of the superior.[6]

As to superior works of art, besides evaluating their interdimensional excellences, art criticism in the sense and spirit above suggested may have two other uses for appreciation. To persons who have not experienced the works in question, the terminal evaluations of such criticism may provide useful starting-points. The danger here is that the evaluations of the critic may become prepossessions, inhibiting the free personal reactions of the appreciator. But this danger can be avoided if these evaluations are taken as hypotheses, not as dogma—as value apprehensions to be tested and to be accepted only in terms of one's own vivid experience. To persons who have experienced the works in question, criticism in the present sense may be useful in a different way. It may bring out interdimensional, as well as terminal, values which were missed in prior experience. It may also help to make more explicit any judgments previously formed or, by the challenge of its analyses, stimulate the appreciator to re-experience the works and check and retest his perceptions in the light of the critic's experiences. Finally, criticism of superior works can be useful in suggesting general methods of appreciating works of art of all types, as when a stimulating critical analysis of a series of fine paintings suggests a general method of critical appreciation of all types of paintings—indeed, even of all types of works of art.[7]

Art criticism in the sense intended in this discussion can also be of considerable use to creation. Although creative activity in the arts is based on a number

---

[6]A simple example, and there are literally thousands, would be Margaret Marshall's critical review of John Steinbeck's *Cannery Row (Nation,* CLX [January, 1945], 75-76). The example is simple because the critic deals only with expressive features of the novel, but it is very effective in distinguishing for the reading audience a bit of chaff from the wheat of literature.

[7]A. C. Barnes, *The Art in Painting* (New York: Harcourt, Brace & Co., 1925, 1928, 1937), and Thomas Munro, *Great Pictures of Europe* (New York: Coward-McCann, Inc., 1930), contain critical analyses of this type.

of unconscious factors, it is rarely, if at all, a merely automatic process. It also employs reflective guidance, and often artists can improve here immensely. An artist may choose subjects not well suited to his talents or be unaware of certain possibilities of his peculiar idiom. He may become careless and imperceptibly relax his standards or be puzzled by the general direction of his growth. By analyses of specific works, the good critic can illumine all these things, as well as encourage all the fine things. The labor of the creative artist is one long ceaseless process of self-discovery in his art, and the keen and able critic who also appreciates the nature and hardship of creation can assist and accelerate this process in many ways.

It is probably true that the majority of artists, particularly recent artists schooled in the romantic tradition, furiously resent critics, feeling that critics generally are envious, incompetent, and parasitic people who see art from the outside only. Critics are people incapable of understanding or coming to close grips with the problems of creation. Otherwise, they would not be critics, but artists themselves. This view ignores the fact that many of the best critics are and have been creative artists. But the view is certainly correct to this extent, that, artists or nonartists, good critics are very rare. The great scarcity of good critics, however, should not blind one to the considerable usefulness to creation that good criticism can have when it does occur. The chief business of good criticism is reflective, analytic object judgment, such as the artist himself must perform to some extent on his works if he is to profit markedly from his own creative experience. Moreover, the good critic usually possesses to a far greater extent than the majority of artists those powers of abstraction, comparison, and generalization that make possible superior reflective object judgment. If critics too frequently have used these powers ignorantly or offensively, the good critic can use them constructively and as a respectful mentor of the artist. Indeed, criticism has frequently championed artists vigorously and intelligently against immense obstinate and ignorant opposition, as the *Neue Zeitschrift für Musik* championed Schubert, Chopin, and Weber; Griepenkerl, Berlioz; Ruskin, Turner; or Gustave Jeffrey, Cézanne.

Good criticism can also contribute to creation in general, as well as in specific, ways. If artists refuse to learn from critical analyses of their own works, they frequently do learn from sage and penetrating analyses of the works of other artists, particularly the works of rival artists or of the greater artists of the past. By seeing wherein others have succeeded or failed, artists may renew in their own mind the aims of their undertakings and augment these aims by lessons drawn from the present and the past. Furthermore, good criticism can disseminate a body of ideas and foster an atmosphere favorable to the best creative work. By provocative and trenchant analyses of artistic problems and achievements, not only can good criticism influence artists directly or indirectly, but it can help to develop a wider and more discriminating audience for the arts, which demands and relishes the best that artists can create[8] and rejects the counterfeit works of spurious talents.

Finally, art criticism in the above sense can be of considerable use as a source of knowledge. This is particularly apparent when one remembers that the full range of art criticism in this sense would include the genetic and immanent phases. These phases clearly can contribute richly to our knowledge of the origins and properties of works of art, while the judgmental phase, although its sole aim is not the enunciation of propositions universally valid, can nevertheless formulate estimates of the interdimensional and certain dimensional values of works of art which have general validity. That the total body of propositions thus resulting sums up to a science, the science of criticism, as some might claim, is largely a matter of terminology. If a narrow meaning of science is preferred, e.g., a science is a body of statements based upon controlled experiment and capable of formulation in mathematical terms, this knowledge is clearly not a science. If a broader meaning of science is allowed, e.g., a science is a body of statements based on experience and capable of verification by competent observers, this knowledge at its best is a science. At its best it is based on analytic aesthetic experience and is verifiable by all persons competent to undertake criticism in the present sense of the term.

Art criticism can contribute to philosophy as well as be a science in the broader sense just mentioned. I have said that a philosophy of art implies a theory of art criticism. It is equally true that criticism of art implies a philosophy. All criticism proceeds in terms of certain broad assumptions about the nature and purport of fine art which constitute what the critic believes the arts should offer human beings. These assumptions underlie and control the critic's approach to works of art and generate the expectations governing his diverse particular procedures. Without such a philosophical substratum, indeed, art criticism would be helpless. It would lack intelligible direction or goal. It would be unaware of what art or works of art are and so of what criticism should seek to estimate in regard to them.

Critics, it is true, rarely state explicitly their general assumptions about art and are often unconscious of them. Nevertheless, as necessary to criticism, these assumptions can be found in their writings, and the philosopher can often learn much from detecting and formulating them. In a sense the business of the art critic and the philosopher of art is the same, the reflective analysis of fine art, and the philosopher should be something of a critic and the critic something of a philosopher. The difference between the two is that the critic is primarily concerned with the analysis of particular works of art, artists, schools, and

---

[8]Cf. *Paul Cézanne, letters* Eng. trans. by Marguerite Kay, ed. John Rewald (London: Bruno Cassirer, 1941), p. 248, on the value to the creative artist of a public of intelligent amateurs.

periods, while the philosopher is primarily concerned with the general nature and importance of art. But, just as the philosopher's concern with the general involves some consideration of the particular, so the critic's concern with the particular involves at least some vague conceptions of the general. These general conceptions can be analytically separated from the particular and often contain general insights into art that the philosopher might never have reached except for the critic, since the philosopher does not have the detailed concern with the particular that first called forth these insights as premises or framing assumptions of the analyses of the critic.

VII. A Historical Retrospect

It may help to set our theory of art criticism in a proper light to take a brief glance at certain historical positions. Art criticism, we have said, has three phases — a genetic, an immanent, and a judgmental phase — and invariably, we might add, it involves all three phases to some extent as parts of one complex total activity.

During a given historical period, however, one phase or more tends to be dominant, and during the early "modern" era — the era of classicism, embracing the seventeenth century and the largest part of the eighteenth — the judgmental phase was dominant. Fine art, the classicist believed, should conform to certain fixed canons and universal laws, and the chief business of art criticism is to measure particular works of art by their conformity to these canons and laws. The classicist identified art with fine workmanship, and to this extent, of course, he was right. But he identified fine workmanship mainly with the achievement of a certain limited type of pattern or form. In consequence, when he propounded his canons and laws, they turned out to be such criteria as the three unities of the drama, the "classical" rules of musical harmony, the Greek orders à la Palladio, the revived canon of Polyclitus, the golden section, the serpentine line; and at once works of art were found or produced that ignored or broke these criteria and yet were marvelously effective aesthetic objects.

In this early modern era, opposition to the prevailing classicist creed was to be found in the writers belonging to the so-called "School of Taste"[9] and in Hutcheson, Hume, and Kant, all of whom denied that beauty was conformity to rational concepts and that artistic excellence was mere consistency with authoritative rules and laws. Art, Kant held, was founded on genius not on rules, beauty was a matter of "taste." And from these beginnings, which were especially vigorous in the late eighteenth century, the modern romantic conception of art sprang to full flower, and the juridical emphasis in criticism

---

[9]Cf. Joel E. Spingarn, *Critical Essays of the Seventeenth Century* (Oxford: Clarendon Press, 1908), I, lxxxviii – cvi; see also my article, "Taste and Its Education," in *Encyclopedia of the Arts* (New York: Philosophical Library, 1946), pp. 996 ff.

associated with classicism ceased to be the dominant factor in all except academic and ultra-conservative critical circles.

During the next one hundred and fifty years, the heyday of modern romanticism, the immanent and genetic phases of criticism received most emphasis. Romanticism itself directly favored an immanent type of criticism. The artist as genius was viewed by the romantic as the maker of the law, a free creative titan. To hold up rules for his guidance or to measure him à la Beckmesser was sheer pedantry and arrogance. The first business of the critic should be to follow sympathetically in the footsteps of genius and feel in his own soul the manifold nuances of the experience portrayed by the artist. Criticism should be a record of personal adventures among masterpieces, and the ultimate aim of the critic should be to create a work of art from works of art; to give an intimate and expressive interpretation of the immanent features of the creations of genius; and to be a keen, suggestive, imaginative, and finished writer in the manner of Walter Pater and George Moore.

Romanticism, however, was by no means the only cultural force affecting criticism in the late eighteenth, nineteenth, and early twentieth centuries. There was the enormous expansion of science, especially the extension of exact science to living and growing things, as in biology, under the unifying concept of evolution. This development stimulated the use of the genetic or historical method in every field, and the critical study of the arts was no exception. One of the first results in art criticism was to produce well-documented and increasingly accurate scholarly records of the outer facts about artists and works of art, an enormous historical erudition.[10] In addition, there were the attempts, by Taine and the Marxists among others, to explain these facts by various genetic or historical principles. With the growth of psychology and the appearance of psychoanalysis, the genetic emphasis was extended by a more inward approach to art and artists. The result was the numerous case histories and psychoanalytic biographical studies that are the commonplaces of recent criticism.

There is no doubt that the very best criticism of these hundred and fifty years has had very great merits. The genetic approach has immensely increased the exactness of our knowledge of the sources and historical conditions of works of art and has immensely broadened our conception of the motivation of artists. If, sometimes, the outer facts turned up have seemed trivial and the inner divinations far-fetched, this approach has nevertheless yielded considerable subtle commentary and illuminating exegesis to our understanding of the backgrounds of art. The immanent approach at its best has had equal merits. It has resulted in numerous excellent expositions and elucidations of the aesthetic

---

[10]Germany was the center of this new industry, of which American academic studies in literature by the professoriat and graduate scholars of the universities constitute one of numerous later by-products.

values of specific works of art and has stressed the importance of basing criticism on firsthand personal experience. It has also set a high standard of literary excellence for criticism and has kept alive, in the face of the scientific avalanche, the similarities of criticism to art.

Nevertheless, both these modern developments have had a serious defect. They have failed to provide an adequate canon of judgment to replace the discredited criteria of the classicist. The chief canon of many leading romanticists, for example, was personal feeling. A critical judgment is describing one's personal feelings, one's pleasure in, or repugnance for, the public object. A critical judgment is simply a statement of an honest prejudice and rests upon nothing more solid or objective than the spontaneous sentiments that occur to one in the contemplation of the object.[11] The difficulty with this canon is that personal feelings about objects are conditioned by one's sensitivity and imagination, one's interest and knowledge. And, no matter how exuberantly or gracefully one may state these feelings, criticism will be blind, tangential, irrelevant, or erroneous if one is deficient in sensitivity, imagination, interest, or knowledge. Much more than strong feeling is needed as a basis for a judicious estimate of the values in a work of art, and this "more" is a knowledge of the value possibilities which it is proper to require of a work of art and an awareness of a work's intrinsic aspects and of the actual stature of these aspects in relation to the value possibilities.

The geneticist often tried to dodge the whole problem of standards. He made no judgments, he said; he described facts. He merely showed the soil from which certain works of art sprang. And, of course, this was his chief contribution and his main task. But his work usually employed or involved standards of judgment. Otherwise, it would have ceased to be art criticism, as so much latter-day scholarship derived from the genetic outlook has. Moreover, geneticists whose orientation to art was through history, psychology, or genetic philosophy rather than through natural science, often stated these standards explicitly. The most characteristic of these standards were two: the intention of the artist and the standards and needs of the time of the artist. A work of art is good if it fulfils the intention of the artist, the motives of the individual behind it. And a work of art is good if it fulfils the standards and needs of its time or of the society from which it springs. Neither of these criteria is very impressive.

In judging works of art in terms of the intention of the artist, the geneticist was, of course, accepting the romanticist's general premise, which elevates the creative artist above any "objective" rules. This league with romanticism, however, did not greatly strengthen the geneticist's hand. Indeed, the criterion of intention is inherently defective on many counts. The intentions of artists are

---

[11]Cf. Anatole France, *La Vie Littéraire* (Paris: Calmann-Lévy, 1889-92). Preface; see also H. L. Mencken, *Prejudices* (New York: A. A. Knopf, 1919-27).

often difficult to determine and, once determined, are often multiple – e.g., the artist was aiming to make money, to amuse himself, to pay off in satire a long-standing grudge, to add to the list of his works. The criterion of intention leaves us in some cases with no basis for judgment and in other cases with too many bases, unless we limit it in these cases to the specific aesthetic intention that the artist obviously had in fashioning the particular work. Even with this limitation and supposing that the aesthetic intention of artists is always knowable, difficulties arise. Many works of art have undertones and overtones not contained in the specific aesthetic intention that the artist obviously had in fashioning a given work, and sometimes these undertones and overtones are much more interesting than what the artist actually intended. Should these be excluded from an estimate of what the work is for critical judgment? The criterion of intention, strictly interpreted, implies that they should, since these undertones and overtones are not part of the intention or of the fulfilment of the intention of the artist. But in that case criticism would necessarily be an inadequate judgment of what there is in the public object for aesthetic perception. Furthermore, the specific aesthetic intention of an artist may be trivial, e.g., gracefully to say as little as possible as long as possible, and the artist may succeed perfectly in this intention, saying nothing gracefully for a very long time. The criterion of intention would imply that the result is as perfect a work of art as possible, since it completely fulfils the intention behind it. But, obviously, such a work falls far short of what a work of art can be as an aesthetic object.

Similar remarks apply to the second criterion – fulfilment of the standards and needs of the time of the artist. There is the great difficulty of determining what these standards and needs are and, since they are usually multiple, which ones should be chosen as bases of judgment. And, once this is settled, if it can be settled, other difficulties arise. Many works of art that are considered masterpieces today violated prevailing standards of their day and, instead of serving prevailing needs, lay relatively neglected until later epochs. Moreover, a work of art may fulfil prevailing standards and needs perfectly. But, if these standards and needs are superficial and ephemeral, the work will be superficial and ephemeral, although it should be as perfect as a work of art can be and hence the very opposite of superficial and ephemeral, if this second criterion were right. In general, the standards and needs of an era supply only a very limited basis for the judgment of artistic excellence. In some cases they may be important. For example, they may help in judging the social expressiveness of a work, as the intention of the artist may help in judging a work's personal expressiveness. But, as a canon for judging a work completely or perennially, the standards and needs of its era provide a hopelessly provincial criterion, which in many ways is much less useful than either the romantic or the genetic criterion previously criticized.

VIII. Summary and Conclusions

Art criticism, then, consists of exegesis, immanent description, and judgment with a view to rendering a documented and suggestive estimate of the aesthetic values of works of art. Its most basic task is judgment or relating the aesthetic properties of a work to a scheme of possible aesthetic values relevant to artistic creations. Exegesis relates the aesthetic properties of a work to the work's causal origin and setting; description relates these properties to the actualities of a work's being. Judgment, however, relates them to the best possible relevant values and is therefore the definitive element in an estimate of the aesthetic excellence of the properties.

Judgment of works of art has two major tasks. The first is to evaluate the interrelation of the dimensions of a work of art, to detect incongruities, inconsistencies, and failures of implementation, to attend to a work to determine whether its dimensions combine with and amplify one another, e.g., whether the form, the function, the expressive spirit, the materials and site of a building, co-operate in a voluminous and harmonious effect. The basic criterion of judgment here is integrity, the union of all aspects of a work of art into an integral ensemble with densely interior relational values. This principle of interdimensional integrity replaces the traditional classical criteria of form in our account.

The second task of judgment is to appraise the terminal features of a work of art. These termini—materials, form, expression, and function—exist outside art, which is merely a particular integrated realization of them within a larger relational setting. How far are these termini, as realized in a work of art, adequate to the aesthetic possibilities of art? How far are they the refined and clarified aesthetic foci that art at its best can provide? Besides dealing with a different question, this second task of judgment differs from the first in another respect. It cannot be performed entirely in abstraction from the temperament of the critic. One can estimate whether a given dimension fits in with and reinforces another, independent of one's temperamental affinity for either dimension. But in any wide and searching estimate of the adequacy of termini as refined and clarified foci of intrinsic perception, temperamental affinities—a preference for one type of refinement or clarification over another—are bound to enter. It is the individual values of works of art—what makes Bach not Ravel and Ravel not Bach—as well as the universal values that make art worth while, and these individual values are bound to tinge one's experience of the termini and elicit different responses from differently tempered individuals and different estimates of the termini.

This circumstance does not bar the way to the discernment and enunciation of terminal values of universal scope. Considerable agreement on the comparative refinement and clarification attained by diverse works of art—the comparative width and depth and coherence of their termini for perception—still remains possible. But it does make untenable the common conception of art criticism as concerned exclusively with the formulation of judgments which are all universally valid as they stand. The view we have urged is that the aim of art criticism in the region of terminal values is to formulate estimates that, if not universally valid as they stand, will lead diverse percipients to a discovery of the exact stature of the terminal values for their own experience. The main function of criticism is to be suggestive, not legislative here. This recognition of temperament as a limitation upon terminal universality takes the place in our theory of the traditional romantic recognition of personal feeling as a vehicle for projection of the evaluations of the critic.

We may say, then, that the judgmental phase of art criticism has two tasks — to measure the *integrity* in perception and to suggest the *richness* for perception of a work of art, communicating these findings in such a way that the informed and qualified percipient can learn the interdimensional values of the work and is led to discover more completely the exact terminal values of the work for his own experience. In brief, the aim of art criticism is to evaluate a work of art for perception generally, in so far as this can be done successfully by a given temperament.

In concluding this account of art criticism, I should like to comment on a conception of it that critics sometimes offer in explanation of its current shortcomings. A great deal of art criticism today is contained in newspaper and magazine reviews, which for most people are "previews" of works of art. Some critics have complained that properly to fulfil their function of giving a foretaste or preview they would have to reproduce the actual work of art, which is impossible in most cases. The music critic of a daily newspaper cannot by words which are his medium literally reproduce a concert that he heard today and his readers may hear tomorrow. To do that he would have to employ means utterly different from those available to him. Hence his criticism is foredoomed to failure.

This conception of art criticism as literal reproduction of works of art seems a rather odd interpretation of its nature. Literal reproduction of works of art, in whole or in part, it has usually been thought, is the business of the manufacturer of phonograph records, the copyist, the photographer, and the printer and has only an incidental illustrative role in art criticism. The main business of the art critic who writes for a reader who has not yet experienced a given work would rather seem to be to formulate his reactions to the work in terms useful to his reader. Not to reproduce the work of art, but to reproduce or give his observations and judgments of it: this would seem to be the critic's primary business. That this is difficult to do well in words — that, in general, it is difficult to communicate well any thought or experience in words — is, of course, not to be denied. But that the critic should aim primarily to reproduce a work of art itself, instead of to communicate his understanding and judgment of it, seems a rather naïve misconception of the business of art criticism.

The Educative Function of Criticism

JEROME STOLNITZ

At the beginning of his now classic *Shakespearean Tragedy,* A. C. Bradley describes the purposes of his critique. Here Bradley shows himself to be, not merely a critic, but also a critic who is thoughtfully concerned about the methods and functions of criticism. To this extent, he is a philosopher of art criticism.

Bradley has one goal above all:

Nothing will be said of Shakespeare's place in the history either of English literature or of the drama in general. . . . I shall leave untouched, or merely glanced at, questions regarding his life and character, the development of his genius and art, the genuineness, sources, texts, inter-relations of his various works. . . . Our one object will be what . . . may be called dramatic appreciation; to increase our understanding and enjoyment of these works as dramas.[1]

Thus Bradley shuns various kinds of contextual criticism.[2] His studies of the tragedies are, for the most part, intrinsic criticism. As he recognizes, this

From Jerome Stolnitz, *Aesthetics and Philosophy of Art Criticism* (Boston: Houghton Mifflin Company, 1960), pp. 493-501. Reprinted by permission of the author and Houghton Mifflin Company. Some minor changes in the footnotes have been made for this edition.
[1] A. C. Bradley, *Shakespearean Tragedy* (London: Macmillan, 1952) p. 1.
[2] "Contextual" criticism studies the circumstances, notably psychological and historical, in which the work of art originated and its effects upon society and the future development of the art. "Intrinsic" criticism, by contrast, studies the work of art in itself, as an object of aesthetic appreciation.

involves analysis of the plays. But analysis can also be justified by the purpose of criticism:

> The dissecting processes . . . are still, and are meant to be, nothing but means to an end. When they have finished their work (it can only be finished for the time) they give place to the end, which is that same imaginative reading . . . of the drama from which they set out, but a reading now enriched by the products of analysis, and therefore far more adequate and enjoyable.[3]

Art criticism is sometimes interpretive and sometimes judicial.[4] These critical functions are important in themselves. But, in all areas of value, the chief reason for analysis and evaluation is to enrich our future value-experience. So the chief function of art criticism is to make aesthetic experience better than it would otherwise be, to make it, as Bradley says, "more adequate and enjoyable." What is gained in human enjoyment is the ultimate, and the best possible justification for criticism.

Criticism makes aesthetic experience better by making aesthetic perception more discriminating. It enables us to see what we had not seen before. We can now discern and therefore respond to all that is richly contained within the work. Criticism calls our attention to the sparkle or charm of the sensory matter, the subtlety of form and the way in which its formal structure unifies the work, the meaning of symbols, and the expressive mood of the entire work. Criticism gives us a sense of the work's "aesthetic intention,"[5] so that we do not make illegitimate demands upon it. Criticism also develops aesthetic "sympathy" by breaking down the prejudices and confusions which get in the way of appreciation. It explains the artistic conventions and social beliefs of the artist's time. It relates the work of art to the great world and shows its relevance to our own experience.

In these and many other ways, criticism is *educative*. It teaches, but it does not simply impart knowledge. Directly or indirectly, it instructs perception, thought, feeling, and imagination, so that they can all lean toward the work of art sympathetically and knowingly.

Thus the critic performs an indispensable function in our aesthetic lives. He is the seer and guide. It has been said that the great artist must create the audience for his works, but he rarely does so without the great critic. The critic directs perception to the values of new and unfamiliar art and thereby encourages its acceptance. Many artists have achieved fame largely because of the educative activity of the critic. Ruskin performed this service for the painter Turner, the late Olin Downes for Sibelius, the critic-editor Robert Bridges for

---

[3]Bradley, *Shakespearean Tragedy*, p. 2.
[4]"Interpretive" criticism seeks to clarify the meaning and structure of the work of art. "Judicial" criticism estimates the relative goodness or badness of the work.
[5]"Aesthetic intention" is a metaphoric way of referring to the total effect that the work is supposed to have on the aesthetic percipient.

the poet G. M. Hopkins. Probably the best example is that which we have already studied, i.e., the achievement of Roger Fry, in educating an entire generation to appreciate Post-Impressionistic painting and sculpture.

In the last chapter, we studied some of the major kinds of criticism. All of them can be educative, in different ways. I want to show this for each kind of criticism in turn.

Criticism by rules[6] begins by classifying the work in a certain *genre*. This in itself can be aesthetically educative. To call a poem a "lyric" or an "elegy" already gives us a sense of its aesthetic intention. It helps us to "set" ourselves appropriately as we begin to read. We expect a certain expressive "tone," and, when the work is highly traditionalized, we are in a position to understand its stylistic and formal conventions. Moreover, the application of rules to the work picks out salient details in it. Our perception can become more discriminating as a result. Then the evaluation which results from judging by the rules has the same educative function as all evaluation, viz., it tells us the kind and degree of value we can expect to find in the work. This too influences our aesthetic "set." Criticism by rules tells us both what the object "is" and "what it is worth."

Contextual criticism, we have seen, is strongest in dealing with subject matter, symbol, conceptual theme — all the elements which point beyond the work to "life" — weakest in dealing with the "purely" artistic elements of medium and form. If we take it at its best — as we should take all criticism — contextual criticism can be invaluable. For some works, indeed, contextual criticism is absolutely indispensable. It does a large part of the job of interpretive criticism. The knowledge which it discloses helps toward a coherent "reading" of the work. But neither the knowledge nor the interpretation can be educative if it remains detached from aesthetic experience. The knowledge must be absorbed into the "equipment" with which the percipient meets the work. "Ideal aesthetic knowledge, absolutely ready response, would bury the whole system of discriminations in our nerves and our habits."[7] Further, the interpretation which the contextualist helps to build must be translated into our perception. The aesthetic spectator has to "structure" the work as it unfolds before him — he must distinguish what is of primary importance from that which is only secondary, he must decide how the parts are interrelated and where the climax falls, etc. The artist, of course, gives leads to the spectator. But a work can be interpreted in different ways, as we have seen more than once. The artist cannot dictate rigidly how the work shall be apprehended. Ultimately the viewer or listener must do the job of active, creative perception. The contextualist critic cannot do it for him, but he can contribute much.

---

[6]"Criticism by rules" is found throughout the so-called "neo-classical" criticism of the sixteenth, seventeenth, and eighteenth centuries.
[7]D. W. Prall, *Aesthetic Analysis* (New York: Crowell, 1936), pp. 57-58.

The contribution of the impressionist[8] is quite different. He deliberately shuns contextual knowledge and he gives no formal interpretation. And yet— unless his "impressions" are wildly irrelevant—his critique can also be educative. His moods, images, and thoughts, as he describes them, can suggest the richness of the work. By indirection, they call attention to the properties of the work which have stimulated them. The impressionist also educates when he, so to speak, makes impressionists of *us,* i.e., when he encourages us to approach the work with a fertile imagination. Too many of us are intimidated or inhibited by works of art. We hesitate to think any thoughts or feel any emotions other than the "proper" ones that we have read or heard about. The impressionist can make our perception more supple, inventive, and alive. Finally, and best of all, the impressionist often infects us with his own enthusiasm for the work. Perhaps more than any other kind of critic, his writing has zest and gusto. It has the interest of any intense, personal statement. Other kinds of criticism often seem to be lifeless by contrast. They may analyze carefully and judge scrupulously, but the whole business seems mechanical and prosaic. When we have finished reading the critique, we still have no interest in looking at the work for ourselves. The impressionist often stimulates such interest. We approach the work, after having read him, not only sympathetically, but eagerly. The measure of the critic's success is the spontaneity and delight of our experience.

"Psychological intention" can be educative for some, though not all, works of art. When the critic asks, and can answer, the question, "What was the artist trying to do?" he makes us more sympathetic to the work. The question is especially pertinent when the work is in a radically new style or form. People have an unfortunate tendency to dismiss such works offhand. "Psychological intention" gets us to understand the artist's purpose, and this is the first step in seeing that what he has achieved may be worth while. "Aesthetic intention" is, of course, educative under any circumstances. We must have some sense of what the work is "trying to do" if we are to look at and respond to it appropriately. But since "aesthetic intention" refers to immediacies of experience, it is not readily described. It generally eludes conceptual description. Hence the critic must often resort to suggestive, metaphoric language to convey the intention. Many of the best critics have excelled in this kind of writing. James Agate says of Tchaikovsky's Fifth Symphony that it is "drenched with self-pity." "But," he goes on, "I like listening to it just as I like looking at a fuchsia drenched with rain."

Finally, intrinsic criticism, such as the New Criticism,[9] is clearly educative

---

[8]"Impressionist" criticism records and describes the ideas, images, and emotions aroused in the critic by the work of art.

[9]The "New Critics" of the twentieth century, such as Eliot, Ransom, and Brooks, see the poem as a formal patterning of the explicit meanings and the emotional and cultural overtones of the words which make it up, and of the interactions between them.

because it guides perception to what is hidden beneath the surface of the work. By disclosing the meanings embodied in the work, it makes our experience more subtle and, as Bradley says, "more adequate."

Thus each kind of criticism is educative, in its own way. But "the common reader," the person who takes some interest in art and wants to increase his interest, must do this job, too. Criticism by itself is never enough. It is no substitute for direct aesthetic awareness. We traduce criticism and we rob ourselves of enjoyment if we forget this. Sometimes people gain information from the critic, but they fail to work this information into their discrimination of the work. They are satisfied just to be able to talk plausibly about the work. Sometimes they read the critic's account of his own experience, but they make no attempt to experience the work for themselves. Criticism is educative, ultimately, only in its end product—felt aesthetic experience. Criticism can be educative, therefore, only when the percipient makes the effort of aesthetic attention and sympathy.

T. S. Eliot is probably the foremost critic of our time. But he speaks for the enlightened "common reader" here:

So the critic to whom I am most grateful is the one who can make me look at something I have never looked at before, or looked at only with eyes clouded by prejudice, set me face to face with it and then leave me alone with it. From that point, I must rely upon my own sensibility, intelligence, and capacity for wisdom.[10]

Just as no one kind of criticism has a monopoly on educative usefulness, neither is any kind of criticism foolproof against being *anti*-educative. Any critical method, instead of sharpening discrimination and encouraging interest, can have just the opposite effect.

Criticism by rules can, in various ways, blur the uniqueness of the work of art. By classifying works into *genres,* such criticism stresses the similarities of the work to other works, rather than its differences. There is a real danger that the critic will, therefore, overlook what is distinctive about *this* work. The reader will, accordingly, perceive the work as a stereotype. His responses will be the mechanical, habitual ones developed by other works in this *genre;* he will fail to see the work as a fresh and unique object. Moreover, the application of rules places greater weight upon the parts of the work than upon the whole. Unless the critic's judgment is balanced by attention to the whole, he will, indeed, "murder to dissect." He will fail to show how the parts contribute to what Pope calls "the full result of all." His reader will have knowledge of details, and evaluations of each of them, but aesthetic appreciation requires, above all, a sense of the whole. Only so can the percipient "set" himself to

---

[10]T. S. Eliot, "The Frontiers of Criticism," in *On Poetry and Poets* (London: Faber & Faber, 1957), p. 117.

respond appropriately. And only so can he interpret each detail, and give it its place in a coherent unity.

The danger in using contextual criticism is obvious. It is pointed up in the writings of many of the contextualists. It is, of course, that the critic will give us knowledge *about* the work and nothing more. Such critics fail to show — sometimes they seem not to care — how this knowledge is relevant to the interpretation and appreciation of the work. The unwary reader learns the contextual facts and thinks that this is enough. But he may then use the work simply to pick out elements which illustrate these facts — "This is where the composer's love affair went sour," and so on. Since many of the contextual facts have no aesthetic relevance whatever, he often spends his time looking for things in the work that simply are not there. Contextual criticism is profoundly antieducative when it results in diverting attention from the art-object to its context.

The impressionist critic can also divert attention from the work of art. If this writing is exciting or attractive, as it often is, the reader takes the critique to be an end in itself and loses sight of the work. If the critique is simply a wild flight of fancy, as it sometimes is, he learns nothing of the intrinsic properties of the work. Moreover, even when the critique is aesthetically relevant, it is usually one-sided. The impressionist excels in giving an evocative description of the work's total quality or "flavor." But he tends to be weak on details. Hence the critique does not increase our discrimination. One who is under the influence of an impressionist critic often experiences a vague, generalized mood, in the face of the work, but he fails to see the details which would make his emotions more varied and more specific.

"Psychological intention" is part of the context of the art-object. Criticism in terms of it is therefore subject to the same perils which we have just noted in contextual criticism generally.

It would seem, however, that intrinsic criticism would have to be educative. For it confines itself to what is within the work, and it makes the work more significant to us. Yet even when all of its analysis of meaning remains "inside" the work — as it does not always do, in the New Criticism — such criticism can still be antieducative, though in a rather subtle way.

The ingenious and imaginative critic can, as we have seen, find many different overtones of meaning within the work. An expert critic will be able to demonstrate how each of these is grounded in the words of the poem or drama. Still, his detailed exposition of meanings may be *too* complex to be of help in aesthetic perception. The percipient is unable to assimilate all of these meanings into his experience. Once again, we must remind ourselves that the aesthetic experience is signally different from the critical experience. We can comprehend each of the meanings which are spelled out piecemeal by the critic. But these meanings cannot always be worked into the aesthetic object. The rhythm of aesthetic perception is brisk and urgent, by contrast to the pace of analysis. The rhythm will be slowed down or collapse altogether, if the reader attempts to distinguish each of the meanings disclosed by the critic. As Ransome says, in criticizing one of the New Critics, the "movement of the poem" must come off faster"[11] than the critic allows it to do. Aesthetic attention attempts to grasp an object in its immediacy. The work which is weighted down with a vast superstructure of interpretation is too lumpy and complex to be grasped. It is unable to make a direct, immediate impact.

Consider the student taking a course in literature, in which the instructor and the textbook use the methods of the New Criticism. After a short while he comes to see how superficial his earlier reading of the poem or novel was. He missed the deeper levels of meaning, the "more" which the New Criticism always finds in literature. And yet, just because he was not aware of the complexity of the work when he first read it, he could seize it as a concrete unity, and in some degree, feel its imaginative and emotional excitement. After he has studied critiques of the work, he is far better informed than before. Yet all of the meanings which he has learned cannot be absorbed into the aesthetic body of the work. All too often, therefore, his reading of the novel becomes a process of *recognizing* the meanings, one after the other. The work therefore loses its vitality and excitement.

Thus, it is not enough for the criticism to be "relevant" simply in the sense that the critique sticks to what is in the work. To be educative, it must also be "relevant" in the sense that what is learned can enter into and intensify aesthetic experience. Criticism is anything but educative when it disperses aesthetic interest and transforms it into a cognitive exercise.

What follows from this, I need hardly say, is not that there should be *no* explication of meanings at all. That would be silly, for it would deprive us of all the educative gains of intrinsic criticism. The moral is, rather, that the critic should always bear in mind the aesthetic experience which his reader is going to have. The critic must remember the salient differences between analysis and aesthetic perception. And he must therefore remember the needs and limitations of aesthetic perception. Consequently, he must himself set limits to his explication. He should try to make perception more intelligent and informed; but he should not so overload it that it cannot function at all.

We can generalize this conclusion to apply to all kinds of criticism. We have found that they can all be antieducative in different ways. There is no infallible remedy for this. But criticism is more likely to be educative when the critic seeks always to honor his responsibility to his reader's future experience. All the errors of criticism which we have just discussed result from forgetting this. The critic becomes absorbed in himself, or infatuated with his methods, or he is really more interested in scholarship than the enjoyment of art. A critic can assist and guide the spectator only if he remembers what aesthetic awareness is

---

[11]John Crowe Ransom, *The New Criticism* (Norfolk: New Directions, 1941), p. 123.

like, how it proceeds and what it seeks. Whatever his methods, the critic must ultimately bring about "formation in the receptive mind of a whole condition of feeling and awareness,"[12] a "condition" which will enable the percipient to respond to the work of art acutely and intensely.

Aesthetic experience comes first, in importance and value. It is the goal or end of criticism. Criticism is an aid and a means, not an end in itself.

From this follow some further guiding principles for criticism.

The critic must always recognize that his interpretation and value-judgment must be tested in aesthetic experience. They do not prove themselves. They are proved when the interpretation can be used fruitfully within aesthetic awareness, and when the judgment tallies with the goodness that people actually feel in their encounter with the work. Hence there is no room for finality or infallibilism in art criticism. A critique is, or should be, a hypothesis, not a dogmatic verdict.

Since it is a hypothesis, it is always subject to revision. The critic, like the rest of us, must keep going back to the work. Unless he holds to his pet interpretation inflexibly, he will almost inevitably change it, as he discriminates details which he had not seen before and gains new insights. If you will look back at the passage quoted from Bradley at the beginning of this chapter, you will find him saying of critical analysis that "it can only be finished for the time." The critic who forgets this pays the price of narrow and shortsighted criticism.

Moreover, the critic should choose his methods and value-criteria in the light of aesthetic experience. He must adapt his procedures to the nature of the aesthetic object. Old standards often will not be relevant in judging new and different works. As an aesthetic percipient, he must make every effort to see what is good in the work; as a critic, he must select or, often, devise techniques of analysis which explain the work's goodness. Hence the critic's methods and criteria must be flexible, not rigid. And they should be varied, not limited, in order to take account of the endless diversity of works of art.

The critic who recognizes the richness of works of art will also recognize that many interpretations of a work, not his alone, are legitimate. Accordingly, many value-judgments are sound. Different observers find different values in the work. Aesthetic experience is the goal. Any interpretation which is relevant and coherent, and which abets genuine aesthetic experience, must be respected. For this reason, too, dogmatism is unjustified in criticism.

But there is another reason, the final reason, for humility in criticism. Works of art are inexhaustibly rich. There is no limit to what they will give to those who approach them with disinterested love and sympathy. No single interpretation can capture and distill the aesthetic goodness of the work, not even the partial goodness which it has on this interpretation alone. Neither can a whole

---

[12]I. A. Richards, *Practical Criticism* (New York: Harcourt, Brace, 1952), p. 333.

host of interpretations ever sum up all of the values which the work may disclose. No amount of critical talk suffices. The critic who respects the precious uniqueness of the work knows and will gladly admit that there is more still to be said. There will always be more to be said. And no matter how much we say about the work of art, "at the hypothetical limit of attention and interest there will always remain, quite untouched, the thing itself."[13]

[13]R. P. Blackmur, "A Critic's Job of Work," in *The Double Agent* (New York: Arrow Editions, 1935), p. 276.

*Criticism and the Problem of Intention**

RICHARD KUHNS

The cult of personality has been under attack in the Western critical symposia as well as in the Eastern party congresses. The cry of "personal heresy" has been as damning in criticism as in politics. Whether maintaining an interest in the personality of the artist is merely a doctrinal heresy or a serious methodological fallacy is not clear, but both of these accusations have been made. Out of the dispute has grown a large literature concerned with the place of intention in the interpretation and evaluation of works of art; at the bottom of the arguments are some perplexing philosophical problems. This is an attempt to clarify those problems. I will first consider what may be meant when the term "intention" is used in reference to art; then I will ask what constitutes an explanation in criticism; finally, I will offer a reconstruction of the term "intention" which will, I hope, make it a more useful category in the theory and practice of criticism than it has heretofore been.

I. Various Uses of "Intention"

In contemporary criticism the disputes over artistic intention are due not so much to the fact that critics use "intention" in different senses, but rather to the

From the *Journal of Philosophy,* Vol. LVII, No. 1 (1960), pp. 5-23. Reprinted by permission of the author and the *Journal of Philosophy.*
*This study was completed under a grant from the Columbia University Council for Research in the Humanities.

fact that "intention," in whatever sense it is used, functions in different ways in different theories. In surveying the uses of "intention" it should be kept in mind that "use" here implies type of category as well as sense.

A. The Intention of the Artist

When we talk about the intention of the artist we usually mean one of two things: (1) that the artist aims at a certain result, or (2) that the artist's purpose is to convey a meaning.

1. The Artist's Intention as Aiming at a Result. In this sense, to speak of the intention of the artist is to refer to his performance as a mental process and a manipulation of the medium for some end. (*a*) The most controversial usage here is that which assumes the artist has his work in his head prior to the forming activity with the medium. Croce and Collingwood are often accused of holding this view.[1] (But Collingwood does emphasize the importance to the artist of working out his feelings through the handling of the medium.)

Interpretations which assume this position claim that what the artist conceives in thought is more important than what he does with the medium. But the position might be modified to state: (*b*) the artist has an intention in the sense that he aims at a specific effect which he knows of before the actual construction in the medium, but the precise way he will come to state it is as yet unknown to him, for this must be discovered in the medium. If either of these positions is assumed by the critic he commits himself to separating the idea in the artist's mind from the medium which is taken to be a vehicle of expression. Further, the critic assumes he can give a special kind of explanation for the work; e.g., "The artist painted this in order to convey his deep sense of loss," or "He wrote this poem because he had been impressed with the fact of ineradicable evil." Clarity demands that the critic consider carefully whether he thinks the artist uses the medium simply as something to embody his thoughts and feelings, or whether there is an important element of discovery in working the medium.

In making a distinction between what is in the artist's mind and the finished product the critic may wish to point out that (*c*) the artist's intention was non-artistic—"He produced this work in order to achieve fame," or "Behind this work was a need to resolve a neurotic conflict." Such explanations are of a curious kind, but are found frequently in critical writings. They assume, as do (*a*) and (*b*), that the critic has access to the artist's psychic dispositions. Indeed, there may be evidence for such statements, but they have to do with biography and history, not with art criticism as such.

A more tentative position would be one that maintained: (*d*) the artist has an

---

[1] John Hospers, "The Concept of Artistic Expression," *Proc. Arist. Soc.,* Vol. LV (1954-55), pp. 313-344.

intention in the sense that his behavior is purposive, though not purposeful as in (*a*), (*b*), and (*c*). The artist behaves as if he knew his goal beforehand in a conscious way, though it is questionable if he really does. This sense of intention is sometimes assumed (occasionally, for example, by Plato) because we want to distinguish cases of purposeful behavior where there is a consciously entertained goal from purposive behavior where conscious intention is either absent or questionable.[2] One of the criticisms directed against the theory of expression is that it assumes too often that the artist works in a purposeful way, when in fact he works in a purposive way. Psychoanalytic theories, too, are unclear about the purposive and the purposeful in creation.

The positions so far outlined imply that the critic can perform his task adequately only if he can compare the finished work with the artist's goals (conscious or unconscious) prior to the work. A further implication is that the evaluation of the work requires an assessment of how well the artist accomplished what he set out to do, or how well the work exhibits the aritst's needs at the time of creation. Criticism of this kind places high value on artisanship (i.e., the artist's ability to get his purposes embodied in the medium) and expressive power (i.e., the artist's ability to convey his emotions). The critic who looks upon art as contrivance, expression, or sublimation usually assumes one of the above senses of intention.

2. The Artist's Intention as the Conveying of a Meaning. To speak of the artist's intention is sometimes to speak of the artist's meaning. T. M. Gang has pointed out that to ask for the meaning of a literary work is sometimes to ask for a statement of the literal content, sometimes to ask for its "message." The critic is more apt to assume that the artist could give a paraphrase than that he could give the message, "For we are more inclined to believe that an author knows the weak significance of his words, than that he knows the strong. We sometimes talk as if a work could possess a strong meaning without the author's wish, or even against his wishes."[3] Much literary criticism is devoted to an explication of the text, seeking the plain meaning of the words. And some criticism is concerned with interpretation, i.e., getting at the message which may go beyond the plain, literal sense. It is important that the critic be clear about the way in which he invokes the author when giving an interpretation. One way to use the author is to assume that his work is meaningful in some private sense, and that full understanding requires the revelation of the private sense. Another, and more legitimate, use is to see the author as a kind of ideal spectator: what would the work mean to him, given his outlook and his assumptions? Gang has noted that there are cases where private use of

---

[2]The distinction between "purposeful" and "purposive" is discussed in W. E. Agar, *A Contribution to the Theory of the Living Organism,* Melbourne University Press, 2nd edition, 1951. For a discussion of how this distinction can be logically maintained, see I. Scheffler, "Thoughts on Teleology," *Brit. Jour. for the Phil. of Science,* Vol. LX (1959), pp. 265-284.
[3]"Intention," *Essays in Criticism,* Vol. VII (1957), pp. 175-186.

language makes it necessary to look for something other than the meaning of terms set by common usage; this requires going to the artist rather than to his contemporary audience.[4]

When we inquire into the intention of the artist we must be sure we understand the kind of data we seek. Are we asking for the psychological conditions that were the cause of the work, or are we asking what the artist thought he was up to, or are we asking what the artist meant? It has just been pointed out that to ask for the intention in the sense of the meaning allows us to ask, "What is the purpose of such and such an element in the work?," or to ask, "What did the artist (as the ideal beholder) understand by such and such an element?," without necessarily referring to private psychic information. It is evident that the referent of intention can shift from the author's motivation to the meaning of the work.

There is an interpretation of artistic intention that should be noted before considering "intention" as referring to the work of art. In contemporary stylistics there is a school, leaning heavily on the expressionist theory of Croce, whose most noted members are Vossler, Spitzer, and (with a somewhat different approach) Alonso. The method they employ is sometimes called "Stilforschung" or "la stylistique de l'individu." The aim of the method is to discover the "psychic forces" responsible for the stylistic peculiarities of the work. The psychic forces are sometimes interpreted in a personal sense, sometimes in a rather impersonal sense. The critic seeks to penetrate to what Spitzer has called "the psychological etymon, the radix in his [the author's] soul."[5] This is accomplished by means of the "philological circle": a careful reading and rereading of the text until peculiarities of structure and style impress themselves upon the reader, the generalizing of these traits, and the relating of them to the artist's psyche. Finally, the text is further explored in the light of the stylistic and psychological hypotheses formulated originally. The work of art is regarded as an expressive system. Such a system, Alonso claims, "embraces everything from the internal constitution of the work to the suggestive power of the words and the aesthetic efficacy of rhythmical interplay. And by 'internal constitution' I am referring to that world which in his poems, in his tragedy, or in his novel, the poet shapes out of his sentiments and thoughts."[6]

The search for intentions does not demand that there be confirming information about the artist's psychic dispositions in letters and contemporary journalism, but simply that the mind behind the work be taken as a necessary part of the work. The assumption is that the work of art, as an *expressive* synthesis of

---

[4]*Ibid.,* p. 181. The example given is Blake. Gang is referring to some remarks of F. W. Bateson in "Intention and Blake's Jerusalem," *Essays in Criticism,* Vol. II (1952), pp. 105-114. See also F. W. Leakey, "Intention in Metaphor," same journal, Vol. IV (1954), pp. 191-198.
[5]Leo Spitzer, *Linguistics and Literary History,* Princeton, Princeton University Press, 1948, p. 13.
[6]Amado Alonso, "The Stylistic Interpretation of Literary Texts," *Modern Language Notes,* Vol. LVII (1942), pp. 489-496.

materials, presents us with a "living impression," the "mind of the author," as Croce puts it. But the mind is in the work, is the work. There is no need, in fact it is impossible, to find a separate, real mental experience behind the work. In studying the "expressive system" which is the work of art, this school of stylistics finds the intention of the author in his expressive conduct, i.e., in the work itself.[7]

B. The Intention of the Work of Art

When it is said that intention is relevant to the evaluation of a work of art, it is sometimes meant that the work itself exhibits an intention. In this context there are three usages of "intention." The first refers to the work of art as a purposive or organic whole; the second refers to the fact that a work of art seems to make demands upon the beholder; the third refers to the belief that works of art exhibit processes or ends which are supra-personal. The first is found in organicist interpretations of art; the second in Gestalt theories of art; the third in idealist theories of art.

1. The Work of Art Has an Intention, i.e., is an Organic Whole. "There can be," writes Kant, "purposiveness without purpose, so far as we do not place the causes of this form in a will, but yet can only make the explanation of its possibility intelligible to ourselves by deriving it from a will."[8] The purposiveness we attribute to art is discovered in the fact that the elements of the object cohere in such a way that a satisfactory experience results, i.e., we feel pleasure. How can it be, Kant asked, that an experience which is fundamentally one of feeling can yet be the foundation for an objective evaluation? This is possible, he believed, only if it can be shown that an object, non-conceptual in its organization, yet somehow purposive, is the stimulus for a judgment of taste. The purposiveness we find in art is an attribution we make when we reflect upon the forms of nature and art. A work of art is like a natural object: it seems to be composed for some end, though Kant is careful to make clear that the purposiveness of both art and nature is ideal, not real.[9]

2. The Work of Art Has an Intention, i.e., Makes Certain Demands upon the Beholder. In the writings of contemporary Gestalt psychology and of critics influenced by it a work of art is considered to have an intention because the beholder responds to the work in a peculiar way. One prominent art historian who uses intention in this way is Panofsky. Man-made objects, he maintains, demand to be experienced in a particular way because their style

---

[7]For a discussion of this school and others see S. Ullmann, *Style in the French Novel,* Cambridge, University Press, 1957; P. Guiraud, *La Stylistique,* Paris, Presses Universitaires de France, 1957; H. Hatzfeld, "Recent Italian Stylistic Theory and Stylistic Criticism," *Studia Philologica et Litteraria in Honorem L. Spitzer,* Bern, Franke Verlag, 1958, pp. 227-244.

[8]*Critique of Judgment,* sec. 10 (J. H. Bernard's translation).

[9]*Ibid.,* Introduction, sec. viii; Dialectic, sec. 59.

"bears witness to artistic intentions." Intentions can properly be defined only by reference to a choice between alternative ways of solving an artistic problem. Thus verification for statements about intentions is to be found in art history and style analysis. And the need to provide verification comes from the "re-creative" experience of the beholder in which intentions are immediately perceived.[10]

Philosophers, too, have analyzed intention phenomenologically. One of the best examples is to be found in the writings of David Prall, who devoted a book to the articulation of directly apprehended artistic qualities, relationships, and intentions.[11] To speak of the intention of a work of art from this point of view is to exhibit the way in which the sensuous elements in combination give rise to the distinctive affective qualities of the whole. The work is seen to move towards a terminal condition, and the coöperation of the parts in the achievement of this final condition is directly apprehended in experience. The parts of the work exist for the specific end to which they contribute.

Sometimes the macroscopic properties of an artistic style are spoken of as exhibiting an intention. For example, it is said that "The intention of the Baroque style was to break up space," or, "The use of local color in the romantic novel had as its intention the exploration of new words and their undisclosed linguistic possibilities." In his essay, "Perspective as Symbolic Form," Panofsky characterizes the art of the middle ages as one "whose historical mission was to fuse into a genuine unity what had previously appeared as a plurality of individual things."[12] To refer to gross stylistic features as exhibiting an intention is to try to account for the fact that we find in style the manifestation of artistic purposes which go beyond that of an individual artist. This suggests a third use of "intention": works of art may have an intention of a supra-personal kind.

3. The Work of Art Has an Intention, i.e., It Manifests Supra-personal Purposes. This use of intention is well known from the writings of Schopenhauer and Hegel, as well as from the writings of the Jungian school. Jung rests his interpretation of art on the distinction between a problem-solving art ("contrived art") and spontaneous art which results from the "autonomous complex." The concept of intention as applied to the work of an individual is irrelevant to spontaneous art. The only way we can speak of intention in this case is if we mean it to refer to a supra-personal force. If the artist cannot let the forces of autonomous creativity work through him he produces contrived art. Such art exhibits the intention of the calculating artisan, and is as a consequence impoverished. In contrast, great art exhibits the intention of

---

[10]E. Panofsky, "Art as a Humanistic Discipline," *Meaning in the Visual Arts,* New York, Anchor Books, 1955, pp. 1-25.

[11]*Aesthetic Analysis,* New York, Crowell, 1936.

[12]*Vorträge der Bibliothek Warburg,* 1924-25.

an apparently "foreign impulse" that uses the artist and cannot be controlled by him.[13]

The difference between Panofsky's and Jung's interpretation of art results from a fundamental difference in their explanations of human creativity. The issue here is rather like that between reductionists and vitalists, a dispute prominent in the 19th century which has today been carried over into realms other than biology. Panofsky will admit intention only in the sense of an effort to solve a problem. Jung will admit that in the case of contrived art, but will admit it only in an entirely different sense in the case of spontaneous art. For Panofsky the recognition of intention depends upon a thorough grasp of art history and sensitivity to style. For Jung recognition of intention is a spontaneous response to symbols having a universal significance; the content of art produced by the autonomous complex consists of symbols drawn from the collective unconscious which set up reverberations in the unconscious of the beholder.

There is one way in which the intention of the work of art might be spoken of which does not fit into any of the above examples. This is a normative usage; to speak of the intention in this way is to specify what a work of art ought to do or be. For Plato a work of art has an intention in that it ought to exhibit moral and intellectual content of a certain kind. The value of the work depends not upon the end for which it was created, but upon the end in fact achieved. If the end is moral enlightenment, the work is praiseworthy. Plato and those like him, who wish to discover the true end of art, presuppose that the intention, in the sense of "the proper end," can be stated.

II. What Constitutes an Explanation in Criticism?

The several usages of "intention" differentiated above show how misleading it is to talk of an "intentional fallacy." However urgent the need to dismiss intentions from criticism in one or another sense, the complexity of the term's use would indicate that one might well want to keep it in the critical vocabulary, provided a sufficiently clear and fruitful definition could be worked out.

If we ask what is taken to be an explanation in criticism we shall see, I believe, why critics have disputed the relevance of intention to criticism, and we shall see also that ultimately intention can be a useful category in critical analysis. However, before a reconstruction of intention can be offered, there are two issues that require examination. They will throw light on the assumptions which critics make in terms of which they take different stands on the importance of intention to criticism. The first is the extent to which we do as a

---

[13]"Contributions to Analytical Psychology," quoted in Vivas and Krieger, *The Problems of Aesthetics,* New York, Rinehart, 1953, p. 169. See also, Erich Neumann, "Art and Time," *Man and Time, Papers from the Eranos Yearbooks,* London, Routledge & Kegan Paul, 1958, pp. 3-37.

matter of fact concern ourselves with the artist's intentions when we try to give an explanation of a work of art. The second is the kind of object we assume a work of art to be when we give an explanation. The first will require a brief phenomenological survey; the second a brief exposition of a confusion concerning "form."

We frequently ask ourselves what the artist wanted to do or realize when we perceive a work of art. Such questions come to mind when a difficulty is encountered, when we are puzzled by a detail in the work, when one part of the work is not consistent logically or affectively or aesthetically with another part. Here are questions one critic has put in reading Shakespeare's "Troilus and Cressida":

> Application of the 'historical method' does not, however, explain completely the difficulties of this strange play. It does provide an indispensable startingpoint, but it does not reveal why Shakespeare selected this unpleasant theme—for it could, as we shall see, hardly have been treated in a pleasant fashion in his day—or why, though managing it technically as a comedy, he chose to offer so little relief to the intensity of the shadows. Nor does it make clear his conception of the whole. His version is like to no other; what effect did he aim to produce? How did he mean his play to be understood?[14]

A less sophisticated commentator may forge on to answer such questions; a popular edition of Shakespeare's plays published at the beginning of the century included as part of the preface for each play a section entitled, "The Poet's Purpose in this Play." In the preface to "Measure for Measure" we read: "It was his indignation at this hypocritical virtue [of the Puritans] that led him to write 'Measure for Measure.' He treated the subject as he did because the interests of the theatre demanded that the woof of comedy should be interwoven with the severe and somber warp of tragedy."[15]

When we ask, "How did he mean his play to be understood?," it is because we believe (rightly or wrongly is not at issue here) that the poet was aiming at something which if known to us would either make the organization of the play apparent, or show us the way in which it fails. And we believe this to be legitimate because we feel we are in the presence of a mind responsible for a purposeful human act when we confront the work. Admittedly, the "person" may be an artistic "persona," but the phenomenological fact remains.

Even when we are not puzzled we are apt to make inferences from the work to the artist's intentions and personal characteristics. Bernard Berenson, for example, after considering the painting of Piero della Francesca, offers this comment: "One is almost compelled to conclude that Piero was not interested in human beings as living animals, sentient and acting. For him they were existences in three dimensions whom perchance he would have gladly ex-

---

[14]William Witherle Lawrence, *Shakespeare's Problem Comedies,* New York, Macmillan, 1931, p. 124.
[15]Booklovers Edition, New York, The University Society, 1901.

changed for pillars and arches, capitals, entablatures and facets of walls."[16] Berenson's generalization results from an acquaintance with the artist's entire output and his inference has nothing of the curiosity about the artist's private life which questions about intentions frequently display. His response is a natural one, however, for it takes characteristics of Piero's art and sees them as consequences of an attitude and a preference. We cannot help seeing human performances in this way.

Knowledge about the artist's personal interests, problems, life history, and psychic peculiarities are much sought after. The reason for this is not, as C. S. Lewis suspects, because we believe that "all poetry is *about* the poet's state of mind,"[17] but rather because we sometimes find that this information gives us clues to what is in the work itself. We cannot deny the obvious interest in artistic personalities for its own sake; artists are frequently interesting people whom we wish to know—which is to say, we wish to see how their work and life fit together. It is wrong to deny *a priori* the possible relevance of personal information to the artistic experience itself. There is a long tradition in Western art which links the life of the artist to his productions. It finds its exemplifications in the stories of the childhood of famous artists so common in the Renaissance, in the theories of genius so important to the 18th and 19th centuries, and in the romantic views of art that are maintained to this day. It is indeed possible that for many people the art-work and the art-life are part of a whole "object" which claims attention in the beholder's experience.[18]

It may be the case that knowledge of artistic aims will help us to evaluate a work of art. One job the art historian performs is to get the information we need in order to know what standards are relevant in appraising an object. I do not wish at this time to question such inquiries and the conclusions made on the basis of them; in fact they are a part of many critics' work, as the following comment upon an ivory panel of the late fourth century indicates:

There is a positive intention behind [these features of 'sub-antique' art]. . . . There is in this carving an almost deliberate protest against realism. The sculptor makes it clear that he has no confidence in formal beauty and naturalism. He disregards the laws of nature; he shows that he is not interested in such things as three-dimensional space and the autonomy of the human body. For these he substitutes other values. His concern is the abstract relationship between things rather than the things themselves.[19]

It is a fact, then, that questions about the artist's intentions often do concern us when we perceive a work of art. While these are the result of immediate

---

[16]*Piero della Francesca or The Ineloquent in Art,* New York, Macmillan, 1954, p. 5.
[17]*The Personal Heresy,* London, Oxford University Press, 1939, p. 2.
[18]See E. Kris, "The Image of the Artist," *Psychoanalytic Explorations in Art,* New York, International Universities Press, 1952, pp. 64-84. Also, E. Zilsel, *Die Entstehung des Geniebegriffes,* Tübingen, Mohr, 1926.
[19]E. Kitzinger, *Early Medieval Art in the British Museum,* London, The British Museum, 1940, pp. 13-14.

perplexities and inferences which we entertain, they are raised in the hope that an answer to them will resolve difficulties in the work and thereby allow us to enrich our experience of it. The critic who follows his naive disposition to ask such questions believes (though he may be mistaken) that he can give a better explanation if he can discover what the artist intended. However, in pursuing this line of inquiry the critic may misunderstand what it is that forces him to raise such questions. Since he feels, as we all do, the presence of a creative intellect in his experience of the work he believes that he can clarify his perception if he finds out how that intellect functioned, how it looked upon its work. In doing this he shifts his attention from the work to a hypothetical mind responsible for the work. Yet the awareness of an intention is generated by the work, not by something behind and beyond it.

The critic who deviates from the work to the artist's conscious or unconscious intention ignores the artistic fact for what he assumes to be a more meaningful psychological fact. However, he must fabricate or infer the second, while the first is directly available to him. When the critic turns to the artist's intention he turns away from the artistic intention. An explanation in criticism requires the second; it may be able to ignore the first.

When we look at the questions that are asked on the basis of direct experience we find that we do wonder about the intention of an artist, a style, and even a society. But what we idly entertain and the many things about which we are naturally curious give us no ground for a theory of criticism as such. To strengthen theory we must give an interpretation of fundamental categories, such as intention, that will make them relevant to the job of criticism. It will be argued below that the most relevant and fruitful meaning of "intention" is to be found in construing it as referring to the kind of experience the work of art realizes for the beholder through its maintenance of a focal effect.

If a critic is to give a satisfactory explanation of a work of art he must have some idea of the kind of object he is dealing with. One answer to the question, "What kind of an object is a work of art?," is to be found by looking at the history of philosophies of art. There many answers are proposed; but they are not answers that help us because they are usually interested in stating the ultimate nature of a work of art. To be told that art is a manifestation of will, or a kind of play, or the objectification of the beautiful, and the like, cannot help the critic because he still must analyze the specific object confronting him. He must know what it is that characterizes works of art as perceptual objects.

The term most frequently used to describe the peculiar characteristic of a work of art is "form." There is no need to examine the many meanings that have been associated with that term; we need only note that critics tend to use it in two fundamentally different ways. These usages reflect beliefs, frequently unexamined, about what kind of object a work of art is, or at least how a work of art ought to be considered. One usage implies that a work of art is a structure whose parts and relationships the critic must map; the other usage implies that a work of art has a peculiar function which the critic must analyze in terms of its effect upon the beholder. It is, of course, possible to deal with a work of art in both of these manifestations, but critics tend to select one or the other for their primary concern.

In its most common sense, "form" refers to the structure of the work of art; all objects have a form in this sense on the condition that we can distinguish elements and their relationships in what is perceived. Obviously works of art have a structure, since they are systematically organized objects; and the structures peculiar to art can sometimes be isolated and talked about apart from the objects exhibiting the structure. Thus we speak of sonata form, sonnet form, and the like.

This first usage of "form" might be called its analytical sense. I will refer to it as the "structure" of the work of art in order to distinguish it from a normative use of "form" which I will refer to as "aesthetic form." When "form" is used in this second sense the critic usually wishes to denote by it the kind of experience a work of art makes possible. In recent years several attempts have been made to use form in this way because of a dissatisfaction with form taken simply as structure. To say a work of art has form in the sense of aesthetic form is to say that it is organized to achieve a certain end, viz., the production of an experience with special qualities. The three writers who have done most to develop this sense of form are Abercrombie, Burke, and Dewey.[20]

Those who take form in the first sense would give a different answer to the question, "What constitutes an explanation in criticism?," than would those who take form in the second sense. For the critic who sees form as structure, an explanation would be a description of the elements and their interrelationships to be found in an object. For the critic who sees form as aesthetic form, an explanation would be the discovery and justification of a function. The former claim an objectivity and precision for their explanations that they say the latter can never achieve. The latter claim that they are concerned with what is most important in art, the effect a work has upon a beholder, the end for which a work is designed. They disagree about the relevance of historical data because they disagree about what is the legitimate scope of an explanation. As a consequence they have been wary of talking about intentions either because intentions are too closely related to historical matters irrelevant to understanding a work of art qua art, or because intentions carry one out far beyond the verifiable meanings that can be discovered by paying close attention to the elements of the object.

I wish to show that the concept of intention can be a useful one, though it

[20]L. Abercrombie, *The Idea of Great Poetry,* London, Martin Secker, 1925; K. Burke, *Counterstatement,* New York, Harcourt Brace, 1931; J. Dewey, *Art as Experience,* New York, Minton Balch, 1932. For an elaboration of this point see my "Professor Frye's Criticism," this JOURNAL, Vol. LVI (1959), pp. 745-755.

requires reinterpretation if it is to be useful. I want to show that on methodological grounds it is not necessary to think of intention as being correlated in a one to one manner with specific terms of the work; and, finally, I want to show that intention can be most useful if taken in conjunction with style.

III. Intention Reconsidered

A work of art is a system in which a variety of parts function together to maintain a whole. The question that critics ask, and the problem about which they disagree, is, What constitutes the whole? Is it the immediately perceived object? Is it something entertained in the imagination after the sensuous given has been worked upon and elaborated by the beholder? It has been suggested that a distinction ought to be made between the "work of art" and the "aesthetic object" to differentiate the experience of two beholders with the same object, and to account for the different experiences of one person on two confrontations. This implies that the whole is not determined by the given; but then to what extent ought the beholder to go beyond the given? To what extent ought he to be aware of the object's place in its historical tradition? T. S. Eliot has said, "No poet, no artist of any art has his complete meaning alone."

Where ought the boundaries of relevance to be laid down? The simple answer is that the boundary is established for us when the object makes sense, or gives us pleasure, or satisfies us, in whatever vague way we mean "satisfies." But the critic cannot accept that kind of answer, for though we may all know when we are pleased or satisfied, we don't know whether our satisfactions are impoverished ones or not. One of the critic's tasks is to show us the difference between a full satisfaction and an impoverished satisfaction.

Because art objects are the purposive work of intelligent agents they can properly be called "functional wholes." By functional whole is meant an organization of parts which are interdependent; i.e., the significance or qualitative peculiarities of each part are functions of the significance and qualitative peculiarities of the other parts. This has sometimes been expressed by saying that no part of a work of art can be changed without seriously affecting the whole. However, this common assumption is highly dubious. In many cases we can change a part of a work of art without seriously affecting the whole. Yet alterations do change the work in its specific details and thus do change to some (perhaps slight or irrelevant) extent the experience we have of the work. Within limits changes can be made without altering the basic organization and fundamental meaning of the work; but if we go outside those limits the work is seriously affected. This suggests that a work of art is a functional whole in a peculiar sense, not in a strictly logical sense, but in a looser or weaker sense.

There is a difference between the values of the parts of a work which if changed would not alter the over-all effect of the work, and the values of the elements of a work which if changed would alter the over-all effect of the work.

One way of stating this is to say that within limits it is possible to change the parts and the relationships between the parts of a work of art without changing the *style* of the work. The style remains as a kind of organization of elements capable of sustaining a constant "focal effect."[21] I will call the focal effect which the style sustains the *intention* of the work of art.

When in aesthetic theory or critical practice a writer speaks of a work of art as an "organic unity," or as exhibiting "unity in variety"; when it is said that a work of art is a "functional whole," or that no part of a work of art can be changed without seriously altering the whole, what is meant is that a work of art is an object the parts of which are *interdependent*. A strict definition of interdependence can be given, following Oppenheim and Grelling, if we say that: "A class of functions ϕ will be called interdependent when and only when every element f of ϕ depends on the complementary class consisting of all elements of ϕ except f."[22]

A definition of "dependence" can be given as follows: If for each pair $[x_1, x_2]$ such that $f_1(x_1) = f_1(x_2)$ for all f_1 other than f, then $f(x_1) = f(x_2)$. Therefore, a class of functions $(f_1, f_2 \ldots f_n)$ is interdependent if the value of any one function depends on the values of the other $n - 1$ functions.

Although it is possible, I believe, to interpret the style of a work of art as a family of variables, values, and functional relationships, the system they define is not an interdependent one in the strict logical sense. But there is good reason to begin with a rigorous statement of interdependence, for only then can we, by comparison, know what we mean when we say that the elements of a work of art are interdependent in a weaker sense, and therefore that a work of art is, in a weaker sense, a functional whole. If we are to talk meaningfully about a work of art in these terms we must determine (1) what we mean by an element of a work of art; (2) what we mean by a functional relationship among the elements of a work of art; (3) what we mean by the values of the variables functionally related.

What we mean by an element depends upon the medium and the purpose of the analysis. If we were to analyze a painting by Pissarro we might want to discriminate each spot of paint and refer to it as an element in order to show how the painting is built up to achieve its effect. Or if we were examining a Brueghel depiction of various proverbs we might discriminate as elements each figure, house, tree, recognizable object, in the painting.

In the case of an aural medium we might wish to call an element a note, a melody, a phrase, a theme, depending upon our purpose in conducting the

---

[21]The term "focal effect" is taken from G. Sommerhof, *Analytical Biology*, London, Oxford University Press, 1950.

[22]"Logical Analysis of 'Gestalt' as 'Functional Whole,'" reprinted for members of the Fifth International Congress for the Unity of Science, Cambridge, Mass., 1939. This would have appeared in the 9th volume of *Erkenntnis*, but the volume never appeared in print. I am indebted to Professor Ernest Nagel for the copy I have seen.

analysis. The same holds for literature: a phoneme, a word, a sentence, a paragraph, a scene, a chapter, each of these might properly be referred to as an element of the work. As a rule in critical practice, an element is that discriminable part of a work, phenomenally considered, which if changed would cause a change in the focal effect.

This makes it obvious that functional relationships between elements are hard to identify. What can we mean when we say that one element in a Pissarro painting is a function of the value of another element in the painting? What can we mean when we say that a functional relationship holds between two elements of a poem, a sonata? If to be a functional whole a system must have interdependent elements, and if by interdependence we mean a relationship of the sort logically defined, then clearly works of art are not functional wholes. The values of the variables in a work of art are certainly not interdependent in the same sense that the volume and pressure of a fixed volume of a gas are interdependent. There is no quantitative way in which the variations of the values of the variables can be measured. And yet we do believe that in some sense the elements of a work of art are functionally related, and we do find that the values of the variables are related in such a way that a phenomenal change in one leads us to feel that a phenomenal change in at least some of the others is required.[23]

But when we say "required" we mean it in a phenomenological sense, not a logical sense. The relationships of dependence and interdependence that we believe characterize a work of art are at best analogous to the logical relationships defined above. It is a looser sense of dependence and interdependence that we speak about in the case of works of art.

When we say that the elements of a work of art depend upon one another we mean that the medium is structured in such a way that the act of composition in the medium is controlled by (1) a set of rules, (2) the artist's style. For a medium such as language there are rules of grammar and syntax; for a medium such as sound there are rules of harmony, tonality, and rhythmic structure; for the plastic media there are rules of perspective, color, and organization of the figure.[24] Though these rules change, it is possible, when we know the rules in terms of which the artist works, to give a precise definition of dependence and interdependence for that artist's work. We could predict what changes would be made in at least some other elements of a work if one specific

---

[23]It is necessary to distinguish real from phenomenal changes. for it is possible that a real change would have no appreciable phenomenal effect.

[24]It must be understood that "rules" need not be explicitly formulated; they may be conventions of the time or school, or regularities in the artist's means of structuring the medium. For an important discussion of this see, Jan Mukařovský, "Standard Language and Poetic Language," *A Prague School Reader,* translated by P. Garvin, Washington, D. C., The American University Language Center, 1958.

element were changed. But the rules are not exhaustive of the structuring principles. In addition there is the artist's style. Here we cannot predict with any high degree of probability what the value changes of the variables would be, given a specific value change in one variable. However, we can say this: the values assigned to the variables will be controlled by the artist's style, for the style is an organization of the medium responsible for the maintenance of a constant focal effect. The constant focal effect is the intention of the work of art. It is in this looser sense that we can say the work of art is a functional whole: the values of the variables are so related that a change in one value will determine a range of values of the other variables such that the range will be a domain of values capable of sustaining the artistic intention.

Finally, it must be asked, what kind of relationship is there between the elements of a work and its intention? There is in some sense a causal relationship between the elements and the end product, but it is not a relationship of such a kind as permits us to say element x is responsible for the end product. Rather, it is all the elements in their partial interdependence and dependence which are responsible for the focal effect. But when we analyze a work of art we find an object of such complexity that it is impossible to discover more than series of interrelated elements. That is, a work of art is like a net-work of causal chains in which we can distinguish certain elements as intimately related to one another; but the series of such closely related elements may not be intimately related to one another. Yet they function together to sustain the focal effect.

It is evident that the intention of the work enjoys a certain independence in respect to the specific variables and their values. The intention has a stability so that as one variable takes a certain value, at least some of the other variables take compensating values out of a determined domain in order to sustain the focal effect.

We can now return to the question we started with: to what extent ought the critic to be concerned with intention? Let it be said first that as a matter of fact, when we consider our experience with works of art, we are not interested except in a biographical sense with the artist's intention, if by intention we mean what the artist consciously entertained when he set to work. This is not to say, as has been pointed out, that we do not wonder about the artist's life, his thoughts, and motives. But when we attend to a work of art the psychological conditions, in any verifiable sense, that gave rise to the product are of secondary concern.

However, we are concerned with the intention of the work in the proper artistic sense of intention: what the work sustains as a certain kind of experience, its focal effect. The artistic intention may or may not be what the maker was aiming at. His intention, psychologically speaking, may have been quite different from what the work effects. But it is the artistic intention that matters for criticism. It may be that the intention of the work is what the maker would inevitably effect with his handling of the medium because of social and cultural factors, but this, too, is extraneous to criticism.

When we speak of the intention of the work of art we are quite justified in leaving out of account the psychological, social, and cultural factors that obtained at the time of the work was created because the work of art is, properly speaking, a closed system free from *unspecified* outside influences.[25]

It is up to the critic to determine where he will set the framework or boundaries of relevance for his analysis of the art work. He may wish to consider the work as a closed system in a very restricted sense, or as a closed system in a broader sense. Where he sets the boundaries will depend upon the kind of object he is examining and his critical presuppositions. But wherever he sets his boundaries, he will consider the work of art as a system whose organization is definitional within those boundaries. Once he has defined the system he can treat it as a closed system. This does not mean that the system is free from outside influences; it is closed only in the sense that for purposes of analysis it is regarded as free from *unspecified* outside influences.

The disagreements among critics come from two perplexities about setting up boundary conditions: (1) an uncertainty about whether one is justified in treating a work of art as a closed system in the sense just stated; (2) an uncertainty about whether different boundary conditions can be tolerated. If it were realized that different sets of boundary conditions can legitimately be established, then critics could argue fruitfully about the relevance of the events and relationships which they include in their systems. To do this they must specify the boundaries of relevance which they have set; failure to do this implies that only an interminable analysis will do. The boundaries, however, cannot be determined *a priori,* something that, unfortunately, critical theories predispose us to do. The boundaries of relevance will be at least partly determined by the intention of the work of art.

What of the confusion that results from a belief that a system cannot be considered as a closed system but must be considered as including a variety of causal events such as cultural norms, Weltanschauungen, unconscious psychological processes, and the like? A given series of events, E_1, E_2 ... E_n, can properly be said to cause an end state—e.g., the finished work of art. The events can be extended to include social, cultural, and psychological factors as well as the immediate response of the artist to the medium he is shaping. But the intention of the work can be considered as independent of any one or more of these determining factors. This independence is claimed not because the ordinary sense of causation is inapplicable to artistic products, but because the end product is determined by the sum total of these factors as they work together. The intention is produced by a set of variables which take a possible

---

[25]This discussion of a work of art as a "closed system" is taken from G. Sommerhof, *op. cit.,* pp. 84-85.

range of values due to an undetermined number of antecedent events. The intention cannot be said to be the direct effect of any one cause, whether the artist's specific life experience at time t_1, or his unconscious wish at time t_2, or the social demands at time t_3.

Thus, following Sommerhof,[26] we might term the functional relationships that obtain among the variables "undetermined functions." By undetermined function is meant one for which there exists no known formula enabling the value of a dependent variable to be calculated from that of an independent variable. Except in very simple cases, the relationships between variables in a work of art will be undetermined functions.

The critic is free to set the boundaries of relevance for the system he is to explicate. What he has to work with is the system, conceived of as a concatenation of variables each with a domain of values, and the intention of the system, conceived of as the specific kind of experience the work of art realizes. A central, and most difficult, task for him is to establish the dependence of the intention upon the style of the work. What the critic wants to discover is the relationship between (1) his experience with the work of art and (2) the objective values and functional relationships which define the elements of the work of art and which together establish a system open to the inspection of any member of an audience. In short, he wants to establish the dependence of intention upon style where the functional relationships between style-variables are undetermined. But this problem must be reserved for another occasion.

---

[26]*Op. cit.*, pp. 83-84.

The Historian as Critic

JAMES S. ACKERMAN

We overhear an argument between a critic and a historian of art; the critic says "You are interested only in facts about works of art and not in quality; you approach it as a document of civilization rather than the creation of an individual spirit." The historian replies "You are so preoccupied with your own reactions that you cannot see it in its proper perspective; you are not concerned with the facts, and what you write is not criticism but inferior literature." The critic mumbles something about "dry objectivity," the historian something about "sloppy subjectivity," and they part, the one bearing with him the object, the other its qualities. Between them they have torn it apart, body from soul, as they might say. They are not the most inspired representatives of their profession, and we trust that their betters will put it back together again; but even they might be able to collaborate in that reconstruction if they were not so bemused by their rigid and rather old-fashioned concepts of subjectivity and objectivity.

The isolation of art history from art criticism in recent times is due largely to a conviction that a clear distinction can be made between facts and feelings about works of art, that we make sound "objective" observations at one moment and unreliable "subjective" evaluations at another. The separation is grounded in an outmoded psychology of perception that entirely isolates the

From James S. Ackerman and Rhys Carpenter, *Art and Archaeology*. © 1963, by permission of Prentice-Hall, Inc., Englewood Cliffs, New Jersey, and the author.

work of art (object) from the observer (subject) by assuming the latter to be the passive recipient of emanations from the former. Thus, certain stimuli are attributed to the object and regarded as "real"—fit subject for scientific investigation—while the effect of these stimuli in the subject are attributed to individual emotions and are regarded as ephemeral and unworthy of scholarly attention. The argument is wrong because we cannot distinguish clearly "objective" from "subjective" factors in visual perceptions, and because nearly every conclusion we make about works of art bears the stamp of our personality, experience, and system of values, though in varying degrees.

We cannot say with certainty of the object that it conveys a particular message to the subject because we know that every subject gets a somewhat different message. The subject, in receiving his message, is not a sponge absorbing an invariable signal issuing from the source, but a contributing agent who sees in any object—whether or not it is a work of art—what his experience predisposes him to expect and to receive, and what his imagination prompts him to add or to alter. Therefore, what a work of art communicates can be described only in terms of an interaction between an object and a subject; it communicates nothing at all unless someone is there to look at it. In other words, there are no aesthetic objects, only physical objects, which, when observed, are capable of stimulating an aesthetic *event*.

This process may be clarified by a tautology; since our responses to visual objects are entirely within us, all of them are "subjective." On the sole basis of our own experience of the objects, we cannot designate some of our responses as "objective." But in making *statements about* responses, we distinguish as "objective" those that we believe will correspond with the experience of other people—provided they understand our premises and are supplied with the relevant information. In other words, we do not know intuitively what is objective; we learn it from our experience of the way others in our culture articulate their responses; and, as the term *objective* implies, we assume that when people proceeding on similar premises and information make or are willing to accept the same statement about some feature of an object, this feature is an inherent characteristic of that object.[1] So subjectivity and objectivity are not different, much less polar states of mind, traceable to distinct portions of the brain and separated in our experience; perceptions are complex wholes that cannot be divided neatly into categories. But communication is greatly facilitated if we use these concepts to estimate what statements will be more readily communicable (objective) and what statements—those dependent on individual experience and sensitivity—will be less readily communicable (subjective).

---

[1] For a statement to be "objective" it must be acceptable in the cultural context in which it is made, though it need not be true. "The sun moves about the earth" was an objective statement before 1550 but not after. It would still be objective to an aborigine, who proceeds on different premises and more restricted information.

Criticism, then, like other forms of communication, could be thought of as an attempt to objectify subjective responses. In criticism we try to induce others to perceive works of art as we do, and the problem is simplified by our prediction that one sort of statement, which can be made in conventional terms, will be taken as relatively "objective" ("This building is thirty feet high and is made of brick"), while another demands more refined gifts of exposition and an audience capable of responding to them ("This is one of the most powerful of Rembrandt's portraits"). Statements about responses that cannot be communicated or shared by others ("This picture reminds me of my mother," or the esoteric metaphors of much contemporary critical journalism) are more relevant to autobiography or literature than to criticism; they convey information about the critic, not the work of art.

Let us think of critical practice in terms of a spectrum extending from the most readily communicable statements to those that are the most individualized and difficult to transmit. At one end of the spectrum we represent the work of art as an object to be examined in terms of its physical properties, materials and the techniques used to make it; at the other we represent the work as a unique experience that demands the greatest powers of understanding and communication. Somewhere between these two we may place statements referring to the formal and symbolic structure (e.g., composition and subject matter) of the work — its conventional character — which we examine by analyzing conventions shared by groups of artists or characteristic of the work of single artists. Statements about physical character generally are called empirical; those about conventional character analytic, and those about the total import of the work of art intuitive or valuative. Such distinctions, however, are justifiable only as a means of classifying types of discourse; they do not define separate areas of experience. In our perception of works of art the response to size, materials, color, composition, meaning, mood and quality comes as a complex whole, not as the accumulation of distinct percepts. Indeed, any single aspect of a work of art tends to function in isolation quite differently from the way it functions in the total context. Therefore, while it is convenient to develop differentiated means of speaking of particular aspects of a work of art, the work can be represented ultimately only as a totality that corresponds to our total experience of it. It can be understood only partially by scholarship that represents it simply in terms of its more communicable aspect or by criticism that represents simply its more affective and individualized aspects.

For purposes of identification and classification we represent works of art in terms of physical properties such as size, shape, and materials. Statements about such characteristics are the most easily communicable because they can be referred to readings from conventional instruments that everyone agrees to accept as standards of measurement. Some of these — such as the record of dimensions — may come as near to perfect communicability as human beings can get, but they are few. In a catalog of drawings, for example, each entry starts with a statement of the dimensions of the sheet, the material of which it is composed, the tools and media used in making the drawing, and the incidence of identifying clues such as watermarks on paper or the identification stamps put on by earlier collectors. But, while the first of these data may come near to being free of individual variation, since they require no more than attentive readings from a calibrated scale, the others are increasingly open to interpretation. The limits of empirical description are indeterminate; the cataloger's desire to support an impression that the drawing is extremely precious, or perhaps that it is a copy, may prompt him to read an unclear clue in whatever way will suit his argument. There are no data so self-evident that they cannot be influenced by an unconscious invasion of will.

The classification of objects according to their physical properties usually is not regarded as an aspect of criticism, but it is not really a separable function. The very properties defined in this way may excite a response that is quite inaccessible to empirical measurement. Though we are unlikely to be moved by reading the dimensions of a drawing in a catalog, they symbolize proportions that can affect our response to the work when we actually see it; physical properties may be a substantial factor in our appreciation of objects made of precious stones and metals, or in techniques such as mosaic, enamel, the glazing of oil pigments, or stained glass; even common materials may awaken affective associations in a particular culture—most of us are attracted by thatched roofs and cobblestones. Whether the pleasure we get from these natural or manufactured charms can be attributed to the enjoyment of art rather than the influence of personal taste depends on whether the artist does anything to promote it. In any case it is like most physical pleasures, accessible to nearly everyone without the exercise of much effort.

Physical properties are relevant to criticism in another way. The critic's knowledge of the physical potentialities of the materials employed in any work of art must be sufficient to acquaint him with the problems they pose to the artist (e.g., the strength of marble in tension and compression is relevant to a discussion of the design of Greek temples). Furthermore, the physical condition of works of art—their present state in relation to their original state—is always relevant to interpretation. Sometimes condition can be determined by the naked eye; but laboratory techniques and historical documents often are a necessary preamble to responsible criticism. A typical example is the detection of the later repainting of old pictures by X-ray and cleaning or by reference to the history of pigment media, to contemporary reproductions and literary descriptions.

A technique usually is harder to classify and define than the materials it employs; when we examine a mural we may be sure that it is done with earth pigments in a binding medium on plaster, but not always sure that the technique is fresco (painted on wet plaster) rather than secco (painted on dry plaster); the ink and paper of a print are easily classified, but we may mistake an etching for a drypoint. Techniques, though they may remain more or less the same for millennia and in diverse cultures (e.g., the throwing of ceramic pottery on wheels), are the inventions of man and are subject to change at will, as materials are not. We can therefore speak of the history of a technique. Although techniques are more variable than materials, they are less variable than the formal or symbolic conventions of style, and for this reason are more difficult to objectify than the former and less than the latter. Domes built on pendentives, engraved gems, or cast bronze statues are found in many cultures and in arts of diverse styles; techniques are more stable than forms and symbols because they are involved in the entire technology of a society, and are less subject to variation by individual choice. Radical shifts of style often take place without changes in technique (e.g., in fresco painting) but rarely do radical shifts of technique fail to accompany changes in style. New tools suggest new forms, as is obvious in the art of recent times from steel frame skyscrapers to paintings executed with plastic paint dripped from cans. Conversely, the artist's vision of a new form stimulates the development of a new technique, as in Romanesque times, when the desire to vault churches stimulated the revival of skilled masonry work. In general, the artist is more likely to anticipate the technology in less industrialized societies; but in all art there is a close link between technical means and artistic end.

Later in this chapter I suggest that there are certain conventions of formal organization and symbolization characteristic of the style of a time and place, and comparable individualized conventions characteristic of the style of individual artists. The same may be said of technique. When we speak of "a" technique, we mean the accepted modus operandi with certain tools and materials (it also may be necessary to define the stage in the development of this technique). When we speak of "Rembrandt's technique," we mean the particular artistic personality which that individual reveals in manipulating the standard tools. In this sense, a technique, such as etching, is never the same in different hands; Rembrandt's etching technique differs significantly from that of his contemporary Seghers. Critical representation of the individualized aspect of technique draws us far from empirical discourse. To discuss it at all, we need a substantial knowledge of the range of potentialities offered by that technique, as well as a sensitivity to the nuances of style in the artist. Statements about technique in this sense demand much more of the critic and of his audience than those I have discussed so far.

Techniques, like materials, may be pleasing or displeasing in themselves; some people prefer engravings to paintings, some like the way sculptors leave the imprint of their touch on clay, or the way architects expose the bracing in half-timber buildings. The expression of such preferences seldom constitutes responsible criticism because they are imposed upon and not stimulated by particular works of art. But when the artist handles his techniques in such a way that our attention is drawn to them and we are forced into an unfamiliar response (early twentieth century collage was a shocking revision of the relation of technique to form and content), then our reaction is relevant to the particular work and therefore to criticism.

Communication of the symbolic and formal structure of works of art already is a more complex task than the exposition of physical character and technique. Ordinarily we can identify the subject matter of a figurative work of art with so little conscious effort that the process seems to be as self-evident as the measurement of size and shape. We are unaware of the substantial contribution we must make out of our own experience before we can call a configuration of red, ochre, white, and black oil pigments on canvas surface the head of a woman, or when we say that behind this head is an expanse of distant hills. We just forget to say or to think that the artist has arranged his materials in accordance with certain conventions that — providing we also are familiar with them — make it possible for us to realize the illusion of a woman's head and of a three-dimensional spatial extension related to that "head." Only when the formal conventions used or invented by the artist are *unfamiliar* to the observer (that is, when the observer is not trained to contribute to an illusion) is he likely to see a picture in terms of the configuration of pigments on a surface. Under these circumstances, he becomes aware of the differential between the physical and the communicative character of the work. Today, through museums, photography, and the press, sophisticated observers have been trained in so many conventions that they rarely lack the key to an unfamiliar work. But not long ago there were many earnest amateurs who could not perceive the head or the bottles in Cubist portraits and still lifes. In time the grammar of Picasso and Braque became so familiar that the same observers could "read" the pictures even if they did not comprehend what they had read. I speak of grammar and of reading because I think of the conventional aspect of style as a means of communication, a kind of language, within which symbolic and formal conventions are organized into coherent constructs similar to a grammar. To be able to apprehend the import of a work of art, whether it be a painting or a poem, we must first learn its language.

But knowing how to "read" the language is only a first step; it is not equivalent to understanding what is said in that language. As we pass from the measurement of physical characteristics to the decipherment of the language — from empirical to analytical exposition — we arrive at a stage that requires more learning and experience but not necessarily more critical skill or sensitivity. We may call this the province of linguistic analysis, and go on to examine two aspects of it: the interpretation of symbolic and of formal conventions.

Symbols cannot be divorced from their form either in creating or in experiencing a work of art, and the separation of "form" from "content" has caused confusion in criticism. But so long as we are speaking of conventions the distinction not only is permissible but necessary for description, because the life of symbols and the life of forms has not been everywhere coexistent in history. Some symbols (such as those for the Holy Ghost or the Virtues and Vices) pass through varied forms, while formal conventions (such as those of late antique sculpture or Gothic manuscript illumination, which were used for pagan and Christian themes alike) are applied to symbols of different, even conflicting significance.

Formal conventions are those that govern the use of the sense stimuli available within a medium and a technique (color, shape, texture, line, light-and-dark relationships) and the disposition of those stimuli according to a certain structure or relationship (composition, scale, interval, proportion). Techniques and materials impose their own limitations that become channeled into conventions (most notably in architecture, which is dependent on a technology not wholly controlled by the architect). The over-all range of color, stroke, or of compositional scheme in painting becomes fixed in conventions; a complex of such conventions constitutes the formal component of style. The great artist is often a maker — and the lesser artist a taker — of conventions, but even he most often works with reference to an established practice. And, while his innovations may effect one aspect of it — perhaps even its over-all shape — they do not sweep away the edifice. Much of today's abstract art, for example — despite its apparent antihistoricism — is done with pigments on rectangular canvases of a Renaissance scale and proportion, or is cast in traditional bronze or plaster according to ancient techniques; and even the artists who seem to be the most licentious work consistently, even rigorously, within self-imposed criteria.

The fact that a picture induces in us the illusion of a woman in a landscape we owe to our ability to grasp certain conventions: in an Egyptian fresco, we might distinguish a woman from a man by skin color; in a Greek-vase, a single tree alongside the woman might imply a landscape; even the linear and aerial perspective that suggests depth in a Renaissance landscape is a convention that we must learn to interpret.

Symbolic conventions are effective when the artist and the observer share the association of a particular concept with a particular form. They may be established for any aspect of human experience that is susceptible to visual symbolization. Obviously this means that they are competent to convey far more complex meanings than "woman" and "landscape." In most art of past ages the identity of the woman would have been an essential feature of the symbolism. If she represented the Virgin Mary, a particular patrician lady, or a character from a poem, the observer's understanding of the picture's import would depend in part upon his knowledge of the religious significance of the Virgin, or the social and historical milieu of the sitter, or the narrative in the poem. Symbolic conventions, that is, can be imposed upon or sought out by the artist from the symbolic activities of civilized man other than those of the spatial arts.

As the artist combines components of formal conventions such as color and texture into a composition, so he combines isolated symbols (a virgin, halo, throne, angels, a child) into a structure of meaning. (For example, in a "santa conversazione" the Virgin and Child are shown enthroned and flanked by a small company of saints and angels.) If the artist is to convey a narrative he may need conventions not only for relating the dramatis personae one to another and to a specific setting but for suggesting temporal as well as spatial relationships (the action represented on the left may "precede" the one represented on the right; a figure may be "moving" from left to right); or even temporal-spatial ones as in the "simultaneous" representation of different views of one object in Cubism.

Reference to Cubism calls to mind the fact that symbolic conventions, far from being restricted to illusionistic representations like the lady in the landscape, are even more apparent in so-called abstract art. *Abstract* is an imprecise term; *all* symbolic conventions are abstract; we use the word simply to define art in which the conventions are not designed to produce an illusion of the common-sense world. In Cubism or in Byzantine art the conventions are rooted in objects of everyday experience, and in much of contemporary art they are not. But we cannot say that nonobjective art is without symbolic conventions, because that would mean that its language conveyed no meaning, that it was mere gibberish. The symbols of nonobjective art also refer to everyday experience; not to the experience of physical matter but of space, tension, lightness and darkness, rhythm, gesture and other incorporeal percepts. Since these experiences are not identified with fixed forms in the world of nature, the conventions for symbolizing them must be learned entirely from the art itself. That there are such conventions and that they are part of a structure as clear as in any art of the past is indicated by the fact that the styles of contemporary art are as distinct and as recognizable as those of the past. The symbolism of these artists, like that of many contemporary poets and novelists, is often personal; but when it is effective it is because the artist provides in his work the clues to its decipherment; his language then becomes a public language. Rarely in the arts today does a familiarity with the symbolic conventions from religion, poetry, or history contribute, as it has in the past, to our comprehension. We may bring our knowledge of Christianity to bear upon the "reading" of a crucifixion, but the conventions of abstract art are made only by artists.

Just as materials and techniques may be enjoyed for their own sake, so may conventions. We can like Japanese prints or idyllic landscapes generically, be fascinated with the story of the prodigal son, or prefer nonobjective art. I suppose a majority of the pictures on the walls of American homes were bought because the owners like or are accustomed to their formal or symbolic conventions, or because a certain prestige accrues to the art that exemplifies whatever conventions the social milieu may prize. In other words, those pleasures that derive from conventions define taste or fashion and, since they are excited by works of art irrespective of their individual quality, tend to be volatile.

As the linguist studies basic elements (phonemes, words) and their combination in complex structures (syntax, grammar), the critic studies colors, symbols, or architectural orders, and their combination into compositions, stories, or buildings. The method is analytic; it demands more experience and learning than the description of physical character, but less than the synthetic or evaluative criticism required for the exposition of the individualized aspects of works of art.

One function of criticism, however, lies in a range between the analytic and the synthetic; the study of the style of individual artists. Artists develop distinctive conventions or traits that can be detected in anything they do, even through radical shifts of technique and structure. The individual conventions make it possible for us to recognize the author of a work of art because they evoke an image of other works we have seen by the same person; in much the same way we recognize the handwriting or the footstep of an acquaintance. These conventions are distinctive enough to aid us in attributing anonymous works to artists whose style is familiar, and even in selecting from a body of anonymous works those that were done by the same unknown hand. Judgments of this kind are the foundation for further art historical and critical activity, particularly in the study of styles such as those of the past four hundred years, in which individuality is prized. By analytic method, we may categorize all the traits of an artist that appear significant to us, and apply the categories to questionable works.

But, while the analysis of individual traits is easily objectified and apparently "scientific," it is not of itself reliable; if it were, copies and forgeries would never pass for originals (indeed, copyists and forgers often assemble in one work more of a master's characteristic conventions than we can find in any authentic product). This is because the sense of individual style also is based on the peculiar over-all tone or quality that can be found in anything a particular artist does; the relative role of quantitative evidence and intuitive "feel," by which we apprehend the quality of the whole, are as indeterminate in our judgment of artistic individuality as in our judgment of the people we meet.

An individual style is like a personality; in defining it we do not necessarily make judgments of value; bad habits are as revealing as good ones; great artists have off-days, and supposedly inferior ones can perform brilliantly. If judgments of this kind are to be trustworthy, they must be based upon a body of knowledge and experience first, of the individual artistic personality and second of the degree to which that personality may be differentiated from others like it. But knowledge and experience may be of no avail; in the study of art as in life there are good and poor, honest and dishonest judges of character, and the latter may be even more learned and experienced than the former. The judgment of personality is a factor of the judge's personality, and it cannot be made empirical. What makes it possible to proceed further on the basis of attributions reached in such an "unscientific" way is the fact that the wrong conclusion can be rejected rather easily even when we are not equipped to improve upon it, and the right one may be confirmed slowly by virtue of having survived a succession of challenges. It is like hiring a man on the recommendation of a personnel expert; if he is poorly equipped for the job we soon discover it, though we may be unable to recommend a better candidate; but if he is fully qualified, the proof emerges only gradually as he is confronted by a variety of new problems.

I have suggested that the idiosyncratic traits of an artist are not necessarily marks of quality; they serve to individualize good and bad art alike, and may be found in fashion drawings as well as in masterpieces. Yet individual habits may be a factor in our enjoyment of a work of art; we may like those of a given artist as we like, say, a certain violinist or conductor, more or less independently of the works in which we see or hear them displayed. Western criticism has put a high premium on individuality, with the result that idiosyncracies may be not simply accepted but actually sought. The premium placed on the casual and revealing gesture in recent abstract art has been pursued on such a scale that a would-be mark of individuality paradoxically has become a convention. In products of cultures more tightly organized than ours, the individual trait is absorbed into the group trait, but the difference is not significant for criticism. Chinese bronzes and Egyptian statues reveal a definable personality, but it is more collective than individual.

In sum, while the traits of artistic personality, like conventions, may be represented analytically, we cannot construct an image of the way they are integrated in an artist's work—as the historian must in solving problems of authorship—without a sense of the total personality, the spirit as well as the "hand." This brings us further into the range of intuitive criticism.

As we proceed from studying the physical character of the work of art to the traits of personality revealed by the artist, we pass from aspects that are the least individualized to those that are the most. Objects of comparable size and material are found in many cultures; certain symbols or modes of composition are found in many works but within only one culture; while a particular handling of line and color may be found in the art of only one person. The final stage in the critical process is the exposition of the uniqueness of the single work of art. This uniqueness already is implied in a negative sense in empirical and analytic observations, which equip us to say that a certain material, technique, or symbol is *not* found in other works by the same artist or in the same culture. But if we want to represent it in positive sense, we no longer can objectify our statements by proving them against conventional standards of measurement or by comparing two or more works of art. So the process of articulating the uniqueness of the individual work generally is called subjective or intuitive. I call it synthetic, since it no longer defines a trait or component of the work, but its total import for the observer.

As a student I was warned that statements that cannot be readily objectified or proved by techniques of comparison are "unsound." Perhaps good advice for students, but maturer scholars might measure it against a proposition of information theory, that the most easily communicable message conveys less information than the more complex and individualized one. So we value most highly the work of art or of criticism that stimulates responses in us that expand our realm of experience beyond its customary limits. We therefore think of the superior work of art as one that "rises above" its material, technical, and conventional exigencies, and of the superior critic as one who is able to crown his empirical and analytic exposition with revealing syntheses. The difficulty of such synthetic criticism is that it must employ conventional language — as the artist employs his conventional tools — to surpass the limits of convention. Words in their normal functions carry us only to the border of artistic creativity; to penetrate beyond is itself a creative act.

Ordinarily criticism is content to describe effects but not causes of the experience of works of art. For example, Chartres Cathedral is "uplifting," a Rembrandt portrait has a "profound humanity." But what is being described is largely the reaction to conventions. *All* Gothic cathedrals could be called uplifting, and *all* competent Baroque portraits of sad old men, humane. The issue for the critic is why and how Chartres and the Rembrandt portrait are more so. No inventory of separate elements will answer that question, for anything that can be detached from its context can become a convention that a follower could emulate. It is a question of the import of the whole. The work of art is a product of the artistic personality at a given moment; to judge it in terms of its parts would be equivalent to judging a person's expression of feeling by his gesture or his facial configuration or his words or their tone but not by the entire effect. At this point we may abandon the simile of artistic and human personality, for they communicate in different ways. It is not necessary to be a good man in order to make a good statue, or to be a Christian in order to design Chartres; Rembrandt was not known to be a good judge of character. Great art is the transfiguration of commonplace experience by a vision that belongs to art and not by love, faith, philosophy, or other virtues or accomplishments of personality in the usual sense.

To convey the uniqueness of a work of art the critic requires first a sensitivity to and understanding of the work and second the creative capacity to turn his visual experience into verbal discourse. What he describes is the experience of his encounter with the work; but if his description contains too much of his own contribution to the encounter, what he says will be meaningful only to him and will not enlighten his readers. Conversely, if he submerges himself with the intention of "letting the work speak for itself" his intervention becomes superfluous; the work might as well speak directly to the reader. The first of these flaws was attributed to the typical critic at the start of this chapter, and the second to the typical historian.

The historian who wants to avoid the problem of synthesis restricts his attention to physical description and to the analysis of conventions. In recent times, the study of conventions has been fragmented into specialties: formal analysis, iconography (the study of symbolic conventions) and connoisseurship (the study of individual traits). This restriction is adequate for tracing the history and evolution of style, because it operates with the extrinsic characteristics of works of art. But it implies a renunciation of the attempt to discover and reveal in a single work of art anything but the traits it shares with other works or with other aspects of the culture that produced it, so that its individuality can be defined only on negative grounds, and its significance can be measured only mechanically in terms of its influence in establishing new conventions.

By comparing the single work to others in the same milieu, we can make a quantitative account of the extent to which it is distinguishable from others that observe like conventions. But a qualitative account is important for historical as well as critical activity—not the number of unique traits, or the degree of uniqueness of any one, but the impact of the whole that can be experienced but that cannot be tabulated. This force is the only basis for distinguishing mere innovations or idiosyncrasy from substantial artistic achievement.

I cannot define the nature of this experience in the abstract because it is the outcome of an encounter of a particular observer and a particular work of art in which both contribute to an aesthetic event. If the observer's understanding of the work is a function of his knowledge, his habits of perception and sensitivity, then there is no meaning in questions such as "What is the aesthetic experience?" Maybe this is why the literature of aesthetics over the centuries has failed to agree upon even the most fundamental rules for answering questions of this kind.

Still, without defining what art is, we realize that we get from it something different than from other forms of communication. We do learn how men of greater genius and sensitivity than ourselves visualize reality, but we gain something beyond information and intellectual enrichment, which we speak of as emotional or spiritual. In this, our relationship to art resembles our relationship to people, in that it may be intimate, shocking, or passionate; but more than most human relationships, it also generates reactions rooted in our physical form and functions. Our responses to symmetry, rhythm, scale, for example, are keyed to the structure of the body and the beat of the heart. So, unlike any other products of the imagination (e.g., in philosophy, science, law) art is a medium for the communication of human feeling. Because there is a consistency to human feelings and physical structure throughout all time and irrespective of cultural differences, this peculiar province of art is by no means inaccessible to critical communication.

If, as I have suggested, the entire range of criticism involves the objectification of subjective responses, then the attempt to articulate judgments of quality or value cannot be evaded as especially ephemeral or unreliable. These judgments are integral factors in our responses; we may form them more distinctly than other responses. They are not, then, in a distinct realm of experience. Indeed, value distinctions cannot be avoided even by the most "scientific" historians. The decision that one theme is more promising than another in initiating new research, the selection of one work rather than another to illustrate the achievement of an age or of an artist, are based on such distinctions.

This is not to say that every judgment is equally valid. We call some responsible, by which we mean that the critic clearly articulates the grounds on which they are made and demonstrates persuasively how his conclusions may be justified within his terms. Others, which we call irresponsible, are merely the assertion of private responses reflecting mere bias or the unconscious inheritance of the principles of someone else. So the danger of misleading evaluation is paradoxically the greatest in those who believe they are not judging at all.

Suspicion among scholars of the problems of evaluation comes from a justified mistrust of shifting standards of taste. But the issue of taste need not enter. Our taste is a response to materials, techniques, or conventions exclusive of their embodiment in works of art. Since it is not stimulated by specific works, it resides entirely within us, and whether it makes a specific work more or less pleasing to us, it may not help us to see it or, if we are engaged in criticism, to suggest its unique nature. What matters in communicating our judgments is not whether we like or dislike a work of art but whether we do or do not find in it a synthesis that surpasses convention.

While historians and critics alike benefit from considering the entire range of the spectrum of criticism, there are aspects of each vocation that justify the distinction we make between them. History is more concerned with the reconstruction of the context in which works of art are produced; criticism more with the articulation of responses to works of art in relation to current modes of thought. But the difference is one of degree rather than of kind; criticism takes the lead in the study of contemporary art because the special tools of history are difficult to use profitably amid the profusion of data. Where data are sparse, as in the study of extinct civilizations, effective criticism is impossible without substantial historical preparation (e.g., the evaluation of a primitive or prehistoric work without knowledge of the function it served, the meaning of its symbolic conventions, or the distinction between the conventions of the group and those of the individual artist). So, where historical data are profuse, criticism takes the initiative, aiding the historian to distinguish relevant from irrelevant data (critical judgments have prompted historians to document extensively the art of Picasso and Le Corbusier, while thousands of "lesser" contemporaries, even successful ones, go unrecorded); where they are sparse, archaeology and history take the initiative, uncovering sufficient information on the context of works of art to support responsible criticism. In practice, the contrast is more extreme: between journalistic criticism as the arbiter of taste and the empirical research of archivists, editors of sources, catalogers, etc. But the extremes are not equivalent; the former is an ephemeral luxury, while the latter is the essential foundation of the historical disciplines.

Somewhere between, criticism and history merge in a superior alloy; its composition cannot be quite constant, for every critic-scholar must mix it according to his own recipe. Some will lean more toward conveying the individuality of works of art, others more toward the problems of culture or style. The former may select the art that they are able to experience most fully, while the latter may penetrate unexplored reaches to discover even in strange and uncongenial art fresh facets of the human imagination. But, however composed, the alloy is stronger than its component metals.

IV

THE PROBLEM OF DEFINING, EXPLAINING,

AND EVALUATING NEW MEDIA:

FILM

Introduction

This section is intended as an area of specific application for the book's major concerns. However, it is also a plea for recognition of film as a significant art form. That the importance of film is being recognized is evidenced by a number of attempts both abroad and in this country to incorporate film study into the curriculum.[1] But as might be expected, problems are being encountered in definition, explanation, and evaluation.[2]

"Whether we like it or not," writes Erwin Panofsky, "it is the movies that mold, more than any other single force, the opinions, the taste, the language, the dress, the behavior, and even the physical appearance of a public comprising more than 60% of the population of the earth." Were the movies to be outlawed, says Panofsky, the social consequences would be catastrophic, whereas cessation of the work of traditional artists would be noticed only by a few. As the considered reflection of a distinguished scholar, such remarks have special significance.

In "Style and Medium in the Motion Pictures," Panofsky explains the unique qualities of the movies and in addition supplies a justification for the

---

[1]The recent impetus for screen education derives from England and the efforts of UNESCO. However, there is increasing activity in this country which already has resulted in a number of promising projects, including the founding of an American Film Institute and a National Screen Education Committee, an American counterpart to the British Society for Education in Film and Television. If it is wondered why discussions of television are not included in this section, it is because the conditions for producing and viewing television do not differ *radically* from those of film though, of course, some distinctions are in order. Further, television relies increasingly on film and video-tape, this latter permitting much the same approach to production that is found in moviemaking. Television, of course, does affect the *kind* of film that is made specially for it. Some problems that arise in explaining the nature of television may be found in Evalina Tarroni, "The Aesthetics of Television," in A. W. Hodgkinson (ed.), *Screen Education* (New York: UNESCO Publications Center [NAIP], 1964).

[2]For example, consider Sigfried Kracauer's thesis in *Theory of Film: The Redemption of Physical Reality* (New York: Oxford University Press, 1960), p. 300, that "The cinema can be defined as a medium particularly equipped to promote the redemption of physical reality. Its imagery permits us, for the first time, to take away with us the objects and occurrences that comprise the flow of material life." Then compare to Rudolf Arnheim's contention that "genuine realism consists in the interpretation of the raw material of experience by means of significant form and that, therefore, a concern with unshaped matter is a melancholy surrender rather than the recovery of man's grip on reality." In "Melancholy Unshaped," *The Journal of Aesthetics and Art Criticism,* Vol. XXI, No. 3 (Spring 1963), p. 297. Now what is the nature of cinema?

contention that film is a legitimate art form. According to Panofsky, the development of this contemporary art form represents the spectacle of a new medium becoming increasingly conscious of its possibilities and limitations. The potential of the film, it is claimed, was determined by its beginnings; contrary to precedent, moving pictures were not the product of an artistic urge, but the by-product of a technical invention. Due to their origin, moreover, in a sphere untouched by traditional art forms and the higher cultural values, early movies became a type of folk art, vehicles for the primordial categories of success or retribution, sentiment, sensation, pornography, and crude humor. After unsuccessful attempts to imitate respectable stage plays, movie makers discovered that the only promising future for the new medium lay in the further development of its folk art character and in the exploitation of its unique and specific capability for the *dynamization of space* and the *spatialization of time*. This potential for a novel space-time organization had two implications: one for the spectator and another for the relationship between sound and spoken word and the screen image.

The moviegoer, in contrast to the theater audience, occupies his seat only physically. As a subject of an aesthetic experience he is in perpetual motion as his eye identifies with the lens of the camera. This identification opened up unique possibilities for the experiencing of strong emotions, augmented by the fact that psychological states could be projected directly on the screen. In the relationship between sound and action the film also differs from the stage play. Even silent movies were never mute, since they were accompanied by music and narration. The advent of the talkies marked a break chiefly in acting style. But even with the added soundtrack, the main emphasis remained visual, and the dialogue, or script, had to conform to the principle of coexpressibility. The script's merit does not depend on its quality as a piece of literature, but on its capacity to be integrated with the events on the screen. Good film scripts, unlike good theatrical plays, do not necessarily make interesting reading.[3] Just as the screen-play has no existence independent of its performance, so the characters have no existence outside the actors. A film is written for a specific producer, director, and cast. Those involved in its production, moreover, work in a fashion comparable to that of the plastic artist, that is, piecemeal, discontinuously, and according to the most efficient use of materials rather than according to the order evident in the finished product. Because a movie is brought into being by a cooperative effort in which each contribution has the same degree of permanence, it is the nearest modern equivalent to the medieval cathedral.

Finally, movies are commercial art, hence must obey the requirement of communicability, which makes them potentially more vital and effective — for

---

[3]The screen plays of Ingmar Bergman and Arthur Miller are exceptions. See Hollis Alpert, *The Dreams and the Dreamers* (New York: The Macmillan Co., 1962), p. 247.

better or for worse — than noncommercial art. Today, Panofsky states, only the film does justice to that materialistic interpretation of the universe which pervades our civilization, since its materials consist of physical objects and persons, not of a neutral medium. Materialistic and commercial though they may be, the movies do satisfy the canons of art. Their problem is to manipulate unstylized reality in such a way that the result has style, and this is a proposition no less legitimate and no less difficult than any proposition in the older arts.

The selection by the noted film critic James Agee, "What Hollywood Can Do," attempts the explanation of film from the vantage point of the busy writer for the weekly magazine. The most obvious categories of criticism in Agee's review stress story-line and the quality of the acting. The evaluation of the script once again illustrates the subservience of the dialogue to the visual image. Agee writes: ". . . the scenes are so planned, and the lines so laid down, that every action and reaction, every motion and everything that is seen, is more central, eloquent than the spoken lines." Agee's criticism also concentrates on the more purely visual qualities evident in set design and camera work. With respect to the latter, he speaks in terms of will, creative energy, taste, power, and expressiveness, words rich with aesthetic meaning.

It should be evident that the style of film criticism varies according to the conditions under which it is written. Hence the intellectual monthly or quarterly gives rise to a form of reflective criticism absent in the dailies and weeklies. A sample of this type of criticism is found in the next selection by Robert Warshow.

Two of the observations made by Panofsky, that the film is a vital art form and that it has its roots in folklore, are borne out by Warshow's "Movie Chronicle: The Westerner." The Westerner, unquestionably the most successful form of American movies, conforms to an easily recognizable pattern. The message and significance of the film are always embodied in a single individual, the Western hero; the conflict of good and evil takes on the form of a duel between two men; and merit is a matter of personal deportment in situations characteristic of Westerners. The hero is a lonely, reposeful figure, rarely visibly employed and never working hard to "get ahead." He is associated with the open land and horses, symbols of moral and physical freedom. In a Western movie, the function of realism can only be to incise the lines of the pattern more clearly. It is spoiled, claims Warshow, by attempts to introduce social drama and aestheticizing tendencies. What makes it possible for the pattern to retain its appeal through countless repetitions is the special character of the film medium where physical differences between objects and protagonists are of immense importance.

Why does the Westerner impinge so vividly on our imaginations? Because, says Warshow, it is perhaps the only art form that represents violence responsibly. One of the characteristics of contemporary civilized opinion is the denial of the value of violence. This has led not to a reduction of violent acts, but to the abandonment of control, leaving the celebration of violence to the irresponsible cultural underground of the gangster film, crime stories, and television. The Westerner, by contrast, links violence with responsibility in two ways. First of all, the hero "does what he has to do," he feels a moral obligation. Yet, no matter what his justification, we are not made to forget that he is a killer of men. And in a good Westerner the hero will gain tragic stature by his own awareness of his inevitable guilt and of the limits of his moral ideals. Frequently he no longer believes in the drama but continues to act out his role perfectly. Secondly, the moment of violence must come in its own time and according to its special laws, which include great self-restraint and a minimum of brutality, or else it is valueless. There is, throughout, a sense of decorum which reminds us of the possibility of a significant life-style in an age that is pretending style has no meaning.

The problem of presenting violence responsibly is perceptively discussed by Martin S. Dworkin in "*The Desperate Hours* and the Violent Screen." In an essay that can stand as a model for a certain kind of film criticism, Dworkin examines two versions of a recurring film melodrama, the theme of the invaded community, or of good held captive by evil. In assessing certain films expressing violence, it should be noted that Dworkin ascribes blame and praise not only on aesthetic but also on moral grounds. Mayhem in the movies is too overladen with social significance to permit the luxury of moral detachment. That is, the manner in which the relation of means and ends is handled in a film cannot be ignored, claims Dworkin, once it is admitted that the action on the screen does in fact influence our behavior after we leave the theater.

According to Dworkin, *The Desperate Hours* is a film superior to *Teen-Age Crime Wave* owing to the ways in which the former's imagery and symbology are contrived to establish empathic and imaginative identification on the part of the audience with the major protagonists, this implicative power being the unique capacity of film. Otherwise, the subject matter of the two films is the same. Compared to *Teen-Age Crime Wave*, the nature of the good and its statement in *The Desperate Hours* is neither obvious nor ineptly expressed. In the latter, the use of violence as a means is argued with far greater aesthetic and moral restraint, as if out of respect not only for the materials of the medium but also for the sensibilities of the members of the audience participating in the desperate measures of the film. The matter being stated with force and clarity, says Dworkin, we can appreciate the more what has been done to stimulate understanding of the real perplexity of the situation.

To repeat the question of an earlier essay: Does *The Desperate Hours* say anything important? According to Dworkin, yes; it says man is responsible for his acts and that violence is at best an evil means. Or more precisely, these are the inferences Dworkin makes, since works of art themselves are not assertions. In this connection it will be helpful to point out again the aesthetic-moral character of Dworkin's appraisal. It is not simply the sensory, formal, and technical aspects of the film that are judged but also its dramatic content. The pedagogical question is whether pupils should be encouraged to make such judgments or whether only formal, aesthetic judgments should be stressed. Many would argue, and I believe rightly so, that the moral dimensions of art criticism should not be neglected in art instruction. However, the development of the capacity to make aesthetic-moral judgments will demand a more rigorous intellectual diet of art education than is now required by the schools.

Moving from Hollywood to a consideration of European films, the problem of explication is compounded because of cultural variations and a greater emphasis on symbolic meaning. But why is it, asks Norman N. Holland, that opaqueness of meaning notwithstanding, enigmatic films such as *The Seventh Seal, La Dolce Vita,* and *Last Year at Marienbad* do in fact appeal to moviegoers? In "Three Puzzling Movies: And a Guess at Their Appeal," Holland attempts to answer this question. The puzzling movies, he claims, contain two sources of perplexity which are, at the same time, purveyors of enjoyment. In the first place, we are uncertain as to the overall meaning of these films; and secondly, we find it difficult, if not impossible, to detect a continuous scene-by-scene narrative. Because we feel that somehow the film must "mean" something, that sooner or later the pieces will fall into place, we are free to give ourselves to the immediate experience of the purely visual, or aesthetic, aspects. Because, on the narrative level, we are seeing cryptic outward actions but are not permitted to become aware of the underlying emotional motivations, we assume a role similar to that of the child who observes but does not understand adult behavior. But with a sophisticated adult audience childlike bafflement is translated into the sort of aesthetic and intellectual puzzle that adults enjoy and that they feel confident they can solve.

This anthology concludes with two brief articles by Martin S. Dworkin in which the problem of knowledge in the arts is once again a central consideration. In *The Family of Man* we have evidence, Dworkin states, of having learned to understand a new language — the language of film and photography. Almost completely without written text, this unique exhibition successfully communicated a philosophy of man. However sentimental that philosophy may be, countless persons around the world received, and continue to receive, the clarity of its message. Dworkin attributes this instance of successful communication to the perfection of the medium of photography and to the influence of cinematic techniques in the design of the exhibition, suggesting that the chief significance of the exhibition lies in the way it reveals the influence of film on photography.[4]

---

[4]*The Family of Man,* of course, can be viewed from different perspectives. Jacques Barzun, for example, interprets the content of the exhibition as a typical example of the betrayal of Intellect. "Whatever is formed and constituted (the work seems to say) whatever is adult, whatever exerts power, whatever is characteristically Western, whatever is unique or has a name, or embodies

Finally, the particular form of knowing characteristic of art is discussed in "The Vanishing Diary of Anne Frank." According to Dworkin, we are conditioned to certain ways of knowing, but some occurrences, such as the atrocities committed by the Nazis, fall outside all familiar frames of reference. They are labeled "inconceivable," "impossible," "fantastic," and they tend to be altered or overlooked. We have difficulty in gaining knowledge of such things. But, Dworkin maintains, we may receive considerable aid from the arts: "... an articulate vision, as in a work of art, can create the conditions of knowing, giving form to the inaccessibly, bewilderingly complex and various realities that must be grasped."

The conditions of knowing were present in the diary of Anne Frank. But this diary, Dworkin points out, is not a work created by the girl. It *is* the girl, a very complex, questioning, maturing adolescent. The various dramatizations of the diary, however, in an effort to bring Anne Frank closer to their audiences, betrayed the spirit of the diary by making the girl recognizable. The movie in particular cast her as the easily identifiable type of the adolescent, and this popularization of the work effected a qualitative change. The possibility of knowledge, in other words, was sacrificed to simple recognition. While the diary could bring the reader to a feeling of personal bereavement, the effect of the play and movie did not go beyond a general sadness and pity.

---

the complexity of thought, is of less interest and worth than what is native, common, and sensual; what is weak and confused; what is unhappy, anonymous, and elemental." In *The House of Intellect* (New York: Harper and Brothers, 1959), p. 29. Contrariwise, Dwight Macdonald thinks the show communicates the Midcult message "that although there are real Problems (death, for instance), it's a pretty good old world after all." In *Against the American Grain* (New York: Random House, 1962), p. 45. Actually at issue is the problem of formulating relevant standards for judging the products of a democratic mass society. For some comments in this regard, see Martin S. Dworkin, "Seeing for Ourselves: Notes on the Movie Art and Industry, Critics, and Audiences," *Arts in Society*, Vol. II, No. 4 (1964), pp. 138-44. In discussing the illusion of freedom in the creation and selection of mass produced media products, Dworkin writes that "The relation of freedom and responsibility is no less vital a matter for constant elucidation here than in any other realm of action. In the nature of this relationship, involving the technological, commercial, aesthetic, political, and moral dimensions of the movies will be found the foundations for valid standards of filmic quality — the only standards, in fact, which will enable us to control what we do to ourselves in the theaters." (p. 142)

Style and Medium in the
Motion Pictures

ERWIN PANOFSKY

Film art is the only art the development of which men now living have witnessed from the very beginnings; and this development is all the more interesting as it took place under conditions contrary to precedent. It was not an artistic urge that gave rise to the discovery and gradual perfection of a new technique; it was a technical invention that gave rise to the discovery and gradual perfection of a new art.

From this we understand two fundamental facts. First, that the primordial basis of the enjoyment of moving pictures was not an objective interest in a specific subject matter, much less an aesthetic interest in the formal presentation of subject matter, but the sheer delight in the fact that things seemed to move, no matter what things they were. Second, that films—first exhibited in "kinetoscopes," viz., cinematographic peep shows, but projectable to a screen since as early as 1894—are, originally, a product of genuine folk art (whereas, as a rule, folk art derives from what is known as "higher art"). At the very beginning of things we find the simple recording of movements: galloping horses, railroad trains, fire engines, sporting events, street scenes. And when it had come to the making of narrative films these were produced by photographers who were anything but "producers" or "directors," performed by people

From Erwin Panofsky, "Style and Medium in the Motion Pictures," *Critique,* Vol. I, No. 3; reprinted in Morris Weitz (ed.), *Problems in Aesthetics* (New York: The Macmillan Company, 1959), pp. 526-42. Reprinted by permission of the author.

who were anything but actors, and enjoyed by people who would have been much offended had anyone called them "art lovers."

The casts of these archaic films were usually collected in a "café" where unemployed supers or ordinary citizens possessed of a suitable exterior were wont to assemble at a given hour. An enterprising photographer would walk in, hire four or five convenient characters and make the picture while carefully instructing them what to do: "Now, you pretend to hit this lady over the head"; and (to the lady): "And you pretend to fall down in a heap." Productions like these were shown, together with those purely factual recordings of "movement for movement's sake," in a few small and dingy cinemas mostly frequented by the "lower classes" and a sprinkling of youngsters in quest of adventure (about 1905, I happen to remember, there was only one obscure and faintly disreputable *kino* in the whole city of Berlin, bearing, for some unfathomable reason, the English name of "The Meeting Room"). Small wonder that the "better classes," when they slowly began to venture into these early picture theaters, did so, not by way of seeking normal and possibly serious entertainment, but with that characteristic sensation of self-conscious condescension with which we may plunge, in gay company, into the folkloristic depths of Coney Island or a European kermis; even a few years ago it was the regulation attitude of the socially or intellectually prominent that one could confess to enjoying such austerely educational films as *The Sex Life of the Starfish* or films with "beautiful scenery," but never to a serious liking for narratives.

Today there is no denying that narrative films are not only "art" — not often good art, to be sure, but this applies to other media as well — but also, besides architecture, cartooning and "commercial design," the only visual art entirely alive. The "movies" have re-established that dynamic contact between art production and art consumption which, for reasons too complex to be considered here, is sorely attenuated, if not entirely interrupted, in many other fields of artistic endeavor. Whether we like it or not, it is the movies that mold, more than any other single force, the opinions, the taste, the language, the dress, the behavior, and even the physical appearance of a public comprising more than 60 per cent of the population of the earth. If all the serious lyrical poets, composers, painters and sculptors were forced by law to stop their activities, a rather small fraction of the general public would become aware of the fact and a still smaller fraction would seriously regret it. If the same thing were to happen with the movies the social consequences would be catastrophic.

In the beginning, then, there were the straight recordings of movement no matter what moved, viz., the prehistoric ancestors of our "documentaries"; and, soon after, the early narratives, viz., the prehistoric ancestors of our "feature films." The craving for a narrative element could be satisfied only by borrowing from older arts, and one should expect that the natural thing would have been to borrow from the theater, a theater play being apparently the *genus proximum* to a narrative film in that it consists of a narrative enacted by persons that move. But in reality the imitation of stage performances was a comparatively late and thoroughly frustrated development. What happened at the start was a very different thing. Instead of imitating a theatrical performance already endowed with a certain amount of motion, the earliest films added movement to works of art originally stationary, so that the dazzling technical invention might achieve a triumph of its own without intruding upon the sphere of higher culture. The living language, which is always right, has endorsed this sensible choice when it still speaks of a "moving picture" or, simply, a "picture," instead of accepting the pretentious and fundamentally erroneous "screen play."

The stationary works enlivened in the earliest movies were indeed pictures: bad nineteenth-century paintings and postcards (or waxworks à la Madame Tussaud's), supplemented by the comic strips—a most important root of cinematic art—and the subject matter of popular songs, pulp magazines and dime novels; and the films descending from this ancestry appealed directly and very intensely to a folk art mentality. They gratified—often simultaneously— first, a primitive sense of justice and decorum when virtue and industry were rewarded while vice and laziness were punished; second, plain sentimentality when "the thin trickle of a fictive love interest" took its course "through somewhat serpentine channels," or when Father, dear Father returned from the saloon to find his child dying of diphtheria; third, a primordial instinct for bloodshed and cruelty when Andreas Hofer faced the firing squad, or when (in a film of 1893-94) the head of Mary Queen of Scots actually came off; fourth, a taste for mild pornography (I remember with great pleasure a French film of *ca.* 1900 wherein a seemingly but not really well-rounded lady as well as a seemingly but not really slender one were shown changing to bathing suits—an honest, straightforward *porcheria* much less objectionable than the now extinct Betty Boop films and, I am sorry to say, some of the more recent Walt Disney productions); and, finally, that crude sense of humor, graphically described as "slapstick," which feeds upon the sadistic and the pornographic instinct, either singly or in combination.

Not until as late as *ca.* 1905 was a film adaptation of *Faust* ventured upon (cast still "unknown," characteristically enough), and not until 1911 did Sarah Bernhardt lend her prestige to an unbelievably funny film tragedy, *Queen Elizabeth of England*. These films represent the first conscious attempt at transplanting the movies from the folk art level to that of "real art"; but they also bear witness to the fact that this commendable goal could not be reached in so simple a manner. It was soon realized that the imitation of a theater performance with a set stage, fixed entries and exits, and distinctly literary ambitions is the one thing the film must avoid.

The legitimate paths of evolution were opened, not by running away from the folk art character of the primitive film but by developing it within the limits of its own possibilities. Those primordial archetypes of film productions on the folk art level — success or retribution, sentiment, sensation, pornography, and crude humor — could blossom forth into genuine history, tragedy and romance, crime and adventure, and comedy, as soon as it was realized that they could be transfigured — not by an artificial injection of literary values but by the exploitation of the unique and specific possibilities of the new medium. Significantly, the beginnings of this legitimate development antedate the attempts at endowing the film with higher values of a foreign order (the crucial period being the years from 1902 to *ca.* 1905), and the decisive steps were taken by people who were laymen or outsiders from the viewpoint of the serious stage.

These unique and specific possibilities can be defined as *dynamization of space* and, accordingly, *spatialization of time*. This statement is self-evident to the point of triviality but it belongs to that kind of truths which, just because of their triviality, are easily forgotten or neglected.

In a theater, space is static, that is, the space represented on the stage, as well as the spatial relation of the beholder to the spectacle, is unalterably fixed. The spectator cannot leave his seat, and the setting of the stage cannot change, during one act (except for such incidentals as rising moons or gathering clouds and such illegitimate reborrowings from the film as turning wings or gliding backdrops). But, in return for this restriction, the theater has the advantage that time, the medium of emotion and thought conveyable by speech, is free and independent of anything that may happen in visible space. Hamlet may deliver his famous monologue lying on a couch in the middle distance, doing nothing and only dimly discernible to the spectator and listener, and yet by his mere words enthrall him with a feeling of intensest emotional action.

With the movies the situation is reversed. Here, too, the spectator occupies a fixed seat, but only physically, not as the subject of an aesthetic experience. Aesthetically, he is in permanent motion as his eye identifies itself with the lens of the camera, which permanently shifts in distance and direction. And as movable as the spectator is, as movable is, for the same reason, the space presented to him. Not only bodies move in space, but space itself does, approaching, receding, turning, dissolving and recrystallizing as it appears through the controlled locomotion and focusing of the camera and through the cutting and editing of the various shots — not to mention such special effects as visions, transformations, disappearances, slow-motion and fast-motion shots, reversals and trick films. This opens up a world of possibilities of which the stage can never dream. Quite apart from such photographic tricks as the participation of disembodied spirits in the action of the *Topper* series, or the more effective wonders wrought by Roland Young in *The Man Who Could Work Miracles,* there is, on the purely factual level, an untold wealth of themes as inaccessible to the "legitimate" stage as a fog or a snowstorm is to the sculptor; all sorts of violent elemental phenomena and, conversely, events too microscopic to be visible under normal conditions (such as the life-saving injection with the serum flown in at the very last moment, or the fatal bite of the yellow-fever mosquito); full-scale battle scenes; all kinds of operations, not only in the surgical sense but also in the sense of any actual construction, destruction or experimentation, as in *Louis Pasteur* or *Madame Curie;* a really grand party, moving through many rooms of a mansion or a palace. Features like these, even the mere shifting of the scene from one place to another by means of a car perilously negotiating heavy traffic or a motorboat steered through a nocturnal harbor, will not only always retain their primitive cinematic appeal but also remain enormously effective as a means of stirring the emotions and creating suspense. In addition, the movies have the power, entirely denied to the theater, to convey psychological experiences by directly projecting their content to the screen, substituting, as it were, the eye of the beholder for the consciousness of the character (as when the imaginings and hallucinations of the drunkard in the otherwise overrated *Lost Weekend* appear as stark realities instead of being described by mere words). But any attempt to convey thought and feelings exclusively, or even primarily, by speech leaves us with a feeling of embarrassment, boredom, or both.

What I mean by thoughts and feelings "conveyed exclusively, or even primarily, by speech" is simply this: Contrary to naïve expectation, the invention of the sound track in 1928 has been unable to change the basic fact that a moving picture, even when it has learned to talk, remains a picture that moves and does not convert itself into a piece of writing that is enacted. Its substance remains a series of visual sequences held together by an uninterrupted flow of movement in space (except, of course, for such checks and pauses as have the same compositional value as a rest in music), and not a sustained study in human character and destiny transmitted by effective, let alone "beautiful," diction. I cannot remember a more misleading statement about the movies than Mr. Eric Russell Bentley's in *The Playwright as Thinker,* p. 289: "[The potentialities of the talking screen] differ from those of the silent screen in adding the dimension of dialogue—which potentially is poetry." I would suggest: "The potentialities of the talking screen differ from those of the silent screen in integrating visible movement with dialogue which, therefore, had better not be poetry."

All of us, if we are old enough to remember the period prior to 1928, recall the old-time pianist who, with his eyes glued on the screen, would accompany the events with music adapted to their mood and rhythm; and we also recall the weird and spectral feeling overtaking us when this pianist left his post for a few minutes and the film was allowed to run by itself, the darkness haunted by the monotonous rattle of the machinery. Even the silent film, then, was never mute. The visible spectacle always required, and received, an audible accompaniment which, from the very beginning, distinguished the film from simple pantomine and rather classed it—*mutatis mutandis*—with the ballet. The advent of the talkie meant not so much an "addition" as a transformation: the transformation of musical sound into articulate speech and, therefore, of quasi pantomine into an entirely new species of spectacle which differs from the ballet, and agrees with the stage play, in that its acoustic component consists of intelligible words, but differs from the stage play and agrees with the ballet in that this acoustic component is not detachable from the visual. In a film, that which we hear remains, for good or worse, inextricably fused with that which we see; the sound, articulate or not, cannot express any more than is expressed, at the same time, by visible movement; and in a good film it does not even attempt to do so. To put it briefly, the play — or, as it is very properly called, the "script" — of a moving picture is subject to what might be termed the *principle of coexpressibility*.

Empirical proof of this principle is furnished by the fact that, wherever the dialogical or monological element gains temporary prominence, there appears, with the inevitability of a natural law, the "close-up." What does the close-up achieve? In showing us, in magnification, either the face of the speaker or the face of the listeners or both in alternation, the camera transforms the human physiognomy into a huge field of action where — given the qualification of the performers — every subtle movement of the features, almost imperceptible from a natural distance, becomes an expressive event in visible space and thereby completely integrates itself with the expressive content of the spoken word; whereas, on the stage, the spoken word makes a stronger rather than a weaker impression if we are not permitted to count the hairs in Romeo's mustache.

This does not mean that the scenario is a negligible factor in the making of a moving picture. It only means that its artistic intention differs in kind from that of a stage play, and much more from that of a novel or a piece of poetry. As the success of a Gothic jamb figure depends not only upon its quality as a piece of sculpture but also, or even more so, upon its integrability with the architecture of the portal, so does the success of a movie script — not unlike that of an opera libretto — depend, not only upon its quality as a piece of literature but also, or even more so, upon its integrability with the events on the screen.

As a result — another empirical proof of the coexpressibility principle — good movie scripts are unlikely to make good reading and have seldom been published in book form; whereas, conversely, good stage plays have to be severely altered, cut, and, on the other hand, enriched by interpolations to make good movie scripts. In Shaw's *Pygmalion,* for instance, the actual process of Eliza's phonetic education and, still more important, her final triumph at the grand party, are wisely omitted; we see — or, rather, hear — some samples of her gradual linguistic improvement and finally encounter her, upon her return from the reception, victorious and splendidly arrayed but deeply hurt for want of recognition and sympathy. In the film adaptation, precisely these two scenes are not only supplied but also strongly emphasized; we witness the fascinating activities in the laboratory with its array of spinning

417

disks and mirrors, organ pipes and dancing flames, and we participate in the ambassadorial party, with many moments of impending catastrophe and a little counterintrigue thrown in for suspense. Unquestionably these two scenes, entirely absent from the play, and indeed unachievable upon the stage, were the highlights of the film; whereas the Shavian dialogue, however severely cut, turned out to fall a little flat in certain moments. And wherever, as in so many other films, a poetic emotion, a musical outburst, or a literary conceit (even, I am grieved to say, some of the wisecracks of Groucho Marx) entirely lose contact with visible movement, they strike the sensitive spectator as, literally, out of place. It is certainly terrible when a soft-boiled he-man, after the suicide of his mistress, casts a twelve-foot glance upon her photograph and says something less-than-coexpressible to the effect that he will never forget her. But when he recites, instead, a piece of poetry as sublimely more-than-coexpressible as Romeo's monologue at the bier of Juliet, it is still worse. Reinhardt's *Midsummer Night's Dream* is probably the most unfortunate major film ever produced; and Olivier's *Henry V* owes its comparative success, apart from the all but providential adaptability of this particular play, to so many *tours de force* that it will, God willing, remain an exception rather than set a pattern. It combines "judicious pruning" with the interpolation of pageantry, nonverbal comedy and melodrama; it uses a device perhaps best designated as "oblique close-up" (Mr. Olivier's beautiful face inwardly listening to but not pronouncing the great soliloquy); and, most notably, it shifts between three levels of archaeological reality: a reconstruction of Elizabethan London, a reconstruction of the events of 1415 as laid down in Shakespeare's play, and the reconstruction of a performance of this play on Shakespeare's own stage. All this is perfectly legitimate; but, even so, the highest praise of the film will always come from those who, like the critic of the *New Yorker,* are not quite in sympathy with either the movies *au naturel* or Shakespeare *au naturel.*

As the writings of Conan Doyle potentially contain all modern mystery stories (except for the tough specimens of the Dashiell Hammett school), so do the films produced between 1900 and 1910 pre-establish the subject matter and methods of the moving picture as we know it. This period produced the incunabula of the Western and the crime film (Edwin S. Porter's amazing *Great Train Robbery* of 1903) from which developed the modern gangster, adventure, and mystery pictures (the latter, if well done, is still one of the most honest and genuine forms of film entertainment, space being doubly charged with time as the beholder asks himself not only "What is going to happen?" but also "What has happened before?"). The same period saw the emergence of the fantastically imaginative film (Méliès) which was to lead to the expressionist and surrealist experiments (*The Cabinet of Dr. Caligari, Sang d'un Poète,* etc.), on the one hand, and to the more superficial and spectacular fairy tales à la Arabian Nights, on the other. Comedy, later to triumph in Charlie Chaplin, the still insufficiently appreciated Buster Keaton, the Marx Brothers and the pre-Hollywood creations of René Clair, reached a respectable level in Max Linder and others. In historical and melodramatic films the foundations were laid for movie iconography and movie symbolism, and in the early work of D. W. Griffith we find, not only remarkable attempts at psychological analysis (*Edgar Allan Poe*) and social criticism (*A Corner in Wheat*) but also such basic technical innovations as the long shot, the flashback and the close-up. And modest trick films and cartoons paved the way to Felix the Cat, Popeye the Sailor, and Felix's prodigious offspring, Mickey Mouse.

Within their self-imposed limitations the earlier Disney films, and certain sequences in the later ones,[1] represent, as it were, a chemically pure distillation of cinematic possibilities. They retain the most important folkloristic elements — sadism, pornography, the humor engendered by both, and moral justice — almost without dilution and often fuse these elements into a variation on the primitive and inexhaustible David-and-Goliath motif, the triumph of the seemingly weak over the seemingly strong; and their fantastic independence of the natural laws gives them the power to integrate space with time to such perfection that the spatial and temporal experiences of sight and hearing come to be almost interconvertible. A series of soap bubbles, successively punctured, emits a series of sounds exactly corresponding in pitch and volume to the size of the bubbles; the three uvulae of Willie the Whale — small, large and medium — vibrate in consonance with tenor, bass and baritone notes; and the very concept of stationary existence is completely abolished. No object in creation, whether it be a house, a piano, a tree or an alarm clock, lacks the

---

[1] I make this distinction because it was, in my opinion, a fall from grace when *Snow White* introduced the human figure and when *Fantasia* attempted to picturalize The World's Great Music. The very virtue of the animated cartoon is to animate, that is to say endow lifeless things with life, or living things with a different kind of life. It effects a metamorphosis, and such a metamorphosis is wonderfully present in Disney's animals, plants, thunderclouds and railroad trains. Whereas his dwarfs, glamourized princesses, hillbillies, baseball players, rouged centaurs and *amigos* from South America are not transformations but caricatures at best, and fakes or vulgarities at worst. Concerning music, however, it should be borne in mind that its cinematic use is no less predicated upon the principle of coexpressibility than is the cinematic use of the spoken word. There is music permitting or even requiring the accompaniment of visible action (such as dances, ballet music and any kind of operatic compositions) and music of which the opposite is true; and this is, again, not a question of quality (most of us rightly prefer a waltz by Johann Strauss to a symphony by Sibelius) but one of intention. In *Fantasia* the hippopotamus ballet was wonderful, and the Pastoral Symphony and "Ave Maria" sequences were deplorable, not because the cartooning in the first case was infinitely better than in the two others (*cf.* above), and certainly not because Beethoven and Schubert are too sacred for picturalization, but simply because Ponchielli's "Dance of the Hours" is coexpressible while the Pastoral Symphony and the "Ave Maria" are not. In cases like these even the best imaginable music and the best imaginable cartoon will impair rather than enhance each other's effectiveness.

Experimental proof of all this was furnished by Disney's recent *Make Mine Music* where The World's Great Music was fortunately restricted to Prokofieff. Even among the other sequences the most successful ones were those in which the human element was either absent or reduced to a minumum; Willie the Whale, the Ballad of Johnny Fedora and Alice Blue-Bonnet, and, above all, the truly magnificent Goodman Quartet.

faculties of organic, in fact anthropomorphic, movement, facial expression and phonetic articulation. Incidentally, even in normal, "realistic" films the inanimate object, provided that it is dynamizable, can play the role of a leading character as do the ancient railroad engines in Buster Keaton's *General* and *Niagara Falls*. How the earlier Russian films exploited the possibility of heroizing all sorts of machinery lives in everybody's memory; and it is perhaps more than an accident that the two films which will go down in history as the great comical and the great serious masterpiece of the silent period bear the names and immortalize the personalities of two big ships: Keaton's *Navigator* (1924) and Eisenstein's *Potemkin* (1925).

The evolution from the jerky beginnings to this grand climax offers the fascinating spectacle of a new artistic medium gradually becoming conscious of its legitimate, that is, exclusive, possibilities and limitations—a spectacle not unlike the development of the mosaic, which started out with transposing illusionistic genre pictures into a more durable material and culminated in the hieratic supernaturalism of Ravenna; or the development of line engraving, which started out as a cheap and handy substitute for book illumination and culminated in the purely "graphic" style of Dürer.

Just so the silent movies developed a definite style of their own, adapted to the specific conditions of the medium. A hitherto unknown language was forced upon a public not yet capable of reading it, and the more proficient the public became the more refinement could develop in the language. For a Saxon peasant of around 800 it was not easy to understand the meaning of a picture showing a man as he pours water over the head of another man, and even later many people found it difficult to grasp the significance of two ladies standing behind the throne of an emperor. For the public of around 1910 it was no less difficult to understand the meaning of the speechless action in a moving picture, and the producers employed means of clarification similar to those we find in medieval art. One of these were printed titles or letters, striking equivalents of the medieval *tituli* and scrolls (at a still earlier date there even used to be explainers who would say, *viva voce*, "Now he thinks his wife is dead but she isn't" or "I don't wish to offend the ladies in the audience but I doubt that any of them would have done that much for her child"). Another, less obtrusive method of explanation was the introduction of a fixed iconography which from the outset informed the spectator about the basic facts and characters, much as the two ladies behind the emperor, when carrying a sword and a cross respectively, were uniquely determined as Fortitude and Faith. There arose, identifiable by standardized appearance, behavior and attributes, the well-remembered types of the Vamp and the Straight Girl (perhaps the most convincing modern equivalents of the medieval personifications of the Vices and Virtues), the Family Man, and the Villain, the latter marked by a black mustache and walking stick. Nocturnal scenes were printed on blue or green film. A checkered tablecloth meant, once for all, a "poor but honest" milieu; a happy marriage, soon to be endangered by the shadows from the past, was symbolized by the young wife's pouring the breakfast coffee for her husband; the first kiss was invariably announced by the lady's gently playing with her partner's necktie and was invariably accompanied by her kicking out with her left foot. The conduct of the characters was predetermined accordingly. The poor but honest laborer who, after leaving his little house with the checkered tablecloth, came upon an abandoned baby could not but take it to his home and bring it up as best he could; the Family Man could not but yield, however temporarily, to the temptations of the Vamp. As a result these early melodramas had a highly gratifying and soothing quality in that events took shape, without the complications of individual psychology, according to a pure Aristotelian logic so badly missed in real life.

Devices like these became gradually less necessary as the public grew accustomed to interpret the action by itself and were virtually abolished by the invention of the talking film. But even now there survive — quite legitimately, I think — the remnants of a "fixed attitude and attribute" principle and, more basic, a primitive or folkloristic concept of plot construction. Even today we take it for granted that the diphtheria of a baby tends to occur when the parents are out and, having occurred, solves all their matrimonial problems. Even today we demand of a decent mystery film that the butler, though he may be anything from an agent of the British Secret Service to the real father of the daughter of the house, must not turn out to be the murderer. Even today we love to see Pasteur, Zola or Ehrlich win out against stupidity and wickedness, with their respective wives trusting and trusting all the time. Even today we much prefer a happy finale to a gloomy one and insist, at the very least, on the observance of the Aristotelian rule that the story have a beginning, a middle and an ending — a rule the abrogation of which has done so much to estrange the general public from the more elevated spheres of modern writing. Primitive symbolism, too, survives in such amusing details as the last sequence of *Casablanca* where the delightfully crooked and right-minded *Préfet de Police* casts an empty bottle of Vichy water into the wastepaper basket; and in such telling symbols of the supernatural as Sir Cedric Hardwicke's Death in the guise of a "gentleman in a dustcoat trying" (*On Borrowed Time*) or Claude Rain's Hermes Psychopompos in the striped trousers of an airline manager (*Here Comes Mister Jordan*).

The most conspicuous advances were made in directing, lighting, camera work, cutting and acting proper. But while in most of these fields the evolution proceeded continuously — though, of course, not without detours, breakdowns and archaic relapses — the development of acting suffered a sudden interruption by the invention of the talking film; so that the style of acting in the silents can already be evaluated in retrospect, as a lost art not unlike the painting

421

technique of Jan van Eyck or, to take up our previous simile, the burin technique of Dürer. It was soon realized that acting in a silent film neither meant a pantominic exaggeration of stage acting (as was generally and erroneously assumed by professional stage actors who more and more frequently condescended to perform in the movies), nor could dispense with stylization altogether; a man photographed while walking down a gangway in ordinary, everyday-life fashion looked like anything but a man walking down a gangway when the result appeared on the screen. If the picture was to look both natural and meaningful the acting had to be done in a manner equally different from the style of the stage and the reality of ordinary life; speech had to be made dispensable by establishing an organic relation between the acting and the technical procedure of cinephotography — much as in Dürer's prints color had been made dispensable by establishing an organic relation between the design and the technical procedure of line engraving.

This was precisely what the great actors of the silent period accomplished, and it is a significant fact that the best of them did not come from the stage, whose crystallized tradition prevented Duse's only film, *Cenere,* from being more than a priceless record of Duse. They came instead from the circus or the variety, as was the case of Chaplin, Keaton and Will Rogers; from nothing in particular, as was the case of Theda Bara, of her greater European parallel, the Danish actress Asta Nielsen, and of Garbo; or from everything under the sun, as was the case of Douglas Fairbanks. The style of these "old masters" was indeed comparable to the style of line engraving in that it was, and had to be, exaggerated in comparison with stage acting (just as the sharply incised and vigorously curved *tailles* of the burin are exaggerated in comparison with pencil strokes or brushwork), but richer, subtler and infinitely more precise. The advent of the talkies, reducing if not abolishing this difference between movie[2] and stage acting, thus confronted the actors and actresses of the silent screen with a serious problem. Buster Keaton yielded to temptation and fell. Chaplin first tried to stand his ground and to remain an exquisite archaist but finally gave in, with only moderate success (*The Great Dictator*). Only the glorious Harpo has thus far successfully refused to utter a single articulate sound; and only Greta Garbo succeeded, in a measure, in transforming her style in principle. But even in her case one cannot help feeling that her first talking picture, *Anna Christie,* where she could ensconce herself, most of the time, in mute or monosyllabic sullenness, was better than her later performances; and in the second, talking version of *Anna Karenina,* the weakest moment is certainly when she delivers a big Ibsenian speech to her husband, and the strongest when she silently moves along the platform of the railroad station while her despair takes shape in the consonance of her movement (and expression) with the movement of the nocturnal space around her, filled with

---

[2]Professor Panofsky asks that "movie" be inserted here (ed.).

the real noises of the trains and the imaginary sound of the "little men with the iron hammers" that drives her, relentlessly and almost without her realizing it, under the wheels.

Small wonder that there is sometimes felt a kind of nostalgia for the silent period and that devices have been worked out to combine the virtues of sound and speech with those of silent acting, such as the "oblique close-up" already mentioned in connection with *Henry V:* the dance behind glass doors in *Sous les Toits de Paris;* or, in the *Histoire d'un Tricheur,* Sacha Guitry's recital of the events of his youth while the events themselves are "silently" enacted on the screen. However, this nostalgic feeling is no argument against the talkies as such. Their evolution has shown that, in art, every gain entails a certain loss on the other side of the ledger; but that the gain remains a gain, provided that the basic nature of the medium is realized and respected. One can imagine that, when the cavemen of Altamira began to paint their buffaloes in natural colors instead of merely incising the contours, the more conservative cavemen foretold the end of paleolithic art. But paleolithic art went on, and so will the movies. New technical inventions always tend to dwarf the values already attained, especially in a medium that owes its very existence to technical experimentation. The earliest talkies were infinitely inferior to the then mature silents, and most of the present technicolor films are still inferior to the now mature talkies in black and white. But even if Aldous Huxley's nightmare should come true and the experiences of taste, smell and touch should be added to those of sight and hearing, even then we may say with the Apostle, as we have said when first confronted with the sound track and the technicolor film, "We are troubled on every side, yet not distressed; we are perplexed, but not in despair."

From the law of time-charged space and space-bound time, there follows the fact that the "*screen play*," in contrast to the theater play, *has no aesthetic existence independent of its performance, and that its characters have no aesthetic existence outside the actors.*

The playwright writes in the fond hope that his work will be an imperishable jewel in the treasure house of civilization and will be presented in hundreds of performances that are but transient variations on a "work" that is constant. The script-writer, on the other hand, writes for one producer, one director and one cast. Their work achieves the same degree of permanence as does his; and should the same or a similar scenario ever be filmed by a different director and a different cast there will result an altogether different "play."

Othello or Nora are definite, substantial figures created by the playwright. They can be played well or badly, and they can be "interpreted" in one way or another; but they most definitely exist, no matter who plays them or even whether they are played at all. The character in a film, however, lives and dies with the actor. It is not the entity "Othello" interpreted by Robeson or the entity "Nora" interpreted by Duse; it is the entity "Greta Garbo" incarnate in a figure called Anna Christie or the entity "Robert Montgomery" incarnate in a murderer who, for all we know or care to know, may forever remain anonymous but will never cease to haunt our memories. Even when the names of the characters happen to be Henry VIII or Anna Karenina, the king who ruled England from 1509 to 1547 and the woman created by Tolstoy, they do not exist outside the being of Garbo and Laughton. They are but empty and incorporeal outlines like the shadows in Homer's Hades, assuming the character of reality only when filled with the lifeblood of an actor. Conversely, if a movie role is badly played there remains literally nothing of it, no matter how interesting the character's psychology or how elaborate the words.

What applies to the actor applies, *mutatis mutandis,* to most of the other artists, or artisans, who contribute to the making of a film: the director, the sound man, the enormously important cameraman, even the make-up man. A stage production is rehearsed until everything is ready, and then it is repeatedly performed in three consecutive hours. At each performance everybody has to be on hand and does his work; and afterward he goes home and to bed. The work of the stage actor may thus be likened to that of a musician, and that of the stage director to that of a conductor. Like these, they have a certain repertoire which they have studied and present in a number of complete but transitory performances, be it Hamlet today and Ghosts tomorrow, or Life with Father *per saecula saeculorum.* The activities of the film actor and the film director, however, are comparable, respectively, to those of the plastic artist and the architect, rather than to those of the musician and the conductor. Stage work is continuous but transitory; film work is discontinuous but permanent. Individual sequences are done piecemeal and out of order according to the most efficient use of sets and personnel. Each bit is done over and over again until it stands; and when the whole has been cut and composed everyone is through with it forever. Needless to say that this very procedure cannot but emphasize the curious consubstantiality that exists between the person of the movie actor and his role. Coming into existence piece by piece, regardless of the natural sequence of events, the "character" can grow into a unified whole only if the actor manages to be, not merely to play, Henry VIII or Anna Karenina throughout the entire wearisome period of shooting. I have it on the best of authorities that Laughton was really difficult to live with in the particular six or eight weeks during which he was doing—or rather being—Captain Bligh.

It might be said that a film, called into being by a co-operative effort in which all contributions have the same degree of permanence, is the nearest modern equivalent of a medieval cathedral; the role of the producer corresponding, more or less, to that of the bishop or archbishop; that of the director to that of the architect-in-chief; that of the scenario writers to that of the scholastic advisers establishing the iconographical program; and that of the actors, cameramen, cutters, sound men, make-up men and the divers technicians to that of those whose work provided the physical entity of the finished product, from the sculptors, glass painters, bronze casters, carpenters and skilled masons down to the quarry men and woodsmen. And if you speak to any one of these collaborators he will tell you, with perfect *bona fides,* that his is really the most important job — which is quite true to the extent that it is indispensable.

This comparison may seem sacrilegious, not only because there are, proportionally, fewer good films than there are good cathedrals, but also because the movies are commercial. However, if commercial art be defined as all art not primarily produced in order to gratify the creative urge of its maker but primarily intended to meet the requirements of a patron or a buying public, it must be said that noncommercial art is the exception rather than the rule, and a fairly recent and not always felicitous exception at that. While it is true that commercial art is always in danger of ending up as a prostitute, it is equally true that noncommercial art is always in danger of ending up as an old maid. Noncommercial art has given us Seurat's *Grande Jatte* and Shakespeare's sonnets, but also much that is esoteric to the point of incommunicability. Conversely, commercial art has given us much that is vulgar or snobbish (two aspects of the same thing) to the point of loathsomeness, but also Dürer's prints and Shakespeare's plays. For, we must not forget that Dürer's prints were partly made on commission and partly intended to be sold in the open market; and that Shakespeare's plays — in contrast to the earlier masques and *intermezzi* which were produced at court by aristocratic amateurs and could afford to be so incomprehensible that even those who described them in printed monographs occasionally failed to grasp their intended significance — were meant to appeal, and did appeal, not only to the select few but also to everyone who was prepared to pay a shilling for admission.

It is this requirement of communicability that makes commercial art more vital than noncommercial, and therefore potentially much more effective for better or for worse. The commercial producer can both educate and pervert the general public, and can allow the general public — or rather his idea of the general public — both to educate and to pervert himself. As is demonstrated by a number of excellent films that proved to be great box office successes, the public does not refuse to accept good products if it gets them. That it does not get them very often is caused not so much by commercialism as such as by too little discernment and, paradoxical though it may seem, too much timidity in its application. Hollywood believes that it must produce "what the public wants" while the public would take whatever Hollywood produces. If Hollywood were to decide for itself what it wants it would get away with it — even if it should decide to "depart from evil and do good." For, to revert to whence we started, in modern life the movies are what most other forms of art have ceased to be, not an adornment but a necessity.

That this should be so is understandable, not only from a sociological but also from an art-historical point of view. The processes of all the earlier representational arts conform, in a higher or lesser degree, to an idealistic conception of the world. These arts operate from top to bottom, so to speak, and not from bottom to top; they start with an idea to be projected into shapeless matter and not with the objects that constitute the physical world. The painter works on a blank wall or canvas which he organizes into a likeness of things and persons according to his idea (however much this idea may have been nourished by reality); he does not work with the things and persons themselves even if he works "from the model." The same is true of the sculptor with his shapeless mass of clay or his untooled block of stone or wood; of the writer with his sheet of paper or his dictaphone; and even of the stage designer with his empty and sorely limited section of space. It is the movies, and only the movies, that do justice to that materialistic interpretation of the universe which, whether we like it or not, pervades contemporary civilization. Excepting the very special case of the animated cartoon, the movies organize material things and persons, not a neutral medium, into a composition that receives its style, and may even become fantastic or pretervoluntarily symbolic,[3] not so much by an interpretation in the artist's mind as by the actual manipulation of physical objects and recording machinery. The medium of the movies is physical reality as such: the physical reality of eighteenth-century Versailles — no matter whether it be the original or a Hollywood facsimile indistinguishable therefrom for all aesthetic intents and purposes — or of a suburban home in Westchester; the physical reality of the Rue de Lappe in Paris or of the Gobi Desert, of Paul Ehrlich's apartment in Frankfurt or of the streets of New York in the rain; the physical reality of engines and animals, of Edward G. Robinson and Jimmy Cagney. All these objects and persons must be organized into a work of art. They can be arranged in all sorts of ways ("arrangement" comprising, of course, such things as make-up, lighting and camera work); but there is no running away from them. From this point of view it becomes evident that an attempt at subjecting the world to artistic prestylization, as in the expressionist settings of *The Cabinet of Dr. Caligari* (1919), could be no more than an exciting experiment that could exert but little influence upon the general course of events. To prestylize reality prior to tackling it amounts to dodging the problem. The problem is to manipulate and shoot unstylized reality in such a way that the result has style. This is a proposition no less legitimate and no less difficult than any proposition in the older arts.

---

[3] I cannot help feeling that the final sequence of the new Marx Brothers film *Night in Casablanca* — where Harpo unaccountably usurps the pilot's seat of a big airplane, causes incalculable havoc by flicking one tiny little control after another, and waxes the more insane with joy the greater the disproportion between the smallness of his effort and the magnitude of the disaster — is a magnificent and terrfying symbol of man's behavior in the atomic age. No doubt the Marx Brothers would vigorously reject this interpretation; but so would Dürer have done had anyone told him that his "Apocalypse" foreshadowed the cataclysm of the Reformation.

What Hollywood Can Do

JAMES AGEE

December 7, 1946

What Hollywood Can Do

The Best Years of Our Lives, a misfired title seems to have started as a gleam in Samuel Goldwyn's eye when he saw in a mid-war issue of *Time* a picture and article about returning veterans. At a later stage it was a verse novel by MacKinlay Kantor called *Glory for Me* — not a very good title either. Robert E. Sherwood turned this into a screen play; the director William Wyler and the cameraman Gregg Toland and a few hundred others turned the screen play into a movie. The movie has plenty of faults, and the worst of them are painfully exasperating; yet this is one of the very few American studio-made movies in years that seem to me profoundly pleasing, moving, and encouraging.

The story is of a sort that could have been, and often remains, just slick-paper fiction at its most sincere, and that could also have become, and occasionally suggests, a great and simple, limpid kind of fiction which few writers of serious talent seem able to attempt or even to respect, at present. An ex-bombardier (Dana Andrews), an ex-infantry sergeant (Fredric March), and an ex-sailor (Harold Russell) meet for the first time as they return to their home city, part to undertake the various pleasures and problems of their return, and meet again at various subsequent times as their lives and relationships shake down into new shape.

The bombardier, a highly intelligent proletarian, can find nothing better in the way of a job than his old place in a drugstore. He finds, too, that he and the girl he married just before he went overseas no longer get along. The sergeant, who was once the kind of nervously well-married, vocationless, rather sensitive business man, too good for his job, who tries to sweep along his uneasiness in a momentum of alcohol, clowning, fairly sophisticated wit, and his real but seldom focused affections, finds that none of that has changed for the better. He is made vice-president of his bank, in charge of G.I. loans, and spends a good deal of his time drunk. The sailor, who has lost both hands and has learned to use a pair of hooks quite well, returns to the gentlest and most touching depths of the lower middle class. His chief problem is the girl he had always expected to marry; another is his extreme uneasiness about everybody's attempt to be good about his hooks; a hideous complication is that he is at once intuitively very perceptive and sensitive, and hopelessly inarticulate, and that most of the people he returns to are equally well-meaning and unsophisticated.

At its worst this story is very annoying in its patness, its timidity, its slithering attempts to pretend to face and by that pretense to dodge in the most shameful way possible its own fullest meanings and possibilities. Perhaps one shouldn't kick too hard at a "mere" device, but I feel very dubious about the invention of a nice bar in which the veterans keep meeting each other, perhaps because I suspect that one of the dodged truths is that, once they become civilians again, most men of such disparate classes or worlds would meet seldom, with greater embarrassment than friendliness, and that the picture is here presenting, instead of the unhappy likelihood, a hopeful and barely plausible lie. I feel a good deal of interest in the love affair that develops between Andrews and the banker's daughter, played by Teresa Wright, but again they have made it easy for themselves by showing Andrews's wife to be a bag, and they atone for this convenience only in part by making her as well-meaning and sympathetic and essentially innocent as, in terms invented for her, she could be. Thanks to much of the writing and all of the playing, this illicit affair is by implication remarkably real and mature; but in action, in the good old inevitable Sunday School way, the extra-marital activities are limited to a single Andrews-Wright kiss and a boy-friend, for Andrews's wife, lolling in his shirtsleeves; and it is the wife who asks for a divorce.

Or again, they pretend to hit the banker's predicament between the eyes, and allow him to tell off his careful world which doesn't want to make loans to veterans without collateral in a speech which, on the movie scale of things, is reasonably bold. They even have the firmness to let March have the last word on that issue; he says that with nearly every loan without collateral he will have to put up the same fight all over again. Yet one is emotionally left with the impression that he has cleverly and lovably won his fight and will win it on every subsequent occasion, and the hints that his own bread and butter are and will be increasingly in jeopardy if he keeps his courage are so discreet as to be all but inaudible. As a footnote to this his boss, played by Ray Collins, is represented, not with the cool realism which could here have been so good and so nearly unprecedented in an American movie, but in the kind of skillful caricature which, like so much of Gilbert and Sullivan, makes every punch a kind of self-caress.

The only boss types represented cruelly are the manager and floorwalker of a chain drugstore — that is, men in a job predicament in which they are as much bullied as bullying; and it is not shown that they are bullied. The only business type who is represented with what seems like perfect justice is the father of the sailor's sweetheart, a specialized, fussy, feminine little man who nervously tries to badger the sailor about his plans for the future. Or for still another major fault — and here direction and playing are as much to blame as the script — the very interesting and, for movies, new character of the banker is only hinted at, not solidly presented. Only the psychologically sophisticated can gather from the film that his marriage is only nominally happy and is actually precarious, and that the people who made the movie may possibly be on to this; and March's benders, though extremely well done in their way, are staged with all but frantic gratitude as broad comic relief, as if professional entertainers who were also good artists were on these occasions very glad to betray their responsibilities as artists for the sake of getting a little bit of sure-fire — and commercially much-needed — fun into the show.

In fact, it would be possible, I don't doubt, to call the whole picture just one long pious piece of deceit and self-deceit, embarrassed by hot flashes of talent, conscience, truthfulness, and dignity. And it is anyhow more than possible, it is unhappily obligatory, to observe that a good deal which might have been very fine, even great, and which is handled mainly by people who could have done, and done perfectly, all the best that could have been developed out of the idea, is here either murdered in its cradle or reduced to manageable good citizenship in the early stages of grade school. Yet I feel a hundred times more liking and admiration for the film than distaste or disappointment.

December 14, 1946

It seems to me that the movie's basic weaknesses are in the script — or are more likely, in the writer's knowledge of all that he would have to go easy on as a part of the rather remarkable bargain by which he got away with all that he managed to. Yet this is a most unusually good screen play. Although the dialogue has a continuous sheen of entertainment slickness it is also notably well-differentiated, efficient, free of tricks of snap and punch and over-design, and modest in its feeling for how much weight it should carry on the screen; and most of the time there is an openness about the writing which I don't doubt every good screen writer tries for but which few achieve. By openness I mean simply that the scenes are so planned, and the lines so laid down, that every action and reaction, every motion and everything that is seen, is more centrally eloquent than the spoken lines. The movie thus has and takes its chance to be born in front of the camera, whereas the general run of screen plays force what takes place before the camera to be a mere redigestion of a predigestion.

With a director and camera man in charge so gifted as Messrs. Wyler and Toland it is impossible to guess which of them, or Mr. Sherwood, is most to be thanked for the great force, simplicity, and beauty of some of the scenes and countless of the camera set-ups; so it is purely my hunch, with apologies in advance, that the real heroes in this film are Wyler and Toland, with invaluable assists credited to the set designer and art director, who provide some of the best stages for the action that I have ever seen in a movie. I can't think of a single shot of Toland's that doesn't show the amount of will, creative energy, and taste, and doesn't add with perfect power and modesty its own special kind of expressiveness, which of course ought to be evident in every shot in every good movie, and which of course plenty of people try for without more than spasmodically achieving. I can't remember a more thoroughly satisfying job of photography, in an American movie, since *Greed*. Aesthetically and in its emotional feeling for people and their surroundings, Toland's work in this film makes me think of the photographs of Walker Evans. Toland either lacks or subsumes any equivalent intellect, irony, and delight in the varieties of texture, edge, meaning, mystery, and shape in clothing and in all inanimate things; but it is a question how much such powers of perception could be used in telling a story in motion.

William Wyler has always seemed to me an exceedingly sincere and good director; he now seems one of the few great ones. He has come back from the war with a style of great purity, directness, and warmth, about as cleanly devoid of mannerism, haste, superfluous motion, aesthetic or emotional over-reaching, as any I know; and I felt complete confidence, as I watched this work, that he could have handled any degree to which this material might have been matured as well as or even better than the job he was given to do. His direction of the nonprofessional, Harold Russell, is just an exciting proof, on the side, of the marvels a really good artist can perform in collaboration with a really good non-actor; much more of the time it was his job to get new and better things out of professionals than they had ever shown before. One conspicuous failure — good as it is in its regrettable way — is March in his drunk scenes; and Myrna Loy, as his wife, is surprisingly uneven. But March is far outside his normal habits, and very good indeed, in, for instance, his interview with Dana Andrews over the question of the March daughter. And such a scene as that in which the sailor's father helps him get ready for bed seems to me so quietly perfect that I would set it in the world with the best fiction, or poetic drama, or movies that I know.

Almost without exception, down through such virtually noiseless bit roles as that of the mother of the sailor's fiancee, this film is so well cast and acted that there is no possible room to speak of all the people I wish I might. I cannot, however, resist speaking briefly, anyhow, of Teresa Wright. Like Frances Dee, she has always been one of the very few women in movies who really had a face. Like Miss Dee, she has also always used this translucent face with delicate and exciting talent as an actress, and with something of a novelist's perceptiveness behind the talent. And like Miss Dee, she has never been around nearly enough. This new performance of hers, entirely lacking in big scenes, tricks, or obstreperousness — one can hardly think of it as acting — seems to me one of the wisest and most beautiful pieces of work I have seen in years. If the picture had none of the hundreds of other things it has to recommend it, I could watch it a dozen times over for that personality and its mastery alone.

I can hardly expect that anyone who reads this will like the film as well as I do. It is easy, and true, to say that it suggests the limitations which will be inevitable in any Hollywood film, no matter how skillful and sincere. But it is also a great pleasure, and equally true, to say that it shows what can be done in the factory by people of adequate talent when they get, or manage to make themselves, the chance.

Movie Chronicle: The Westerner

ROBERT WARSHOW

They that have power to hurt and will do none,
That do not do the thing they most do show,
Who, moving others, are themselves as stone,
Unmoved, cold, and to temptation slow;
They rightly do inherit heaven's graces,
And husband nature's riches from expense;
They are the lords and owners of their faces,
Others but stewards of their excellence.

The two most successful creations of American movies are the gangster and the Westerner: men with guns. Guns as physical objects, and the postures associated with their use, form the visual and emotional center of both types of films. I suppose this reflects the importance of guns in the fantasy life of Americans; but that is a less illuminating point than it appears to be.

The gangster movie, which no longer exists in its "classical" form, is a story of enterprise and success ending in precipitate failure. Success is conceived as an increasing power to work injury, it belongs to the city, and it is of course a

From Robert Warshow, *The Immediate Experience* (New York: Doubleday & Company, Inc., 1962), pp. 135-54. Reprinted by permission of Joseph Goldberg, Trustee of Robert Warshow. © 1962 by Joseph Goldberg. "The Westerner" first appeared in *Partisan Review*, Vol. XXI, No. 2 (March-April 1954).

form of evil (though the gangster's death, presented usually as "punishment," is perceived simply as defeat). The peculiarity of the gangster is his unceasing, nervous activity. The exact nature of his enterprises may remain vague, but his commitment to enterprise is always clear, and all the more clear because he operates outside the field of utility. He is without culture, without manners, without leisure, or at any rate his leisure is likely to be spent in debauchery so compulsively aggressive as to seem only another aspect of his "work." But he is graceful, moving like a dancer among the crowded dangers of the city.

Like other tycoons, the gangster is crude in conceiving his ends but by no means inarticulate; on the contrary, he is usually expansive and noisy (the introspective gangster is a fairly recent development), and can state definitely what he wants: to take over the North Side, to own a hundred suits, to be Number One. But new "frontiers" will present themselves infinitely, and by a rigid convention it is understood that as soon as he wishes to rest on his gains, he is on the way to destruction.

The gangster is lonely and melancholy, and can give the impression of a profound worldly wisdom. He appeals most to adolescents with their impatience and their feeling of being outsiders, but more generally he appeals to that side of all of us which refuses to believe in the "normal" possibilities of happiness and achievement; the gangster is the "no" to that great American "yes" which is stamped so big over our official culture and yet has so little to do with the way we really feel about our lives. But the gangster's loneliness and melancholy are not "authentic"; like everything else that belongs to him, they are not honestly come by: he is lonely and melancholy not because life ultimately demands such feelings but because he has put himself in a position where everybody wants to kill him and eventually somebody will. He is wide open and defenseless, incomplete because unable to accept any limits or come to terms with his own nature, fearful, loveless. And the story of his career is a nightmare inversion of the values of ambition and opportunity. From the window of Scarface's bulletproof apartment can be seen an electric sign proclaiming: "The World Is Yours," and, if I remember, this sign is the last thing we see after Scarface lies dead in the street. In the end it is the gangster's weakness as much as his power and freedom that appeals to us; the world is not ours, but it is not his either, and in his death he "pays" for our fantasies, releasing us momentarily both from the concept of success, which he denies by caricaturing it, and from the need to succeed, which he shows to be dangerous.

The Western hero, by contrast, is a figure of repose. He resembles the gangster in being lonely and to some degree melancholy. But his melancholy comes from the "simple" recognition that life is unavoidably serious, not from the disproportions of his own temperament. And his loneliness is organic, not imposed on him by his situation but belonging to him intimately and testifying to his completeness. The gangster must reject others violently or draw them violently to him. The Westerner is not thus compelled to seek love; he is prepared to accept it, perhaps, but he never asks of it more than it can give, and we see him constantly in situations where love is at best an irrelevance. If there is a woman he loves, she is usually unable to understand his motives; she is against killing and being killed, and he finds it impossible to explain to her that there is no point in being "against" these things: they belong to his world.

Very often this woman is from the East and her failure to understand represents a clash of cultures. In the American mind, refinement, virtue, civilization, Christianity itself, are seen as feminine, and therefore women are often portrayed as possessing some kind of deeper wisdom, while the men, for all their apparent self-assurance, are fundamentally childish. But the West, lacking the graces of civilization, is the place "where men are men"; in Western movies, men have the deeper wisdom and the women are children. Those women in the Western movies who share the hero's understanding of life are prostitutes (or, as they are usually presented, barroom entertainers) — women, that is, who have come to understand in the most practical way how love can be an irrelevance, and therefore "fallen" women. The gangster, too, associates with prostitutes, but for him the important things about a prostitute are her passive availability and her costliness: she is part of his winnings. In Western movies, the important thing about a prostitute is her quasi-masculine independence: nobody owns her, nothing has to be explained to her, and she is not, like a virtuous woman, a "value" that demands to be protected. When the Westerner leaves the prostitute for a virtuous woman — for love — he is in fact forsaking a way of life, though the point of the choice is often obscured by having the prostitute killed by getting into the line of fire.

The Westerner is *par excellence* a man of leisure. Even when he wears the badge of a marshal or, more rarely, owns a ranch, he appears to be unemployed. We see him standing at a bar, or playing poker — a game which expresses perfectly his talent for remaining relaxed in the midst of tension — or perhaps camping out on the plains on some extraordinary errand. If he does own a ranch, it is in the background; we are not actually aware that he owns anything except his horse, his guns, and the one worn suit of clothing which is likely to remain unchanged all through the movie. It comes as a surprise to see him take money from his pocket or an extra shirt from his saddlebags. As a rule we do not even know where he sleeps at night and don't think of asking. Yet it never occurs to us that he is a poor man; there is no poverty in Western movies, and really no wealth either: those great cattle domains and shipments of gold which figure so largely in the plots are moral and not material quantities, not the objects of contention but only its occasion. Possessions too are irrelevant.

Employment of some kind — usually unproductive — is always open to the Westerner, but when he accepts it, it is not because he needs to make a living, much less from any idea of "getting ahead." Where could he want to "get ahead" to? By the time we see him, he is already "there": he can ride a horse faultlessly, keep his countenance in the face of death, and draw his gun a little faster and shoot it a little straighter than anyone he is likely to meet. These are sharply defined acquirements, giving to the figure of the Westerner an apparent moral clarity which corresponds to the clarity of his physical image against his bare landscape; initially, at any rate, the Western movie presents itself as being without mystery, its whole universe comprehended in what we see on the screen.

Much of this apparent simplicity arises directly from those "cinematic" elements which have long been understood to give the Western theme its special appropriateness for the movies: the wide expanses of land, the free movement of men on horses. As guns constitute the visible moral center of the Western movie, suggesting continually the possibility of violence, so land and horses represent the movie's material basis, its sphere of action. But the land and the horses have also a moral significance: the physical freedom they represent belongs to the moral "openness" of the West — corresponding to the fact that guns are carried where they can be seen. (And, as we shall see, the character of land and horses changes as the Western film becomes more complex.)

The gangster's world is less open, and his arts not so easily identifiable as the Westerner's. Perhaps he too can keep his countenance, but the mask he wears is really no mask: its purpose is precisely to make evident the fact that he desperately wants to "get ahead" and will stop at nothing. Where the Westerner imposes himself by the appearance of unshakable control, the gangster's pre-eminence lies in the suggestion that he may at any moment lose control; his strength is not in being able to shoot faster or straighter than others, but in being more willing to shoot. "Do it first," says Scarface expounding his mode of operation, "and keep on doing it!" With the Westerner, it is a crucial point of honor *not* to "do it first"; his gun remains in its holster until the moment of combat.

There is no suggestion, however, that he draws the gun reluctantly. The Westerner could not fulfill himself if the moment did not finally come when he can shoot his enemy down. But because that moment is so thoroughly the expression of his being, it must be kept pure. He will not violate the accepted forms of combat though by doing so he could save a city. And he can wait. "When you call me that — smile!" — the villain smiles weakly, soon he is laughing with horrible joviality, and the crisis is past. But it is allowed to pass because it must come again: sooner or later Trampas will "make his play," and the Virginian will be ready for him.

What does the Westerner fight for? We know he is on the side of justice and order; and of course it can be said he fights for these things. But such broad aims never correspond exactly to his real motives; they only offer him his opportunity. The Westerner himself, when an explanation is asked of him (usually by a woman), is likely to say that he does what he "has to do." If justice and order did not continually demand his protection, he would be without a calling. Indeed, we come upon him often in just that situation, as the reign of law settles over the West and he is forced to see that his day is over; those are the pictures which end with his death or with his departure for some more remote frontier. What he defends, at bottom, is the purity of his own image—in fact his honor. This is what makes him invulnerable. When the gangster is killed, his whole life is shown to have been a mistake, but the image the Westerner seeks to maintain can be presented as clearly in defeat as in victory: he fights not for advantage and not for the right, but to state what he is, and he must live in a world which permits that statement. The Westerner is the last gentleman, and the movies which over and over again tell his story are probably the last art form in which the concept of honor retains its strength.

Of course I do not mean to say that ideas of virtue and justice and courage have gone out of culture. Honor is more than these things: it is a style, concerned with harmonious appearances as much as with desirable consequences, and tending therefore toward the denial of life in favor of art. "Who hath it? he that died o' Wednesday." On the whole, a world that leans to Falstaff's view is a more civilized and even, finally, a more graceful world. It is just the march of civilization that forces the Westerner to move on; and if we actually had to confront the question it might turn out that the woman who refuses to understand him is right as often as she is wrong. But we do not confront the question. Where the Westerner lives it is always about 1870—not the real 1870, either, or the real West—and he is killed or goes away when his position becomes problematical. The fact that he continues to hold our attention is evidence enough that, in his proper frame, he presents an image of personal nobility that is still real for us.

Clearly, this image easily becomes ridiculous: we need only look at William S. Hart or Tom Mix, who in the wooden absoluteness of their virtue represented little that an adult could take seriously; and doubtless such figures as Gene Autry or Roy Rogers are no better, though I confess I have seen none of their movies. Some film enthusiasts claim to find in the early, unsophisticated Westerns a "cinematic purity" that has since been lost; this idea is as valid, and finally as misleading, as T. S. Eliot's statement that *Everyman* is the only play in English that stays within the limitations of art. The truth is that the Westerner comes into the field of serious art only when his moral code, without ceasing to be compelling, is seen also to be imperfect. The Westerner at his best exhibits a moral ambiguity which darkens his image and saves him from absurdity; this ambiguity arises from the fact that, whatever his justifications, he is a killer of men.

In *The Virginian,* which is an archetypal Western movie as *Scarface* or *Little Caesar* are archetypal gangster movies, there is a lynching in which the hero (Gary Cooper), as leader of a posse, must supervise the hanging of his best friend for stealing cattle. With the growth of American "social consciousness," it is no longer possible to present a lynching in the movies unless the point is the illegality and injustice of the lynching itself; *The Ox-Bow Incident,* made in 1943, explicitly puts forward the newer point of view and can be regarded as a kind of "anti-Western." But in 1929, when *The Virginian* was made, the present inhibition about lynching was not yet in force; the justice, and therefore the necessity, of the hanging is never questioned — except by the schoolteacher from the East, whose refusal to understand serves as usual to set forth more sharply the deeper seriousness of the West. The Virginian is thus in a tragic dilemma where one moral absolute conflicts with another and the choice of either must leave a moral stain. If he had chosen to save his friend, he would have violated the image of himself that he had made essential to his existence, and the movie would have had to end with his death, for only by his death could the image have been restored. Having chosen instead to sacrifice his friend to the higher demands of the "code" — the only choice worthy of him, as even the friend understands — he is none the less stained by the killing, but what is needed now to set accounts straight is not his death but the death of the villain Trampas, the leader of the cattle thieves, who had escaped the posse and abandoned the Virginian's friend to his fate. Again the woman intervenes: Why must there be *more* killing? If the hero really loved her, he would leave town, refusing Trampas's challenge. What good will it be if Trampas should kill him? But the Virginian does once more what he "has to do," and in avenging his friend's death wipes out the stain on his own honor. Yet his victory cannot be complete: no death can be paid for and no stain truly wiped out; the movie is still a tragedy, for though the hero escapes with his life, he has been forced to confront the ultimate limits of his moral ideas.

This mature sense of limitation and unavoidable guilt is what gives the Westerner a "right" to his melancholy. It is true that the gangster's story is also a tragedy — in certain formal ways more clearly a tragedy than the Westerner's — but it is a romantic tragedy, based on a hero whose defeat springs with almost mechanical inevitability from the outrageous presumption of his demands: the gangster is *bound* to go on until he is killed. The Westerner is a more classical figure, self-contained and limited to begin with, seeking not to extend his dominion but only to assert his personal value, and his tragedy lies in the fact that even this circumscribed demand cannot be fully realized. Since the Westerner is not a murderer but (most of the time) a man of virtue, and since he is always prepared for defeat, he retains his inner invulnerability and his story need not end with his death (and usually does not); but what we finally respond to is not his victory but his defeat.

Up to a point, it is plain that the deeper seriousness of the good Western films comes from the introduction of a realism, both physical and psychological, that was missing with Tom Mix and William S. Hart. As lines of age have come into Gary Cooper's face since *The Virginian,* so the outlines of the Western movie in general have become less smooth, its background more drab. The sun still beats upon the town, but the camera is likely now to take advantage of this illumination to seek out more closely the shabbiness of buildings and furniture, the loose, worn hang of clothing, the wrinkles and dirt of the faces. Once it has been discovered that the true theme of the Western movie is not the freedom and expansiveness of frontier life, but its limitations, its material bareness, the pressures of obligation, then even the landscape itself ceases to be quite the arena of free movement it once was, but becomes instead a great empty waste, cutting down more often than it exaggerates the stature of the horseman who rides across it. We are more likely now to see the Westerner struggling against the obstacles of the physical world (as in the wonderful scenes on the desert and among the rocks in *The Last Posse*) than carelessly surmounting them. Even the horses, no longer the "friends" of man or the inspired chargers of knight-errantry, have lost much of the moral significance that once seemed to belong to them in their careering across the screen. It seems to me the horses grow tired and stumble more often than they did, and that we see them less frequently at the gallop.

In *The Gunfighter,* a remarkable film of a couple of years ago, the landscape has virtually disappeared. Most of the action takes place indoors, in a cheerless saloon where a tired "bad man" (Gregory Peck) contemplates the waste of his life, to be senselessly killed at the end by a vicious youngster setting off on the same futile path. The movie is done in cold, quiet tones of gray, and every object in it—faces, clothing, a table, the hero's heavy mustache—is given an air of uncompromising authenticity, suggesting those dim photographs of the nineteenth-century West in which Wyatt Earp, say, turns out to be a blank untidy figure posing awkwardly before some uninteresting building. This "authenticity," to be sure, is only aesthetic; the chief fact about nineteenth-century photographs, to my eyes at any rate, is how stonily they refuse to yield up the truth. But that limitation is just what is needed: by preserving some hint of the rigidity of archaic photography (only in tone and décor, never in composition), *The Gunfighter* can permit us to feel that we are looking at a more "real" West than the one the movies have accustomed us to—harder, duller, less "romantic"—and yet without forcing us outside the boundaries which give the Western movie its validity.

We come upon the hero of *The Gunfighter* at the end of a career in which he has never upheld justice and order, and has been at times, apparently, an actual criminal; in this case, it is clear that the hero has been wrong and the woman who has rejected his way of life has been right. He is thus without any of the larger justifications, and knows himself a ruined man. There can be no question of his "redeeming" himself in any socially constructive way. He is too much the victim of his own reputation to turn marshal as one of his old friends has done, and he is not offered the sentimental solution of a chance to give up his life for some good end; the whole point is that he exists outside the field of social value. Indeed, if we were once allowed to see him in the days of his "success," he might become a figure like the gangster, for his career has been aggressively "anti-social" and the practical problem he faces is the gangster's problem: there will always be somebody trying to kill him. Yet it is obviously absurd to speak of him as "anti-social," not only because we do not see him acting as a criminal, but more fundamentally because we do not see his milieu as a society. Of course it has its "social problems" and a kind of static history: civilization is always just at the point of driving out the old freedom; there are women and children to represent the possibility of a settled life; and there is the marshal, a bad man turned good, determined to keep at least his area of jurisdiction at peace. But these elements are not, in fact, a part of the film's "realism," even though they come out of the real history of the West; they belong to the conventions of the form, to that accepted framework which makes the film possible in the first place, and they exist not to provide a standard by which the gunfighter can be judged, but only to set him off. The true "civilization" of the Western movie is always embodied in an individual, good or bad is more a matter of personal bearing than of social consequences, and the conflict of good and bad is a duel between two men. Deeply troubled and obviously doomed, the gunfighter is the Western hero still, perhaps all the more because his value must express itself entirely in his own being—in his presence, the way he holds our eyes—and in contradiction to the facts. No matter what he has done, he *looks* right, and he remains invulnerable because, without acknowledging anyone else's right to judge him, he has judged his own failure and has already assimilated it, understanding—as no one else under-stands except the marshal and the barroom girl—that he can do nothing but play out the drama of the gun fight again and again until the time comes when it will be he who gets killed. What "redeems" him is that he no longer believes in this drama and nevertheless will continue to play his role perfectly: the pattern is all.

The proper function of realism in the Western movie can only be to deepen the lines of that pattern. It is an art form for connoisseurs, where the spectator derives his pleasure from the appreciation of minor variations within the working out of a pre-established order. One does not want too much novelty: it comes as a shock, for instance, when the hero is made to operate without a gun, as has been done in several pictures (e.g., *Destry Rides Again),* and our uneasiness is allayed only when he is finally compelled to put his "pacifism" aside. If the hero can be shown to be troubled, complex, fallible, even eccentric, or the villain given some psychological taint or, better, some evoca-tive physical mannerism, to shade the colors of his villainy, that is all to the good. Indeed, that kind of variation is absolutely necessary to keep the type from becoming sterile; we do not want to see the same movie over and over again, only the same form. But when the impulse toward realism is extended into a "reinterpretation" of the West as a developed society, drawing our eyes away from the hero if only to the extent of showing him as the one dominant figure in a complex social order, then the pattern is broken and the West itself begins to be uninteresting. If the "social problems" of the frontier are to be the movie's chief concern, there is no longer any point in re-examining these problems twenty times a year; they have been solved, and the people for whom they once were real are dead. Moreover, the hero himself, still the film's central figure, now tends to become its one unassimilable element, since he is the most "unreal."

The Ox-Bow Incident, by denying the convention of the lynching, presents us with a modern "social drama" and evokes a corresponding response, but in doing so it almost makes the Western setting irrelevant, a mere backdrop of beautiful scenery. (It is significant that *The Ox-Bow Incident* has no hero; a hero would have to stop the lynching or be killed in trying to stop it, and then the "problem" of lynching would no longer be central.) Even in *The Gunfighter* the women and children are a little too much in evidence, threatening constantly to become a real focus of concern instead of simply part of the given framework; and the young tough who kills the hero has too much the air of juvenile criminality: the hero himself could never have been like that, and the idea of a cycle being repeated therefore loses its sharpness. But the most striking example of the confusion created by a too conscientious "social" realism is in the celebrated *High Noon.*

In *High Noon* we find Gary Cooper still the upholder of order that he was in *The Virginian,* but twenty-four years older, stooped, slower moving, awkward, his face lined, the flesh sagging, a less beautiful and weaker figure, but with the suggestion of greater depth that belongs almost automatically to age. Like the hero of *The Gunfighter,* he no longer has to assert his character and is no longer interested in the drama of combat; it is hard to imagine that he might once have been so youthful as to say, "When you call me that — smile!" In fact, when we come upon him he is hanging up his guns and his marshal's badge in order to begin a new, peaceful life with his bride, who is a Quaker. But then the news comes that a man he had sent to prison has been pardoned and will get to town on the noon train; three friends of this man have come to wait for him at the station, and when the freed convict arrives the four of them will come to kill the marshal. He is thus trapped; the bride will object, the hero himself will waver much more than he would have done twenty-four years ago, but in the end he will play out the drama because it is what he "has to do." All this belongs to the established form (there is even the "fallen woman" who understands the marshal's position as his wife does not). Leaving aside the crudity of building up suspense by means of the clock, the actual Western drama of *High Noon* is well handled and forms a good companion piece to *The Virginian,* showing in both conception and technique the ways in which the Western movie has naturally developed.

But there is a second drama along with the first. As the marshal sets out to find deputies to help him deal with the four gunmen, we are taken through the various social strata of the town, each group in turn refusing its assistance out of cowardice, malice, irresponsibility, or venality. With this we are in the field of "social drama" — of a very low order, incidentally, altogether unconvincing and displaying a vulgar anti-populism that has marred some other movies of Stanley Kramer's. But the falsity of the "social drama" is less important than the fact that it does not belong in the movie to begin with. The technical problem was to make it necessary for the marshal to face his enemies alone; to explain *why* the other townspeople are not at his side is to raise a question which does not exist in the proper frame of the Western movie, where the hero is "naturally" alone and it is only necessary to contrive the physical absence of those who might be his allies, if any contrivance is needed at all. In addition, though the hero of *High Noon* proves himself a better man than all around him, the actual effect of this contrast is to lessen his stature: he becomes only a rejected man of virtue. In our final glimpse of him, as he rides away through the town where he has spent most of his life without really imposing himself on it, he is a pathetic rather than a tragic figure. And his departure has another meaning as well; the "social drama" has no place for him.

But there is also a different way of violating the Western form. This is to yield entirely to its static quality as legend and to the "cinematic" temptations of its landscape, the horses, the quiet men. John Ford's famous *Stagecoach* (1938) had much of this unhappy preoccupation with style, and the same director's *My Darling Clementine* (1946), a soft and beautiful movie about Wyatt Earp, goes further along the same path, offering indeed a superficial accuracy of historical reconstruction, but so loving in execution as to destroy the outlines of the Western legend, assimilating it to the more sentimental legend of rural America and making the hero a more dangerous Mr. Deeds. (*Powder River,* a recent "routine" Western shamelessly copied from *My Darling Clementine,* is in most ways a better film; lacking the benefit of a serious director, it is necessarily more concerned with drama than with style.)

The highest expression of this aestheticizing tendency is in George Stevens' *Shane,* where the legend of the West is virtually reduced to its essentials and then fixed in the dreamy clarity of a fairy tale. There never was so broad and bare and lovely a landscape as Stevens puts before us, or so unimaginably comfortless a "town" as the little group of buildings on the prairie to which the settlers must come for their supplies and to buy a drink. The mere physical progress of the film, following the style of A *Place in the Sun,* is so deliberately graceful that everything seems to be happening at the bottom of a clear lake. The hero (Alan Ladd) is hardly a man at all, but something like the Spirit of the West, beautiful in fringed buckskins. He emerges mysteriously from the plains, breathing sweetness and a melancholy which is no longer simply the Westerner's natural response to experience but has taken on spirituality; and when he has accomplished his mission, meeting and destroying in the black figure of Jack Palance a Spirit of Evil just as metaphysical as his own embodiment of virtue, he fades away again into the more distant West, a man whose "day is over," leaving behind the wondering little boy who might have imagined the whole story. The choice of Alan Ladd to play the leading role is alone an indication of this film's tendency. Actors like Gary Cooper or Gregory Peck are in themselves, as material objects, "realistic," seeming to bear in their bodies and their faces mortality, limitation, the knowledge of good and evil. Ladd is a more "aesthetic" object, with some of the "universality" of a piece of sculpture; his special quality is in his physical smoothness and serenity, unwordly and yet not innocent, but suggesting that no experience can really touch him. Stevens has tried to freeze the Western myth once and for all in the immobility of Alan Ladd's countenance. If *Shane* were "right," and fully successful, it might be possible to say there was no point in making any more Western movies; once the hero is apotheosized, variation and development are closed off.

Shane is not "right," but it is still true that the possibilities of fruitful variation in the Western movie are limited. The form can keep its freshness through endless repetitions only because of the special character of the film medium, where the physical difference between one object and another—above all, between one actor and another—is of such enormous importance, serving the function that is served by the variety of language in the perpetuation of literary types. In this sense, the "vocabulary" of films is much larger than that of literature and falls more readily into pleasing and significant arrangements. (That may explain why the middle levels of excellence are more easily reached in the movies than in literary forms, and perhaps also why the status of the movies as art is constantly being called into question.) But the advantage of this almost automatic particularity belongs to all films alike. Why does the Western movie especially have such a hold on our imagination?

Chiefly, I think, because it offers a serious orientation to the problem of violence such as can be found almost nowhere else in our culture. One of the well-known peculiarities of modern civilized opinion is its refusal to acknowledge the value of violence. This refusal is a virtue, but like many virtues it involves a certain willful blindness and it encourages hypocrisy. We train ourselves to be shocked or bored by cultural images of violence, and our very concept of heroism tends to be a passive one: we are less drawn to the brave young men who kill large numbers of our enemies than to the heroic prisoners who endure torture without capitulating. In art, though we may still be able to understand and participate in the values of the Iliad, a modern writer like Ernest Hemingway we find somewhat embarrassing: there is no doubt that he stirs us, but we cannot help recognizing also that he is a little childish. And in the criticism of popular culture, where the educated observer is usually under the illusion that he has nothing at stake, the presence of images of violence is often assumed to be in itself a sufficient ground for condemnation.

These attitudes, however, have not reduced the element of violence in our culture but, if anything, have helped to free it from moral control by letting it take on the aura of "emancipation." The celebration of acts of violence is left more and more to the irresponsible: on the higher cultural levels to writers like Céline, and lower down to Mickey Spillane or Horace McCoy, or to the comic books, television, and the movies. The gangster movie, with its numerous variations, belongs to this cultural "underground" which sets forth the attractions of violence in the face of all our higher social attitudes. It is a more "modern" genre than the Western, perhaps even more profound, because it confronts industrial society on its own ground — the city — and because, like much of our advanced art, it gains its effects by a gross insistence on its own narrow logic. But it is anti-social, resting on fantasies of irresponsible freedom. If we are brought finally to acquiesce in the denial of these fantasies, it is only because they have been shown to be dangerous, not because they have given way to better vision of behavior.*

In war movies, to be sure, it is possible to present the uses of violence within a framework of responsibiltiy. But there is the disadvantage that modern war is a co-operative enterprise; its violence is largely impersonal, and heroism belongs to the group more than to the individual. The hero of a war movie is most often simply a leader, and his superiority is likely to be expressed in a denial of the heroic: you are not supposed to be brave, you are supposed to get the job done and stay alive (this too, of course, is a kind of heroic posture, but a new — and "practical" — one). At its best, the war movie may represent a more civilized point of view than the Western, and if it were not continually marred by ideological sentimentality we might hope to find it developing into a higher form of drama. But it cannot supply the values we seek in the Western.

Those values are in the image of a single man who wears a gun on his thigh. The gun tells us that he lives in a world of violence, and even that he "believes in violence." But the drama is one of self-restraint: the moment of violence must come in its own time and according to its special laws, or else it is valueless. There is little cruelty in Western movies, and little sentimentality; our eyes are not focused on the sufferings of the defeated but on the deportment of the hero. Really, it is not violence at all which is the "point" of the Western movie, but a certain image of man, a style, which expresses itself most clearly in violence. Watch a child with his toy guns and you will see: what most

---

*I am not concerned here with the actual social consequences of gangster movies, though I suspect they could not have been so pernicious as they were thought to be. Some of the compromises introduced to avoid the supposed bad effects of the old gangster movies may be, if anything, more dangerous, for the sadistic violence that once belonged only to the gangster is now commonly enlisted on the side of the law and thus goes undefeated, allowing us (if we wish) to find in the movies a sort of "confirmation" of our fantasies.

interests him is not (as we so much fear) the fantasy of hurting others, but to work out how a man might look when he shoots or is shot. A hero is one who looks like a hero.

Whatever the limitations of such an idea in experience, it has always been valid in art, and has a special validity in an art where appearances are everything. The Western hero is necessarily an archaic figure; we do not really believe in him and would not have him step out of his rigidly conventionalized background. But his archaicism does not take away from his power; on the contrary, it adds to it by keeping him just a little beyond the reach both of common sense and of absolutized emotion, the two usual impulses of our art. And he has, after all, his own kind of relevance. He is there to remind us of the possibility of style in an age which has put on itself the burden of pretending that style has no meaning, and, in the midst of our anxieties over the problem of violence, to suggest that even in killing or being killed we are not freed from the necessity of establishing satisfactory modes of behavior. Above all, the movies in which the Westerner plays out his role preserve for us the pleasures of a complete and self-contained drama—and one which still effortlessly crosses the boundaries which divide our culture—in a time when other, more consciously serious art forms are increasingly complex, uncertain, and ill-defined.

"The Desperate Hours" and the
Violent Screen

MARTIN S. DWORKIN

The Desperate Hours and *Teen Age Crime Wave* are major and minor versions of a recurring melodrama, in which a family or community — here the former — is imprisoned or besieged by criminals. There have been at least two other films in recent years with closely similar themes: *Suddenly,* in which Frank Sinatra and two henchmen held a family at bay while they prepared for an attempt to assassinate the President; and *The Night Holds Terror,* written, directed, and produced by newcomer Andrew Stone, in which three homicidal desperadoes seized the home of a young couple. The theme of the invaded community has been represented recently in a larger number of films including *The Wild One, Violent Saturday, The Phenix City Story* — and *The Blackboard Jungle,* which purportedly tried to treat real problems of education and juvenile deliquency with frankness, but patently exploited the form, as well as the rationale of the entrenched-hoodlums melodrama. Western films, of course, have as one of their leading motives the struggle to rid a town or territory of badmen in control, and often include, or even focus upon situations in which small groups of people are beleaguered.

The theme of the good held captive by evil is ancient, as is the dramatic device of analogizing between society in the large and in microcosm. We may

From *Shenandoah*, Vol. XI, No. 2 (1960), pp. 39-48. Reprinted by permission of the author. This article was first printed in the *Queen's Quarterly*, Vol. LXIII, No. 3 (1956).

add, too, that it is no new thing for films to debate the use of violence – nor, to be sure, for them to seem to decry the brutality they actually glorify. But it is significant that the screen should be so preoccupied now. (It is practically impossible to count how often the embattled family or community theme has appeared on television. The family-held-hostage, particularly, offers opportunities for closet melodrama uniquely suited to the intimacy and focalized framing of the medium). In fact, the nature as well as the number of these films suggests that we may be reaching a climax in the latest cycle of screen violence. At least, at this point it may be possible to clarify what we mean when we judge a film to be gratuitously violent – and, perhaps, to suggest ways of recognizing the effects violent films have upon us.

If we like, we may see *The Desperate Hours* and *Teen Age Crime Wave* as representing the best and the worst of their type – comprising a kind of dialectical statement. It is as if the movies were carrying on their own debate, under the pressures which have been exerted recently by government, religious, educational – and even film industry groups, concerning the nature and quantity of brutality on the screen. And this debate reflects the ambiguity of popular attitudes – at least as much as the movie violence itself expresses destructive forces, or wishes, or tendencies at work in our society. It may be true, as Paul Rotha and Richard Griffith have asserted, that the spate of crime and gangster films after World War II was directed toward "a public weary of the conflict, but so steeped in violence that anything else seemed tame." But the critique of violence in the films themselves suggests doubts, as well as compulsive surfeit – even as the shooting, slugging, and other melodramatized mayhem continues. When and whether a man should use his fists, or draw his guns, or reach for the rifle over the mantel – or call the police, are questions constantly asked, and answered, in the movies. But they bear a formal resemblance, and have a certain analogical pertinence to questions of how we may deal with many problems, local, national, and international. In the ways in which many people deal with issues such as the use of nuclear weapons, total war, preventive war, and the value of allies and international agencies for peace, it is possible to discern refractions of the images of conflict of typical crime and Western movie melodramas.

These images are conventionally contrived to involve the audience in such ways that the principal actors are its protagonists. The deliberate intention is to establish empathic participation. The heroine's anguishes and fulfillments, the hero's struggles and triumphs, are designed to incarnate prototypical experiences of the imagination in those who watch. The unique, enormous power of film, and its televised manifestation, lies in this incomparable capacity to implicate people; at once expressing their imaginations, as participating in a kind of collective imagination, and providing the imagery and symbology whereby their participation is articulated.

The theme and execution of *The Desperate Hours* and *Teen Age Crime*

Wave purpose an especially excruciating implication of our sensibilities. Both films establish a situation of primordial challenge, in which a family is captivated by violent criminals, its members held as hostages for each other's survival. Both confront decent people with the need to fight — exemplifying the integral necessity which film industry voices have submitted as the justification of violence in films. Both dramatize a crucial, and symbolically elemental threat to the basic unit of society, as well as subjecting its members to a battery of provocations. Decency is not only vexed and incited to act, but forced to preserve itself.

The quality of the two films, of course, is incomparable. *The Desperate Hours* is perhaps the outstanding film of its kind. From Joseph Hayes's screenplay, after his own novel and stageplay, it is produced and directed by William Wyler, who disposes a virtuoso's armament of cinema techniques. In the swift and clear delineation of distinctive characters, in his economy in counterposing them to achieve a drama of immediate engrossment, continuing suspense, and considerable subtlety, Wyler offers a demonstration of screen directing that should recreate his reputation among those who do not remember his *The Little Foxes,* or *The Best Years of Our Lives.* Frederic March completely personifies that significantly unusual protagonist: the embattled father, shocked into sustained, ferocious warfare for his family. Humphrey Bogart (who established the type of the gangster holding a group hostage in *The Petrified Forest)* as completely projects the criminal: deadly, fiercely vigilant, wholly immoral. The opposition of these two characters rises at moments to true heroic pitch — not the least because both March and Bogart possess the rare dramatic presence that can vivify and dominate the screen by itself.

In contrast to *The Desperate Hours'* proficiency, *Teen Age Crime Wave* sometimes gives the impression of having been jerrybuilt on its few sets, from a script concocted by the director and the actors as they went along, borrowing elements from sensationalist films about juvenile delinquents, jailbreak movies, cops-and-robbers chases, and — most significantly — family-held-hostage melodramas. By the time the two juvenile hoodlums, overacted with incredible ineptitude by Tommy Cook and Mollie McCart, have overcome the officers taking the latter to reform school together with the unjustly implicated Sue England, it is apparent that every act of brutal, criminal behavior is going to be relished, even as it is avowedly condemned. By the time the two have been driven from the home of Kay Riehl, James Bell, and their son, Frank Griffin, which they have dominated at pistol-point, we are as sick of Cook's performance as we are of the insufferable punk he portrays. The film obviously, if ineptly, intends us to be pleased when Miss McCart is shot as her just desert, and Cook gets his in a beating by Griffin, after an inexplicable retreat to an observatory. Crime does not pay, and the good guys are people who administer the beatings in the end.

The matter is not so clear in *The Desperate Hours.* The criminals here are not malevolent upstarts, but truly dangerous men: the cold, fiercely cunning Bogart; his young brother, Dewey Martin—perturbed by his first contact with the respectability he has been conditioned to despise, but dangerous out of the only loyalty he knows; and the hulking, brutish Robert Middleton—a homicidal monster with the mind of a stupid child. From the moment we know of them, in a remarkable shot from the inside of an automobile, with only a hand showing and a cold voice selecting the home to be invaded for a temporary hideout, we know that these men are really dangerous, completely criminal. In fact, the conventional melodrama of improbable triumphs is explicitly repudiated, as March struggles to convince his nine-year-old son, Richard Eyer, that the guns in the hands of the criminals are real, and that attempted heroics, "movie-style," will get loved ones killed. The mutual concern of the rest of the family: March's wife, Martha Scott, and their daughter, Mary Murphy, is convincing— not only because the criminals are so credibly dangerous, but because the dilemma is so agonizing.

March has to scheme and battle against Bogart and the other two—and against the police. For him, police intervention means the death of his loved ones—whether at the hands of the criminals, or in the crossfire. Concerning the issue of whether or not to go to the police, there has been some critical debate. Bosley Crowther, in the New York *Times,* remarked that the whole story was unrealistic because March did not notify the authorities at his first opportunity. In reply, to point up the reality of March's agonized choice, writer Joseph Hayes wrote the *Times,* citing the true instance of a criminal who killed a child he was using as a shield, because a policeman fired at him, despite warnings. Within the story of the film, however, the issue is academic. March's house is finally surrounded by police, but he is allowed to go in alone—following a debate of two police viewpoints: the one interested only in getting the criminals, no matter if innocents are hurt; the other, movingly represented by Arthur Kennedy, arguing for March's right to try to save his family, and for a concept of police work not at odds with the decency it is supposed to protect.

The final showdown, then, opposes the protagonists of decency and of evil in the traditional single combat of the conventional melodrama. Martin, Bogart's younger brother, has gone off alone earlier—in a first venture into independence—and has been killed, ingloriously wounded by state police, and then run over by a huge trailer-truck in a scene that is deliberately gruesome to emphasize the tragic waste of his life. Middleton, the moronic giant, has been tricked by March into getting his arm caught in the front door, and, running from the house in uncontrollable pain, has been shot down by the police. Only Bogart is left, with a gun he thinks is loaded pointed at the head of March's little boy. At March's command, the boy runs—and Bogart discovers what March has known: that the gun is empty. In March's hand is the revolver the criminals had used to menace the household, loaded. Bogart taunts March to shoot; although beaten, he savors March's hesitation. March insists that now, for the first time, he understands the mind of a killer like Bogart. The latter, however, senses otherwise, sneering, "You don't have it in you." March cannot, and does not pull the trigger. Almost with contempt, the criminal lets himself be driven out of the house, into the fire of the massed police guns.

The bad guys are killed by the police, the regularly constituted agency for violence against violence. In Joseph Hayes's final script, this legal violence had been sardonically depicted: it was apparent that Bogart could have been captured, but was shot down by Kennedy, against whom the criminal had sworn vengeance years before. But perhaps to provide a final fillip to Bogart's figure of heroicized malevolence, Wyler now has him fling his empty pistol at a police floodlight, smashing it. It is the final gesture of a gangster-king, out of the archaic *Götterdämerungen* epoch of gangster films, in which the Muni-Cagney-Bancroft-Robinson-Bogart underworld titans made their exits to the orchestration of shattering glass and cascading shots. This end, however, does emphasize the stature of the antagonist March has overcome. And if it is a moment of obvious braggadocio, it is also one of final, complete futility.

For the meaning of the film, however, it is a moment almost of anticlimax. The melodramatic confrontation of good and evil has already occurred—in traditional style, but with quite untypical resolution and significance. In the final chase and combat between the hoodlums and the hero in *Teen Age Crime Wave*—as in almost all melodramas of violence—the intentional meaning is clearly the direction of audience implication so that there is triumph, release, and pleasure in the beating given the bad guy. In *The Desperate Hours,* good must triumph over evil, too—but what the *good* is, and the manner of its victory, are conceived with a most unusual consistency. At least, the dilemma of ends and means is given a clearer statement than in most melodramas, and is resolved with much less of the meretriciousness that gives the audience axiomatic outcomes and sanctified brutalism: a dubious morality won through cheap thrills.

At the climactic instant—the classic moment of crime and Western melodramas, when the hero has drawn his gun and is prepared to kill with the perfect proficiency of unequivocated rectitude—March does not shoot. It is not that Bogart is unarmed, and so can cheat the movie hero's game, according to its little-boys' laws. He is still, unremittingly dangerous. March does not shoot *because we do not want him to.* There is no mistaking Hayes's and Wyler's intention. The scene might have come out differently—with consequent transformation of the film's meaning. Nor would March have had to pull the trigger.

Out of a myriad memories of other movies, we can imagine Bogart lunging at March—the pistol skittering across the floor out of reach—a desperate scramble to grasp it—vise-like grips and terrible grimaces (dolly to close-up)—heroic haymakers crashing against one chin, then the other—the door splintered off its hinges—the berserks battling on the landing, bursting through the balustrade to fall to the floor below—the last, colossal, deliberately-directed Sunday-punch, dropping the beaten Bogart in a heap, that tries to rise, only to collapse in utter vanquishment—the emergence of the bloodied, magnificently bedraggled March through his front door, into the floodlights of the admiring police and the arms of his loved ones.

Such an outcome, with its salutary purge for costive spirits, would have been according to the rules of movie melodrama, which make it the hero's right—even duty—to beat up or kill the evil adversary at the proper moment. And when he does either, the audience does it with him—and thereby hangs the crucial equivocation of the controversy over "excessive" brutality on the screen. It isn't the brutality of the evil protagonists that is really at issue, generally speaking. This is usually made clearly repugnant: it is the behavior whereby the bad guys show they are bad. The issue arises out of the audience's empathic association with the hero, personifying good and right—and being violent, at the least, about it. If it were only a matter of some especially suggestible moviegoers leaving the theatres to emulate the villains and their methods the issue would be simple and clear—as it has been during those occasional cycles of films deliberately glorifying crime.

Recalling Aristotle's definition of evil as having a deficient, not an efficient cause (that was evoked by Aquinas against the perennial Manichees), the problem here refers to the conditional nature of good, as the end of human conduct. For the moral rectitude of the movie hero is apodictic: by definition, as it were. But what he does to achieve the right—and what the audience does with him, and, later, because of him—is far less certainly good. Those in the film industry who have justified heroic violence because it is on the side of right at least implicitly presuppose that it is an evil: necessary, as in warfare and in situations of mortal challenge to the good; but an evil, nevertheless. What is "excessive" violence on the screen then becomes a matter of quantity—and perhaps of taste. But it is not one of principle, since any violence admittedly is at best a bad means towards a good end. This solution makes possible the considerable hypocrisies of films which have first denoted violence as evil, then established it as necessary, then have reveled in it. The guns spit and the heads crack; but the dead and maimed are only evildoers after all—and it makes a glorious victory.

That the solution amounts to no more than doing the wrong thing for right reasons—the end justifying the means—is not evaded on the screen. The necessary evil is easily made a lesser one, within the fictional melodramas enacted. But off the screen, where the movies may have their actual outcomes, dispersed through infinities of possible behavior and transmuted by illimitable differences of character, the lesser evil may become the principal one. What gloriously defeated unqualified villainy in the dream may merely drive some sordid motive towards some dubious good, in the real world of imperfect protagonists and ambiguous purposes. It is not vital here to be concerned with establishing the movies as either causing or expressing violence in society. They may do both, of course, in different dimensions of analysis, each with its own order of evidence and proof. All that need be admitted is that the film penetrates and informs our thoughts and habits after we leave the theatres, to emphasize the importance of the way in which the issue of ends and means is raised on the screen. And we may appreciate the more what Hayes and Wyler have done in *The Desperate Hours* — despite the foregone machine-gunning at the close — to evoke recognition of the real perplexity of the matter, and to state it with force and clarity.

For the argument from the necessity for screen violence to hold water, it must be made clear — not only logically, within the story, but empathically, in those committed vicariously within the film's drama — that violence is no better than an expedient. When it becomes, by design or indirection, an occasion for empathic satisfaction, it is revealed as an end in itself — and no amount of "industry statesmanship" or press-agent's casuistry can argue the implications away. That violence may be a necessary resort in our lives is not at issue here, but its representation on the screen. Once this is recognized, the frequent confusion of violence with the requirements of "realism" can be clarified. Men do kill and beat each other with bestial ferocity, outside the theatres, everywhere. But actual violence is rarely dramatic, at first hand. Even in war, after the parades are marched, the filthy, day-to-day business of soldiering begins, and glory is something in the press dispatches: something to color memories, formed in images of plays and pageants. On the screen, what is called "realistic" violence is quite stylized, in one mode or another, in order for us to view it as having dramatic meaning. When this formal structure is absent, what we see appears as senseless, sordid, and tragically trivial as the Brownian movements of mobs in newsreels, erratically rushing here or there in some cause or other, without character or plot, and with a topical significance that has to be explained to us by the narrator, for mobs are all alike, and their passionate importances ephemeral. The newsreel images are "realistic," to be sure, but undramatic without the super-imposition of headlines, narrated captions — or the format of the newsreel itself, designed to equate breathlessly the minute and the momentous, while snatches of nondescript, manufactured music assign the proper emotional tenor to each sequence.

The "necessity" for film violence — as for any other filmic element — is established by film form, as it is recreated in each instance. And each instance, according to the purposes of its makers, will determine the style — "realistic," "romantic," or even "fantastic" — in which the violence is depicted. To argue the necessity for screen violence except in terms of dramatic intentionality is fallacious; the most frequent argument from the requirements of "realism" is usually meretricious. How much violence there is in a film, and the force of its emotional battery, is a matter of intention — hence of control, incarnation, artistry. Screen violence is *created,* and we may speak properly of there being too much of it, as if film makers can do something about its quantity and quality — not only without sacrificing their artistic and moral responsibilities, but in order to fulfill them.

The climactic moment of *The Desperate Hours* is a critical point in the course of film entertainment during the past ten years. Again, the audience, personifying society, decency, has been implicated in a desperate situation, and has had to concur in desperate measures. But at the moment of intentional nudity, it is made responsible for its acts, rather than provided with heroic surrogates. Hayes and Wyler achieve razor-sharpness of empathic focus, and the audience makes its choice — not only as it does, ineluctably; but as it must, desperately.

The Puzzling Movies: Their Appeal

NORMAN N. HOLLAND

Late in 1958, Janus Films released on a largely unsuspecting American public Bergman's *The Seventh Seal* and so started a flood in the art theaters of what seems to be a new genre in film, "the puzzling movie": *Hiroshima, Mon Amour, La Dolce Vita, Les Amants, Les Cousins, The Magician, L'Avventura* — to name but a few of these films, most of which almost dazzle with their richness, their sheer filmic excellence. As a genre, they represent perhaps the only sustained group of films after the advent of sound to be truly and overwhelmingly visual: these films look good like a cinema should.

Arthur Schlesinger, Jr., has recently suggested they are creating a new "Movie Generation" to replace those of us who grew up, cinematically, on the popcorn and cheesecake Hollywood classics of the thirties.[1] Another reviewer calls these films the "undergraduate movies," and there is much truth in the adjective, if we extend it to include not only the four-year kind, but also the perpetual undergraduates on the other side of the lectern. These are indeed films that make their chief appeal to the academic and the intellectual.

But why do they appeal to anybody? If you stand outside an art theater as the audience comes out from a "puzzling movie," you will hear over and over again in a variety of phrasings and degrees of profanity, "What was *that* all

From *The Journal of the Society of Cinematologists,* Vol. III (1963), pp. 17-28. Reprinted by permission of the author and *The Journal of the Society of Cinematologists.*
[1]Arthur Schlesinger, Jr., "When the Movies Really Counted," *Show,* III (No. 4, April, 1963), 125.

about?" As a local joke has it, one Harvard undergraduate to another, "Have you seen *Last Year at Marienbad*?" The other, slowly, thoughtfully, "I — don't know." The feeling these films almost invariably leave us with is, "It means something, but just what I don't know," and the question I am asking is, Why should that feeling of puzzlement give us pleasure.

It doesn't, of course, to everyone. Popular as these films may be among intellectuals and academics, there are plenty of people who find them simply boring. At a somewhat more sophisticated level (I am thinking of the usual reviewer for the daily paper), we hear two kinds of complaint. First, these films make just one more statement of the moral and social confusion of the century. Second, we are likely to find a sexual indignation, for these films are rather strikingly casual about such matters. There were, for example, the two proper Bostonian ladies who went to see *The Virgin Spring*. During that appalling rape scene, one leaned over to the other and whispered, "You know, in Sweden, things are like that." And, in fact, sex in these films does tend to be either rape or mere amusement, a kind of bedroom Olympics in which neither the Russians nor the Americans stand a chance — only Common Market countries.

Sex and *mal de siècle,* certainly these films have them in abundance, but the quality that still stands out is the puzzlement they create. Contrast a film-maker like Eisenstein. He uses montage, symbolism, and the rest not very differently from the way the makers of the puzzling movies do, but Eisenstein aims to communicate his socialist and Marxist message; his symbols serve that end. The maker of the puzzling movie, on the other hand, as much as hangs out a sign that says, "Figure it out — if you can." His symbols serve not so much to communicate as to suggest or even to mystify. (Think, for example, of the devilfish at the end of *La Dolce Vita* and all the different interpretations of it.) Yet, despite the intentional mystification, we take pleasure in them just the same — these films are puzzling in more than one sense.

In particular, there are two ways they puzzle us. They puzzle us as to their meaning in a total sense. They puzzle us scene-by-scene simply as to what is going on in a narrative or dramatic way. Let me consider, first, our puzzlement as to meaning — Why should these films, that seem almost to hide their own meaning, please us?

To answer that question, it helps to take a detour by way of the joke, an humble, but useful route through aesthetic problems, for the joke will serve as a model or prototype for more respectable literature. Jokes, for example, cartoons, limericks, all have a "frame," as serious literature does, and the frame leads us into an attitude of playful attention, a special combination of involvement and distancing, the aesthetic stance, just as the appearance of a poem on the page does or entering a theater to see a film. Jokes present us with the problem of form in a more acute way than even poetry does: no form, no joke, but clearly form alone is not what makes a joke funny. Jokes have content, that is, rational thought, social and moral purpose, but, clearly, editorial content is not what makes a joke funny, either. Rather, jokes get their response from some complex interaction of form and content, as, no doubt, the puzzling movies do.

In particular, jokes often have the same riddling quality as, say, a film by Antonioni. We have to solve some little problem before we "get" the joke—for example, the old saying, "A wife is like an umbrella—sooner or later one has to take a taxi." The riddling form of the joke does two things. First, it draws and holds our attention to the joke. In the case of the puzzling movie, it draws and holds our attention to the film. Second, the riddling form binds our processes of intellection, creating a state of tension or damming up. The riddling form busies us with solving the riddle and so enables less relevant, less presentable thoughts prompted by the joke to sneak up on us, to take us unawares, as it were. So with the puzzling film: its enigmatic promise of "meaning" not only draws and holds our attention to the film; it also distracts us from the real source of our pleasure in the film, the thoughts and desires it evokes.

This, modern psychology tells us, is the real function of form in art. The neo-classic critics used to say form justifies content. A modern psychological critic would say, intellectual content justifies form, and then form justifies emotional content. That is, in the case of the joke, its promise that there will be an intellectual meaning, a "point," enables us to relax and enjoy a playing with words and ideas that we would ordinarily dismiss as childish or insane: intellectual content justifies form. At the same time, the play with words and ideas acts as an additional and preliminary source of pleasure. The pleasure in this play unbalances the usual equilibrium between our tabooed impulses and our defenses, and it provides the extra to topple those defenses—we laugh. In other words, the point (or intellectual content) of the joke justifies the form; then the pleasure we take in form allows another kind of content to break through, and we gratify some sexual or aggressive impulse we would ordinarily hold in check.

The same process seems to operate with the puzzling movie. The feeling we have is: "This means something, but I don't know what." "This means something," the first part of our reaction, acts like intellectual content in the joke—it justifies form; it bribes our reason to accept the incoherent stream of images or the incoherent narrative of the puzzling movie. Then, our pleasure in those images, the sheer visual beauty of the films in this genre, acts like form: it allows us to enjoy the forbidden content of the film.

But what is this forbidden content? In the joke-situation, we can usually identify the hidden impulse of hostility or obscenity that the joke works with. The content of the puzzling movie is not so easy to get at.

We can get a clue, though, from the adverse reactions to the films. Those reviewers and audiences for whom the puzzling quality doesn't work complain of two things: the casual attitude toward sex; the feeling that the films express in a peculiarly negative way the moral confusion of the age. For the disappointed critics of these films, the form didn't work, and the fantasies prompted by the film came through raw and repulsive: sexual promiscuity and a fear of moral confusion.

The sexual angle is the easier to see. These films are extraordinarily free about such matters — I am thinking of such scenes as Jeanne Moreau's taking a bath in *Les Amants* and *La Notte;* the striptease in *La Dolce Vita;* the scenes of lovemaking in *Hiroshima;* rape in *The Virgin Spring, Through a Glass Darkly,* or *Marienbad.* In effect, the puzzling quality of the films gives us an intellectual justification for gratifying the simplest of visual desires, looking at sexy things. This, I hasten to add, is a crude, first-order effect, but nevertheless a very important part of the appeal of even these very sophisticated and intellectual films. Or, for that matter, their lack of appeal — read Bosley Crowther.

In effect, the puzzling movies are an intellectual's version of the old DeMille Bible epic, where we gratify our sexual desires by watching the wicked Assyrians, Philistines, Romans, or whomever carry on their grand pagan orgies, but we are justified by the ponderously moral content of the film. The Biblical frame allows us to gratify almost shamelessly the seventh and least of the sinful impulses. I say, "us," but no doubt I do you an injustice: no proper intellectual would be fooled by the crudity of the moral sop in the DeMille biblio-epic, and this is not the kind of form the puzzling movie gives us. The puzzling movie presents itself as an intellectual and aesthetic problem rather than a moral one, and then perhaps it does fool the intellectual in the same amiable way that jokes and works of art do: the puzzling movie engages his intellectual attention and lets the dark underside of the self (which even intellectuals have) gratify its chthonic wishes.

We can see the process *in statu nascendi,* as it were, in Leslie Fiedler's remarkable review of a "nudie" movie, *The Immoral Mr. Teas.*[2] Mr. Fiedler, I presume, has reached the end of his own innocence and knows what he is doing. Even so, he looks at this film and finds in it "ambiguity," "irreality," "a world of noncontact and noncommunication." He treats this jolly and ribald movie as an index to the American national character, illustrates from it American attitudes toward the body, and (most strikingly) contrasts the nudity in *The Immoral Mr. Teas* with the more humane nudity in *Room at the Top* and *Hiroshima, Mon Amour.* In other words, Mr. Fiedler's astute analysis has erected such an intellectual "meaning" for this film (though it is scarcely above the level of a stag movie) that any self-respecting intellectual could go see it with a clear conscience and a blithe spirit — of analysis. Mr. Fiedler does it with criticism; the puzzling film-maker does it with his camera; but, in either case, the intellectual promise of "meaning" justifies the simpler and more primitive pleasure.

---

[2]Leslie A. Fiedler, "A Night with Mr. Teas," *Show,* I (No. 1, October, 1961), 118-119.

Leslie Fiedler treats *The Immoral Mr. Teas* in intellectual and aesthetic terms, whereas the "meaning" that justified the content of the Biblical epic was its religious and moral "message." This shift from moral message to intellectual "meaning" is itself a source of pleasure in the puzzling movie, particularly for the intellectuals to whom the puzzling movie makes its chief appeal. After all, moral and religious issues have a strong and perhaps frightening emotional overtone. Aesthetic and intellectual "meaning" seems much more manageable. The notion that the moral confusions of this most trying of centuries can be shifted over to the very kind of aesthetic and intellectual puzzle that highbrows are adept at is itself a very comforting hope indeed. And again, confirmation of this source of pleasure comes from those in the audience who find no pleasure in this displacement: the films clearly deal with moral problems, but for those in the audience who cannot accept their translation of moral issues into intellectual ones, the puzzling movies seem merely to express moral problems without answering them, and these critics say the films just prove the sickness of the century.

So far, then, we have found three sources of pleasure in the way these films puzzle us as to meaning. First, we feel that somehow this film "means something," and that promise of content, a "point," enables us to take pleasure in the seemingly incoherent and puzzling visual form of the film. That preliminary visual pleasure in form combines with a less acceptable source of visual pleasure in content: peeping at some very erotic scenes. The combination of these pleasures from form and from content unbalance and override our usual inhibitions. At the same time, these films displace moral and social inhibition into aesthetic and intellectual demands for "meaning," something that intellectuals at least find much easier to resolve, and the puzzling quality so provides still a third source of pleasure.

This kind of economic analysis, however, seems highly abstract. Somehow, we are missing some of the essential quality of these films. Let's see if we can get closer by looking at the second source of puzzlement: not now as to total "meaning," but scene by scene, the simple narrative riddle of, What's going on?

I have suggested that one of the brute, root sources of pleasure in these films is simply that of looking at sexual scenes. Yet sex in these films has a peculiar and special quality. I mentioned Jeanne Moreau's bath scenes in *Les Amants* and *La Notte*—the first occurs in the context of a casual affair; in the second, her husband is simply bored by the sight. Similarly, the husband is bored by Romy Schneider's long and lovely bath scene in the Visconti episode of *Boccaccio 70,* a visual feast but an emotional fast. The striptease in *La Dolce Vita* and virtually all the sex in that film is without any emotion but simple desire. Again, there is simply lust or hate in the rape scenes of *The Virgin Spring* or *Rocco and his Brothers*. The same quality shows in those seductions tantamount to rapes by the heroine of *Through a Glass Darkly* and by the nymphomaniac at the hospital in *La Notte*. The opening love scenes of

Hiroshima, Mon Amour set out another casual love affair; the woman's voice drones on the sound track throughout the sequence much as the narrator's voice drones on in *Marienbad* debating with himself whether he took the woman by force or not. *The Seventh Seal,* perhaps the finest film in the genre, seems to vary this emotionless pattern, but not really: Bergman isolates sex *cum* love in the juggler and his wife, those who escape Death; while the knight and his wife, the squire and his girl rescued from rape, the blacksmith's wife seduced by the actor, they all show the same dogged lovelessness which seems to be the distinctive feature of human relationships in the puzzling movie.

This emotionlessness does not confine itself to sexuality, either. Think, for example, of the cryptic face of Max von Sydow in *The Seventh Seal* or Monica Vitti's classical mask in the Antonioni trilogy. These films are cryptic on the simple level of, What's he thinking? What's he feeling? The suicide of Steiner in *La Dolce Vita* reveals some underlying emotional reality his aesthetic and intellectual life had screened, but what? The disappearance of Anna in *L'Avventura,* her earlier cry of "Sharks!" in the swimming sequence — these tell us something about her inner life, but what? The long, circling walk of the lovers in the last third of *Hiroshima, Mon Amour,* the fashion-plate style of *Marienbad,* the disguises in *The Magician,* all show us cryptic outward actions as a substitute for inner emotions not revealed.

All through the puzzling movies, in other words, we are seeing events without understanding their meaning, particularly their emotional meaning. We are simply not permitted to become fully aware of what is going on emotionally. This sensation, though, is not by any means a new one, special to the puzzling movies. In fact, these films duplicate an experience we have all had, one which was at one time irritating, even frightening, a constant reminder of our own helplessness in the face of forces much bigger than we. I am thinking of the child's situation, surrounded by a whole range of adult emotions and experiences he cannot understand. "What's that man doing, Mommy?" is a not inappropriate comment on the whole genre of "puzzling movies."

Typically, the child does not even have the words with which to grasp these adult emotions and experiences, a circumstance these films duplicate by happenstance. That is, they are all foreign-language films which put us again in a position where the big people, the ones we see on the screen, have all kinds of complex experiences which they speak about in a language we cannot understand (at least those of us who bestowed our time in fencing, dancing, and bear-baiting instead of the tongues). Even for those who spent some time with the tongues, these films make us regress, grow backward, into children a second way by their intentionally visual and filmic quality. They take us back to the picture-language of the comic strip, of children, and of dreams.

There is still a third way these films take us back to the child's frame of mind: in sexuality. The child's dim awareness of adult sexuality very much resembles the sexuality of the puzzling movies. He can see or, more usually, imagine the physical act, but he cannot feel the whole range of complex emotions and experiences the adult knows as love. Rather, the child understands the act of sex as something associated with violence and danger, as we see it, for example, in *The Virgin Spring, Rocco and his Brothers, La Dolce Vita, Hiroshima, Mon Amour, Last Year at Marienbad, Les Cousins,* and the rest. The child is aroused at his sexual fantasies and a bit afraid at his own arousal, as indeed we ourselves tend to be at a puzzling movie. Further, the child's general uncertainty about the adult world finds a focus for itself in his uncertainty, arousal, and fear at this particular area of adult life — sexuality. It serves as a nucleus for his total puzzlement at adult emotions and actions, just as the sexuality in the puzzling movies serves as the nucleus of the total atmosphere of mysterious, baffling emotions and motivations.

In various ways, then, the puzzling quality at the story level of these films takes us back to a childhood situation of puzzlement, but presents it now as an intellectual and aesthetic puzzle rather than an emotional one in real life. "This event obviously says something about the emotional life of these people, but I don't know what, and its only a film anyway." The film puzzles, disturbs, presents us with an emotional riddle, but puts it in an intellectual and aesthetic context. Further, it transforms the emotional puzzle into precisely the kind of puzzle that an "undergraduate" audience might feel it could solve, an intellectual and aesthetic puzzle, instead of an emotional one. In other words, not only do these films take us back to childhood disturbances; they seem to say we can master those disturbances by the strategies of our adult selves, our ability to solve aesthetic and intellectual puzzles.

The puzzling movies hold out to their intellectual audiences the possibility of mastering childish puzzlement by the defenses of the adult intellectual. For example, most intellectuals have a good deal of curiosity. The reason psychologists offer is that their early attempts to solve the puzzles of childhood became a way of life. In technical jargon, infantile curiosity became sublimated into the intellectual and aesthetic curiosity of the adult. Now the puzzling movie comes along and enables us to do or think we can do just what our life-style has been wanting to do all along: solve the riddle of emotions and sexuality by purely intellectual means. Would that we could!

The puzzling movies play into the intellectual's life-style in another way. Academics and intellectuals often present the appearance to other people of "cold fish," the reason being that it is very typical of the highly intellectualized person that he puts up a barrier between sensuous emotional experience and the intellectual problems with which he concerns himself. The puzzling movie enables him to do this again — to put aside the emotional mysteries of the film and see it coldly, in intellectual terms. In short, the puzzling movies, precisely because they are puzzling, take us, as any great work of art does, along the whole spectrum of our development from infancy to adulthood; or, at least, they do for most of their "undergraduate" audience.

There is, though, one special reaction that deserves notice: some critics feel no uncertainty at all—at least on the narrative level. The usual review of an Antonioni film, for example, in a film magazine or a literary quarterly will tell you scene by scene and scowl by scowl what each of the characters is thinking at every given moment.[3] For this kind of person, there is no mystery in the puzzling movie, or, more properly, his careful observation of the film enables him to say that he has seen everything there is to be seen. There is no mystery —he understands the emotional riddle. This response offers a variant but no less pleasurable way of overcoming that residue of childish bafflement in us— instead of shifting it to an adult intellectual problem, the critic simply says it doesn't exist at all: there is no puzzle. I have seen it all and understood it all; there is nothing to be puzzled—or frightened—by. And this procedure is no less satisfying than the other ways the puzzling movie works.

To bring them all together, the puzzling movie turns its puzzling quality into pleasure in two large areas. First, it presents itself as an aesthetic mystery: What does it "mean"? As in a joke, the oblique promise of a "point" enables us to relax our demand for coherence and take pleasure in the incoherent visual form of the film. Then, that visual form lets us take pleasure in the sexual content and, at the same time, shifts any moral qualms we might have to intellectual and aesthetic qualms. Second, the puzzling movie presents us with a mystery on a simple narrative or dramatic level: What's going on? This second kind of mystery duplicates a child's feeling of bafflement at the adult world around him, but translates that pre-verbal emotional bafflement into an aesthetic mystery that a sophisticated, intellectual audience, no longer children, can feel confident about solving.

There is a lesson here about movies in general, for all movies take us back to childhood. They give us a child's pleasure in looking at things, which we, as film critics, respond to in our demand that the film be true to its medium, that it be visual. Similarly, the film takes us back to a pre-verbal stage of development; and, again, as critics, we demand that the picture make its point, not through words on the soundtrack, but through pictures. Most important, however, there is that certain feeling people have, that looking at a film is somehow "passive." In fact, of course, the film involves no more passivity than reading a novel or watching a play, and yet there is something akin to passivity in the cinematic transaction.

Wolfenstein and Leites, in their classic study of the psychology of the movie audience, find part of that sensation of passivity in the audience's "peering with impunity" at the big people on the screen:

---

[3]See, for example, Joseph Bennett, "The Essences of Being," *Hudson Review*, XIV (1961), 432-436, on *L'Avventura;* or, in general, Ian Cameron, "Michaelangeo Antonioni," *Film Quarterly*, XVI (No. 1, Fall, 1962, Special Issue), 1-58, particularly 37-58.

What novels could tell, movies can show. Walls drop away before the advancing camera. No character need disappear by going off-stage. The face of the heroine and the kiss of lovers are magnified for close inspection. The primal situation of excited and terrified looking, that of the child trying to see what happens at night, is re-created in the theater; the related wish to see everything is more nearly granted by the movies than by the stage. The movie audience is moreover insured against reaction or reproof from those whom they watch because the actors are incapable of seeing them. The onlooker becomes invisible.[4]

The actors, in short, can't fight back, and that is one way the film seems a "passive" medium.

The other side of the coin is that we can't provoke the actor. Unlike the stage situation where the length of our laughter, the solemnity of our listening will affect the actor's performance; unlike the television situation where we can turn the box off, get up for a beer or whatnot, we have no such effect on the film which grinds away its twenty-four pictures a second as relentlessly as Niagara Falls. We are powerless, as we were when we were children, to change the doings of the "big people." Now, though, we are immune; the giants on the screen cannot affect us, either. Our regression is safe, secure, and highly pleasurable.

This regression to the safe but powerless child, it seems to me, is the reason people feel watching a film is somehow "passive": the big people cannot act on us; we cannot act on them. This regression, of course, is a key source of pleasure not only in the puzzling movies, but in all films, and especially those which, like the puzzling movies, make their appeal visually, that is, those in which the pre-verbal element of the film is especially strong.

In fact, we could define filmic achievement in terms of what it does with this visual, pre-verbal element in the situation of safe helplessness induced by the motion-picture situation. In the case of silent comedy, the action on the screen says to us, in effect, "This mysterious pre-verbal world of violence and disaster is really harmless—it's all right." Eisenstein's films and others of the montage school say, "This mysterious pre-verbal world you see is meaningful. You understand it, and you respond to it emotionally and morally." The puzzling movie says to us, "This mysterious pre-verbal world you see, though you don't understand it, still, it can be solved." The puzzling film pleases us because it is, in the last analysis, as all art is, a comfort.

---

[4]Martha Wolfenstein and Nathan Leites, *Movies: A Psychological Study* (Glencoe, Ill.: Free Press, 1950), p. 289.

"The Family of Man"

MARTIN S. DWORKIN

No exhibition of photographs has received the interest and acclaim accorded *The Family of Man,* conceived and created by Edward Steichen — himself one of the greatest photographers — with the assistance of Wayne Miller. At New York's Museum of Modern Art, where Steichen is director of the department of photography, the exhibition attracted more than a quarter of a million visitors during its three-month stay early in 1955. The response grew enormously on its tour of the United States of America. In Minneapolis, Dallas, Cleveland, Philadelphia, Baltimore, and Pittsburgh, larger crowds than had ever attended museum exhibitions were counted. As the full-size edition continued traveling during 1957 and 1958, to Los Angeles, San Francisco, Toronto (Canada), and other cities, several smaller versions were also circulated, reaching unnumbered people who thereby had their first experience of formally presented art.

In Europe and Asia, *The Family of Man,* presented under the auspices of the United States Information Agency, impressed new multitudes — both as the

From *Fundamental and Adult Education* (UNESCO), Vol. X, No. 4 (1958), pp. 177-80. Based on an article published originally in *The Progressive* magazine, Vol. XIX, No. 9 (August 1955), pp. 25-26. This article has also been published in *International Education: A Documentary History,* David G. Scanlon, (ed.) (New York: Bureau of Publications, Teachers College, Columbia University, 1960), pp. 191-96. Reprinted by permission of the author.

most ambitious use of photographs hitherto attempted, and by its theme of the inherent community of mankind. In addition to first-hand impact upon viewers, the exhibition has exerted incalculable influence in publications throughout the world, which carried accounts and commentaries, often considerably illustrated. A book containing all the pictures and thematic texts has, in fact, become one of the most successful illustrated volumes ever published.

That a collection of photographs could excite such a response has been judged an absolute proof of the vitality of photography as a medium of artistic expression and communication. Some critics and photographers have been dubious about the theme or organic concept—as well as about Steichen's selection of photographs and way of ordering them into a unitary whole. But *The Family of Man* has been nothing if not popular. The public apparently understands the concept, and likes it, while enjoying the experience of looking at a large number of photographs carefully arranged in a museum or exhibition hall.

In fact, the greatest importance of *The Family of Man* lies in this understanding, or successful communication of ideas—evidence of the coming to maturity of a language and the refinement of means of using it. Nobody is puzzled about the theme, and no critic complains about recondite meanings. If Steichen's philosophy of man is essentially fuzzy, and the show relentlessly sentimental in consequence, this is all eminently clear. What is not understood is *why* it is all so clear. The space of museums has been used to present 503 photographs from 68 countries, organized deliberately to convey a particular message—and it has worked. If this seems unremarkable, it is only because we have learned so much so well—albeit in a time so amazingly short that people still young may recall its beginning.

Steichen has been the leader in experimenting with the form of the photographic exhibition as a vehicle for ideas. His earlier shows: *In and Out of Focus, The Exact Instant,* and particularly *The Korean War,* pictorially illuminated specific themes. *The Family of Man* articulates a generalized philosophy. The photographs are arranged in groups, and presented around lyrical epigrams or proverbs out of many cultures: Homer, Lao-tze, Shakespeare, Deuteronomy, Einstein, Montaigne, the Kwakiutl Indians, James Joyce, Genesis, the Pueblos, the Bhagavad-Gita, the Charter of the United Nations. The prevailing temper is joyous, rhapsodic—represented by Eugene Harris's repeated *leitmotiv* picture of a happy Andean piper boy. Each group subtheme advances the observer along the general argument of the exhibition, expressed in a prologue by Carl Sandburg—who is by happy co-incidence Steichen's brother-in-law. Man, it is declared, belongs to a single family, whatever his culture, or colour, or nation, or variety of circumstance.

The pictures take this up at once. Man everywhere is equally naked in nature —symbolized by Wynn Bullock's striking photograph of a nude child asleep in a forest glade, embedded in new leaves and surrounded by primeval ferns. Man loves, he weds, he begets children, tenderly treated — who grow, and play, and show those fears and angers that presage adult conflicts. He works, and his labour in the earth nourishes him; he sings and dances, laughs and celebrates, studies and ponders, courts and converses, dies and mourns and marks his passing. But life flows on, and there is agony, hunger, misery — and dreams of hope, humility, and reverence for deity.

People are fundamentally good and kind; but they struggle, they need justice from themselves, the mutual concern of self-government. For a soldier's corpse in a blasted earth, there is Sophocles's question, 'Who is the slayer, who the victim? Speak.' And to answer, there are only people, everywhere, forming their multitudes, singly, so different and alike. The United Nations Assembly represents their hope organized; the atomic cataclysm the potentiality of obliteration, futility. At the end again are the children, playing: embodiments of a new world, as in W. Eugene Smith's classic photograph of a little boy and girl walking hand in hand through woods into sunlight.

This 'text' is given almost wholly in pictures alone. The thematic epigrams are strophic guides, marking the stanzas. Such deliberate use of pictures is no longer novel; this is precisely the point to be noted. The achievement of *The Family of Man* lies in its linguistic sophistication, rather than origination. Not long ago, the exhibition would have been generally abstruse — or even unintelligible — for most of the people who comprehend it immediately today. Its use of photographs, and of a museum's space to present them, follows and pre-requires an expanding familiarity with the terms and grammar of a complex pictorial language — itself one of the unique developments in communication of our century.

The first element of this language is photography, whose images of the world have become part of everyday vision in the past hundred years. But its visual syntax has developed only in a generation or two — looking back from the picture magazines, *Life, Look,* and their myriad counterparts everywhere, which revolutionized journalism in the 1930's; to the upheaval in spatial design that stirred a little more than sixty years ago, and produced a new painting, sculpture, architecture — and a new format for presenting words and pictures, the modern magazine page-spread; to that organic element that imparts more than unitary meanings to the pictures when they are grouped together: *montage,* that was learned from the motion picture.

The Family of Man, in fact, is the most spectacular demonstration in recent years of the influence of the cinema in the visual arts. The photographs are not exhibited in the old, salon manner of the pictorialists, derived from ways of looking at paintings — each separately framed and contained, in form as well as content. They were selected and ordered to create a picture story — much as picture stories are synthesized in magazines and books. Each section, in its own room or part of the museum display, corresponds to a 'spread' in a picture magazine — and, especially, to a sequence in a film, with the vital filmic element of time suggested by a pictorial rhythm that is analogous to the rhythm created in editing a motion picture.

The eye leaps from one photograph to the next — not haphazardly, but by design. The mind associates its images — not in any accidental pattern of fragments, but in a *gestalt* or configuration, or form-relationship, that was deliberately intended, and deliberately created by careful choice and discard, juxtaposition and emphatic isolation. If we had not learned, since we were children, to follow the montage or combination of separate shots in a movie, we would be unable to 'read' the picture story — in a museum display, or in magazines and newspapers, or even in comic strips, which are so filmic as to resemble the story boards or visual synopses used in the production of motion pictures.

The eye moves around the typical magazine story-spread according to the design in which the pictures have been arranged — and this layout is the practical application of principles that were developed during modern artists' exploration of relations in two- and three-dimensional space. We may regard the abstractions of the *De Stijl* movement — exemplified by van Doesburg, Huszár, and most famously, Piet Mondrian — as Western sophistications of the linear simplicities of Japanese graphic design and architecture. But they have had profound practical consequences — as in providing the formal idiom wherein to arrange the structural elements of steel and glass, in Lever House or the United Nations; or the discipline whereby the eye may travel over the precisely mapped routes of advertising display — or, reading a magazine story, from pictures to text, or from pictures to pictures, in an exact, orderly manner.

The Family of Man exhibition was designed to reapply this discipline to three-dimensional space. As Paul Rudolph has created the basic installation, the viewer is directed to walk and see in a way quite similar to that whereby the eye moves over a picture magazine or book. But the design of a picture story, whether on paper or on walls or partitions in a museum, serves only to provide direction for the appreciation of content. And the modern language of photographs, that has become one of the great tongues of the earth, depends upon a grammar which we had to master first in order to comprehend the movies. It is a language in whose terms we may formulate our knowledge of the world, and speak of it to others. It has orders of coherence, and requires a discipline for determining clarity and evaluating meaning. It does not simply reproduce reality, in an exact likeness, but recreates it according to a continually elaborating iconography.

The pioneer director, D. W. Griffith, who made *Birth of a Nation* and *Intolerance,* originating most of the essential elements of cinematic form, once remarked, 'The moving picture, although a growth of only a few years, is boundless in its scope and endless in its possibilities. . . . The task I'm trying to achieve is above all to make you see.' How much we have learned to see in the way of the cinema, albeit far from the theatres and their quickening screens, may be the deepest meaning of Steichen's *The Family of Man*.

The Vanishing Diary of Anne Frank

MARTIN S. DWORKIN

Men of my unit went into two of those places the Nazis had efficiently called 'concentration camps,' but for which there are other names: Buchenwald, near Weimar, and Ohrdruf, near Gotha. What struck the mind, and remained, was the unbelievable. The greater the horror, the more it was necessary to select details to make the whole have some reality. At Buchenwald, amid the fantastic complex of gas chambers and furnaces, the great sheds filled with human debris piled to the roofs, what seemed to affect the men most of all were some strange decorative plaques. A day or so afterwards, when an article in the service newspaper *Stars and Stripes* identified the objects as mounted pieces of tattooed human skin, the reaction was not quite melodramatic revulsion, but a more sudden, self-conscious formation of what had actually been seen. The journalistic account put things into place; the sentences, with their plain words and terse phrases, made the entire experience into something that had happened. One man rushed over to say that the things described in the article were the things he had held in his hands. Now, he knew that his experience had been real, and he knew what it was he had experienced.

At Ohrdruf, some indignant civilians from the neighbourhood were being put

From *Blackfriars* (London), Vol. XLV, No. 523 (January 1964), pp. 22-29. This article was first published in *Quadrant* (Australasian Association For Cultural Freedom, Sydney) Vol. IV, No.1 (Summer 1959-1960), pp. 75-81. Reprinted by permission of the author.

to work digging graves and burying the bodies left untidily about when the camp was hastily abandoned by the guards. There were corpses with blackening gouges in the sides and back. One or two walking cadavers, their filthy rags flapping, explained that some of the starving inmates of the camp were able to eat the livers and other organs of those who died. Then, much as guides denoting sights of interest to passing tourists, they pointed out the ingenious arrangement whereby the furnaces of the crematoria heated the buildings of the commandant's headquarters. On the way out of the camp, one of the soldiers began saying that it all hadn't been real, that what we had just seen was a lot of propaganda. A few of the others in the jolting truck took this up, explaining why they did not choose to remember.

There are subjective limits to fact, as well as objective. The ways of knowing in which we are indoctrinated can alter or overlook occurrences, just as they give them the form in which they are knowable. It takes sensitivity, and sometimes — as any newspaper editor or professor of history can testify — a lot of training, to recognize the significance of the unfamiliar: the 'fantastic,' the 'impossible,' the 'inconceivable.' The very size of the horror the Nazis had perpetrated was difficult to make into a fact, into something that could be known. Millions of people, torn out of civilized living; collected and shipped like cattle; their bodies duly numbered and tattooed; marched in dehumanized gangs to insect labours; penned up and stripped and gassed and burned and powdered and scattered or packaged for fertilizer; their belongings sorted and stacked; the fillings of their teeth dug out of their dead jaws and melted into bullion. By now, we say we know these things. But how can we know them? One person who is bereaved of one beloved does not know how the world goes on. Millions of people. Many of us, of course, do not care. But for those who can care there is the problem of how to know. And it is here that an articulate vision, as in a work of art, can create the conditions of knowing, giving form to the inaccessibly, bewilderingly complex and various realities that must be grasped. It is in this sense, of the problem of bringing all who can care to the state of personal bereavement, that we must read and judge the diary of Anne Frank, and consider its dramatizations on stage and screen.

The existence of this book, that it was written and that it was preserved, is itself a fantastic event. There is no exact way of measuring its effect; we can only cite its translation in twenty-one languages, its distribution in ninety-five countries — figures comparable today only to those tabulating the successes of diligently popularized trivia. The statistics alone say nothing of the meaning of the book as an experience to the millions upon millions of separate readers. Only in some grandly indefinite way can we speak of how this journal of one single young girl may affect the individuals who read it; of how it has come to incarnate the anguish of the shadowy, uncountable myriads of separate persons who were unspeakably degraded, tortured, and obliterated. And this indeterminacy is carried into the dramatized versions, with their inevitable transformations of the images the book evokes in each private, unique reading.

The problem of the play and film goes deeper than that easily laboured old difficulty of whether it is possible to transcribe a book to stage or screen without ruining or cheapening its qualities. We may grant that each dramatization is a separate work, requiring judgment on its own merits first of all, with reference to its source secondary, albeit necessary. But each transcription, however excellent, must also be seen in that dreadful light of memory which is a kind of nimbus about the book. In that light, the original diary itself can appear incredible — too good to be what it is, too perfectly appropriate to have been left to a miraculous chain of chances: to be written in precisely this, exquisitely artless way; to remain intact in a pile of rubbish, while libraries and the records of centuries were lost; to be rediscovered in time to become a monument. A triumph of the book is that it has the grandeur to stand alone and undeniable as a work out of the enormity of what happened. In the light of actuality, and of its own unparalleled quality, all doubts and cavils about its authenticity are irrelevant.

But they return in considering the dramatizations — not any dramatizations, on principle, but these particular ones, on their merits. Not that the play and the film are not skillful, absorbing, eloquent in theme and execution in a drama and cinema pervaded by shrill irresponsibility and slick inconsequence. From its opening late in 1955, the play, by Frances Goodrich and Albert Hackett, has won a reception perhaps unique in theatrical history. Audiences in more than thirty countries have approached it with a deference, and even reverence, rarely accorded any kind of play-acting, no matter how serious. The film produced and directed by George Stevens from the screen play by Goodrich and Hackett, is likely to enjoy a wider response. In fact, it may be expected to heighten the intimacy of participation for many, according to the unique, quintessential nature of the movies as vicarious experience.

But it is in this intimacy, in this skillfully-engendered exercise of identification, that the film, following the play, perpetrates a fundamental falsity — that is not simply untrue to the spirit of the book, but projects back upon it unreasonable, ungrounded dubieties. Out of what must be seen as a carefully considered effort to universalize the imagination of a particular young girl, there emerges a picture of an imagination that is recognizable because it is all too familiar. The particular Jewish girl, born in Germany and raised in Holland, deeply, if still youthfully educated in the European literary tradition, with the meaning of her Jewishness vivid in every instant of her life, emerges as an apotheosized, yet theatrically conventional adolescent. The person of the play and film is knowable, but not in any way ambiguous, as is the author of the book. As a dramatized cliché, she may induce an illusion of recognition. But the very ease with which the audience is enabled to know her every mood and manner measures the mystery that is evaded — and enters a new doubt that so carefully commonplace a character could have created so richly individual a work, that has become the torch to light up the faces of all the unknown dead in the dark spaces of our hearts.

It is not simply a matter of performance, but of conception. The authors of the play and film were confronted by an enormous technical difficulty. The book consists entirely of the impressions of the girl who is the principal of the drama. All the characters are seen through her eyes. Their speech is as she recorded it or recreated it. The book is a diary: subjective, capricious, marked by unexpected divagations and tantalizing brevities, changes of attitude and explorations of new paths of reasoning as a child was growing into puberty. The play and film transpose the viewpoint. The audience no longer sees and hears and feels via the sensibilities of the girl, but observes her as the protagonist of an ordered drama.

In principle, of course, this may be wholly legitimate and even dramaturgically necessary — unless one were to argue the sovereign possibility that the book itself be somehow retained and personified — perhaps as a continuing narration. By whatever device, such retention might preserve and project not only the distinctive imagery, but the asides, the mercurial malices and freshets of sentiment, the passionate dissections of motives and outcomes — determinedly juvenile and yet so consistently astute; and, perhaps most important, the constant, characteristic literary allusions, criticisms, and even quotations.

The book is not something that was written *about* the girl, her family and companions in hiding from the enveloping horror. The book *is* the girl; it is all we have of the girl. And the book, *Anne Frank,* is profoundly, passionately intellectual, emerging from the intellectual and spiritual vitalties of a Jewish family which talked and read and sang together in several languages, wrote poetry in honour of festive occasions, argued about judgments of history and works of art, fought throughout its vigil, in constant fear, discomfort, and privation, to preserve not only its existence and essential virtue, but actually as well as symbolically the entire humane tradition of knowledge and humility, intellect and spirit, laughter and charity.

The book is not the Anne Frank played on stage by Susan Strasberg, and on screen by her much less skilled imitator, Millie Perkins. The girl portrayed is a signally American figure of thoughtless youth. In 1955, one of the few critics who regarded the play unfavourably, Algene Ballif, wrote in *Commentary* that the Anne on stage was 'still another image of that fixed American idea of the adolescent, the central imperative of which is that this species of creature is not to be taken seriously. (Unless, of course, he becomes a delinquent.)' In the Goodrich and Hackett versions of the book, the central poignance has been subtly diluted, in order to give it a familiar soft-drink flavour. The character of Anne is simplified to afford easy recognizability. The situation of the people in the secret hide-away is played out as a melodrama with an implied tragic ending, around a conventionally central love story. In place of the deepening maturity of the girl, as revealed by the diary's always self-critical record of her changing observations, there is a progressive theatricalism carried over to the screen from the stage. If there is any gain in formal coherence and popular comprehension, there is a grievous loss in spiritual complexity — and in fundamental credibility.

The manner of the stress upon melodrama and romance is decisive here, and not any preconception of how a performable work might be constructed from the book. The possibility of alternative dramatizations, in fact, came up in a long and bitter litigation conducted against Kermit Bloomgarden, producer of the play, Anne's father Otto Frank, and others, by Meyer Levin. Levin, author of *The Old Bunch, In Search,* and *Compulsion,* had prepared an adaption of the diary in 1953, with a notable emphasis upon the Jewish character of the story, and an avowed purpose to retain as much of Anne Frank's own language as possible. Levin's charges of 'fraud and deceit' in the disposition of his prior claims to rights to dramatize the diary were not sustained in court. But a jury did award him the more-than-symbolic sum of $50,000 for damages suffered in the inclusion of some of his original material in the version that was produced.

The merits of Levin's dramatization versus that of Goodrich and Hackett are not at issue here. But the evidence in the case of the deliberate shift of emphasis away from the Jewish spirit of the book, and from its particular literary character, is of great significance. Once again, the choice of tactics in popularizing a complex work has effected a qualitative change in the work itself. To persons who may never read the book, the Anne Frank of the play and film may be an adequately moving image: not so brilliantly unique that she could not be any girl in the audience; not so specifically Jewish that she could not be a member of any group that might be suffering some transient persecution. To these people, this Anne Frank may not represent the millions of Jews who were obliterated, as much as the popular image of youth's indictment of the adult world, that perpetually interferes with the romantic fulfilment of adolescent dreams.

It may be another example of the inexorable punctuality of accident, that the book found in the rubbish of a place where a group of Jews had hidden from the Nazis happened to be the diary of a young girl. And it may be that the force of circumstances in our time has truly exacerbated the perennial anguish of youth in worlds it does not make. Of all the Jeremiads ever heard and unheeded, the most poignant and damning may be the cries of the young, the innocents. But there is something symptomatic of the reigning juvenilism of our present popular culture in the way the play and film of the diary of Anne Frank transform its existence and meaning.

On stage, under Garson Kanin's direction, the melodrama and the romance were thematically dominant, but the theatrical distance from the setting and characters offered the possibility of perspective. From this distance, for example, it appeared that the Goodrich and Hackett dramatization set off the conventionalized adolescence of Anne by magnifying her own idealized image of her father. We may overlook invidious speculations arising during the controversy over the Levin version as to how much the stage Otto Frank had affected the actual Otto Frank in his decision to support the Bloomgarden production. But it must be said that the emergence of the father as so all-wise, all-prudent a figure of force, despite the restraint of Joseph Schildkraut's superb performance, adds more to the melodrama than to the sense of re-created actuality. In one aspect, the power of the father in the play grows in proportion as the power of the book is diluted in the dramatized character of Anne.

On screen, the camera's elimination of distance in the theatre, particularly in the use of close-ups, increases the imbalances of the play's transcription of the book. The least expression on the girl's face is not simply enlarged, but completely fills the enormous CinemaScope frame. Her scenes with the boy, which on stage already exaggerated the delicate, hesitant, and by no means paramount relationship described in the book, on screen become climatic — and misleading. The choice of Miss Perkins for the role of Anne itself says much about the conception of the book to be realized on screen. Her resemblance to the surviving likenesses of Anne is as the movies traditionally would have it: every similar feature distinctly prettier, and in ways quite according to topical, fashion-model modes of beauty. Her inexperience as an actress is treated as an advantage, with her limited but quite exhausting repertoire of lisps, pouts, and other mannerisms made to protest her sincerity in a role requiring from childish tantrum to grown-up introspection. Her age points up one of the ways whereby American movies during the past decade have catered to the self-glorification of adolescent audiences.

It is no accident that consistently places actors and actresses in their twenties and even older in roles of adolescents, but the reflection on screen of fantasied behaviour, making propaganda for actual behaviour in a deadly roundabout. The popular image of the adolescent, moreover, requires performers of greater age and experience for satisfactory dramatic projection and vicarious fulfilment. When this fashionable representation of adolescence is injected into the dramatizations of the diary of Anne Frank, what remains of the book vanishes before our eyes. In its place, we are left with quite another work. The play and film may possess many qualities that are comparatively worthy. But what they make of the heroine can have no more than fictional bearing upon the true tragedy of Anne Frank, the little girl who died, one among millions.

That tragedy had begun to be evaded at the moment it was discovered — and the evasions have persisted, perhaps just because the dreadful evidence proved so much. And the play and the film of the diary of Anne Frank are themselves evasions — although made by dedicated people with excellent intentions, and the courage to be serious at the rites of entertainment. For, the more fully the individuals in the audience are brought to imagine themselves in the place of the heroine, according to the design of the dramatizations, the more truly do they evade real confrontation of the archetypal victim. To only pity the girl, her family and companions in hiding is evasion enough. To be projected into vicarious participation in the particular, formally conventional romance and melodrama, however, leads to the inversion of pity to pity of self: to the purging of guilt, responsibility, and even memory in a catharsis of sweet sadness.

Sadness is not enough. The saddest truth of all is that a vast proportion of those seeing the play and film know little of even the facts of the extermination of six million Jews by the Nazis, and will not be led to knowledge in the theatres. The film reviewer of a leading family weekly, that happens to be Catholic in direction, can write a reverent appreciation of the Stevens production of *The Diary of Anne Frank* for the same issue in which a letter is published asserting that there was not one gas chamber in any German concentration camp, and that it is an 'old propaganda myth that millions of Jews were killed by the national socialists.' The letter applauds the opinions of one of the weekly's regular columnists, to the effect that continued concern with the Nazi atrocities is unwarranted defamation of persons of German descent everywhere, and that 'the rehashing of such bitter memories would hardly help . . . (a tourist) . . . enjoy his holiday in Germany.' The story of the little Jewess in the movie will not make Christians of these people, if the sacred drama of that other Jew has not done so by this time.

A CONCLUDING NOTE

The purpose of this volume has been twofold: to highlight the problems and operations of defining, explaining, and evaluating art and to underline the importance of understanding the nature of content and its uses in art instruction. Now content or subject matter, it was suggested in the Preface, consists of important topics and leading ideas under discussion in relevant disciplines of thought and action. Assuming that aesthetics is a relevant discipline from which to derive content, the question once again arises, what are the basic topics of art education? Only a start can be made here in answering this question. But insofar as the selections in this volume are concerned, certain topics recur, albeit in slightly different form depending on a writer's orientation. In particular, the topics of "aesthetic experience," "the work of art," "artistic communication," "artistic intention," "artistic style," "artistic knowledge," "artistic expression," and "artistic form" stand out.

From the point of view of art instruction, perhaps the most important of these are "aesthetic experience" and "the work of art." The reason for saying this is that a theory which asserts propositions about the character and nature of aesthetic experience and the form and style of works of art has also generally decided on the issue of the cognitive status of art and on whether in order to grasp aesthetic meaning it is necessary to have knowledge of artists' intentions.

But if "aesthetic experience" and "the work of art" are the central topics of art instruction, the major task in their analysis and clarification involves investigation and elucidation of the nature of "aesthetic criticism." For whether it is the artist deciding what to do next, the beholder animating the expressive aspects of the artist's product, the critic weighing a work's merit, or the museum director installing an exhibition to best effect, *criticism* is of the essence.

If it is reasonable to hold the foregoing, then the clarification of the patterns or models of aesthetic criticism is the fundamental problem of philosophical analysis in art education, and the cultivation of the special kinds of discipline attending aesthetic criticism in its various contexts defines the distinctive purpose structure of teaching and learning in the arts. From an awareness and acceptance of these assertions a directive for research emerges. Research in art education will be most fruitful and relevant when the aesthetic critical response is studied within the framework of a theory or theories of art and aesthetic experience. And when research turns to aesthetic theory for assistance and guidance, it will encounter problems in definition, explanation, and evaluation. Hopefully, this volume may make coping with these problems less mystifying.

Appendix I
The Criticism of Criticism

THOMAS MUNRO

An Outline for Analysis Applicable to Criticism of Any Art

NOTE: This questionnaire is intended as a checklist of considerations which are often relevant in the analysis and appraisal of a piece of critical writing. It is adapted for use in the preparation of books and courses on aesthetics, the history and theory of criticism, and related fields. While the questions are given in a systematic order, it is not implied that this is necessarily the best order for use in any given case. The nature of the critical work being studied, or of the problem in hand, may suggest a different order as preferable. Nor is it implied that all the questions should be asked in every case, or answered with equal fullness. In each case, certain ones will appear as especially important, while others may be answered briefly or omitted. It is not implied that answers to all these questions will provide the basis for a complete understanding or final evaluation of the critical work. Such a final judgment may never be possible. Many other questions, not here included, may be more important in particular cases. But a careful application of those listed may assist the student in working out a balanced, comprehensive, preliminary study.

From the *College Art Journal,* Vol. VII, No. 2 (Winter 1958), pp. 197-98. Reprinted by permission of the author and the *College Art Journal.*

I. The *piece of criticism* to be analyzed: title or other identification of the text. (E.g., a complete essay or excerpt from longer work, journalistic criticism, general theory, history, biography, advertising, propaganda. Date and place published; conditions and occasions for writing and publishing it.)

II. Its *author;* the *critic* or evaluator. (Significant facts about him and his predispositions; personality, education, special interests and attitudes as elsewhere shown. Social, cultural, intellectual, religious, philosophic background.)

III. *Artist* or artists whose work is criticized. Significant facts: e.g., their date, place, school or style of work; nature of their other works.

IV. *Work or works of art* criticized or evaluated: particular objects or performances; general types or styles of art discussed; periods, traits, specific details.

V. *Main evaluative or affective terms* applied to the text; to what or whom; in what specific ways. (What verdicts, judgments, attitudes, conclusions expressed? Mostly favorable or unfavorable? Extremely or moderately so? Uniformly or with some exceptions? Calmly and objectively or with emotion such as contempt, anger, sarcasm, rapturous or sentimental adulation?).

VI. *Standards* used by the critic or implied in his evaluation; principles, theories of artistic or moral value. His tastes in art and in related matters. Explicitly stated or tacitly assumed? How defended? Criteria of excellence or improvement; reasons for praising or denouncing; concepts of desired or desirable qualities, effects, functions, purposes of this type of art. Rules for good art accepted by the critic. Cultural and ideological background of these standards (social, historical, religious, philosophical, political, etc.).

VII. *Arguments and evidences* given by the critic to show how these standards apply to the present case. Defense of judgments expressed. Authorities invoked. Sources of evidence. References to the work of art itself, indicating how it exemplifies certain qualities regarded as especially good or bad, strong or weak, beautiful or ugly, great or trivial, original or imitative, etc.

VIII. Alleged *effects and consequences* of the work of art or some parts or aspects of it, on those who observe it. What kinds of *immediate experience* or psychological effect does it tend to produce, according to the critic? (E.g., pleasant or unpleasant, interesting or boring, exciting, soothing, amusing, sad, terrifying, stimulating, elevating, depressing). Does it tend (according to the critic) to arouse anger and resentment, religious devotion, pity and sympathy, or some emotional attitude? Some disposition to a certain kind of action or attitude? What *deferred or indirect* effects, as on character, education, morality, religious faith, elevation or debasement of mind, mental health, citizenship, success in life? Are these effects considered important enough to determine the total value of disvalue of the work of art?

IX. On *whom or what kinds of person* is the work of art said to have these effects? (E.g., adults, children, men, women, soldiers, foreigners, invalids?) On people in general, without restriction? Under what *circumstances?* (E.g., in school, church, evening entertainment? In foreign exhibition, performance or translation?)

X. Does the *critic himself* claim to have *experienced* such effects or *observed* them in others? When and how? What evidence does he give for believing them sure or probable in future? How conclusive is this evidence?

XI. General modes of *thinking, feeling and verbal expression* exemplified in the criticism as a whole. How manifested; in what proportion and degree? (E.g., polemic, interpretive, factual, explanatory, judicial, personal, impressionistic, autobiographical, scientific, hedonistic, art-for-art's-sake, moralistic, mystical, propagandistic.)

XII. Special personal *motivations* and *influences* which may have affected the critic's attitude and judgment. (E.g., friendship or enmity toward the artist; extreme prejudices; connection with political, religious, socio-economic, or other groups which might tend to bias judgment; fear of or desire to please powerful authorities.) What evidence exists for this? To what extent, if at all, does it seem to invalidate the criticism?

XIII. *Strong and weak points of the criticism as an evaluation* of the artist or work of art. Do you find it convincing or not? Why? Is it enlightening, informative, helpful in perceiving, understanding, appreciating, or sympathizing with the work of art? Fair or unfair? Logical and adequately documented? Based on adequate personal experience and verifiable knowledge? Vague or clear? Thorough, profound, superficial, trivial, or perfunctory? Strongly individual and subjective or the opposite?

XIV. *Literary or other merits or demerits of the criticism.* (Aside from the question of its correctness as evaluation, or its factual truth as description and interpretation.) Does it read well as a literary composition in its own right? For what qualities? (E.g., of style, imagery, colorful personality, etc.) What faults does it have as literature? Is it poetic, humorous, informative, enlightening? The expression of an attitude one can respect even though disagreeing?

XV. *Summary estimate* of its nature and value. Which of the above questions and answers have been given most weight in reaching this estimate of the critical writing? Why?

Appendix II
A Questionnaire for Picture-Analysis

THOMAS MUNRO

This outline is intended for the use of readers who may wish to analyze pictures for themselves, from the standpoint of form, with more than ordinary care and thoroughness. It consists of a series of questions, to be read through and answered in the presence of any given picture. Its aim is to aid in detailed, systematic observation, through directing the reader's attention to the many different elements which go to make up a complex design. In addition, it aims to help the reader make up his own mind about a picture's merits, through taking up one by one several points on which it can be judged. For a beginner it may be well to answer all or most of the questions in the order given, with about the same degree of care. Later on, he will discover that for different pictures, different questions are most important. He will learn to "size up" a new picture more quickly in a general way, and will alter his plan of analysis to suit. If he sees that color is most important in the work at hand, he will concentrate his attention on the use of color; if line, he will stress that. The analyses given in this book follow no set order, and mention only the qualities that seem most important in each case; to do otherwise would be useless and tedious. But at first the untrained observer is apt to look only for the few qualities in painting with which he is familiar. His main effort should be to keep

From Thomas Munro, *Great Pictures of Europe* (New York: Coward-McCann, Inc., 1930), pp. xxii-xxxii. Reprinted by permission of the author and Coward-McCann.

looking at the same picture from different points of view, to find if possible some important qualities he has been overlooking.

A. First Impressions of the Picture as a Whole

1. What is most striking, interesting or unusual about the picture at first sight? What is most pleasing? Least pleasing? Why?

2. What seems to have been the artist's chief aim or interest in this picture? (E.g., line or color pattern, dramatic narrative, facial expression, religious or other associations.)

3. Is the picture at first sight more interesting for its design or for the subject represented? What, in general, is most noteworthy about each? Does the picture seem to combine and harmonize both of these kinds of appeal?

4. Of what main parts or elements is the design composed? In what general way are they put together? (E.g., three solid figures arranged in a pyramidal group against a flat contrasting background.)

5. What lines, colors, shadows, masses or other elements in design are most conspicuous? Are some of them (e.g., a certain angle, or a certain shade of red) repeated several times, with only slight variation? Are two or more very different colors, shapes of line or other elements contrasted with each other?

B. Line

1. Are the outlines of things conspicuous? Do they stand out as separate, detached strokes of the brush, distinct from areas on both sides of them? Do they appear only as edges or contours of surfaces or objects? Are such contours sharp and clear-cut, or blurred by soft shadows or gradual color blends? Are there wholly isolated lines, which do not serve to mark the limits of any area of light or color?

2. Are the lines rhythmic, full of repeated shapes? Is their general appearance smooth, flowing, graceful, delicate, flexible, undulating, swirling? Is it rough and jagged, stiff, angular, heavy or static? Is it weak, aimless, confused? Different in different places?

3. What particular linear theme, if any, such as a characteristic curve, seems to dominate in the design? Does it dominate through frequent repetition, or through large size, or other emphasis? Where is it repeated? Is it slightly varied in size, shape or direction, or through being embodied in differently lighted or colored objects?

4. What other very different linear theme is there? (E.g., a series of sharp angles as contrasted with a series of flowing curves.) How is this one repeated and varied? Are some lines intermediate in shape between the two, serving as gradual transitions between them? Are there more than two definite themes?

5. Are these themes combined in a single, unified pattern? How? (E.g.,

through being arranged in symmetrical opposition, intertwined in a continuous arabesque, fitted together into a pyramid or circle, or caught up in some general swirling or zig-zag movement.) Does this pattern extend through the whole picture, or is it limited to certain parts? Is it independent of the spots of color, solid objects and other factors, or do these also join in the same arrangement?

6. Are the linear contours of things reproduced from nature with great accuracy? (E.g., bodily proportions, perspective.) In minute, elaborate detail, or with some simplifications and emphasis? With great alteration or distortion?

7. Is the result to bring out some rhythm or pattern? To bring out some distinctive feature of the object represented, as in a caricature, or a portrait that accents some peculiarity of physique or personality? To represent some action or situation more tersely? To express some definite emotion or mood of the artist?

C. Light and Dark

1. Are there distinct light areas and dark areas? Where? Are the light parts concentrated or scattered? The dark?

2. Is there strong contrast between one and the other, from extreme to extreme? Are there only a few definite shades, or many intermediate degrees of lightness and darkness? Are transitions between them sudden, sharp-edged, or soft and gradual?

3. Do the lightest spots when looked at together, or the darkest spots when looked at together, combine to form a pattern? (E.g., do they stand out as indicating parts of a triangle, circle, spiral or some other definite shape?) Do all the different shades combine into one complex pattern?

4. Is there an effect of real illumination, as from the sun or a lamp? Are the light spots of the picture made chiefly by reflected highlights or direct gleams from a source of light? Are the dark spots formed by cast shadows? Partly or entirely in other ways, as by white and black garments, or tree-trunks against snow?

5. Are the shadows soft, velvety, delicate, full of subtle gradations, faint reflections, vaguely suggested shapes and textures? Dense, black, murky, flat and shiny? Are the highlights also subtly graded in intensity, or bare and uniform?

6. Is there an effect of outdoor sunlight, moonlight, lamplight? From one concentrated source? If from more than one, how are the reflections and shadows from them distinguished or blended? Is the light direct, intense, diffused, clear, broken, filtered through leaves, flickering, cloudy, dulled, glaring?

7. Is an effect produced of soft, pervasive atmosphere, luminous glow, or rich surface texture? By subtle light gradations alone, without the aid of color?

Are light transitions closely bound up with those of color, or independent?

8. Is some kind of illumination represented with great accuracy, as it would appear in a real scene? Are lights or shadows intensified, made unnaturally bright or dark? Are shadows omitted, or placed where they could not possibly fall? Made sketchy, rough, fragmentary? Are long streaks of light and shadow used as lines to define contours or directions of movement?

9. Is the result realistic? Is it to bring out some pattern or the shape of some important object? Does the quality of light produce some distinctive emotional tone, such as gloominess, cheerfulness, weirdness, mystery, agitation?

D. Color

1. What is the immediate general effect of the picture's coloring at a distance, without regard to details of pattern or representation? Is it dull, dark, sombre, bleak or bare? Is it vivid, intense, clear, pure, jewel-like? Warm or cool? Crude, violent, barbaric, clashing, glaring? Dingy, muddy, acid, tawdry? Quiet, subdued, soft, delicate? Rich, gorgeous, rainbow-like? Monotonous, confused, tiresome? Do different parts of the picture vary notably in these respects?

2. When a particular small area of color is looked at closely, does it seem monotonously uniform within its own limits? Is it rich, iridescent, shot through with glints of light, subtly varied in tint? Is it built up of various films of paint, the lower showing in places through the upper? Of contrasting small brush-strokes side by side? Of colors partly but not wholly blended? Do different areas vary in these respects? Does it make much difference how far away one stands?

3. What hue or tint is dominant, most important? Because of its brightness? Its wide distribution? Its central or focal position? What color is next in importance? What minor notes of color are there? Are there many different hues?

4. Is each different color enclosed within definite linear boundaries? Strongly contrasted with its neighbors? Do some colors, or all, blend into each other gradually, as if melting and overflowing linear boundaries? Do they blend completely, into one almost uniform surface, or is there a moderate amount of contrast?

5. In regard to each principal hue employed: where is it repeated in separate spots? What variation is there between the spots of a certain color? Where is it made lighter? Darker? More intense? Duller? Where is it mixed a little with another tint? With still a different tint? (E.g., a green which varies here toward blue, there toward yellow, somewhere else toward violet.) Are some areas neutral, intermediate between two principal contrasting hues? Are some intermediate in shade, and in intensity, between the principal color-areas? If not, is the result monotonous? Confused? Clashing?

6. Do the scattered spots of a certain color combine to form a pattern when looked at together? Is this pattern otherwise indicated, as by linear outlines, or does it depend on color alone, so that it would disappear in a photograph? What sort of pattern is it, as to complexity, and method of interrelating parts?

7. Do color repetitions link together parts of the picture that would be otherwise unrelated? Do color contrasts help distinguish parts that would otherwise be vague or confused? Are some parts of the picture unincluded in the main color-pattern?

8. Does the juxtaposition of certain colors seem to affect the quality of each? E.g., when a hand is placed over one area, do its neighbors seem different? Less luminous? More or less agreeable? Do areas which are weak or unpleasant in color, when examined individually, become satisfying when seen as parts of a group? Could individual areas be much altered in color without weakening the effect of unity?

9. Do the colors rise to a climax of richness, intensity or brightness at some point or points? Are there minor as well as major accents and climaxes? Do other colors contrast with them and lead up to them in continuous, orderly progressions?

10. Are there fairly distinct subordinate groups or color-chords, combinations which occur together repeatedly in small areas? How are they related to each other through the picture? How varied? Is the picture built up of distinct sections or panels, each a distinct pattern or texture in itself? (E.g., are some sections of a uniform flat color, others striped, shadowed, flowered, mottled?) Are there repetitions of similar sections?

11. Does color seem to be a superficial, unnecessary addition, laid on after the picture has been basically constructed of lines, lights and darks? How much would the picture lose in black and white?

12. Is color realistic, made to seem an inseparable part of objects, permeating their inner substance, through subtle variations of light and tint? Are the distinctive qualities of different substances brought out clearly? (E.g., a hand as contrasted with stone or wood.) Are certain textures (e.g., metallic, silky, woolly) repeated, varied and contrasted as themes?

13. Are the colors blended into a soft, deep, translucent atmosphere? Is it warm, Venetian, glowing, red-and-gold? Cool, blue, pale, clear, crystalline, fresh, silvery? Dense, hazy, misty, dim? Shimmering, sparkling, glittering? Does the atmosphere serve to unify all parts of the picture? Are certain parts unincluded within it?

14. Are shadows dead, shallow, muddy grays or browns? Richly tinted, but the same in general hue as the highlights? Contrasting in hue? (E.g., rose highlights with olive shadows.) With what effect on realism? General richness of texture? Definite pattern?

15. Is emphasis placed on the surface reflections of sunlight on colored objects? Is broken-color technique used? Is the local, intrinsic color of any

object altered by reflection from other colored surfaces? (E.g., a yellow dress by grass near it.) Is the result realistic? More than naturally brilliant?

16. Does the coloring help express some distinctive mood or emotion? (E.g., gay, martial, funereal, weird, austere, majestic, agitated.) Is this consistent with the rest of the picture? With the usual associations of the subject?

E. Mass

1. Do objects appear to stand out from their backgrounds as solid, three-dimensional masses? In clear-cut, high relief? In low relief? Are they delicate, fragile, lacy? Soft, vaporous, vague, shapeless? Are some or all objects flat? (E.g., silhouettes against a fire.)

2. Do various objects differ much in degree of solidity? Does this help emphasize important objects, or balance weights?

3. Are the various parts of an individual object (e.g., separate garments and limbs) clearly distinct, or do they blend gradually? Do they produce an effect of design through repeating a certain kind of plane, such as triangular folds in a garment?

4. Is the illusion of solidity produced by light and shadow alone? By perspective? By the advancing or receding quality of certain colors?

5. Are the shapes and contours of objects accurately represented? In detail, or with selective emphasis to bring out essentials, such as the basic structure of the body?

6. Are shapes distorted to bring out some pattern? (E.g., by elongating limbs, or exaggerating muscles, to produce a repetition of similar shapes.) Are they flattened, to bring out surface pattern of lines and colors?

7. Are shapes distorted to accent some peculiarity in the thing represented, such as strength, fatness, agility? To express some emotion such as pain, ecstasy or frenzied effort?

F. Space

1. Do all parts of the picture appear to be at the same distance from the eye, or is there an illusion of deep space and different distances? Is there a shallow inward view, stopped at a short distance, as by a curtain or wall? A definite, large area, like a public square, or a vista that recedes into infinite distance?

2. How is the illusion of depth, if any, produced? By converging perspective lines, lights and shadows, variations in size, different degrees of distinctness, color-contrasts?

3. Are the relative distances of objects clear or vague? Clearer nearby? Unnaturally clear, even in the distance?

4. Is the surface of the picture divided into similar parts, such as triangles, rectangles, ellipses?

5. Does some one figure or other object dominate the picture, through size, conspicuous light or color, or position at focus of converging lines? At or near the center? Is symmetry preserved, exactly or approximately? Is the main part far to one side? If so, is balance restored by some compensating factor on the other, such as a bright light or color, or several small objects? Is balance definitely destroyed? Does this seem unintentional, or consistent with the spirit of the whole, as in a deliberate effect of unrest or casualness?

6. Is there a distinct division into foreground, middleground and background? With more than natural contrast in light or color?

7. Is the arrangement of objects in space haphazard? Could they be shifted without weakening the unity of the whole? Are they vague, confused, in relative position?

8. Is there a definite, step-by-step recession away from the eye? At fairly regular intervals, with rhythmic effect? In groups, or individually?

9. Are some regions in deep space over-crowded? Are some empty, bare, uninteresting? Are objects distributed through the area taken in, to fill it and mark it off clearly?

10. Are the planes of different objects arranged in space at different angles, to make a design? (E.g., roof-tops, hills, dishes on a table.) With definite repetition, variation, contrast?

11. Are natural laws, such as perspective and gravitation, ignored in any way? (E.g., by raising horizon line or corner of table; showing together various moments or aspects of a scene, which could not be seen together in nature.) For a decorative purpose, as to give a tapestry-like flat background? For expressive or narrative reasons?

12. Are some figures represented as moving in space? With convincing illusion of movement, or stiffly and woodenly? According to natural laws, or in impossible, fantastic ways?

13. Are the suggested movements of various figures related together in some way? Only as representing elements in the same story? By some continuous rhythm of lines or masses? Do light and color contrasts help the sense of movement? Are the movements mainly in unison, in opposition, in confusion? Do they lead up to some emphatic, significant gesture or attitude as a climax? (E.g., the dead body in a *Pieta;* the ascent in an *Assumption*.) Do they produce an effect of dynamic design, as in an organized group dance? With excessive regularity, or with variation and contrast?

G. Unity of Design

1. Which of the above factors, and which quality in its use, seems to contribute most to the intended effect of design? Which seems to be most original, and in what way? Which are notably weak? Imitative?

2. Does some one factor stand out in isolation from the whole? With an

effect of conflict or confusion? Of intended emphasis or specialized, limited mode of appeal? Are the other factors unrelated, inconsistent, or merely subordinated?

3. Do line, light, color, mass and space all cooperate actively and harmoniously? Do all the particular qualities, rhythms and subordinate patterns noted above contribute definitely to one cumulative effect?

Appendix III
The Categories of Painting Criticism

MONROE C. BEARDSLEY

The Categories of Painting Criticism. We have sorted out the following kinds of nonnormative critical statement about paintings. The question is whether there are other nonnormative statements that critics would make about paintings, for which no category is provided here.

I. Description: statements about the characteristics of the painting in itself.
  A. Statements about the parts of the work
    1. Statements about elementary areas ("This is blue")
    2. Statements about complex areas ("This is an oval-shaped array of pink dots")
  B. Statements about relations between parts
    1. Statements about relations between elementary areas ("This blue is more highly saturated than that")
    2. Statements about relations between complex parts: these are statements about *form,* which include
      a. Statements about large-scale relations ("This side of the painting balances that side"): *structure*
      b. Statements about recurrent small-scale relations ("This shape of brush stroke appears throughout"): *texture* or, roughly, *style*

From *Aesthetics: Problems in the Philosophy of Criticism* by Monroe C. Beardsley, © 1958, by Harcourt, Brace & World, Inc., and reprinted with their permission, and that of the author.

    C. Statements about regional qualities of the whole or parts

        1. Statements about nonhuman qualities ("This has a triangular dominant pattern"—which can also be considered a *structure*-statement—or "This is unified")

        2. Statements about human qualities ("This is vigorous")

II. Statements about the likeness of the painting to other objects in the world

    A. Statements about representation, including

        1. Depiction ("This represents a horse")

        2. Portrayal ("This represents Bucephalus")

    B. Statements about suggestion ("This suggests a windmill")
       (Symbol-statements are subclasses of representation-statements and suggestion-statements)

    C. Statements about mere likeness ("This line is similar to a line on a human palm")

Note that all true statements about the relation of the painting to other things, other than its causes and effects, are here understood as similarity-statements. Those in groups A and B are generally called "interpretations" of the painting, and there seems to be no serious danger in this usage.

ROBERT GESSNER

I. OBJECTIVE ELEMENTS:
   1. Animate life (actors, persons, animals).
   2. Makeup.
   3. Costume.
   4. Inanimate objects.
   5. Locale.
   6. Light.
   7. Color.
   8. Size (closeup, medium, long shots).
   9. Perspective.
       (a) Linear (line, point, mass, depth).
       (b) Optical (lenses).
   10. Voice.
   11. Music.
   12. Sound.

From "Cinema and Scholarship," _The Journal of the Society of Cinematologists,_ Vol. III (1963), pp. 78-9. Reprinted by permission of the author and _The Journal of the Society of Cinematologists_. Also see Robert Gessner. "Seven Faces of Time: An Aesthetic for Cinema," in G. Kepes (ed.), _The Nature and Art of Motion_ (New York: George Braziller, 1965), pp. 158-67.

II. COORDINATIVE FACTORS:
    13. Subject movement (normal, fast, slow, reverse).
    14. Frame movement (pans, trucks, tilts, zooms).
    15. Editing.
        (a) Continuous (continuity).
        (b) Simultaneous (crosscut).
        (c) Accelerated (montage).
        (d) Past (flashback).
III. SUBJECTIVE QUALITIES:
    16. Descriptive.
    17. Narrative.
    18. Informational.
    19. Symbolic.

Note: beyond 19 lies the intangible part of talent and taste. Direction is a humanistic control of the whole, not an indivisible factor in itself. Similarly, acting is a combination of elements, factors, and qualities.

BIBLIOGRAPHY

The Bibliography is not intended to be exhaustive, and selections reprinted in the text have not been repeated. The books listed under (VI) contain references to the standard literature of art education.

I. Logic, Critical Thinking, and Intellectual Discipline

Beardsley, M. C. *Practical Logic.* Englewood Cliffs, N. J.: Prentice-Hall, Inc., 1950.

Broudy, H. S. "Mastery." In B. O. Smith and R. H. Ennis (eds.). *Language and Concepts in Education.* Chicago: Rand McNally & Co., 1961.

Cohen, M. R., and E. Nagel. *Introduction to Logic and Scientific Method.* New York: Harcourt, Brace & Co., Inc., 1942.

Dewey, J. *How We Think.* Rev. ed. Boston: D. C. Heath & Co., 1933.

Ennis, R. H. "A Concept of Critical Thinking," *Harvard Educational Review,* Vol. XXXII (Winter 1962), pp. 81-111.

Hullfish, H. G., and P. G. Smith. *Reflective Thinking: The Method of Education.* New York: Dodd, Mead & Co., Inc., 1961.

Kimball, S. T. "Darwin and the Future of Education," *The Educational Forum,* Vol. XXV (November 1960), pp. 59-72.

Kneller, G. F. *Logic and Language of Education.* New York: John Wiley & Sons, Inc., 1966.

Langer, S. K. *An Introduction to Symbolic Logic.* 2nd ed. New York: Dover Publications, Inc., 1953.

Little, W. W., *et al. Applied Logic.* Boston: Houghton Mifflin Co., 1955.

Popper, K. R. *The Logic of Scientific Discovery.* New York: Basic Books, Inc., 1959.

Raup, R. B., *et al. The Improvement of Practical Intelligence.* New York: Harper and Brothers, 1950.

Robinson, R. *Definition.* London: Oxford University Press, 1954.

Scheffler, I. *Conditions of Knowledge.* Chicago: Scott, Foresman and Co., 1965.

Wertheimer, M. *Productive Thinking.* New York: Harper & Row, Publishers, 1959.

II. Anthologies and General References

Argan, G. C. "Art." In *Encyclopedia of World Art*. Vol. I. New York: McGraw-Hill Book Co., Inc., 1959. Columns 764-810.

Aschenbrenner, K., and A. Isenberg (eds.). *Aesthetic Theories*. Englewood Cliffs, N. J.: Prentice-Hall, Inc., 1965.

Assunto, R., *et al.* "Criticism." In *Encyclopedia of World Art*. Vol. IV. McGraw-Hill Book Co., Inc., 1961. Columns 114-48.

Elton, W. (ed.). *Aesthetics and Language*. New York: Philosophical Library, 1954.

Hofstadter, A., and R. Kuhns (eds.). *Philosophies of Art and Beauty*. New York: Modern Library, 1964.

Kennick, W. E. (ed.). *Art and Philosophy*. New York: St. Martin's Press, 1964.

Kepes, G. (ed.). *Education of Vision*. New York: George Braziller, Inc., 1965.

Langer, S. K. (ed.). *Reflections on Art*. Baltimore: John Hopkins Press, 1958.

Levich, M. (ed.). *Aesthetics and the Philosophy of Criticism*. New York: Random House, 1963.

Margolis, J. (ed.). *Philosophy Looks at the Arts*. New York: Charles Scribner's Sons, 1962.

Philipson, M. (ed.). *Aesthetics Today*. New York: Meridian Books, 1961.

Rader, M. (ed.). *A Modern Book of Esthetics*. 3rd ed. New York: Holt, Rinehart and Winston, Inc., 1960.

Salerno, L., *et al.* "Historiography." In *Encyclopedia of World Art*. Vol. VII. New York: McGraw-Hill Book Co., Inc., 1963. Columns 507-59.

Sesonske, A. (ed.). *What Is Art? Aesthetic Theory from Plato to Tolstoy*. New York: Oxford University Press, 1965.

Spirito, U., *et al.* "Esthetics." In *Encyclopedia of World Art*. Vol. V. New York: McGraw-Hill Book Co., Inc., 1961. Columns 28-75.

Stolnitz, J. (ed.). *Aesthetics*. New York: The Macmillan Co., 1965.

Sypher, W. (ed.). *Art History: An Anthology of Modern Criticism*. New York: Vintage Books, 1963.

Tomas, V. (ed.). *Creativity in the Arts*. Englewood Cliffs, N. J.: Prentice-Hall, Inc., 1964.

Vivas, E., and M. Krieger (eds.). *The Problems of Aesthetics*. New York: Holt, Rinehart & Co., 1953.

Weitz, M. (ed.). *Problems in Aesthetics*. New York: The Macmillan Co., 1959.

Wilson, R. N. (ed.). *The Arts in Society*. Englewood Cliffs, N. J.: Prentice-Hall, Inc., 1964.

Whyte, L. W. (ed.). *Aspects of Form*. New York: Pellegrini & Cudahy, 1951.

III. Works of Special Interest

Aldrich, V. *Philosophy of Art*. Englewood Cliffs, N. J.: Prentice-Hall, Inc., 1963.

Arnheim, R. *Art and Visual Perception*. Berkeley: University of California Press, 1957.

Clark, K. *The Nude*. New York: Doubleday Anchor Books, 1959.

Fallico, A. *Art and Existentialism*. Englewood Cliffs, N. J.: Prentice-Hall Inc., 1962.

Gombrich, E. H. *Art and Illusion*. New York: Pantheon Books, Inc., 1960.

Greene, T. M. *The Arts and the Art of Criticism*. Princeton: Princeton University Press, 1940.

Hofstadter, A. *Truth and Art*. New York: Columbia University Press, 1965.

Hospers, J. *Meaning and Truth in the Arts*. Hamden, Conn.: Archon Books, 1964.

Jenkins, I. *Art and the Human Enterprise*. Cambridge: Harvard University Press, 1958.

Kaelin, F. E. *An Existentialist Aesthetic*. Madison: University of Wisconsin Press, 1962.

Kubler, G. *The Shape of Time*. New Haven: Yale University Press, 1962.

Langer, S. K. *Problems of Art*. New York: Charles Scribner's Sons, 1957.

Margolis, J. *The Language of Art and Art Criticism*. Detroit: Wayne State University Press, 1965.

Munro, T. *Toward Science in Aesthetics*. New York: The Liberal Arts Press, Inc., 1956.

Osborne, H. *Aesthetics and Criticism*. London: Routledge & Kegan Paul, Ltd., 1955.

Parker, D. H. *The Principles of Aesthetics*. New York: Appleton-Century-Crofts, 1946.

Pepper, S. C. *The Basis of Criticism in the Arts*. Cambridge: Harvard University Press, 1945.

Randall, J. H., Jr. *Nature and Historical Experience*. New York: Columbia University Press, 1958.

Read, H. *The Forms of Things Unknown*. New York: Meridian Books, 1963.

Sypher, W. *Four Stages of Renaissance Style*. New York: Doubleday Anchor Books, 1955.

Von Simson, O. *The Gothic Cathedral*. New York: Harper Torchbook, 1964.

Woelfflin, H. *Principles of Art History*. Translated by M. D. Hottinger. 7th ed. New York: Dover Publications, Inc., n.d.

IV. Aesthetics and Art Education

Ames, V. M. "Aesthetics." In R. Ulich (ed.). *Education and the Idea of Mankind*. New York: Harcourt, Brace & World, Inc., 1964. Pp. 227-48.

Arnstine, D. G. "Shaping the Emotions: The Sources of Standards for Aesthetic Education," *The School Review*, Vol. LXXII (Autumn 1964), pp. 242-71. Reprinted in *The Journal of Aesthetic Education*, Inaugural Issue (Spring 1966), pp. 45-69.

_____. "Needed Research and the Role of Definitions in Art Education," *Studies in Art Education*, Vol. VII (Autumn 1965), pp. 2-17.

Beittel, K. R. "Curriculum Experimentation in Art Education as Seen Through Recent Research." In P. C. Rosenbloom (ed.). *Modern Viewpoints in the Curriculum*. New York: McGraw-Hill Book Co., Inc., 1964. Pp. 113-28.

Broudy, H. S. *Building a Philosophy of Education*. 2nd ed. Englewood Cliffs, N. J.: Prentice-Hall, Inc., 1961. Chapter 9.

_____. *Paradox and Promise*. Englewood Cliffs, N. J.: Prentice-Hall, Inc., 1961. Pp. 155-65.

_____. "Contemporary Art and Aesthetic Education," *The School Review*, Vol. LXXII (Autumn 1964), pp. 394-411.

_____. "Aesthetic Education in the Secondary School," *Art Education*, Vol. XVIII (June 1965), pp. 24-30.

_____. "Aesthetic Education in a Technological Society," *The Journal of Aesthetic Education*, Inaugural Issue (Spring 1966), pp. 13-23.

_____, B. O. Smith, and J. R. Burnett. *Democracy and Excellence in American Secondary Education*. Chicago: Rand McNally & Co., 1964. Chapters 9, 13, 15. Excerpt, "The Exemplar Approach," reprinted in *The Journal of Aesthetic Education*, Inaugural Issue (Spring 1966), pp. 113-21.

Burt, C. "The Appreciation of Beauty" [Review of C. W. Valentine, *The Experimental Psychology of Beauty*], *The British Journal of Educational Psychology*, Vol. XXXIII, Part 2 (June 1963), pp. 194-201. Reprinted in *The Journal of Aesthetic Education*, Inaugural Issue (Spring 1966), pp. 71-84.

Dudley, L., and A. Faricy. *The Humanities: Applied Aesthetics*. 3rd ed. New York: McGraw-Hill Book Co., Inc., 1960.

Ecker, D. W. "Teaching Machines and Aesthetic Values," *Studies in Art Education,* Vol. III (Spring 1962), pp. 8-15. Reprinted in *Educational Theory,* Vol. XII (July 1962), pp. 170-77.

_____. "The Artistic Process as Qualitative Problem Solving," *The Journal of Aesthetics and Art Criticism,* Vol. XXI (Spring 1963), pp. 283-90.

_____. "Some Inadequate Doctrines in Art Education and a Proposed Resolution," *Studies in Art Education,* Vol. V (Fall 1963), pp. 71-81.

_____, and E. W. Eisner. *Readings in Art Education.* New York: Blaisdell Publishing Co., 1966.

_____, and E. F. Kaelin. "Aesthetics in Public School Art Teaching," *College Art Journal,* Vol. XVII (Summer 1958), pp. 382-91.

Eisner, E. W. "Knowledge, Knowing and the Visual Arts," *Harvard Educational Review,* Vol. XXX (Spring 1963), pp. 208-18.

_____. "Education and the Idea of Mankind," *The School Review,* Vol. LXXIII (Spring 1965), pp. 30-47.

_____, and D. W. Ecker. *Readings in Art Education.* New York: Blaisdell Publishing Co., 1966.

Feldman, E. B. "The Educational Value of Aesthetic Experience," *Harvard Educational Review,* Vol. XXI (Fall 1951), pp. 225-32.

_____. "The Nature of the Aesthetic Experience." In J. J. Hausman (ed.). *Report of the Commission on Art Education.* Washington, D. C.: National Art Education Association, 1965.

_____. "Works of Art as Humanistic Inquiries," *The School Review,* Vol. LXII (Autumn 1964), pp. 309-18.

Harris, D. B. *Children's Drawings as Measures of Intellectual Maturity.* New York: Harcourt, Brace & World, Inc., 1963.

Hastie, R. (ed.). *Art Education.* National Society for the Study of Education. Sixty-fourth Yearbook. Part II. Chicago: The University of Chicago Press, 1965.

Hausman, J. J. "Research on Teaching the Visual Arts," In N. L. Gage (ed.). *Handbook of Research on Teaching.* Chicago: Rand McNally & Co., 1963. Chapter 22.

Kaelin, E. F., and D. W. Ecker. "Aesthetics in Public School Art Teaching," *College Art Journal,* Vol. XVII (Summer 1958), pp. 382-91.

Kaelin, E. F. "Aesthetics and the Teaching of Art," *Studies in Art Education,* Vol. V (Spring 1964), pp. 42-56.

Kimball, S. T., and J. E. McClellan. *Education and the New America.* New York: Random House, 1962. Pp. 301-3.

Langer, S. K. "The Cultural Importance of the Arts." In M. F. Andrews (ed.). *Aesthetic Form and Education.* Syracuse: Syracuse University Press, 1958. Reprinted in *The Journal of Aesthetic Education,* Inaugural Issue (Spring 1966), pp. 5-12.

Lanier, V. "Schismogenesis in Contemporary Art Education," *Studies in Art Education,* Vol. V (Fall 1963), pp. 10-19.

Marantz, K. "Indecent Exposure," *Studies in Art Education,* Vol. VI (Autumn 1964), pp. 20-24.

Munro, T. *Art Education: Its Philosophy and Psychology.* New York: The Liberal Arts Press, 1956.

―――. "The Interrelation of the Arts in Secondary Education." In T. Munro and H. Read. *The Creative Arts in American Education.* Cambridge: Harvard University Press, 1960.

―――. "'Beautification' Reconsidered," *The Journal of Aesthetic Education,* Inaugural Issue (Spring 1966), pp. 85-100.

Phenix, P. *Philosophy of Education.* New York: Henry Holt & Co., 1958. Chapter 24.

―――. *Realms of Meaning.* New York: McGraw-Hill Book Co., Inc., 1964. Pp. 139-85. Excerpt, "Esthetic Meaning," reprinted in *The Journal of Aesthetic Education,* Inaugural Issue (Spring 1966), pp. 101-4.

Read, H. *Education Through Art.* 3rd ed. New York: Pantheon Books, 1958.

―――. "The Third Realm of Education." In T. Munro and H. Read, *The Creative Arts in American Education.* Cambridge: Harvard University Press, 1960.

―――. *The Redemption of the Robot.* New York: Trident Press, 1966.

Reimer, B. "The Development of Aesthetic Sensitivity," *Music Educators Journal,* Vol. LI (January 1965), pp. 33-36.

Smith, P. G. *Philosophy of Education.* New York: Harper & Row, Publishers, 1964. Chapters 6, 7. Excerpt, "The Structures of Productive Disciplines," reprinted in *The Journal of Aesthetic Education,* Inaugural Issue (Spring 1966), pp. 105-11.

Smith, R. A. "The Structure of Art-Historical Knowledge and Art Education," *Studies in Art Education,* Vol. IV (Fall 1962), pp. 23-33.

―――. "The Liberal Tradition of Art Education," *Studies in Art Education,* Vol. IV (Spring 1963), pp. 35-44.

―――. "The Mass Media and John Dewey's Liberalism," *Educational Theory,* Vol. XV (April 1965), pp. 83-93, 120.

―――. "Patterns of Meaning in Aesthetic Education," *Council for Research in Music Education,* Bulletin No. 5 (Spring 1965), pp. 1-12.

_____. "Images of Art Education," *Studies in Art Education,* Vol. VII (Autumn 1965), pp. 56-61.

_____. "The Aesthetic Dimension of Environmental Responsibility," *School Arts,* Vol. LXV (April 1966), pp. 20-22.

_____. "Aesthetic Education at the University of Illinois," *The Journal of Aesthetic Education,* Inaugural Issue (Spring 1966), pp. 123-26.

Valentine, C. W. *The Experimental Psychology of Beauty.* London: Methuen & Co., Ltd., 1962.

Villemain, F. "Democracy, Education and Art," *Educational Theory,* Vol. XV (January 1964), pp. 1-14, 30. Reprinted in *The Journal of Aesthetic Education,* Inaugural Issue (Spring 1966), pp. 25-43.

Whipple G. M. (ed.). *Art in American Life and Education.* National Society for the Study of Education. Fortieth Yearbook. Chicago: The University of Chicago Press, 1941.

V. Film and Television

Arnheim, R. *Film as Art.* Berkeley: University of California Press, 1957.

Eisenstein, S. *Film Form and The Film Sense.* Edited and translated by J. Leyda. New York: Meridian Books, 1957.

Fischer, E. *The Screen Arts: A Guide to Film and Television Appreciation.* New York: Sheed & Ward, 1960.

Fulton, A. R. *Motion Pictures: The Development of an Art from Silent Films to the Age of Television.* Norman: University of Oklahoma Press, 1960.

Hodgkinson, A. W. (ed.). *Screen Education.* New York: UNESCO Publications Center (NAIP), 1964.

Jacobs, L. *The Rise of the American Film.* New York: Harcourt, Brace & Co., Inc., 1939.

Knight, A. *The Liveliest Art.* New York: Mentor Books, 1957.

Kracauer, S. *Theory of Film.* New York: Oxford University Press, 1960.

Lingren, E. *The Art of the Film.* 2nd ed. New York: The Macmillan Co., 1963.

Mallery, D. *The School and the Art of Motion Pictures.* Boston: National Association of Independent Schools, 1964.

Manvell, R. *Film.* Baltimore: Penguin Books, 1946.

Peters, J. M. L. *Teaching About the Film.* New York: UNESCO Publications Center (NAIP), 1961.

Rotha, P. *The Film Till Now.* New York: Twayne Publishers, Inc., 1960.

Schramm, W. (ed.). *The Effects of Television on Children and Adolescents.* New York: UNESCO Publications Center (NAIP), 1964.

Skornia, H. *Television and Society*. New York: McGraw-Hill Book Co., Inc., 1965.

Smith, R. A. "Film as Significant Art," *Screen Education* (London), Vol. XXXII (January-February 1966), pp. 3-11.

_____. "Film Appreciation as Aesthetic Education," *The Educational Forum*, Vol. XXX (May 1966), pp. 483-89.

Stewart, D. C. "The Study of Motion Pictures in Colleges and Universities," *The Educational Record*, Vol. XLI (Winter 1965), pp. 33-67.

Spottiswoode, R. *A Grammar of the Film*. Berkeley: University of California Press, 1950.

Talbot, D. (ed.). *Film: An Anthology*. New York: Simon & Schuster, Inc., 1959.

Tyler, P. *Magic and Myth of the Movies*. New York: Henry Holt & Co., Inc., 1947.

Wolfenstein, M., and N. Leites. *Movies: A Psychological Study*. Glencoe, Ill.: The Free Press, 1950.

VI. Some Standard Texts in Art Education

Barkan, M. *A Foundation for Art Education*. New York: The Ronald Press, 1955.

Conant, H. *Art Education*. Washington, D. C.: Center for Applied Research in Education, 1964.

Conrad, G. *The Process of Art Education in the Elementary School*. Englewood Cliffs, N. J.: Prentice-Hall, Inc., 1964.

DeFrancesco, I. *Art Education: Its Means and Ends*. New York: Harper & Brothers, 1958.

Faulkner, R., E. Ziegfeld, and G. Hill. *Art Today*. 4th ed. New York: Holt, Rinehart & Winston, Inc., 1963.

Gaitskell, C. D. *Children and Their Art*. New York: Harcourt, Brace & World, Inc., 1958.

Jefferson, B. *Teaching Art to Children*. Boston: Allyn and Bacon, Inc., 1959.

Lanier, V. *Teaching Secondary Art*. Scranton: International Textbook Co., 1964.

Logan, F. W. *Growth of Art in American Schools*. New York: Harper and Brothers, 1955.

Lowenfeld, V., and W. L. Brittain. *Creative and Mental Growth*. 4th ed. New York: The Macmillan Co., 1964.

McFee, J. *Preparation for Art*. San Francisco: Wadsworth Publishing Co., 1961.

Pearson, R. M. *The New Art Education*. Rev. ed. New York: Harper and Brothers, 1953.

Schinneller, J. A. *Art: Search and Self-Discovery*. Scranton: International Textbook Co., 1961.

Ziegfeld, E. (ed.). *Education and Art*. New York: UNESCO, 1953.

CONTRIBUTORS

Walter Abell, Late Professor of Art, Michigan State University

James S. Ackerman, Department of Fine Arts, Harvard University

James Agee, Late Author and Film Critic

Monroe C. Beardsley, Department of Philosophy and Religion, Swarthmore College

Max Black, Department of Philosophy, Cornell University

Harry S. Broudy, Department of History and Philosophy of Education, University of Illinois

Martin S. Dworkin, Author, Film Critic, and Lecturer, Teachers College, Columbia University

Edmund B. Feldman, Department of Art, University of Georgia

Robert Gessner, Department of Communications and Motion Pictures, New York University

E. H. Gombrich, Warburg Institute, University of London

D. W. Gotshalk, Retired, Department of Philosophy, University of Illinois

Arnold Hauser, Author, resides in London, England

Norman N. Holland, Department of English, University of Buffalo

John Hospers, Department of Philosophy, Brooklyn College

Richard F. Kuhns, Department of Philosophy, Columbia University

Thomas Munro, Curator of Education, Cleveland Museum of Art

Erwin Panofsky, Institute for Advanced Study, Princeton University

Israel Scheffler, Professor of Philosophy and Education, Harvard University

Frank Sibley, Department of Philosophy, Cornell University

B. Othanel Smith, Department of History and Philosophy of Education, University of Illinois

F. E. Sparshott, Department of Philosophy, University of Toronto

Jerome Stolnitz, Department of Philosophy, University of Rochester

Leonard F. Swift, Professor of Education, Hofstra University

Contributors

J. O. Urmson, Fellow, Corpus Christi College, Oxford

Robert Warshow, Late Author and Film Critic

Morris Weitz, Department of Philosophy, The Ohio State University

Paul Ziff, Department of Philosophy, University of Wisconsin

INDEX

509